MW00396562

ASPA Classics

Conceived of and sponsored by the American Society for Public Administration (ASPA), the ASPA Classics series publishes volumes on topics that have been, and continue to be, central to the contemporary development of the field. The ASPA Classics are intended for classroom use, library adoptions, and general reference. Drawing from the *Public Administration Review* (*PAR*) and other ASPA-related journals, each volume in the series is edited by a scholar who is charged with presenting a thorough and balanced perspective on an enduring issue.

Each volume is devoted to a topic of continuing and crosscutting concern to the administration of virtually all public sector programs. Public servants carry out their responsibilities in a complex, multidimensional environment, and each collection will address a necessary dimension of their performance. ASPA Classics volumes bring together the dialogue on a particular topic over several decades and in a range of journals.

The volume editors are to be commended for volunteering to take on such substantial projects and for bringing together unique collections of articles that might not otherwise be readily available to scholars and students.

ASPA Classics

Local Government Management:
Current Issues and Best Practices
Douglas J. Watson and Wendy L. Hassett, eds.

Local Government Management

Current Issues and Best Practices

An ASPA Classics Volume

Edited by

Douglas J. Watson and Wendy L. Hassett

M.E.Sharpe
Armonk, New York
London, England

Library of Congress Cataloging-in-Publication Data

Local government management : current issues and best practices / edited
by Douglas J. Watson, and Wendy L. Hassett.
    p. cm. — (ASPA classics)
Includes bibliographical references and index.
  ISBN 0-7656-1127-9 (cloth: alk. paper) ISBN 0-7656-1128-7 (pbk.: alk. paper)
  1. Local government. I. Watson, Douglas J. II. Hassett, Wendy L.
III. Series.
  JS78.L654 2003
  352.14′0973—dc21

                                                                  2003000340

Printed in the United States of America

The paper used in this publication meets the minimum requirements of
American National Standard for Information Sciences
Permanence of Paper for Printed Library Materials,
ANSI Z 39.48-1984.

BM (c) 10   9   8   7   6   5   4   3   2
BM (p) 10   9   8   7   6   5   4   3   2

CONTENTS

LIST OF TABLES, FIGURES, AND BOXES

Tables

Figures

Boxes

PART 1

RELATIONS BETWEEN ELECTED OFFICIALS AND PROFESSIONAL STAFF

Since the earliest public administration literature in the United States, the issue of the relationship between elected officials and professional staff has been paramount. Woodrow Wilson and Frank Goodnow wrote extensively on this subject, as have numerous scholars in the decades that followed their pioneering work. Generally, scholars have used the policy-administration dichotomy as the theoretical construct to describe or explain the relationship between those elected to identify and enunciate the will of the people and those hired to carry out the will of the people, as presented to them by those elected.

Much of the literature on the policy-administration dichotomy has centered on council-manager government for two reasons. One is that it personifies the dichotomy so much more clearly because of the superior position the elected council holds relative to the manager. Mayor-council government, based on the concept of separation of powers, does not lend itself nearly as well to an evaluation of the policy-administration dichotomy as does council-manager government. The second reason is that public administration scholars probably have a stronger interest in the professional public administrators who fill the positions of city managers. Therefore, many of the articles included in Part 1 of this volume evaluate the relationship between elected officials and professional staff in the context of council-manager government.

We begin with Karl A. Bosworth's "The Manager *Is* a Politician" (chapter 1), which was previously published in *Public Administration Review* in 1958. Bosworth reviews three historic styles of city managers and concludes that all three types of managers play a key role in the policy process. His three types are the Administrator Manager, the Policy Researcher and Manager, and the Community Leader and Manager.

Bosworth noted that city managers and their professional association, then known as the International City Managers' Association (ICMA), had only recently acknowledged a policy role for city managers. He pointed out that, historically, proponents of council-manager government "have feared that the role of active policy leadership would bring discredit to the form of government" (p. 7). Several decades before his time, Bosworth recognized the key role that managers play as community and policy leaders. His advice to city managers: "City managers, whichever role they wish to follow, must seek to be among the best politicians in town, for their work deals with the satisfaction of the wants of people who have the privilege of discussing and voting about this work" (p. 9).

Richard J. Stillman II continues the debate that Bosworth had begun on the manager as politician (chapter 2). In 1977, Stillman wondered in his title whether city managers were professional helping hands or political hired hands. Bosworth, and Norton Long before him, concluded that managers were the best politicians in town because of their influence over budgetary matters, personnel decisions, and ability to advise their city councils. While Stillman did not completely dispute Long and Bosworth, he refined their conclusions by recognizing that differences among managers' work environments determine the extent of their policy involvement. He observed: "Increasingly city managers seem to take an activist view of their community policy roles, but three variables—city size, politics, self-definition of leadership roles—largely seem to determine the extent and nature of a manager's policy activity" (p. 18). Stillman concluded that managers cannot totally embrace either role of politician or professional. They must "cautiously and continuously tread a middle ground between the two poles of politics and expertise" (p. 20).

Nelson Wikstrom addresses another common misconception about council-manager government (chapter 3). The prevalent textbook view of council-manager mayors was restrictive and titular. Mayors were nothing more than ceremonial representatives of their local governments. In his 1979 study of the role of mayors in Virginia cities, Wikstrom uncovered a very strong policy role played by the mayors in Virginia. Over the next two decades, the mayor was recognized in the literature as the central political and policy leadership position in council-manager governments. Wikstrom concluded that not only did mayors exert strong policy leadership, but that the city managers with whom they worked preferred a mayor who provides "policy leadership and direction, and bears a strong sense of political responsibility for the resolution of controversial social issues confronting the community . . ." (p. 31). He concluded that the emergence of mayors as policy leaders in council-manager governments was a positive development.

James H. Svara adds considerably to the understanding of the relations between elected officials and professional staff (chapter 4). In his 1985 article, "Dichotomy and Duality: Reconceptualizing the Relationship Between Policy and Administration in Council-Manager Cities," Svara concluded that the traditional conception of the policy-administration dichotomy was inadequate to explain the complex relationship that existed between elected officials and city managers. In his study of five North Carolina cities, he realized that there are four dimensions to the relationship rather than two. He described the roles of the elected official and the city manager as mission, policy, administration, and management and decided that both positions had some role in all four dimensions, even though the first two were primarily the spheres of the elected official and the latter two the spheres of the city manager.

The general conclusion in the literature is that city managers are taking on a greater policy role. However, James M. Banovetz foresees a very different future for city managers than that described by most scholars (chapter 5). In his 1994 article, he concluded that in the future, city managers would be in positions similar to professional baseball managers : "City managers of the future may find that their job, like their job tenure, is more similar to that of baseball managers than to political leaders, and that the resulting insecurity, as well as job demands, will cause them to focus on managerial rather than policy responsibilities" (p. 51). Banovetz opined that the reversion to a stronger managerial role and a lessened policy role is based on the changing political reality. He identified four periods in the twentieth century where public perceptions of government moved from "corrupt" (1900–14), to "should be limited" (1915–35), to "is paternalistic" (1935–65), to "is excessive" (1965–present). Political leaders in the United States grew up in this last period when government was viewed with hostility and mistrust. The new political leaders want a more direct and active role in government that requires that managers "match their technical competence with human relations skills" (p. 58).

Robert S. Montjoy and Douglas J. Watson review the writings of the early reformers and conclude that there are two dichotomies—the policy-administration dichotomy and the politics-administration dichotomy (chapter 6). Clearly, the literature over the decades has documented the role in policymaking that city managers play. However, an equally important role for city managers is to restrict the intrusion of particularistic politics into the management decisions of the city government. The manager serves as a gatekeeper for the department heads who are doing their jobs based on the best professional practices and not in response to the political demands of elected officials. In their 1995 article, Montjoy and Watson concluded that the politics-administration dichotomy "is still a live issue for council-manager government" (p. 71) because it serves as a guidepost for managers in their dealings with their councils and in handling employee-council relations. It is one of the few weapons that a manager can use "to resist the particularistic tendencies in our political system" (p. 71).

James H. Svara, writing again in 1999 (and published here as chapter 7), identified changing conditions that caused differences in the traditional relationships between elected officials and city managers in thirty-one large American cities that use council-manager government. In his survey of elected officials and appointed administrators in these cities, Svara found that four of five viewed the working relationship between them as very good or good. However, he noted that a "change in council members' behavior and preferences is occurring" (p. 76). Specifically, Svara found that council members tend to be concerned with specific, short-term matters and not with long-range policy. "It is possible that the city manager has become more active in mission and policy than previously, but another explanation is that the manager's policy activity is more obvious as council members pay less attention to goal setting" (p. 77) he concluded. Managers have become what Svara described as the "activist-initiator" while the elected officials are more consumed with their roles as ombudsmen, current problem solvers, and overseers of the manager's work.

CHAPTER 1

THE MANAGER *IS* A POLITICIAN

KARL A. BOSWORTH

Upper governmental bureaucrats everywhere live under the imperative of thinking of the continued justification of the activities of their bureaucracies. What are the possible ways of modifying
programs and methods? How appealing to whom are the alternatives? What are the dangers to be
avoided? Are the achievements impressive? Is there a firm and possibly growing body of public
awareness, satisfaction, and support? These and similar considerations haunt the thoughts of the
prudent governmental officer. What he does with these thoughts may depend upon the form of
government and political system within which the officer works.

Council-manager government, by placing the manager directly in public view, accentuates
public interest in how this kind of bureaucrat operates as a political leader. Not only is he
inevitably in public view, but the range of his operations is broad, and the fate of his community
may be determined in part by the public goals his thoughts lead him to set for his government.
Recent awareness of the broad roles in policy leadership admitted by some city managers has
raised the question as to whether council-manager government is developing now as an acceptable political system. In other words, given this bent, is it still a popular government or is there a
danger that an undemocratic political system is being contrived?

It is the view here that the relatively recent willingness of city managers to admit generally
that they are community leaders does not reflect a marked change in their role. City managers,
abetted particularly by the International City Managers' Association, have been concerned about
the image of themselves presented to the public. The role of the manager has been, after all, in the
process of being structured; and the fortunes of the managers and the Association depended upon
public acceptance of a described role.

The description of the role as it affects policy leadership has varied from time to time and place
to place. Looking at three "styles" of city managers as these roles have been described will, I think,
point up the relatively minor nature of the recent changes. One should not think of these "styles" as
a historical series. Although some case might be made for a historical trend, the emphasis here is on
the presence of policy initiating elements in all the styles of manager that have been described.[1]

The Administrator Manager

One stylized view of the city manager has so sought to emphasize his role in internal administration as to leave no room for policy initiative. In this view, he just carries out administrative duties
such as hiring, setting up the tasks, reviewing the work, and looking for the ways of getting more

From *Public Administration Review*, vol. 18, no. 3 (Summer 1958), pp. 216–222. Copyright © 1958 by
American Society for Public Administration. Reprinted with permission.

production from the same input or the same production from less input. Of course he also makes up the budget, and therein, if nowhere else, he is in politics.

A manager could, and a few have tried to, provide a council with budget estimates in which there was no firm proposal but rather a pricing of amounts of programs with supplementary programs priced in a fashion so that the council could buy as much or as little as it chooses. But the firm, balanced budget is the rule, and in such a proposal the manager says to the tax-saver that the city "needs" stated amounts for various programs and to the spender that the city "can get by" on the stated totals. The saver must find some program from which he can make deductions, if he would tinker with the proposal, while the spender has either to do the same or to propose the raising of taxes. Even if a manager has had budgetary guidance from the council, he cannot ordinarily escape some public responsibility for his proposed budget: "He didn't include anything new for us," or "They got nearly everything they wanted." Whether such statements emanate from employees or from others interested in programs, they are the essence of politics.

Let us not depreciate the manager's role as an internal administrator, for that is one of the plan's principal justifications. However, even in this role the administrator-manager is likely to set goals whose achievement may impress people with the desirability of the plan and the ability of the manager; good politics, in other words. Short-run goals may include the rewriting of some of the city's contracts for services or insurance with a view toward savings or improved service or coverage. These can be matters of policy as well as administration, and if one of the changes proves to be controversial, this is politics. A longer run goal may be the transformation of a mediocre department into a technically proficient one—a change, if accomplished, resulting in changes in the quality of the services and almost unavoidably in the quantity and kinds of service. The effective city policy has changed whether the change has been noticed or not.

It is difficult not to imagine our administrator hearing of state legislation which compels or allows the city council to make some new decision and transmitting this information to the council, along with administrative advice and the news about other cities initiating a service locally unknown; but these items may, if desired, be saved for the next "style" of city manager.

The Policy Researcher and Manager

The manager may have learned that all policy issues have their administrative aspects, and that he, as administrative expert, should advise the council on the ramifications of their proposals, including the budgetary consequences. It is likely, further, that in comparison with council members, the manager is highly informed about municipal affairs and about sources of municipal information and how to mine these sources. The council will insist that the manager enlighten their deliberations.

In this role, the manager who is also a policy researcher will contrive to know about what is coming up in a council meeting from sources other than his desk so that he can be somewhat prepared with relevant information. He will further seek to school the council to refer to him for study and report nearly all issues which anyone wants seriously to consider. Councilmen, impressed with the manager's expertise and concerned with their own responsibilities, fall readily into the pattern of asking his assistance.

It should be noted that these policy proposals may come from anywhere: councilmen, other individuals and organizations in the community, or the manager. It has long been accepted that managers should bring overt policy ideas to the council. This was implicit in the manager's presumed expertise in municipal affairs. He had had more opportunity than the council to learn about alternative and supplementary municipal services or regulations, and he could be expected to give attention to the channels of current municipal information.

The standard role of managers, in fact, goes well beyond the passive or reactive patterns suggested above. The manager has been expected, like any good mayor, to study the problems, programs, and facilities of *his* city and to make proposals to the council on these matters. Any perusal of the several editions of *The Technique of Municipal Administration*, including chapters devoted to administrative research, planning, and particularly programming, shows that the International City Managers' Association has been hoping for a strong measure of city-statesmanship in its managers. The current word is that it is one of the responsibilities of the manager to see that issues of the maintenance, discontinuance, and initiation of program elements be systematically reviewed by the legislative body.[2] It is, of course, official dogma that the manager be in a position to participate in long-term planning as well as the planning of programs for current operations.

The researcher-manager acknowledges all the while that he is the council's man. He works for the council. He studies the proposals they refer to him and reports to the council. He initiates policy studies for presentation to the council. He advises the council; warns it and even argues with its members. Others may read or listen, but the role is structured in relation to the representative body. He is aware of the community, but he works for the council. They hired him; he works for them; they are responsible for the decisions.

Although our manager is the council's man, he gives attention to public relations. He seeks to have the city avoid offending the public unnecessarily. He wants all elements of the administration to present an appearance of courtesy, consideration, and effective operation. He seeks through news channels and reports to get city accomplishments told to the public. Many managers also seek ways to get some communication from the public. Systems for handling complaints aid the manager in gauging public expectations as well as in reviewing operations. And managers everywhere explain to publics the council-manager form of government, an inevitably self-referring form of communication.

It may be important to note two models of this researcher-manager style differentiated by their policy presentations. One seeks to emphasize factual materials, stating alternative policies and predicting the consequences of following each. He seeks to avoid making recommendations. The other model, perhaps at the council's insistence, or perhaps by personal inclination, presents his policy proposals as recommendations, with reasoned factual support but a minimum of "confusing alternatives." This could be an important enough difference to merit thinking of the recommender as a separate style of manager. However, the manager with facts and alternatives does make recommendations—as in his budget. And he will surely weigh the values of his council and community in considering alternatives to present to the council. Interest in economy of time and of effort in explanation will lead even the cautious manager to prejudge a great many policy issues for council.

The Community Leader and Manager

Throughout the history of the movement, some city managers have ventured into overt community leadership in the settlement of public problems. Through the same period, some students and proponents of the plan have feared that the role of active policy leadership would bring discredit to the form of government. Although the argument has never terminated, the common doctrine has described the manager in clear and continuous subordination to council, expressing his activist political inclinations upon and through council. A minor variation would include the mayor as an alternate in the intermediate role.

In the last ten years, however, there have been numbers of instances in which managers have admitted or proclaimed the broader role for themselves, and there is now a common doctrine of valid, if limited, manager initiative in policy information. Different ones would draw the limitations variously, so the picture of this manager is less precise.

Even the latest edition of *The Technique of Municipal Administration* states that "The city manager is free to act as a community leader in the great majority of municipal policies which do not involve political controversies."[3] The 1958 edition also gives what may be the key to the newly described role:

> A manager can often serve effectively as a community leader without heading a committee or taking direct leadership in civic programs. By searching out and discovering the many real leaders existing in the community, interesting them in new improvements for the community, and keeping them supplied with new ideas and encouraging them to work together, he can achieve far more than by direct leadership of his own.[4]

Managers are thus expected to study the informal power structures of their communities and to use the persons in these channels of influence insofar as they will cooperate to achieve the managers' goals. This may be simply a more candid expression of what experienced managers have commonly done, or it may emerge from a more sophisticated perception of the distribution of influence. In any case, relevant power may rest elsewhere than in the council and the managers are seeking to use it.

What are other characteristics of this style of manager? He accepts without question the role of city emissary to state and federal government organs, including legislative committees, to state and national professional and civic associations, and to other municipal governments. To some he will express the city's point of view and with others he may negotiate for his city.

He will pay particular attention to all organized groups in his community, partially as a means of making the acquaintance of the natural leaders of these groups. "It is the manager's job to provide facts, offer council, encourage and tactfully to guide community groups in the planning of worthwhile improvements."[5] The telephone numbers of the executive directors of associations presuming to speak for the interests of commerce, health, welfare, education, industry, religion, labor, good government, and real estate, among others, ought to be readily at hand. These executives may include most of his cohorts outside his administrative team, for they and the manager may have adjacent goals as well as similar methods of operation.

He may seek to participate in the meetings of boards and commissions of his own government and, whenever possible, the meetings of boards of special districts covering his city. "Personal contacts by the manager with various county officials open the door for unannounced leadership."[6]

When he has acquired acceptance in the community power structure, his opportunities for influence will broaden and he is likely to be consulted by groups making plans for any segment of the community.

> In this concept a manager can and should deal with political parties on much the same basis as other interest groups. By avoiding any sign of preference or of dealing in personalities, a constructive influence can be had.[7]

What are the limits to this role? In one sense, the question is unanswerable, for managerial leadership "is a function of the instant, the setting, and the personalities."[8] In another sense, the community-leading manager is limited by his sense of appropriate behavior for his role as servant of the public. In yet another sense, although conscious of his power, the manager must remember that his power is a result of the tolerance for him of the present city council and any council membership which may soon be elected. Any Tuesday night could be the last, particularly the meeting following election of a new council. No one suggests that managers should depart from their traditional watchful obliviousness to these elections, although a few will admit that they seek to develop possible candidates for the council among board and commission membership.

Are There Serious Risks?

The city managers in any of these styles are not simply master mechanics of bureaucratic routine. Even our administrator-manager had better be able to sense the public pulse at budget time. And he may have more difficulty predicting public satisfaction with his planned administrative achievements than does the community leader who feels free to try his ideas on his local acquaintances. City managers, whichever role they wish to follow, must seek to be among the best politicians in town, for their work deals with the satisfaction of the wants of people who have the privilege of discussing and voting about this work.

There are risks to popular government in council-manager cities. A manager could convince his council and significant elements in the community that only by his nonpartisan, objective mind can the city problems of first, second, and third importance be identified and only through his skilled, impartial analysis can the correct solutions be found. The special risk here is that the values the manager uses in making these decisions will reflect those of some limited group within the city rather than values representative of his city.

There are risks that the administrative mind will successfully insist that matters decided shall stay decided; that some newly proposed facility cannot be considered because it is not in the six-year capital outlay plan; or that any undesired change in operation cannot be considered because "we have a policy on that." Managers cannot be blamed for hoping that complex issues may be considered fully, decided upon, and that the decision stick. But it should be the manager's discretion which determines when decisions shall be reconsidered.

There are risks that a city's effective policies may be determined increasingly through processes of negotiation between the city and other governments, and with banks, utilities, development and other corporations, professional and business groups, and unions. If the manager is an uninstructed ambassador in these negotiations, his negotiating premises partially may foreclose later consideration by his governing body of alternative policies to those on which negotiation has been concluded.

These are real risks, but the risks of concentrated political leadership are not limited to council-manager cities. We are thus thrown back to the question of whether the values of managers will represent those of their communities and whether the local political and representative system will enforce some correspondence between popular wishes and governmental performance.

With regard to the political systems in council-manager cities, it may well be time to give thought to both informal and formal arrangements. If only stooges for some manager-supporting power combine are elected to the council, or if the system has made the ardent practice of political leadership unprofitable for all save the manager, or if the political system is incapable of expressing either discontent or contentment, or if a competing point of view to the government position cannot gain intelligent expression, it is time to be inventive. Perhaps there is need for a tax benefits association, with research staff, publicists, and publications, as well as a taxpayers' association. Perhaps it needs to be recognized that local parties are not going to develop and that charter groups are commonly going to confuse the public about the manager plan by asking the voter for support of the plan or the manager rather than support of a program of current policies.[9]

Perhaps thought needs to be given to findings suggesting that the nonpartisan election does not readily permit the registration of protest and perhaps permits no clear indication of assent.[10] Perhaps it can be remembered that our national political parties are federations of state and local parties, that political parties have demonstrated a capacity to express ideals with some contrast, and that not only "nice people" but most of the talented ones who are aspirants for elective office are now accustomed to working in parties. Although we have had enough of faith in gimmicks, perhaps it is time to think of some system which will assure the representation of both parties on the council—where this is feasible—rather than no parties. If we want a political system which will diffuse the public attention now placed on the manager as political leader, perhaps we should ask the parties for assistance in providing public discussion from some variety of points of view. In any case, care needs to be given to the selection of a governing body. It may decide to govern; or in the absence of a manager it may have to govern for a time.

Governments depend greatly upon the values held by their important bureaucrats, and democratic governments depend on the capacity of these bureaucrats to sense the values of the communities the governments serve. There appears to be a basis for some belief that government employment, including the manager profession, attracts individuals whose values seem realizable in service to the public, in contrast to more dramatic or more pecuniarily promising roles. Helping to achieve public goals, to "do some good," is appealing. A stronger than usual ethical sense may be present.[11] The training of these people is likely to be highly inculcating and reinforcing of values of personal integrity, fair play, just dealing, and appreciation for the rights and views of others.

The leadership of the International City Managers' Association has used its literature and conferences to seek to maintain in managers values consistent with their roles in democratic government. The injunctions to walk uprightly before men, compassionately before the weak, and humbly before the council stand out in the tracts.[12] The personal moral tragedies among managers must be relatively few, judging from the small publicity of such events.

The problems with regard to the values of managers are in part concerned with their own values and in part concerned with those of the community. A risk is that as the manager becomes an upper-income citizen he will have preferences like an upper-income citizen, that he may learn to think like those with whom he lunches, or to think that no good idea could come from a source that has seemed not to appreciate him. These risks are probably no greater, however, in the administrative leader manager than in the other styles, for the leader in his varied community contacts must sometimes listen. The manager's staff and department heads may also be correctives for his preferences.

City manager dogma used to include the notion that the plan of government was appropriate only for those cities that wanted this form of government—cities whose people were willing to sacrifice some of the fun of political controversy and patronage for the benefits of a skilled management. Without exploring in detail the boundaries set by such criteria, it may be possible to suggest that cities in which there are very strong and deep disagreements over values test, perhaps beyond reasonable expectation, the possibility of any career general executive representing in his decisions the preferences of the community. Similarly, in communities where the relevant local government values shift, as a result of population mobility or new problems, or where the electoral system results in frequent changes in the value components of the community being represented, the capacity of any manager to sense and move with the changing dominant values of his community may be tested beyond his or the council's endurance. Can a particular manager shift back and forth in his preference system as the majority on the council shifts from labor to conservative inclinations? Probably in situations such as these one should not expect the manager to stand exposed and alone.

These calculations undoubtedly leave most of the suburbs, many independent cities, and some central cities appropriate grounds for the manager plan. And where managers are used, let us think of them as officers of general administrative direction *and* political leadership, for that is what they are.

Notes

Publishers' note: ICMA changed its name in 1969 from International City Managers' Association to International City Management Association and again in 1990 to the International City/County Management Association. All three names are used throughout this book, depending on the publication date of the article being reprinted.

1. For a historical view noting relevant changes in the managers' "Code of Ethics," see Hugo Wall, "Changing Concepts of Managerial Leadership," *Public Management* 36 (March 1954): 50–53. Compare Douglas G. Weiford, "Changing Role of the City Manager," *Public Management* 36 (August 1954): 170–172. For a view of kinds of city managers in terms of occupational sociology, see George K. Floro, "Types of City Managers," *Public Management* 36 (October 1954): 221–225. Any attempt to think about the roles of managers must depend heavily upon the work of Harold A. Stone, Don K. Price, and Kathryn H. Stone (and others) done in the late 1930s and, especially, their book, *City Manager Government in the United States* (Public Administration Service, 1940). They seemed to weigh more heavily than one would today the formal responsibility of the council, and they seemed to have had a clearer distinction between policy and administration than can be mustered today, but one cannot much project their insights.

2. *Institute for Training in Municipal Administration* (4th ed., International City Managers' Association, 1958), p. 109.

3. Ibid., p. 31. In a book of biblical character coming from many hands one should not expect all statements to agree with that quoted.

4. Ibid., p. 32.

5. "Leadership Functions of the Manager," *Public Management* 37 (March 1955): 53. This is a report prepared by a group of managers for discussion at the Fortieth Annual Conference of ICMA held December 5–8, 1954.

6. Ibid., p. 52.

7. Ibid., p. 54.

8. Ibid., p. 53.

9. The Stone, Price, Stone findings on this point sound quite contemporary. See chap. 12.

10. Charles R. Adrian, "Some General Characteristics of Non-partisan Elections," *American Political Science Review* 46 (September 1952): 766–776.

11. A professor may be indulged in some judgments about his students. Consideration is being given to methods for studying the values of administrators of various sorts.

12. "Relations of the Manager with the Public," *Public Management* 37 (April 1955): 77–83, esp., p. 79.

CHAPTER 2

THE CITY MANAGER:

Professional Helping Hand, or Political Hired Hand?

RICHARD J. STILLMAN II

Nearly one hundred million Americans reside in cities served by city managers or chief administrative officers (CAOs). Today, 2,655 city managers and CAOs are appointed by city councils as full-time administrators of their community governments. In a typical council-manager plan city, a small council made up of five, seven, or nine representatives, generally elected on a nonpartisan, at-large basis, serves as the chief policy-making body of the city principally through its legal powers of approving city ordinances, personnel policies and budgetary appropriations.[1] The council appoints a chief executive officer, a city manager, or CAO who generally serves without tenure "at the council's pleasure."

A complex working relationship evolves between the elected legislative policy makers on council and the appointed chief administrator. Under the manager plan, the mayor generally performs part-time ceremonial functions, with the manager assuming full-time, day-to-day responsibilities over all or most line functions of local government. CAOs normally have fewer direct line departments of the city to supervise by comparison to managers, though both managers and CAOs exercise vital and powerful roles through budget preparation and personnel recruitment, as well as through formal and informal advisory activities with council.[2]

The "professional" nature of managers' work in terms of their on-the-job activities, skills, experience, training, and career is legally prescribed by most council-manager city charters, as well as promulgated as official doctrine by the International City Management Association (ICMA), the professional association of city managers and CAOs. For instance, the typical council-manager charter that outlines the manager's job reads: "As chief administrative officer, the city manager provides professional counsel to the city council. . . . His work is performed with professional independence. . . ." The introduction to the ICMA's Code of Ethics for managers also emphasizes that one of their primary purposes is ". . . to strengthen the quality of urban government through professional management."[3]

However, political scientists over the last two decades, drawing on sophisticated community power studies and decision making analyses, have evolved another view of managers and CAOs strikingly different from that of traditionally autonomous professions subject to an independent code of ethics, peer group review, and their own standards of expertise. Rather, a manager is viewed from this perspective as one of the chief actors in community politics, response to local interests and decision makers and, in turn, influencing the general course of city affairs.

From *Public Administration Review*, vol. 37, no. 6 (November/December 1977), pp. 659–670. Copyright © 1977 by American Society for Public Administration. Reprinted with permission.

In the words of Norton Long, managers are in reality "politicians for hire," or as Karl Bosworth put it more concisely, simply "politicians" who derive their considerable influence within city hall and the community at large from their control over budget preparation, personnel appointments, and formal as well as informed council advisory functions.[4] For this "realist school of political scientists, the very term "professional" simply disguises one of the best politicians in town, and, as they view it, "professional" is both a meaningless and deceptive term that fails to describe a manager's "real" activities and functions.

This chapter will attempt to sort out the two prominent but seemingly contradictory views of managers/CAOs—that of "professional helping hands" versus "political hired hands"—by beginning with a brief look at their unique triad of historic values which did much to create their contemporary occupational identity confusion.

The Business Corporation, Neutral Expertise, and Pragmatic Reform

Unlike other public officials, city managers were originally conceived as the centerpiece of a normative reform theory or "model" for restructuring and redirecting the very purposes of local government. Thus, the manager's occupation was at its very inception deeply enmeshed within a peculiar frame of political values that was the handiwork, not of a seasoned public official nor profound political thinker, but of a relatively obscure New York City businessman, twenty-eight-year-old Richard S. Childs, who pursued a part-time hobby of municipal reform. Shortly after graduating from Yale College, Childs in 1904 with another prominent Progressive of that day, Woodrow Wilson, set out to rid cities of boss rule by promoting the "short ballot" idea, which sought to improve and rationalize voting processes through shortened ballots. He later was attracted for similar reasons to "the commission plan," first popularized in Galveston, Texas, but in 1909 his eye fell accidentally on an experiment in Staunton, Virginia, that had recently hired "a manager" as chief full-time administrator.[5] From his one-room New York City short ballot office, Childs soon produced a steady stream of anonymous articles and stories praising the virtues of city manager government as superior to the commission plan (giving the mistaken impression that the manager plan was already in widespread operation). Childs wielded a powerful pen that made him a virtuoso at publicizing manager government. News editorials and after-dinner speakers soon were repeating his catch-phrases that became stock-in-trade programs of the Progressive municipal reformers. By 1918, one hundred cities, one as large as Dayton, Ohio, had adopted "the manager plan." Ironically, while all this occurred, the man who claimed to be "the plan's inventor" remained so inconspicuous that no one had ever heard of him at the first meeting of city managers (I doubt few managers today have ever heard of Richard Childs).

To Childs's credit, however, he recognized early that to mobilize support for the idea it "must be condensed to a catch-phrase first, even if such a reduction means lopping off many of its vital ramifications and making it false in many of its natural applications." Childs had an undeniable knack at simplification and promotion, yet as a Progressive reformer, Childs also had a genuine and vital concern about the need for better local government by means of widening popular participation in community affairs through structural change. The manager plan was his prime vehicle of structural reform that, as Don Price rightly observed,[6] rested on the manipulation symbols then dominant (and still I would venture to argue popular today) in American culture—the business corporation, neutral expertise, and pragmatic reform.

These three fundamental values behind the plan I would argue operate simultaneously on three levels: at the first level in engendering popular support and public acceptance for the plan and hence creating the very occupational role a manager performs in a community; at a second level in influencing the particular and unique formal structure within which a manager's job is performed; and on a third level in giving rise to the persistent and fundamental value problems associated with this line of work. Table 2.1 illustrates the "interrelatedness" among the three fundamental values of the plan and the three levels of "impact" upon the city management occupation. While much of Table 2.1 is self-explanatory, I would argue that the enduring and critical value problems of city managers depicted under Level Three stem frequently from the difference between the popular expectations of the plan (Level One) and the practicalities of governance that managers encounter in making the plan work (Level Two). The business model, for instance, which sells well to voters by establishing a council-manager government on the basis of a business corporation and which sharply separates policy from administration, is in practice a terribly difficult, if not an impossible dichotomy to achieve on a daily working basis, because, as numerous political scientists have noted,[7] so much policy "slips and slops" into administration that the distinction between the two becomes both fuzzy and blurred.

Similarly, the second value of neutral expertise implicit in a manager's official title may warm the hearts of voters because of its apolitical symbolic appeal, but neutrality on the practical level of running cities is extraordinarily hard to achieve in pluralistic communities where a five-man council may indeed have five different opinions about any issue it faces. Also, the value of pragmatic reform may sell the plan well, but sometimes at a price, in that managers are expected to achieve the humanly impossible under the plan, such as reducing taxes in an inflationary economy.

In short, the persistent disparity between the ideals implicit in the plan—ideals that, of course, make the very existence of a city management occupation possible—and the human practicalities of day-to-day operational problems of urban governance force managers to assume perpetually a sort of schizophrenic double identity—"a professional identity," one defined by law in city charters and given popular credence from the general public's support of "the plan"—and a "political identity" that requires them to exercise a great deal of savvy of an astute politician in terms of "fitting" the ideals of the plan into a real world. No other public official is forced to operate within a legacy of this sort of a triad of values that causes persistent tensions and identity crises in terms of his/her own self-image.

The Shape of City Management Today: Its Contemporary Values and Social Trends

What is the shape of the city management field today? In what directions is it evolving? While I do not pretend to offer up a list of all changes that are occurring within city management (the diversity of the field makes a comprehensive listing impossible), among the eight most noteworthy major trends over the last two decades that influence the direction of this line of work as well as the individual roles of managers are the following:

1. A continued popularity and growth of managers/CAOs and a rise in the multiplicity of their responsibilities but with a concomitant "dispersion" of their authority.

Since World War II, an average of sixty-five cities annually have adopted council-manager government. War and depression have slowed the growth of the plan, but the relative prosperity of the 1960s and 1970s with demands of growing city/suburban populations for better municipal services and new federal money from revenue sharing has helped to spur the growth rate of city management. Furthermore, with the broader ICMA criteria for general management recognition established in 1969, a record 159 communities were recognized as approved council-manager cities in 1973, and 110 were approved in 1975. The statistical growth of the plan of course leads

Table 2.1

[Fundamental Values and Their Impacts]

Triad of values implicit in "plan"	Means for impact	Level one: Symbolic and popular appeal of "plan's" values to voters	Level two: Structural "impact" of "plan's" values on city management practitioners today	Level three: Critical operational issues posed for managers by values of the "plan"
Corporate value	Formal model for city government enacted by law in council-manager charters	Pattern of local government modeled on business corporation denoting central values of economy/efficiency	Provides a formal bureaucratic hierarchy for local government with a sharp differentiation between policy-making role of council and administrative authority of manager	Clear-cut idealized dichotomy between politics and administration poses perpetual and complex practical problems of relations between manager and council in matters of governance, policy formulation, and cooperative direction
Neutral expertise	City charter that establishes a professional city manager's post	Word "manager" denotes energetic, nonpolitical leadership	Centralizes decisional authority and responsibility in *one* individual who takes a "communitywide approach" to solving city problems	Complex problems associated with finding the "public interest" or "community good" in order to apply neutral expertise in achieving a pluralistic community's desired goals
Pragmatic reform	Immediate demands for improvements and changes in local government by city council and community when "plan" is adopted	The council-manager plan denotes a reform measure designed to generate specific changes in government as well as as general civic progress	Council-manager government serves to respond to specific community needs by reforming community government structure and providing improved and "effective" municipal services	Reformers have frequently oversold the plan by promising the manager can do the impossible, like lower taxes, and so forth

to increased occupational opportunities for city management practitioners. As indeed recent surveys have shown, managers themselves remain relatively optimistic about the future expansion of their field.[8]

As the plan itself has grown, so too have managerial responsibilities widened. New demands for their expertise applied to new areas like environmental protection, affirmative action, pollution control, and energy conservation have contributed to significantly expanding their roles, activities, and interests. Managers, like front line soldiers on the battlefield, are frequently the first public officials to face the assault of new issues and innovations affecting government, and thus are frequently the first to learn how "to cope" with the new problems.

Along with rising responsibilities, managers have faced in recent years a concomitant "dispersal of authority," due on one side from the rapidly increased "intrusion" over the last decade by federal/state authorities into what once was the manager's pretty much exclusive "turf." The intergovernmental layer cake that turned into a marble cake has meant the dispersal of the once clear lines of authority of managers over their own internal administrative functions. Federal and state oversight and interest in city government has risen, thanks largely to its generous fiscal support which usually has strings attached.

The challenge to managerial authority comes equally from below as well. Public employee unions' growing demands at the bargaining table for better pay and working conditions made unions now equal or almost equal partners with managers in setting administrative priorities and policies for communities. Similarly, new minority participation in local government further has served to widen the circle of citizenry in the community decision-making processes, and further serves in "fuzzing" the manager's traditional authority. As one manager who recently resigned his post in one small community told the newspapers on his departure:

> I have a philosophy that local government doesn't have as much effect on city government as regional and state policies. Most of the policies the city implements don't originate locally . . . and 95 percent of the revenue the city receives, including where it is obtained and how it can be spent, is controlled by the state and federal government. Local government is an ebbing entity . . . that is becoming increasingly diverse and complicated.[9]

2. In response to the growing cross-pressures on managers from "above" and "below," the traditional core values of their occupation have also been significantly broadened from an emphasis on technique-oriented engineering efficiency to more general public management based upon recent social science knowledge.

One of the best barometers of the widening concerns and values of city management is found by an examination of the most widely used educational publication of the ICMA's Municipal Management Series (commonly referred to as the Green Book Series, which first appeared in 1934). These green books for forty years have attempted to outline "the best" practices of the field of local government administration, covering such subjects as police administration, planning, fire protection, community health, and public works. The "flagship" of the green books has traditionally been *The Technique of Municipal Management.* In its last edition in 1958 its expressed purpose was "to define the job of management in municipal administration and to suggest techniques and practices which will help municipal officials." This book, as its title suggested, was something of a how-to-do-it manual for city managers, and its chapters enumerated many of the best techniques for efficient internal management of local administration, including sections on: "Techniques of Directions," "Programming Municipal Services," "Administrative Planning and Research," and "Administrative Measurement."

The 1974 edition of this book, edited by James M. Banovetz of Northern Illinois University, was retitled *Managing the Modern City,* and adopts a much broader perspective of the subject for training practitioners. Drawing on the last two decades of organization theory, decision making, and human relations, the new edition attempts to relate modern social science research to the practical world of municipal affairs. In contrast to the 1958 edition, representative chapters cover such topics as: "The City: Forces of Change," "Environment and Role of the Administrator," "Decision Making," "Leadership Styles and Strategies," "Administrative Communication," and "Administrative Analysis." New emphasis is placed on computer technologies and intergovernmental relations, as well as PPBS. Clearly in the years that transpired between this book's 1958 and 1974 revisions, the vertical and horizontal dimensions of city management values and interests were considerably broadened and extended.

3. Despite the growth of the city management field and its ever-widening concerns, city managers remain a fairly small, homogeneous occupational group with a strong small town–suburban orientation.

City managers as a social group from their very beginnings have shown consistent homogeneous social patterns: white, male, in their early forties, middle-class, Protestant. Their incomes have grown over the years (currently averaging $19,962 per year) and their remuneration compares favorably with other professionals today—the average lawyer now earns $22,000 and a school superintendent $20,000.[10] But blacks, women, young, or religious minorities are found only in token numbers in the city management field. The heavily suburban, small-town setting in which most manager plans function is one of the chief causes for the small numbers of minorities by comparison to other professional groups.[11]

4. Managers increasingly are better trained with less engineering-oriented education, combining both an "administrative generalist" and "specialist" background.

Managers have always been a well-educated group of men. Even in 1934, Ridley and Nolting reported 64 percent of them held baccalaureate degrees; in 1975 an ICMA survey showed 76 percent having bachelors degrees, and 48 percent of these had masters degrees.[12] An even higher percentage of their assistants (86 percent) today have baccalaureate degrees. In recent years there has been a noticeable shift, however, away from engineering as the preferred preparation for city management. In 1934, 77 percent of managers held bachelor degrees in engineering, but today that figure is only 18 percent, with 34 percent of modern managers majoring in political science or government and 78 percent of those who hold masters degrees obtaining them in the field of public administration. Today only 3 percent of managers' advanced degrees are in engineering.

A generalist management background in public administration seems now to be the preferred training for the field and also may be an indication for the reduced demands on the part of city councils for technicians as opposed to administrative generalists. Most managers now cite the more administrative generalist educational areas as being the most useful job preparation for city management, particularly the fields of budgeting and finance, administration and organization theory, public relations, and personnel. Also, informal specialization in narrow skill categories of solid waste removal, collective bargaining, or grantsmanship is found among many managers. Increasingly, a generalist administrative education coupled with "skill specialties learned on-the-job" seems to be the most common training background for city management. No doubt, the advanced degree gives the practitioner a professional image while the on-the-job training gives the pragmatic skills for coping with daily hazards of occupational survival.

5. While there is still no prescribed professional career pattern in city management, informal common career patterns have developed that seem to prefer the "in-and-outer" administrative generalist.

Statistics show career patterns informally have developed in the city management field. Most managers take their first jobs in the field in their late twenties or early thirties, frequently after working as an assistant city manager or with a consulting firm in city management. Their average local government service is thirteen years, while their average tenure in a single city is five years. More than a third of the managers today were alerted to the field by college or graduate training, and another third by a job after school.

Generally, most seem to "drift" into the field from many jobs, but primarily most have been experienced administrators prior to becoming city managers: 29 percent had some previous experience in government service, 47 percent had prior business administration experience, and 16 percent had some engineering background before taking their first job in the field. Unlike most careers, breadth of experience in different types of challenging administrative jobs in public and private agencies is encouraged, even preferred, and so city management remains one of the few "open fields" that a person can enter comparatively late in life without having been specifically trained. Indeed, many do take up city management as a second career after service in the military or private industry.

6. *Managers see themselves as "career professionals," though not all are "careerists."*

Surveys of managers emphasize that the chief perception they hold of themselves and their community roles places them squarely in the "professional category." While only 23 percent of managers view themselves as in an established profession like law or medicine, 75 percent see themselves as in a new professional field, akin to diplomacy or school superintendency. Less than 2 percent claim that their line of work is not professional at all. Moreover, they reflect an optimism about the future of their careers, with more than half believing that there will be increasing numbers of cities adopting city management form of government.[13]

However, recent surveys of managers also find that not all managers can be classed as "careerists" in their field. Only one-quarter of the managers spend most of their working careers as city managers. Better than one-half of the managers are more accurately classed as administrative generalists or "in-and-outers" moving into and out of city management from and to a wide variety of jobs in both business and government. A quarter of the managers must be categorized as "local appointees" or "hometown boys" who took the job because it was easily available to them. Local appointees by definition have no aspirations beyond the local horizons. The high percentage of in-and-outers and local appointees within city management is perhaps ultimately due to the political hazards, as Paul Ylvisaker aptly described: "A manager's job tenure is only secure until the next council meeting."

7. *The professional association of city managers, the International City Management Association (ICMA), has significantly broadened its outlook and scope of activities in recent years, but nonetheless, remains a weak voluntary association with little or no influence over the entrance, promotion, training standards, and ethical performance of individual city managers.*

In the late 1960s, the ICMA undertook several important reforms which were healthy as a whole for the urban management field: it moved its national headquarters to Washington, DC, staffed its ranks with new leaders, enlarged its research and training programs, adopted a new code of ethics, and changed its name from "manager" to "management" association in order to include administrative professionals in the many related management fields of local government.[14] Yet, in spite of its intense new look of the last decade, the ICMA, unlike the American Bar Association or American Medical Association, exercises no control over the entrance or promotion into the field of city management. And while the ICMA has a code of ethics and publishes the popular Green Book Series, and *Public Management*, it enforces neither ethical nor educational standards for city managers.

The ICMA can recommend and indeed does actively encourage such standards, but the hiring and firing of managers remains squarely with independent local city councils across the nation. The limited extent to which managers are aware of any peer group influence in their field was demonstrated by a recent survey that asked managers to rank the top three city manager practitioners—few could even name one person.[15]

8. *Increasingly city managers seem to take an activist view of their community policy roles, but three variables—city size, politics, self-definition of leadership roles—largely seem to determine the extent and nature of a manager's policy activity.*

While Richard Childs and other early founders of the manager plan stressed "a neutral expert role" for the city manager, a number of community power studies written by political scientists over the last two decades seem to agree that the city managers today are not merely inconspicuous public administrators, but rather their empirical analyses conclude that managers play very influential roles in determining public politics within their respective communities.[16]

After a careful analysis of several council-manager cities in Florida, Gladys Kammerer and her associates found "no managers . . . who were not involved in making, shaping, or vetoing policy proposals." A similar study, conducted in North Carolina by B. James Kweder, pointed out that ". . . in many cities the city manager clearly emerges as a person who has the greatest influence on what is happening at every stage of the policy-making process." Aaron Wildavsky's *Leadership in a Small Town*, which examined decision making in Oberlin, Ohio, revealed that the city manager was frequently the central figure in determining the important outcome of community policy issues. Oliver P. Williams and Charles R. Adrian made similar observations in two out of the four Michigan cities they studied: "the city manager was the key leadership figure and policy innovator." Even surveys of managers themselves show a remarkable shift away from a view of themselves as neutral experts and toward a proactive policy involvement.[17]

While contemporary political scientists and surveys of managers' own views on their policy roles have concluded that managers are no longer merely neutral administrators, the extent and scope of a manager's policy-making role seem to be also very much influenced by three key variables. The first, as would be expected, city size, is an important factor determining a manager's policy involvement. Large city managers, because of the urban diversity and sizes of their city resources, are more inclined to be involved with broader, more abstract policy matters such as shaping the city budget, advising city councils, negotiating with unions, dealing with inter- and intra-governmental matters—policy issues akin to those of large corporation executives.

On the other hand, small town managers whose role involves more technical matters like parking, snow removal, sewer repair, and the like are involved more frequently with the mundane technical side of administration. Limited staff assistance and fewer resources force small town managers to solve on their own many diverse technical as well as nontechnical problems of communities. Like small businessmen, small city managers must not only make up their financial accounts, but also stock the store themselves.

The political environment of the community also decisively shapes the policy role that managers play in their communities. Edward C. Banfield and James Q. Wilson classed manager cities in five categories ranging from small homogeneous, "faction-free" cities to large, highly factionalized communities.[18] Those cities they found with a high degree of political conflict force managers frequently into roles of "negotiators" and "conflict resolvers," while the more homogeneous communities or those with the large stable majorities provide managers with greater consensus on policy matters and, therefore, give managers a freer hand in finding effective and efficient techniques for implementing agreed-upon goals.

As John Bollens and John Ries have pointed out,[19] managers tend to fare better in those homogeneous, growing communities as opposed to stable or declining cities with considerable political conflict. The former group of cities demand technical competence to cope with their growth, which is the premium stock-in-trade skill of managers, while the latter type of city, one enmeshed in continuous political combat, requires an able politician more versed in the arts of negotiation and compromise rather than efficient administration.

Ronald Loveridge, in his excellent role analysis of San Francisco Bay area city managers, emphasized a third important determinant influencing policy involvement among city managers: that is, self-definition of their own leadership role. Professor Loveridge's analysis found four classes of managers in terms of how they perceived themselves as "activists" in their policy roles in communities:[20]

A. *Political Leaders* who take the broadest view of their policy role and see themselves as idea men and change agents in communities. These managers espouse a political readiness to act as plaintiffs for good government and the public interest.

B. *Political Executives*. This group of managers believes they should be policy innovators and leaders yet they are less willing to stick their necks out in pushing councilmen toward major policy decisions. They take a more pragmatic and less moralistic view of their political roles as managers.

C. *Administrative Directors* are convinced that managers should actively participate in the policy process but, nevertheless, they articulate a reluctance to be a novel administrator or open community leader. They tend to be preoccupied with the art of the possible, stressing the constraints and the problems, the council's authority as opposed to the manager's expertise.

D. *Administrative Technicians* define their policy roles within the narrowest context with a focus on administrative or housekeeping functions. They see themselves as staff advisors who are clearly subordinate to city councils and rather than proposing or instituting changes, they view themselves as curators of the established goals.

Professor Loveridge's fourfold classification of the self-perceptions of management leadership roles influences very directly the breadth or narrowness of the managers' goals, strategies, and results which they expect to achieve in community government. Loveridge argues the "political leader-type" frequently has the best contemporary education in public administration and exhibits great willingness to introduce new ideas for making broad city improvement projects by openly soliciting or "playing politics" with council members for their votes on various issues. At the other extreme, Professor Loveridge points up that "administrative technicians" have very often limited formal managerial training and are more inclined to view their own roles in communities as strictly subservient to the city council's wishes. While city size is not found to be correlated with "type of managerial style," Professor Loveridge believes there may be a certain self-selection process that occurs, with cities seeking out managers and managers seeking out cities most compatible to their own particular favored style of public management.

Taking Stock of the Occupation

What can be said about city manager professionalism from the standpoint of the foregoing summary of current statistical and social trends in city management? Can managers be classed as "professionals" or not? What are attributes that favor as well as prevent ranking city management as a professional career? Table 2.2 shows them to have a foot on both sides of the fence.

Table 2.2 should emphasize clearly that city managers are different from other public professionals. They have developed into a clear-cut occupational field as administrative generalists in city management—but they are a Janus-faced occupation that looks simultaneously in the directions of "professionalism" with its peer group–defined norms of expertise and behavior as well as being very much in politics with primary orientation toward and demands for community responsiveness and accountability.

Managers cannot totally embrace either role of professional or politician. If managers became neutral experts without reference to the political facts of life, they would jeopardize their own survival, but if they became politicians without responsible knowledge or expertise in urban affairs, they [would] jeopardize their credibility and worth to the public they serve. In short, managers cautiously and continuously tread a middle ground between the two poles of politics and expertise.

Table 2.2

[Professional and Nonprofessional Attributes of City Managers]

Attributes favoring professional status	Attributes favoring nonprofessional or political status
General influence on American life Significant and growing in terms of numbers of managers/CAOs with increasing job responsibilities	"Dispersing authority" due to increased participation of federal/state action in local government and new minority/union participation
Ethos and outlook Outlook characteristically of an administrative generalist	Exercise of administrative/leadership skills highly dependent upon and subject to shifting political nature of community life, causing the bulk of managers to be "in-and-outers"
Informal social background of managers Homogeneous/middle-class occupation with professional-level salary	Social make-up of city management, especially influenced by parochial small town, suburban political pressures
General educational preparation Survey shows increasing college/graduate educational preparation	No required degree or certification to obtain employment
Core skills necessary on the job Informally favors administrative generalist background with preference for skills of budgeting, personnel, and management, as well as newer specialties like energy conservation or federal grantsmanship (which depends on needs of individual communities)	No skills specified by law for employment
Career patterns An informal route of career advancement developing for many managers through assistant managerships, consulting work, business, or related government careers	None legally or formally specified
Lifetime occupation Possibility for all managers	The bulk of managers are "in-and-outers"—moving across a broad range of comparable administrative-type jobs
Self-perception of occupation Most managers see themselves akin to public professional groups like diplomats or school superintendents	Less than one-quarter of managers believe that they are "an established profession" like law or medicine
Peer-group influence of professional association—the ICMA The ICMA informally promotes professional and ethical codes of conduct through training programs, meetings, and publications	No formal control by the professional elite or professional association relative to entrance, work standards, promotions in profession, nor does ICMA attempt to enforce an ethical code of behavior on the practitioner; employment of manager remains subject to local council's decision
Degree of professional autonomy in relation to politics and community affairs Classic theory of the manager plan as well as most manager charters view managers as neutral experts in municipal affairs	Reality of management role deeply affected by nature and distribution of community politics; extent and scope of manager involvement in policy leadership is influenced by (1) community size, (2) degree of political conflict, and (3) self-definition of leadership styles
Conflict or possible competition with other professional groups In theory managers are viewed as the chief professional administrator in charge of various professional services	In reality possibilities exist for wide array of conflict with community professional as well as minority and union groups

The Future of the City Manager: As an Envoy of the Potomac?

What does the future hold for the city management field? If the past seventy years of unabated growth of the "manager phenomenon" is any guide to the future, the prominence and influence of city managers, individually and collectively, in the context of American community life will no doubt continue, even expand. The technological and social complexities of modern urban life increasingly require their specialized administrative talents in coping with the myriad of insistent problems like energy, pollution, crime, minority recruitment, urban planning, and mass transit. Moreover, as the local public sector is pressed urgently by citizen and federal government alike to deal with these kinds of problems, city managers and their counterparts—CAOs, county managers, town managers, city administrators—with their central and full-time responsibilities on the local scene for planning, budgeting, personnel selection, and advice to council will remain the indispensable link between the conceptualization and achievement of community goals.

At the same time, strong countervailing pressures in the opposite directions, away from the extended application of professional expertise, are at work in the city management field. Growing demands for widespread citizen participation, minority employment, and union involvement—in short, widening political representation—are constant pressures on city managers and urban government as a whole. Managers are now and will remain at the delicate fulcrum point where these fierce twin cross-pressures for both narrow expertise and wider citizen representation meet and are balanced.

Yet, on the horizon is the ominous and rapidly growing intergovernmental intrusion "from above" with which most managers (like most local public officials) must contend. Greater federal and state presence on the local scene unquestionably will mean an ever-increasing dispersal of the manager's real authority over internal community functions. Many managers already spend a third or more of their time on intergovernmental matters, and this percentage seems to be growing every year.

Our cultural mythology of "home rule" to the contrary, American city managers may indeed play at the present time a role more akin to the French Prefect in responsiveness to the national capitol's dictates and demands than we or even they care to imagine. Today Washington's "unseen hand" is as invisible and omnipresent as ever was Adam Smith's.

The hard fact is, so long as local government continues to ebb as an entity in the national structure of governance, for better or worse, we may expect managers in service more as envoys of the Potomac than of Peoria. And no doubt in response to this shifting locus of authority, the traditional twin images of the manager as "a professional helping hand" and "political hired hand" will have to be recast to fit the new political realities of this line of work. Certainly these future changes will demand a reappraisal of traditional managerial functions, educational preparation, career orientation, professional associations, and the like, though the old political mythology and verities of managers' roles changes slowly, if at all.

Notes

The author wishes to thank the following individuals who kindly took the time to review and comment on this chapter: Professor Ronald O. Loveridge, University of California, Riverside; David Arnold, director of publications, International City Management Association; David Bauer, chief administrative office, New Haven, Connecticut; James Buell, assistant city manager, Bakersfield, California; and Marjorie Sauer, assistant to the academic vice president, California State College. Vice President Phillip Wilder and Dean Richard Wallace at Cal State Bakersfield generously provided research and travel funding for the author's work.

1. It is important to emphasize at the outset the distinction between the "manager plan," which is essentially a theory of local government, and the "city manager," which is a recognized and established public service occupation. This chapter focuses principally on the latter subject though, of course, the "plan" and "occupation" are closely related.

2. In recent years the distinction between CAOs and managers in terms of their functions and authority has grown increasingly "fuzzy," and since the ICMA includes CAOs (along with "kindred spirits" like town managers, city business managers, etc.) now in their membership, this chapter also will lump them together within the city management field. For a separate discussion of CAOs, read Edwin O. Stene, "Historical Commentary," in *Public Management* (June 1973): 6; Charles R. Adrian, "Recent Concepts in Large City Management," in Edward C. Banfield (ed.), *Urban Government* (New York: Free Press, 1969); and James B. Hogan, *The Chief Administrative Officer* (Tucson: University of Arizona Press, 1976).

3. My unproven observation is that four very real pressures are constantly upon managers moving them in the direction of increased professionalism in terms of their work substance and attitudes: (1) greater numbers of higher educational institutions throughout the nation, specifically schools of public administration and public affairs, are turning out increasing numbers of students with professional administrative skills and outlook; (2) an increasing competition for a limited number of openings in the city management field helps to ensure a high quality "crop" of managers (particularly true in the tight white collar labor market today); (3) well-trained and upwardly mobile managerial staffs found in most middle-sized and large cities constantly press both expertise and professionalism upon managers; and (4) city managers' regional associations, perhaps even more than the national ICMA, serve informally as "professional informational exchanges" and a very important avenue for many managers in terms of keeping their professional expertise current.

Readers will note throughout my chapter that I back off from trying to define the actual substance of city management professionalism for in my view it leads into a hopeless semantic bog that is represented by the essay of Robert Kline and Paul Blanchard, "Professionalism and the City Manager: Examination of Unanswered Questions," *Midwest Review of Public Administration* (July 1973): 163–175.

4. Norton Long, "Politicians for Hire?" *Public Administration Review*, vol. 25 (June 1965), p. 119; Karl A. Bosworth, "The City Manager Is a Politician," *Public Administration Review*, vol. 18 (Summer 1958): 216–222; and for both a lively and more contemporary essay following this line of reasoning written by a city manager, read: William V. Donaldson, "Continuing Education for City Managers," *Public Administration Review*, vol. 33 (November/December 1973): 504–508. For an excellent insight into the role of city managers in the budgetary process, refer to Arnold J. Meltsner, *The Politics of City Revenue* (Berkeley: University of California Press, 1971), pp. 51–60.

5. For the unusual story of the development of the council-manager plan, read John Porter East, *Council-Manager Government: The Political Thought of Its Founder, Richard Childs* (Chapel Hill: University of North Carolina Press, 1965); and Richard J. Stillman II, *The Rise of the City Manager, A Public Professional in Local Government* (Albuquerque: University of New Mexico Press, 1974).

6. Don Price, "The Promotion of the City Manager Plan," *Public Opinion Quarterly* (Winter 1941): 570–571. There is considerable controversy in the historic literature over Childs's actual role in the development of the manager plan. Price terms Childs's role as "a manipulator of symbols"; Herbert Emmerich saw it as "an inventor of the plan"; but Childs liked to describe himself as the "minister" who performed the marriage between the commission and manager plans. My own view is that Richard Childs is best understood from the historic perspective as a child of the American Progressive Era and its reformist spirit.

7. There is an immense literature on this subject. Perhaps one of the best and most thoughtful analyses of this issue is found in Clarence E. Ridley, *The Role of the City Manager in Policy Formulation* (Chicago: International City Managers' Association, 1958). For more current views of this subject, read Arnold J. Meltsner; Timothy A. Almy, "City Managers, Public Avoidance, and Revenue Sharing," *Public Administration Review*, vol. 33, no. 1 (January/February 1977): 19–27; and Robert P. Boynton and Deil S. Wright, "Mayor-Manager Relationships in Large Council-Manager Cities: A Reinterpretation," *Public Administration Review*, vol. 31, no. 1 (January/February 1971): 28–35.

8. See Stillman, p. 73. For the high degree of general satisfaction with this field by its practitioners even among those who leave city management altogether, read Fremont J. Lyden and Ernest G. Miller, "Why City Managers Leave the Profession: A Longitudinal Study in the Pacific Northwest," *Public Administration Review*, vol. 36, no. 2 (March/April 1976): 175–181.

9. Sali and Walt Damon-Ruty, "Former Taft City Manager Tells Viewpoints," *The Bakersfield Californian* (March 10, 1977), p. 33. I realize that this issue of the dispersal of authority of city managers and of all public professionals in general is an important subject that deserves considerably more attention than I have given it.

Certainly the subject deserves book-length treatment rather than a few paragraphs. In my view one of the best books to date to treat this subject in relationship to cities as a whole is Norton Long, *The Unwalled City: Reconstituting the Urban Community* (New York: Basic Books, 1971).

10. Survey data drawn from the following sources: Laurie S. Frankel and Carol A. Pigeon, *Municipal Managers and Chief Administrative Officers, A Statistical Profile, Urban Data Service Reports,* vol. 7, no. 2 (Washington, DC: International City Management Association, February 1975); Richard J. Stillman, chap. 4; *Directory of Recognized Local Governments, 1977* (Washington, DC: ICMA, 1977); *The Directory of Assistants* (Washington, DC: ICMA, 1977); and Robert Huntley and Robert MacDonald, "Urban Managers: Organizational Preferences, Managerial Styles and Social Policy Roles," *Municipal Yearbook* (Washington, DC: ICMA, 1975), pp. 149–159.

11. No large city over 500,000 (except Cleveland) has ever adopted the manager plan, and Cleveland threw it out after two years. Several manager plan communities, though, adopted it prior to growing over 500,000. Most large cities like New York, San Francisco, and New Orleans have opted instead for vesting administrative authority in a CAO or deputy mayor. Perhaps large-city municipal problems are less administrative and more political, so voters prefer to have a strong mayor "on top" and an administrator "on tap" rather than the reverse under manager government. The classic debate over the application of the manager plan to large cities appeared in the pages of the *Public Administration Review* between Wallace S. Sayre, "The General Manager Idea for Large Cities," vol. 14 (Autumn 1954): 253–258 and John E. Bebout, "Management for Large Cities," vol. 15 (Summer 1955): 188–195.

12. Clarence Ridley and Orin Nolting, *The City Manager Profession* (Chicago: University of Chicago Press, 1934). Also for good early statistics on city managers, see Joseph Cohen, "The City Manager as a Profession," *National Municipal Review* (July 1924): 391–411. Certainly the most significant determinant of managerial selection are the attitudes and preferences of city councilmen. For one of the best discussions of this subject, read Efraim Torogovnik, *Determinants in Managerial Selection* (Washington, DC: ICMA, 1969). In the Torogovnik study public administration ranked first as the preferred background of managers by councilmen, with business administration and engineering second and third respectively.

13. Here I can be criticized for sidestepping the whole issue of what constitutes city manager professionalism, but as I pointed out in note 3, in my view one enters a hopeless semantic bog when one attempts to define this term. The important point I feel is that most managers believe themselves to be professionals, even though the substance of their professionalism has never been adequately defined.

14. For an extended account of the significant changes that have occurred within the ICMA during the last decade, read Stillman, chap. 3. I must also emphasize that I do not want to leave the impression from this chapter that the ICMA is totally impotent with regard to enforcement of professional standards; indeed, from time to time it does expel members for the most flagrant violations of its professional code of conduct. For a recent case of expulsion, see *ICMA Newsletter* (February 28, 1977), p. 1. Nevertheless, I feel my point still stands that ultimate authority for enforcement of professional standards rests not with the ICMA but local city councils.

15. Stillman, p. 74.

16. For the rather complex evolution of thinking on this subject over the last seventy years, refer to Stillman, ibid., chaps. 1–3. I should qualify this point somewhat by pointing out that while "the early founders" like Childs did stress a neutral role for managers, the early managers hardly approached their work in a neutral manner. Indeed, not handicapped by federal or state guidelines and mandates as are modern city managers, early managers probably exercised considerably more control over internal city matters and were not hesitant to exercise very broad policy initiatives over many areas of city activities, see particularly the early chapters of Leonard White, *The City Manager* (Chicago: University of Chicago Press, 1926). Today perhaps the real change is that the managers' own view of their policy roles (as reflected by the ICMA's Code of Conduct) better reflects their actual community policy involvement. The paradox today may be that this proactive ideology may vastly overestimate their real power and authority over community affairs, given their general "dispersal of authority."

17. The results of the Stillman survey of city managers, pp. 73–74, contrasts sharply on this subject by comparison with the 1934 Ridley and Nolting survey.

18. Edward C. Banfield and James Q. Wilson, *City Politics* (New York: Vintage, 1963), pp. 168–186.

19. John C. Bollens and John C. Ries, *The City Manager Profession: Myths and Realities* (Chicago: Public Administration Service, 1969). More recently, the Bollens–Ries thinking has been refined further by Cortus T. Koehler in "Policy and Legislative Oversight in Council-Manager Cities," *Public Administration Review,* vol. 33, no. 5 (September/October 1973): 433–441. Koehler divides councilmanic policy oversight into three types: "average," "blind faith," and "politician," and depending on the composition of these type of councilmen in the makeup of any council, the degree of managerial autonomy over policy issues is thus determined.

20. Ronald O. Loveridge, *City Managers in Legislative Politics* (Indianapolis: Bobbs-Merrill, 1971). Unquestionably the Loveridge book is one of the best on city managers to appear in recent years. Timothy A. Almy, "Local-Cosmopolitanism and U.S. City Managers," *Urban Affairs Quarterly* (March 1975): 243–272, is an interesting and useful essay that builds further upon Loveridge's typology by utilizing Gouldner and Merton's localism-cosmopolitanism concepts. Professor Almy demonstrates empirically how the local versus cosmopolitan backgrounds of managers significantly shape their policy roles.

Further Reading

The two outstanding classics on the city manager and the city manager plan, which are still useful in terms of providing historical perspectives on the development of the city management field, are Leonard White's *The City Manager* (1926) and Harold Stone, Don Price, and Catherine Stone, *City Manager Government in the United States* (1940). Two interesting early statistical surveys of managers are found in Joseph Cohen's "The City Manager as a Profession," *National Municipal Review* (July 1924); and Clarence Ridley and Orin Nolting, *The City Manager Profession* (1934). For the best current surveys on contemporary city managers, read Ronald O. Loveridge, *City Managers and Legislative Politics* (1971); John Bollens and John Ries, *The City Manager Profession: Myths and Realities* (1969); and Richard Stillman, *The Rise of the City Manager: A Public Professional in Local Government* (1974), John Porter East's *Council Manager Government: The Political Thought of Its Founder, Richard Childs* (1965) is the most authoritative and thorough analysis to date of Childs's thought, ideas, and involvement with the development of the manager plan.

CHAPTER 3

THE MAYOR AS A POLICY LEADER IN THE COUNCIL-MANAGER FORM OF GOVERNMENT:

A View from the Field

NELSON WIKSTROM

Textbook descriptions of the role of the mayor in the council-manager form of municipal government invariably describe the mayor's role in a titular and restrictive fashion. One widely adopted text states: "There is often . . . a mayor, who performs ceremonial functions as head of the local government. He may preside at meetings of the council, represent the city on public occasions, and sign legal documents for the city."[1] Another notes: "The mayor or president of the city or village normally performs only ceremonial functions and presides over the council. He has no administrative powers except in the case of an emergency, and no vote."[2] In a similar appraisal, a third text states: "There is often a presiding officer for the city council who is given the title of mayor. He is a regular voting member of the council but usually possesses no more administrative authority than any other council member; he simply presides at meetings. The only other functions of the mayor are ceremonial."[3] These descriptions of the mayor's role are in accordance with the role recommended for the mayor by the National Municipal League, the most forceful advocate of the council-manager plan, in its *Model City Charter:* "The mayor shall preside at meetings of the council, shall be recognized as head of the city government for all ceremonial purposes and by the governor for purposes of military law but shall have no administrative duties."[4]

I would like to advance the proposition that the aforementioned descriptions of the mayor's role are undiscerning, simplistic, and represent undue generality, for each fails to acknowledge that the mayor may play an aggressive policy-making leadership role. Three basic factors appear paramount in accounting for why authors of municipal government and politics textbooks have commonly failed to portray the mayor's role in a more expansive fashion. Undoubtedly the usual limited and perfunctory formal duties assigned to the mayor by most municipal charters, that of serving as a titular spokesman for the city and presiding over council sessions, have structured the nature of the descriptions advanced. Reflective of the theoretical underpinnings of the plan, few council-manager charters specifically assign broad policy or administrative responsibilities to the mayor. Second, initial and present day advocates of the plan have emphasized that policy-making is the collective enterprise of a council, with the mayor exercising no leadership role in any particular singular fashion. Finally, textbook descriptions of the role of the mayor in the

From *Public Administration Review*, vol. 39, no. 3 (May/June 1979), pp. 270–276. Copyright © 1979 by American Society for Public Administration. Reprinted with permission.

council-manager form of government have remained consistent over the years simply because the mayor's role has not been the object of much systematic empirical inquiry.

Although there is a relative lack of past research concerned with the subject, a few studies have investigated, either directly or obliquely, the mayor's role and the resultant findings serve to challenge the belief that the mayor plays no leadership role. Charles Adrian found in his examination of governmental leadership and decision making in three middle-size (50,000–80,000) council-manager cities in Michigan that although the mayor usually was "no more likely to serve as a policy leader than is any other councilman"[5] this was not true in one community where the mayor did exercise a leadership role.[6] Edward C. Banfield and James Q. Wilson postulate in their typology of council-manager relations that in some communities political realities force the mayor to take the initiative on policy matters both within the council and before the public.[7] Gladys Kammerer discerned in her investigation of city manager tenure in Florida that the mayor's role is significantly enlarged if he (she) is directly elected. Mindful of her findings, Kammerer recommended that, in order to ensure that the basic tenets of the plan are not violated, mayors be chosen by their council colleagues.[8] Drawing a somewhat contrary conclusion, David A. Booth, as a result of his investigation into the operation of council-manager government in small cities, maintains that it is preferable for the mayor to be popularly elected since this might well serve to increase the political acceptability of the plan and voter turnout.[9] Jeffrey Pressman found in his review of past mayoral leadership (or lack thereof), in the council-manager administered city of Oakland, California, that the role of the mayor varied, in a restrictive or expansive fashion, according to the personality of the mayor and the extent to which he determinately engaged in "pyramiding" his resources, such as formal position and powers, prestige, and saliency, on behalf of leadership and influence.[10] Finally, one is reminded of the central leadership role of the mayor of Oberlin, Ohio, as portrayed by Aaron Wildavsky in his work *Leadership in a Small Town*.[11]

The most systematic investigation concerning the mayor's role in the council-manager form of government was carried out by Robert Boynton and Deil Wright, as part of their larger inquiry into mayor-manager relationships. On the basis of data tabulated from questionnaires sent to the managers of forty-five cities with populations in excess of one hundred thousand and a subsequent discussion held with a smaller number, Boynton and Wright concluded in regard to the mayor's role: "The behavior of the mayors as governmental leaders . . . varies considerably from the model and from legal prescriptions."[12] Elaborating upon their findings they observed:

> The major differences between the mayor as imagined and the mayor as an active institution in contemporary urban life are not to be found in the differences between formal power and its informal exercises. The differences are to be found, rather, in the consequences for leadership that flow from the position of mayor and from the exercise of these powers— whether formal or informal.[13]

The aforementioned findings suggest that we have been wedded to a description of the mayor's role in the council-manager form derived primarily from formal charter provisions and the normative requirements of the plan's proponents, rather than from empirical observation and experience. As Boynton and Wright figuratively state:

> The images of the offices of the American mayor and the city manager found in the literature of public administration and political science are related to the realities of those offices in much the same way as Smokey the Bear is related to the grizzly bear of the Northwest. The literary figures are benign, simplified caricatures of complex and not completely tamable realities.[14]

We need to gain a better understanding of the mayor's role in order to assess better the appropriateness and future viability of the council-manager form, and especially its resourcefulness to respond to the demands of complex urban political life.[15] This concern is underscored by the fact that the council-manager plan is presently utilized by 47 percent of all municipalities in the United States with populations in excess of 10,000, with the preponderance of communities between 25,000 to 500,000 employing the plan.[16]

We can posit that the mayor's role in any one community is the product of demographic, institutional or structural, political, and personal factors. Demographic variables include population size and the prevailing degree of ethnic and political conflict. Evidence indicates that mayors in large communities, with their usual heterogeneous population base and broad array of political interests, play a more significant political role in managing political conflict and reconciling competing political demands, than their counterparts in smaller localities. Institutional or structural variables include: the electoral arrangements by which the mayor gains office—whether directly elected by the citizenry or chosen by council colleagues; the length of the mayor's tenure of office and opportunity to seek an additional term; and formal entrusted duties, responsibilities, and privileges of the mayor, including the right to vote and the exercise of the veto power. For example, some scholars such as Kammerer, stress that the mayor who is directly elected by the citizenry enjoys greater power and influence, than those chosen by their council colleagues.[17] Further, from a formalistic perspective, it is reasonable to infer that a mayor who enjoys the prerogative to veto legislation passed by council has more than an equal role in the policy-making process. Political variables which serve to structure the role of the mayor include: the desire to seek reelection or higher elective office, and the resultant need to maintain or gain additional political support; the relationship with council colleagues and the manager; and the involvement in local partisan political activity. In addition, the role of the mayor is shaped by the nature of the issues before council and the configuration of a community political power. Finally, the mayor's role is a function of his or her personal attributes, the desire to exercise political leadership, and the manner in which the mayor defines his or her role.

Focus and Methodology of This Study

This study examines the role of city mayors in Virginia, where the council-manager plan has long enjoyed a favored position. The city of Staunton retained the first manager in 1908 and in the succeeding years *all* forty-one cities in the state have adopted the plan. This investigation did not attempt to assess the impact of all factors which appear to be instrumental in shaping the role of the mayor, but rather it was confined to setting forth an explanation of the mayor's role as a function of selected aspects of the above stated demographic, structural, political, and personal variables: (1) the kinds of individuals, in terms of socioeconomic attributes, who serve as mayors; (2) reasons mayors advance for seeking the office; (3) the manner in which mayors define and implement their role; (4) formal and informal sources of mayoral power; (5) role expectations of the mayor held by members of council; (6) mayor-manager relationships; (7) citizen demands made of mayors, and (8) miscellaneous factors. A twofold methodology was utilized. Initially an examination was made of all municipal charters to ascertain the method by which the mayors are selected and the extent of their formal powers and duties. Second, interviews were sought with each of the forty-one city mayors and managers. Interviews with mayors were designed to elicit data on their socioeconomic attributes, the extent to which and why each sought the office, how each defined and carried out his or her role, and the manner and extent to which each interacted with the manager. Interviews with managers focused on their relationships with their respective mayors and their perspectives of their mayor's role. A total of thirty-two mayors and a like number of managers were interviewed representing a completion rate of 78 percent.[18] Four of the mayors and four of the managers interviewed held office in core cities located in metropolitan (SMSA) areas, seven mayors and seven managers held office in suburban cities, while the remaining twenty-one mayors and an equal number of managers were situated in small independent cities. The population size of these communities is as follows: five between 100,000–250,000; three between 50,000–100,000; four between 25,000–50,000; eleven between 10,000–25,000; while the remaining nine communities have populations ranging from 5,000–10,000. As the above data substantiates, the overwhelming number of mayors and managers interviewed in this study were office holders in either medium or small cities.[19]

Mayors: A Socioeconomic and Political Profile

Mayors were, for the most part, well-educated, white, married males of middle age drawn from the business and professional ranks of the community and predominately identified with the Democratic Party. Specifically, of the thirty-two mayors interviewed, only three were black males and two were white females. By age grouping, 78 percent were between forty and fifty-nine, 19 percent were over sixty, and one person was under thirty. In the aggregate, mayors were better educated than the general population. No less than 56 percent graduated from an institution of higher learning. Of this number, a majority (55 percent) further obtained an advanced academic or professional degree. It is of note, however, that the formal education of 41 percent of the mayors did not exceed the high school level, and one mayor never attended either elementary or secondary school. About 47 percent of the mayors were involved in business enterprise, while 35 percent were professionals, serving as doctors, dentists, educators, or lawyers. Somewhat surprising was the fact that only four, or about 13 percent, were lawyers. Occupational positions of a semiskilled variety were held by 10 percent, and another 10 percent were retired. Exactly half of the mayors were Democrats, 16 percent were Republicans, while the remaining 34 percent indicated no partisan preference. The preponderance of mayors who were Democrats reflected the traditional Democratic loyalties of Virginia.

In summary, Virginia mayors basically share the socioeconomic and political attributes of their counterparts throughout the nation, although in the aggregate they are more oriented toward the Democratic Party.[20] Even though one cannot establish a determinate relationship, the socioeconomic characteristics of Virginia mayors and the array of personal skills associated with these characteristics, particularly those acquired from an extensive amount of formal education, are the kinds of skills which would seem to be required to assume a role of political leadership. It is significant, in terms of political recruitment, that the largest segment of mayors were gainfully employed in business while a paucity of mayors were lawyers, in contrast to the usual dominant position of the latter group in state legislatures and Congress.[21]

Tenure and Quest for Office

The procedure by which Virginia mayors gain office and their term of office vary. In thirty municipalities, of which only three conduct their elections on a partisan basis, mayors are chosen by their council colleagues and serve a two-year term. In eleven cities the mayor is directly elected; in only two of these are mayoral candidates identified by party label. Most directly elected mayors serve a four-year term; however, in one locality the tenure of office is three years while in another it is two years. All mayors may seek unlimited terms of office.

Sixty-nine percent, or twenty-two of the mayors were in their first term, 16 percent in their second, while the balance were serving their third or more terms of office. The large segment of first-term mayors reflects the tendency of rotating the position of mayor among council members in those localities where the mayor is chosen by his or her colleagues. Sixteen mayors, including seven directly elected, actively sought the office, while the others maintained that, responding to a sense of civic duty, they reluctantly agreed to serve after being prevailed upon by their council colleagues or other political associates. It is instructive to note the *primary* motivating reason advanced by those mayors who actively sought the office: 57 percent were desirous of exercising general political leadership or leadership on behalf of certain programmatic goals; 13 percent were eager to end factionalism and bring about a more unified council; 18 percent sought the office because of the prestige involved; while only 12 percent felt it was their civic duty to serve.

At the time each was interviewed, twenty-two of the thirty-two mayors had decided to seek an additional term of office. An overwhelming majority, 82 percent, were so inclined simply because they wished to retain a position of political leadership in order to ensure the realization of certain programmatic goals. Only 18 percent sought retention of their office for reasons relating to civic duty or prestige.

To summarize, a distinct majority (70 percent) of individuals in Virginia who either initially sought or wished to retain the office of mayor were motivated by their desire to exercise political leadership; a minority (30 percent) were primarily attracted by the ceremonial trappings of the position or felt it was their civic duty to serve. This is consistent with the finding of a nationwide investigation which found that few individuals seek the office of mayor because of the supposed prestige gained.[22] The position of mayor in Virginia cities is viewed by most of those who seek the office, or wish to retain it, as a central vantage point through which they can influence the policy process.

General Mayoral Leadership

Interviews with mayors substantiate the impression that the usual definition of the mayor's role as gleaned from charter provisions is excessively restrictive and fails to recognize the exercise of broad mayoral leadership. Sixty-nine percent of the managers stated that the role of the mayor is of greater significance than would be inferred from appropriate charter provisions. To a large degree this is the result of the way in which the mayor defined and implemented his or her role. As set forth in Table 3.1, 84 percent of the mayors perceived that their dominant role was that of providing political leadership for a single or multiple array of purposes. Only 16 percent restricted their role to that of presiding over council meetings and carrying out public representational duties. This normative conception that mayors entertain of their role in most instances is consistent with their overt political behavior: Exactly two-thirds of the managers assessed that the mayor functions as a political and policy leader, while only one-third relegated the mayor's role to that of a more circumscribed nature.

Reflective of their policy leadership role, two-thirds of the mayors, in addition to seeking the support of their council colleagues, actively sought public endorsement of favored projects or policies. These projects or policies most often involved downtown renewal or redevelopment, voter approval of bond referendums to provide funding for the extension of water and/or sewer lines, or the construction of a municipal facility. Mayors also sought public support for policies relating to recreation facilities and services, city-county merger or annexation, education, comprehensive local planning, and a variety of other concerns.

Table 3.1

Mayors: Dominant Normative Role (*N* = 32)

Role	Number	Percent of total
Provide political leadership/realize goals	8	25.0
Provide political leadership/relate government to citizenry	4	12.5
Provide leadership to council	4	12.5
Provide leadership to council/facilitate communication between council and manager/assure that manager is following council policy	11	34.0
Preside over council/represent the city	5	16.0

Although the formal powers of Virginia mayors are usually limited,[23] mayoral leadership is facilitated by a number of factors and developments. First, because mayors occupy a formal position they are the beneficiaries of status and authority denied to their council colleagues. As Richard Neustadt has written in a different, though not totally dissimilar context, status adds something to one's ability to persuade and exercise leadership.[24] Furthermore, in those eleven communities where the mayors are directly elected by the citizenry their status is even somewhat greater because of demonstrated popular support.

Second, mayoral leadership is given further impetus because most mayors, interpreting their role in an active-position fashion, devote an extensive amount of time to the office involving on the average about twenty hours per week, although some mayors expend a much greater amount of time. Given the fact that the office of mayor is usually formally set forth as only a part-time position the amount of time mayors apply to the office is considerable. Third, an overwhelming majority, specifically 84 percent, of the managers prefer that the mayor adopt an aggressive policy leadership position, rather than a more retiring and, hence, less involved role. On the whole, managers prefer a mayor who provides policy leadership and direction, and bears a strong sense of political responsibility for the resolution of controversial social issues confronting the community involving such matters as education and other human services; issues which are not commonly susceptible to a decision-making process largely based on managerial or technical consideration.

Fourth, because of the visibility of the mayor and widespread popular ignorance of the mechanics of the council-manager form, even in Virginia where the plan has enjoyed long and extensive utilization, citizens often direct their concerns about municipal services and requests for assistance to the mayor. It is in this sense that the mayor, usually far in excess of any other member of council, functions as a local ombudsman. Sixteen percent of the mayors spend more than ten hours per week listening to and dealing with citizens inquiries and complaints; 50 percent between three and ten hours, while only 34 percent report devoting less than three hours per week to this activity. Fifth, mayoral leadership is facilitated by the trend throughout Virginia of providing the mayor with an office in the city hall and some measure of assigned staff. Indeed, three mayors enjoy full-time personnel assistance. Sixth, the requirements of horizontal and vertical intergovernmental relations, especially involving grantsmanship, necessitates the interaction of the mayor and other political actors representing various components—local, regional, state, or national—of the federal system. In addition, mass media, especially the press and television, has made for more visible mayors; visibility that most mayors skillfully exploit on behalf of mayoral leadership and their pursuit of policy goals. Finally, and most significantly, mayors emerge as policy leaders because of their leadership role in council deliberations, a subject to which we now turn.

Mayoral Leadership of Council

Practically all Virginia mayors preside at council meetings and formally exercise a legislative role equal to that of their colleagues. However, this equalitarian perspective of the mayor's role in many communities conflicts with reality. Two-thirds of the mayors are of the view that their legislative role is of greater policy impact than as is suggested by the charter. The mayor's role in the legislative process is tactically recognized by about two-thirds of the managers who first informally discuss with the mayor a major issue before submitting a policy recommendation to the council.

Formal resources and procedural prerogatives facilitate mayoral leadership in the policy-making process. As Boynton and Wright remind us, the mayor "is not only a member of the council, he is its presiding officer with certain rights and duties in relation to the legislative process. . . ."[25] Similar to their colleagues, mayors have the right to vote, except for six directly elected mayors who may only vote in the case of an evenly divided council. Five popularly elected mayors may veto legislation, which can be overridden by a two-thirds vote of council. The mayor's duty of presiding over council sessions in conjunction with his or her involvement in the preparation of council agenda (66 percent of the mayors participate in agenda formulation) allows the mayor to advocate energetically his or her policy goals. In addition, these goals may be the subject of special council sessions which an overwhelming majority of mayors call on a rather frequent basis. Furthermore, where the council makes use of committees, the formal or customary power of the mayor to establish committees and designate their membership enables him or her to place in key positions like-minded political allies sharing similar policy goals.

In reality, informal considerations are of even greater import in ensuring the usual centrality of the mayor in the policy-making process. Mayors usually play a more influential role than their colleagues because of their prior council experience, greater awareness of issues, closer working relationships with the manager, and desire to exercise leadership. Moreover, in any group situation someone must undertake the leadership role and especially in those communities where the mayors are chosen by their council colleagues, the mayor, as Arthur Bromage noted some years ago, is the most logical person,[26] to fulfill this role.

Congruent with their legislative leadership stance, practically all mayors take the lead in promoting consensus when the council is divided over policy matters. In addition, two-thirds of the mayors perceive that council members substantially rely upon their advice when voting on major policy issues, an assessment which does not appear to be overly excessive if the perceptions of managers are taken into account. When queried on the policy leadership role of mayors, two-thirds of the managers sensed that council members usually followed the policy posture of the mayor and one-quarter of the managers even went as far as to state that the mayor *dominates* the policy-making process. The mayor's legislative leadership role is only supplanted in those instances where another member of council has developed or possesses particular policy expertise or undermined when the council is divided by permanent factions. Finally, 56 percent of the mayors believe that they are primarily responsible for ensuring that the manager is implementing the policies of council. Investing the mayor with this responsibility enhances his or her stature in the policy-making process.

Concluding Commentary

A majority of mayors in Virginia, irrespective of charter provisions, function as policy leaders through their mobilization of formal and informal resources of power. Only a minority of mayors fit the usual description advanced by textbooks or urban government and politics. The precise

Table 3.2

Mayors: Average Weekly Contact Times with Manager[a] (N = 32)

Contact times per week	Number of cases
Daily	20
Four times	6
Three times	2
Twice	3
Once	1

Note: [a]Exclusive of formal and informal council meetings.

role of each mayor is determined by the manner in which he or she defines and implements his or her role, the role of other political actors, and overall political circumstances. On the basis of this study it seems reasonable to assume that many mayors throughout the United States functioning in the council-manager framework exercise strong policy leadership.

The exercise of mayoral leadership does have some important implications for the council-manager form of government. Suffice it to say, managers are required to adopt a posture which is appreciative of and congruent with an expansive mayoral role. The viability of the plan in any community is, at least, partially dependent upon the success to which the mayor and manager, without negating the importance of council generally, establish a productive working relationship. In a sense, council-manager government has evolved into teamwork governance; mayors and managers need and depend upon each other. This mutual interdependence is clearly underscored by the data contained in Table 3.2 setting forth the average weekly frequency with which the mayor converses with the manager either in person or over the phone, apart from council meetings. This extensive amount of mayor-manager interaction occurs for several reasons. On the one hand, these usual daily exchanges are partially due to the legislative oversight responsibilities of the mayor and they allow him or her to ascertain if the manager is faithfully implementing the policies adopted by the council. On the other hand, these media relate to the mayor's advisory function of setting forth and interpreting for the manager the political mood of the council and the larger community. It should be noted, however, that this mayor-manager contract is not a recent development but one which has, because of the increasing importance of local government and the needs of mayors and managers, evolved [as] more vital. As long ago as 1939 Harold C. Stone, Don K. Price, and Kathryn H. Stone in their assessment of the city manager government of Lynchburg, Virginia, noted the unique relationship then prevailing between the mayor and the manager:

> The present mayor, for example, devotes some time each day to city business, usually spending an hour or two around noon at the city hall. He personally looks over improvements that the manager is recommending, usually on Sunday afternoon, in order to be well informed about them. He may personally advise the manager on matters such as the policy of collecting delinquent taxes, or participate in the work of committees that guide the development of other policies. He thinks of his job as twofold: to keep an eye on the work of the manager for the council so as to lead the discussion on the manager's recommendations; and to be a public relations adviser to the manager, warning him about the attitude of the public in matters of policy.[27]

Second, mayoral leadership has further undermined that cardinal principle of the plan which stresses the sharp distinction between policy making and administration. In a general sense the distinction was always artificial, since, as Paul Appleby and Dwight Waldo have reminded us, policy making and administration are part and parcel of a whole approach, often difficult to distinguish one from the other.[28] We have long recognized that the manager is an integral, if not dominant, actor in the policy-making process; this study suggests that we must also acknowledge that mayors often acting on behalf of solicitous councils seeking information about the implementation and success of a policy, not uncommonly will involve themselves in broadly defined administrative, managerial, or personnel matters. Ordinarily, Virginia mayors do not limit their discussions with managers to narrowly defined policy matters. Similarly, Boynton and Wright found that in one-quarter to one-third of the cities in their survey the mayor operated in the bureaucratic arena.[29]

Finally, we may conclude that the emergence of mayors as policy leaders in the council-manager form is, on balance, a positive development. Assertive mayoral leadership may serve to correct the perceived imbalance of executive-legislative relations in the plan with the mayor serving as a countervailing force to the manager in the policy process. In addition, by mayors exercising a more visible and significant role this serves to render the plan more "democratic" (making it resemble a skew version of the mayor-council with a chief administrative officer form), thus raising the possibility that the council-manager form will be utilized by a greater proportion of "unreformed" large cities, where its employment has been limited.

Notes

I wish to acknowledge that funding for this study was provided by the Committee for the Grants-in-Aid Program for Faculty, Virginia Commonwealth University.

1. Robert L. Lineberry and Ira Sharkansky, *Urban Politics and Public Policy*, 2d ed. (New York: Harper and Row, 1974), p. 110.

2. Charles R. Adrian and Charles Press, *Governing Urban America*, 3d ed. (New York: McGraw-Hill, 1968), pp. 204–205.

3. William S. Schultz, *Urban and Community Politics* (North Scituate, MA: Duxbury Press, 1974), p. 272.

4. National Municipal League, *Model City Charter*, 6th ed. (New York: The League, 1964), p. 6.

5. Charles R. Adrian, "Leadership and Decision-Making in Manager Cities," *Public Administration Review* 18 (Summer 1958): 213.

6. Ibid., p. 210.

7. Edward C. Banfield and James Q. Wilson, *City Politics* (New York: Vintage Books, 1966), p. 178.

8. Gladys M. Kammerer, "Role Diversity of City Managers," *Administrative Science Quarterly* 8 (March 1964): 442.

9. David A. Booth, "Are Elected Mayors a Threat to Managers?" *Administrative Science Quarterly* 12 (March 1968): 589.

10. Jeffrey L. Pressman, "Preconditions of Mayoral Leadership," *American Political Science Review* 66 (June 1972): 511–528.

11. Aaron Wildavsky, *Leadership in a Small Town* (Totowa, NJ: Bedminister Press, 1964), especially pp. 236–252.

12. Robert Paul Boynton and Deil S. Wright, "Mayor-Manager Relationships in Large Council-Manager Cities: A Reinterpretation," *Public Administration Review* 31 (January/February 1971): 29.

13. Ibid.

14. Ibid., p. 28.

15. One is reminded of the now classic exchange between Wallace Sayre and John Bebout concerning the applicability of the council-manager plan for large core cities which appeared in the *Public Administration Review* over twenty years ago. See Wallace Sayre, "The General Manager Idea for Large Cities," *Public Administration Review* 14 (Autumn 1954): 253–258; and John E. Bebout, "Management for Large Cities," *Public Administration Review* 15 (Summer 1955): 188–195.

16. Specifically the percentage of cities arranged according to population size utilizing the council-manager form of government is as follows:

Population size	Percent of cities employing council-manager form
Under 10,000	29
10,000–24,999	37
25,000–49,999	66
50,000–99,999	70
100,000–249,999	69
250,000–499,999	54
500,000–999,999	28
1,000,000 and above	0

Note: The above data was derived from information contained in *The Municipal Yearbook 1978.* See International City Management Association, *The Municipal Yearbook 1978* (Washington, DC: The Association, 1978), p. xiii.

17. Kammerer, op. cit., p. 426.

18. These interviews were completed in 1976–77.

19. Although the findings reported in this study are primarily derived from interviews with mayors and managers holding office in small- and medium-size cities this does not necessarily restrict the implications of these findings to such situated cities. As David A. Booth notes: "As an existing and integral element of twentieth century life, the small unit of government holds special interest for the social scientist, particularly when it is capable of demonstrating, on a small scale, certain concepts and theories of municipal management which are operational at other levels." See Booth, *Council-Manager Government in Small Cities* (Washington, DC: International City Managers' Association, 1958), p. 2.

20. For comparative data, see National League of Cities, *America's Mayors and Councilmen: Their Problems and Frustrations* (Washington, DC: The League, 1974), p. 30.

21. Regarding the usual dominance of lawyers in Congress and state legislatures, see William J. Keefe and Morris S. Ogul, *The American Legislative Process*, 4th ed. (Englewood Cliffs, NJ: Prentice-Hall, 1977), pp. 118–120.

22. National League of Cities, op. cit., p. 38.

23. Only the municipal charter of Charlottesville provides sweeping powers to the mayor. Section 2–70 states:

> The mayor shall be the chief executive officer of the city and shall advise with the city manager and supervise the administration of the affairs of the city by the city manager.
>
> He shall have the power to investigate the acts of the city officers and employees, have access to all books and documents in their offices and may examine them and their subordinates on oath. Evidence given by persons so examined shall not be used against them in any criminal proceedings.
>
> The mayor shall exercise a general supervision over all the city's rights, franchises, properties and affairs, departments, and offices.

24. Richard E. Neustadt, *Presidential Power: The Politics of Leadership* (New York: Wiley, 1976), especially pp. 101–125.

25. Boynton and Wright, op. cit., p. 32.

26. Arthur W. Bromage, *Urban Policy Making: The Council-Manager Partnership* (Chicago: Public Administration Service, 1970), p. 25.

27. Harold A. Stone, Don K. Price, and Kathryn H. Stone, *City Manager Government in Lynchburg* (Chicago: Public Administration Service, 1939), p. 23.

28. See Paul Appleby, *Policy and Administration* (University of Alabama Press, 1949); and Dwight Waldo, *The Administrative State* (New York: Ronald, 1948).

29. Boynton and Wright, op. cit., p. 31.

CHAPTER 4

DICHOTOMY AND DUALITY:

Reconceptualizing the Relationship Between Policy and Administration in Council-Manager Cities

JAMES H. SVARA

For almost a hundred years, those interested in public affairs have grappled with the perplexities of the relationship between policy and administration. Woodrow Wilson's formulation, simplified over time as the dichotomy of policy and administration, defined the terms for discussing the relative roles and proper contributions of elected officials and appointed staff in policy making for half a century. Since 1945, the model of separate spheres of authority has been attacked, rejected, and seemingly destroyed. The challenge has been three-pronged: conceptual, with redefinition of the key terms accompanying the behavioral movement in political science; empirical, as the evidence mounted of extensive contributions of administrators to policy; and normative, expressed most dramatically in the New Public Administration which proclaimed that administrators should make policy to promote values rarely advanced by elected officials. Yet, despite the challenges, the dichotomy model has persisted for two reasons. First, it is partially accurate in describing the relationship between elected officials and administrators. Second, the model provides a normative base, rooted in democratic theory, for assessing the appropriateness of behavior. Alternative formulations either have not provided such prescriptions or contradict democratic theory. It is necessary to recast the policy-administration dichotomy in a form that is normatively and empirically tenable.

The purpose of this chapter is to reconceptualize the relationship between policy and administration in council-manager cities. References will be made to research on other levels of government and other institutional forms in cities, but the primary data source is interviews with elected and administrative officials and citizen leaders in the five cities in North Carolina with populations of more than 100,000—Charlotte, Durham, Greensboro, Raleigh, and Winston-Salem.[1]

In the interviews, mayors, councilors, and administrators described their roles in traditional terms which presumed a dichotomy of functions. A majority perceived separation and asserted its value to the operation of the system, yet they frequently referred to instances that deviated from that division, and 41 percent of the respondents indicated that there was some form of "mixture," either staff in policy or councilors in administration.[2] Several explanations for these findings are possible. Perhaps the majority ignored the deviations of practice from their preferred conceptual model. Perhaps the theory and meaning of key concepts is so unclear that observers interpret the

From *Public Administration Review*, vol. 45, no. 1 (January/February 1985), pp. 221–232. Copyright © 1985 by American Society for Public Administration. Reprinted with permission.

same phenomenon differently. Finally, perhaps there is separation and mixture at the same time. The discussion that follows suggests that each of these explanations is partially correct, and seeks to develop an alternative model that will clarify the conceptualization of council-manager relationships. The concepts "policy" and "administration" are each broken down into two component functions, and data are presented to show how councilors and managers are both involved in some functions and largely excluded from others. The new model simultaneously accommodates division and sharing of responsibility in the governmental process.

The next two sections of this chapter will trace the paths that led to the new model. The first was ultimately a dead end, although much was learned along the way by reviewing the "existing" models in the literature for understanding the relationship of policy and administration. These models have the problems of either poor fit with empirical research or normative blind spots, but each contributed to the new model. The second path was the trail of evidence from the interviews that meandered over the landscape of policy and administration, ignoring any boundary lines. The new model suggests where a boundary can typically and ideally be drawn, and notes some common deviations. The concluding section will consider the implications of the model for administrative ethics, council activities, and future research.

Review of Other Models

Discerning the alternative models which guide our thinking about the activity of elected officials and administrators in policy and administration is not easy to do. Among the alternatives to "dichotomy," the activity of administrators in policy has received much more attention in the literature than that of elected officials in administration, even though both are forms of "mixture." Further complicating differentiation is the uneven emphasis on prescription and description. Prescriptive formulations stand out with greater clarity as models, because it is neater to specify how things should be than to describe how they are. Finally, only the "dichotomy" model is explicitly developed in the literature. The reader is certainly aware of the excessive license that can be exercised in specifying the implicit.

Putting these difficulties aside, four models have been delineated. To magnify the distinctions, even at the risk of distortion, each model is given a descriptive title and translated into a graphic representation showing how that model divides responsibility for policy and administration between elected officials and administrators.[3]

The *Policy-Administration Dichotomy Model* represented the mainstream of thought through the 1930s as reflected, for example, by Wilson and Goodnow, and was reinforced by Simon's value-fact dichotomy in the 1950s and Redford's concept of "overhead democracy" in the following decade.[4] It continues to dominate thinking, if not practice, about the division of roles in local government with reformed institutions. The major elements of this primarily normative model are emphasis on democratic control of government and the rule of law. Policy is made by elected officials and implemented by administrators. Under these conditions, administrative discretion is permissible and expected—Doig has noted that Wilson stressed the need for administrators to exercise "great powers"[5]—but cannot extend to the formulation of policy. Insulation of administrative staff from elected officials is important both to eliminate corruption and also to avoid the inefficiency that results when elected officials interfere with the "details of administration." The basis for division of responsibility between elected officials and administrators, illustrated in Figure 4.1a, is essentially separation.

The *Mixture in Policy Model*, which emerged from the post-war behavioral revolution in political science, depends heavily on the redefinition of key terms and the shift in research on

Figure 4.1   **Existing Models of Relationship Between Elected Officials and Administrators in Governmental Process**

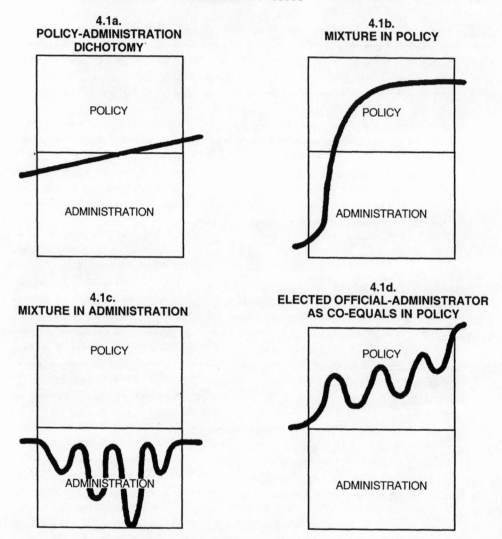

4.1a.
POLICY-ADMINISTRATION DICHOTOMY

POLICY

ADMINISTRATION

4.1b.
MIXTURE IN POLICY

POLICY

ADMINISTRATION

4.1c.
MIXTURE IN ADMINISTRATION

POLICY

ADMINISTRATION

4.1d.
ELECTED OFFICIAL-ADMINISTRATOR AS CO-EQUALS IN POLICY

POLICY

ADMINISTRATION

In each figure, the heavy line marks the boundary between the spheres of elected and appointed officials. All of the space

— *above* the line is responsibility of *elected officials.*
— *below* the line is responsibility of *administrators.*

policy making that accompanied the transformation of the discipline. One cannot be certain how "The Study of Administration" would have been changed if Wilson had read Easton, Dahl, and Sayre,[6] but certainly it makes a difference to define politics as a distributional process in which administrators, among others, make value choices and allocate resources. With this reconceptualization, the scope of what constituted policy behavior was broadened considerably at the same time that the scale of governmental activity and the size of the bureaucracy were also expanding greatly. This model emphasizes "policy mixture" because insulation of administration is carried over from the "dichotomy" model, but policy is viewed as the mixture of efforts by elected officials and administrators with the latter sometimes dominant. Administrators have extensive opportunity to set policy—initiating proposals, exercising discretion, manipulating expertise, writing budgets, and determining the delivery of services—and through implementation they shape policy formulated by elected officials.[7] Administrators have considerable resources which give them power in dealings with elected officials, and, indeed, it is a common theme that neither the legislature nor the executive is capable of controlling the bureaucracy.[8] Thus, there is a complete intermixture of roles in policy but virtual autonomy of administrators within their sphere is presumed, as illustrated in Figure 4.1b. In contrast to the first model, this one largely ignores normative issues, although, as Schick notes, legislative meddling has been proscribed in the quest for "administrative purity."[9]

The *Mixture in Administration Model* is the logical antithesis to the former as another alternative to the "dichotomy" model. It emphasizes activity by legislators in administrative affairs. The relationship is portrayed in Figure 4.1c, which shows legislative probes into the depths of administration, such as influence over hiring or the award of contracts. The logic of the model, but not the extreme interference, is reflected in the recent reassertion of legislative prerogatives and increased activity in administration through measures such as oversight and legislative vetoes designed to curb the presumed excesses of an "uncontrolled bureaucracy."[10] Although the model does not address normative issues, it is conceivable that one could make the case for limited, positive involvement by legislators in administration.

The *Elected Official-Administrator as Co-Equals in Policy Model* shares many of the characteristics of the "policy mixture" model, but adds a normative dimension. As formulated by the New Public Administration movement,[11] this model asserts the ethical obligation of administrators to promote the values of equity and participation and to oppose actions by elected officials which would be adverse to the interests of the politically powerless. The movement sought to address the deficiencies in the policy process that result from unrepresentative legislative bodies and the uneven level of political organization and participation among citizens by expanding the role of professional administrators. The presumed legitimacy of administrators as political actors was a "radical break" from traditional democratic theory,[12] and, thus, stands in stark contrast to the dichotomy model with respect to responsibility for policy. Not only is administrative insulation expected, but also administrators are urged to construct mechanisms for policy making and administration which bypass elected officials and establish direct linkages between governmental staff and the public. The illustration of this model in Figure 4.1d, therefore, features administrative intrusion in policy but no reciprocal control by elected officials. Although support for this model has waned with the decline in political activism and shrinking budgets, the underlying logic of administrators as the driving force in government persists.[13] Furthermore, the ethical commitment of administrators to protect the public interest even without the prodding of elected officials has endured.[14]

Assessing the Models. The models can be assessed in terms of their consistency with evidence from other studies and their utility in handling normative questions concerning the proper division between elected officials and administrators. The "dichotomy" model, as noted in the introduction, ignores the accumulation of evidence that administrators do make policy and value choices of great consequence. The "mixture in policy" model, however, suggests greater administrative control than is warranted. Ripley and Franklin argue that bureaus are weak in agenda setting: "Very rarely will they join the debate over what the government should or should not address at the broadest level."[15] Also, legislators maintain much tighter control over some areas of policy than others,[16] and administrative influence over middle-range policy decisions concerning budgeting and service delivery may be misinterpreted as broad policy-making authority. Kaufman has dismissed the supposed rising power of the uncontrolled bureaucracy as a "raging pandemic," and controls over bureaucracy by elected officials have recently become more salient, indicating that the degree of administrative autonomy may be overdrawn.[17] Further, this model as well as the dichotomy model ignores that legislators may take part in "administrative" decisions and have a legitimate role to play in examining how policy is translated into programs. The "mixture in administration" model is, of course, contradicted by the high—if somewhat exaggerated—level of administrative insulation from legislative intrusion resulting from institutional changes in American government and the increased power of administrators. The model also fails to specify the proper limits of legislative activity in the administrative sphere. Finally, the "elected official-administrator co-equal" model shares the shortcomings of the "policy mixture" model with respect to empirical fit. It does provide normative guidance to administrators as policy makers, but its prescriptions do violence to democratic theory and the rule of law. Furthermore, it slights the significance and extent of the formal authority of elected officials.

Beyond these empirical and normative problems, we are burdened with such imprecise definitions of the central concepts that distinctions between office and function are difficult to make. One cannot conclude, as Meier does, that the only distinction between "policy" and "administrative" decisions is who makes them.[18] It is essential to the task at hand to discriminate precisely among functions in the governmental process without presuming who discharges them.

The New Model

The first task in elaborating the new model is to consider the nature of policy and administration. They are intertwined yet can also be viewed as linked to more general elements in the governmental process which are distinct. Deciding what to do entails determining mission and detailed policy, on the one hand, and getting the work done involves administration and management, on the other. Whereas the responsibility for the "extreme" functions of mission and management is largely dichotomized, responsibility for policy and administration is shared and the activities themselves are difficult to separate. These concepts will be defined and operationalized for council-manager city governments, illustrated with findings from the study cities and occasional references to other forms and levels of government.

Mission

Mission refers to the organization's philosophy, its thrust, the broad goals it sets for itself, and the things it chooses not to do. It is the determination of "what government should or should not address at the broadest level" to use Ripley and Franklin's phrase again.[19] In city government, aspects of mission include the scope of services provided, philosophy of taxation and spending, policy orientation, for example, growth versus amenities, and constitutional issues, such as charter changes, annexation, and relations with other local governments. Mission may be explicit or implicit, resulting from significant decisions or nondecisions.

It is the responsibility of elected officials to determine mission. This is clearly the normative requirement of democratic theory, and, although exceptions are common, practice usually follows theory. City managers, despite their influence over policy, "find themselves," Loveridge observes, "regardless of personal choice, responsive and accountable to major community demands, interests, and values" translated in large part by the city council.[20] The manager's recommendations and advice about what a city can do surely influence councilmanic conclusions about what it should do, but in the cities studied, the council still determines the city's basic purposes. Naturally, it is the elected officials who occupy the public and adversarial roles associated with setting mission goals, because, as Lynn observed in national politics, shaping broad policy and the struggle over ends "is played in the open rather than behind the scenes and entails a willing involvement in controversy and the power to persuade and dramatize.[21] In this arena, professional administrators are uncomfortable and ineffective actors, unless the council has endorsed the initiative under consideration.

This is not to suggest that administrative staff are either absent from or powerless in setting mission. A great deal of the planning and analysis of trends done by staff is directed toward mission questions, if the government maintains a proactive stance and undertakes comprehensive administrative planning.[22] The manager and staff can also exert a negative force to resist change in mission. An extreme form of this influence—the "bureaucratic veto" described by Lupsha[23]—was not observed in the North Carolina cities. Still, in several cities, some respondents noted that the manager's resistance to program expansion into nontraditional human services represented an obstacle that partially prevented council initiatives in these areas. Thus, the manager is not powerless, but mission is largely the sphere of the council.

Policy

Policy refers to middle-range policy decisions, for example, how to spend government revenues, whether to initiate new programs or create new offices, and how to distribute services at what levels within the existing range of services provided. Interaction is common in policy, as administrators give advice and make recommendations to elected officials. Staff discretion, influence over the budget, and determination of formulae for distributing services are extensive and councils are sometimes viewed as mere rubber stamps of managerial decisions about initiation or elimination of programs. Examination of each of these manifestations of staff activity in policy making, however, reveals a pattern of sharing: the council is not alone in making policy but neither is the manager uncontrolled.

The extent of managerial discretion was considered to be appropriate—neither too great nor too limited—by most of the respondents in this study. Only 20 percent felt that the manager had too much discretion overall, and only 10 percent felt that the manager acted with too much independence in program creation or elimination. Program change has clear policy implications, and managers do not take liberties in this area by acting without councilmanic direction.

Opinions concerning the extent of council involvement in a variety of areas, including responsibility for shaping service distribution and the budget, are presented in Table 4.1. Staff influence over setting the formulae for allocating services, that is, who and what areas of the city get how much of a service, is extensive in the North Carolina cities, just as has been observed in other cities. Only 21 percent of the respondents viewed the council as being very involved in this activity, and slightly more felt that the council was not very involved. The remainder—57 percent—felt the council was involved to some extent. Councilors argued that they had a hand in service allocation in other ways, at the time of program creation or major change, through budget review, or in their follow-up of citizen complaints. Still, answering the essential political question of "who gets what" is largely a staff endeavor within the parameters set by and under the watchful eyes of the council.

Similarly, subject to review and ratification of the council, the budget is set by administrative staff, although the extent of their latitude should not be overstated. Only 14 percent of the

Table 4.1

Council Involvement in Governmental Activities (N = 58)

	How much involved (%)				
Area/Rank*	Very	Some	Not very or none	Don't know	Total
A. Budget formulation/5	14	33	52	0	99
B. Budget review and approval/1	88	7	5	0	100
C. Service delivery/6	9	53	36	2	100
D. Hiring or promotion decisions about staff/7	2	7	90	2	101
E. Determining formula for allocating services/4	21	57	22	0	100
F. Handling complaints from citizens/2	45	43	10	2	100
G. Handling complaints from employees/8	0	26	67	7	100
H. Developing policies for internal management/3	33	41	24	2	100

*Rank is determined by the proportion responding "very much" involved.

respondents felt that the council was very involved and more than half said the council was not very involved in budget formulation, that is, preparing the budget proposal. This is a significant finding, because once the budget is constructed, the extent of change by the council is very small. Almost all of the respondents considered the council to be very involved in budget review and approval. The size and complexity of the document, however, and the pressure of time to approve it give whoever prepares the budget considerable influence over the conduct of city affairs for at least the upcoming year.

These considerations support the view that budgeting is a staff function but several forms of control exercised by councils make budgeting more a joint enterprise than is often concluded. First, most councils set budget limits, particularly a mandated tax rate, which served as a powerful constraint for administrators in preparing the budget. Second, approval of new or expanded revenue sources had to come from councils, and staff sought guidance from councils early in the budget process about whether such changes would be acceptable. Third, several of the councils set goals for the year in January which provide the framework for staff in preparing the budget document. In addition to specific directions, the shape of the budget is largely determined by prior programs in particular and the city's mission in general.

Thus, the pattern that emerges is a mixture of responsibility for policy usually involving determination of general form or limits by council and the specific content of policy by staff. Conclusions that stress either council or staff dominance or exclusion are not supportable in these cities.

Administration

Administration refers to the specific decisions, regulations, and practices employed to achieve policy objectives. As one would expect, administration is largely the domain of the bureaucracy. There are, however, four aspects of legislative action in administration: specification of techniques to be employed, implementing decisions by legislators, intervention in service delivery, and legislative oversight.

First, much attention is given to the vagueness of some legislation which leaves administrators free to set policy, but other legislation spells out in detail how a program is to be implemented. Lynn observes that congressional committees are sometimes "as much concerned with how their purpose was to be achieved as with the purpose itself," and Schick classes the trend toward lengthier and more detailed laws as one of the manifestations of a "resurgent" Congress trying to reestablish control over the bureaucracy.[24] In the study cities, similar practices were used to provide more detailed directions to the city manager about program content and execution, especially over controversial issues or matters of great interest to councilors.

Second, some specific implementing actions are carried to legislative bodies for final decision, such as application of a zoning ordinance to a particular case or approval of locations for scattered site housing. Council members choose to take a hand in others. Planning, zoning, housing, and development activities commonly involved the council in detailed examination of particular cases. Further, administrative actions may be "appealed" to legislative bodies. The congressional veto, which permitted legislators to step into the administrative process, has recently been prohibited by the Supreme Court, but city councils have frequent opportunities to participate in implementation of programs, particularly through their committees. Although these actions are carried out by legislators, they are essentially "administrative" in character.

Third, there are a variety of acts of intervention by individual councilors and the council collectively. Less than 10 percent of the respondents saw the council as being very involved in service delivery, but over half considered it to be somewhat involved. The most common example of intervention is handling citizen complaints. Almost half the respondents felt that councilors were very involved in complaint handling (the second highest rank among the eight areas covered), and only 10 percent viewed this as an area in which there was little councilmanic involvement. Councilmanic intervention was only rarely considered to be necessary to secure an adequate staff response to inquiries coming directly from citizens. Still, many councilors felt that their attention to the matter could make a difference especially by influencing "close calls" by staff in interpreting rules. Whether their help is needed or not, however, councilors are increasingly adopting an ombudsman role, acting as a consumer advocate for constituents to assure fair and sensitive treatment for citizens in dealings with staff. As one manager put it, councilors feel "a strong sense of responsibility for services and the way they are delivered." Complaint handling was viewed as a way to make administrative behavior more "responsive" and citizen oriented.

Fourth, legislators in the oversight function examine the conduct of programs to determine whether implementation is consistent with policy, whether programs are being administered appropriately, and what results are being accomplished. Oversight is typically associated with state legislative or congressional activity, where the amount and depth of oversight is increasing.[25] The councils in the study cities, in contrast to their state and national counterparts, do not undertake much formal oversight activity. Although councilors typically indicated that they engaged in oversight through their other responsibilities, a third of the respondents did not consider oversight to be adequate. Although one manager replied, "Lord, yes!" when asked whether there was sufficient oversight, another indicated that the council could not fulfill this function because they lacked clear standards to use in measuring program performance.

In sum, although program implementation is largely a staff responsibility, the strong policy implications of administration produce a lively interest and wide-ranging involvement by elected officials. In some areas, councilors may be too involved, especially when they make implementing decisions and act as ombudsmen, and in another area, that is, oversight, not active enough. Nonetheless, involved they are in the administrative sphere.

Management

Finally, management refers to the actions taken to support the policy and administrative functions. It includes controlling and utilizing the human, material, and informational resources of the organization to best advantage. It also encompasses the specific techniques used in generating services. Management is largely devoid of policy, even though management systems are not neutral in their effect on internal distribution of resources in the organization. Management is the province of the manager. The council is, however, involved in this sphere to some extent. It ratifies some management changes and occasionally initiates others.

Rarely does the council interfere with details of management, in contrast to its interests in the details of administration. Whereas who gets services is a legitimate question for councilors to ask, who gets a job or a contract is not. Almost all agreed that the council keeps out of staff hiring or promotion decisions, and 63 percent indicated little involvement in handling employee complaints. Typically, this activity was limited to passing employee concerns to the manager without taking sides. Staff respondents indicated that councilors also stayed out of purchasing and contract procedures, and when required by state statute to approve large purchases, tended to follow staff recommendations.

The council is quite interested, however, in questions of management "policy" and in the performance of the manager and the organization. Over a third of the respondents indicated that the council was very involved in developing policies for internal management, such as affirmative action and salary programs, and three-quarters felt that the council was at least somewhat involved. Thus, management policy was the third highest ranking area of council involvement. Councils were also quite active in initiating study or prompting the manager to make changes in management areas, such as merit pay plans, staff reorganizations, grievance procedures, zero base budgeting, and minority hiring and purchasing procedures in city contracts. The council respects managerial prerogatives, and it relies on his or her proposal as the basis for action, tending to withhold approval and seek revisions rather than substitute its own version if the manager's proposal is not acceptable. Although they do it, councilors are hesitant to enter the area of management. Making suggestions is common, but some councilors view the need to propose management changes as an indication that the manager is not doing the job and is failing to innovate. The council is most comfortable acting on its interest in management style, organizational structure, and operations in its appraisal of the manager's performance, usually in closed sessions held annually.

With some variations, all the study cities have strong management and smoothly functioning, efficient operations. For the most part, the boundary between elected officials and administrators in handling management is clear. Councils do act in the management area in the ways described. There could be wider recognition, however, that the city council can play a legitimate role in reviewing management, supporting improvements, making suggestions, and acknowledging organizational accomplishment, while still leaving the manager free to manage.

The Model

Mission, policy, administration, and management are the four functions of the governmental process. Although each blends into the other to form a continuum from "pure" policy to "pure" management,[26] each function has been distinguished conceptually. The division of responsibility between elected and administrative officials can be represented graphically by marking a line through a diagram similar to those used earlier but with the addition of zones for mission and management. The patterns observed in the study cities are summarized in Figure 4.2. The legislative body dominates mission formulation although the manager plays an advisory role in developing proposals and analyzing conditions and trends. In policy, the manager has a slightly larger space than the council because of the large amount of policy advice and policy setting by

Figure 4.2 **Mission-Management Separation with Shared Responsibility
for Policy and the Administration**

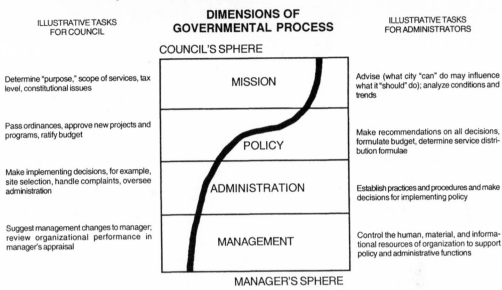

ILLUSTRATIVE TASKS
FOR COUNCIL

**DIMENSIONS OF
GOVERNMENTAL PROCESS**

ILLUSTRATIVE TASKS
FOR ADMINISTRATORS

COUNCIL'S SPHERE

Determine "purpose," scope of services, tax level, constitutional issues — MISSION — Advise (what city "can" do may influence what it "should" do); analyze conditions and trends

Pass ordinances, approve new projects and programs, ratify budget — POLICY — Make recommendations on all decisions, formulate budget, determine service distribution formulae

Make implementing decisions, for example, site selection, handle complaints, oversee administration — ADMINISTRATION — Establish practices and procedures and make decisions for implementing policy

Suggest management changes to manager; review organizational performance in manager's appraisal — MANAGEMENT — Control the human, material, and informational resources of organization to support policy and administrative functions

MANAGER'S SPHERE

The curved line suggests the division between the Council's and the Manager's spheres of activity, with the Council to the *left* and the manager to the *right* of the line.

The division presented is intended to roughly approximate a "proper" degree of separation and sharing. Shifts to either the left or right would indicate improper incursions.

administrators, but the larger "quantity" of managerial policy making does not alter the council's ultimate responsibility for all policy. Staff has the much larger role in administration, although the council makes a substantial contribution to this sphere. Management is the sphere of the manager with council contributions limited to suggestions and assessment through appraisal of the manager. Thus, conceptually and in these cities empirically, there is a dichotomy of mission and management, but policy and administration are intermixed to the extent they are a duality, distinct but inseparable aspects of developing and delivering government programs.

The diagram suggests the "average" division among the five cities, which can be regarded as "typical," and, for reasons to be discussed below, represents a hypothetically "ideal" division of authority. The size of the spheres is not based on absolute values at this stage in the development of the model, but rather is intended to be suggestive of tendencies in council-manager relations. One can make relative distinctions and compare different jurisdictions or note shifts of responsibility in a single city over time.

The variations among the five study cities are marked, although the differences fall within a narrow range that does not fundamentally shift authority for any functions. Four patterns can be abstracted from the research. The "Strong Manager" pattern is suggested by Figure 4.3a, in which the boundary line is shifted to the left, and the manager's space for action is larger in all functions. The council becomes a "board of directors" which relies on the manager's advice concerning mission and grants him or her extensive discretion in all other areas. The opposite is the "Council Dominant" pattern in Figure 4.3b, in which the line is shifted to the right. The "Council Incursion" pattern, illustrated in Figure 4.3c, results from a council that probes more deeply in all areas

Figure 4.3 **Deviations from Typical Division**

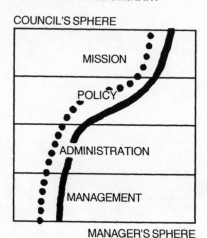

4.3a
STRONG MANAGER

COUNCIL'S SPHERE

MISSION

POLICY

ADMINISTRATION

MANAGEMENT

MANAGER'S SPHERE

4.3b.
COUNCIL DOMINANT

COUNCIL'S SPHERE

MISSION

POLICY

ADMINISTRATION

MANAGEMENT

MANAGER'S SPHERE

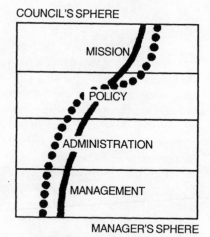

4.3c
COUNCIL INCURSION

COUNCIL'S SPHERE

MISSION

POLICY

ADMINISTRATION

MANAGEMENT

MANAGER'S SPHERE

4.3d
COUNCIL-MANAGER STANDOFF

COUNCIL'S SPHERE

MISSION

POLICY

ADMINISTRATION

MANAGEMENT

MANAGER'S SPHERE

than in the typical model, yet is not consistently assertive in all areas. The incursive council makes administrators wary of offering any proposals concerning mission and is unpredictable in its reactions to policy recommendations from staff. It accepts many recommendations but in some cases undercuts extensive staff preparations and sets off to make its own policy decision. The council probes persistently but somewhat haphazardly into administrative matters, and dabbles in management. Thus, the boundary line is "ragged" in this situation. The "Manager-Council Standoff" pattern, illustrated in Figure 4.3d, is produced by a strong manager and assertive council who check and contain each other with neither the council establishing clear control nor the manager securing the discretion he or she wishes. The manager may play a larger role in mission—particularly in a veto capacity—and in policy where recommendations are presented in such a way that the council has difficulty not accepting them, even though they feel uncomfortable doing so. The council, on the other hand, imposes administrative constraints on the manager in order to gain some control and probes into management.

These alternative patterns illustrate the variability of relationships, and the usefulness of the model in charting them. A task for future research is to devise measures that will delineate more precisely the division of responsibility in each function for council-manager and other forms of government.[27]

Conclusion: Implications of the Model

The dichotomy-duality model in which there is a separation of responsibility for mission and management, with sharing of policy and administration has implications for administrative ethics, council roles, and future research. Each will be briefly explored.

The ethical precepts suggested by the model could be called the Neotraditional Public Administration, because they combine elements of the long-standing as well as the new emphases in the field. Administrators should recognize the authority of elected officials to determine mission and are obligated to advance the mission of the organization through actions taken in policy, administration, and management. Within the framework of controls provided by mission goals, the manager should exercise discretion and can do so without becoming an autonomous actor. The manager seeks to promote openness and fairness and to assure that existing services are allocated equitably. The manager should administer programs in a way that is consistent with mission and policy, seeking to prevent administrative actions which subvert policy intent, and should provide sufficient information on performance to permit the council to assess the administration of policies and programs. Finally, the manager is committed to efficiency and improved productivity, and, as essential conditions for effective administration and efficient management, asserts the right to control the internal management of the organization and to resist interference from outside. These guidelines at once set high standards for managerial attainment, promote the integrity and discretion of the manager, and safeguard democratic principles. This is an advance over the dichotomy model which prescribed behavior for a pure but powerless manager, on the one hand, or the mixture in policy and coequal models which gave the manager license to be powerful but at the cost of political purity and democratic control.[28]

Second, councils should define their purpose and spend their time somewhat differently than they typically do. Council members feel overworked yet unable to fulfill their responsibilities. The model suggests that they should do more of some things and less of others. In the former category is attention to mission and broad policy and to oversight to ensure that the goals of the organization are being advanced, both citywide and in particular neighborhoods. They should add to their strong interest in holding down tax rates a broader concern for the quality of management and look to the manager for ways to enhance efficient and effective organizational performance. Their burden is lightened by recognizing and encouraging full managerial participation in policy making and extensive discretion in decision making and implementation. On the other hand, they should do less detailed policy making, discourage the referral of implementing decisions and administrative appeals to the council, avoid picking over isolated details of administrative performance, and dispense with unnecessary errand running for constituents, while promoting a high level of staff accessibility and responsiveness to citizen inquiries and complaints. By shifting allocation of time and attention in these ways, councilors can free time for the more substantial tasks without worrying that the bureaucracy is being let off the lease.

Third, research should be directed into a number of areas highlighted by the model. The content of mission, how it is developed and changed, and the relationship between general goals and specific policy should be examined more fully. The forms and impact of administrative involvement by councils through specification of methods, implementing decisions, complaint handling, and oversight requires much more attention. Between council and manager, the role of the mayor is largely unknown, and the distinct contributions of this official to each of the functions deserves more study.[29]

Further, patterns of interaction among official actors should be reexamined. The model indicates that conflict is not inevitably the underlying condition of city government. Although the view is widespread that contentious promotion of self-interest by all participants dominates the urban political process,[30] it is possible for officials to interact positively within a framework that balances discretion and control for both councilor and administrator. When the ideal division of responsibility is found, the situation more closely approximates a cooperative model of urban governance than the conflict model which has dominated the conceptualization of city politics. It is possible for city governments to develop policies that anticipate problems instead of merely generating "political resultants" in reaction to crisis. Administration and management can make the policy-making process "work" in the sense that the political will of elected officials is faithfully translated into programs and services that are provided equitably and efficiently to citizens. Thus, the "manageable" city is as much a possibility in theory and practice as the "ungovernable" city, and we should carefully examine the conditions associated with each.

In conclusion, there is not a complete separation of policy and administration as the discredited but tenaciously surviving traditional model has held. Nor is there a complete intermingling of the two which precludes the division of responsibilities between elected officials and administrative staff and obviates the possibility of maintaining democratic control over the governmental process. There is a clear division between the formulation of mission and broad policy for the organization by elected officials, which creates a framework of goals within which all other activities take place, and the management of the organization by administrative staff. The manager must be free to create and maintain a system of rational management practices that direct staff and resources toward the accomplishment of the city's goals to ensure both efficient and effective operation. Between mission and management, detailed policy making must be a joint concern and councilors should recognize and encourage the full contribution of staff to policy making. The execution of policies requires the experience and expertise of administrative staff and should be primarily their concern, but councilors must direct attention to the way policies are being translated into action through general oversight. The dichotomy of mission and management with shared responsibility for policy and administration provides, therefore, not only for the division of responsibility that makes best use of the distinctive talents and resources of councilors and administrators but also ensures that the conditions for democratic government are preserved.

Notes

Portions of this chapter were presented at the annual meeting of the American Political Science Association in Chicago and the Urban Affairs Conference of the University of North Carolina in Raleigh in 1983. I would like to acknowledge the invaluable research assistance provided by Cheryl Coller, formerly a student in political science at the University of North Carolina, Greensboro and currently a graduate student in planning at Georgia Institute of Technology, and financial support from the University Research Council.

1. In each of the cities, interviews were conducted with the mayor and a sample of councilors chosen to balance at-large and district members and socioeconomic and racial characteristics of constituents; the manager and assistant manager for operations, and the directors of budgeting and planning; and leaders who would have

opportunity to observe council-manager relations—the presidents of the League of Women Voters and the NAACP, the staff director of the Chamber of Commerce, and the local government reporter from the major daily newspaper. The total number of respondents was sixty-five.

2. Respondents were asked, "Considering experience in [city], would you say that the council is responsible for policy and the manager is responsible for administration, or is there some mixture of responsibility?"

3. The boundary between spheres in the alternatives to the dichotomy model is indicated with a curving line intended to suggest a pattern of division in the absence of more precise measurements.

4. Woodrow Wilson, "The Study of Administration," *Political Science Quarterly* 2 (1887) [reprinted in *Classics of Public Administration*, ed. Jay M. Shafritz and Albert C. Hyde (Oak Park, IL: Moore, 1978), pp. 3–17]; Frank J. Goodnow, *Politics and Administration* (New York: Macmillan, 1990); Herbert Simon, *Administrative Behavior*, 2d ed. (New York: Macmillan, 1957); Emmette S. Redford, *Democracy in the Administrative State* (New York: Oxford University Press, 1969). Paul P. Van Riper, "The American Administrative State: Wilson and the Founders—An Unorthodox View," *Public Administration Review* 43 (November/December 1983): 478–479, questions the direct influence of Wilson on the work of scholars before 1950.

5. Jameson W. Doig, "'If I See a Murderous Fellow Sharpening a Knife Cleverly . . .' The Wilsonian Dichotomy and the Public Authority Tradition," *Public Administration Review* 43 (July/August 1983): 292–304.

6. David Easton, *A Systems Analysis of Political Life* (New York: Wiley, 1965); Robert A. Dahl, "The Science of Public Administration," *Public Administration Review* 7 (Winter 1947): 1–11; Wallace S. Sayre, "Premises of Public Administration: Past and Emerging," *Public Administration Review* 18 (Spring 1958): 102–105.

7. For examples of administrative influence through budgeting, service delivery, and professional expertise in local government, see John P. Crecine, *Governmental Problem-Solving* (Chicago, IL: Rand McNally, 1969); Kenneth P. Mladenka, "The Urban Bureaucracy and the Chicago Political Machine: Who Gets What and the Limits to Political Control," *American Political Science Review* 74 (1980): 991–998; Robert S. Lineberry, *Equality and Urban Policy* (Beverly Hills, CA: Sage, 1977); and Melvile C. Branch, "The Sins of City Planners," *Public Administration Review* 42 (January/February 1982): 1–5.

8. For review of the literature of bureaucratic control, see Kenneth J. Meier, *Politics and the Bureaucracy* (North Scituate, MA: Duxbury Press, 1979).

9. Allen Schick, "Congress and the 'Details' of Administration," *Public Administration Review* 36 (November/December 1976): 517.

10. Ibid.; James L. Sundquist, *The Decline and Resurgence of Congress* (Washington, DC: Brookings, 1981).

11. Frank Marini, ed., *Toward a New Public Administration: The Minnowbrook Perspective* (New York: Chandler, 1971); H. George Frederickson, *New Public Administration* (Tuscaloosa: University of Alabama Press, 1980).

12. Lewis C. Mainzer, *Political Bureaucracy* (Glenview, IL: Scott Foresman, 1973), p. 72.

13. B. Guy Peters has attempted to determine whether "the bureaucracy was capable of providing a viable government—meaning both policy direction and routine management—for a society" in "The Problem of Bureaucratic Government," *Journal of Politics* 43 (1981): 56–82 (quotation p. 65).

14. Rayburn Barton, "Roles Advocated for Administrators by the New Public Administration," *Southern Review of Public Administration* 3 (1980): 463–486. Both the National Association of Schools of Public Affairs and Administration in its guidelines for masters programs and the American Society for Public Administration have shown strong interest in elevating professional ethics.

15. Randall B. Ripley and Grace A. Franklin, *Bureaucracy and Policy Implementation* (Homewood, IL: Dorsey, 1982), p. 32.

16. Meier, chap. 4.

17. Herbert Kaufman, "Fear of Bureaucracy: A Raging Pandemic," *Public Administration Review* 41 (January/February 1981): 1–9.

18. Meier, p. 49.

19. Ripley and Franklin, p. 32; Laurence E. Lynn, Jr., *Managing the Public's Business* (New York: Basic Books, 1981), p. 146, calls the resolution of such issues the "high game."

20. Ronald O. Loveridge, *City Managers in Legislative Politics* (Indianapolis, IN: Bobbs-Merrill, 1971), p. 173.

21. Lynn, p. 147.

22. John K. Parker, "Administrative Planning," in *Managing the Modern City*, ed. James M. Banovetz (Washington, DC: International City Management Association, 1971), chap. 10.

23. Peter Lupsha, "Constraints on Urban Leadership, or Why Cities Cannot Be Creatively Governed," in *Improving the Quality of Urban Management*, ed. Willis D. Hawley and David Rogers, *Urban Affairs Annual Reviews* 8 (1974).

24. Lynn, p. 18; Schick, pp. 525–526.

25. Joel D. Aberbach, "Changes in Congressional Oversight," in *Making Bureaucracies Work*, ed. Carol H. Weiss and Allen H. Barton (Beverly Hills, CA: Sage, 1980), pp. 65–87.

26. Paul Appleby, *Policy and Administration* (Tuscaloosa: Alabama University Press, 1949); John B. Richard, "Politics In/And/Or/But Administration," *Public Administration Review* 35 (November/December 1975): 647–651; and Cheryl Miller Colbert, "An Empirical Analysis of Policy in Administration: Bureaucratic/Administration Participation in Policy Process," paper presented to the Southern Political Science Association, 1982.

27. The model should be applicable to mayor-council systems as well. Political executives would play a much larger role in the formulation of mission and policy, and would be extensively involved in administration and management, although in the latter two areas, the boundaries between the executive and administrative staff are difficult to establish. A second boundary line could be added to mark off the sphere of the mayor, who would take responsibility from both councilors and staff. As a consequence, the scope of responsibility for legislators would be substantially smaller than in the council-manager form.

28. The standards seek, as Warwick does, to strike a balance between what he calls "administrative Darwinism" and "Weberian Idealism." Based on the observations in the North Carolina cities, the standards are attainable. See Donald D. Warwick, "The Ethics of Administrative Discretion," in *Public Duties: The Moral Obligations of Government Officials*, ed. Joel L. Fleischman, Lance Leibman, and Mark H. Moore (Cambridge, MA: Harvard University Press, 1981), pp. 93–127.

29. For exploratory research in this area, see James H. Svara and James W. Bohmbach, "The Mayoralty and Leadership in Council-Manager Cities," *Popular Government* 41 (1976): 1–6.

30. Douglas Yates, *The Ungovernable City* (Cambridge, MA: MIT, 1977).

CHAPTER 5

CITY MANAGERS:

Will They Reject Policy Leadership?

JAMES M. BANOVETZ

Ever since Karl Bosworth opined that "The City Manager Is a Politician" (Bosworth 1958), many local government administrators and scholars have embraced that job description, suggested that Woodrow Wilson's politics-administration dichotomy was invalid, and predicted a growing political-policy role for city and county managers in the future (Frederickson 1989; Stillman 1974; Loveridge 1971; Sherwood 1976; Newland 1979; Graves 1982; Mikulecky 1980; Gaebler 1983). Even the best contemporary discussions of the city management profession[1] have reiterated this evolutionary process: Ammons and Newell (1989) recently noted that the "politics–administration dichotomy . . . continues to erode in practice . . . in the constant quest for the leadership necessary to solve the problems of the nation's cities" (170), and Svara (1990) predicted that "a continuing shift toward the policy and political roles (for city managers) is likely since younger and professionally trained managers are likely to devote more time to them and less to the management role" (181).

City managers, too, report that such a shift is occurring. Ammons and Newell (1989) found that, in 1988, 56 percent of city managers in their study reported that the policy role was the most important for success in their jobs, whereas Wright in 1965 found only 22 percent of the city managers giving such a response (Ammons and Newell 1989).

Despite such evidence, however, there is now reason to speculate that this trend might not continue, but rather that the city manager's role in the early twenty-first century might be more like the role of managers in the mid-twentieth century than of managers in recent decades. City managers of the future may find that their job, like their job tenure, is more similar to that of baseball managers than to political leaders, and that the resulting insecurity, as well as job demands, will cause them to focus on managerial rather than policy responsibilities.

To be sure, the city manager's job has changed during the course of the twentieth century, and the typical manager's job description has included a growing list of policy responsibilities. Keller (1989) argues that city managers must be "chief executives of appropriate interorganizational network economies and polities"; Newland (1979) has charged the manager to be a futurist; Mikulecky (1980) has labeled the manager a diplomat in intergovernmental relations; and Toffler (1980) has called the manager a broker of interests. Gaebler (1983) has used the term *entrepreneur* to describe the manager's role, and the International City/County Management Association (ICMA) itself has suggested that the title *city manager* might give way to the label *city coordinator*

From *Public Productivity & Management Review*, vol. 18, no. 4 (Summer 1994), pp. 313–324. Copyright © 1994 by Jossey-Bass. Reprinted with permission.

(Rutter 1980). The ICMA prediction may have been right, but for the wrong reasons: city managers may be city coordinators, but managerial coordination will take precedence over policy coordination.

Trend Conflict

The difference between these two perspectives is rooted in different interpretations of trends. Scholars and practitioners who predict a growing policy role for city managers do so on the basis of a linear extension of the manager's evolving role. Although frequently used, this methodology is based on the perilous assumption that the environment is stable. It presumes that the circumstances in which city managers operate—the forms of government, political attitudes and values, political behaviors, citizen expectations, socioeconomic trends, organizational milieus, and work patterns—will remain relatively constant or change in a parallel linear manner.

The notion that the city manager's role will revert to a stronger managerial focus, with a lessening of its policy focus, is predicated on evidence that the managerial environment will not stay stable; indeed, it is not stable now. The assumption of linearity in policy roles assumes a constancy in relationships between managers and their bosses—elected mayors, city council members, county board presidents, and county board members—that simply does not exist. The political behaviors of such elected officials are themselves undergoing changes that are more dialectic than linear in nature.

City managers are fond of saying that their term of office "extends until the next council meeting." The accuracy of this assertion necessarily (and intentionally, given the precepts of democratic theory; see Mosher 1982) makes the manager's role a function of the behavior and expectations of elected council members. The "behavior and expectations" are evolving in a dialectic fashion, and the same behavior and expectations may force managerial roles to deviate from the linear pattern sketched by scholars and practitioners.

Dialectic Evolution of Council Behavior

The behavior of elected local government officials, and thus the role development of city management, has been profoundly affected by four distinct sets of public attitudes toward government, each of which was rooted in its own period of twentieth-century history. These attitudes, summarized in Table 5.1, have run the gamut from revulsion toward government to reliance upon government as a paternalistic guarantor of personal and economic well-being.

Attitudes toward government in the early twentieth century were products of the corruption of the late nineteenth century. (For a discussion of this early history and its impact on the council-manager plan of local government, see Judd 1979.) Partisan machine politics and its accompanying corruption led voters, and especially the emerging middle class, to distrust government and restrain it through legal controls. These controls were written into restrictive state laws and further embellished by narrow construction in the interpretation of governmental powers. At the local level, popular hostility toward government led to the formation of suburban governments, where the new middle class could separate itself from the big-city machines and enjoy control over neighborhood governments. In this environment, the council-manager plan was sold to local voters on the basis of (1) its structural parallels with contemporary business models, and specifically the business corporation,[2] which gave the plan validity in terms of the middle-class values of economy and efficiency, and (2) the dichotomy between politics and administration, noting that the council-manager plan guaranteed administrative expertise divorced from political considerations.

Table 5.1

Public Attitudes Toward Government

Era	Public perception	Exemplifying factors
Early twentieth century	Government is corrupt	Spoils system Machine politics "Shame of the Cities"
1915–1935	Government should be limited	Dillon's rule Substantive due process Reform legislation
1935–1965	Government is paternalistic	New Deal Great Society War on poverty Civil rights
1965–present	Government is excessive	Antiwar (Vietnam) Demonstrations Taxpayers' revolt Reaganism

Attitudes toward government changed markedly with the onslaught of the depression and the postwar economic expansion. The New Deal spawned the expectation that government had a responsibility to provide economic well-being for all, including responsibility to provide educational opportunity, economic security, housing, health care, transportation, recreation, and civil rights (Frisch and Stevens 1971, 13–21). The attitudes stemming from these changed popular expectations also affected cities, which found themselves responsible for an ever-increasing range of human services; city managers found themselves supervising a growing list of programs and responding to a widening spectrum of citizen demands (Banovetz 1971, 18). The popularity of the council-manager plan expanded rapidly during this and the following era as popular suspicion of government was replaced with popular demands for more government. The people's mood had swung from popular distrust of government to popular enthusiasm for it, from dialectical thesis to antithesis.

The turbulent decade of the 1960s brought the dialectical synthesis. Popular support for government programs and services did not lessen, but the people revolted against the "excesses" of government. Reacting to the turbulence associated with U.S. involvement in the Vietnam War, government-ordered desegregation plans, increasingly burdensome taxes, and the expanding scope of government regulatory activity, people viewed the role of government in society as too pervasive.

In short, public attitudes toward government are now a synthesis of high expectations for personal benefits and strong convictions that the scale and cost of government activity must be substantially reduced.

Linear Evolution of the Managerial Role

In his description of the "rise" of the city manager profession, Stillman (1974) described several eras in the profession's history, eras that relate in interesting ways to changing public expectations of government. He divided the profession's evolution into four periods. The first, 1914–1924, was the period when the profession established its identity, culminating in the approval of its first code of ethics in 1924, which described the profession's role in strictly administrative terms. In the second period, 1924–1938, the profession reflected the values of the scientific management philosophy; it culminated with the amendment of the code of ethics in 1938 to establish clearly the politics-administration dichotomy and to suggest a role, but a strictly limited role, for the manager as an adviser to the council.

Whereas the first two periods reflected public interest in a limited government, the second two periods reflected the changing public mood toward government. The third period, 1938–1952, was described by Stillman as a period during which the profession went through an identity crisis as it sought to reconcile its precepts to "the New Political Realism." It culminated in 1952 revisions to the code of ethics that defined the manager as "a community leader (who) submits policy proposals to the council and provides the council with facts and advice on matters of policy." The fourth era began in 1952 and was marked by 1969 code amendments that continued to delineate a political role for the manager.

Stillman's analysis should be updated to take account of the ICMA's 1980 pronouncement on the profession's future, which suggested a much more proactive and forceful role for the profession in addressing the problems of local governments during the remaining decades of the century and beyond (Rutter 1980).

These trends are set forth and embellished in Table 5.2. The city manager's executive functions and the change in informal descriptive titles significantly parallel the job's changing and expanding responsibilities. Although city managers have been loath to acknowledge this operational job title change in public, many do so in private conversation.

Unfortunately, the extent to which the linear progression in managerial role (see Table 5.2) has already occurred may be sufficiently extreme to provoke a counterreaction in the opposite direction, a dialectic antithesis. Such a reaction is made more likely by the changes occurring in the behavior of the managers' bosses, local elected officials.

Changes in Elected Official Behavior

However, no matter how clearly managers see or want a more active policy-making role for themselves, that role will not emerge unless it is compatible with the political expectations of the public and their elected representatives. The city management profession, with its history of resignations and terminations, has learned that lesson only too well.

Predicting the public's future expectations for government bears some similarity to predicting school enrollments. Enrollments can be predicted into the near future with some degree of certainty because children are born some years before they enroll in school. Similarly, public expectations of government can be predicted in advance with some (albeit less) certainty because those expectations are based on attitudes and values that are formed in advance. People acquire their political attitudes and values during youth and young adulthood, arguably between the ages of fifteen and twenty-five. The attitudes and values learned during those ages become the basis for political expectations and behaviors that shape public policy when those persons reach the ages when they are most likely to be politically active and hold public office, the ages between thirty-five and sixty. Thus attitudes and values formed at an early period of life become operative in government at a later period of life.

Viewed from this perspective, the political role expansion of the city manager from 1952 to the present, and particularly between 1960 and 1985, can be attributed to the elected city officials who developed their political attitudes and values when government was viewed as paternalistic, a source of support and service. People with such political attitudes welcomed city

Table 5.2

Evolution of the City Management Profession

Era	Manager's job focus	Descriptive job title
1914–1924	Administrative technician Eliminate corruption Establish scientific management methods	City administrative officer
1924–1938	Administrative technician Organization director Policy leader	City administrator
1938–1952	Organization leader Policy adviser	Chief administrative officer
1952–1980	Organization leader Policy adviser and initiator Intergovernmental manager Program initiator Decision-making catalyst	Executive officer
1980–present	Coordinator of administrative operations Policy initiator and coordinator Decision-making catalyst Community development leader Policy and program evaluation	Chief executive officer

managers who could help government deliver more of the services being desired. This reaction was in marked contrast, however, to the much slower growth of city management in the period 1914–1952, when city councils were populated by people who were in favor of limited government, people who had been raised to view government with suspicion. Such persons were much less willing to trust the management of their local affairs to an "outsider."

This dialectic swing in popular attitudes toward government has occurred again. As Table 5.1 suggests, a new generation has emerged in American public life, a generation that grew up viewing government with hostility and mistrust. Just as past generational changes affected the city management profession and city manager roles, so, too, will the hostility and mistrust of the generation now being elected to public office.

The post-1960s generation experienced yet another change that will affect, and is affecting, evolutionary trends. It is a generation with a new and stronger sense of political efficacy and commitment. Political activities associated with the antiwar movement and civil rights demonstrations gave participants a sense of personal, individual empowerment to bring about government change. It opened new avenues for popular participation in government and encouraged markedly increased levels of political activism by people from all walks of life and at all levels of government. This generation is empowered by its youthful experiences to take a more personal and active role in government at all levels.

This sense of empowerment, of the ability of the individual to make a personal mark upon government, will not diminish with age. Braungart and Braungart (1991), in a life-history study of former activist leaders, suggest that "a political generation takes a lifetime to end. Although the collective-activist phase of their youth ceased more than two decades ago, the spirit of the 1960s political generation endures. Whether these men and women who led SDS and YAF in the

1960s viewed their earlier experiences as 'life transforming' or a 'learning experience,' they continue in their middle-age years to try to implement their youthful values—in high public office as well as in 'little niches'" (297).

Sociological studies of generational impacts confirm that sociopolitical orientations tend to endure over the life span (Alwin and Krosnick 1991; Braungart and Braungart 1991; Krosnick 1991); historical evidence also documents the cyclical nature of political change in the American polity and the ability to base predictions for the future on such changes (Smith 1990). Changes in the political attitudes and behaviors of the American electorate are coming, and their coming will significantly affect the role of the city manager in council-manager government.

Some of these changes have already come, and they are presenting problems for council-manager government. The makeup of city councils has changed: the membership of such bodies is more diverse, and the behavior of the members is different. Many more council members are being elected from districts: more and more city managers are finding that they must shift to accommodate ward-based politics, which brings new, and many more, stresses.

The role of the mayor in council-manager government has also been changing. As early as 1979 city managers were discussing the impact of the "strong mayor/manager" form of government at their annual meeting. More recently, the *Municipal Yearbook* (1988) has noted a convergence of the council-manager plan and the mayor-council plan, noting "excellent prospects for the further interchange of aspects of structure and function" (9). Svara (1990, 181) has also noted this convergence and the likelihood that it will bring increased conflict in council-manager cities.

Ehrenhalt (1991) has identified still another pattern of change that will have an impact on city managers and their roles, and that, in fact, may have a decisive impact on managerial involvement in policy processes. Ehrenhalt has found that elected office holders have changed in nature. They have changed from persons elected to office with the support of parties or groups in the community to persons who gain election as a result of personal incentive and effort. They have changed from persons whose primary occupation was in the private sector and who held public office as a community service to persons whose primary time and energy commitment is to public office and only secondarily to other professional activity. They have changed to increasingly include those who have been willing to make a major investment of time and talent to gain and exercise political influence. Such people typically want more than to serve the community; they want to make a significant difference.

Ehrenhalt describes the new style of office holder in the following terms:

> Seeking and holding office take up more of a politician's time than they did a generation ago. It is much harder now to combine politics and a career in private life. . . .
>
> People in local government—city council members, county commissioners, and their equivalents—nearly all have some discretion in how much time they devote to their work. . . . Local politicians can hold down private jobs and most of them do. But a variation on Gresham's law has come to operate in local politics: full-timers drive part-timers out of circulation. The city councilman who spends his days building political coalitions, meeting with constituents, and cultivating financial support sets a standard of political sophistication that colleagues pretty much have to meet if they are going to stay effective or even stay in office. Once a city council attracts its first full-time member, it is on the way to becoming a de facto full-time institution, even if it does not think of itself as one.
>
> What matters . . . is ambition. Political careers are open to ambition now in a way that has not been true in America in most of this century. . . . The real barriers are the burdens that a political career has come to impose on people who pursue it—the burdens of time,

physical effort, and financial sacrifice. Politics is a profession now, not just in Congress, but in many state legislatures and in countless local governments, where a casual part-time commitment used to suffice. . . .

Every individual is a faction unto himself. [Ehrenhalt 1991]

Such a public office holder is not a linear extension of political predecessors but the antithesis of elected local officials of a generation ago. Yet this new breed of office holder is becoming increasingly familiar to city managers; it is a kind of office holder to whom city managers must adapt if they wish to survive as policy leaders.

City Manager Adaptations

Some city managers are adapting to, and will survive in, this new political environment. Particularly well suited will be those in cities sufficiently well staffed to employ professionals as department heads and management assistants and in middle-management positions; those who enjoy the policy game; and particularly those sufficiently fortunate to avoid too many of Ehrenhalt's new breed of politicians on their councils. But many others will have difficulty: they will not have sufficient staff support; they will have difficulty adapting to the multiple, and often conflicting, demands of the political activists on the council; and they will hesitate to risk their job in an uncertain employment market.

Newell, Glass, and Ammons (1989) have already uncovered evidence of change in city manager policy activity that, although it does not involve less attention to policy, does suggest a difference in approach: "As the political environment of council-manager cities has changed, city managers have apparently relinquished the mantle of community leadership to elected officials while not only spending more time on but regarding as more important the policy role, which encompasses policy development and council relations."

Managers of the future will increasingly face the dilemma of the baseball manager. With no control of the people above them in the organizational hierarchy, with limited choice and control over those whom they must manage, and with publicly visible responsibility for organizational success, they will find themselves the easy target of those, on the council and in the community, who have reason to find fault with organizational performance. Just as the unhappy owners of losing baseball teams find it easiest to fire the manager, so too will dissatisfied city council members find that "firing the manager" offers a quick, convenient way to give constituents the impression that they are taking charge of events and moving to make improvements.

In such a milieu, many—perhaps most—city managers will "hunker down" in their jobs, focus their energies on delivering services and resolving citizen complaints, and avoid, whenever possible, entanglement with the personalities on the council. Such managers may still list "involvement in policy" as their primary activity, but it will be a kind of involvement that is much different from that of their predecessors in the 1970s and 1980s. It will not be a proactive involvement that seeks to identify policy needs, detail policy alternatives, and encourage optimization in decision making. Instead, it will be a reactive involvement, addressing issues that arise from other sources, waiting for council direction before charting alternatives, and willingly accepting "satisficing" solutions.

Managers are, after all, only human. Faced with increasing political uncertainty and the possibility of imminent job loss, they will sacrifice rationality for incrementalism in decision making; work diligently more to avoid mistakes than to achieve success; perfect standard routines rather than assume the risks of innovation; and seek anonymity rather than leadership. In short, they will become government bureaucrats. In the process, they will have lost their distinctive place in the field of public management, their ability to be "unique in the degree to which they can rather openly assert their special quality and status in the exercise of leadership" (Sherwood 1976, 586).

Implications for Professional Development

The city management profession, in short, may find that its role in local government ceases to advance in a linear fashion, building on past achievements. Instead, it may begin to experience dialectic change similar to the pattern characteristic of society's political values and leadership. If it does, the manager of the future will represent a synthesis of the administrative officer of the pre-1938 era and the policy activist/leader of the present era. Such a managerial role will be very different from what will occur if Svara's vision of "a continuing shift toward the policy and political roles" is realized.

In either event, managers of the future will need more sophisticated and developed "political skills" if they are to survive and succeed. Whether they are "hunkered down" trying to avoid dismissal by politically ambitious council members or aggressively, perhaps even politically, providing policy leadership, they will have to take a page from the book of the nineteenth-century government reformers who learned that structural reform, by itself, does not resolve the problems of local government. Rather, reformers found that "the missing ingredient was a need for wider human understanding and concern. . . . All the reasoning in the world that the reformers' policies of efficiency and economy would benefit the masses would not, did not, and could not compensate for a lack of contact, caring, and empathy. These were all qualities that these same masses met and recognized in probably the majority of the precinct and ward leaders of the political machine" (Griffith 1938).

These qualities continue even now to be projected by successful political leaders. Unless city managers of the future can project these same qualities, they are not likely to survive the future milieu projected either by Svara or this chapter. If they are to play aggressive policy and political roles, then they must project the qualities of successful public leaders; if they are to survive as government bureaucrats in a position not unlike that of baseball managers, then they must portray the caring and empathy needed to give each of their individual council members a sense of personal fulfillment and political success.

To prepare for such roles, managers must match their technical competence with human relations skills. The field of administration has long recognized the need for such skills in working with subordinates. The literature, from Mary Parker Follett to contemporary OD (Organization Development) theorists, is replete with admonitions regarding the human factor in management. What is now needed is the development of OD-type skills, competencies, and methodologies for dealing with organizational superiors—with the council members, other political leaders; members of local advisory boards and commissions, neighborhood organization leaders, and the proverbial taxpayers who make demands on city hall.

These OD skills will be different from those employed in the technology of making the organization work. Although people are always people, relationships are not always the same. The people above the manager in the organization may be just as human as those below, but their relationships are vastly different.

Managerial relationships with elected officials are changing as the behavior—the objectives, involvement, and expectations—of elected officials changes. New OD-type competencies and insights must be developed so that city managers can adjust to, capitalize on, or simply survive in whatever changing role is now emerging for their profession.

Notes

1. County managers, professional twins of city managers, have come into their own as local government administrators in recent years, but for simplicity's sake this article will use the more widely accepted generic term *city managers* to refer to city and county management professionals.

2. Judd (1979, 104–109) describes the theme used by proponents of council-manager government to sell the plan to Dallas voters in 1930: "Why not run Dallas itself on a business schedule by business methods under business management? . . . The city manager plan is after all only a business management plan. . . . The city manager is the executive of a corporation under a board of directors. Dallas is the corporation. It is as simple as that. Vote for it." The voters did.

References

Alwin, D., and J. Krosnick. 1991. "Aging, Cohorts, and the Stability of Sociopolitical Orientations over the Life Span." *American Journal of Sociology* 97, no. 1: 169–195.

Ammons, D., and C. Newell. 1989. *City Executives.* Albany: State University of New York Press.

Banovetz, J. 1971. *Managing the Modern City.* Washington, DC: International City Management Association.

Bosworth, K. 1958. "The City Manager Is a Politician." *Public Administration Review* 18: 215.

Braungart, J., and R. Braungart. 1991. "The Effects of the 1960s Political Generation on Former Left- and Right-Wing Youth Activist Leaders." *Social Problems* 38, no. 3: 297.

Ehrenhalt, A. 1991. *The United States of Ambition.* New York: Times Books, pp. 14, 15, 18, 272–273, 276.

Frederickson, H. 1989. *Ideal and Practice in Council-Manager Government.* Washington, DC: International City Management Association.

Frisch, M., and R. Stevens. 1971. *American Political Thought.* New York: Charles Scribner's Sons.

Gaebler, T. 1983. "The Entrepreneurial Manager." *Public Management* 65, no. 1: 14.

Graves, C. 1982. "Guidelines for the Black Urban Administrator." *Public Management* 65, no. 6: 15.

Griffith, E. 1938. *A History of American City Government: The Conspicuous Failure, 1970–1900.* New York: Praeger.

Judd, Dennis R. 1979. *The Politics of American Cities: Private Power and Public Policy.* Boston, MA: Little, Brown.

Keller, L. 1989. "City Managers and Federalism." In *Ideal and Practice in Council-Manager Government*, ed. H. Frederickson. Washington, DC: International City Management Association.

Krosnick, J. 1991. "The Stability of Political Preferences: Comparisons of Symbolic and Nonsymbolic Attitudes." *American Journal of Political Science* 35, no. 2: 547–576.

Loveridge, R. 1971. *City Managers in Legislative Politics.* New York: Bobbs-Merrill.

Mikulecky, T. 1980. "Intergovernmental Relations Strategies for the Local Manager." *Public Administration Review* 40, no. 4: 379.

Mosher, F.C. 1982. *Democracy and the Public Service*, 2d ed. New York: Oxford University Press.

Municipal Yearbook 1988. Washington, DC: International City Management Association.

Newell, C., J. Glass, and D. Ammons. 1989. "City Manager Roles in a Changing Political Environment." In *Ideal and Practice in Council-Manager Government*, ed. H. Frederickson. Washington, DC: International City Management Association.

Newland, C. 1979. "Future Images: Urban Diversity and Democracy." In *Municipal Yearbook 1979.* Washington, DC: International City Management Association.

Renner, T. 1990. "Appointed Local Government Managers: Stability and Change." In *Municipal Yearbook 1990.* Washington, DC: International City Management Association.

Rutter, L. 1980. (for the ICMA Committee on Future Horizons of the Profession), *The Essential Community: Local Government in the Year 2000.* Washington, DC: International City Management Association.

Sherwood, F. 1976. "The American Public Executive in the Third Century." *Public Administration Review* 36, no. 5: 586.

Smith, T. 1900. "Liberal and Conservative Trends in the United States Since World War II." *Public Opinion Quarterly* 54: 479–507.

Stillman, R., II. 1974. *The Rise of the City Manager.* Albuquerque: University of New Mexico Press.

Svara, J. 1990. *Official Leadership in the City.* New York: Oxford University Press.

Toffler, A. 1980. "New Worlds of Service." *Public Management* 62, no. 1: 8.

CHAPTER 6

A CASE FOR REINTERPRETED DICHOTOMY OF POLITICS AND ADMINISTRATION AS A PROFESSIONAL STANDARD IN COUNCIL-MANAGER GOVERNMENT

ROBERT S. MONTJOY AND DOUGLAS J. WATSON

For as long as there have been city managers their roles in politics and the policy process have been issues of paramount concern to practitioners and scholars. The centerpiece of this discussion has been the dichotomy of politics and administration, the doctrine that administration could and should be institutionally separate from politics. Applied to the council-manager form of government, a strict version of this doctrine would place the manager in a role of a neutral expert who efficiently and effectively carried out the policies of the council.

Over the years, a number of scholars have suggested that such a strict interpretation might not be what early proponents of a dichotomy had intended (Golembiewski 1977, 9–11; Cooper 1984, 80–84; Waldo 1984, 222–225). Nevertheless, the idea of an institutional separation has persisted and has been the foil for numerous studies. In a review of the literature, James Svara found consistent evidence that, almost throughout the history of the council-manager plan, managers have played an active role in the policy process. Yet instead of being settled, the issue has been "periodically rediscovered" (Svara 1989, 77).

Svara attributed the dichotomy's persistence to its partial descriptive accuracy and to its normative appeal as a guide for administrative behavior consistent with democratic theory. His own reconceptualization of council-manager relationships as a mission-management continuum appears to improve on the descriptive accuracy of the dichotomy without abandoning the idea of role separation (Svara 1985; 1989).

John Nalbandian (1991) takes a stronger position. He argues that politics has transformed the role of the city manager from that of neutral expert to community leader and problem solver. The dichotomy persists not as a guide to behavior but as an intellectual device connecting practice to theory. He seeks to replace this function of the dichotomy with an expanded base of professional values for city managers.

We agree with Svara and Nalbandian that the dichotomy of policy and administration, as traditionally interpreted, prescribes roles that are neither practical nor desirable in council-manager government. On the other hand, we think that few would wish to abandon the dichotomy of politics and administration as a bulwark against certain forms of particularism, such as special

From *Public Administration Review*, vol. 55, no. 3 (May/June 1995), pp. 231–239. Copyright © 1995 by American Society for Public Administration. Reprinted with permission.

favors in hiring or contracting decisions. Must we throw out the baby with the bath water? The answer depends upon what we mean by the dichotomy and how we intend to use the concept.

We focus on the politics-administration dichotomy as a professional standard in council-manager government, not as a description of actual behavior. In this we follow Herbert Simon's normative interpretation of the dichotomy (1967, 88). The debate over its utility should rest, we think, on both normative issues (the values served) and empirical issues (whether such a standard can actually affect behavior in desired ways). Under this perspective, evidence that some behavior falls short of the standard is not, in itself, grounds for abandoning the standard. On the other hand, if a standard proscribes behavior, such as participation in the policy process, which is necessary to the job, then the standard may be of no value or even of negative value because it robs practitioners of legitimacy. So, it is crucial to examine exactly what the standard is and what behavior it advocates.

This chapter is divided into two principal parts. In the first, we reinterpret the dichotomy. In the second, we explore the implications for council-manager government.

Reinterpreting the Dichotomies

We make the case that it is reasonable to base an interpretation of the dichotomies on the writings of Woodrow Wilson (1887) and Frank Goodnow (1900) because of their historical connection with the council-manager plan. The dichotomy of *policy* and administration was a conceptual distinction underlying a theory of democratic accountability. It was not intended as a guide to behavior. The dichotomy of *politics* and administration was intended as a behavioral prescription directed against contemporary practices of machine politics. The reformers' arguments apply as well to the broader issue of particularism in government, which is as relevant today as it was a century ago. The institutional ban on particularistic politics in administration was not a ban on discretion, as long as administrators were accountable. The reformers' theory of accountability required a concentration of power, which was not achieved in the governments of their day because of the constitutional separation of powers. If there is an exception to the separation-of-powers problems, it is to be found in council-manager government.

Wilson, Goodnow, and the Council-Manager Plan

We focus on the writings of Wilson and Goodnow because they preceded the adoption of the council-manager plan and because both authors were active in associations that subsequently promoted the plan. For this reason, we will not consider later work, such as that of Gulick and Urwick (1937), which emphasized the scientific aspects of management to the exclusion of politics (Graham and Hays 1986, 24–25).

The council-manager plan was born during an era of reform, muckraking, and scientific management (Stillman 1974, 25). The most influential of the reform associations was the National Municipal League, formed in 1895. Its primary goal was to develop structural changes in city government to make it less prone to corruption. Although the league's first model city charter in 1898 advocated the strong mayor form of government, its members were soon drawn to the commission form of municipal government, which was founded in Galveston, Texas, following the disastrous hurricane of 1900. Five elected commissioners acted as a body for legislative matters, but they individually managed the various municipal departments. The plan proved popular, and only a decade after its adoption in Galveston, over 160 American cities were operating under the commission form. This scheme had abandoned the separation of powers, but critics charged that it spread administrative functions and failed to give any central direction to the city (Holli 1974, 147–148).

Staunton, Virginia, appointed the first city manager in 1908. This innovation caught the attention of reformer Richard S. Childs (1965), who refined the idea and became the chief advocate of the council-manager plan. In 1912, Sumter, South Carolina, became the first city to adopt the pure council-manager plan as Childs espoused it. Shortly thereafter, in 1915, the National Municipal League adopted the plan for its Model City Charter.

The council-manager plan can trace its intellectual lineage through Childs to Wilson, Goodnow, and other reformers of the day. Childs had joined with Wilson and James Bryce to found the Short Ballot Organization in 1909. He served with Frank Goodnow on the board of the National Municipal League when that organization adopted the council-manager plan for its model charter.

The point of this discussion is that Wilson and Goodnow had an opportunity to influence the development of the council-manager plan and not vice versa. They wrote about governments characterized by separation of powers. As a result, the dichotomies picked up some theoretical baggage which is not relevant to council-manager government. So we proceed by unpacking the baggage in search of the essential pieces.

Two Dichotomies

Much of the confusion, we believe, comes from Goodnow. He gave the title *Politics and Administration* (1900) to a book in which he devoted much attention to the distinction between policy making and administration. Was his dichotomy between politics and administration or between policy making and administration, or were politics and policy making interchangeable for him? In fact, it is difficult to tell what he really meant, but we offer an interpretation based on the assumption of two dichotomies—a conceptual dichotomy between policy and administration and an institutional dichotomy between politics and administration.

Goodnow began his treatise with a conceptual argument. He attacked the familiar premise of three basic functions of government—executive, legislative, and judicial. Instead, he argued, there were but two: the expression of the popular will and the execution of that will. The three traditional powers were derived from the two functions, and each of the three branches of the United States government combined in different measure both the expression and the execution of the popular will. Most judicial activity, for example, was the application of law in specific cases, that is, an execution of the public will (Goodnow 1900, 9–13).

At this point in its development, the dichotomy was an analytical construct, a division of governmental powers into two instead of the three. As such, it had the same intellectual posture as Montesquieu's tripartite division of powers before it was institutionalized in the United States Constitution.

We have not answered the question of whether this expression of the public will was policy making or politics or both. It would seem to include elements of both because the public will is expressed in the form of policy, and politics is involved in that process. In order to make a finer distinction between politics and policy, we must consider the second dichotomy.

"The field of administration is a field of business. It is removed from the hurry and strife of politics. . . . Administration lies outside the proper sphere of politics. Administrative questions are not political questions" (Wilson 1887, 18). These statements certainly do advocate a separation of politics and administration, but what they would mean in practice depends upon the definitions of the key terms. Rosenbloom (1984, 104) points out that Wilson actually dealt with two different types of politics, one focused on partisanship and patronage, the other on policy making. The distinction is important. If politics includes all of what we know as policy making, then the dichotomy would, indeed, bar administrators, presumably including city managers, from participation in that process. If, on the other hand, the term refers to something else, the same conclusion does not necessarily hold.

Clearly, Wilson wished to separate patronage politics from administration. He demonstrated this concern in the sentence immediately following the previously cited quotation: "Although politics sets the tasks for administration, *it should not be suffered to manipulate its offices*" (Wilson 1887, 18, emphasis added). Whether Wilson advocated a dichotomy of policy making and administration is another issue. "Regardless of what he wrote in 'The Study of Administration,' the implications of his later work are unavoidable: administrators were politicians; they must have the freedom to make ethical decisions" (Miewald 1984, 17).

Goodnow's writing on this point offers a possible explanation for much of the confusion on the dichotomy. He used both "politics" and "policy" to refer to the expression of the popular will and "administration" to refer to the execution of that will. This usage is a source of considerable confusion, as noted above. Does politics mean patronage or does it mean policy making, or are the three concepts indistinguishable?

The answer may lie in the dictionary definition of politics that he offers near the beginning of *Politics and Administration:*

> The act or vocation of guiding or influencing the policy of a government through the organization of a party among its citizens—including, therefore, not only the ethics of government, but more especially, and often to the exclusion of ethical principles, the art of influencing public opinion, attracting and marshalling voters, and obtaining and distributing public patronage, so far as the possession of offices may depend upon the political opinions or political services of individuals. (Goodnow 1900, 19)

This statement yields two important points. First, politics is definitionally limited to that part of the policy-making process, "the act or vocation of guiding or influencing the policy of a government," which is accomplished through a particular method, "the organization of a party among its citizens." Second, the application of that method explicitly includes patronage.

This definition is consistent with Wilson's usage, and it offers a simple and attractive solution to the interpretation of Goodnow. We have to conceive of his "expression of the public will" as the entire policy-making process, including elections. Politics is that part of the process related to political parties. Patronage was a common element in party organization of the time. Indeed, Rosenbloom (1993) points out that the dichotomy was a weapon in a struggle against political bosses and the system of political ethics they represented. As we shall try to show, however, the removal of partisanship and patronage from administration does not necessarily equate to an institutional separation of all policy making from administration.

We do not claim that this is the only interpretation possible from the entire text of the reformers' works. Certainly, other readers have reached different conclusions. We have simply shown that there is evidence for our interpretation. At this point, rather than going through a line-by-line analysis to show what Goodnow really said, we will rest our case on the meaning of the terms in the fundamental argument that he made for an institutional dichotomy.

The objection to mixing politics and administration was twofold: it interfered with the accurate expression of the will of the state, and it interfered with the efficient administration of that will (Goodnow 1900, 37–38). The former problem came from people voting on the basis of discrete personal benefits as opposed to principle. The latter problem came from administrators using the resources of their offices for the benefit of a particular party or class rather than the efficient execution of the state will (i.e., policy). This statement can be seen as a generalization of the problem of the urban machine, such as the Tweed ring in New York, about which Goodnow (1888) had already written.

Goodnow's argument, it seems to us, helps to clarify the definitional issue. How can politics interfere with the accurate expression of the state will if the two terms are synonymous? The argument makes sense only if we take politics to mean patronage, or other particularistic benefits, in this case.

If this interpretation is correct, we are left with two dichotomies. The first is conceptual, dividing the functions of government into the expression of a will and the execution of that will. The second is operational, the doctrine that the filling of administrative offices (those primarily concerned with execution of the will) should not be used by candidates to attract support in the contest for electoral offices.

Particularism

It may be objected that equating politics with patronage makes the institutional dichotomy irrelevant to most merit systems in use today. To answer that objection, we must broaden the concept from patronage to particularism, which is an organizational decision based on some criteria other than the official goals of the organization (Perrow 1986, 6–9).

The urban political machine shows that particularism extend beyond patronage. Banfield and Wilson (1963, 115–127) define the machine as an organization that uses specific, material inducements to maintain support, and they documented a much more complex network of personal obligations than simply the trading of jobs for votes. Patronage employees were important, not just because they and their families would vote for the machine but also because they would provide small particularistic services that created feelings of personal obligation on the part of clients. Even if the service were appropriate under formal rules, it could be delivered in such a way as to create a feeling of personal obligation.

Particularistic politics are not limited to urban machines. Recent allegations of influence peddling (Abscam, the Keating Five, and the Whitewater investigation) illustrate both the variety and persistence of particularism. We know of several mayor-council cities in our home state of Alabama that routinely give each council member a portion of the budget to distribute as he or she sees fit.

Formal theory also suggests inherent incentives for particularism. The extensive rational choice literature on voting participation argues that the policy benefits of an election are rarely sufficient to induce participation (e.g., Downs 1957; Aldrich 1993). Personal obligations created by particularism are a means by which elected officials can avoid the free-rider problem and gain active political support (Fiorina 1977).

Finally, and probably most important, we do not have to invoke sophisticated strategies to explain the persistence of particularism. People depend on personal relationships in their everyday lives, and most of them do not go through rigorous courses in rational-legal authority structures when they are elected to office, especially at the local level. What could be more natural than a city council member, for example, responding to a citizen's problem by going to the public servant involved and trying to get her or him to take action? It seems reasonable to conclude that particularism is worth concern today as well as in Goodnow's time.

In this section, we have attempted to make two points. First, Goodnow's argument is not logically limited to political patronage. It applies to all forms of particularism in public organizations. Second, particularism was not an exclusively nineteenth-century phenomenon. The incentives for it are inherent in human relationships and in politics. We now turn to a consideration of how the reformers sought to combat particularism.

Discretion and Accountability

If the goal was to insulate administration from particularistic politics, what was the method? The merit system was a step. Was the elimination of discretion another?

Jameson Doig (1983) has made a persuasive argument on this point. Far from shackling administration, the reformers wanted to empower it. "The idea for us is a civil service cultured and self-sufficient enough to act with sense and vigor, and yet so intimately connected with the popular thought, by means of elections and constant public counsel, as to find arbitrariness or class spirit quite out of the question" (Wilson 1887, 22). Doig argues that the reformers' frequent business analogy carries with it the notions of leadership and daring that characterized public perceptions of the successful entrepreneur at that time. While seeking to eliminate particularism, the reformers also had the goal of providing for a vigorous administration.

What is to prevent abuse of power by a vigorous administration? The answer would seem to come from the reformers' well-known views on accountability. "Large powers and unhampered discretion seem to me the indispensable conditions of responsibility. . . . There is no danger in power, if only it be not irresponsible. If it be divided, dealt out in shares to many, it is obscured; and if it be obscured, it is made irresponsible" (Wilson 1887, 20). As this quotation from Wilson demonstrates, the reformers favored the concentration of power if it could be held accountable.

Their mechanism for accountability was an administrative hierarchy reporting to elective, policy-making institutions. Nothing in their system prevents the exercise of discretion within the bounds of higher policy, nor is there anything to preclude attempts to influence higher policy, as long as those attempts stay within the hierarchically established chain of command. Thus, Goodnow could envision a system of officials with progressively smaller policy roles as one moves down the pyramid. He divided the administrative function into three subfunctions: the executive function, which is charged with the general execution of the law; the *quasi*-judicial and semiscientific functions of applying technical knowledge to specific cases (property assessment or building code enforcement); and the purely clerical and ministerial functions of simply carrying out the "orders of superiors in whose hands is the determination of general questions of administrative policy" (Goodnow 1900, 88).

Whereas Goodnow had consistently contended that the general functions of the expression and execution of will could not be allocated exclusively to separate institutions, he apparently felt that these subfunctions could be sufficiently segregated so that he could begin to speak of the officers and positions to which they would be assigned.

> In the semi-scientific, quasi-judicial, clerical, and ministerial divisions of the administrative system provision should be made for permanence of tenure, if efficient and impartial administration is to be expected, and if questions of policy are to be determined in accordance with the popular will. In its higher divisions, that is, those where the incumbents of offices have a determining influence on questions of policy, and particularly in case of the executive head, permanence of tenure should be avoided. Provision should in these cases be made for political control if it is hoped to secure the decision of questions of policy by bodies representative of the people. (1900, 91)

It would seem clear from this statement that Goodnow anticipated policy making within the administrative offices. Reference is even made to policy determination within the lower divisions, among the semiscientific and *quasi*-judicial workers whose job it is to make decisions in concrete cases. "In these cases much must be left to official discretion, since what is demanded of the officers is not the doing of a concrete thing, but the exercise of judgment" (1900, 81). The picture presented here seems closer to a policy continuum, such as that found by Svara, than to a dichotomy.

Thus, it seems to us, one reasonable interpretation of Goodnow's doctrine is not the elimination of discretion (the dichotomy of policy making and administration) but the elimination of particularism (the dichotomy of politics and administration). By what means? Although one could try to eliminate the particularistic use of discretion by the elimination of all discretion, such a process would not be very efficient, even if it were possible, because it would deprive the organization of "the exercise of judgment." Goodnow and Wilson seem to have rejected that alternative in favor of two other methods: (1) civil service reform to eliminate the principal means of effecting particularism and (2) accountability through hierarchy. The latter method raises another question that the reformers had to address: accountability to whom?

The Concentration of Power

At this point, the reformers' argument ran afoul of fragmented power in the U.S. political system. Fragmentation took many forms—the long ballot, independent boards and commissions, committee government in Congress—but the most basic of these was the constitutional separation of powers. Independent powers broke the chain of accountability at the broad policy (lawmaking) level by creating multiple masters for the bureaucracy. Rather than presenting administration with the singular expression of will upon which Goodnow based his argument, the Constitution imbued each branch with different values (Rosenbloom 1983). The absence of a singular power center prevented the establishment of a hierarchy which could both direct and empower its agencies. Hence Norton Long's famous observation some years later: "It is clear that the American system of politics does not generate enough power at any focal point of leadership to provide the conditions for an even partially successful divorce of politics from administration. Subordinates cannot depend on the formal chain of command to deliver enough political power to permit them to do their jobs" (Long 1949, 204).

The reformers were aware of this problem and advocated various mechanisms to consolidate power. John Rohr has pointed out that Wilson actually envisioned a parliamentary (cabinet) government and wrote with such a system in mind (Rohr 1986, 63). Goodnow saw the political party as a potential solution within the existing constitutional order. Parties could unite at least the executive and the two houses of the legislative branch, thereby concentrating power and completing the chain of accountability to the electorate.

The dichotomy (as an analytical construct) can be interpreted as Goodnow's attempt to legitimize the role that parties would have to play in the reformers' solution to the accountability problem. Having determined that there were but two functions of government, he could then argue that one would have to be superior to the other in order to provide harmony in government. In a popular government, this would have to be the expression of will. In the American system, no single branch of government could exercise this control, but a party could (Goodnow 1900, 24–25). Thus party government could, in principle, solve the accountability problem.

A unified government, again in principle, could receive policy recommendations and advocacy from a variety of sources (including officials who were also charged with administrative duties), formulate clear and consistent policies, transmit those policies through the hierarchy, hold the hierarchy accountable for implementation, and make itself accountable to the electorate. If the hierarchy is to have any discretion in implementation, it must exercise that discretion in support of the official policies. Otherwise, implementation of the official policy will be diluted and accountability will suffer. Thus, the hierarchy must be free, insofar as possible, from extraneous influences. Hence, the institutional dichotomy of politics, meaning particularistic influences, and administration.

This is an admittedly idealized vision of bureaucratic accountability, not a description of actual conditions. It is certainly not a novel idea. We would simply suggest that it may be what the reformers had in mind by the dichotomy. Patronage politics was to be banned from administrative offices because of its deleterious effects on the expression and execution of the public will. Policy making was not banned, but it had to conform to hierarchical lines. Thus, for example, an interest group that lost at the broad policy-making level could not subsequently alter the policy by influencing implementation at a lower level. While such an idea may seem farfetched today, it might not be so obviously out of place in a system that had a true center of power and a mechanism for protecting the hierarchy.

The model that Goodnow and other reformers advocated can be viewed as a prescription designed to promote accountability, efficiency, and impartiality by buffering the bureaucracy from the political environment. Does it work? Not at the national and state levels, certainly not to the extent that the reformers would have liked. There, political parties have never been able to overcome the separation of powers, and the sheer size and complexity of government weaken hierarchical control and support. Under such circumstances civil service reform may be a necessary but not a sufficient condition.

Should this failure lead to a rejection of the dichotomy as interpreted here? Not necessarily. An alternate conceptualization, the tripartite division of powers, was already institutionalized in our Constitution and supported by court interpretations and an alignment of interests built up over a century of government. Pitting the reformers' dream against this imbedded system should not be regarded as a critical test.

If there is an exception to Long's generalization, it is most likely to be found at the local level in the council-manager form of government. The separation of powers does not apply there, and the system was designed to serve the same purposes as Goodnow's model, though sometimes with different means. So we turn to a consideration of the council-manager form in order to ask whether our interpretation of the dichotomy has utility there.

Dichotomy in Council-Manager Government

In tracing the implications of the above reasoning for council-manager government, our basic argument is that by concentrating power in the legislative body, council-manager government satisfies the intent of the conceptual dichotomy, giving expression of the public will control over the execution of that will. A body which is sure of its own authority is free to allow subordinates as much discretion and as large a policy role as seem appropriate. The institutional dichotomy comes into play, not between the council and the manager, but in the relationship between council members and the administrative hierarchy. As we shall try to show, the reasoning of the reformers supports requirements that (1) directions from the council come in the form of official policy and (2) that neither individual members nor the whole council bypass the manager in giving directions to the staff. The maintenance of this system, we think, requires both the rules embodied in council-manager charters and the professional standards of the International City/County Management Association.

The Council-Manager Plan

The basic elements of the plan are familiar. An elected council exercises the legislative function and hires a city manager who serves at the pleasure of the council. The manager is in charge of a staff that performs most of the functions of the city. The council-manager plan avoids the separation-of-powers problem by clearly establishing legislative supremacy. This arrangement is consistent with Goodnow's maxim that the expression of will should be superior to the execution of the will. In this respect, it is also analogous to the cabinet system which Wilson so admired. While it fails to produce an electoral mandate for party government, at least the council-manager plan does not institutionalize different values in competing power centers. In principle, there is unity of command and a clear chain of accountability up through the administrative hierarchy to the manager, who is accountable to the council. Again in principle, this arrangement satisfies the intent of the conceptual dichotomy, legislative supremacy.

The model charter reflects the reformers' antipathy to patronage and their desire to channel policy direction through the hierarchy. The council may not demand the appointment of officers or employees under the manager, and they may not give orders to those officers or employees (National Civil League 1989, 12). Child's explanation of these provisions shows his desire to enforce the hierarchy.

> The managers, of course, often have to defend their proper prerogatives as chief of staff. They must preserve discipline, and city business must be moved up to the council through orderly channels. The council members must be carefully and tactfully headed off from personal interferences in departments under the manager for, if such ways become common, one councilman begins to enjoy foreknowledge or special advantages over the rest and they will resent it. Likewise, municipal employees must be restrained from going over the head of the manager to lobby in the council against his programs or discipline. (Childs 1965, 25)

Applying the Reinterpreted Dichotomies

The above statement does not preclude a policy role for the manager. In fact, the manager would seem to qualify as an executive under Goodnow's classification. Executives could have "a determining influence on questions of policy." Hence they should not have job tenure but be subject to political control. If one follows the logic of the reformers, the lack of tenure is a strong indication that a position was supposed to be involved in the policy process.

Early charters gave the manager a voice in policy making. That of Dayton, Ohio, the first sizable city to adopt the plan, includes under powers and duties of the city manager "to recommend to the commission for adoption such measures as may deem necessary or expedient," in addition, the manager was "to attend all meetings of the commission, with the right to take part in the discussion but having no vote" (Mabie 1918, 56). Similar provisions were put in the charter of Springfield, Ohio, the second largest city to have adopted the council-manager plan by 1913 (Bromage 1970, 34). The Model City Charter adopted in 1916 contained language identical to that of the Dayton charter. As Svara commented, there has never been any question but that the manager was a policy leader (1989, 70).

Our interpretation of the policy-administration dichotomy is consistent with Svara's finding. We have argued that this was a conceptual dichotomy used to justify legislative supremacy, which is already accomplished in adoption of the council-manager plan. It does not preclude a role for the manager in policy making.

On the other hand, the council-manager plan does attempt to create an institutional dichotomy between politics and administration if one interprets "politics" to mean patronage and particularistic influence. Recall Perrow's definition of particularism as decisions based on criteria other than the goals of the organization. Who sets the goals of the organization? The council has ultimate authority to do so, but only when it is acting as a council. The above requirements are designed to force the council to act through official policy. They do not prevent the council from influencing administration through fairly detailed policy, but they do force the council to act as a body, rather than as individuals, and to take a public position on its directions, being subject to electoral accountability for the same.

We can interpret the institutional dichotomy as an effort to prevent staff participation in particularistic politics. Although politicians might promise favors to supporters, they could not use the staff to deliver on these promises except in the form of official policy adopted by the council and passed through the manager. By the same logic, staff could not give or accept particularistic favors.

What of staff involvement in the policy process? Could they take the initiative? Could they advocate changes? Our interpretation would suggest that they could, so long as their policy activities stayed within the channels provided by the hierarchy. It is hard to imagine an administrator possessed of broad powers who is precluded from advocating policy changes to her or his superior. Yet authoritative policy decisions must stay within the bounds of the hierarchy to ensure accountability and legislative supremacy.

Our interpretation removes the policy-administration dichotomy as a clear dividing line between the council, on the one hand, and the manager and staff on the other. The council is capable of directing the bureaucracy through very detailed policy if it chooses to do so. We are left with a policy-administration continuum, which is what Svara found. That continuum must, however, be confined within existing lines of authority if our interpretation of the politics-administration dichotomy is correct. What this means in practice is that managers can participate in the policy process, exercise as much discretion as the council will allow, and still hold a clear line against particularistic requests directed to themselves or to members of the staff.

This conclusion leads to another question. Who or what is to define and enforce the roles that the different parties must play? We address that issue in the next section.

Making the Dichotomies Work

Despite his rejection of the dichotomy as traditionally conceived, Svara found that councils and managers were able to work out meaningful role differentiation in many cities. We would suggest that the explanation for meaningful role differentiation may lie with city managers, who belong to a profession that has its own norms and socialization processes. They have a vested professional interest in making the system work, and they are in a pivotal position to manage council-staff relations. They can help to determine the degree of council involvement in the various governmental functions that Svara outlined, by putting their jobs on the line if necessary. The potential for employment elsewhere and the importance of their standing with the profession may influence their behavior.

The role of the manager in the structuring of council-staff relations has not received the attention devoted to direct manager-council relations. We would argue, however, that it is as important. In a 1984 ICMA survey, 54 percent of the managers responding said they always resisted council involvement in administration while only 40 percent said they always played a leading role in policy making (Green 1987, 3). With Svara's reconceptualization, perhaps future surveys will differentiate among types of council involvement.

The role of the manager adds a new dimension to Goodnow's theory. He wanted job tenure to avoid patronage. The staff in council-manager cities have that. He advocated party government to concentrate power and ensure accountability. The council-manager plan concentrates formal power through legislative supremacy (although some may object that nonpartisan elections diminish the electoral accountability of the council to the citizenry). But Goodnow had no mechanism other than exhortation to ensure that the participants played their proper roles. The institutionalization of the values that he advocated in a profession whose members occupy the pivotal role between elected officials and career employees is a powerful addition. For this reason, the way in which they interpret the dichotomy as a guide to behavior is very important.

For the sake of an analogy let us return for a moment to the separation of powers in our national government. That doctrine is imbedded in our Constitution, just as council-manager-staff relationships are prescribed in charters. Yet the founding fathers did not rely on the words of the Constitution, alone, to enforce their scheme. They built in a system of checks and balances among equal institutions so that each could protect itself from encroachment by the other. Are there analogous provisions in council-manager government?

In one sense the answer is no. Councils and managers are not equal. Councils can replace managers at will. The manager is the party most likely to understand how the system is supposed to work, but what incentive is there for the individual manager to risk angering council members by standing up for the system?

The city-county management profession, on the other hand, has a strong interest in making the system work. By adopting and promoting professional standards, it can influence the behavior of managers and councils. That is why we think it would be dangerous for the profession to abandon its heritage in the form of the dichotomy. It is quite clear that the traditional interpretation of the dichotomy is untenable as a guide to behavior. We have offered an alternate interpretation which, we believe, is both reasonable and relevant.

Conclusion and Implications

The case that we have presented is a very traditional one of accountability through hierarchy. In itself, it is certainly not a novel argument. Where we differ from much of the literature on council-manager government is in the contention that this is what the works of Wilson and Goodnow imply.

We found two dichotomies. One was an analytical construct, a division of government powers into two (the expression of will and the execution of will), rather than three (legislative, executive, and judicial). From this starting point, Goodnow was able to justify his call for accountability through hierarchy and party government. We see nothing in this dichotomy which prohibits a policy continuum as long as the lines of ultimate authority are clear. The second dichotomy, the attempt to ban particularistic influences from administration, was a necessary corollary to the first.

This system cannot work where power is institutionally divided at the top. Council-manager government avoids this problem, but that fact alone will not make the system work. We suggest that the role of the manager is critical in maintaining the system, and that the standards of an organized profession are critical in sustaining the manager.

We hasten to add that such a system is not necessarily an unadulterated good. It has the advantages and disadvantages of bureaucracy as an organizational form, without the prejudicial connotations that often accompany the word in our society (Goodsell 1985). It seeks to avoid the kind of rampant pluralism of which Lowi (1969) complained, although by a different method than the "juridical democracy" which he proposed. It would deny particularistic benefits as a basis of political participation. While the new public administration might approve of broader discretion, it would probably disapprove of the plan's insistence on hierarchy. Citizens' advice could be accepted but the transfer of authority to citizens' groups would disrupt the system of accountability, as Victor Thompson has pointed out (1975, 65–86). In principle, at least, the decision to adopt such a system is a decision to elevate certain values at the expense of others.

There are both normative and empirical questions to ask about council-manager government. Framing the discussion in terms of the dichotomy as traditionally interpreted is both irrelevant and misleading. It is irrelevant because the reformers almost certainly conceded a policy-making role to top executive positions like those of the city manager. It is misleading because the rejection of the dichotomy on the basis of findings that managers *do* make policy dismisses without consideration those aspects of the dichotomy that *are* relevant to council-manager government.

Our purpose has been to demonstrate that the politics-administration dichotomy, as we have interpreted it, is still a live issue for council-manager government. It is important for the theoretical reasons expressed by Wilson and Goodnow. It is also important as a guidepost for managers, both in their individual dealings with councils and in their structuring of employee-council relations. Finally, it may serve as one of the few weapons, as Rosenbloom (1993) termed it, that a manager can use to resist the particularistic tendencies in our political system. Hence, the dichotomy, as we have interpreted it here, remains important as a normative standard in the profession of local government management.

References

Aldrich, John H. 1993. "Rational Choice and Turnout." *American Journal of Political Science* 37 (February): 246–278.

Banfield, Edward C., and James Q. Wilson. 1963. *City Politics.* Cambridge, MA: Harvard University Press.

Bromage, Arthur W. 1970. *Urban Policy Making: The Council-Manager Partnership.* Chicago: Public Administration Service.

Childs, Richard S. 1965. *The First 50 Years.* New York: National Municipal League.

Cooper, Phillip J. 1984. "The Wilsonian Dichotomy in Administrative Law." In *Politics and Administration,* ed. Jack Rabin and James S. Bowman. New York: Marcel Dekker, pp. 79–94.

Doig, Jameson. 1983. "'If I See a Murderous Fellow Sharpening a Knife Cleverly. . .': The Wilsonian Dichotomy and the Public Authority Tradition." *Public Administration Review* 43 (July/August): 292–304.

Downs, Anthony. 1957. *An Economic Theory of Democracy.* New York: Harper and Brothers.

Fiorina, Morris. 1977. *Congress: Keystone of the Washington Establishment.* New Haven, CT: Yale University Press.

Golembiewski, Robert. 1977. *Public Administration as a Developing Discipline.* New York: Marcel Dekker.

Goodnow, Frank G. 1888. "The Tweed Ring in New York City." In *The American Commonwealth,* ed. James Bryce. London: Macmillan, pp. 335–353.

———. 1900. *Politics and Administration.* New York: Russell and Russell.

Goodsell, Charles T. 1985. *The Case for Bureaucracy: A Public Administration Polemic,* 2d ed. Chatham, NJ: Chatham House.

Graham, Cole Blease, and Steven W. Hays. 1986. *Managing the Public Organization.* Washington, DC: CQ Press.

Green, Roy E. 1987. "Local Government Managers: Styles and Challenges." ICMA *Baseline Data Report* 19 (March/April): 1–11.

Gulick, Luther, and L. Urwick, eds. 1937. *Papers on the Science of Administration.* New York: Institute of Public Administration.

Holli, Melvin G. 1974. "Urban Reform in the Progressive Era." In *The Progressive Era,* ed. Lewis L. Gould. Syracuse, NY: Syracuse University Press, pp. 133–151.

Long, Norton E. 1949. "Power and Administration." *Public Administration Review* 9: 257–265. Reprinted in *Classics of Public Administration,* ed. Jay M. Shafritz and Albert C. Hyde. 1987. Chicago: Dorsey Press.

Lowi, Theodore. 1969. *The End of Liberalism.* New York: W.W. Norton.

Mabie, Edward Charles. 1918. *City Manager Plan of Government.* New York: H.W. Wilson.

Miewald, Robert D. 1984. "The Origins of Wilson's Thought: The German Tradition and the Organic State." In *Politics and Administration*, ed. Jack Rabin and James S. Bowman. New York: Marcel Dekker, pp. 1–30.

Nalbandian, John. 1991. *Professionalism in Local Government.* San Francisco, CA: Jossey-Bass.

National Civic League. 1989. *Model City Charter*, 7th ed. Denver, CO: National Civic League Press.

Perrow, Charles. 1986. *Complex Organizations: A Critical Essay.* New York: Random House.

Rohr, John A. 1986. *To Run a Constitution: The Legitimacy of the Administrative State.* Lawrence: University Press of Kansas.

Rosenbloom, David H. 1983. "Public Administration Theory and the Separation of Powers." *Public Administration Review* 43 (May/June): 219–227.

———. 1984. "Reconsidering the Politics-Administration Dichotomy: The Supreme Court and Public Personnel Management." In *Politics and Administration*, ed. Jack Rabin and James S. Bowman. New York: Marcel Dekker, pp. 103–118.

———. 1993. "Have an Administrative Rx? Don't Forget the Politics." *Public Administration Review* 53 (November/December): 503–507.

Simon, Herbert A. 1967. "The Changing Theory and Changing Practice of Public Administration." In *Contemporary Political Science: Toward Empirical Theory*, ed. Ithiel de Sola Pool. New York: McGraw-Hill.

Stillman, Richard. 1974. *The Rise of the City Manager.* Albuquerque: University of New Mexico Press.

Svara, James H. 1985. "Dichotomy and Duality: Reconceptualizing the Relationship Between Policy and Administration in Council-Manager Cities." *Public Administration Review* 45 (January/February): 221–232.

———. 1989. "Policy and Administration: City Managers as Comprehensive Professional Leaders." In *Ideal and Practice in Council-Manager Government*, ed. H. George Frederickson. Washington, DC: ICMA, pp. 70–93.

Thompson, Victor A. 1975. *Without Sympathy or Enthusiasm: The Problem of Administrative Compassion.* University: University of Alabama Press.

Waldo, Dwight. 1984. "The Perdurability of the Politics-Administration Dichotomy: Woodrow Wilson and the Identity Crisis in Public Administration." In *Politics and Administration*, ed. Jack Rabin and James S. Bowman. New York: Marcel Dekker, pp. 219–233.

Wilson, Woodrow. 1887. "The Study of Admnistration." *Political Science Quarterly.* Reprinted in Jay M. Shafritz and Albert C. Hyde, 1987. *Classics of Public Administration*, 2nd ed. Chicago: Dorsey Press, pp. 10–25.

CHAPTER 7

THE SHIFTING BOUNDARY BETWEEN ELECTED OFFICIALS AND CITY MANAGERS IN LARGE COUNCIL-MANAGER CITIES

JAMES H. SVARA

Council-manager governments in the United States have been an important venue for observing the general relationship between politics and administration. Although the roles of the mayor and council members, on the one hand, and the city manager and staff, on the other, have sometimes been viewed as strictly separate, officials have blended democracy and professionalism in ways that maintain distinct but shared roles. It is possible, however, that changing conditions in local government may create pressures that alter official roles and the relative contributions of officials. This is particularly likely in large cities about which the question has perennially been asked whether the council-manager form of government is viable. Although the council-manager form has been most commonly used in moderately small to moderately large cities, only in recent decades have many cities that use council-manager government grown into "large" cities.[1] Now over two-fifths of cities exceeding 200,000 in population use the council-manager form. This study focuses on these thirty-one cities.[2] The group includes five cities at or near the million population mark—Dallas, Phoenix, San Antonio, San Diego, and San Jose. All of these as well as twenty-three of the other twenty-six are sunbelt cities. Although the sunbelt has been viewed as relatively placid and homogeneous, its cities have become ever more diverse places with intense interest group politics (Ehrenhalt 1991; Benest 1991).

Determining whether roles are shifting presumes norms against which to measure current attitudes and behavior. As a starting point, we will presume that elected officials set broad goals and ultimately approve most policy decisions, oversee program accomplishment, and appraise the city manager's performance but refrain from direct involvement in implementation and service delivery or in specific management decisions. City managers advise the council on the city's direction, propose policies, and handle implementation and organizational management.

Empirical research has shown that officials generally fill these roles in a coordinated way and, as cause and consequence of coordination, maintain a positive relationship. The question to be explored is whether these characteristics are changing and whether the conceptual model needs to be revised in large cities where one finds a high level of political activity that may strain the coordination of roles and cooperative relationship among officials.

From *Public Administration Review*, vol. 59, no. 1 (January/February 1999), pp. 44–53. Copyright © 1999 by American Society for Public Administration. Reprinted with permission.

Changing Roles and Relationships in Large Council-Manager Cities

It has long been presumed that the council-manager form of government faces special challenges in large cities,[3] and there are several reasons to expect unique circumstances in such cities. They are more heterogeneous, and the media magnify political affairs. The problems large cities face tend to be more complex, more interrelated, and more difficult to handle. In general, the political environment of the large city is highly charged. Some argue that the council-manager form is not well suited to manage conflict (Banfield and Wilson 1963) and that a strong elected executive is needed in such cities (Gurwitt 1993, versus Blodgett 1994). As a consequence, relationships may be strained and the coordinated division of roles may break down in large council-manager cities.

These expectations have never been tested in systematic research on the performance of council-manager government in large cities. To fill this gap, a questionnaire was distributed to the mayor and council members and to the city manager, deputy and assistant city managers, and the department heads in finance, public works, and police in the large council-manager cities.[4] Initial mailings were sent in 1995 with follow-up requests in early 1996. For council members, it is possible to compare results with responses in a 1989 national survey of elected officials in cities over 200,000 in population.[5] Some important comparisons can also be made with the attitudes of council members and administrators from six moderately large council-manager cities who were interviewed in 1985 (from Svara 1990).[6]

The response rate for this survey was 44 percent for council members and 42 percent for administrators. This moderate level of response is understandable given the heavy responsibilities of officials in large cities. In addition to the written questionnaires, personal interviews that solicited comments on the survey results were conducted with selected council members and administrators in four of the cities in 1977.[7] There was general agreement that the findings represent prevailing attitudes among elected officials and administrators, and the interviews offered insights into the reasoning of council members and administrators underlying the survey findings.

Council-Manager Roles and Relationships

There is clear continuation of the cooperative relationship among these officials despite the impression based on comments by city managers that tensions are rising in large cities. In their responses to the survey, four out of five council members and administrators view the working relationship among officials in city government as very good or good. Only 4 percent feel that relations are not very good or negative. When the relationship between the city council and the city manager alone is considered, there is almost unanimous agreement by council members and administrators that the relationship is good (see Table 7.1). Most also view the relationship of the mayor and council as positive. Over 70 percent of the council members agree that the council provides sufficient direction and overall leadership to city government as do 60 percent of administrators, and two-thirds of both groups *disagree* that the council is too involved in administration. Three-quarters of both groups also agree that the council's appraisal of the city manager is satisfactory in depth and frequency. Thus, there is evidence of cooperative relationships and coordination of roles.

Other indicators, however, of the city council's role performance deviate from normal expectations in council-manager government:

- Seven in ten feel that the council focuses too much on short-term problems and gives too little attention to long-term concerns.

Table 7.1

Assessment of Roles and Relationships by Council Members and Administrators

	Council members	Administrators
Cooperation		
The council and city manager have a good working relationship	91*	90
The council and mayor have a good working relationship	74	77
Coordination of roles		
The council provides sufficient direction and overall leadership to city government	71	60
The council is too involved in administrative activities (disagree)	66	65
The council's appraisal of manager's performance is satisfactory in depth and frequency	72	77
Performance in roles		
The council has difficulty making clear decisions	44	59
The council focuses too much on short-term issues and gives too little attention to long-range concerns	68	73
Intervention by a council member is necessary to get staff response to citizen complaints	55	6
Council members try to get special services and benefits for their constituents	70	71

Notes: *Entries are percent that agree with a statement unless indicated otherwise.
$N = 118$ council members and 82 administrators from 31 council-manager cities over 200,000 in population, 1996.

- Over 40 percent of council members and 59 percent of administrators agree that the council has difficulty making decisions.
- Seven in ten agree that council members try to get special services and benefits for their constituents. This is a substantial increase from a 1989 survey of council members in which 55 percent expressed the same opinion (all 1989 figures are from Svara 1991).

Personal interviews with council members suggest that these characteristics are interrelated. The interest in service delivery contributes to the short-term focus of council members and creates a heavy load of decision making. In addition, the wide range of pressing issues that arise in large cities and the impact of the electoral calendar, especially when term limits are used, reinforce the tendency to emphasize current concerns.

On only one measure in Table 7.1 is there sharp divergence in views between the two sets of officials or substantial criticism of administrative staff: 55 percent of council members agree that intervention by a council member is necessary to get adequate staff response to citizen complaints, whereas only 6 percent of administrators agree. In a survey of council members in 1985, only 35 percent considered intervention necessary (Svara 1990, 55) contrasted to the current widespread distrust of staff responsiveness. The view that intervention is needed is more common among council members elected from districts (65 percent) than at-large (45 percent). This attitude that council intervention is needed to help citizens deal with administrative staff who are not sufficiently responsive creates a rationale for extensive attention to constituency services by council members and their staff.

Measures of the council's performance in a range of functions, not included in Table 7.1, reinforce the characteristics already identified. The lowest ratings with less than one-third of council members and administrators giving the council a high rating are for the council's establishing long term goals, overseeing program effectiveness, assessing administrative staff, setting annual objectives, and addressing real problems in the city. A slightly higher rating was given for the effectiveness of the council's performance in the budget process. The strongest ratings are received for providing services to constituents and responding to constituent demands. Over half gave the council high effectiveness ratings in these two areas. The council appears to be a body that provides good overall leadership, but tends to focus on specific, short-term matters. The members are much better at responding to constituent concerns—an essentially reactive mode— than they are at setting long-term goals and priorities.

Thus, the overall division of roles shows coordination, but there are questions about whether the council's relative emphasis on goal setting and service delivery matches traditional expectations in the council-manager form of government.

Levels of Involvement in the Governmental Process

The division of functions described at the beginning of this chapter corresponds to what I have called the dichotomy-duality model (Svara 1985). It describes a pattern in which the council is most involved in setting broad goals or the mission of city government but in which involvement declines over three other dimensions of decisions in the governmental process—policy, administration, and management. The city manager's involvement is the reverse of that of council members. The field research in six moderately large council-manager cities (all over 150,000 population) in the mid-1980s (Svara 1990) and surveys of city managers in North Carolina and Ohio in the late 1980s (Svara 1989), indicated the need for two refinements to the view of how responsibilities are separated and shared. First, the involvement of city council members was closer to the pattern in the *preferences* officials had for council members than in their actual behavior. Council members tended not to play as active a role in mission and policy as they and city managers would have preferred. The second revision from the state surveys of managers was to recognize fairly uniform and high involvement in all four dimensions. In fact, unlike the six-city study, the managers' actual involvement rating was higher than that of the council even in decisions related to the mission of the city.

The 1996 survey in large council-manager cities suggests that a change in council members' behavior and preferences is occurring. There are deviations from the dichotomy-duality pattern as it applies to council members, and a greater contrast between what council members do and their ideal for themselves. Administrators' views of the contribution that council members do and should make have remained fairly constant, but shifts in council member preferences produce greater deviation than previously in the views of the two sets of officials. To make these determinations, officials were asked to estimate the actual and preferred involvement of council members *and* the city manager and staff in eleven specific activities on a scale that ranged from 1.0 for very low to 5.0 for very high.[8] These activities will be grouped into the four dimensions and then examined separately.

The survey results from the council members in the six council-manager cities in 1985 reinforced the view that council involvement is highest in mission and decreases through the other dimensions of decisions (see Figure 7.1 which presents the responses of council members only). These data are drawn from a different sample than the current study (six cities three of which were between 150,000 and 200,000 population), and a larger number of items was used to construct the involvement indices than in the current research.[9] The items used to construct the involvement indices in 1996 are listed in Figure 7.2. Still, the 1985 and 1996 results were based on the

Figure 7.1 **Council Member Ratings of the Involvement of Council and Manager, 1985 and 1996**

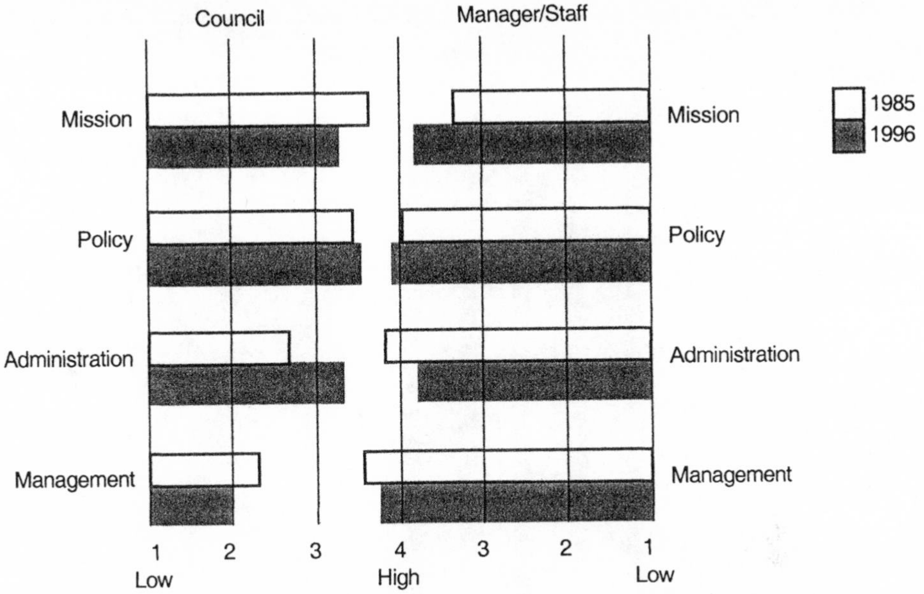

26 council members in six cities in 1985; 118 council members in 31 cities in 1996.

same methodology, and as we shall see the responses from administrators are very similar in both studies. There are, however, these indicators of important changes in the behavior and attitudes of council members:

- Council members are slightly less involved in mission in 1996 than in 1985 and more involved in administration than previously.
- Council members no longer report the greatest involvement in mission in 1996 unlike 1985; in 1996, the highest score was in middle-range policy decisions.
- In 1985, council members viewed the city manager as moderately active in mission but less involved than they were, whereas in 1996 council members viewed the manager's involvement in mission as higher than their own.
- Council members perceive the manager to be more active in policy but less highly involved in administration.

In the mission dimension, there was a net shift of .8—almost one full step on the scale—toward higher relative involvement by the manager and staff compared to the city council when the council's decline (from 3.7 to 3.4) and the manager's increase (from 3.4 to 3.9) were combined. The roles have shifted with the manager perceived to be the source of initiation for mission decisions and council members seeing themselves in a reviewing role. They have moved away from self-perceived leadership in goal setting and long-range decisions. It is possible that the city manager has become more active in mission and policy than previously, but another explanation is that the manager's policy activity is simply more obvious as council members pay less attention to goal setting. Their lower involvement leaves the manager as the visible enunciator of proposals that set goals and address long-range concerns.

Figure 7.2 Involvement of Council in Specific Activities Level Preferred by Council Members and Administrators, 1996

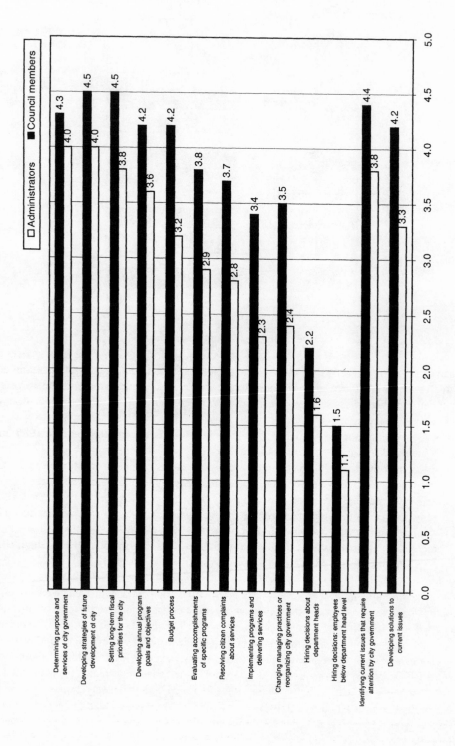

Table 7.2

Council Member and Administrator Ratings of Council Members' Actual and Preferred Involvement, 1985 and 1996

Dimension	Year	Council members[a]			Administrators[b]			Difference in preferred council administrators
		Actual	Preferred	Difference	Actual	Preferred	Difference	
Mission	1985	3.7	4.0	0.3	3.6	3.8	0.2	0.2
	1996	3.4	4.4	1.0	3.4	3.9	0.5	0.5
Policy	1985	3.4	3.6	0.2	3.1	3.2	0.1	0.4
	1996	3.4	4.2	0.8	3.1	3.4	0.3	0.8
Administration	1985	2.7	2.9	0.2	2.7	2.5	−0.2	0.4
	1996	3.2	3.6	0.4	2.7	2.7	0.0	0.9
Management	1985	2.2	2.3	0.1	2.4	2.1	−0.3	0.2
	1996	2.0	2.4	0.4	1.9	1.7	−0.2	0.7
Average	1985			0.2			0.2	0.3
difference	1996			0.7			0.3	0.7

Notes:
[a]These are council members' ratings of their own involvement.
[b]These are ratings by administrators of the council's involvement.
$N = 26$ council members and 68 administrators in six cities in 1985; 118 council members and 82 administrators in 31 cities in 1996.

The preferences of administrators and council members regarding the involvement of the *council* are substantially different, as indicated in Table 7.2 (which repeats the actual council involvement ratings from Figure 7.1), and council members view their current involvement as far less than they would prefer. This is a change from 1985 when the preferences of both groups were similar with only slightly higher preferred involvement by council members.

Council members in both years preferred to be more involved in each dimension, but in 1996 the average difference between actual and preferred involvement was 0.7, compared to an average difference of 0.2 in 1985. In the mission dimension, the difference between actual and preferred involvement is 1.0, that is, they would like to shift from being moderately active reviewers to highly active proponents.

In both years, administrators preferred that the council be more involved in mission—in 1996 much more involved—and in policy and slightly less involved in administration and management.

In 1996, the gap between the level preferred for the council by elected officials and administrators across the four dimensions averaged 0.7 compared to 0.3 in 1985.

The council now prefers much higher involvement across the board. There is preference for almost as much involvement in handling details as in resolving the big picture decisions. These differences in preference represent a potential source of tension over roles between elected officials and administrators.

Table 7.2 also indicates that administrators' ratings of the actual and preferred involvement of council members is essentially unchanged over this period except for lower involvement in management. Administrators generally rate the council's actual involvement at approximately the same level as council members rate themselves. There is a modest gap in the rating of policy involvement in both years, and a discrepancy of one-half step for involvement in administration in 1996. Elected officials may be reflecting the amount of time the activity absorbs and staff reflecting the impact council members' activity has on implementation and service delivery.

In 1985 and 1996, council members' assessments of the actual and preferred level of involvement for the city manager (not presented in a table) were very close to each other, as were those of administrators. In other words, all officials were basically satisfied with the manager's level of activity. In the current survey, the difference between preferred and actual involvement of the manager was 0.1 or less except in administration: council members prefer that the manager play a more active role in administration—4.3 compared to their actual rating for the manager of 3.9. Presumably, the relatively low rating for the city manager reflects the manager's delegation of responsibility to departments for implementation and service delivery. The preference for more involvement may indicate a desire for the manager to take a more direct, hands-on approach in this dimension and be more attentive to service delivery issues about which council members get complaints. One council member's comment that "the city manager should answer my phone" and deal with dissatisfied citizens suggests that they want the manager to get more involved in specific problems as the council members often are.[10] In addition, council members see the manager as their link to staff. They feel that since they appraise only the manager, they cannot deal directly with performance issues within departments or the staff generally except through the manager. Thus, in their view, the manager should be more involved in this area.

When specific activities are examined, there are important similarities and differences in the *preferences* of elected officials and administrators regarding the *city council's* role (see Figure 7.2). Council members and administrators are in agreement about a very active and an active role, respectively, for the council in the activities that make up the mission dimension, for example, determining the purpose and scope of government. The council members prefer almost as high a level of involvement in the budget process and setting annual priorities as in mission decisions whereas administrators prefer less involvement.[11] The gap in preferences continues over evaluation of program results and is even greater in preferences for involvement in implementing programs and resolving citizen complaints. Council members would also like to be much more involved in changes in management practices than administrators would prefer. The former also would like a larger role in personnel decisions than administrators would prefer, although the level council members prefer essentially entails being kept informed rather than reviewing— much less initiating or deciding—personnel decisions.[12] Overall, administrators would prefer that council involvement decrease as activities shift from the general and strategic to the specific and operational. Council members' preferences for involvement recede somewhat but remain relatively high in policy and administrative actions as well as those dealing with reorganization and change in management policy. Thus, when these differences in preferences are considered, there is a bulge in the middle activities with council preferences deviating most from those of administrators in dealing with the more specific and concrete matters.

Figure 7.2 also includes two activities that fall outside those that can clearly be assigned to the four dimensions—identifying current issues that require attention by the city and developing solutions to them. Such issues can cut across and combine the dimensions, as when an allegation of police mistreatment of a citizen sparks discussion of the philosophy of law enforcement, budget allocations to the police, community policing policies and programs, and hiring, manpower allocations, and disciplinary practices in the police department. Such issues generate a *current problem agenda* that coexists with and at times may overshadow the ongoing work of city government. Both council members and administrators report that the city council is actually more highly involved in identifying current issues than they are in all but one of the other activities examined.[13] As indicated in Figure 7.2, administrators prefer that this involvement be fairly high, whereas council members would like to be even more active. Furthermore, council members want to be almost as involved in developing the solutions as in identifying the issues, whereas administrators would prefer that council members back off and respond to proposals developed by the city manager and staff. When preferences of the council members for administrators (not included in Figure 7.2) are examined, council members are willing to accept an active role by administrators in developing solutions along with their own active involvement.

In practice, council members are most engaged in *specific, operational, current* matters with highest actual involvement in resolving citizen complaints (3.7 is their rating of actual involvement) and identifying problems that require attention (3.7). They are more involved in solving current problems and budget review (3.5) than in setting long-term (3.4) or annual direction (3.4). In the administrative arena, they are more active in resolving specific complaints (3.7 as noted above) than in evaluation (2.8).

Administrators prefer involvement for the council that corresponds to the dichotomy-duality pattern, which emphasizes the long-term over the current and which stresses that involvement in administrative decisions should be lower than in mission and policy and should focus on assessing effectiveness of performance. Administrators also prefer to maintain the adviser-reviewer distinction between the city manager and the city council. Council members, although the variations in their preferences display the same relative ordering as those of administrators, want it all. They aspire to be leaders in mission, initiators and full partners in policy, and active reviewers and proponents in administration and management policy change. They also want to be more informed about major administrative appointments. These aspirations contrast with the actual practice of taking a hands-on approach to emerging issues and specific policy and administrative decisions while deferring to the manager and staff when it comes to framing goals and broad policy.

There are a number of factors that constrain the capacity of council members to change their behavior and to greatly expand their level of activity in all aspects of the governmental process. The pressures of constituency affairs and concerns about reelection or pursuit of higher office cause council members to emphasize short-range concerns. Term limits, where used, reinforce this tendency although the orientation is common even without term limits. Council members spend a considerable amount of time in their official position already—they report spending an average of thirty-six hours per week in the position. Already half feel that long hours are a serious problem and even more complain that the position takes too much time away from family. Elected officials would like to be super-policy makers and ombudsmen, but in actuality they devote more attention to short-range concerns.

The manager and staff assume a larger role in goal setting and, in interviews, suggest that council members are not particularly interested in creating a policy framework. By their ratings of the actual and preferred involvement, council members indicate that they perceive the city manager's extensive involvement in mission and policy and accept it. As one city manager characterized the situation, the council has essentially decided that "mission is something managers do." City managers stress general policy, and councils focus on alterations, adjustments, and exceptions that respond to current circumstances and political pressures. Although they would like to be more broadly involved, council members are activists or doers rather than broad policy makers, and ombudsmen-style overseers rather than evaluators. Council members would like to determine the long-range future of the city as well as guiding it in a more immediate sense, but, if they must choose one or the other, most focus on the latter.

Causes, Consequences, and Implications

Two factors can be offered to explain these findings. First, persons filling elected office at the local level are now more likely to be electoral activists rather than trustees who hold their office primarily as a service to the community (Prewitt 1970). An "electoral activist" is someone who tries to help his or her community by seeking to be chosen by citizens as their spokesperson and representative. Being successful entails not a passive approach of simply "doing a good job," but rather an active approach to building support from constituents—primarily the residents of a district from which most are elected. This in turn requires gaining attention and recognition through the media, assisting constituents, and being an ombudsman to solve the problems that concern them (Heilig and Mundt 1984). It is natural, therefore, that council members will place greater emphasis on the representational rather than the governance aspects of the position.

Second, council members are ambivalent about making policy decisions, particularly when they are general and long-term. In their preferences, they would like to be highly involved in determining the mission of their cities, but do not want to abandon—indeed they want to expand—their activity in middle-range policy and administrative matters. It appears that council members want to maintain greater control by being involved in determining the details of policy and implementation (Box 1995, 720–725); they are concerned about "the devil in the details." They also seek to avoid final commitments and keep their options open as programs are being carried out as a way of coping with cross-pressures from the media and interest groups. The electoral cycle focuses the attention of elected officials on the near-term rather than the long-term, and term limits when used increase the sense of urgency.

Council members may also be distracted by the current political agenda of problems that need to be solved and have difficulty making other major long-term decisions at the same time. The response to these pressing issues is an indicator of the current council style of decision-making. Whereas managers would be inclined to study an issue to determine the underlying problem and consider a range of options for dealing with the problem, council members want to "experiment," as Nalbandian (1994) has suggested. The logic may be "let's try this and, if it doesn't work, we'll try something else, but let's do something." It is telling that council members prefer to be almost as involved in solving these problems as in identifying them.

The findings of the research have important implications for the way we think about respective roles of officials in government and about the nature of the politics-administration relationship. There is scant evidence of any elements of dichotomy in the council-manager relationship in the large cities at the present time. In retrospect, it was not appropriate to use the dichotomy in the "dichotomy-duality" label for characterizing the data from 1985 which were reported here. As we have seen, there was shared responsibility in developing mission even if the manager's involvement was somewhat lower than the council's. In the present study, council members perceived the city manager to be more involved than they are in formulating mission (as did administrators). By clinging to the concept of dichotomy, the extent of shared responsibility is obscured.

In both periods, the extensive sharing suggests that the relationship of elected officials and administrators is best understood as a complementarity—a model of interaction in which administrators respect the control of elected officials, and at the same time there is interdependency and reciprocal influence between elected officials and administrators who fill distinct but overlapping roles in policy and administration. In council-manager government, complementarity is found between a board of governors responsible for policy direction and oversight and an accountable CEO who guides the formation of policy and directs the organization.[14] Within that framework, there are several and potentially shifting ways that the contributions from elected officials and administrators can be blended.

The 1985 data revealed the continuation (presumably) of a traditional pattern in council-manager government that might be called the *ratifier-proposer* pattern.[15] The council took the lead in ratifying mission decisions in the positive sense of validating and legitimizing them. Managers were actively involved in policy, as the council looked to the manager for guidance before committing to a course of action. The council was more content to oversee policy accomplishments in general terms and to refer constituent complaints to staff. Change was already evident in the mid-1980s with some activist mayors creating citizen hotlines to handle complaints and some district council members stressing the ombudsman role, but attitudes about actual and preferred roles with receding council involvement across the four dimensions reflected the ratifier-proposer pattern.

Presumably this pattern can still be found, but currently in large cities the mix is different. The interaction in large cities might be called the *activist-initiator* pattern. Council members are active proponents of policies to solve current problems. City managers are extensively involved in developing broad-range, long-term, and citywide proposals as well as continuing to be very active in proposing middle-range policies. There is much closer scrutiny of the details of manager's proposals, and policy decisions by the council are often provisional and temporary with requirements that the manager check back to report on progress and get additional guidance. In the administrative realm, council members emphasize the ombudsman role (also an activist orientation focused on solving individual problems), whereas city managers stress making systems work better. In management, the council promotes change in management methods, for example, more privatization, and wants a hand in or to be informed in advance about key decisions. Beyond appraising the city manager, they would like to know more and have more impact on management below the level of manager.

This pattern does not represent a reversal of roles between elected officials and administrators, although it is not surprising that local government managers would perceive it in that way (Morgan and Kass 1993). The extensive involvement of city managers in policy is not new (see, for example, White 1926, and Stone, Price, and Stone 1940). What is different in the current pattern is the need for city managers to be the source of broad policy initiation. Furthermore, they must be the subtle but persistent force to raise and bring long-term policy issues to resolution.[16]

On the surface, these tasks seem to extend beyond the limits of legitimacy for administrators in a democratic system. Some managers have been trapped into thinking that separation of spheres is the norm by the persistent dichotomy construct (Golembiewski and Gabris 1994). In a survey of practices conducted by ICMA in 1996,[17] city managers demonstrated this ambivalence about roles. Virtually all local managers identify community needs and initiate policy proposals (86 percent) although one-third question the desirability of doing so. Nine in ten promote policy discussion among council members, but 55 percent do not consider this action to be desirable. They are uncomfortable promoting team building on the council—only 29 percent think it is a desirable practice—but 81 percent undertake such efforts.

Complementarity provides the basis for legitimizing these practices, that is, making them justifiable. The interaction between city managers and elected officials is so extensive and the interface is so close that the behavior of city managers necessarily affects the democratic process. Policy making would be far different if the city manager did little beyond filling a management role, just as it is different—broader, more purposeful, more informed, and more inclusive—when the city manager acts positively as an accountable policy initiator who stimulates open policy discussion by the council. It is not a departure from the model of council-manager government for city managers to behave in this way; indeed such behavior is consistent with the features of the form intended by its founders (Svara 1998).

Elected officials would like to be more active in virtually all areas. The realities of their office, however, produce emphasis on the constituency orientation, and the conditions in their cities and their electoral aspirations and circumstances reinforce a focus on immediate problems. Elected officials must realistically examine the tradeoffs required in reordering their priorities and spending their time differently. City managers can help by acknowledging the difficulty of elected office and the value of what council members actually do, and Morgan and Kass (1993, 185) suggest that they do. Council members help to keep the city in touch with the electorate, they serve as a pressure valve that helps to moderate the tension of distraught constituents, they draw attention to specific breakdowns in systems and problems with services, they promote consideration of a wider range of alternatives than professionals might raise, and they deal with the political realities that surround many city government actions. Large cities have serious current problems that must be attended to even if they are a distraction from long-range concerns and cannot be "solved."

The boundary line is increasingly blurred and shifting in ways that include more of what might be considered to be administration and management in the council's sphere and more of mission formulation in the city manager's. Whereas elected and administrative officials were familiar and comfortable with the ratifier-proposer pattern, they are still working out relationships and redefining roles as more council members are activists and managers are required to be not just policy formulators, guides, and advisers but initiators as well.[18] Some might argue that the distinction in roles is eroding, that the basic division between governors and CEO is being lost, but I would contend that this is not the case. City council members may devote less attention to creating a framework of goals, but they put more emphasis on setting the agenda for action. City managers still look to the city council for authoritative direction even though they must do more to frame the options and at times press the council for resolution. City council members still rely on the manager and staff for professional support in achieving their objectives at the same time that they want to be broadly involved themselves. Elected officials respect the manager's need to be the head of the municipal organization, but they offer input to and seek to be informed about administrative and management decisions. Furthermore, they will intervene on behalf of constituents when they feel it is needed.

If both sets of officials start their consideration of respective roles with a recognition of shared but distinct responsibilities, it will be easier for them to come to grips with the shifts that are occurring. They should seek not a "restoration" of an artificial division of roles or the former shared roles with which administrators were conformable but rather look for new ways to sustain the cooperative and supportive relationship that has been a foundation of council-manager government. All in all, this result is being achieved in the largest cities that use this form of government despite the stresses and uncertainties officials are experiencing. Since many of the strains reflect the nature of the times rather than large size alone, it is likely that council members and city managers in many cities are making the same adjustments.

Notes

1. The common impression that council-manager government is a small-town form is misleading. A majority of cities in the 50,000–100,000 size range have used the form since 1955; a majority in the 25,000–50,000 range did so by 1965. The council-manager form is more commonly used in cities over 100,000 (almost half) than it is in cities with populations between 2,500 and 10,000.

2. The 200,000 figure was used as the minimum population for the large city category in a survey of city council members conducted in 1989 (Svara 1991). According to *The Municipal Year Book, 1995*, 41 percent of cities over 250,000 in population use the council-manager form.

3. In 1922, two speakers at the city managers' annual meeting debated the question "Is City Manager Government Applicable to Our Largest Cities?"

4. The research was supported by a grant from College of Humanities and Social Sciences at North Carolina State University. City managers in the informal Large City Executive Forum offered some suggestions and feedback about the study.

5. See Svara (1991). A sample of council members in cities between 25,000 and 200,000 was surveyed along with all the council members in the large cities. The response rate for council members from large cities was 43 percent.

6. In that study like the present one, surveys of council members and the city manager and—in that case all department heads—were conducted. The response rate in the six council-manager cities was 48 percent for council members and 63 percent for department heads.

7. Three cities were in the West and one in the Midwest. Interviews were completed with fifteen council members and two staff members for elected officials and with the city manager or assistant managers in each city. In one city, a meeting was held with all department heads.

8. In the questionnaire, the scale was presented as follows: How would you rate the overall level of involvement by the city council and the city manager and staff in the areas listed below? For each consider both the actual current level of involvement and amount of involvement you would prefer for each in the future using the following scale:

> 1 = very low: not involved but may receive a report on actions of others;
> 2 = low: minimum review or reaction;
> 3 = moderate: advising or reviewing;
> 4 = high: initiating, proposing, actively reviewing and revising, instructing, or strongly defending;
> 5 = very high: handle entirely although others may be informed of your actions.

9. In both studies—the 1985 research reported in Svara (1990) and the current research—council members and the city manager and department heads (selected heads in 1996) were surveyed. Three of the original six items were used to measure involvement in mission, three (with budget formulation and budget review combined into budget process) of the original eight items for policy, five (with making specific decisions that are part of large projects, delivering services to citizens and specific decisions about delivering services combined into implementing programs and delivering services) of the original seven items for administration, and three of the original eight items for management.

10. The only specific activity in which the council members rate their involvement as higher than the manager's is resolving citizen complaints.

11. Although the figures for actual involvement are not included in Figure 7.2, administrators want the council to be more involved than they actually are in the activities through evaluating programs (with the exception of budget process where actual and preferred are the same) as well as in identifying issues and developing solutions; they prefer them to be less involved than currently in the remaining activities.

12. It should be noted, however, that 42 percent prefer an intermediate or higher level of involvement, that is, 3.0 or higher. Such council members presumably would favor advice and consent authority, as one council member proposed in an interview.

13. The level of involvement was 3.70 for identifying current issues compared to 3.74 for resolving citizen complaints. These figures on actual involvement are not included in Figure 7.2.

14. The division of functions and the scope of activity by administrators is affected by the structural form of government but complementarity applies to either elected executive, for example, strong mayor-council, or governing board forms if professional administrators are present.

15. The relative contributions in this pattern are essentially those of the dichotomy-duality pattern I had previously proposed. At that time, it seemed important to retain some reference to the dichotomy concept because of its presumed historical importance, but I have subsequently argued that the dichotomy is an "aberration" and not the founding concept of public administration or the council-manager form (Svara 1998).

16. City managers in the large and small cities alike also report that it now takes more effort to persuade council members to follow their own or their predecessors' policy until they explicitly choose to change the policy.

17. The survey, developed by ICMA's Council-Manager Plan Task Force, was sent to 2,787 jurisdictions. The response rate was 47 percent.

18. In the past and presumably in smaller cities still, some managers have confined their policy role to providing proposals at the request of the council and commenting on their proposals. In the survey of managers in North Carolina and Ohio, half rated their own involvement as moderate to low in their self-assessment on the mission dimension and 30 percent did so on the policy dimension (Svara 1989). This relationship might be called the director-implementer pattern.

References

Banfield, Edward C., and James Q. Wilson. 1963. *City Politics*. New York: Vintage Books.
Benest, Frank. 1991. "Marketing Multiethnic Communities." *Public Management* 73 (December): 4–14.
Blodgett, Terrell. 1994. "Beware the Lure of the 'Strong Mayor.'" *Public Management* 76 (January): 6–11.
Box, Richard C. 1995. "Searching for the Best Structure for American Local Government." *International Journal of Public Administration* 18: 711–741.
Ehrenhalt, Allan. 1991. *The United States of Ambition*. New York: Times Books.
Golembiewski, Robert T., and Gerald Gabris. 1994. "Today's City Managers: A Legacy of Success-Becoming-Failure." *Public Administration Review* 54, no. 6: 525.
Gurwitt, Ronald. 1993. "The Lure of the Strong Mayor." *Governing* 8: 36–41.
Heilig, Peggy, and Robert J. Mundt. 1984. *Your Voice at City Hall*. Albany: State University of New York Press.
Morgan, Douglas F., and Henry D. Kass. 1993. "The American Odyssey of the Career Public Service: The Ethical Crisis of Role Reversal." In *Ethics and Public Administration*, ed. H. George Frederickson. Armonk, NY: M.E. Sharpe, chap. 9.
Nalbandian, John. 1994. "Reflections of a 'Pracademic' on the Logic of Politics and Administration." *Public Administration Review* 54, no. 6: 531–536.
Prewitt, Kenneth. 1970. *The Recruitment of Political Leaders*. Indianapolis, IN: Bobbs-Merrill.
Stone, Harold A., Don K. Price, and Kathryn H. Stone. 1940. *City Manager Government in the United States*. Chicago: Public Administration Service.
Svara, James H. 1985. "Dichotomy and Duality: Reconceptualizing the Relationship Between Policy and Administration in Council-Manager Cities." *Public Administration Review* 45, no. 1: 221–232.
———. 1989. "Policy and Administration: Managers as Comprehensive Professional Leaders." In *Ideal and Practice in City Management*, ed. H. George Frederickson. Washington, DC: International City Management Association, 70–93.
———. 1990. *Official Leadership in the City: Patterns of Conflict and Cooperation*. New York: Oxford University Press.
———. 1991. *A Survey of America's City Councils*. Washington, DC: National League of Cities.
———. 1998. "The Politics-Administration Dichotomy Model as Aberration." *Public Administration Review* 58, no. 1: 51–58.
White, Leonard. 1926. *The City Manager*. Chicago: University of Chicago Press.

PART 2

USING TAX DOLLARS WISELY: BUDGETING AND FINANCIAL MANAGEMENT

If local government managers do not employ and control successfully the financial resources they have, they are likely to fail. This failure will result in a lack of confidence by the public in the government and will impact negatively the elected officials for whom they work. For that basic reason, financial management is of utmost importance to governmental managers. In addition, the local government's ability to accomplish its mission is reflected in the quality of its budgeting and other financial management practices. Of course, as many experts have observed, budgeting reflects the values and policy choices of the public, the politicians, and professional public administrators.

While budgeting receives the most attention from scholars because of its importance in translating community values into policy and spending choices, other elements of financial management are also very important. Debt management, tax fairness, capital improvement programming, legal requirements, accounting standards and financial reporting, internal controls, purchasing, and performance measurement are also extremely important to the effective and efficient use of taxpayers' dollars by local governments. Professional financial managers must have an understanding of these practices and standards if they are to advise effectively local government managers and elected officials. The articles selected for inclusion in Part 2 reflect the broad area of financial management in local government. Of course, this complicated field of study with its many aspects cannot be covered completely even by the best journal articles. However, the articles we present here will give the reader a broad knowledge of financial management and will lead him or her to other valuable sources of further information.

W. Bartley Hildreth (chapter 8) describes the balancing acts that chief financial officers (CFOs) for local governments must perform "as they adjust the competing financial concerns to public policy" (p. 103). Hildreth presents an overview of the challenges facing CFOs in developing and implementing budgets that gain efficiency, achieve effectiveness, manage capacity, provide timely service, maintain quality, make investments, achieve the benchmark, make appropriate market disclosures, maintain adequate public communications, and mobilize invisible assets. He describes the differences between "bottom-up" budgeting and "top-down" budgeting and argues that the latter is needed to break the theoretical and practical grip that incrementalism has on local government budgeting. Hildreth also argues that budgets should focus on the work process rather than follow departmental lines. "CFOs must visualize finance as more than a system of transactions but as a vehicle for enhancing decisions," he concluded.

Budget reform is of constant interest to academic and practicing public administrators. Irene S. Rubin (chapter 9) examined how six cities identified and adopted budget reform based on the level of their political reform. She categorized two of the cities (Dayton and Phoenix) as "more reformed" based on their acceptance of council-manager government, at-large elections, and accountability through openness of administrative processes and documents. Two cities (Rochester and Tampa) were considered as having intermediate levels of reform because they possessed some of the elements of reform and two others (St. Louis and Boston) were labeled as least reformed cities because they are "traditionally decentralized, politicized mayor-council cities." Rubin concluded that the more-reformed cities adopted budget reforms more quickly than the intermediate cities and the intermediate cities adopted the reforms more quickly than the least reformed cities.

Carol W. Lewis (chapter 10) explored the norm, concept, and practice of budgetary balance in large American cities and presents her research in a case study of Bridgeport, Connecticut. Lewis's research revealed that at least twenty states require municipalities to have balanced annual budgets either by statute or by state constitution. However, almost all of the respondents to her survey replied that they are required to have balanced budgets even though many could not point to a legal requirement. She concluded that having a balanced budget is a norm accepted by local government managers and elected officials. When Bridgeport's mayor attempted to have his city declare bankruptcy under the federal Bankruptcy Code, the courts rejected the city's argument and forced the city to operate within its revenue. Lewis points out that there are many ways to achieve formal balance compliance so she cautions against using budgetary balance as a single criterion by which to judge the financial status or success of a municipality.

Local governments can establish priorities for spending in various ways, as Aimee L. Franklin and Brandi Carberry-George review in their 1999 study of budgeting practices in Texas cities (chapter 11). Resource limitations and increased expectations for better and more services are forcing local decision makers to examine how they set priorities for spending. The authors review three frameworks for budgeting that are prominently featured in the financial management literature: incremental, performance, and community values. They argue that even though local governments use different decision-making frameworks, a budget theory can be developed if researchers understand better the sequence for budget approval, number and type of participants, and reference resources used in the budget process. In their study of Texas cities, the authors identified five different budget approval sequences that could be arranged along a continuum: Council-only, Council Public, Public Participation, Planning, and Multi-Planning. They identified the "Big 4" participants in the budgetary process as the council, mayor, city manager, and department heads but found that there are other players who have direct involvement in budgeting in Texas cities. The most commonly used reference source for decision making was budget requests followed by new statutory mandates and performance measures. The authors concluded that Texas cities were most likely to use a combination of the three decision-making frameworks and that they were moving away from a single framework.

An important tool that local governments have in achieving their goals is the ability to borrow for major infrastructure needs. W. Bartley Hildreth, in a 1993 *Public Administration Review* article (published here as chapter 12), explained why some municipal borrowers were more successful when they ventured into the capital market than were other cities. He concluded that experience in the capital markets is an important factor, as is having qualified participants on the local government's financial management team. Hildreth described for readers the roles played by various participants in the issuance of debt, such as the issuers, investors, underwriters, financial advisers, bond counsels, trustees, credit rating agencies, voters, monitors, and controllers. This inside look at the intricacies of the municipal bond market provided a valuable service to students of local government management because most managers only learn these things through experience. Hildreth concluded that managers should develop a well-planned strategy when entering the capital market. Without an effective strategy, it is likely that the local government manager will cost his municipality money through higher interest rates or unfavorable repayment schedules.

Susan A. MacManus (chapter 13) explores the rising cost of litigation for local governments and its impact on the budgets of California cities. Because local governments are perceived to have "deep pockets," they are good targets for individuals, businesses, and lawyers who decide to settle disagreements through litigation. She found that one-third of the cities surveyed reported that their budgets were impacted "a lot" by litigation while another 53 percent "a little." Only 14 percent said litigation had no impact on their budgets during the past year. Because litigation costs are very difficult to predict, many cities (43 percent) passed budget amendments to deal with the unexpected costs of litigation or judgments. MacManus reported that there was a link between bond ratings and litigation costs even though the number of cities that were downgraded or expected to be downgraded because of litigation was relatively small. Insurance costs have also risen for many California cities. The functional areas most negatively impacted are police, streets, employee salaries, parks and recreation, and planning. The importance of MacManus's study is that other cities throughout the country should expect the rising cost of litigation to result in even greater budgetary and financial uncertainty.

CHAPTER 8

FINANCIAL MANAGEMENT:

A Balancing Act for Local Government Chief Financial Officers

W. BARTLEY HILDRETH

Introduction

Citizens expect their governments to do needed activities but within fiscal constraints.[1] Financial management seeks to carry out this fiscal imperative. The private economy generates the wealth that elected representatives of the public extract in part to provide for public goods and services. Public law prescribes the form of this taxation, the method of getting other forms, and the handling of these resources once they are in the custody of the public treasury. Further, the budgeting process offers a structured means for gaining a modicum of political consensus on how to address goals for the upcoming fiscal period. Civic results, therefore, hinge on the jurisdiction's financial management. Managing local finance requires more than the accounting of funds, however. Chief financial officers (CFOs) have to do a fiscal balancing act within the local body politic, requiring strategic integration of budgeting, accounting, and financial management in pursuit of the public good.

Balancing Process and Results

Public budgeting reflects the values of those involved in making the allocation. This means that there is no one best way to conduct budgeting or to judge the outcome. By default, the focus turns to the study of the process of budgetary decision-making and the results of those decisions. Looming on the near horizon, however, is a serious attempt by many to hold governments accountable for their service delivery and the accomplishment of articulated goals.

The process of budgetary decision-making examines the relationship of participants and the sequencing of those decisions. Two broad theories capture that thinking: "bottom up" and "top down" approaches to fiscal decision-making (LeLoup 1988).

Traditional "bottom up" budgeting emanates from fragmented decision-making with significant influence by program managers who build the budget from the bottom up, one line-item at a time. Although both operating and capital budgets follow a linear sequence, the behavior of each budgetary actor relates to the behavior of others in the process (Kiel and Elliot 1992; Forrester 1993). Decision-makers, moreover, adopt simplifying rules to limit the scope of analysis.

From *Public Administration Quarterly*, vol. 20, no. 3 (Fall 1996), pp. 320–342. Copyright © 1996 by Southern Public Administration Education Foundation, Inc. Reprinted with permission.

Stable fiscal environments allow relationships to develop and mature, often with recognizable rules and predictable results governing the budgetary debate. Despite its rejection as a general explanatory theory of budgeting (Berry 1990), incrementalism retains a theoretical and practical grip on the field of local government budgeting (Hendrick 1989, 1992a, 1992b; Rubin 1992).

In "top down" budgeting, top leaders impose macro constraints, by that limiting the role of lower-level managers in setting fiscal goals. A program may receive notice that it will lose its funding or can only propose a budget of a certain level. This preempts a program's desire to define its own budget and offers an opportunity for more comprehensive thinking about broad fiscal policy, forcing micro-level tendencies to yield to macro goals. Besides, macro-budgeting offers a way to respond to resource scarcity since a dynamic environment interrupts routine patterns of decision-making. Macro-decisions, however, can imperil the fiscal health of a local government that otherwise follows fiscally sound practices. Orange County, California, for example, declared bankruptcy in 1994 because of its aggressive investment practices. In 1996, the city of Miami, Florida, declared a fiscal emergency due to central finance problems.

Traditionally, the results of budgetary decisions appear as dollar allocations. Incremental budget theory posits that history decides budget results, meaning that past funding levels are likely to extend into future allocations. Specifically, in a bottom-up process, the budget of each successive organizational level is an aggregation of lower-level decision (Hendrick 1992b). In contrast, a centralized, top-down decision-making environment holds that primary decisions are on the total budget size and broad priorities and all other decisions flow from these macro choices. Still, the focus remains on budget change over time as well as in comparison with others. In such cases, it suggests that public agencies are less concerned with program accomplishments than with spending totals. Public constraints on taxing, borrowing, and spending naturally spring from citizens expressing their dissatisfaction with such results (O'Sullivan, Sexton, and Sheffrin 1995).

A contrary focus on what the dollar buys—not just on the formatting of the budget or dollar level—is now taking hold. Tight revenues compel managers to examine all spending patterns and performance and measure success against the stated mission and objectives. As part of this new calculus, governments have to reconsider their roles in the provision and production of each service (Oakerson 1987). In such an environment, however, CFOs must guard against the temptation of producing a skewed financial analysis to justify a preconceived idea (Hildreth 1983).

Reconciling Expenditures to Revenues

Balancing revenues against expenditures is the demanding requirement of public budgeting. Insatiable spending demands run up against constrained resources. Nevertheless, public officials have to make tough tradeoffs between spending and taxing options.

Revenues

The power to tax is a key point of distinction between a governmental entity and other organizational forms. Public revenue structures, however, vary from fixed rate tax levels to pricing of private goods publicly produced (e.g., toll roads, utility service). Since many resource flows are dedicated for particular purposes, an accounting system has to record and track each dollar into and out of the appropriate earmarked account. This promotes accountability to the citizens, users, and others and complicates financial reporting practice by requiring lengthy end-of-year financial statements summarizing transactions for each specialized set of accounts.

Aggressive efforts to increase the reach of taxes and fees can run into practical, if not legal, challenges. Taxpayers have to guard their pocketbooks because public officials frequently search for new revenues (Meltsner 1971). As commerce flows across legal borders, however, it becomes difficult to assess and collect particular taxes. For example, the growth in interstate sales through mail orders and over the Internet renders impotent a growing share of the local sales tax pending a national coordinated solution. Other revenue sources must pass constitutional hurdles such as in an interpretation of when a taxing method violates the interstate commerce clause.

Whatever the taxing scheme, it imposes an economic burden on individuals and businesses and these burdens vary by circumstances. A property tax, with differential appraisal and classification methods, affects people differently. Similarly, consumption tax burdens vary by consumption habits and the exemption from taxation of items such as food. An area ripe for political exploitation is the burden on fixed-income individuals caused by utility service fees increases. Relying upon transferred profits from cash-rich government enterprises (such as an electric utility) may help lower property taxes, but it also spreads the burden differently than might occur with a general property tax. As electric utilities, for example, face retail distribution competition, these subsidies may vanish, requiring the general fund to generate substitute funding. As a result, the burden will shift. Compounding the problem is that local governments lag the states in judging the burden of various revenue schemes.

Taxpayers signal dissatisfaction through their unwillingness to pay. Citizens want more services but at a lower cost, quite a conundrum for public officials seeking public support for programs (Glaser and Hildreth 1996). However, for officials to go around fiscal limits is to risk public retribution upon discovery of this subterfuge (Hildreth 1994). Revenue flows drive the budget. Overly optimistic revenue projections are the precursors of serious financial problems (Martin 1982). A community dependent upon a single industry for a major share of the tax base is particularly vulnerable. Caution also extends to communities with a concentrated economy measured by the share of the tax base owned by the top ten taxpayers (Hildreth and Miller 1994).

Expenditures

Money is a means to a desired end. It takes money to pay for a worker's time, to get equipment and machinery, and to pay for fuel and other essential supplies. The budget has to reach beyond these purchases and return added value to the citizens. Generally, taxpayers tolerate taxation to receive a bundle of services but increasingly make strident calls for results and limits. Performance accountability is one response. To compound matters, however, officials have to adjust public services continually to a changing community. Governments, dependent upon flexible budgets premised on customers paying as they use a service, have to adjust spending accordingly. Adding complexity is the high percentage of budget devoted to personnel costs, a fact that limits discretion and influences budget results (Hendrick 1992b). Moreover, budget systems can influence the incentive of parties to conserve resources (Klay 1987). Despite protections against incremental budgeting, many government programs get almost what they did in the prior year, although an aggregate view may mask significant changes within the budget (Hendrick 1989).

Particular types of public spending, especially in physical and social infrastructure, can influence the local economy (Lansing 1995). This arises because commerce depends upon a well-managed transportation network of streets and bridges, a sufficient water supply and adequate sewage treatment, and effective public safety services (e.g., police, fire, and emergency medical services). Quality of life measures, such as parks, green space, libraries, and cultural attractions, also assume importance in attracting and nurturing the engines of economic growth. Some of these expenditures represent developmental functions of the local budget (Peterson 1981) which coincidentally rank high as a spending preference of mayors (Longoria 1994).

Budget Balance

Budgets seek to reconcile expenditures to revenues. Resolving taxing and spending decisions jointly allows taxpayers to understand the tradeoffs and to avoid the illusion of not paying for services. The pressure point is the forecast of expected revenues. Communities using overly optimistic revenue forecasts may do so to avoid tradeoffs only to face cutbacks in midyear (Rubin 1982). In contrast, when the goal is to have a year-end fund balance, the tendency is to underestimate revenue. Revenues over estimates, therefore, fail to [lessen] the fund balance. On the other side, unanticipated spending needs may arise from unanticipated service demands to changes in political priorities. Quite frequently, therefore, the original adopted budget does not hold with formal revisions required during the fiscal year (Forrester and Mullins 1992).

Matching Assets to Liabilities

An organization wanting to remain a going concern needs to have and maintain assets sufficient to cover liabilities. The balance sheet reveals the monetary value of assets, liabilities, and equity as of the close of a financial period—a snapshot on a particular date. More than an accounting issue, however, the relationship of assets and liabilities is at the heart of organizational viability.

Things of monetary value held by an organization are assets. Cash held in the treasury is a very liquid asset but the city hall building gotten with past funds is no less an asset although an illiquid one. A dedicated, service-oriented public workforce is an asset, but its value is not posted on the balance sheet since humans are rented not owned.

Fixed assets, namely property, plant and equipment, require valuation and protection from loss. Few governments, however, completely value the built infrastructure that predates the most recent record-keeping system. To place a replacement value on the extensive network of infrastructure elements exceeds the practical needs of most local governments. Municipal electric utilities, however, must deal with stranded investments in generation capacity as deregulation of retail service takes hold.

Cash, the most liquid of all assets, can become illiquid by its manner of investment. The citizens of Orange County, California, awoke to this fact in late 1994. There, an elected treasurer caused the county to file for federal bankruptcy due to an aggressive investment strategy that failed. While this case was severe, poor investment strategies are not that uncommon in local government finance. For example, Toledo and several other Ohio local governments made investment mistakes in the mid-1980s, followed by another group in the mid-1990s that made the same type of poor investment as did Orange County. As Miller (1987) notes, however, the meaning of loss and its implications vary.

Every asset has a claim against it, either by owners of the organization or by those to whom something is owed. An asset with a corresponding unpaid claim is a liability. Examples include a box of pencils received but not paid for and the first week of a biweekly payroll for employees. Generally accepted accounting principles provide guidance on how to handle such claims. Local governments, both large and small, are prone to overlook the basics of accounting, however (Advisory Commission on Intergovernmental Relations 1985).

The balance sheet may not reveal all financial liabilities. An extensive textual review of supplemental liabilities is in the "Notes to the Financial Statements." Long-term obligations that commit the governmental jurisdiction to payments in the future years but do not rise to the definition of a liability for financial reporting purposes emerge from a review of the notes. Therefore, for example, a capital-lease purchase contract may give the government a legal way to avoid paying the lease payments by that rendering the lease payment outside the definition of liability. To the market, however, this is a legal artifact to get around the legal definition of long-term debt, not a legal loophole for use by public officials (Hildreth 1994).

Each asset has an offsetting claim but there is a big difference between a claim by external parties and one by the owners or clients. Insolvency is the condition when total liabilities exceed a fair valuation of assets. More common is technical insolvency or a "maturity matching" problem which occurs when a government is unable to pay debts as they come due in the normal course of business. New York City faced this situation in the mid-1970s and had to restructure its finances quickly to avoid more serious problems. In contrast, Orange County's insolvency led it to file for bankruptcy.

The market expects an organization's fiscal assets to exceed liabilities, not just be equal, and for most governments this is the case. Even in the face of severe fiscal stress, insolvency may not be at risk. For example, Bridgeport, Connecticut, wanted to declare bankruptcy but the federal court dismissed the filing. The court ruled that, although the city had budget deficits, it was not insolvent, by that failing a prerequisite for filing for municipal bankruptcy (Lewis 1994).

Covering Payments with Cash

It takes cash to pay a bill. Liquidity is the availability of cash to meet payroll demands. Forecasting cash inflows and outflows for the upcoming fiscal period helps catch potential liquidity problems. One approach for dealing with an interim shortage of cash is to use short-term borrowing. Cash-flow borrowing can cause a problem when the funds are repaid in a different year than when borrowed. Cleveland fell into this trap in 1979, leading to a default on general obligation one-year notes.

Before entering into any obligation, local governments have either to have the cash on hand or forecast its availability within the fiscal year. Most states allow their local governments to spend against budget revenues. There is a risk that these revenues will not appear. Moreover, when revenues fall short of expectations, budgets quickly fail the balancing test and require budget revisions to correct the situation. Just because an item has been budgeted, however, does not mean that cash will be there on time to allow that expenditure. Program managers find it quite discouraging to find out that they cannot fill a new position authorized in the budget because the general cash flow situation has changed (Hildreth 1993a).

Reconciling Short- and Long-Term Plans

Budgets give a very limited view of a community's civic life. For a specified period (usually 12 months), policy-makers have to define what will be done and at what public price. This fosters a tradeoff of one budget year against all future ones. A fund balance accumulated over several years, for example, is susceptible to use by current spenders. Adding new employees or increasing the pay of the existing workforce may bolster today's public employees but escalate future costs. A similar result flows from deferred maintenance. Saving a few maintenance dollars in one year can lead to higher repair bills later.

Operating and capital budgets provide an opportunity to examine rationally short- and long-term fiscal plans. Practice falls short of theory, however (Forrester 1991, 1993; Starling 1986).

Large budget decisions linger in a community, such as starting a new landfill, clearing a blighted part of downtown or extending water lines to an outlying development. Furthermore, stable taxes benefit economic development because such strategies allow businesses to make long-term investment decisions. Similarly, a prudent fund balance helps cushion temporary disruptions to the public fisc.

Due to the time lag between making a decision and seeing the results, policy-makers have to make hard decisions early. It takes time to see public assets or to privatize contracts. To change the frequency, much less the scale of a service, requires planning. Changing the frequency of a service includes, for example, steps to cut the grass only after it reaches a higher height or to sweep the streets less frequently. It does not take long to change the frequency of a service once officials make the decision. Changing the scale of a service, in contrast, represents actions to consolidate services and to eliminate unnecessary levels of supervision, actions that require more complicated and time-consuming approval steps. There is a tendency to avoid taking some of these more controversial actions. An all-too-common local way to deal with fiscal stress is to draw down the fund balance and invoke an across-the-board cut. Containing the fiscal shock internally this way only delays the inevitable data for making service changes and the receipt of the fiscal dividend (Donaldson 1988).

Achieving Results

Budgeting deals with money and gains its mystique from that linkage. A major sense of accomplishment comes from adopting and achieving a balanced budget. Yet, there are other financial and nonfinancial measures of interest to finance officers as sampled below.

Financial Measures

Balance the Budget. Budget laws and tradition define the meaning of a balanced budget rule. Lewis (1994) identifies only twenty states that place municipalities under a constitutional or statutory burden to balance the budget but most large cities face local rules requiring one. A more important point is whether the budget has to be balanced at the end of the year or merely upon submission by the executive and/or at the time of legislative adoption. Furthermore, a budget submission may be in balance but only because it relies upon an unrealistic revenue forecast or a requested, but not yet approved, tax rate increase. Lewis (1994) reports that only about one-third of the one hundred most populous cities in the United States must balance the budget at year-end!

Obtain a Positive Variance. Officials often strive for a positive variance between what was budgeted and the actual results. In terms of revenues, this means collecting more than the amount forecasted at the beginning of the year. In contrast, a positive expenditure variance translates into spending less than planned. An intended strategy of lowball revenue forecasts and inflated spending plans can yield larger than expected end-of-year fiscal balances. However, while an excess of revenues (and sources of funds) over expenditures (and uses of funds) may give a fleeting sense of accomplishment to top financial officers, ultimately it weakens confidence in the fiscal process by finance managers, elected officials, taxpayers, and service recipients. If fiscal managers manipulate the process to mask intended strategies, the budgetary process can lose its consensus-forming advantages. Besides, the capital market may reward a municipality for meeting its balanced budget target not by enlarging (or diminishing) the fund balance (Giroux and Apostolou 1991).

Maintain a Fund Balance. Governments show their error tolerance but preserve financial flexibility from one fiscal period to the next by maintaining a fund balance (McCollough and Frank 1992). Credit rating agencies pay attention to this decision although there are no precise guidelines for the desired size (Allan 1990; Moody's Investors Service 1993). It is possible to understate the usable fund balance on the balance sheet by claiming that the fund balance is unreserved but designated. Usually this is merely an arbitrary label meant only to mask the true size. Instead, it is appropriate to label the fund balance "unreserved, undesignated." After debating the level of a minimum fund balance, that amount would remain safe from all claimants until meeting specified policy conditions. Otherwise, hiding large amounts in arbitrary, technical labels fuels cynicism and undermines full fiscal disclosure.

Invest Nonrecurring Funds. While matching recurring revenues to continuing expenditures is what general budgeting is all about, using a one-time revenue windfall to cover normal expenditures is a recipe for a structural budget imbalance in later years. An alternate course of action is to invest the windfall using only the dividend from the principal each year or dedicating the windfall for capital construction so that the benefits accrue over time (Hildreth 1988).

Avoid Enterprise Subsidies/Transfers. Municipalities often operate one or more businesslike enterprise operations such as water, sewer, and electrical systems. An enterprise fund's narrow purpose and rate-making discretion contrast starkly with the tight general fund. The pressure, therefore, is to transfer excess utility funds into the general fund. A counterbalance is that lenders of borrowed money typically impose legal covenants requiring rates to cover yearly expenses plus a cushion. Moreover, as competitive rate pressures intensify on each utility, these subsidies will give way to general fund shortfalls. Transfers can go in the opposite direction with the General Fund subsidizing a money-losing public enterprise. Creditors are alert to this fact and factor in this threat to the general fund.

Stabilize Finances over Time. Fluctuating tax rates complicate business and individual tax planning just as undependable public service interrupts daily routines. Besides, a balanced budget promised on a stable tax rate, if not a lower one, is a powerful political signal.

Achieve Competitive Advantage. Community leaders and the media frequently draw comparisons between their community and others. Tax rate comparisons are very common but offer only one narrow view of what makes a community unique, distinctive, and attractive to growth and investment. A community must assess its factor endowments—namely location, human capital, and local wealth—and plan accordingly (Schmidt 1993). Denver, for example, made major investments in downtown event facilities and a new international airport and that strategy is successful.

Maintain Intergenerational Equity. Each yearly set of taxpayers should pay its own way and not push the burden for current services onto a future taxpayer generation. Thus, deferred maintenance of public infrastructure, unfunded pension liabilities, and poorly considered debt repayment schedules illustrate how one spending generation can foist its costs onto another one. In contrast, an accumulated fund balance accrues to the benefit of a future generation.

Obtain a Low Cost of Capital. The goal of capital acquisition is to obtain the needed money at the lowest cost (Hildreth 1993b). Most issues of debt seek to influence that cost by adopting policies and practices that mirror the recommendations of bond rating agencies. While this is good, it appears that a growing and diversified local economy is the real path to higher bond ratings (Loviscek and Crowley 1990). If so, there may be little a borrower can do in the short term to improve its rating (Coe 1994).

Preserve Debt Capacity. A community can afford only so much long-term debt in spite of any legally allowed debt limit. Therefore, it helps to assess local debt capacity and preserve some flexibility within the economic limit (Hildreth 1996a). Interjurisdictional debt coordination recognizes that the same debt base supports various political subdivisions and that it is the aggregate that matters most to taxpayers (Hildreth and Miller 1994).

Nonfinancial Measures

A budget is more than a listing of allocated money. It conveys the mix of programs and services authorized for a fiscal period. In essence, the budget publicly defines the boundaries of operational tasks as suggested by the following measures.

Gain Efficiency. Production requires the transformation of some mix of acquired labor, capital, materials, and technology into a desired good or service. A typical approach is to count the outputs and compare these results to the costs of production by that gaining a cost per unit. Many governments have developed expertise in applying these measures.

Achieve Effectiveness. Effectiveness addresses whether the organization is doing the right thing, not just doing better what has been done in the past. This imposes a burden on the organization to identify its goals and to measure movement to that target. Applying these types of measures is difficult but there are many governments working toward this goal.

Manage Capacity. An operating system can handle only so much work. Yet, governments have a great tendency to build excess capacity and to design redundancies into operating procedures. Internal audit controls foster a separation of duties in handling cash, for an example. Also, the construction of excess water and sewer treatment capacity imposes cost but no benefits on today's ratepayers. This excess capacity may be a form of risk aversion, a way to avoid another lengthy building cycle with its tough political debate, difficult financial tradeoffs, complicated building procedures, and frequent delays.

Provide Timely Service. Consumers honor a private enterprise when it provides a desired and timely product with the firm tallying its rewards in sales and profits. Governments, however, display a callous disregard for the time of their citizens/customers. Budget allocations seldom depend on achieving service goals measured by time. Other than in public safety response time, few performance indicators consider time a key target.

Maintain Quality. Customers want a fair value for their money. A value-added activity is one that contributes to customer satisfaction with implications for fiscal policy. Foul smelling water, for example, is a clear indicator of a quality problem that can influence a user's willingness to pay for system improvements (Hildreth 1996b).

Make Investments. A community has to foster its private economy or else it risks economic stagnation, even ruin. Every tax has an economic effect, potentially aiding or harming the economic actors upon whom the community depends. Spending decisions also influence economic invest-ments. It starts with responsible fiscal policy but rests on a viable local (and even regional) economic base defined by many as economic growth. Achieving that goal requires attentive tax and spending decisions (Governor's Tax Equity Task Force 1995).

Achieve the Benchmark. Measures of success are not easy to agree upon in the provision of public goods. One way to measure success is to benchmark a community to its peer group or to successful organizations generally. The work on benchmarking is incomplete. Correcting this failing of public management deserves the highest priority of both scholars and practitioners. Otherwise, public attention will shift exclusively to the one area where comparisons are readily available: tax rates.

Make Appropriate Market Disclosures. Local governments with outstanding long-term debt—or plans to issue debt in the future—must consider market demands for information (Hildreth 1996b). Issuers of debt must formally reveal certain matters upon the issuance of debt, make continuing disclosure each year after that, and reveal particular events when they occur. Failure to make these commitments can render it difficult, if not impossible, to enter the national capital market. Fur-thermore, it can result in a violation of securities law.

Maintain Adequate Public Communications. Public executives and policy leaders have a re-sponsibility to the citizens and taxpayers to provide continuing information about public poli-cies and plans. The tendency to use technical language in budgets make this important fiscal document unintelligible for the average reader and even the local media (Swoboda 1995). A budget serves as an opportunity to present fiscal plans in a way that expresses the tradeoffs made in doing the public's business and the expected results from using the public's funds. Citizens in Maricopa County, Arizona, and Miami, Florida, have learned that an award-winning budget (as in receipt of a distinguished budget presentation award from the Government Finance Officers Association) says little, if anything, about the accuracy of the numbers.

Mobilize Invisible Assets. Not all assets are valued in monetary terms and carried on the balance sheet (Itami 1987). Termed invisible assets, these items help define the community. For example, the willingness to pay taxes when elected representatives present propositions to the voters is a sign of community consensus. Repeated ballot failures signal an unhappiness with the local public agenda but overuse of the tax base can lead to economic flight. Another invisible asset is the organizational culture with an atmosphere of tight control likely to prevent effective uses of personal incentives and entrepreneurial behavior. Third, a tradition of providing added value for the tax dollar fosters trust in local leaders. Credit-rating firms have a difficult time measuring these and other invisible assets but does not prevent them from probing.

Work to Be Done, Not Location

Local governments, like most organizations, prominently display and budget by the organiza-tional chart. Employees spend most of their careers within one department, fostering loyalty, expertise, and stability (even rigidity). Budgets follow departmental lines, each department a small island, sovereign and separate from the others. This translates into competition among and between departments for scarce dollars, both the new increments of dollars and the existing share of the total budget (Tucker 1981). Even in a program budget orientation the same aggregation problems reappear with the department remaining the focus of attention.

A contrary approach is to focus on the work process. A work process involves many employee activities that consume time and costs. To control costs, therefore, requires a focus on activities. Each step in the activity chain should add value or else it becomes a candidate for elimination. While organizations rigidly follow departmental structures, work flows across departmental boundaries, creating costs in each department. Budgets neatly compartmentalize expenditures and mask any attempt to derive the true cost of a service. Accounting systems must adapt and capture cost at each step in the process, allowing managers to see the total costs, not just a segment. The goal is to track costs as the organization renders the service (Kehoe et al. 1995; Stoner and Werner 1993; Ostrenga et al. 1992).

CEOs must visualize finance as more than a system of transactions but as a vehicle for enhancing decisions (Hildreth 1989). What are the budget implications of saving one day in a permit approval process or reducing by a half-minute the average response time for emergency services? Most municipal budgets do not allow readers on their own to make these "what if" analyses. Thus, the budget is not the dynamic choice-forcing tool it could be.

Balancing Control with Incentives

Budgeting and finance is a staff function and that conveys its most disturbing quality—its distance from the productive services that add value to the life of a community and its citizens. Central budget offices can no longer micro manage the budgets of direct service departments, taking the budget review role to the extreme. To steer the future fiscal strategy of a local government requires a shift from a dominant fiscal control orientation to one interested in responsive service delivery.

The chief financial officer has the duty to implement the chief executive's fiscal agenda and enhance the fiscal allegiance of program managers. A control philosophy predominates in most fiscal operations. The budget office structures the budgetary process, using terminology and designs of its choice. It translates fiscal trends and threats into visible budget figures that program managers must overcome. Every action of any monetary term provides valuable information to hold executives and managers accountable for results. Moreover, accounting and auditing controls provide powerful signals on acceptable management behavior. As a result, the finance officer is a central clearinghouse for things that matter in the life of an organization (Gargan 1987b). With the information flow comes power but it does so at the expense of program managers (Giroux, Mayper, and Daft 1986). The viability of such a command and control system is under severe challenge in today's dynamic environment.

A contrary approach gives program managers discretion but tied to responsibilities. The first step is to replace the notorious "use or lose" incentive, deriving from the yearly stocking of a department or program with an approved budget amount. After competing and winning against all the other potential claimants for funds, the program must deliver the planned services for the agreed-upon "price" (the budgeted level). To have slack in the budget raises questions about the sincerity of the budget request and the reliability of the approval process to detect excess funds embedded in the requests (Merchant 1985). Besides, there is an opportunity cost for not having those funds available to allocate for higher priority purposes. As a result, program directors have little incentive to feign economic savings because it could make the program susceptible to cuts in upcoming budget periods (Wildavsky 1964). Therefore, there is a rush to spend the funds before the end of the fiscal year perhaps by buying computer equipment or other one-time purchases.

To advance an incentive to save, a local government might allow a budget unit to carry over unspent funds (or at least a share of it) into the next fiscal year. This could allow a program manager to make more judicious use of these hard-earned funds. Complicating this move, however, is the prevailing practice of reverting all departmental unspent funds to a general fund balance at year-end. A perverse practice is to hide money in departments up front, knowing that savings will fall to the fund balance at year-end.

After a period of centralized purchasing requirements, the population is swinging back to more discretion by worksite supervisors. Municipalities find that the number of people who have to sign off on small dollar purchases often outweighs the benefits. As a result, some governments now allow purchases below a certain amount (e.g., $500, $1,000, or $5,000, depending upon the size of the budget) without preapproval and with a city's credit card. The credit card has the added benefit of providing a document trail for use in post-auditing.

To encourage more program discretion calls for a change in the role of the central budget. Department heads instigate most spending initiatives by translating service demands into actual programs. In turn, the capital budget office serves as a gatekeeper to the money, a powerful counterweight to program heads. This places the budget office in a veto role rather than a partner to the program experts. Finance officers build barriers to avoid getting "blindsided" by program managers. All too frequently, finance officers learn late in the legislative process that the fiscal consequences of an action (perhaps even supported by the chief executive) has escaped attention. Stopping the initiative at this late stage is difficult, even if the chief executive was under the mistaken impression that the proposal had undergone the required fiscal review. To avoid such missteps, municipalities build elaborate fiscal approval sequences, backed up by memorandums and assorted details that make decision-making quite complex and time-consuming.

An improvement to the centralizing tendency is to empower the program head with the fixed expertise to anticipate likely fiscal questions by preparing a better initial proposal. This places the budget office in a consulting role rather than a gatekeeper. In this arrangement, the program manager engages the fiscal office only when needed. For this scheme to work, however, program managers must become better policy analysts and fiscal managers, and have to set aside their myopic program advocacy role for a shared vision of the organization (Hildreth 1989).

Local Customs, Market-Based Guidelines

Over time local financial patterns are ingrained as a way of life. Incrementalism in budgetary decision "favors old claims over new ones" (Schick 1988, 61). Upon questioning why a particular practice is done a certain way, the refrain is "that is just the way we've always done it." While these cobwebs of the past can retard innovative behavior, they also serve to make people stick to a well-trodden comfortable path even if it is going in the wrong direction. In contrast, unreasonable objectives can push units to improve on the past even if the results fall short of that unreasonable objective (Riordan 1992).

One challenge to local tradition is the rapid pace of efforts to compare local practice to comparative benchmarks. This ranges from the use of seasoned business executives to analyze government operations (Hildreth and Hildreth 1989) to more systematic efforts to advance market metaphors in government activity.

The local customs of public finance are yielding to professional norms and standards. Moving from an internal or local focus to one that is more cosmopolitan or external can infuse new thinking into an organization and its strategic planning (Bruton and Hildreth 1993). Fundamentally, state and local laws compel minimal behavior while professional practice may demand additional steps. For example, state laws require the auditing of local accounts every other and on a cash basis of accounting. However, governmental units desiring to borrow capital market are expected to have a yearly audit prepared according to generally accepted accounting principles, known as GAAP. In such a situation, GAAP does not replace the cash-basis reporting requirement, it just requires an additional set of practices and financial statements. However, if a local governmental unit lacks the capital to do minimal fiscal practice, then it is unlikely to achieve the higher order improvements (Gargan 1987a).

Finance officers improve their professional standing, if not also their government's, by preparing financial documents that meet peer review criteria. The budget and the Comprehensive Annual Financial Report (the audit) are core financial documents and each is measurable against established guidelines. Budget allocations are political decisions and thus not subject to outsider review, nor is the accuracy of the data tested, as Miami and Maricopa County citizens have learned. Instead, the peer review is of the documents as a financial plan, an operations guide, a management device, and a communications vehicle (Andrus 1993). To meet GAAP guidelines requires that a government prepare a Comprehensive Annual Financial Report and issue it within six months of the fiscal year's end.

Another peer review area fosters development and adoption of formal cash management and investment policies as a way to respond to the Orange County situation. Emerging on the horizon is an attempt to develop "best practice" guidelines in all areas of public budgeting so that state and local government officials and finance professionals will have a common set of principles that define performance expectations (Government Finance Officers Association 1993). Also the effort by GFOA to award the "certified public finance officer" designation upon the demonstrated mastery of five substantive test areas is likely to shape the future of professional development and the education of CFOs in government.

An additional area of market expectation and now federal regulatory review is in disclosure practices regarding the issuance of municipal securities. Selling bonds in the national capital market has long required preparation and distribution of an offering circular known as an "official statement," although the comprehensiveness of it has grown in recent decades. These governments now have to agree to provide continuing disclosure material to investors in those bonds plus certain market events, including defaults and other potential impairments of obligations to pay, demand immediate dissemination to the broad market.

Moreover, elected officials can no longer delegate to appointed executives or hired experts the responsibility for meeting securities law. In addressing the Orange County debacle, federal securities regulators issued findings against the elected county supervisors for inadequate oversight despite the officials' reliance on a team of legal, financial, and administrative experts (Securities and Exchange Commission 1996). As a result, elected officials have to know what it is they are agreeing to do when they allow the government unit to issue debt. Elected officials cannot accept the recommendations of professionals without conducting their own review of the facts. This latest development presages a change in the relationship between elected officials and professional finance officers.

Conclusion

The fiscal agenda of a public organization permeates all of its policies and programs. Success is measured in more than dollars. Without a monetary metric, however, the budget has little meaning. A program advocate or department head can do little without dollars to spend. Furthermore, for any organization to remain a going concern, assets must equal or exceed liabilities, and cash has to be available to cover the bills. These are the easy parts of finance.

Finance officers have to examine the long-term implications of contemporary decisions. Innovative and cost-conscious managerial behavior is at a premium as is measuring services against market benchmarks. All of this emphasizes the delicate balancing act facing finance officers as they adjust the competing financial concerns to public policy. To accomplish this goal, finance officers have to change from the controller of transactions (the bean-counter role) to the more demanding job of fiscal strategist.

Note

1. An earlier version of this chapter appears in Jack Gargan, ed., *Handbook of Local Government Administration* (New York: Marcel Dekker, 1997).

References

Advisory Committee on Intergovernmental Relations. 1985. *Bankruptcies, Defaults, and Other Local Government Financial Emergencies.* Washington, DC: Author.

Allan, I.J. 1990. "Unreserved Fund Balance and Local Government Finance." *Research Bulletin.* Chicago: Government Finance Officers Association.

Andrus, A. 1993. "GFOA's Budget Awards Program: New Directions Planned for 1994." *Government Finance Review* 9: 11–14.

Berry, W.D. 1990. "The Confusing Case of Budgetary Incrementalism: Too Many Meanings for a Single Concept." *Journal of Politics* 52: 167–196.

Bruton, G., and W.B. Hildreth. 1993. "Strategic Public Financing: External Orientations and Strategic Planning Team Members." *American Review of Public Administration* 23: 307–317.

Coe, C. 1994. "Obtaining a Better Bond Rating: A Case Study." In *Case Studies in Public Budgeting and Financial Management,* ed. A. Khan and W.B. Hildreth. Dubuque, IA: Kendall/Hunt.

Donaldson, G. 1988. *Strategy for Financial Mobility.* Boston: Harvard Business School Press.

Forrester, J.P. 1991. "Multi-Year Forecasting and Municipal Budgeting." *Public Budgeting and Finance* 11: 47–61.

———. 1993. "Municipal Capital Budgeting: An Examination." *Public Budgeting and Finance* 13: 85–103.

Forrester, J.P., and D.R. Mullins. 1992. "Rebudgeting: The Serial Nature of Municipal Budgeting." *Public Administration Review* 52: 457–473.

Gargan, J.J. 1987a. "Local Government Financial Management Capacity: A Political Perspective." *Public Administration Quarterly* 11: 246–276.

———. 1987b. "The Knowledge-Interest Context of Local Public Finance: Judgments of City Finance Officers." *International Journal of Public Administration* 9: 245–272.

Giroux, G.A., and N.G. Apostolou. 1991. "The Market Reaction to the Information Content of Municipal Surplus/Deficit Ratios." *Public Budgeting and Financial Management* 3: 487–514.

Giroux, G.A., A.G. Mayper, and R.L. Daft. 1986. "Organization Size, Budget Cycle, and Budget Related Influence in City Governments: An Empirical Study." *Accounting, Organization, and Society* 11: 499–519.

Glaser, J., and W.B. Hildreth. 1996. "A Profile of Discontinuity Between Citizen Demand and Willingness to Pay Taxes: Comprehensive Planning for Park and Recreation Investment." *Public Budgeting and Finance* (Winter): 94–111.

Government Finance Officers Association. 1993. "National Budget Symposium: Report of Proceedings." Chicago: Author.

Governor's Tax Equity Task Force. 1995. Topeka, KS: Office of the Governor.

Hendrick, R. 1989. "Top-Down Budgeting: Fiscal Stress and Budgeting Theory." *American Review of Public Administration* 19: 29–48.

———. 1992a. "Budget Reform in the 1980s: The Compatibility of Design and Practice." *Public Budgeting and Financial Management* 4: 611–644.

———. 1992b. "Budgetary Tradeoffs Under Top-Down and Bottom-Up Budgeting." *Public Budgeting and Financial Management* 4: 327–358.

Hildreth, W.B. 1983. "Applying Professional Disclosure Standards to Productivity Financial Analysis." *Public Productivity Review* 7: 269–287.

———. 1988. "The Politics of a Windfall: Allocating Special Offshore Oil and Gas Receipts in Four Southern States Facing Fiscal Retrenchment." *International Journal of Public Administration* 11: 581–600.

———. 1989. "Financial Strategy." In *Handbook of Strategic Management*, ed. J. Rabin, G.J. Miller, and W.B. Hildreth. New York: Marcel Dekker.

———. 1993a. "Budgeting the Work Force: Influences, Elements, Disclosure Strategies, and Roles." *International Journal of Public Administration* 16: 985–1014.

———. 1993b. "State and Local Governments as Borrowers: Strategic Choices and the Capital Market." *Public Administration Review* 53: 41–49.

———, ed. 1994. "Certificates of Participation in Brevard County: A Local Political Issue and Its Implications for the National Municipal Bond Market." *Municipal Finance Journal* 15: 50–74.

———. 1996a. "State and Local Government Debt Issuance and Management Service." Austin, TX: Sheshunoff Information Services.

———. 1996b. "Addressing Customers' Capital Improvement Preference: A Study of Water Utility Net Benefits." In *Public Works Administration: Modern Public Policy Perspectives*, ed. L. Brewer. Newbury Park, CA: Sage.

Hildreth, W.B., and R.P. Hildreth. 1989. "The Business of Public Management." *Public Productivity Review* 12: 303–321.

Hildreth, W.B., and G.J. Miller. 1994. "Can the Riverside Community Afford a Massive Debt Financed Capital Improvement Program?" In *Case Studies in Public Budgeting and Financial Management*, ed. A. Khan and W.B. Hildreth. Dubuque, IA: Kendall/Hunt.

Itami, H. 1987. *Mobilizing Invisible Assets*. Cambridge, MA: Harvard University Press.

Kehoe, J., W. Dodson, R. Reeve, and G. Plato. 1995. *Activity-Based Management in Government*. Arlington, VA: Coopers and Lybrand.

Kiel, L.D., and E. Elliot. 1992. "Budgets and Dynamic Systems: Change, Variation, Time, and Budgetary Heuristics." *Journal of Public Administration Research and Theory* 2: 139–156.

Klay, W.E. 1987. "Management Through Budgetary Incentives." *Public Productivity Review* 41: 59–74.

Lansing, K.J. 1995. "Is Public Capital Productive? A Review of the Evidence." Economic Commentary: Federal Reserve Bank of Cleveland, March.

Lewis, C.W. 1994. "Budgetary Balance: The Norm, Concept, and Practice in Large U.S. Cities." *Public Administration Review* 54: 515–524.

LeLoup, L.T. 1988. "From Microbudgeting to Macrobudgeting: Evolution in Theory and Practice." In *New Directions in Budget Theory*, ed. I.S. Rubin. Albany: State University of New York Press.

Longoria, T. Jr. 1994. "Empirical Analysis of the City Limits Topology." *Urban Affairs Quarterly* 30: 102–113.

Loviscek, A.L., and F.D. Crowley. 1990. "What Is in a Municipal Bond Rating?" *Financial Review* 25: 25–53.

Martin, J.K. 1982. *Urban Financial Stress: Why Cities Go Broke*. Boston, MA: Auburn.

McCollough, J., and H. Frank. 1992. "Incentives for Forecasting Reform Among Local Finance Officers." *Public Budgeting and Financial Management* 4: 407–429.

Meltsner, A.J. 1971. *The Politics of City Revenue*. Berkeley: University of California Press.

Merchant, K.A. 1985. "Budgeting and Propensity to Create Budgetary Slack." *Accounting, Organizations and Society* 10: 201–210.

Miller, G.J. 1987. "Will Governments Hedge Interest Rate Risks?" *Public Administration Quarterly* 11: 297–313.

Moody's Investors Service. 1993. "Key Factors in Moody's Credit Analysis of Tax-Supported Debt." *Perspective on Municipal Issues* (April 15).

Oakerson, R.J. 1987. "Local Public Economics: Provision, Production, and Governance." *Intergovernmental Perspective* 13: 20–24.

Ostrenga, M.R., T.R. Ozan, R.D. McIllhattan, and M.D. Harwood. 1992. *The Ernst and Young Guide to Total Cost Management*. New York: John Wiley.

O'Sullivan, A., T. Sexton, and S. Sheffrin. 1995. *Property Taxes and Tax Revolts*. New York: Cambridge University Press.

Peterson, P.E. 1981. *City Limits*. Chicago: University of Chicago Press.

Riordan, T.A. 1992. "Management by Unreasonable Objectives." *Municipal Finance Journal* 13: 83–90.

Rubin, I.S. 1982. *Running in the Red: The Political Dynamics of Urban Fiscal Stress*. Albany: State University of New York Press.

———. 1992. "Budget Reform and Political Reform: Conclusions from Six Cities." *Public Administration Review* 52: 454–466.

Schick, A. 1988. "An Inquiry into the Possibility of a Budgetary Theory." In *New Directions in Budget Theory*, ed. I.S. Rubin. Albany: State University of New York Press.

Schmidt, R.H. 1993. "Regional Comparative Advantage." *FRBSF Weekly Letter* (October 29).

Securities and Exchange Commission. 1996. "Report of Investigation in the Matter of County of Orange, California as it Relates to the Conduct of the Members of the Board of Supervisors" (Release 36761). Washington, DC: Author.

Starling, J.D. 1986. *Municipal Coping Strategies: As Soon as the Dust Settles*. Beverly Hills, CA: Sage.

Stoner, J.A.F., and F.M. Werner. 1993. *Finance in the Quality Revolution*. Morristown, NJ: Financial Executives Research Foundation.

Swoboda, D.P. 1995. "Accuracy and Accountability in Reporting Local Government Budget Activities: Evidence from the Newsroom and from Newsmakers." *Public Budgeting and Finance* 15: 74–90.

Tucker, H.J. 1981. "Budgeting Strategy: Cross-Sectional Versus Longitudinal Models." *Public Administration Review* 6: 644–649.

Wildavsky, A. 1964. *The Politics of the Budgetary Process*. Boston, MA: Little, Brown.

CHAPTER 9

BUDGET REFORM AND POLITICAL REFORM:

Conclusions from Six Cities

IRENE S. RUBIN

Big City Budgeting

Municipal budgeting, especially in larger cities, has changed over the last twenty years. A variety of tools like program formats, long-term revenue and expenditure projections, management-by-objectives (MBO), zero-based and target-based budgets, capital budgeting, and strategic planning have become commonplace (Poister and Streib 1989). A surprising large number of cities are using some performance monitoring (242).

Why does budgeting change? Budget formats and processes develop over time, as new tools are adopted, altered, and incorporated into the standard repertory in response to changes in resources levels and the spirit of the times. The relative emphasis on spending controls, managerial efficiency, and program planning (Schick 1966) is influenced by the current rate of growth in revenues, the rate of growth of expenditures in the previous period, and the pressure on government to solve infrastructural and social problems.

Literature about changing budget formats and processes emphasizes trends across time rather than variation between governmental units. Yet some cities responded earlier and more whole-heartedly to program budgeting, zero-based budgeting, or performance measures than others. The topic of this article is how cities differ in their use of budget reforms depending on the level of their political reform.

The concept of political reform is multidimensional. In this study, a city with a council-manager form of government and at-large elections for council seats is considered more reformed. Less-centralized cities with weak mayoral control and strong department heads are considered less reformed. The importance of patronage employees and the choice of friends of the mayor as key administrators are also considered indicators of the level of political reform. More politicized cities, where electoral politics play an important part in policy and administrative decisions, are considered less reformed. Political reform also has a historical dimension; a city that has alternated between a manager and a mayor or that has recently given up the manager form of government is considered less reformed than a city that has a long, unbroken tradition of city-manager government. In less-reformed cities, accountability is provided more through elections and the person of the mayor; in more reformed cities, accountability is provided more through the openness of administrative processes and documents.

From *Public Administration Review*, vol. 52, no. 5 (September/October 1992), pp. 454–466. Copyright © 1992 by American Society for Public Administration. Reprinted with permission.

Box 9.1
The Study

The four alternatives grew out of (but were not tested in) six case studies representing varying degrees of political reform. Two were city-manager cities with traditions of reform (Dayton, Ohio, and Phoenix, Arizona); two were mayor-council cities, with some reformed elements (Rochester, New York, and Tampa, Florida); and two were traditionally decentralized, politicized mayor-council cities (Boston, Massachusetts, and St. Louis, Missouri). Each pair of cities represented different regions of the country.

The case studies combined interviews with documentary materials, such as charters, budgets, capital improvement plans, constitutional constraints, and newspaper accounts. There were thirty-eight interviews, with several informants interviewed twice. Key informants included the staff members who were most responsible for the introduction of major budget changes, current budget directors, department heads and/or their assistants, city managers and/or their assistants, and the mayors and/or their assistants. The questions asked included the role in the budget process of the mayor, the council, the departments, and the budget office; the timing and nature of any changes in the budget process or format; the reasons for these changes; and how the changes were implemented.

The reforms studied included Planning-Programming-Budgeting Systems (PPBS), performance evaluation, productivity programs, zero-based (ZBB) and target-based budgets (TBB), and capital budgeting. The study also looked at the extent to which all municipal spending was described in one budget (consolidation) in a relatively easy to understand format.

Budget reforms have been adopted in cities with varying degrees of political reform, but they do not seem to fit decentralized, highly political cities. The reforms have included central financial controls over departments and evaluation of departmental performance, and they have emphasized openness and accountability. They have linked the budget with policy-based planning goals. Long-term financial planning challenges the ad hoc nature of political deal making. The top-down nature of some of the reforms defies the independence of powerful departments. The openness of evaluation created political vulnerability to the press and opposition candidates, and the transparency and comprehensiveness of reformed budgeting threatens the traditional secrecy of decision making in more political cities.

If this image of a mismatch between less-reformed cities and budget reform is correct, one would expect cities with a weaker reform tradition to avoid budget reforms or adopt them selectively or implement reforms in ways that reduce their potential threat value. However, the possibility remains that the level of political and structural reform may make little difference to the adoption of budget innovations. Cities with different levels of political reform may adopt the same budget reforms because they are responding to similar environmental pressures. Or they may adopt similar budget reforms, but for different reasons. This chapter explores the relationship between political reform and the adoption of budget reform by examining these four alternatives (see Box 9.1).

The first alternative is that cities avoid some reforms and pick others that suit their political characteristics. Target-based budgeting, with its more lump-sum allocations, might be welcome in cities with strong departments and weak budget offices. More centralized cities would presumably choose budget processes that made explicit tradeoffs between programs. Cities with strong departments may be unable to adopt budget systems that request extensive information from the departments, especially information that departments see as threatening.

The second alternative is that cities adopt the same reforms, but implement them at different levels, depending on the degree of political reform. Less-reformed cities might not fully implement reforms that require more control over the departments, or that expose politicians to negative publicity. Performance measures might be implemented in such a way that departmental goals are always achieved 100 percent, so the departments are not threatened and politicians are not vulnerable to public criticism. Reforms requiring more openness of decision making may be less fully implemented in more politicized cities. For example, the budget may be less integrated, with more separate decision processes, each addressing a separate political constituency.

The third alternative is that, regardless of the level of political and structural reform, cities have been experiencing similar environmental threats, including declining federal aid, recessions, and tax revolts, and have adopted similar patterns of budgeting to help them solve these problems. Different budget reforms are intended to solve particular problems, and, when the problems change, an informed staff picks the appropriate budgeting system. For example, if lack of public confidence in government fuels a tax revolt, then budget processes may need to emphasize public accountability and more public input into budget priorities.

The fourth alternative is that cities with different levels of reform have been adopting similar budget reforms, but for different reasons. For example, a more-reformed city may adopt target-based budgeting because it helps deal with financial uncertainty, whereas a more decentralized city might adopt it because it helps deal with conflicts between the budget office and the departments. Cities that are less reformed might adopt program and performance measures because they give the mayor more policy control over the departments. Cities that are more reformed might adopt program and performance measures because they promise to improve efficiency.

The Case Studies

Reformed Cities: Dayton and Phoenix

Dayton was the first of the large cities to adopt the council-manager form of government, in 1913, and it has maintained this form of government to the present. The five-member commission (which serves as a council) is elected at large. The mayor, who is separately elected, is one of the five commissioners. Central control over the departments is very strong. Throughout the years, Dayton has been an early adopter of new management techniques.

The city of Dayton's major budget changes began in 1968, when it was chosen (because of its reputation for good management) as part of a national experiment to introduce the Planning Programming Budgeting System (PPBS) to five states, five counties, and five cities. The city had automated its financial system and recast the budget in program format, with descriptions of activities and work-load measures by 1971. The budget split people between programs, which became problematic when the city had to make cutbacks. Cutting a program meant cutting a part of a person's salary (Woodie 1989). The city reorganized in early 1975, so that programs did not include fractional people.

The public, irritated at service cuts, refused to support tax increases, forcing more cuts. In 1974, after taxes were put in the budget office, the budget director decided to spell out the level of services the city would provide and the taxes necessary to provide those services at that level for five years. The proposal was approved by the public, and the city was bound by a five-year plan.

The city had to demonstrate that it had done what it promised over the last five years in order to get public approval of revenue for the next five years. The city manager set up a series of measurable, verifiable, and attainable objectives in 1974. Quarterly reports of accomplishments were circulated to the neighborhoods and the press. High-level objectives were printed in the budget; level-two objectives were reported to the manager and department heads; and level-three objectives were reported only to program directors. Initially, the budget director chose the most important issues, then that decision shifted to the council. The program director was then restructured around council goals so council members could see how their goals were being accomplished in the budget.

By 1975, as part of the effort to make budgets accountable, the budget process was consolidated. The capital and operating budget processes were integrated and any separate funds were brought on budget. Capital projects and departmental equipment were listed separately in the budget, but capital projects were also listed with each program so the total expenditures of each program were clear.

To make the budget reflect public priorities, the city gathered citizen input on budget priorities. As the former budget director put it, "we wanted to pass the tax, so we were going to become responsive" (Woodie 1989). The public continues to approve tax levels by wide majorities.

Most of Dayton's budget changes were in place by 1975 and remained, with minor tinkering, until 1990. Between 1989 and 1990, property tax revenues declined and grant revenue declined sharply, while other key revenue sources grew slowly. The city responded by drawing down a rainy day fund. By spring of 1991, the city adopted spending targets (target-based budgeting) to help keep expenditures down. The budget office used revenue estimates to help fashion ceilings for the departments; within those limits, substantial decision making authority was decentralized to the departments.

To summarize, Dayton's early adoption of PPBS reflected the reformed nature of city management and willingness to try new techniques. The city modified the program budget structure to facilitate cuts. When tax increases were rejected by the public, the city responded by making budgeting more open and bringing citizens into the budget process earlier in the decision making. The city set goals, costed them out, and got public approval for them. Performance measurement was a required part of the agreement; the city had to be able to show it had done what it promised to do. The recession of the early 1990s caused several years of draw downs in reserves. The city responded by changing the budget system to one that would systematically hold down expenditures to the level of revenues—target-based budgeting.

Phoenix is a little less politically reformed than Dayton. It adopted the council-manager form of government in 1914; it was among the first dozen cities to do so (Luckingham 1989). However, the first city manager proved too reformed for the business elite, as he attacked patronage positions, introduced competitive bidding, encouraged municipal ownership, and actually collected license fees. He was fired, and the powers of the city scaled back (Luckingham 1989, 71). In 1948, the powers of the manager were again strengthened, and members of the business and social elite formed the Charter Government Committee to slate candidates. This coalition dominated city government until about 1975 (150). In 1982, the city voted to change from at-large to district elections in an effort to make government more responsive and democratic (Luckingham 1989, 223). The level of reform is still high. As one department head described it,

> The mayor here is the chairman of the council, but the manager runs the city. The council members are prohibited from giving directions to the department heads; they have no appointments; everything is professional staff. We win recognition every year, we run like a business. It's the opposite of the older, eastern cities, with patronage and political intervention. (Public Works Director, Phoenix, December 1990)

Phoenix's budget changes began in 1970, as part of an effort to improve productivity. A group of engineers was added to the budget department, doubling its size. In 1971 and 1972, as part of the continuing effort to enhance productivity, PPB was introduced. The industrial engineering continued while staff tried to produce citywide goals and program analysis reviews, which were effectiveness studies. The effectiveness studies stayed with the budget office, but the engineering studies later went to the auditor's office.

In 1977, the city adopted zero-based budgeting. This changed to a target-based budget only to revert to zero-based budgeting during fiscal stress of the late 1980s and early 1990s.

The citywide goals statement, which had been part of PPB, evolved into two parts, an MBO type performance achievement system and a long range strategic plan. Work on the strategic plan began in 1985. Currently, there are three levels of planning, which are only loosely integrated with each other and the budget. One is a departmental planning process, the second is a citywide corporate plan, and the third is a community-based long-term plan which only partly involves the city in implementation.

The engineering focus on productivity gradually changed to an employee-development focus with quality circles. At the department level, Phoenix's five-year plans replaced the old program analysis reviews and are focused less on effectiveness and what the departments are doing and more on where they are going.

Why were these changes adopted? One informant described the initial engineering efficiency drive as a response to fiscal stress in the late 1960s (Manion 1990). Private sector people on the council said that business handled its problems using industrial engineering so the city should too. Once in place, the efficiency emphasis suggested the importance of studying effectiveness as well. The same consultants who recommended efficiency measures in the late 1960s, also recommended the adoption of PPB. PPB was getting a lot of publicity then, so the city picked it up; it fit their need to judge effectiveness.

PPB did not give the city adequate tools to handle cutback. The oil embargo and the recession of 1973 and 1974 forced the city to make cuts by attrition and reduce the number of vehicles purchased, without much reflection on the impact on operations. By 1976, the city tried to raise the sales tax. The voters rejected the $10 million tax hike in February 1977, the middle of a fiscal year. The budget director at the time, Charles Hill, argued, "We needed a new way to set priorities, so I educated myself to use zero-based budgeting" (Hill 1990). He used the ability of PPB to delineate service impacts in order to implement zero-based budgets.

The recession of 1980 and 1981–1982 caused another round of cutbacks. The at-large council cut out some popular neighborhood projects. These specific service cuts combined with underfunding of service expansion as the city rapidly increased its area. Many neighborhoods and areas of the city felt neglected. These citizens wanted services; many of them supported the change to election of council members by district in 1982 because the district system promised more responsiveness to neighborhood needs.

> The former budget director argued that the change to district elections did have some impact on budgeting. "Neighborhood coalitions became more powerful, and affected budgeting. Capital budget on construction—we began to produce reports on each district. We informally set aside a sum for council add-ons after the manager's budget, for recreation, school officer, and the like. That is the way the council adapted their budgets, add-ons after the manager's budget. With the manager's full understanding that that was the way it would work. It grew each year until last year it reached $2 million in add-ons for various programs." (Hill 1990)

If there are difficult policy choices in the budget, a budget hearing takes place in every district. The Public Information Office works up a sound and slide show to present the budget. The budget officer attends to answer questions, and the mayor and the district council member listen to the public comments. The elected officials can take what they hear from the public to help them formulate their moderate add-ons to the manager's proposal.

> The capital budget process, which is somewhat separate, reflects a desire to get public support early in the budget process. "There is a 200 member citizen bond committee. The departments prepare needs studies and take them to the citizens' councils, there are ten or twelve of them, for different areas, like police. They review the departments' needs and develop recommendations for what is taken to the voters. The council then decides. . . . The budget office updates the capital improvement plan for the council. . . . We continue to work with the citizens' committee as advisory. We take the preliminary capital improvement plan to them, to see that it meets with the citizens' intent." (Tevlin 1990)

When the city manager was asked what factors influenced budget processes, he offered three. First, the city staff tried to keep up with national trends and modern practice. Second, the city tried to adapt to pressures from the council or the community to respond to community needs. Third, the staff continually evaluated their own budget processes to see what could be improved. The manager elaborated on the second of these reasons for changing the budget process. "As community needs have arisen, and trust has ebbed and flowed between the community and the city . . . we try to make the process more open when trust is low and give the council more input. When there is more trust, we have short cut the process" (Fairbanks 1990).

The city manager downplayed the importance of fiscal stress in determining the budget process, in part because some fiscal stress had been present during each of the preceding twelve years. He agreed, however, that the budget process did help find different ways to cut the budget.

Phoenix's zero-based budgeting evolved into target-based budgeting. Prioritization occurred at the margins with new revenue, but most of the base remained intact from year to year. However, Phoenix was particularly hard hit by overbuilding in real estate and a drop in real estate values and was further threatened by the possibility of declining state aid in the early 1990s. As the city wrestled with financial problems, the Chamber of Commerce warned that there could be pet projects in the base budgets and departments might be bringing projects to the council that the council could not cut. In response, the mayor called for a comprehensive budget review. The departments were divided into five groups; all the programs in one group would be examined in year one, all the programs in a second group would be reviewed the next year, and so on, until all the programs had been reviewed. Staff portrayed the process as an opportunity to educate the council, but the council surprised them by cutting an additional $20 million during the first year of the more intensive review.

The comparison between Dayton and Phoenix is interesting. Both were early adopters of PPB. During the middle 1970s, each city responded to recession and price increases with a proposed tax increase and both were defeated at the polls. Dayton reacted by strengthening the planning end of PPB, setting goals with the public, and linking them to the budget, creating a kind of contract. Phoenix, in a similar situation, strengthened its capacity to rationally cut back and engaged in nearly continual cuts of some sort for the next twelve years. It alternated between a zero-based and a target-based budget system. It did not add strategic planning until 1985, and it took five years to get the process running. Even then, the planning process was only loosely linked to the budget. Although Phoenix was generally ahead of the curve in anticipating and reacting to fiscal stress, it was sometimes behind the curve in planning for its enormous, rapid growth and in responding to community demands.

Intermediate Levels of Reform: Rochester and Tampa

From the turn of the century to 1922, Rochester was a Republican city under a political boss. Supporters of the manager system were able to take advantage of the boss's death and the disarray in the Republican party to push through the council-manager system in 1925. By 1931, the city's expenditures increased greatly as a result of the unemployment burden of the depression and an ambitious capital improvement program. Republicans, pointing to greatly increased debt, failure to balance the budget, and increased tax bills, won the election, restoring the old political machine (Mosher 1940).

When the machine-oriented administration refused to accept the financial advice of the business community in 1932, bankers and businessmen successfully demanded a new city manager, a mayor of their choice, and a continuing voice in the affairs of the city. "The bankers had the whip hand, since they could refuse the city credit" (Mosher 1940, 44). The manager system lasted from 1932 until 1986.

Most of the staff and many of the procedures from the manager period were retained after 1986, so the city is part way between the council-manager and mayor-council forms of government. This in-between status is reinforced by a council that has four district and five at-large seats. The city council was openly partisan until the early 1980s, when an open meetings law forbade decision making by party caucus. Departments were powerful under the managers and remained powerful under the mayor.

Staff changed the budget format in the late 1960s, but by 1970, the budget returned to a straight line-item format. Program and performance budgeting were adopted in 1974–75. Fiscal problems had begun several years earlier, but a short interlude of Republican dominance had been characterized by denial of fiscal problems. When the Democrats reassumed dominance in 1974, they inherited a fiscal mess.

One informant described the need for a changed budget format as a response to fiscal stress and a large tax increase. The fiscal problems created a need for a better understanding of the budget. The existing document and systems could not answer the questions that the manager and the budget bureau were asking. Moreover, the need to explain to the council and the public why taxes were being raised so high so quickly required a budget that was open and simple to understand (Myers 1989). The city also needed to explain its financial problems to the county and the state legislature in order to get some financial relief (City of Rochester 1974, M-4).

The new budget format included a program structure, useful descriptions of programs, explanations of changes in programs between the past year and the current year, and workload measures. Over the next few years, measures of success were gradually added. One participant described, "Our attitude was, we would do what worked, we were not wedded to any theoretical system. . . . We borrowed from other budgets. If it was good, we took it" (Myers 1989).

In the mid-1970s, as the city was working on program structures and workload measures, it adopted an engineering-oriented innovation and productivity program. Then the city adopted productivity bargaining with labor, a huge tax hike to balance the budget, and reductions in staffing levels by attrition. However, the city was unable to stabilize finances by 1979. The city was particularly hard hit by the rapid inflation that characterized the end of President Carter's regime. The New York Court of Appeals ruled in the spring of 1978 that the city had improperly excluded certain expenditures from the constitutional tax limit, forcing a last minute revision of the fiscal year 1979 operating budget that resulted in expenditure reductions, service cutbacks, employee terminations, and new user charges, taxes, and special assessments.

Preparing for 1980, the city found that the level of state aid was uncertain, wage levels depended on arbitration decisions not yet made, and the size of the tax refund the city would have to pay depended on a forthcoming court decision. The county refused to create a refuse district to alleviate the city's burden, and assessed valuation began to decline. The manager wrote in his budget letter, "It was clear we had to prepare for a wide variety of alternatives and produce a budget that could be adjusted to reflect changes in the City's economic situation that were largely outside our direct control. Departments were, therefore, instructed to prepare basic budgets which would enable us to make further reductions if necessary or restore priority items if additional resources became available." (City of Rochester 1979, 2)

This statement in the budget was the first reference to the target-based budgeting that characterized Rochester's budget in the 1980s. Target-base budgeting was initiated as a response to intense uncertainty, but it also handled cuts in a decentralized departmental structure. "They [the departments] understood reductions had to occur. They could be more painful or the best reductions they could get with less pain and more efficiency. We rarely told the departments how to change their budgets . . . they could choose their own poison. They had better knowledge of their operations and were responsible for continuing operations [despite cuts]" (Myers 1989).

After 1986, concurrent with the shift to the mayor-council system, the budget office simplified the budget, eliminating measures that were not being used and working on the performance measures. Although the budget contained good demand and workload measures, only a few programs included results measures in the budget (City of Rochester 1989). The budget director suggested that the city was unlikely to ever have good results measures. "The resources to develop them are not there." He argued, "impact measures take a lot of research, and we may not be ready to share" (Sette 1989).

One informant explained that the political orientation of the city shows up in the performance measures, which are oriented more to workload than to efficiency or outcomes. "You get 25 calls for potholes [demand] you fill 25 potholes [workload]. You used X tons of fill, at $100 a ton [efficiency]. But so what? You filled 25 potholes and that is what matters to citizens. Re-election is the result" (Sette 1989).

Another reason that performance evaluation never became an integral part of the budget was that the departments often did not go along with it. During the 1970s, the city did program evaluations as part of federal grants. Reportedly, the evaluation process caused a lot of anxiety. When the federal grants disappeared, so did the evaluation process. A former budget director described, "The limitation was we couldn't outrun departments that could generate meaningful numbers and understand what it was we were doing. . . . But it wasn't installed from the top down. They had to accept the need" (Robert Myers, October 1989).

The change to a mayor-council city had relatively little impact on the budget process, but there were indications that the budget document itself was considered a little more political and a little more sensitive. The mayor reportedly opposed the inclusion of a list of city goals in the budget because he thought it would look bad if the goals were not accomplished. In the absence of council and public participation, the budget document is a major tool of accountability in Rochester, but it is not clear to city staff if the mayor will continue to keep the budget open.

To summarize, Rochester used budget reform to help explain the city's financial problems to itself, to the public, and to other governmental bodies. After some fifteen years with a performance budget, the city has yet to work out a reasonable set of measures of outcomes. The budget document itself is the major tool of public accountability. It covers most city operations and is reasonably open, reflecting its origins as an attempt to explain the city's financial status. This openness is in tension with the mayor's concerns about leaving his administration vulnerable to public criticism.

The city of Tampa is a somewhat reformed, strong mayor city. The council is composed of three at-large representatives and four district representatives. Department heads and "superchiefs" who manage several departments and link the political and administrative systems are professionals rather than political appointees. Patronage hiring is not a major issue.

The changes in Tampa's budgeting originated with the federal Model Cities program, which required planners to do needs assessments. The planners had to devise city standards for service delivery, so they could know whether a neighborhood was above or below the standard. Then the planners recommended to the mayor a list of projects to meet the needs they had uncovered (Wehling 1991).

In the mid-1970s, Mayor Poe decided to expand the needs assessments and standards of service from grant-funded programs to the whole city, not just to the low-income neighborhoods. The planning office was expanded. The planners wanted program budgets so they could see if the spending they had recommended was resulting in higher service levels. They managed to get program descriptions in the budget in 1975, but the rest of PPB was not implemented. There were no measures of accomplishment of impact, and no analysis (Wehling 1991).

> By the late 1970s, the city was facing financial problems and had to cut the budget. A lot of games were played during cutback. The fire chief would close a fire station in a wealthy neighborhood, knowing it would be restored during the year. Recreation would close a recreation center, or transit would eliminate ten buses. There was no more justification than that, just ten buses. They would negotiate, and take a cut of five instead. (Wehling 1991)

At the beginning of the administration of Mayor Bob Martinez in 1979, the budget office adopted target-based budgeting. The new mayor reportedly liked the target-based system because it gave him more control over the departments and because it was a new process he could identify his administration with. The budget director implemented target-based budgeting because it put the management decisions where he felt they belonged (in the departments) and helped reduce game playing between the departments and the budget office (Desilet 1990). Target-based budgeting gave the departments maximums for their budget requests; the department heads had to decide what to put into the request and what to leave out.

A former staff member in the budget office explained that the year before target-based budgeting was adopted, a midyear shortfall had developed, which was made up from operating lines in the departments that still had unspent funds. Police and public works were especially hard hit. Departments felt the cuts were arbitrary and the budget office staff reportedly felt a little guilty. Target-based budgeting gave credibility to the cutback process because the budget office showed the departments that it had taken a variety of factors into consideration in the assignment of targets. The result was more cooperation and less antagonism between the departments and the budget office.

The current budget director argued that TBB made it easier to prioritize cutbacks. "You get basic policy decisions from the mayor, how to favor the departments, and go from there, how people can manage with that amount, what do they say they can't do, and how critical is that. The powers that be look at that and say how important the unfunded parts are" (Stefan 1990).

Although the city never fully implemented PPB, the needs assessment and service levels analysis that developed under the aegis of planning were integrated into the budget process during Mayor Poe's administration in the later 1970s. The planners made sure the mayor had a list of projects he could recommend that were responsive to the things he gave priority to. Planners created that list by combining policy statements made by the mayor with their own assessments of needs based on service-level analyses (Wehling 1991).

Early in his administration, Mayor Martinez discarded this process because many departments opposed the planning departments' overly large role. After one budget cycle without any way of judging the department's requests, Mayor Martinez reestablished much of the process, but without the dominance of the planning department. The departments had to establish their own standards and document their current needs with respect to the standards. During Martinez's administration, the service-level analysis was closely linked to funding; departments would promise to do a particular amount of service for a particular amount of funding. The mayor could ask for higher standards, or reduce the targets, but budget and performance were linked. Key departments, such as public works, knew almost exactly how much service they could deliver in various programs for particular amounts of money (City of Tampa 1991).

The linkage between the budget and service levels was reportedly weakened under the next mayor, Sandra Freedman, who imposed higher service requirements without additional funding and cut spending targets while expecting service levels to remain the same. Mayor Freedman was familiar with city operations so she found the many hours of meetings with department heads over relatively unchanging service targets tedious. She also opposed service-level analysis because it made her politically vulnerable. When she was running for mayor, "She took the SLA [Service Level Analysis] system and looked at the unmet needs, using them as if the budget should have corrected all of them. It was unfair. But she is so aware of this tactic, and it was used against her, she wants to get rid of it" (Wehling 1991).

Reportedly, what she wanted to put in its place was a simpler list of political goals, such as greater use of partnerships or more emphasis on prevention. There would be no reference to unmet needs. Proposals from the departments would be judged for their contribution to these goals. The mayor could go out to the public and say, "I got the private sector involved, and I got people involved in designing policy." The direction of the shift was from greater emphasis on comprehensive planning to more emphasis on strategic planning.

The difference between mayors is important. Martinez built his popularity on budget cutting, tax reductions, and downtown development. He used the service-level analysis and the target-based budgeting system to achieve those goals. Freedman was more interested in building support by addressing problems such as crime or dirty streets. She took her set of problems from public perceptions, from the people she talked to in the neighborhoods, and from housing, civic, and environmental groups. She did not want some other list of needs. She needed to be able to spend on priority items without destroying the budget, and target-based budgets helped her do that, creating some flexibility for policy redirection within tight budgets. Both mayors were able to use TBB to achieve their goals, but they had different needs for the service-level analysis.

The Least Reformed Cities: Boston and St. Louis

Boston is a strong mayor city, with a very weak council. The council has alternated between at-large and district elections. As of 1983, the city changed to a thirteen-person council, in which nine seats are from districts, and four are at large (Schabert 1989, 133 fn.). Political patronage has been an important part of the municipal government. Mayor Kevin White, who was mayor from 1968 to 1984, reportedly merged his personal machine with the city government. At one time, he employed about 825 people directly loyal to himself, often funded by federal grants and located in different departments and programs (Schabert 1989, 58–60). Superchiefs, who played the role of liaison between the political level and the technical and managerial levels, were generally political appointees and mayoral loyalists, rather than long-term professional employees. Despite the tradition of strong mayors, power has remained fragmented, and some departments have had considerable autonomy.

Boston was one of the early adopters of PPB in 1969 and 1970, but within a few years, the budget returned to a line-item format. In 1986, the city adopted a program and performance budget. Capital budgeting, which has been a separate function in Boston for many years, had a similar pattern of start and stop. Informants attributed the start-and-stop pattern largely to fiscal stress. With respect to the disappearance of PPB, one informant reported,

> The focus at the time was on obtaining more revenue. They were desperate. They were in survival mode. It is hard to think of evaluating programs when you aren't fine tuning. They were making wholesale changes. . . . We got the budget balanced in 1986 and it has been balanced since then. The relatively stable finances gave us a chance to look at program budgeting. The budget was no longer acting as a triage system. (Robert Ciolek 1989)

Similarly, lack of funds derailed the capital budget (Nee 1989). However, the stop-and-go pattern of budget reform also had political roots. "That is life in the big city . . . the Mayor gets out a press release, you have to do it, you don't touch all the bases you need to, to make it work" (Anonymous 1989).

The city's departments were not consulted before the major budget changes in 1986. The performance budget was introduced from the top down. Mayor Flynn, reacting to a reputation of being uninterested in management and responding to a long string of municipal deficits, convened a private-sector task force shortly after his election in 1985. The task force made hundreds of suggestions for improving the accounting system and the operating and capital budgets, most of which the mayor implemented. When asked how the budget office got departmental cooperation, the budget director responded, "We tell the departments they have to do it" (Gottschalk 1990).

Departments resisted the newly centralized capital budgeting process. The director of the capital planning office described, "I was criticized a thousand times over. The mayor always backed me up. . . . The structure had been decentralized and they had their own agendas. I changed the playing field a lot. Most people now see and understand the benefits [of a more centralized system]" (Nee, November 1989).

The implementation of the new budget system depended on the mayor's support. A talented political appointee, the deputy director of fiscal affairs, translated the task force's recommendations into a budget process that matched the personality and needs of Mayor Flynn. He described some of the advantages of the program and performance budget:

> Robert Ciolek: You can make better political decisions when you have good facts. It gives you effective controls over the bureaucracy. It informs and it controls. The budget office can respond to the mayor's direction.
> Author: Are you saying that the budget process makes the departments more responsive to the mayor?
> Ciolek: Yes, that is one of the major reasons why we did it. (Ciolek 1989)

The idea was to help the departments improve their management simultaneously with making them more accountable to the strategic goals of the mayor. The departments listed their goals and then the policy office of the mayor met with each department head. The mayor's goals were incorporated with the performance measures. The departments tried to figure out how to measure the mayor's goals. Several informants reported tension between the mayor's short-term policy objectives and the longer-term objectives of the program budget.

The report on performance measures was treated somewhat politically. It was not widely circulated, because of the fear that the press would pick up the negative aspects and ignore the rest. Despite the limited circulation of the document, departments have set goals low so they can meet all the goals 100 percent. This problem seems to be slowly abating.

Most of the implementation of the program and performance budget was done in one year. The departments and the budget office continued to weed out useless measures and add better ones, but as they were doing that, the city's revenues again became shaky, largely as a function of the state's deteriorating financial condition and a large drop in state aid to the city. The program budget gave little guidance on how to cut the departments, and competition to avoid or minimize cuts was intense. The budget office switched to a target-based budget to help control and minimize this competition for the 1990 budget.

The target-based budget requires the departments to report the impacts of proposed reductions on service levels. These impacts are evaluated for acceptability and for conformity to the mayor's goals. This process gives the departments the opportunity to demonstrate how they will be hurt, and to make a plea for more funds; it also preserves the mayor's policy priorities during cutback.

The initial budget reform was implemented too quickly. Some performance measures were weak, and the budget remained somewhat fragmented. Grants were not incorporated into the operating budget, and a line-item budget alternated with the program budget, page by page. Much attention was focused on making the budget format visually attractive, but there is more to the new budget process than a change in appearance ". . . the process helps in the tactical relationship between the budget office and the departments. It arms the budget office with facts. . . . Its biggest value is to the departments, to help them manage. It also helps the mayor's office tactically . . ." (Ciolek 1989).

St. Louis is the least reformed of the six cities. Budget decisions are primarily the responsibility of the Board of Estimate and Apportionment, composed of the mayor, the comptroller, and the president of the Board of Aldermen, all elected at-large. The council is elected from districts, with no at-large seats. The city government is merged with the county government, the latter controlled by the state. The county positions, referred to as the patronage positions, are not under civil service. Patronage is a hotly discussed issued. The city is poor, and the need for jobs considered so high that some council members do not push for staff that could help them read the budget because they fear the quality of the appointments and the acrimony of the fight to see who will get the jobs.

A highly fragmented power structure and unreformed government are reflected in a highly fragmented budget. The budget director in 1988, Steve Mullin, described the level of fragmentation:

> The municipal government also administers other programs which, at this time, are not subject to review through this primary budget process. They include the Community Development Block Grant Program (approximately $20 million annually), various programs for economic development, various state and federal health programs, the city's revenue collection functions (approximately $3 million annually), the Parking Meter Fund (approximately $2 million annually), the Street Improvement-St. Louis Works Fund (approximately $5 million annually), SLATE federal training programs, and programs for the elderly. Each of these functions is developed independently during the year, and appropriation ordinances are passed by the Board of Aldermen. (City of St. Louis 1988–89)

Despite this fragmentation and severe fiscal problems, in 1989 the budget office introduced a program-and-performance budget that was somewhat integrated with a strategic planning process. However, the budget continued to include a line-item budget.

Although the budget document emerged suddenly, budget changes had been occurring over a long period that gave the mayor some centralized control over a limited set of departments. The first of these changes was a gradual shift from having the budget office report to all three members of the Board of Estimate and Apportionment to having the budget director report only to the mayor. This shift began in the early 1970s and was completed by the early 1980s. The second change had a number of the department heads appointed by and report to the mayor. "St. Louis in the early 1980s was still characterized by department heads who determined their own budgets. Mayor Vincent Schoemehl picked his own department heads and weakened the independence of the commissioners. . . . The mayor transferred some of the commissioners and he persuaded others to be more amenable" (Rubin and Stein 1990, 423).

Once the mayor had some control over the department heads, he strengthened the budget director's control over reviewing departmental proposals and allowed the budget director to formulate the executive budget proposal. The Board of Estimate and Apportionment then reviewed that proposal rather than dealing individually with each department's request. The mayor handpicked young professional budget directors who were familiar with modern budgeting techniques.

When Mayor Schoemehl was first elected in 1981, he brought with him a modified version of MBO. At first, the system did not work very well, because the departments set goals that were too low, the same problem that occurred in Boston. With the help of a consultant, the MBO plan was turned into a motivational tool, to help personnel see the kind of progress they were making toward goals. The goals were not linked directly to pay and evaluation, which may have helped reduce the tendency to set easily achieved goals.

Sometime around 1987, the budget director decided to link the performance measures to the budget and create a program-and-performance budget. By then, the departments had had several years of nonthreatening experience with performance measures, and city staff had experience using visual displays to show progress over time. The performance budget that emerged in 1989 had a multiyear planning dimension and short-term component. Although the budget staff and departments are still struggling to put together additional measures of outcomes, the existing ones are reasonably useful.

During 1987, a new capital budget process was developed. The capital budget process, initiated by an alderman, was in part a response to the declining infrastructure of the city and the difficulty of maintaining a capital budget in the face of pressing operating needs. It was not based on establishing standards or citywide needs; rather, it gathered lists from the departments of their future capital needs and tried to prioritize them. The membership of the capital committee reproduced to some extent the fragmentation of the Board of Estimate and Apportionment, with the mayor, the comptroller, and the president of the Board of Aldermen each having probable control of two or possibly three votes. The five-year plan the capital committee put together was so expensive in comparison to the funds available that it was more a wish list than a budget. Nevertheless, the committee did select projects for the current year's budget and did formulate criteria by which to judge projects.

Part of the motivation for creating the list of projects was to help pass a half-cent sales tax to help pay for capital projects. A consultant had advised the city that voters were more likely to vote for a tax if they knew what they would be getting for it. Despite the existence of the list, the tax was rejected. Without funding, most of the list remained to be carried out; the urgency to meet again and revise the list for the next time was small.

A strategic planning process was also begun in 1987. The strategic planners divided the city into functions and then set goals and achievable, measurable targets for each function. The mayor and his staff chose from among the list of achievable targets a set of projects that could be funded in the near term.

The mayor had been cutting city staff virtually since his inauguration, especially in health and hospitals, and fiscal stress had resulted in delayed maintenance and deteriorating infrastructure. Much grant money went into large downtown economic development projects. These choices resulted in faltering service levels and considerable opposition to the mayor, ultimately contributing to a rejection by the public of the continuation of the three-eighth-cent sales tax, forcing further service cuts.

The mayor must have been aware of the percolating criticism of how he had chosen to cut the budget. The strategic planning process was put in place "to improve the methods of allocating and managing resources to achieve the stated mission of city government" (City of St. Louis Budget 1988–1989, 13). Its intent was to find out the needs of the community, focus government efforts on those needs, and improve effectiveness and efficiency of those efforts. The format of the program and performance budget linked directly to the goals and targets formulated by the strategic planning process, to show how the city was addressing the goals that the public wished the city [to] achieve. The evaluation of performance was not linked directly to the strategic plan, however, although some components of the performance measures addressed some of the goals in the plan. As of 1990, the program and performance report, which had the possibility of demonstrating what the city was doing with public money and possibly helping to win support for a tax increase, was not widely distributed, and the council remained generally unaware of its existence.

Analysis

The case-study cities used similar budget reforms to meet and help handle common environmental threats to some extent, but no one-to-one relationship existed between environmental threats and budget reforms. Environmental threats had little to do with the adoption of PPB or program-and-performance budgets. A stronger case can be made for linking fiscal stress and the adoption of target-based or zero-based budgeting. Budget directors facing cutbacks looked for ways to select and implement cuts. They also sought to defuse the intense budgetary competition resulting from eroding tax bases, reduced state funding, recessions, and defeated tax referenda. Target-based budgeting was also used to hold down property taxes; it responded to a strong antitax sentiment. However, once target-based or zero-based budgeting was in place, the linkage between environmental threat and budget systems was weakened. ZBB and TBB prioritize for either growth or decline. Once cities adopt this form of budgeting, they keep it through good and bad times.

Although the direct link is not that strong, a good case can be made for an indirect link between environmental threat and changes in budgeting process and format. When environmentally caused fiscal stress led a city to go for a tax increase or petition the county or legislature for new revenue sources, the result was an effort to tidy up the budget, to make it clearer, to establish and make concrete the need. This effort often included consolidation of the budget, a five-year revenue and expenditure projection, and larger print, readable formats, glossaries, tables, charts, and narrative descriptions. When the tax increase was turned down by the public in Dayton, and to some extent in St. Louis, the city shifted to trying to get the public more involved in budgetary decision making. In Phoenix, the city tried to live within the narrower revenue limits after a tax increase was turned down, but the public rebelled against the cutbacks in services and slow expansion of services to newer areas of the city, forcing a change in governmental structure and more attention to neighborhood needs in the budget process. Fiscal stress thus creates pressure to improve the accountability of the budget and expand meaningful public involvement in the budget process.

Although some of the similarity in the case-study cities' budget systems resulted from the choice of similar techniques to resolve similar, environmentally imposed problems, the case-study cities sometimes adopted the same budget reforms for different reasons. Dayton adopted PPB as part of a national experiment. Phoenix adopted PPB as part of a productivity drive in response to a stalled economy. Program and performance budgeting was used in less-reformed cities to provide the mayor additional control over the departments in the area of short-term policy goals while it was used in more reformed cities to increase efficiency.

More-reformed cities often adopted reforms because either staff or council members were eager to try out the newest budget practices and make them work. Less-reformed cities were more eclectic, borrowing selectively from other cities to solve specific problems faced by the mayor or the budget office. Budgeting systems were chosen not only for their technical viability and ease of implementation, but also for their match to the personalities and political needs of mayors.

The budget reforms may have looked more similar than they were. In particular, program and performance measures were implemented differentially. Performance measures were fully implemented in Dayton, Phoenix, and Tampa and only partially implemented in Rochester and Boston, neither of which had good measures of outcomes or impact. Generally, more-reformed cities were more determined to implement performance measures and better able to get the departments to cooperate.

Implementation was more problematic in less-reformed cities partly because the budget changes had to be prepared in a hurry, when a new mayor wanted a new system. It took Phoenix five years to implement a strategic planning process; it took Dayton some six years to get its PPB system fully functional, but it took Boston only two years to get its Program and Performance budget up, and most of the implementation was done in the first year. Similarly, the major work of implementing St. Louis's new program and performance budget was over a two-year period. Because of the speed, loose ends were left hanging.

Another problem with implementation of performance measures in less-reformed cities is the fear that they will be used against the mayor or the departments. Mayors in Rochester and Tampa felt vulnerable to bad publicity from opposition on the council if unfilled performance targets were reported in the budget or to the public. In Boston, departments often felt vulnerable if they achieved less than 100 percent of their targets, and performance reports were given limited circulation for fear of bad publicity.

In addition to performance measures, less-reformed cities also implemented program budgeting less fully. Dayton, Phoenix, and Rochester have integrated program budgets. Tampa tried program budgeting briefly and dropped it. St. Louis divides up the budget into two volumes. Volume one is the program budget, with performance measures but no line items; volume two is a departmental line-item budget with lists of personnel positions by program. Boston's budget presentation gives departmental line-item budgets first and then program expenditures.

The dual budgets of the less-reformed cities can be interpreted in different ways. The dual budgets may represent a compromise in which the professional staff improve technical matters and relations between the departments and the budget office while the citywide political decisions are made independently of the budget process much as they always have been. Or the dual structure may include a real (incremental) budget and a symbolic budget intended to improve the appearance of the cities' financial management. Less-reformed cities were generally more likely to use the budget format to communicate symbolically or strategically to the legislature or the county, to get changes in laws or additional revenue, or to shift spending.

Over time, the six cities adopted many of the same reforms, but their overall budget systems evolved in different directions at different times. Dayton and Phoenix adopted PPB; the other cities either tried it and dropped it or did not try it at all. Boston and St. Louis, for much of the period, had traditional line-item budgets. Comprehensive planning characterized Dayton. Tampa recently shifted from comprehensive to strategic planning, while Boston and St. Louis went without a capital plan for years. Boston's recent capital plan was developed under the gun of court mandates. Phoenix adopted a ZBB approach very early, alternating with target budgeting; this fit the city's continuing fiscal stress and inability to raise taxes. Tampa and Rochester were early adopters of target-based budgeting, making this form dominant in the middle group of case studies.

Choices among budget reforms were generally consistent with the level of political reform. More-reformed cities adopted budget reforms that were heavier on planning and comparative programmatic analysis. Cities in the middle generally emphasized techniques that controlled departmental totals and kept the peace with the budget office, while holding down property taxes. The less-reformed cities, until recently, maintained line-item budgeting and virtually no planning. Moreover, when the less-reformed cities did adopt budget reforms, they were more likely to start and stop, based on the availability of revenue and the preferences of the mayor.

The differences in the choice, emphasis, and implementation of budget reforms in cities of varying degrees of political reform are suggestive, but, with the addition of program and performance budgets in Boston and St. Louis and the adoption of target-based budgets in Boston and St. Louis and the adoption of target-based budgets in Boston and Dayton, the cities' budget systems have looked more like each other in the last few years. What might this mean?

One interpretation is that expectations that the level of political reform would structure the adoption of budget reform missed an important dynamic, namely that the level of budget reform may be consciously used to modify the level of political reform, at least in the sense of curtailing highly independent departments. In St. Louis, Mayor Schoemehl used budget reform to help gain some control over the departments; in Boston, the new capital budget process, which had the power of several court mandated changes behind it, forced a new level of centralization on departments. That is not to argue that departments did not resist the changes, or that implementation was not affected, or that the changes might not yet be reversed; only that budgeting can influence the level of centralization. In light of this finding, the fact that the two least reformed cities, St. Louis and Boston, have both dramatically modified their budgets in the last few years, including performance measures, is less difficult to interpret.

The widespread adoption of target-based budgeting reflects not only the widespread conditions of fiscal stress and the usefulness of this budgeting form in setting priorities for expenditures, but also the general applicability of a budgeting system that centralizes fiscal totals and ensures budget balance while decentralizing decision making to the departments and essentially ends budget games between the departments and the budget office. The advantages fell differently depending on whether the city was initially centralized or not. In decentralized cities, it gave the budget office more control over totals; in centralized cities, it gave the departments badly needed autonomy over spending choices. Target-based budgeting builds in the possibility of reallocation, and careful setting of priorities of budget requests at the margins, but it can easily—and comfortably—deteriorate into incremental allocations. Thus it fits in both more- and less-reformed cities, and in the same cities as they choose to be more or less incremental in their decision making. Although the choice of five out of six cities for this type of budgeting seems impressive, it may mask a great deal of variation in how the system is being used and for what purpose.

Some of the most suggestive similarities were not in fact between the particular budget reforms adopted but in the similarities in the pattern of variation within cities between more and less openness to the public and citizen input into the budget. The city manager of Phoenix emphasized the variability of the need to respond to community demands as a major force changing budget processes; neighborhood pressures and the need for citizen participation were important in other cities as well. These pressures resulted not only from declining tax bases and rejection of proposed tax increases, but also from allocation decisions that slighted the neighborhoods, or that weighed business demands for lower taxes more heavily than citizen demands for more services. Dayton seems to have met and resolved that problem with a budget system that endured throughout the period, but other cities experienced more alternation.

Conclusions

Allen Schick (1966) described patterns of changing budgeting from the origin of budgeting in the United States through the adoption of PPB. This article carries the examination forward by looking at budgeting changes in six cities over the last twenty years. The study investigates the variation between cities in their adoption of budget innovations, as well as their evolving similarities. The analysis suggests that the more-reformed cities adopt budget reforms much more quickly, followed by the intermediate, and finally, the least reformed cities. These early, intermediate, and late adopters tend to differ in their motivations and use of reforms. The most reformed cities adopt budget reforms because they are there and to help them adapt to particular environmental threats. The intermediate cities wait to see what works, what can be easily implemented, and what seems to address the specific environmental and technical problems they confront without overly threatening or changing the political structure. The last group, the least politically reformed, use budget reforms to address immediate environmental problems but also to help change the political structure, toward more central control and policy accountability of the departments.

Schick's description of the evolution of budgeting from financial control to managerial emphasis and then to planning, in a developmental sequence, did not apply the shorter time span of my study. The more-reformed cities were more interested in comprehensive planning, the intermediate cities in strategic planning, and the least reformed planned only when forced by courts. The managerial orientation, as reflected in program budgeting and analysis and the potential tradeoffs between programs was also strongest in the most reformed cities, but tradeoffs for policy reasons, as opposed to for efficiency reasons, were dominant in the least reformed cities. How to make the budget responsive to the mayor's short-term policy directions without causing deficits or wreaking havoc with the departments was a key focus of budget reform in the least politically reformed cities. This is not to challenge Schick's formulation, only to add that there may be more than one line of evolution. As budget innovations reach the least politically reformed, the budget reforms are called upon to do different things, which complicates the notion of evolving toward a single goal or model. The second pattern of evolution emphasizes increased accountability of the departments to the mayor and increased accountability of the mayor to the public.

To the extent that the analysis presented here is correct, it provides good news for both budgeters and budget reformers. Budget reforms are widely adopted. They are not just used as window dressing; they are used by pragmatic managers and politicians to solve problems. Moreover, budget reforms turn out not to always be cabooses behind political reform; sometimes, they head the train. They provide an expanded set of options for elected officials who despair of controlling independent departments, and who do not know how to bring back a disaffected public to supporting city government.

Note

This is a revised version of a paper given at the American Political Science Meetings, Washington, DC, September 1991. Some of the field research was funded by the Graduate School at Northern Illinois University.

References

Anonymous. 1989. Asked not to be identified other than as an employee who worked for the city for ten years, interview November 8.

Ciolek, Robert. 1989. Acting director of administrative services and former budget director, City of Boston, interview November 13.

City of Rochester. 1974. Budget letter from city manager Elisha C. Freedman to the city council, May 28, in the City of Rochester Budget for fiscal year 1974–74, p. M–4.

———. 1979. Budget letter from city manager Joe L. Miller to the city council, May 15, in the City of Rochester Budget for fiscal year 1979–1980, p. 2.

———. 1989–1990. Approved budget.

City of St. Louis. 1988–1989. Budget Summary.

City of Tampa. 1991. Public works department budget coordinator, interview January 12.

Desilet, Al. 1990. Former budget director, City of Tampa, interview October 4.

Fairbanks, Frank. 1990. City manager, City of Phoenix, interview December 11.

Gottschalk, Barbara. 1990. Budget director, City of Boston, interview November 9.

Hill, Charles. 1990. Former budget director, City of Phoenix and more recently in charge of strategic planning, interview December 10.

Luckingham, Bradford. 1989. *Phoenix: The History of a Southwestern Metropolis.* Tucson: University of Arizona Press.

Manion, Pat. 1990. Deputy city manager, City of Phoenix, interview December 8.

Mosher, Frederick. 1940. "City Manager Government in Rochester, New York" In *City Manager Government in Seven Cities*, ed. Frederick Mosher, Arthur Harris, Howard White, John Vieg, Landrum Bolling, A. George Miller, David Monroe, and Harry O'Neal Wilson. Chicago: Public Administration Service.

Myers, Robert. 1989. Budget analyst, City of Rochester from 1971–1974 and budget director from 1976–1982, interview October 6.

Nee, Mary. 1989. Director of capital budgeting, City of Boston, interview November 13.

Poister, Theodore, and Gregory Streib. 1989. "Management Tools in Municipal Government: Trends over the Past Decade." *Public Administration Review* 49 (May/June): 240–248.

Public Works Director. 1990. Phoenix, interview December 10.

Rubin, Irene, and Lana Stein. 1990. "Budgeting in St. Louis: Why Budgeting Changes." *Public Administration Review* 50 (July/August): 420–426.

Schabert, Tilo. 1989. *Boston Politics, Creativity of Power.* Berlin: Walter DeGruyter.

Schick, Allen. 1966. "The Road to PPB: The Stages of Budget Reform." *Public Administrative Review* 26 (November/December): 245–256.

Sette, Al. 1989. Budget director, City of Rochester, interview October 5.

Stefan, Jim. 1990. Budget director, City of Tampa, interview October 4.

Tevlin, Andrea. 1990. Acting budget director, City of Phoenix, interview December 10.

Wehling, Roger. 1991. Planner for the City of Tampa, interview January 8.

Woodie, Paul. 1989. Head of the planning department and former head of the budget office when all the changes in budget format took place, interview October 20.

CHAPTER 10

BUDGETARY BALANCE:

The Norm, Concept, and Practice in Large U.S. Cities

CAROL W. LEWIS

The Norm of Balance

The idea of budgetary balance is crucial to contemporary municipal budgeting in the United States. A concise metaphor for good government and a symbol of fiscal integrity and prudence, budgetary balance is pressed into service as a simple, summary measure of overall capacity to govern. A recent article in the *CPA Journal* notes, "The requirement of a balanced budget for governments is widely acclaimed as a means of achieving fiscal prudence and economy" (Granof and Mayper 1991, 28, italics omitted). An article published by Moody's Investors Service proclaims budgetary balance to be "the key urban challenge" for this decade (Kennedy 1991, 1–7).

The focus and clarity inherent in a single dimension no doubt contribute to the concept's prescriptive appeal. Capturing its allure in his nineteenth-century novel *David Copperfield*, Charles Dickens displays its arithmetic elegance: "Annual income twenty pounds, annual expenditure nineteen ninety six, result happiness. Annual income twenty pounds, annual expenditure twenty pounds ought and six, result misery."

In more sophisticated analyses, balance represents more than arithmetic equivalency. Aaron Wildavsky (1992) interprets the chronic federal imbalance as evidence of deep political disagreement. The political functions attributed to balance include consensus building and enforcement. As disciplinarian, balance is "the most important constraint on budgeting" (Rubin 1993, 194). Its absence customarily is interpreted as signaling that political will or political concord is absent as well. For these reasons (and perhaps because so few generalizations hold across municipalities), the conventional descriptive accent in municipal budgeting falls on budgetary balance. Cope (1992, 1099) states, "Most local governments are required by their charters, state laws, or both, to balance their operating budgets." Similarly, Rubin (1993, 198) comments, "Cities, like states, are required to balance their budgets."[1]

Is budgetary balance in fact the ideal and empirical reality portrayed in the prescriptive and descriptive literature on municipal budgeting? The precise meaning and potential impact of budgetary balance vary so widely among jurisdictions that component details are more informative than the generalization. Given possible permutations, how is balance operationalized in different municipalities? What patterns can be discerned?

From *Public Administration Review*, vol. 54, no. 6 (November/December 1994), pp. 515–524. Copyright © 1994 by American Society for Public Administration. Reprinted with permission.

Table 10.1

States Requiring Balanced Municipal Budgets[a]

By Statute	By Constitution
Alabama	Idaho
Connecticut	Virginia
Georgia	Wyoming
Kansas	
Kentucky	
Massachusetts[b]	
Mississippi	
Montana	
New Hampshire	
North Dakota	
Ohio	
Oklahoma	
Oregon	
Pennsylvania	
Rhode Island	
Utah	
Wisconsin	

Source: Search of Lexis database conducted fall 1992 by key words: budget with municipal; budget; fund w/10 balance; deficit; surplus; appropriate; and balance w/10 budget. Supplemented by telephone interviews in selected states in fall 1992.

Notes: [a]Inclusion indicates that the state requirement applies to any or all classes of municipalities. For example, Connecticut's requirement applies only to municipalities with Boards of Finance. Special legislation for an individual city (e.g., New York City) does not trigger inclusion here.

[b]A follow-up telephone survey was conducted in fall 1992. California, Texas, and Ohio, negative on the database search, together account for nineteen (38 percent) of the fifty most populous cities in Table 10.2. According to the Office of the Attorney General in the respective state, Ohio constitutionally requires municipalities to balance their budgets; California has no statewide municipal requirement; and the response for Texas is variable (and confirmed by the Houston respondent's volunteered observation reported in Table 10.2). According to the Division of Local Services of the Massachusetts Department of Revenue, all municipalities, including Boston, must balance their budgets to gain this department's certification of the tax rate and of compliance with the levy limit (Proposition 2-1/2); this indirect approach does not show up on a database search.

To answer these and related questions, database searches and a telephone survey were conducted in fall 1992. Additional telephone calls to finance directors, budget officers, academic experts, and/or other knowledgeable informants were made where discrepancies or ambiguities indicated clarification was needed. Empirical evidence for the hundred most populous U.S. cities confirms and informs the general proposition that municipal budgets must be balanced.

Formal Provisions

As efficient investigation logically begins with the most general applicable rules; here, they are state-imposed budget requirements. The results of the database search of state statutes and constitutions show that at least twenty states require balanced municipal budgets (Table 10.1).[2] The findings necessarily are ambiguous because of: regulatory or backdoor provisions unidentifiable through a search by key words or of statutes (such as in Massachusetts), ambiguity in the law or its application (e.g., Texas), variable treatment of different classes of municipalities (e.g., Connecticut), and the fact that home rule charters supersede state law in some instances (e.g., Virginia and Pennsylvania). Therefore, states not listed in Table 10.1 do not necessarily permit imbalance, and individual cities located in rostered states are not necessarily covered by the general state requirement. Nonetheless, the data in Table 10.1 establish that states prescribe municipal budgetary balance in many cases where the formal, obligatory standard cannot be said to be a norm of municipal budgeting per se.

To supplement and enrich the database search, a telephone survey of finance or budget officers or analysts in the hundred most populous cities in the United States was conducted in fall 1992. Although almost all respondents replied at once that budgetary balance is required, many initially could not pinpoint specifics (and some graciously offered to research the information for the survey). This behavior suggests that balance is an accepted norm even in the absence of known legal requirements. In some instances, moreover, reported data were erroneous or contradictory, although this did not seem at all to the point for some respondents. One veteran finance professional spelled out his view of political and professional reality by explaining that the formal requirement was trivial compared to his community's insistence on balance. These interview experiences bear out that balance is a potent norm in municipal budgeting.

The budgetary balance requirements reported for the hundred most populous U.S. cities are reported in Table 10.2. All of the largest fifty cities and ninety-nine of the hundred leading cities reported a balance requirement of some sort. The legal basis was reported as state law (53 percent) and/or city charter (58 percent). The dominance of California and Texas among the largest cities in Table 10.2, coupled with their absence from Table 10.1, colors any state-by-state analysis. All regions of the country are represented, although New England and the Mid-Atlantic states have relatively few cities on the roster.

Precisely when balance comes into play is one of the more important rules of the game in municipal budgeting. Table 10.2 displays the information for each city. Balance may be required upon submission, when the budget is adopted, for operating results (when a formal year-end deficit in the general fund is prohibited), or in some combination thereof. Each stage spotlights a different institution as responsible for meeting the standard: for submission, it is the executive; for adoption, the legislative body; and for operations, the municipal administration. More than four-fifths of the largest cities report requiring balance upon submission and/or adoption.

Because the constraint is more forceful the later it comes in the process, it is significant that more than one-third (34) of the most populous cities must balance operating results over the course of implementation. In effect, they are required to *rebudget* (Forrester and Mullins 1992a, 1992b). For example, the city charter prohibits a year-end balance in San Francisco, where this provision offsets some credit risk (Table 10.2). "Project and midyear [*sic*] budget imbalances have occurred three years in a row since the city depleted its general fund budgetary balance in fiscal 1991. Previous gaps were closed as the strict city charter dictates" and "[c]harter requirements mandate reserves and reinforce fiscal discipline by requiring [the] controller to withhold appropriations if revenues are insufficient" (Fitch Research 1993b, 1, 3). Conspicuous by its premier population ranking, history of financial disarray, and restrictive balance requirement, New York City must rebalance quarterly to meet the provisions of the state's special legislation. The requirement to balance operating results annually is on the books in 44 percent (22) of the fifty most populous cities, compared with 24 percent (12) of the fifty next most populous cities.

The purpose here is to describe budgetary balance in the largest cities and identify patterns. Data in Table 10.3 bear out that population is not an explanatory variable (no balance requirement correlates significantly with population) but serves solely as the basis for selecting financially and politically interesting cities to describe. Frequency declines as stringency increases, except for adoption. The obvious disjuncture between the third and fourth columns speaks to the relative permissiveness of the balance requirement in the most populous cities.

An across-the-board obligation is the most confining, but it also may diffuse responsibility by widely distributing it. As a tool of mutual restraint affecting strategy and outcomes for *all* participants *at every step*, budgetary balance is required at each of the three stages in the process in almost one-quarter (24) of the hundred most populous cities (see Table 10.3). State law and/or charter provisions apply and (again perhaps because of two states' dominance) no pattern is apparent in the legal source of the comprehensive requirement. Cities in every region of the country operate under a comprehensive balance requirement: Northeast/Mid-Atlantic, two; Southeast, six; Southwest, six; Midwest, six; and the Pacific region running from California to Alaska, four (Table 10.2).

The Balance Model

The fundamental premise that balance describes the desirable relationship between revenues and expenditures is illustrated in simplified terms in Figure 10.1. This relationship is represented as configurations A and F in Figure 10.1. Referring to the Dickens quote, Webber and Wildavsky (1986, 594) define *the Micawber principle:* "it is not the level of income and outgo but their relationship that matters [and] is essential to budgeting." The schematic representation of budgetary balance in Figure 10.1 summarizes the cumulative impact of the annual ritual described by Philip Dearborn (Shiff 1991a). "The process of budgeting is always a difficult one. All budgets start out initially out of balance. . . . The demands for spending always exceed the resources that are available, and this leads to . . . a conflict . . . throughout the budget process, and it leads to very difficult times in balancing budgets . . ." (6–7).

Figure 10.1 depicts how balance theoretically "forces discipline on budget actors" (Rubin 1993, 164) by linking revenue and expenditure decisions. This push toward equivalence does not, however, prescribe which variable(s) to alter, or when. For all its power, balance does not dictate the levels of revenues and spending, but just that they be coupled. In this way, allowance is made for variability in revenue capacity, political and tax preferences, responsiveness, procedures, and other local characteristics.

The link is long term. "Fund balance does not refer to cash balance, nor is it the difference between revenues and expenditures. Rather, fund balance is the cumulative difference of all revenues and expenditures from the government's creation" (Allan 1990, 1). The presumed dynamic underlying municipal budgeting is that a municipality tends over several fiscal periods to move closer toward a balanced relationship, rather than further from it.[3] As Dickens's quote implies, balance usually is revenue driven, but the predictive power presumably holds only over the longer term for a particular jurisdiction, and many permutations are possible in any single fiscal year. Sustained imbalance with excessive revenues logically and empirically stimulates tax cuts. Budgetary imbalance loading on the spending side predictably leads to insolvency in the long term. Configuration E in Figure 10.1 depicts two budgetary patterns heading in this unsustainable direction.

Budgetary balance is only one of many factors contributing to a jurisdiction's capacity and well-being, and says nothing about the quality of life in the community. Because any single measure of financial operations or condition necessarily includes and excludes selected factors and is intrinsically limited, it is useful to bear in mind George Bernard Shaw's (1904, 169) observation, "[T]he balance sheet of a city's welfare cannot be stated in figures. Counters of a much more spiritual kind are needed, and some imagination and conscience to add them up, as well."[4]

Table 10.2

Reported Balanced Budget Requirements in the Most Populous U.S. Cities, 1992–1993

City[a]	Required	By state	By city charter	Other	Stage required Sub-mitted	Adopted	Year end[b]	Population ranking
New York	yes	statute	yes		yes	yes	yes[c]	1
Los Angeles	yes		yes		yes	yes		2
Chicago	*yes*	*statute*	*yes*		*yes*	*yes*	*yes*	*3*
Houston	yes	d		e	yes	yes		4
Philadelphia	*yes*		*yes*		*yes*	*yes*		*5*
San Diego	yes		yes			yes		6
Detroit	yes	statute	yes		yes	yes		7
Dallas	yes	constitution			yes	yes	yes	8
Phoenix	yes	statute					yes	9
San Antonio	yes		yes		yes	yes	yes	10
San Jose	yes	f	yes		yes	yes	yes	11
Baltimore	yes			g	yes	yes		12
Indianapolis	yes	statute			yes	yes	yes	13
San Francisco	yes		yes		yes		yes	14
Jacksonville	yes	statute	yes		yes			15
Columbus, OH	*yes*	*constitution*			*yes*	*yes*	*yes*	*16*
Milwaukee	*yes*		*yes*		*yes*			*17*
Memphis	yes		yes		yes	yes		18
Washington, DC	yes			h	yes	yes		19
Boston	*yes*	*statute*			*yes*			*20*
Seattle	yes	statute			yes	yes	yes	21
El Paso	yes	statute	yes			yes		22
Cleveland	*yes*	*statute*			*yes*	*yes*		*23*
New Orleans	yes		yes		yes			24
Nashville	yes		yes		yes	yes		25
Denver	yes		yes		yes	yes	yes	26
Austin	yes	statute			yes	yes		27
Fort Worth	yes		yes		yes	yes		28
Oklahoma City	*yes*					*yes*	*i*	*29*
Portland	*yes*	*statute*	*yes*		*yes*	*yes*	*yes*	*30*
Kansas City, MO	yes		yes		yes	yes	yes	31
Long Beach	yes		yes				yes	32
Tucson	yes	statute	yes		yes	yes	yes	33
St. Louis	yes		yes		yes	yes		34
Charlotte	yes	statute			yes	yes		35
Atlanta	*yes*	*statute*			*yes*	*yes*		*36*
Virginia Beach	*yes*	*constitution*	*yes*		*yes*	*yes*		*37*
Albuquerque	yes	statute			yes		yes	38
Oakland	yes		yes		yes	yes	yes	39
Pittsburgh	*yes*		*yes*		*yes*			*40*
Sacramento	yes		yes		yes	yes		41
Minneapolis	yes	statute	yes		yes	yes		42
Tulsa	yes	statute			yes	yes	yes	43
Honolulu	yes		yes		yes	yes		44
Cincinnati	*yes*	*statute*			*yes*	*yes*	*yes*	*45*
Miami	yes	statute	yes		yes	yes		46
Fresno	yes		yes		yes	yes		47
Omaha	yes		yes				yes	48
Toledo	*yes*		*yes*		*yes*	*yes*		*49*
Buffalo	yes		yes		yes	yes	yes	50
Wichita	*no*							*51*
Santa Ana	yes		yes		yes	yes		52
Mesa	yes	statute			yes	yes		53
Colorado Springs	yes	statute	yes		yes	yes		54
Tampa	yes	statute			yes	yes		55

City							Rank
Newark	yes	statute				yes	56
St. Paul	yes		yes	yes	yes		57
Louisville	*yes*	*statute*		yes	yes		58
Anaheim	yes		yes	yes	yes		59
Birmingham	*yes*		*yes*	*yes*	*yes*		60
Arlington, TX	yes		e	yes	yes		61
Norfolk	*yes*	*constitution*	*yes*	*yes*	*yes*	*yes*	62
Las Vegas	yes	statute		yes	yes		63
Corpus Christi	yes		yes	yes	yes		64
St. Petersburg	yes	statute		yes	yes		65
Rochester	yes	statute	yes	yes	yes		66
Jersey City	yes		yes	yes	yes		67
Riverside	yes		yes	yes	yes		68
Anchorage	yes		yes	yes	yes	yes	69
Lexington-Fayette	yes	statute	yes	yes	yes		70
Akron	*yes*	*statute*	*yes*	*yes*	*yes*		71
Aurora	yes	statute	yes	yes	yes		72
Baton Rouge	yes	statute		yes	yes	yes	73
Stockton	yes		yes	yes	yes		74
Raleigh	yes	statute		yes			75
Richmond	*yes*	*const., stat.*	*yes*	*yes*	*yes*	*yes*	76
Shreveport	yes		yes	yes	yes		77
Jackson	*yes*	*statute*		*yes*	*yes*		78
Mobile	*yes*	*statute*		*yes*	*yes*	*yes*	79
Des Moines	yes	statute		yes	yes		80
Lincoln	yes	statute			yes	yes	81
Madison	*yes*	*statute*		*yes*	*yes*	*yes*	82
Grand Rapids	yes	f	f	yes	yes		83
Yonkers	yes	statute	yes	yes	yes		84
Hialeah	yes	statute		yes	yes		85
Montgomery	*yes*	*statute*		*yes*	*yes*	*yes*	86
Lubbock	yes				yes		87
Greensboro	yes	statute	yes		yes	yes	88
Dayton	*yes*		*yes*		*yes*		89
Huntington Beach	yes		yes	yes	yes		90
Garland	yes		yes	yes	yes		91
Glendale	yes		yes	yes	yes		92
Columbus, GA	*yes*	*statute*		*yes*	*yes*		93
Spokane	yes	statute			yes	yes	94
Tacoma	yes	statute			yes		95
Little Rock	yes	statute				yes	96
Bakersfield	yes		yes	yes	yes		97
Freemont	yes		yes	yes	yes		98
Fort Wayne	yes	statute			yes		99
Arlington, VA	*yes*	*constitution*	*yes*	*yes*	*yes*	*yes*	100
Total	99	53	58	84	86	35	

Source: Telephone interviews conducted 1992–1993 with finance or budget officials or analysts in reported cities. Population ranking is from U.S. Department of Commerce, Bureau of the Census 1991.

Notes:

[a] Italics indicate that Table 10.1 shows state requires balanced budget from any or all classes of municipalities. Note that city charter may supersede state requirements as in, for example, Philadelphia, Pittsburgh, and Virginia Beach.

[b] Formal year-end deficit is prohibited; operating results must balance, but reserves and/or other tactics may be used to achieve operating balance.

[c] Must rebalance quarterly.

[d] As noted in Table 10.1, state statute is subject to varying legal interpretations.

[e] Independently elected city comptroller certifies availability of funds.

[f] Response of *don't know.*

[g] City ordinance.

[h] Federal law.

[i] May not overexpend appropriations without budget amendment during fiscal year.

Table 10.3

Patterns of Budgetary Balance in the Most Populous U.S. Cities

Population quintile		State required submission	Adoption	Year end	Required at all stages
Lowest	1st	18	15	9	7
	2nd	17	16	8	6
	3rd	17	17	5	3
	4th	20	19	5	5
Highest	5th	12	19	7	3
Total		84	86	34	24

Source: Table 10.2.

Imbalance Versus Insolvency

The recent literature on budgeting (Rubin 1993), fiscal stress and distress (Cope 1992; Mackey 1993; MacManus et al., 1989; Wolman 1983, 1992), urban politics and political economy (Judd and Kantor 1992; Kantor and David 1992), and municipal debt (Sbragia 1983, 1992) offers alternative perspectives on fiscal capacity, stress, and insolvency. Seeming contradictions arise from different definitions and purposes. In *Evaluating Financial Condition*, Groves (1980) usefully distinguishes among four usages: *cash solvency* or short-term liquidity; *budgetary solvency* or fiscal-year balance; *long-run solvency* or balance; and *service-level solvency* that relates to meeting the community's needs and/or demands.

Insolvency and the Bridgeport Bankruptcy Case

The Bridgeport bankruptcy case illustrates the limits of the concept of budgetary balance and how it differs from insolvency. When the mayor of Connecticut's largest city (140,000 population) filed for Chapter 9 protection in June 1991, Bridgeport became the largest general-purpose unit of government ever to petition under the federal Bankruptcy Code (Lewis 1994). Moreover, "the city became a national symbol of urban despair when the former mayor filed for bankruptcy" (Lomuscio 1992).

Finding that the city was not insolvent at the time of the June filing, Judge Alan H.W. Shiff expeditiously dismissed the petition on August 1. (Appeals and cross-appeals to U.S. District Court were pulled and finalized in February 1992, and a stipulation of dismissal approved without prejudice.)

Insolvency is defined in 11 U.S.C. Section 101(32)(C) for purposes of bankruptcy: "with reference to a municipality, financial condition such that the municipality is—(i) generally not paying its debts as they become due unless such debts are the subject of a bona fide dispute; or (ii) unable to pay its debts as they become due. . . ." The jurisdiction bears the burden of proof. The Advisory Commission on Intergovernmental Relations (1985, 39, hereafter ACIR) noted, "The principal unresolved question remains how to define insolvency for purposes of permitting the use of the federal bankruptcy code." The Bridgeport case resolved this core concern. A member of the city's legal team had remarked with evident foresight, "It would be an irony if the city of Bridgeport was [sic] unable to file bankruptcy because it was in too solid financial health" (Scheffey 1991a, 14). Because of the relatively restrictive definition of insolvency used by the court, this is precisely what happened.

Figure 10.1 **The Balance Model**

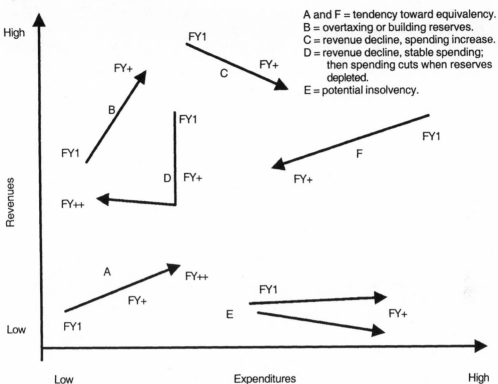

In his memorandum of decision, Bankruptcy Court Judge Shiff (1991b) unequivocally stated, "Bridgeport's insolvency should be judged by a cash flow, not a budget deficiency, analysis." He further determined, "The [c]ity argues that since [*sic*] its expenditures will exceed its revenue, it has satisfied the burden of proving that it is insolvent. The [s]tate counters that if a prospective analysis is used, Bridgeport's solvency should be judged by a cash flow, not a budget deficiency, analysis. I agree with the [s]tate."

Proceeding from an altogether different perspective on insolvency, the city rejected the court's formulation. In its appeal (Bridgeport 1991, 14–15), the city countered,

> The [c]ourt erroneously and without citing any legal precedent concluded that the ability of a municipality to "pay it's [*sic*] debts as they become due" can best and only be determined by a cash flow analysis. The [c]ity proposes that a cash flow analysis is only one, and not the most reliable, measure of a municipality's ability to "pay it's [*sic*] debts as they become due. . . ." The court's cash flow standard is nowhere set forth in the Bankruptcy Act nor in any prior decisions. . . . Rather, the case law disfavors adoption of such an exact standard, and instead requires an analysis of the particular facts and circumstances of an individual case to determine insolvency. . . . Under the [c]ourt-adopted cash flow analysis, Bridgeport indeed may have limited cash on hand at a time when its budget process mandates it reduce spending and/or raise taxes, two nonviable options.

The city's appeal further argued that, "Cash flow analysis is but one part of a fiscal examination, it is not *the* fiscal examination. The [c]ourt erred in focusing so narrowly. . . . The bottom line result of the cash flow analysis is that Bridgeport is in dire financial straits yet will be denied Chapter 9 relief at a time when it is fast approaching a time certain when it will no longer be 'able to pay its debts as they become due.' Such a scenario could not have been contemplated or intended by Congress" (Bridgeport 1991, 18).

Bridgeport's legal team (Bridgeport 1991, 29) interpreted correctly but rejected the ruling. "If a municipality were to be limited by this [c]ourt's restrictively defined insolvency test in its access to the relief intended by Congress to be available through Chapter 9, then clearly Chapter 9 will have extremely limited application and utility." That the city was paying its creditors, covering the payroll, had cash on hand, and a substantial cash reserve (the latter restricted and extraneous to balancing the operating budget) was undisputed. The city's own finance and budget directors testified to these facts in court, and expert participants confirmed them in interviews with this author (Kirshbaum 1992; Robinson 1992; Savitsky 1992). In fact, the city had promised in its initial petition to "guarantee the full payment of its debts with municipal bond holders and trade creditors." The argument concludes (Bridgeport 1991, 29), "In a manner of speaking, the [c]ourt's ruling merely assures that Bridgeport will have money in its pockets when it dies."

Thomas Scheffey, in the *Connecticut Law Tribune* (1991b, 1), colorfully summarized the ruling as having "pegged Chapter 9 as little more than an oddball footnote in bankruptcy law, and not a powerful new tool to unsnarl the fiscal affairs of distressed cities. . . . The ruling sets out a one to two-year test period in which a city must show more than that it's drowning in red ink. It must also be on the verge of exhausting all begged or borrowed cash, and about to start stiffing creditors, within that maximum 24-month period."

The inescapable lesson is that bankruptcy is an unavailing option for ameliorating fiscal stress defined as anything but insolvency and other issues are better addressed in other arenas. According to Bankruptcy Judge Shiff (1991b), broadening bankruptcy's scope is a congressional call: "The flaw in Bridgeport's argument is that the financial difficulties short of insolvency are not a basis for Chapter 9 relief. If such conditions are to be a criteria for municipal bankruptcy, Congress, not the courts, will have to make that change . . ." in the bankruptcy code.

Leaving "the perennial question" of budgetary balance to the political arena, Shiff (1991b, 7) observed, "The answer in the first instance must come from the political process, not the courts. If, however, a city is insolvent . . . [and eligible under law], Chapter 9 may be used . . . but Chapter 9 is not available to a city simply because it is financially distressed."

Connecticut's Attorney General Richard Blumenthal (1991, 6) concurred: "The plain fact is that Chapter 9 does not provide a realistic solution for a major municipality in fiscal crisis. And the reason relates not only to specific provision in Chapter 9—their defects or ambiguities—but more fundamentally to the nature of the financial difficulties faced by our major cities." Adding a political component, Blumenthal discerned, "A federal bankruptcy court clearly lacks—and constitutionally cannot be provided with—two ingredients essential to resolving the fiscal crises that plague our cities today: cash, and power." His conclusion is that "the bankruptcy process provides no real solution to a city facing long term, endemic problems. . . . As sympathetic as we must be to the problems and plight of our cities, bankruptcy isn't the solution."

Prospective Insolvency

The Bridgeport case also clarifies the question of projected insolvency raised by the second clause of the statutory definition. The judge opined, "The conclusion that Section 101(32)(C)(ii) requires a prospective analysis also comports with the purpose of Chapter 9. . . . Cities cannot go out of business. Chapter 9 is intended to enable a financially distressed city to continue to provide its residents with essential services such as police protection, fire protection, sewage and garbage removal, and schools . . . while it works out a plan to adjust its debts and obligations."

A previous case involving the California school district of San Jose had raised the prospect of impending inability to meet financial obligations (Winograd 1985). Here the court found that "the district was unable to meet its debts as they matured for the 1982–83 school year, was unable to balance its budget for the 1983–84 school year, and thus unable to meet its debts as they matured in the 1983–84 school year," and was insolvent for Chapter 9 purposes (ACIR 1985, 39). Allowing for prospective insolvency is evident in the judge's statement that "if you can pay all your bills today, but everyone knows that you can't pay them tomorrow, then you would be eligible." The ACIR (1985, 39) observed, "The anticipated fiscal 1984 budget imbalance in San Jose that was used as a second basis for declaring insolvency also raises doubts about the definition of insolvency. At the time of filing, the school board still had over a year to make adjustments in both the revenue and expenditures sides of the 1984 budget. . . . [T]he claim of an unbalanced budget for 1984 seems somewhat premature."

In contrast, the core of the Bridgeport decision states, "to be found insolvent a city must prove it will be unable to pay its debts as they become due in its current fiscal year or, based on an adopted budget, in its next fiscal year" (Shiff 1991b).

Until this ruling, neither legislative history nor case law specified the duration of the standard—how far into the future the cash-flow standard reaches. The newly minted standard deliberately forecloses premature evaluation by narrowing the window to the current fiscal year *and the next for which a budget has been adopted.* Accordingly, the judge determined, "A prediction at the commencement of this case that Bridgeport will be unable to pay its debts as they become due in the 1992–1993 fiscal year is unreliable. There are many reasons, not the least of which is the uncertainty of its cash position during a fiscal year for which there is not even a proposed budget." The new guideline establishes one fiscal year "as the 'target zone' in which a city must convincingly show it will run out of gas" (Scheffey 1991c, 1).

Although the Bridgeport case clarified the insolvency standard for bankruptcy purposes, the court's ruling probably narrowed access to bankruptcy for the 86 of the 100 most populous cities in the country reported in as legally required to *adopt* a balanced budget (Table 10.3). The second clause of the insolvency test for eligibility is effectively nullified for these cities because they cannot show a duly adopted budget for the ensuing fiscal year as evidence of impending inability to pay debts. Because it is difficult to imagine a court's entertaining admission of other than a legally valid budget—and mandamus proceedings could overturn it—these cities effectively are limited to the first or *current cash* definition of insolvency. The widespread requirement for adopting a balanced budget means that the ruling retreated from the broad access the judge sought. In his first memorandum on Bridgeport, Judge Shiff (1991a, 14–15, citations omitted) declared, "[I]n general bankruptcy laws are to be liberally construed and ambiguities are to be resolved in favor of the debtor, so that the debtor receives the full measure of relief afforded by Congress."

Balance in Bridgeport

Despite city leaders' unwillingness to shift to configuration F in Figure 10.1 and apparent preference for using the federal court to sustain configuration E, Bridgeport is legally obligated to end the fiscal year with a positive operating fund balance. Its experience illustrates the meaning of the stringent requirement for year-end budgetary balance shared by 34 percent of the most populous cities (Table 10.3).

Chapter 6 of the city charter charges the legislative body with responsibility for adopting a balanced budget: "The common council shall have no power to make appropriations in excess of the revenues of the city for any year, and in no case shall the expenses of the city exceed its revenue for any year, except in cases and for purposes for which the bonds are so issued." With respect to taxation, the charter (Chapter 7, Section 95) dictates that "the common council shall, by resolution, set a mill rate for the ensuing fiscal year, which shall, together with other sources of revenues, generate sufficient funds to support the budget adopted by the common council." The mayor as chief executive is responsible for "causing the laws to be executed and enforced within the city" and "to recommend the adoption of all such measures connected with the policy, security, health, cleanliness, and ornament of the city, and the improvements of its government and finances as he shall deem expedient" (Section 24). In 1990, the State Supreme Court ruled that this latter provision "does make it clear that the mayor is charged with oversight responsibility for the city's finances" (*William Hennessy v. City of Bridgeport et al.* 213 Conn, 656).

It was the city's inability to finance its pyramiding operating deficit without state approval that closed off the public credit markets in June 1988 and thrust the city into crisis. The state responded with a special act (*An Act Authorizing the Issuance of Bonds by the Town and City of Bridgeport*, Special Act 88–80, as amended) that created the Bridgeport Financial Review Board to oversee the city's finances, permitted the city to bond its operating deficit, and guaranteed $35 million in city bonds. According to Donald Kirshbaum (1992), the former executive director of the state's financial oversight board for the city, the act requires a strict modified accrual basis of accounting precisely in order to keep the cash flowing; to forestall borrowing from oneself, even an internal service fund may not run a negative balance; revenues must be in cash, in the bank, and the city is not allowed to carry any receivables on the balance sheet.[5]

The city's evidentiary testimony during the bankruptcy proceedings and the subsequent appeal bemoaned the unusually stringent budgetary and accounting practices imposed by the state's special legislation. Using garbled argumentation, the appeal attacked the court's insolvency standard because the city is required to budget on the basis of generally accepted accounting principles (GAAP). "The accrual [accurately, cash] versus the GAP [*sic*] accounting places the [c]ity in a different position when analyzing its cash flow because unlike other municipalities in the state it does not have the ability to carry over any expenses to the following fiscal year. The cash flow analysis with these restrictions and distortions simply should not have been applied in the present situation" (Bridgeport 1991, 10–11). Pointing to a state-imposed basis of accounting more restrictive than for other Connecticut municipalities, the city's leaders (Bridgeport 1991, 16) self-servingly argued that "unlike the other municipalities, [Bridgeport] can only include actual or reasonably expected revenues" and the "accounting method distorts the viability of a cash flow analysis and exposes it as an unreliable measure of the [c]ity's true financial condition. It must be remembered that the [c]ity has a legal obligation to balance its budget within the present fiscal year."

The Discipline of Balance

While pleading for flexibility, city leaders were also making the somewhat perverse argument that they are foreclosed from using the expedients employed in other municipalities to formalistically comply with balance while actually evading it in a given fiscal year. Bridgeport simply must finance current services from current revenues.

Although the fact of balance itself might appear to outweigh the means of achieving it, the tactics actually employed inject policy content into budgetary balance. For example, Fitch (1993a, 2) ranks Cleveland's "[e]ffective budget measures resulting in a return to a positive year-end balance" as among this city's strengths. Such measures include "minimal wage increases for most employees, selective staff reductions, and health-care cost containment." From drawing down reserves or rainy day funds set aside for this very purpose to revenue *enhancements* (e.g., special assessment districts, user charges, service fees), and from *technical* reconciliations (e.g., adjusting the tax base) to David Stockman's notorious *magic asterisk*, anecdotal evidence points to more or less legitimate tactics suitable for the strategy of formalistic compliance with budgetary balance. These tactics are often stamped gimmicks—the stuff of smoke and mirrors—whereby they are painted as scheme or stratagem.

Short-Term Contrivances

Ironically, one purpose of balance is to accommodate the very flexibility these labels censure.[6] Investment rating services appear to value this flexibility in their assessments. According to Standard & Poor's (1993, 22), "The fund balance position is a measure of an [debt] issuer's financial flexibility to meet essential services during periods of limited liquidity. Standard & Poor's considers an adequate fund balance to be a credit strength." To the question about Moody's assessment of large fund balances, Moody's (1993, 9) responds, "Large fund balances often reflect sound financial management, but not always . . . the fund balance is a measure of financial position, but financial structure is important as well."

Addressing correcting imbalance, Moody's recommends (1993, 8), "although such decisions are best made by local representatives, an issuer should keep in mind that strategies can differ for short-term versus long-term objectives. . . . If an operating imbalance is expected to persist, then the response should achieve ongoing budget balance while also maintaining essential service provision and an adequate physical plant." Very much to the point, Moody's (1993, 8) notes, "The reason behind an operating deficit can be more important than the deficit itself."

A long-term perspective is useful. San Antonio, the nation's tenth most populous city, is shown in Table 10.2 as operating under a stringent balance requirement. Although its operations have been balanced through tax increases and discriminating spending cuts, Fitch (1992, 1, 5) identifies a risk: "Future operating surpluses may be harder to achieve given the significant measures taken to realize budgetary balance to date." Table 10.5 indicates that the General Accounting Office (GAO) (1993b) assesses San Antonio as among the "fiscally weakest" cities in its studies.

The literature on budgeting conveniently inventories both prosaic and exceptional techniques short of outright tax increases, service cuts, or cost reductions (Kennedy 1991; Rubin 1993, 164–206; Webber and Wildavsky 1986). Examples of such techniques include: use of reserves; one-shot revenues such as asset sales; shifting costs off the general fund, interfund transfers, and shifting costs to the capital budget; underfunding accrued liabilities such as pensions; delaying deliveries, payrolls, and payments to the next fiscal year; estimation manipulation or distortion; using plugs such as anticipated and even unidentified (and perhaps illusory) savings or revenues; and turning to off-budget entities, indiscernible credit arrangements, loan guarantees, and tax expenditures. Not surprisingly, some entrenched techniques sacrifice efficiency for economy; for example, manipulation of employee benefits may translate into future cost escalations.[7] A testament to ingenuity, this litany accommodates tactics designed for both short-term flexibility and formalistic compliance.

Table 10.4

Nineteen States Requiring Generally Accepted Accounting Principles for Municipal Financial Reporting

Colorado	Kentucky	Nebraska	Oregon
Connecticut	Louisiana	Nevada	Virginia
Illinois	Maine	North Carolina	Wisconsin
Iowa	Massachusetts	Ohio	Wyoming
Kansas	Minnesota	Oklahoma	

Source: Search of Lexis database conducted fall 1992 for generally accepted accounting principles, financial reporting, and by related key words.

Table 10.5

Current Budgetary Imbalance and Credit Rating for Selected Cities, Fiscal Year 1990

	GO bond rating[b]	
Budget as adopted[a]	Moody's	Standard & Poor's
Atlanta	Aa	AA
Baltimore	A1	A
Boston	A	A
Buffalo[d]	Baaa1	BBB+
Cincinnati	Aa	AA+
Cleveland[d]	Baa1	A−
Columbus	Aa1	AA+
Dallas	Aaa	AAA
Denver	Aa	AA
Houston	Aa	AA
Indianapolis	Aaa	NR
Jacksonville	A1	AA
Kansas City	Aa	AA
Memphis[d]	Aa	AA
Milwaukee[d]	Aa	AA+
Minneapolis	Aaa	AAA
New Orleans[d]	Baa	A−
Philadelphia[d]	B	CCC
Pittsburgh	Baa1	A
St. Louis	Baa	BBB
San Antonio[d]	Aa	AA
San Francisco	Aa	AA
Seattle	Aa1	AA
Year-end results[c]		
Cincinnati	Aa	AA+
Columbus	Aa1	AA+
Dallas	Aaa	AAA
Indianapolis	Aaa	NR
Phoenix	Aa	AA+
San Antonio[d]	Aa	AA
Seattle	AA1	AA

Source: Table 10.2; U.S. General Accounting Office (1993b, 112–113); budget data from Dearborn, Peterson, and Kirk (1992, Table 7); and bond ratings from "The Top 50 Cities, 5th Annual Financial Report" (1990, 12–13).

Notes:

[a]In these cities, the adopted budget must formally balance (Table 10.2) and current-year expenditures outstripped current-year revenues in the budget as adopted.

[b]GO signifies general obligation bonds backed by the "full faith and credit" of the jurisdiction.

[c]In these cities, year-end operations must balance (Table 10.2) and a current gap was offset using more or less legitimate devices.

[d]Identified by the U.S. General Accounting Office in 1993 as among the "fiscally weakest" quartile of cities.

As the Bridgeport case suggests, certain tactics derive from the nature of fund accounting, whereby "it is possible to balance the revenues and expenditures of the general fund, to which political attention is paid and to which balanced budget requirements apply, by making discrete transfers among funds or by budgeting selected activities in funds other than the general fund" (Granof and Mayper 1991, 30). The basis of accounting may offer additional maneuverability. Whereas the data in Table 10.4 show that at least nineteen states require generally accepted accounting principles for municipal financial *reporting*, municipal budgets "are generally on a cash or near-cash basis" (Granof and Mayper 1991, 28).

Bridgeport's experience also suggests that estimation procedures are especially fruitful. Projecting a $16 million imbalance for the next fiscal year and a five-year projected deficit of $259 million (Bridgeport 1991, 14), city leaders urged that insolvency be measured by long-term projections. The state alleged that the city's tale was "replete with distortions, inaccuracies, false assumptions and ignored options" (Connecticut 1991, 35). Having allowed consideration of prospective balance, the bankruptcy judge "indirectly set a requirement for credible, complete budget predictions" (Scheffey 1991c, 1). Adjusting estimates and projections is evidently common enough to have provoked legal remedies. For example, the independently elected city comptroller in Arlington, Texas, certifies the availability of funds (Table 10.2). The annotation accompanying Pennsylvania's statute (Section 2–302) specifies, "To prevent over-optimistic estimates by the body which must impose taxes . . . the [m]ayor's estimate of revenue yield is made binding upon the [c]ouncil. Until the budget is balanced, no money may be spent under the annual operating budget."

Current-Year Balance Versus Formal Compliance

Authentic compliance with budgetary balance represents the triumph of technical competence and administrative capacity. Webber and Wildavsky (1986, 592) point out, "The subject of budget balance as a rough equivalence between revenue and expenditure in total could hardly have arisen in modern form before the last 125 years or so, because methods of accounting were too imprecise. . . . [N]ew budgetary devices dominate modern governmental spending. . . . These new budget instruments either do not show up in the budget or, by much reducing the formal budget's size, serve to confuse the calculation of balances." They also ask (592), "Nowadays, presumably, we know how far from this norm [or balance] we have wandered. Or do we?"

Recent research suggests some provocative answers. The declining frequency of current-year surpluses evident since 1988 (GAO 1993b; Lamphere 1990) is attributable to recession, fading or inadequate intergovernmental aid, and other factors, including idiosyncratic community features. In the Bridgeport case, the state (Connecticut 1991, 41–42) cited the National League of Cities' finding that general expenditures exceeded revenues in 1991 for a majority of cities responding to its survey. Citing the same study, the GAO (1992, 56) finds, "Municipal and county [like many states'] fund balances have also been depleted. For example, 59 percent of cities expected to draw down their fund balances in 1991. In addition, 39 percent of the nation's most populous counties and 34 percent of counties under 100,000 population experienced a budget shortfall in fiscal year 1991, thus reducing available local balances." (GAO's own study [1993b] confirmed declining year-end operating budget surpluses at all levels of government.)

In evidentiary hearings, the state's expert witness, Philip Dearborn, testified that, in the preceding two years, at least one-half of the thirty largest U.S. cities had unbalanced budgets in the sense that current revenues outstripped current expenditures and formal balance drew upon various contrivances. His and colleagues' subsequent analysis of financial reports for twenty-eight of the thirty largest cities identifies a current-year imbalance for fiscal year 1990 in twenty-five cities (Dearborn, Peterson, and Kirk 1992, Table 7). As shown in Table 10.5, twenty-three cities of the twenty-five are prohibited from formally adopting an unbalanced budget and seven are prohibited from ending the year with an operating deficit. Corresponding credit ratings confirm the analytic inadequacy of using operating balance in a single fiscal year as the sole or even summary measure of financial performance or condition.

Conclusion

The evidence presented here confirms empirically the pivotal role of balance in municipal budgeting. Findings show that budgetary balance is, in fact, a common legal requirement and, perhaps more importantly, is articulated as an operative norm by participants in the budgetary process. Bridgeport's brief flirtation with bankruptcy cautions against overrating the power of balance as budgetary disciplinarian. Given the many devices for achieving formal compliance, balance need not and often does not translate into equivalency between current revenues and current expenditures.

Municipal budgeting cannot be reduced fruitfully to a single criterion, even one as widely accepted as budgetary balance. Bound by charter and statute, Bridgeport's city leaders unavailingly sought to bypass the strictest of balance requirements *via* federal bankruptcy court. Their contribution to municipal budgeting and "[t]he net gain for bankruptcy law . . . may be just that cities contemplating a bankruptcy know how to plan for it better" (Scheffey 1991b, 1). Although the fiscal woes of many U.S. cities has heightened interest in bankruptcy (Cohen 1991), the case demonstrates that while "persistent balance sheet deficits" are among the several financial warning signs (Standard & Poor's 1989, 12), balance is most usefully distinguished from insolvency and that tactics underlying the balance and other factors warrant attention. Further undercutting the power of a concept whose attraction is related in no small measure to its simplicity, this conclusion calls to mind H.L. Mencken's observation, "For every human problem, there is a solution that is simple, neat, and wrong."

Notes

The author acknowledges Peter Arkins, graduate student in the Master of Public Affairs program, the University of Connecticut, for his exacting research assistance; the generous support of the University of Connecticut's Graduate Research Foundation; and, for reading and commenting upon the draft manuscript, David RePass and Morton J. Tenzer, professors emeriti of the University of Connecticut, and Professor W. Bartley Hildreth.

1. The GAO (1993b, 3) found that all but Vermont and Wyoming among the fifty states have balanced budget requirements. "In most states, the balanced budget mandates apply to enacted budgets or to the governors' proposed budgets. Few balanced budget requirements specifically mandate year-end balance."

2. The ACIR (1993, 46) identified only eight states mandating by constitution or statute that city budgets be balanced.

3. This expectation is predicated upon the presumably universal desire to reduce uncertainty and enhance stability. "Two important goals of local governments are the maintenance of a stable tax and revenue structure and the orderly provision of services to residents" (Allan 1990, 2).

4. In this regard, only Kentucky, Pennsylvania, and Ohio of the thirteen states with statutory provision specify budgetary imbalance among the criteria triggering assistance to local governments with "severe, immediate fiscal problems" (Mackey 1993, 3–6).

5. Section 11 of the act specifies that the financial plan under the aegis of the review board "shall provide for the (1) elimination of all deficits in the general fund; (2) restoration to all funds and accounts, including capital funds and accounts, of any moneys from such funds and accounts that were used for purposes not within

the purposes of such funds and accounts or borrowed from such funds or accounts; (3) balancing of the operating funds in accordance with the provisions of this act."

6. According to the GAO (1993b, 10), "many jurisdictions had fewer year-end budget funds to carry forward to help finance the succeeding year's programs, suggesting a diminished flexibility, at least in the short-run, to increase the funding of current services or undertake major new spending initiatives."

7. "In addition to the hidden costs of benefits, Moody's is seeing salary increases that are partially funded with changes in actuarial pension earnings assumptions, an approach that requires fewer operating fund dollars today. Although this approach may be appropriate for cities with historically conservative assumptions, such changes require careful actuarial scrutiny, and funding levels must be revisited frequently to assure that the more aggressive earnings assumptions are, in fact, being achieved" (Kennedy 1991, 3).

References

Advisory Commission on Intergovernmental Relations. 1985. *Bankruptcies, Defaults, and Other Local Government Financial Emergencies.* Report A-99. Washington, DC: Advisory Commission on Intergovernmental Relations.

———. 1993. *State Laws Governing Local Government Structure and Administration.* Report M-186. Washington, DC: Advisory Commission on Intergovernmental Relations.

Allan, Ian J. 1990. "Unreserved Fund Balance and Local Government Finance." *Research Bulletin.* Washington, DC: Government Finance Research Center of the Government Finance Officers Association, November, pp. 1–8.

Blumenthal, Richard. 1991. "Remarks by Attorney General Richard Blumenthal before the 65th Annual Meeting of National Conference of Bankruptcy Judges." San Francisco, California, October 31.

Bridgeport, City of. 1991. On Appeal from the Judgment of the Bankruptcy Court for the Judicial District of Connecticut, Brief of the Debtor, Appellant City of Bridgeport, filed with United States Bankruptcy Court, District of Connecticut, October 31.

Cohen, Jeffrey. 1991. "Declining Health of U.S. Cities Raises New Interest in Chapter 9." *National Law Journal* (August 5): 15.

Cope, Glenn H. 1992. "Walking the Fiscal Tightrope: Local Budgeting and Fiscal Stress." *International Journal of Public Administration* 5: 1097–1120.

Connecticut, State of, Office of the Attorney General. 1991. Brief by the Appellee/Cross Appellant. Filed on appeal and cross-appeal from orders of the United States Bankruptcy Court for the District of Connecticut, November 15.

Dearborn, Philip M., George E. Peterson, and Richard H. Kirk. 1992. *City Finances in the 1990s.* Washington, DC: Urban Institute, September draft, Table 7.

Fitch Research. 1992. *San Antonio, Texas.* New York: Fitch Investors Service, Inc., July 27.

———. 1993a. *Cleveland, Ohio.* New York: Fitch Investors Service, Inc., April 12.

———. 1993b. *San Francisco, California.* New York: Fitch Investors Service, Inc., April 21.

Forrester, John P., and Daniel R. Mullins. 1992a. *Rebudgeting in Larger U.S. Municipalities,* Baseline Data Report, vol. 23, no. 4. Washington, DC: International City/County Management Association.

———. 1991b. "Rebudgeting: The Serial Nature of Municipal Budgetary Processes." *Public Administration Review* 52 (September/October): 467–473.

Granof, Michael H., and Alan Mayper. 1991. "Current State of Government Budgets." *CPA Journal* 61, no. 7: 28–32.

Groves, Sanford M. 1980. *Evaluating Financial Condition,* Handbook No. 1. Washington, DC: International City Management Association.

Judd, Dennis, and Paul Kantor. 1992. "Introduction." In *Enduring Tensions in Urban Politics,* ed. Dennis Judd and Paul Kantor. New York: Macmillan, pp. 1–8.

Kantor, Paul, and Stephen David. 1992. "The Political Economy of Change in Urban Budgetary Politics: A Framework for Analysis and a Case Study." In *Enduring Tensions in Urban Politics,* ed. Dennis Judd and Paul Kantor. New York: Macmillan, pp. 564–583. Originally published in 1983 in *British Journal of Political Science* 13: 254–274.

Kennedy, Dina W. 1991. "Balancing the Budget: The Key Urban Challenge for the 1990s." *Moody's Municipal Issues.* [Moody's Investors Service] 8, no. 1: 1–7.

Kirshbaum, Donald. 1992. Treasurer's Office, State of Connecticut. Formerly executive director of Bridgeport Financial Review Board. Interviews with author, February 18, Hartford, and by telephone, May 12.

Lamphere, Amy. 1990. "Cities Seeing Red." *City & State* 19 (November): 1, 35.

Lewis, Carol W. 1994. "Municipal Bankruptcy and the States: Authorization to File Under Chapter 9." *Urban Affairs Quarterly* 30, no. 1: 3–26.

Lomuscio, James. 1992. "Another View of Bridgeport's Problems." *New York Times* (March 1), p. CN3. An interview with Bridgeport Mayor Joseph P. Ganim.

Mackey, Scott R. 1993. *State Programs to Assist Distressed Local Governments.* Denver, CO: National Conference of State Legislatures.

MacManus, Susan A., Jessie M. Rattley, Patrick J. Ungaro, William R. Brown, Jr., Scott O'Donnell, Donald L. 'Pat' Shalmy, Norm Hickey, and Denies Jubell. 1989. "A Decade of Decline: A Longitudinal Look at Big City and Big County Strategies to Cope with Declining Revenues." *International Journal of Public Administration* 12: 747–796.

Moody's Investors Service. 1993. "Key Factors in Moody's Credit Analysis of Tax-Supported Debt." *Perspective on Municipal Issues.* Moody's Investors Services, Inc.

Robinson, Richard. 1992. Finance director during bankruptcy filing and through spring 1992 of Bridgeport, CT. Interview with author, February 11, Bridgeport, and by telephone, May 19.

Rubin, Irene, S. 1993. *The Politics of Public Budgeting.* 2d ed. Chatham, NJ: Chatham House.

Savitsky, Linda. 1992. Director of Municipal Finance Services, Office of Policy and Management, State of Connecticut, and executive director of Bridgeport Financial Review Board. Personal and telephone interviews with author, February–September.

Sbragia, Alberta, M. 1983. *The Municipal Money Chase: The Politics of Municipal Finance.* Boulder, CO: Westview Press.

———. 1992. "Politics, Local Government, and the Municipal Bond Market." In *Enduring Tensions in Urban Politics,* ed. Dennis Judd and Paul Kantor. New York: Macmillan, pp. 583–594.

Scheffey, Thomas. 1991a. "Bankruptcy Trial: State's Case Deflates." *Connecticut Law Tribune* 1 (July 29): 14–15.

———. 1991b. "Shiff: Bridgeport's Too Rich to Go Broke." *Connecticut Law Tribune* 1 (August 5): 16–17.

———. 1991c. "Postmortem on Bridgeport's Bankruptcy." *Connecticut Law Tribune* (November 25): 1.

Shaw, George B. 1904. *The Common Sense of Municipal Trading.* Westminister, UK: A. Constable.

Shiff, Alan H.W. 1991a. 129 B.R. 339 (Bankr. D. Conn.). Bankruptcy court judge. Memorandum and Order on the Objection of the State of Connecticut to Chapter 9 Petition. July 22.

———. 1991b. 129 B.R. 339 (Bankr. D. Conn.). Memorandum and Second Order on the Objection of the State of Connecticut to Chapter 9 Petition. August 1.

Standard & Poor's. 1989. *S&P's Municipal Finance Criteria.* New York: Standard & Poor's.

———. 1993. *Standard & Poor's Municipal Finance Criteria.* New York: Standard & Poor's.

U.S. Department of Commerce, Bureau of the Census. 1991. *Statistical Abstract of the United States.* 111th ed. Washington, DC: Government Printing Office.

U.S. General Accounting Office. 1992. *Intergovernmental Relations, Changing Patterns in State-Local Finances.* GAO/HRD-92–87FS. Washington, DC: GAO.

———. 1993a. *Balanced Budget Requirements, State Experiences and Implications for the Federal Government.* GAO/AFMD-93–58BR. Washington, DC: GAO.

———. 1993b. *State and Local Finances, Some Jurisdictions Confronted by Short- and Long-term Problems.* GAO/HRD094–1. Washington, DC: GAO.

Webber, C., and Aaron Wildavsky. 1986. *A History of Taxation and Expenditure in the Western World.* New York: Simon and Schuster.

Wildavsky, Aaron. 1992. *The New Politics of the Budgetary Process.* 2d ed. New York: HarperCollins.

Winograd, Barry. 1985. "San Jose Revisited: A Proposal for Negotiated Modification of Public Sector Bargaining Agreements Rejected Under Chapter 9 of the Bankruptcy Code." 37 *Hasting L.J.* 231.

Wolman, Harold. 1983. "Understanding Local Government Responses to Fiscal Pressure: A Cross-national Analysis." *Journal of Public Policy* 3: 245–264.

———. 1992. "Urban Fiscal Stress." *Urban Affairs Quarterly* 27, no. 3: 470–481.

CHAPTER 11

ANALYZING HOW LOCAL GOVERNMENTS ESTABLISH SERVICE PRIORITIES

AIMEE L. FRANKLIN AND BRANDI CARBERRY-GEORGE

Analyzing Local Government Budgetary Processes in Texas

The 1990s may be remembered as a time in history when government was criticized for not benefiting the "right" people, and politics was often cited as the main consideration in decisions concerning municipal budgets. It has been rather cynically noted that budgetary processes are nothing more than politics, the result of stasis rivalries, voter apathy and interest groups haranguing, leading to the success of the politically powerful over those less powerful.[1]

To test the accuracy of this view, we need to better understand budgetary decision-making processes in local governments. In doing this, it is prudent to look at the similarities and differences. The commonalities are few, but as Bunch and Straussman conclude, a common goal in budgetary creation is to incorporate a set of recommended policies and financial limits that are considered politically realistic.[2] The differences found in each municipality may, on the other hand, reflect individual operating styles and variances in the degree of formalism.

Even though budgetary decision making is an oft-discussed topic, prominent budget theorists lament that the literature is bereft of vital empirical data, particularly in the area of municipal governments. This research attempts to address this lacuna in the hopes of gaining a better understanding of factors that can lead to more effective budgeting processes.[3] This chapter presents results from a testing of propositions concerning the relationship of three variables on the decision-making framework used in a city budget sequence, the participants, and the reference sources. Specifically, the research sought answers to three main questions:

1. Are there commonalities in the sequence of budget approval, the number of actors, and the type of information used to make budgetary decisions?
2. Are there different frameworks, beyond the oft-cited incrementalism, that are dominant in resource allocation?
3. What are the interrelationships between the components of the process and the dominant framework used?

To test these propositions, analysis was conducted on two primary data sources: (1) results from a survey of officials in Texas cities, and (2) secondary analysis of information contained in the *1983* and *1993 County and City Data Book*.[4] The survey was sent via fax and e-mail to all

From *Public Budgeting & Finance*, vol. 19, no. 3 (Fall 1999), pp. 31–46. Copyright © 1999 by Blackwell Publishing. Reprinted with permission.

sixty-eight Texas cities with populations of more than twenty-five thousand in 1990. Responses were received from forty-seven cities for a 70 percent response rate.[5] The results from this research are based on attitudinal and perceptual data gathered from a survey distributed to both the city mayor and the highest ranking appointed official. Eighty-seven percent of the responses used for the analysis were completed by either the city manager or a representative of the budget, finance, community relations, or city secretary's offices; the remaining 13 percent of survey responses were completed by the mayor.

Quantitative analysis of the data occurred in two main stages. First we carried out a descriptive analysis of the variables for budget sequence, number of participants, types of reference sources, and decision-making framework using standard measures of central tendency and dispersion.[6] Then, the bivariate relationships for these variables, as well as four additional control variables (city size, geographical location, age, and form of government), were explored using a cross-tabulation approach. Data distribution problems, small sample size and resulting thin cells, and missing variables for cities that did not exist in 1980 prevent the reporting of measures of association. Included in the survey were open-ended questions requiring a narrative response from the respondent. The responses for these questions were interpreted using an inductive, grounded theory approach. The combination of quantitative and qualitative methods allowed for partial triangulation of results concerning the variables under study.

When reviewing the research results, there are limitations that must be considered. The first limitation concerns the validity of self-reported data obtained through a mail survey. There may be a tendency for respondents to make responses thought to be socially acceptable, rather than providing a true reflection of what occurs. A second limitation is the fact that the perceptions are strictly those of the respondent and may not be an accurate reflection of reality. Third, since the answers reflect the respondent's perceptions, differences based on the specific individual who completed the survey can be expected. For this study, responses were received from two individuals representing the same city for 23 percent of the sample. A side-by-side review of the duplicated responses reveals a fairly high degree of reliability for the majority of the survey questions. Finally, the respondent may not seek clarification of a question or the correct method for responding if it is unclear in a self-administered instrument.

Theoretical Reflections on Budgeting

Understanding resource allocation in municipal budgets first requires familiarity with three main components in a decision-making process—for example, the budgeting sequence, the participants, and the types of reference sources. A review of the literature reveals that local governments have evolved in terms of these factors. The sequence of budget approval is one example. Budget requests, for example, were traditionally created by a limited group of agency administrators. They typically were prepared by the department heads and sent to the city manager and/or the mayor. Then, they were forwarded to the council. This sequence is characterized as a bottom-up approach, and generally is based on what was done previously—supporting incremental budgeting. More recently, Hildreth has argued for a "top-down" process that allows for more public input.[7] This type of budgeting is generally initiated by the elected decision makers and features the identification of goals prior to budget development.

Another area where there has been an evolution in prevailing thought is in the area of participants in the resource allocation process. Much has been written about the commonly held perception that the most important decisions concerning the use of public funds occur behind closed doors in "executive sessions" designed to limit the participation of those who do not have the ear of the most powerful political players.[8] Contemporary authors argue that political influence in municipal governance, common in incremental frameworks described by Wildavsky, is being mitigated through the inclusion of multiple stakeholders in numerous public venues. Such participation, many claim, increasingly occurs in budget processes as well. Using this tactic, elected and appointed official decision makers may keep in touch with the needs and desires of the community they serve.

The amount and nature of information available for budgetary decision making are other areas that have witnessed a great deal of change. Due, in part, to the technological advancements of recent years, there has been an increase in the use of data obtained through core management functions such as strategic planning, performance measurement, and program evaluation during budget reviews.[9] Many authors have speculated that this increased reliance on objective accomplishment data represents an attempt to "manage by fact" and responds to charges concerning the overpoliticization of governmental decision making. While usually perceived as objective, these data may also include subjective information, such as that gathered by public testimony during budget deliberations.

The sequence, participants, and reference sources are three factors that can influence the framework, or conceptual lens that guides the decision process. Hale and Franklin considered three major frameworks that have received attention in budgeting literature. They are incremental, performance, and community values.[10] The incremental framework analyzes the distribution of the marginal change in funding levels from the previous year.[11] Using this method, entrenched interests tend to be the winners in terms of protecting their piece of the budgetary pie, and significant changes are minimized.

A second framework, which periodically resurges in importance, is the performance framework. When using the performance framework, resources are allocated according to the desired level of activity of government programs and the related costs for those services.[12] The performance framework also emphasizes the consideration of previous performance data in establishing a desired level of performance during the resource allocation process. Early underpinnings of the performance framework can be found in the Planning, Programming and Budgeting System included in the Department of Defense in the early 1960s. Contemporary examples include requirements found in the Government Performance and Results Act and similar state and local mandates calling for the use of performance information in budgetary decision making. One common theme in these attempts at performance budgeting is the identification of desired levels of specific outcomes and then, the allocation of funds based on a per unit of accomplishment cost allocation.

The third framework, the community values approach, dictates that decisions regarding the provision of government services and desired levels of outcomes are guided by the views and attitudes of the citizenry regarding the proper role of government in their community. Decisions made under this framework can consider one or more of the following three kinds of issues: (1) should government provide only mandated services, (2) should it provide programs to enrich all of its citizens for the betterment of the society, or (3) should government merely provide a safety net for those in crisis.[13] No matter which of these issues form the basis for decision making, each has a common element in that it responds to the preferences and values of the community.

Despite the plethora of writings proclaiming the dominance of one framework over another, some argue that no identifiable frameworks can be found. Notwithstanding this skepticism, there remains the lure of developing a theory of budgeting. This research elucidates local budgeting processes and demonstrates the possibility of identifying dominant decision-making frameworks.

The results from this analysis show that in Texas, cities do, in fact, consider factors such as performance results and community values, in addition to incremental politics, in their budgetary deliberations.

Components of Local Government Budgeting

In addition to the assumption that these are differences in the framework a local government uses to make decisions on budgetary allocations, the sequence for budget approval, number and type of participants, and reference resources used in the process can also be expected to vary. Understanding the similarities and differences in each of these factors can further attempts to develop a budget theory. An important aspect of this research was attempting to provide answers to questions such as: how budgets are decided; who is involved; and what information is used in this process. Characteristics of responding Texas cities on these variables are presented next.

The survey asked respondents in each city to describe the steps leading to budget adoption. Fifteen cities (32%) provided an excerpt of a previously published document that detailed the formal budget process. Others did not respond to the question ($n = 5$) or elaborate beyond internal budget development and stopped at the point of submission to the council, commission, or mayor ($n = 4$). The representatives of only forty-two of the sixty-eight Texas cities studied and the subjectiveness of self-reported data in an open-ended question should be considered threats to the validity of these findings. What occurs in practice may or may not completely conform to what is contained in the published formal procedures.

To limit the threats to validity due to the varying levels of detail and subjectiveness of the data coding process, both authors independently coded the responses. The first coder used an inductive approach that identified patterns in the responses. The second coder incorporated a deductive perspective using the framework to code the responses. Interrater reliability was 0.8739, indicating high agreement and reduced threats to validity. Despite this limitation, it is interesting to note that 11 percent of respondents describe no public involvement in their city's budget process.

From these responses a new, descriptive typology with five categories was created. Table 11.1 describes each of the different budget approval sequences and shows the corresponding number and percent of cities in each category.

One striking observation from this table is that the first three types represent a more traditional "bottom-up" model that features agency budget preparation followed by elected official deliberation and budget adoption. Further, the Council-only sequence reflects a strong emphasis on the views of the city administrators and elected officials in determining resource allocation, and reports no public involvement in the process. Beginning with the second budget sequence type (Council Public), the views of the public can be heard. However, it is questionable whether this public participation is significant, or merely a formality, due to the fact that it occurs after a preliminary set of budget figures is identified and there is no subsequent council work session after the public hearing(s). Discouragingly, a large number of cities (39%) indicated that they use this sequence in their budgetary process. The Public Participation sequence incorporates citizen input into the process before the council work session and budget adoption. This pattern allows citizens more say in the budget decisions.

The last two budgetary sequences incorporate a "top-down" approach, since goals and funding priorities are identified by elected officials and this information is used by public administrators to guide budget development. The fourth sequence, Planning, involves work sessions with the council and the public to set funding priorities before the administrators create the budget requests. The heaviest public involvement is found in the fifth model, Multi-planning, which

Table 11.1

Prevailing Budget Sequences in Forty-Two Texas Cities*

Sequence type	Description
Council-only (n = 4, 11%)	Department heads to city manager/mayor to council Council work session and budget adoption
Council public (n = 15, 39%)	Department heads to city manager/mayor to council Council work session Public testimony and budget adoption
Public participation	Department heads to city manager/mayor to council Public testimony Council work session and budget adoption
Planning (n = 6, 16%)	Council/public planning process Department heads to city manager/mayor to council Council work session and budget adoption
Multi-planning (n = 5, 13%)	Council/public planning process Department heads to city manager/mayor to council Council work session Public testimony and budget adoption

Note: *The results presented here do not include the four cities that did not elaborate on what occurred once the budget recommendations were presented to the council nor the five cities that did not respond to this question.

accounts for 13 percent of the cities. This model provides multiple opportunities for public input; first, when the goals and objectives are established and then, when the budget is presented to the council. In both the Planning and Multi-planning models, decisions made in the initial planning sessions are later used by the department heads and the city manager or mayor when formulating budget requests.

The five different budget approval sequences can be thought of as a continuum. As you move from the top to the bottom of Table 11.1 you see movement from the least amount of public participation (Council-only) to the most public involvement (Multi-planning). In considering this shift, there is an increasing emphasis on planning and priority setting before budget requests are developed. This trend is suggestive of a bias toward a performance or community values framework and reflects attention to the linkage and alignment of at least two strategic management functions—that is, planning and budgeting.

Another conclusion is that the five types of budget approval sequences can be grouped to represent two different approaches to budget adoption. The first two types can be viewed as an approach where the council is making tentative decisions without direct public input. It may be suspected that these types represent only *symbolic* public participation since the council work session and initial markup of the budget occurs prior to any public input. This type of approach may be favored in cities where the incremental framework is dominant, since under this framework political insiders are theorized to be the ones to determine the allocation of the marginal budgetary changes and public participation is, therefore, superfluous.

At the bottom of the continuum, the remaining three types (Public Participation, Planning, and Multi-planning) can be classified as *participative* since they each emphasize the role of citizen participation through public hearings before either preliminary or final decisions are

Table 11.2

Participants in the Budget Process in Texas Cities

Types of participant groups	Percent reporting participation
Council/Commissioners/Alderpersons	100
Mayor	98
Department heads	96
City manager	94
Citizens	79
Special interest groups	55
Media	34

Note: N = 47.

made. This process suggests that many Texas cities care about citizens' opinions (or at least go through the motions of gathering their input) since these three sequences combine to represent half of the responding cities. This supports Axelrod's conclusion that budgets are a reflection of the aspirations, values, social and economic policies, or simply stated the values, of the community.[14]

Participants

Who participates in the budget process? Survey respondents were given a list of seven common participant groups in the budgetary process. From this list, they were asked to denote all general-ized stakeholder groups who participated in their city's budget discussions. Table 11.2 displays the percentage of cities that reported a particular stakeholder group as taking part in resource allocation deliberations.

This table conveys the dominance of the elected officials and the highest appointed officials since the categories for the council, mayor, department heads, and the city manager were selected by more than 90 percent of all responding cities. Least likely to participate were the media and special interest groups at 34 and 55 percent, respectively. One important observation from this table concerns the role of the public in the decision-making process. Seventy-nine percent of respondents identified citizens as important participants, a figure that is higher than the represen-tation of either the media or the special interest groups.

Respondents were given the opportunity to identify an eighth category of participants not on the original list of seven common stakeholders. The group most frequently included in the "other" category was the budget/planning/finance staffs. A possible interpretation of this finding is that the budget is very complicated and decision makers desire assistance in interpreting the reams of data presented to them.

In considering the combinations of participants selected by the respondents, there were three cities (6%) that *did not* select every one of the "Big 4" (of those that were present in their city)— for example, council, mayor, city manager, and department heads as participants in budget delib-erations. Of this number, it is notable that one city, Longview, selected only the council and mayor out of the seven choices offered even though there are department heads and a manager in this city. The respondent from Tyler (council/manager) did not select the mayor, and the respon-dent from Nacogdoches (commission) did not select the department heads. However, there are other players beyond the "Big 4" who hold important views about resource allocation. It does appear that decision makers in the majority of Texas cities do solicit these views of nonpolitical

Table 11.3

Reference Sources Used for Budgetary Decision Making in Texas Cities

Reference source	Percent reporting use
Budget requests	98
New statutory mandates	89
Performance measures	81
Public testimony	79
Audit results	70

Note: N = 47.

insiders, since more than 80 percent of the responding cities indicated that five or more partici-pant groups normally provided input. This finding is important because it supports the notion that incremental tactics that favor the politically powerful, such as the "Big 4," are not dominant. Instead it appears that the solicitation of the value preferences of other important stakeholder groups is a normal part of the budgetary process, as perceived by survey respondents.

The research also analyzed the relationship between the budget sequence and the number of participant groups. Cities using the "symbolic" participation sequences (Council-only and Coun-cil Public) reported that they included more than the "Big 4" participant groups 68 percent of the time. This finding is interesting since these two sequences do not emphasize the involvement of the public prior to the adoption of the budget. Rather, their participation, if any, seems to merely be a formality.

The remaining three types, which have participation as a fixture in their budget sequence, were more likely to report using more participants in the process. The Public participation, Planning, and Multi-planning sequence types had more than four participant groups in 95 per-cent of the cases. This is expected, since each of these sequences is geared toward public involve-ment in the creation and approval of the budget.

Reference Sources

Another factor that may affect the dominance of one decision-making framework over another is the type of reference sources accessed during budgetary deliberations. For example, do the deci-sion makers rely primarily on objective information (such as performance measures, which would be expected under the performance framework), or is there a bias toward gathering the subjective opinions of the citizenry (as would be preferred under the community values framework)? Re-spondents were asked to indicate the additional reference sources accessed in decision making. Table 11.3 depicts the percent of respondents that identified a particular source.

From this table, it is evident that the most common reference document was reported to be budget requests, followed by new statutory mandates concerning municipal programs. Notably, over three-quarters of the cities also regard performance measures and public testimony as impor-tant inputs when determining how to allocate resources. The choices listed in Table 11.3 reflect mostly objective data; however, nearly eight out of every ten cities reported placing importance on subjective information, such as citizens preferences conveyed through public testimony.

The respondents were given the opportunity to identify other resources, beyond those identified in Table 11.3, used in budget deliberations. Qualitative analysis of these responses reveals that the most frequent references were made to items relating to a larger planning process occurring outside

Table 11.4

Reference Sources and Budget Sequences Used in Texas Cities

	Symbolic (in percent)	Participative (in percent)
Budget requests	94	100
New statutory mandates	90	90
Performance measures	84	84
Public testimony	84	74
Audit results	63	74

Note: $N = 47$.

resource allocation, such as statements of goals and objectives, or a master plan for land use or capital improvements. Forecasts of revenues were cited as another information resource in budgetary deliberations. These forecasts, prepared in support of budget requests, can be viewed as another aspect in the overall planning process. This information supports the importance of linking planning processes with budgetary decision making as reflected in the Planning and Multi-planning sequences, providing further credence to the importance placed on coordinating these strategic management functions.

During the budget process reference sources are frequently used in combination, with more than 90 percent of cities indicating the simultaneous utilization of three or more of those listed. In fact, over one-half of all cities indicated that they consulted varying combinations of five different reference sources. Notably, the respondent from Waco indicated that the only reference source used in budget deliberations was performance measures; they *did not* select budget requests. On the other hand, respondents from Longview and Midland indicated that they used *only* budget requests and new statutory mandates.

As would be expected, the budget requests are used by all cities regardless of the budget sequence, except Waco, which uses the Council-only sequence. As shown in Table 11.4, consideration of new statutory mandates and performance measures was fairly high in all cities, regardless of budget sequence type. However, there were some surprises when considering other reference sources. For example, reference to public testimony was lowest in the participative types with only 74 percent of cities affirming the use of this form of information, whereas 84 percent of the Council-only and Council Public type sequences indicated public testimony was an important source of information. Inclusion of the public in these "symbolic" sequences is interesting since the budget sequence does not provide formal opportunities for this participation. Another unexpected finding was that audit results are used in less than two-thirds of cities with the symbolic sequences and less than three-fourths of the cities using the participative sequences.

Decision-Making Frameworks

The intent of this research was to gain a better understanding of the decision-making frameworks used in Texas cities. To accomplish this, the survey asked respondents to characterize how budgetary decisions are made in terms of the three frameworks. In considering the responses for the community values framework, it is important to remember that this choice can be interpreted to indicate decisions based on three different types of preferences—for example, the provision of only mandated services, the enrichment of the citizenry or the provision of a

Table 11.5

Dominant Decision-Making Frameworks in Texas Cities

Decision-making framework	Percent reporting framework
Incremental	11
Performance	13
Community values	13
Mixed (combination of 2)	32
Hybrid (all three)	32

Note: N = 47.

Table 11.6

Disaggregated Decision-Making Frameworks in Texas Cities

Decision-making model	Percent reporting framework
Incremental framework	53
Performance framework	68
Community values framework	75

Note: N = 47.

safety net. Descriptions given to the survey respondents to assist them in making their selections are provided below:

Incremental	Start with last year's budget and make minor changes
Performance	Examine current and desired performance levels
Community values	Provide funds for those services which government must provide

The results of this invitation to self-characterize indicate that respondents reported the least popular framework to be incremental (see Table 11.5). However, just over one-third of all participants identified just one decision-making approach. Of these, all three of the "pure" frameworks scored no higher than the low teens as a percent of total respondents. The decision-making approaches most frequently identified were a mixed framework that incorporates a combination of two of the three frameworks (32%) and a hybrid framework that incorporates aspects of all three frameworks (32%). These results suggest that municipalities are not limiting themselves to one approach, but rather moving toward more rationalism in the local budget process by blending the three models.[15]

Since responses for the mixed and hybrid frameworks indicated preferences for more than one of the three frameworks, these responses were recoded to analyze the relative prevalence of each of the three basic frameworks. The authors created a coding scheme for disaggregating this data. For example, if a city selected a mixed framework of both incremental and performance, it was coded as "yes" for the incremental framework, "yes" for the performance framework and "no" for the community values framework. Table 11.6 indicates rankings for each framework based on the disaggregated responses. One important conclusion that can be garnered from this table is that slightly less than one-half of the cities indicated that last year's budget is not the starting point and thus, the incremental framework is *not* used at all in their budget processes. This is interesting

Table 11.7

Decision-Making Frameworks and Budget Sequences in Texas Cities (in percent)

	Council-only (n = 4)	Council public (n = 15)	Public participation (n = 8)	Planning (n = 6)	Multi-planning (n = 5)
Incremental		13	13	17	
Performance	25	13		17	40
Community values	50		13	17	
Mixed		53	13	33	
Hybrid	25	20	63	17	60

given the large amount of literature that states that the politics of the incremental framework and budgeting are intermingled and one cannot function without the other. Further, as might be expected at the lowest levels of government, community values are considered by three-quarters of the responding cities.

Understanding Differences Between Cities

Beyond reporting the results obtained for individual variables such as the budget sequence, the number of participants, reference sources utilized, and the decision-making framework a city uses, it is important to examine combinations of these variables. Cross-tabulation procedures were utilized to investigate patterns in: (1) the budget sequence, (2) the number of participant groups, and (3) the kinds of reference sources utilized by type of decision-making framework.

When looking at the cross-tabulation of the budget sequence and the dominant decision-making framework, Table 11.7 indicates that those types that encourage public participation are using either the mixed or the hybrid sequence. The hybrid framework, which contained aspects of incremental, performance, and community values, was most likely to be reported by the Public Participation (63%) and the Multi-Planning (50%) types. The cities using the Planning sequence tended to favor a mixed sequence. The largest number of the Council Public types (53%) stated they use a mixed framework and a majority of the cities using the Council-only sequence favored the community values framework exclusively.

Analysis of the decision-making frameworks overlaid with the number of participant groups in the budgetary process revealed that the community values framework is the most participatory approach, with one-half of the responding cities indicating seven or more participant groups. This finding supports an emphasis on gathering feedback from the public on what the community values are and how they should be represented in city programs. However, as Table 11.8 shows, more than one-third of the cities using the mixed framework (emphasizing two of the three individual frameworks) reported that varying combinations of the "Big 4" are the only participants. In these cities, it is evident that citizen input into the budget approval process is generally not encouraged.

Another area of inquiry was the relationship between the types of reference sources used and the dominant decision-making framework for Texas cities. You would expect all cities employing the performance framework to make use of performance measures in the budget process. As shown in Table 11.9, this assumption was confirmed. Further, it was found that 88 percent of mixed and 93 percent of hybrid cities reported using this information. Another finding that would have been expected was that cities using the incremental and community values framework

Table 11.8

Decision-Making Frameworks and Participant Groups in Texas Cities

Number of groups	2	3	4	5	6	7	8
Incremental ($n = 5$)			20	40	20	20	
Performance ($n = 6$)			17	50		33	
Community values ($n = 6$)				33	17	33	17
Mixed ($n = 15$)	7		27	20	27	13	7
Hybrid ($n = 15$)		13		7	33	40	7

Note: Percent figures are row percents.

Table 11.9

Decision-Making Frameworks and Reference Sources in Texas Cities (in percent)

	Budget request	New statutory mandate	Performance measures	Public testimony	Audit result
Incremental ($n = 5$)	100	80	40	60	60
Performance ($n = 6$)	83	83	100	83	83
Community values ($n = 6$)	100	100	50	83	83
Mixed ($n = 15$)	100	87	88	80	60
Hybrid ($n = 15$)	100	93	93	80	73

reported the lowest level of consideration of performance measures at 40 and 50 percent, respectively. Another assumption of the research was that public testimony would be lowest for cities using the incremental framework. This assumption was also confirmed with only 60 percent of incremental cities reporting that they consider public testimony. The percent of cities using public testimony for every other framework was more than 80 percent.

Conclusion

This research proposes a budget sequence typology based on the perceptions of real world actors, as well as on theory. Beyond identifying the different types of budgetary processors preferred by the respondents from Texas, the typology also leads to the conclusion that though not standardized, the budget processes can be categorized to better understand participation of different stakeholders. In addition, it signals attempts to align strategic management functions such as planning and budgeting. Future research should systematically categorize the budget sequence in a larger sample of municipalities perhaps from more states and with cities of different sizes to confirm the five major types evident in the budget sequence continuum. In addition, perceptual data needs to be confirmed with what appears in the budget (to the degree that it reflects an "objective" reality).

Public participation is proving to be an important factor in budget deliberations with more than three-quarters of the respondents indicating that they use public testimony. The views of other stakeholders are also being sought, with a respectable 34 percent of cities indicating the inclusion of seven or more participant groups. An important finding of this research is that the inclusion of the participants is fairly strong in all budget sequence types and decision-making frameworks. This research indicates that, while the elected and appointed officials are still the major players in budgetary decision making, the role of other participants, in particular the public, is strong in many Texas cities. An interesting question arises when one asks: "What about cities that claim no citizen participation?" Future research needs to extend this work to discover patterns.

Overall, this research found that the decision-making framework that is most likely to be favored by the respondents in Texas cities is a combination one that incorporates aspects of the three frameworks originally proposed. That is, most cities attempt to incorporate the politicalness of incrementalism, the results orientation of the performance framework, and the utility maximization desired under the community values framework. Results from this research indicate that Texas cities are moving away from a single framework orientation as a rule and are incorporating more rational and participative aspects into their budget process. This refutes common wisdom on this topic and suggests a more complicated approach to decision making that emphasizes the injection of more objective performance-related data, as well as the subjective perceptions of nontraditionally dominant participant groups.

This research has uncovered some underlying patterns in the budgetary processes used by local governments in Texas. The results should be replicated with a larger sample of cities to overcome limitations caused by self-reported data and variations in the individual completing the survey. As noted earlier, there were duplicated responses received for roughly one-fourth of the cities included in this study. In assessing the degree of convergence of the responses, the largest differences were noted in the question concerning the dominant decision-making framework. In-depth analysis of these differences does not change the overall results: however, future research of this nature will also serve to increase validity and generalizability of the findings.

Results from this research can encourage dialogue between academics and public policy practitioners in understanding the dynamics of the multiple factors involved in budgetary decision making and further the development of innovative frameworks that have high utility. By providing insights into the resource allocation process, this research can be useful for understanding how cities can structure better budget processes to deal with competing priorities for limited funds.

Notes

1. Steven Falk, "When Budgeting, Focus on Value," *Public Management* 76 (1994): 20; Irene S. Rubin, *The Politics of Public Budgeting: Getting and Spending, Borrowing and Balancing* (Chatham, NJ: Chatham House, 1997).

2. Beverly S. Bunch and Jeffrey D. Straussman, "State Budgetary Processes: The Two Faces of Theory," *Public Budgeting & Finance* 5 (1993): 9–36; Donald Axelrod, *Budgeting for Modern Government*, 2d ed. (New York: St. Martin's Press, 1995).

3. Charles H. Levine, B. Guy Peters, and Frank J. Thompson, *Public Administration: Challenges, Choices, Consequences* (Chicago, IL: Scott Foresman, 1990).

4. U.S. Department of Commerce, Bureau of the Census. *County and City Data Book* (Atlanta, GA: U.S. Census Bureau, 1993 and 1983).

5. Similar to the overall population of Texas cities, the majority of responses were received from cities with less than 100,000 population ($n = 72\%$). Ten cities (21%) that responded had a population between 100,000 and 500,000, and three cities (6%) had a million or more residents. This is very close to the population with the following statistics, with 72, 24, and 4 percent, respectively. The majority of responses came from cities with the council-manager form of government ($n = 79\%$). Surveys returned from Mayor and Commission form of government cities represented 9 and 13 percent of the responses, respectively. Concerning the form of government, the sample percents exactly mirror the proportions found in the population.

6. Susan Welch and John Comer, *Quantitative Methods for Public Administration*, 2d ed. (Fort Worth, TX: Harcourt Brace, 1988); Anselm Strauss and Juliet Corbin, *Basics of Qualitative Research: Grounded Theory Procedures and Techniques* (Newbury Park, CA: Sage, 1990); John Brewer and Albert Hunger, *Multimethod*

Research: A Synthesis of Styles (Newbury Park, CA: Sage, Sage Library of Social Research, vol. 175, 1989); Floyd J. Fowler, Jr., *Survey Research Methods* (Newbury Park, CA: Sage, 1993).

7. W. Bartley Hildreth, "Financial Management: A Balancing Act for Local Chief Financial Officers," Public Administration Quarterly 20 (1996): 320–342. [Reprinted here as chapter 8.]

8. See, for example, William R. Shadish, Jr., Thomas D. Cook, and Laura C. Leviton, *Foundations of Program Evaluation: Theories of Practice* (Newbury Park, CA: Sage, 1991); or Aaron Wildavsky, "The Self-Evaluating Organization," *Public Administration Review* 32 (1972) 509–520; Douglas J. Watson, Robert J. Juster, and Gerald W. Johnson, "Institutionalized Use of Citizen Surveys in the Budgetary and Policy Making Process: A Small City Case Study," *Public Administration Review* 51 (190): 232–239. Literature has also examined the perception that the need for external input is low because of administrative expertise. See, for example, James Q. Wilson, *Bureaucracy: What Government Agencies Do and Why They Do It* (New York: Basic Books, 1989).

9. Robert D. Lee, Jr. "The Use of Program Analysis in State Budgeting," *Public Budgeting & Finance* 17 (Summer 1997): 18–36; Phillip G. Joyce, "Appraising Budget Appraisal: Can You Take Politics Out of Budgeting?" *Public Productivity & Management Review* 20 (June 1997): 384–396.

10. Mary M. Hale and Aimee L. Franklin, "Reevaluating Methods of Establishing Priorities for Governmental Services," *Public Productivity & Management Review* 20 (June 1997): 384–396.

11. The reader should note that there are other definitions or dimensions of the incremental framework contained in the literature. In fact, this concept is often the source of great debate. The operational definition for this research was a "political process that starts with last year's budget and makes minor changes." Aaron Wildavsky, *The New Politics of the Budgetary Process* (Chicago, IL: Scott Foresman, 1988).

12. Executive Office of the President, Bureau of the Budget, *Performance Reporting* (Washington, DC: Government Printing Office, 1950); Neil Carter, Rudolph Klein, and Patricia Day, *How Organizations Measure Success: The Use of Performance Indicators in Government* (London: Routledge, 1994); Public Law 103–92, and Steven D. Gold, ed., *The Fiscal Crisis of the States: Lessons for the Future* (Washington, DC: Georgetown University Press, 1995); John L. Mikesell, *Fiscal Administration: Analysis, and Applications for the Public Sector*, 4th ed. (Fort Worth, TX: Harcourt Brace, 1995).

13. J.M. Grace, *Philosophy of Public Philanthropy: A Conceptual Framework: A Report Prepared for the Tempe Community Council* (Tempe, AZ: Cultural and Human Service Agency Funding, 1995).

14. Axelrod, *Budgeting for Modern Government.*

15. The responses represent the attitudes and perceptions of those completing the survey. This represents a threat to the validity of the results since actual decision-making practices may be based on a different framework, although what people think occurs may be considered by some as a powerful proxy for what actually occurs.

CHAPTER 12

STATE AND LOCAL GOVERNMENTS AS BORROWERS:

Strategic Choices and the Capital Market

W. BARTLEY HILDRETH

State and local governments issue securities to obtain financing for publicly desired projects or activities. A borrower's optimum economic goal is to obtain the lowest cost of capital over the desired repayment schedule. The role of the government's chief financial officer is to design appropriate strategies to achieve this goal within a context of changing market conditions, debt structures, and influences on borrowing choices.

Once considered staid and consistent, state and local government debt instruments—collectively known as municipal securities—now are market-driven decisions. Municipal securities are structured in terms of maturity, denomination, interest (coupon) rate and other features to attract particular investor groups, such as mutual funds. Debt offerings are timed to meet market opportunities, not just the local financing agenda. Further, the security backing the debt is less the full taxing power of the borrower than the ability of an enterprise project to generate revenues to cover debt costs. Taken together, these, and other, practices reveal a dynamic financing arena compounding the search for funds.

Municipal securities have long enjoyed two distinctive qualities—their tax-exempt status and an absence of restrictive federal regulations. Both qualities are now threatened. Unique among investment options, municipal securities pay interest that is traditionally exempt from the U.S. income tax. Although Congress has restricted the tax exemption for certain types of uses over the last two decades, it was not until the U.S. Supreme Court's *South Carolina v. Baker* (1988) decision that it became clear that the Congress, not the Constitution, remains the benefactor of the federal income tax exemption. What Congress grants, it can take away. Although a deceptively simple statement on the surface, it means that Congress can avoid federal income tax losses (also known as tax expenditures) by further curbing or eliminating the tax-exempt nature of municipal securities. This could help generate funds to offset some of the federal budget deficit, but it would do so by abolishing a domestic market dedicated to financing programs and projects approved by state and local governments.

Limited federal regulatory oversight, another hallmark of the municipal market, is threatened also. While corporations face a web of securities laws, issuers of municipal securities have enjoyed little federal interference, short of an issuer committing fraud in a debt offering. The

From *Public Administration Review*, vol. 53, no. 1 (January/February 1993), pp. 41–49. Copyright © 1993 by American Society for Public Administraton. Reprinted with permission.

Securities and Exchange Commission (SEC), spurred by the $2.25 billion Washington Public Power Supply System (WPPSS) default, has turned its attention to the municipal market. Recently, SEC rules have been clarified to state that it is unlawful for investment banking firms to participate in most municipal debt offerings without first investigating the issuer's disclosure documents. The SEC is prohibited by the Tower Amendment of 1975 from *directly* regulating issuers. By placing the regulatory burden on the investment banking community, it is understood, and expected, that the effective burden rests with the governmental debt issuer and the adequacy of the issuer's disclosure documents. As a result of the SEC actions, national standardization of disclosure documents is in the offing.

This article reviews the municipal finance literature and practices to isolate the behavior of issuers. I first review the market behavior of issuers—specifically, differences in terms of the capacity to borrow and the costs of borrowing—and then discuss strategies appropriate to these market concerns. In the second part of the article, the focus is on issuer strategies relative to individuals or groups with a formal stake in state and local debt financing. Once public executives recognize these market features, they can adopt active financial management strategies to exploit the market on behalf of their taxpayers.

The Behavior of Issuers

Governmental jurisdictions are *not* created equal in their ability to borrow or in their cost of borrowing. As political scientist Sbragia (1983, 98) notes, the market is not a "redistributive or compensatory mechanism," rather it rewards the strong and greatly penalizes the weak. As a result, two basic issuance behaviors are observable. First, some issuers borrow more than other issuers. Second, some issuers borrow at lower costs than others.

The Capacity to Borrow

An issuer's capacity to borrow is neither absolute nor static. Rather, debt issuance varies, as tempered by incentives and disincentives. Incentives are based on the need for funds to secure physical assets that will enhance public services while also advancing political agendas and exploiting capital market opportunities.

A leading incentive to borrow arises from a preference to spend. The focus is on what can be purchased or constructed with the capital—physical assets such as buildings, highways, facilities, and other infrastructure items. Whereas capital improvement needs vary by jurisdiction, a series of recent studies document the nation's infrastructure needs (for example, National Council on Public Works Improvement 1988; Office of Technology Assessment 1990). Unmet needs represent a borrower's appetite for capital, if available on the right terms. Plus, the argument that public infrastructure investments have a positive influence on private productivity is the subject of a growing body of research (Cuciti 1991, for example).

Financing a project over time through borrowing overcomes the lack of sufficient up-front capital, a second incentive to borrow. An issuer could husband slack resources by forgoing immediate consumption in order to build a "savings" account. Few governmental entities finance capital improvements out of savings, however. Rather, most jurisdictions use one-time or yearly flows. An immediate and one-time infusion of capital results from external borrowing. In contrast, proceeds from an earmarked tax permit continual restocking of a capital investment account. The charter of Akron, Ohio, for example, dedicates for capital improvement purposes 27 percent of the yearly proceeds from the local income tax. Assured of a yearly base of financial support, capital improvement needs are further enhanced with bond proceeds and other revenue sources, especially federal and state project grants.

Third, borrowing engenders political capital. According to public-choice theory, politicians seek to maximize their self-interest, or reelection probability. The trade currency, political capital, is facilitated by the stock of funds generated from borrowing. In fact, current federal tax law encourages state and local governments to expend bond proceeds quickly, measured in months, thus stripping issuers of the option to borrow at low tax-exempt rates and then invest the bond proceeds in higher yielding taxable investments while delaying expenditure of bond funds— termed arbitrage. Furthermore, being able to construct new facilities, with repayment stretched out over several decades, creates a sort of fiscal illusion. This helps to explain the propensity for capital projects to become a "porkbarrel," or the trading of votes to support projects in various districts. Public choice theory postulates strong incentives to create debt. Research on governors and their propensity to issue debt confirms that debt issuance occurs in time to bolster reelection efforts (Baber and Sen 1986).

Exploiting a changing market constitutes a fourth incentive to borrow. Outstanding debt normally imposes a fixed debt-service cost on the issuer based on factors present at the time of borrowing. Market conditions change; contemporary and prospective views of the market may provide an opportunity to achieve interest savings beyond that found in the original issuance. One method requires calling in old debt at the earliest possible date, using proceeds generated from new debt issued at lower rates. Yet the original debt may contain provisions prohibiting the issuer from redeeming the security prior to its stated maturity, thus negating such a call. Issuers circumvent call restrictions by advance refunding—where funds generated by new debt (at lower rates) are placed in escrow to pay the old debt service as it comes due, not early as with a call. In recent years, debt refunding has accounted for one-fifth or more of the total volume of new bond issues (*Bond Buyer* 1991).

A listing of disincentives to borrow must include legal, political, and economic factors. Leading the list is the legal or structural limit, expressed either in absolute or relative terms. At first glance, it may seem that an absolute prohibition on borrowing is clear (either it is allowed or it is not), but exceptions are possible. For example, the State of Indiana is prohibited from issuing general obligation debt yet it enters the capital markets by having several statutory authorities finance infrastructure and economic development projects on its behalf.

A relative limit permits borrowing, but only up to a certain level. Debt ceilings require issuers to ration their debt appetite. For local governments, a typical ceiling is expressed as a percentage of the assessed value of property within a jurisdiction's boundaries. Issuers circumvent these limits by borrowing against project revenue-generation capability, expected streams of earmarked taxes (e.g., a sales or gasoline tax), or agreements to pay yearly lease payments equal to the debt service on a public-use facility.

To have excess legal capacity to borrow means little if political hurdles are not overcome, a second disincentive to borrow. Gaining approval for a particular debt issuance requires governing-body support, and, where applicable, voter approval and state validation. Navigating these hurdles requires a combination of consensus decision making, careful timing, skilled marketing, and legal preciseness. Generally, voter approval is the most uncertain of the legal hurdles that must be addressed.

Third, an economic disincentive to borrow is the obvious requirement to pay back the borrowed funds, with interest. With a diversified, growing local economy, issuers can borrow against a future, larger tax base. In contrast, some jurisdictions face liquidity problems in handing current spending, much less repaying past borrowing or incurring more long-term obligations. This is especially a problem if no new taxes are levied to support the new borrowing or the tax base is not diversified or growing. This burden to repay requires prospective borrowers to temper their debt creation activities. Confirmation that issuers perform some capital rationing and control is the fact that no general obligation bonds are known to have defaulted since the Great Depression (Davidson 1991). The widespread fiscal stress of state and local governments in the early 1990s warrants careful monitoring, however. Of course, this does not convey much, if anything, about the cost of debt.

The Cost of Borrowing

The market behavior of issuers is characterized by a second phenomena: some issuers borrow at lower costs than other issuers. Why? Although a quick (and incorrect) answer is that the credit rating assigned to the issue greatly determines the interest rate, the rating is really more the result than the cause. Besides, the yields of individual tax-exempt bonds are determined by many variables, including many outside the issuer's control (Cook 1982). This chapter focuses on issuer experience, bidding competition for its debt, frequency, and market competition.

First, debt issuers benefit from market experience. Bland (1985) demonstrates that up to a point, the more experience a municipality has with debt financing, the more likely the municipality will generate interest rate savings. He places the upper limit to this benefit of experience at four prior sales within a ten-year period.

Second, state and local governments benefit from more competition for their bonds. As demand for an issue's securities increase, the issuer's cost of borrowing declines (Cook 1982).

Third, the frequency of the borrowing can impact borrowing costs. One strategy calls for frequent market entries. Lennox Moak, the dean of municipal finance, advocated sales of identical security at intervals of not less than six months (Moak 1982, 161). Consistent with this advice, a study of the secondary market for New York City debt concluded that the city should "establish itself as a seasoned and reliable issuer" (Financial Control Board 1984, 4). A contrasting view emerges from a study of smaller jurisdictions (Bland 1984) in which infrequent issuers gained interest rate savings. The greatest savings accrued to two groups—infrequent issuers borrowing less than half a million dollars and infrequent issuers borrowing large amounts. Based on the research, Bland (1984) advises issues to delay entry into the market until various needs are bundled into a larger, omnibus debt package.

Fourth, an issuer receives a penalty for timing a sale in conflict with other issuers, especially those selling larger amounts. When competitive bids are due at or near the same time for more than one issue within a broad market, issuers are likely to receive fewer bids than might otherwise be the case. This exacerbates some issuer's problems since research reveals that lower rated bonds tend to receive fewer bids, and the bids received have less dispersion (or range) in rates, resulting in higher borrowing costs (Cook 1982).

Although the credit rating services point out that the debt issue determines the rating, higher credit ratings are associated with lower borrowing costs. In addition to designing the bond structure, an issuer has choices in how and when it will sell its bonds, factors that also influence the cost of borrowing.

Relationships and Strategies

Given the fact that most state and local governments can borrow funds under specified circumstances and that their needs vary, opportunities exist for some jurisdictions to adopt deliberate capital market strategies. Identifying debt issuance strategies by following the debt issuance process (i.e., identifying the need, structuring the offering, gaining approval, selling the debt, etc.) is one approach. An alternative approach, and the one adopted here, tracks issuer strategies for dealing with the various participants in the debt issuance process.

Strategic management is premised on purposeful behavior and the recognition that others can have an affect on organizational results (Hildreth 1989). This premise is bolstered by several lines of thinking. Interest group theory holds that public decisions are influenced by an often-shifting set of interested parties. Network political economy, as recently extended into state and local debt issuance by Miller and Hildreth (1988), posits that the various participants involved in a borrowing may have conflicting goals and that results of this team effort may differ from the expectations of a single team member, such as the issuer. This highlights the need to explore in more detail the financing perspectives of each debt issuance participant, such as the executive in charge of the public treasury. Applying Freeman's (1984) stakeholder model of strategic management, government finance executives must deal actively with individuals or organizations who can influence, or be influenced by, achievement of the jurisdiction's objectives. This approach follows the public management school of thinking by assessing debt management choices from the executive's viewpoint, in this case the chief financial officer. Therefore, this chapter attempts to define the need for purposeful behavior on the part of the issuer relative to key participants in capital acquisition. Employing the term participants instead of stakeholders is not meant to signify significant differences in concept, rather it is to follow standard terminology in the debt issuance domain.

Strategies for Dealing with Participants

The municipal market works because of the interactions of various participants. A state or local government, as an issuer, sells a debt instrument or security to an underwriter (also called an investment banker), who then resells the security to an investor (also known as a bondholder). The investor, therefore, loans capital to an issuer; in return, the issuer agrees to pay the investor an agreed-upon interest rate (usually semi-annually) and, upon maturity, to repay the principal.

Several other participants enter into the debt process. A paying agent (or trustee) serves as the conduit for the flow of interest and principal payments between the issuer and the investor. A bond counsel advises the issuer on how to meet all legal requirements to borrow and provides a legal opinion to the investor that the debt instrument meets state and local laws and federal tax law standards. Many governments employ financial advisors to assist in defining capital needs and in structuring and completing the deal. Early in the process, citizens may have to approve the planned borrowing. A state oversight board may have to give its approval. If the issuer desires anything more than local bidders or private placement, private credit rating firms must have an opportunity to pass judgment on the probability of debt repayment.

The issuer has an opportunity to influence each participant's actions and decisions. A review of research and practice will help isolate issuer behaviors.

Issuers

Issuers face many institutional and market hurdles in the borrowing process. A market penalty is assessed for poor timing, as discussed earlier. Most issuers face a lag time (often measured in months) between a decision to borrow and the actual date of borrowing, especially if voter approval is required and the issue is competitively offered for sale. To elude these structural hurdles, issuers utilize several avoidance strategies.

First, to sidestep the hurdles imposed on general obligation borrowing, issuers turn to revenue bonds. During the 1980s, revenue bonds constituted over 65 percent of the yearly dollar volume of municipal bonds (Figure 12.1). By the first half of 1992, revenue bonds had fallen back to pre-1980 levels but still exceeded the issuance of general obligation bonds. Revenue bonds, to a much greater extent than general obligation bonds, may serve as a strategic tool for municipalities facing fiscal strain or limits (Sharp 1986). This is consistent with the extensive expansion of special districts and other statutory authorities—often termed off-budget entities—empowered to issue revenue bonds without placing at direct risk the taxing capacity, or full-faith-and-credit guarantee. In fact, many off-budget entities serve as "conduits," defined as a governmental issuer of securities with an ultimate credit source being a private profit-making or nonprofit organization (Zimmerman 1991). The revenue bond market segment also represents municipalities borrowing in anticipation of future revenue flows (such as collections from nonproperty tax sources such as sales taxes); debt backed by planned, but not guaranteed, lease payments (including certificates of participation); and, other creative security arrangements.

Second, creative debt instruments help issuers take advantage of changing market demands. For instance, where future interest rates are expected to be higher, investors demand a premium to tie up their money in maturities of twenty to thirty years. Issuers who are unwilling to pay the price to sell these long securities can instead sell shorter maturities. Instruments such as variable rate securities allow issuers to borrow long but at near short-term rates.

In many instances, issuers have the authority to sell yearly bond anticipation notes (BANs) as a source of interim financing for capital projects during the construction period. Upon project completion, the expected strategy is to convert the capital financing from short-term notes (BAN) into long-term bonds. Issuers may deviate from this expected conversion strategy. Given that short-term rates are historically lower than long-term rates and that on occasion (such as the early 1980s) long-term rates hover in the double-digits, short-term financing seems sensible, even for completed projects as long as the tax laws permit such practices.

One manifestation of this economic environment is that issuers may roll over BANs year after year to avoid the long-term market, where allowed by law, such as in Ohio. The intended strategy is to wait out the market. However, the more times BANs are rolled over, the more difficult it is for an issuer to obtain interest rate reductions sufficient to offset the accumulated, capitalized interest costs.

A contrary strategy is that by delaying entry into the long-term market, the borrower accrues interest cost savings. As noted earlier, Bland (1985) found evidence supporting this delayed entry strategy. However, his study did not take into account the situation where the prospective *bond* issuer may be incurring and capitalizing interest costs during the delay period by issuing *notes*. Delay imposes costs, not just benefits (Choate 1980).

To be successful, issuers must gain a competitive advantage over other issuers. This is best reflected in the timing of the sale or in the pricing of the offering. As might be expected, timing finesse is easier to accomplish if the choice is negotiated pricing rather than announcing and, after a specified number of days, holding a competitive auction.

Issuers using competitive auctions must be willing to terminate the sale at the last minute by rejecting all bids if the market undergoes a significant change in direction. A highly elastic relationship exists between increases in interest rates and the volume of issuer cancellations and delays (U.S. General Accounting Office 1983). Market conditions can be systemic to all markets or peculiar to the municipal market. Instances of market volatility include legislative consideration to tax interest payments of municipal bondholders in 1968, tax reform initiatives in early 1986; stock market disruptions in 1989, and war news in 1991. A long-set auction consummated at the time of volatility in the market may quickly close favorable windows of opportunity to

Figure 12.1   **Trends in Municipal Securities, 1975–1992**

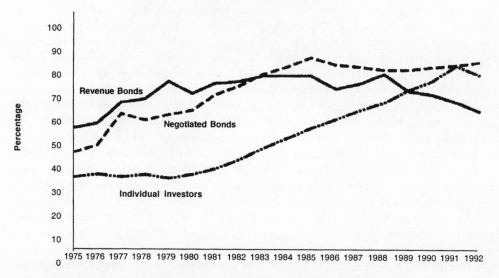

Sources: Bond Buyer, various dates; Board of Governors of the Federal Reserve System, *Flow of Funds Accounts,* Washington, DC, various dates.
Note: Reflects data for first half of 1992.

borrow, resulting in higher than expected borrowing costs. Either canceling a sale at the last minute or rejecting all bids is a serious step. Compelling reasons may exist for proceeding with a sale, especially if the time required to restart the issuance process is long, imposing still further uncertainty and risk.

Traditionally, state and local governments give notice of their plans to issue securities weeks ahead of time, specifying the date and time when bids to purchase are due. New York's Local Finance Law (Section 58.00[2]) breaks with tradition by permitting its municipal corporations to announce to the market a thirty-day window within which the auction may be made. Within this period and with forty-eight hours notice, the municipal corporation can set the time and date for the auction. Alternatively, the issuer can set a time and date for the auction and retain the option to make a change in time and date if done at least forty-eight hours prior to the time originally scheduled. The new schedule has to be with forty-eight hours notice, too. These options permit a borrowing jurisdiction to time its auction with more sensitivity to market conditions, a hallmark of negotiated sales.

Investors

Historically, an issuer had little interest in knowing who actually held its securities, for several reasons. First, issuers sell the security to the underwriter, who then markets them to investors. As a result, the issuer does not deal directly with investors at the sale nor does the issuer know the pool of likely investors, especially individual investors. The common view of the market holds that underwriters serve as salesmen to get a product of demand (by the investor) from a supplier (an issuer) and, in the process, make a transaction profit (measured in fractions of the total value) by linking the buyer with the seller.

A second reason for an issuer's historical inattention to investors is due to the fact that even after the sale, issuers could not find out, even if they inquired, who actually owned the securities. Until 1982, municipal bonds were negotiable instruments, meaning that the last holder could redeem the security with little fear of contrary evidence of ownership. As a result, the issuer had no record of all investors in its securities. The Tax Equity and Fiscal Responsibility Act of 1982 changed the rules, however. Now all municipal securities over one year in maturity must be registered. Although not mandatory for previously issued securities, the investment banking community has responded by converting bearer securities into registered form whenever the securities are traded or come into the possession of institutional investors.

Because issuers are more prone to take an interest in their investors if they know their names, new strategies are possible. Issuers now develop debt issuance plans based on current and prospective investors' interests because the segmentation of the municipal market means investor clienteles are different for short- and long-maturity bonds (Poterba 1986). Tax-exempt mutual funds, for example, need a stock of relatively short-term maturities. Tax-exempt bond funds also are major buyers of municipal securities. The growth of holdings by individuals and mutual funds combined was steady, and pronounced, into the 1990s (Figure 12.1). The early 1992 data reflect competition for tax-exempt income from the remaining holders, including banks and insurance companies.

New financial products, such as "minibonds," allow governmental jurisdictions to alter this bifurcated relationship between issuers and investors. A minibond is a small denomination debt instrument (in $100 or $1,000 units) sold directly to customers. This type of product appears to retail customers, allowing the borrowing government to attract investors it might otherwise be unable to attract.

A more involved investor relations program can help issuers. Some issuers develop strategies to appeal directly to institutional investors, perhaps attempting to offset the perceived, overly critical, bond-rating agencies. Issuers attempt to convey that their credit is stronger than the bond ratings might otherwise suggest. Basically, an issuer seeks to let institutional investors know that it is attentive to the needs of large investors.

Recognizing their market strength, representatives of institutional investors (such as mutual fund companies and insurance firms) along with market analysts from investment banking firms have initiated efforts to require debt issuing jurisdictions to enhance the disclosure of information that might influence the pricing and trading of bonds in the secondary market (that is, after a bond has been issued but before it matures). A key step in this movement is to get issuers to certify that they will satisfy these continuing disclosure concerns, under the implicit threat that this segment of the investor community will not buy the bonds otherwise (Ciccarone 1992). This is important to an issuer because a shrinkage in demand means the cost to issue debt will rise, all other things being equal.

Underwriters

Investment banking firms underwrite the purchase and resale of the securities. Underwriters, as they are called, provide issuers with informed market access because most U.S. state and local issuers tend to rely on outsiders to gauge the market's interest in their securities. Issuers can use competitive auctions to ensure that the bids received from underwriters reflect current market assessments. The overwhelming evidence reveals that competitive bidding promotes more efficient market pricing, meaning that an issuer's interest costs decline as the number of bidders increase (Cook 1982).

A negotiated sale is one where the issuer selects an underwriter to conduct the debt issuance.

This segment of the market has grown to almost 75 percent of all financings (see Figure 12.1). A long line of research indicates that issuers pay an interest rate premium to negotiate the sale rather than to offer it for competitive sale (Cook 1982). Bland shows, however, that an *experienced issuer* (measured by prior market entries) can use negotiation to achieve an interest rate comparable to competitive bid rates (Bland 1985). This finding holds up only if there is little bidding competition, calculated at three bids. So, if the experienced issuer expects more than three bids, then a competitive sale is likely to result in the lowest cost; if the experienced issuer expects no competition for the bonds, then a negotiated sale is less costly. For first-time or very infrequent debt issuers, Bland's advice is to sell "bonds through competitive bidding in order to avoid the heavy penalty placed on inexperience if negotiation is used" (237).

Competitive auctions as practiced in the United States means the underwriter individually or in a group (called a syndicate) bids for all the bonds in the offering. Inzer and Reinhart (1984) suggest that issuers should change this practice and allow the underwriter to bid on parts of the offering, not just the whole offering. This change would allow underwriters to select the optimal bonds for their clients. For this tiered-bidding system to work, however, the issuer would have to assume the risk of having no bidders for particular maturities, resulting in less than the desired amount of proceeds from the sale. To mitigate this result, the issuer would need flexibility in the amount to be offered at each maturity. By accepting more uncertainty, including the exact amount of debt proceeds, Inzer and Reinhart postulate that the issuer should receive lower interest costs, all other things considered. Two recent Nevada bond sales tested the tiered-bidding theory with favorable results. In 1989, the State of Nevada offered $48.7 million in three distinct series of maturity, with separate bids required on each. Interest savings of $36,000 were achieved when two underwriting syndicates bought different parts versus the cost if the syndicate winning two had also won the third series (Lamiell 1989). A Nevada school district used a similar sales structure in 1990, lowering its borrowing cost by more than $160,000 (Walters 1990).

Financial Advisors

A financial advisor, if employed, serves as an issuer's impartial consultant on structuring and selling securities. When an issuer auctions general obligation bonds, the services of a financial advisor are in addition to those of the underwriter. With negotiated sales, the underwriters have the responsibility to optimize debt structure and pricing, both from an issuer's and the underwriter's standpoint. This reduces, but does not entirely eliminate, the need for an independent financial advisor.

Financial advisors press for long-term, comprehensive debt strategy consultations not just the traditional transaction-driven service based on each debt issuance. Issuers utilize financial advisors to "work-out" financial difficulties (such as Cleveland's note default and the recurring fiscal problems in Detroit and Philadelphia) and to enhance market perceptions (such as Boston's multi-year strategy of redefining its economic image). The visibility of financial advisors was most strikingly demonstrated in Philadelphia where, in 1991, a locally based, but nationally known, financial advisor campaigned, but was defeated, in a bid for election as mayor. His failed campaign emphasized his skills in municipal finance. After the election, the victorious mayoral candidate quickly appointed the (defeated) financial advisor's firm to spearhead a review of city finances and to serve as its ongoing financial advisor. By working with the issuer to advance broad fiscal agendas, financial advisors expand their scope of services.

Independent financial advisors seek to segment their industry, separating themselves from investment banking firms providing financial advisory services. A new national association of

independent financial advisory firms is dedicated to enhancing the level of professional credentials of its members and to marketing to issuers the need for independent financial advisors. An
issuer has to realize net economic benefits from such advice (savings in borrowing costs to offset
fees paid to financial advisors) or the total cost of issuance increases as financial advisory fees are
combined with the underwriter's cost, bond rating agency fees, bond counsel fees, and other
transaction expenses.

Bond Counsels

A bond counsel plays a critical role in an issuer's attempt to obtain underwriter and investor
interest in an issue. When tax laws are uncertain, bond counsels hesitate to issue an opinion on
the tax-exempt status of bonds. As the events of early 1986 demonstrated, the market expects a
bond counsel to help screen out unacceptable risks. In early 1986, the United States Senate held
without action the House-passed tax reform bill that included a retroactive effective date of
January 1, 1986, along with significant limits on debt issuance and use of bond proceeds. The
market demanded assurances that issuers would comply with current law, proposed law (that in
the House bill), and potential law (that which had not yet been voted upon). Needless to say,
bond lawyers hesitated to take such a step toward unknown accountability. Because of those
tax-law uncertainties, many issuers were unable to take advantage of an otherwise favorable
interest rate market.

Bond counsel expertise enhances an issuer's financial agenda. A bond counsel can point out
seemingly small nuances in the law permitting the desired public purpose to be debt financed.
Whether the goal is to further a joint public-private capital investment venture or to provide
street lights in nonincorporated areas of a county, presumed legal restrictions are prone to new
interpretations and tests.

When a debt issue is embedded in trouble, the bond counsel can be part of the problem as well
as part of the solution. As bond counsel of record on a bond issue facing imminent technical or
actual default, the bond counsel faces the potential of a liability suit by bondholders, as those
associated with the WPPSS defaulted bonds found out. If a troubled debt issue is dealt with early
enough, the bond counsel can serve as a powerful ally in designing a remedy. Given that the bond
counsel is at risk too, it can work to the issuer's advantage. Because the major bond counsel firms
are also some of the more prominent legal firms in a particular state, if not the region or nation,
their influence runs throughout the various seats of power. For an issue facing troubled times,
bond counsel efforts to secure interlocal, state, and/or federal legislation or assistance can rebound to the jurisdiction's benefit.

Trustees

A paying agent, generally a financial institution, is selected by the issuer to receive and disburse
coupon and principal payments to bondholders. For revenue bonds, however, the same, or a
different financial institution, enters into a more complicated legal duty on behalf of bondholders, serving as a fiduciary to ensure that the issuer follows all bond indenture requirements.

Although all is fine as long as the debt issuer pays principal and interest as specified, the
trustee's role expands as trouble looms. In scenarios concerning troubled revenue bonds, the
trustee must take care to act as if the assets were his own—a fiduciary role (Sawicki 1985). In such
cases, the trustee weighs the consequences of asserting remedial powers, such as to assume
management of the debt-financed project or to "pull the plug"—that is, to declare the bonds due

and payable immediately. In such a situation, an issuer may attempt to position the trustee so that the trustee's success depends upon a cooperative relationship with the issuer instead of the adversarial one envisioned by the remedial powers provisions of the indenture.

By the nature of their position, trustees often detect a change in a debt issuer's repayment status before many others, especially bondholders. A trustee's duty is to report to current (registered) bondholders. By design this gives sellers of the outstanding bonds a market advantage over buyers because of information asymmetrics. To counter this secondary market problem, the trustee industry group (a part of the American Banking Association) encourages its members to provide broad market disclosure of significant events or developments, not just provide the information to current bondholders.

Credit Rating Agencies

Credit rating agencies are paid by the debt issuer to provide an assessment of its risk of nonpayment of borrowed funds. More practically, rating agencies serve as de facto gatekeepers to the broad municipal bond market. For inexperienced or inadequately qualified issuers, either the expected or the actual decision of credit raters can effectively bar an issuer's market entry. Thus, bond ratings are not sought by all debt issuers. Some issuers acknowledge their negative market qualities and rely upon local investors (e.g., local banks), not the broad market of investors. For example, private-purpose revenue bonds, small-sized general obligation bonds, public purpose revenue bonds, and short-term notes often are placed with local investors. If an issuer desires or needs access to the national, or even regional, public market of investors, then an investment-quality rating (the top four rating levels, "Baa" or higher) is necessary. The rating is necessary for both the initial offering of the debt as well as throughout the life of the debt, if the issuer expects any secondary market for that or any future debt issue.

Although credit rating agencies are unlikely to acknowledge their role as market gatekeepers, issuers follow behavioral patterns that substantiate this observation. The hurdle of achieving an investment-quality credit rating leads to at least two observable sets of behavior by issuers: to attempt to *influence* the rating process and/or to *avoid* the rating process, or a part of it.

Avoidance of the credit rating process appears uninviting for all but the smallest issuers. Although a quarter of all municipal bonds are unrated, the total dollar volume of such bonds makes up less than 10 percent of the entire municipal bond market (Petersen 1989). This means there are numerous small dollar-sized bond issues that avoid the rating process.

With two private rating services dominating the market, a second avoidance strategy is to have a single rating, either to avoid a rating agency perceived to be overly critical or merely to stand on the basis of one rating. As to the preference for one credit rating service over another, the two dominant bond rating services enjoy similar dollar volume market shares (Petersen 1989). Furthermore, to assume that one rating saves money is contrary to research that suggests that a second rating lowers an issuer's borrowing cost, even if the ratings are different (Hsueh and Kidwell 1988). In fact, while only about 40 percent of new issues carry ratings from *both* Moody's and Standard & Poor's, this group represents almost 70 percent of the total dollar volume of the municipal market (Petersen 1989).

An issuer has a third option, avoiding a direct rating on its credit quality, in essence, by leasing the credit of a higher-rated institution. Credit enhancement takes the form of bond insurance or a letter of credit facility, whereby a third party guarantees debt service. Bondholders gain added security from the third-party guarantor's credit. Bond insurance also offers economic benefits to issuers (Quigley and Rubinfeld 1991). Research indicates that issuers expecting a rating below the second highest rating class ("Aa") should consider credit enhancement (Reid 1990). As might be expected then, the market for credit enhancement services has grown in recent years (*Bond Buyer* 1991).

Most debt issues carry a bond rating, either their own or a borrowed credit. In fact, a three-year study of debt concluded that only one in ten issues (amounting to 2 percent of the dollar volume) did not enjoy a credit rating either directly or indirectly. Those without some form of credit rating were small issues, averaging $1 million dollars in size (Petersen 1989, 25, 28).

A fourth avoidance behavior is to sell a short-term note to local investors without a rating. The issuer preserves the option to request a rating at some later point, especially at the time of conversion into a bond. An advantage of rolling over the yearly note for several years is that it offers the jurisdiction time to take steps to position itself in a better credit light. Yet rating agencies now assign ratings to notes and look upon increasing amounts of short-term debt in negative terms.

Avoidance of bond ratings may be in the best interests of small governments, for several reasons (Sullivan 1983; Palumbo and Sacks 1987). First, for small-sized bond issues, the fee to obtain a bond rating is a cost of issuance that may not be adequately recovered in interest savings. Second, small governments are unlikely to receive high bond ratings, especially for general obligation bonds. Higher bond ratings are associated with larger-dollar-sized amounts and larger-sized population centers. Thus, small and rural governments face systematic adverse market assessment of credit worthiness (Palumbo and Sacks 1987). Yet in an odd twist, small, rural governments do not have to overcome as much investor suspicion as those borne by a larger jurisdiction. Unlike larger debt issuers who rely on a national investor base, small government bonds often are bought locally; these local investors must trust their own assessment of the debt issuer's credit quality. Thus, a small government may avoid a bond rating and still obtain a reasonable rate of borrowing because local investors know that government's capabilities (Sullivan 1983, 110).

An issuer attempts to *influence* the bond rating decision by enhancing its arguments and the security of the planned issue. Measures to enhance the security backing an issue range from obtaining a third-party guarantee to tightening the financial package, such as putting more up as collateral (e.g., an earmarked sales tax plus sewer user fees for a revenue bond). A guarantee can take the form of a standby letter of credit (primarily for short-term borrowing), a state program (as in Texas where the oil-land-enriched Permanent Fund guarantees local school district borrowings), or private bond insurance. Although a third-party guarantee results in the highest credit rating (an automatic "Aaa" rating in most cases), it does not guarantee that the issuer will borrow at levels commensurate with the highest rating (Bland 1987; Reid 1990).

To enhance its credit quality arguments, an issuer has to document the political, financial, and managerial control necessary to achieve effective public services. This is achieved through such actions as tight financial controls, protection of fund balances, adoption of generally accepted accounting principles (GAAP), adherence to strong financial disclosure practices, and maintenance of political consensus. These steps represent an issuer's preventive or preemptive strategy for dealing with bond rating agencies. That is, issuers attempt to anticipate, and then implement, the more obvious fiscal management policies and practices that credit analysts consider indicators of strong management quality (Doppelt 1985). Generally, actions taken to influence an issuer's credit standing are also effective fiscal management. However, as Detroit was recently told by Moody's Investors Service, strong fiscal management will not offset the negative credit implications of the lack of viable private economic activity (Peirog 1992). Strong economic activity and diversification are the keys to a high bond rating (Loviscek and Crowley 1990).

As part of an enhancement strategy, issuers seek to maintain close contact with the rating agencies to foster harmonious relations and timely disclosure of relevant information. To help advance the spirit of continuous disclosure, issuers share with rating analysts news that could be interpreted as having either positive or negative impact on credit quality. This nurturing of a relationship is very noticeable in the tendency of governors and mayors to visit the raters and to recognize the political, as well as financial, importance of debt strategies, given the credit raters' ability to issue a locally perceived negative or positive signal, as retold by the local media.

Voters, Monitors, and Controllers

Issuers with a requirement to obtain voter or state approval for debt issuance can attempt to influence or avoid some, or all, of these barriers. Voters tend to approve bond elections, at least in terms of a national aggregate trend (*Bond Buyer* 1991). Notwithstanding historical approval trends, some issuers cannot obtain voter approval despite repeated attempts. Needless to say, each bond approval referendum requires a particular marketing campaign. An effective strategy for voter approval tends to be built around a higher perceived, but justified, need coupled with a political-style campaign to motivate citizens to vote for the proposal within a political environment of fiscal trust and accountability.

Issuers show a propensity to avoid onerous debt hurdles, if possible. This is reflected in efforts to: (1) use less-encumbered financing sources, or (2) take steps to remove some of the restrictions. One opportunity arises when the restrictions on issuing revenue bonds are less than those for general obligation bonds. For example, Louisiana local governments must obtain voter approval for general obligation bonds but not for sales-tax-backed revenue bonds; as a result, revenue debt outstanding is significantly higher than general obligation debt. The incentive to utilize revenue bonds is intense in such situations.

Another issuer strategy is to circumvent debt limits. Often this can be accomplished by using "off the debt schedule" financing, such as lease-purchase deals, certificates of participation (COP), or loans from statutory authorities (i.e., a state-created financial conduit agency that issues revenue bonds to generate proceeds to loan to other governmental jurisdictions).

California local governments became major users of COPs because of Proposition 13 restrictions. This innovation spread widely across the country. As the recession of the early 1990s accelerated, investors in COPs grew nervous as public officials publicly questioned the requirement to continue appropriating funds to repay the COPs, knowing that investor comfort in the bonds comes from the issuer's agreement, but not legal requirement, to appropriate yearly funds to repay the investors. This concern was well founded given the 1991 COP default by the Richmond (California) Unified School District and the state's belated questioning of the legality of such borrowing.

Some issuers have two sets of general obligation debt issuance powers. One is greatly restricted in dollar amounts but requires only the governing body's approval—termed unvoted debt in Ohio, for example. The other requires voter approval but has a high ceiling of available borrowing power—termed voted debt in Ohio. Public officials prefer, of course, the flexibility associated with debt merely requiring the approval of the governing body. Thus, one strategy is to carefully select certain projects for placing before the voters, those more attractive and characterized by political consensus. The unvoted debt capacity is reserved for projects where timing is of the essence or the likelihood of voter approval is more suspect. Rationing within the unvoted-debt capacity becomes a significant fiscal strategy. Effective management of the unvoted-debt capacity requires the imposition of internal capital hurdle rules to avoid depleting the slack capacity too quickly.

In summary, issuers adopt strategies to circumvent debt monitors, including the voters. The problem with this behavior is that public officials focus more on how to manipulate state and local debt restrictions than on effective strategies for matching capital needs to the market and the price for borrowed funds (Sbragia 1979; Peterson 1990). In the end, such debt strategies may prove successful, but the issuer may pay the price in significant interest rate differentials whether it is due to delay, issuance of revenue bonds, or other factors.

Conclusion

This chapter suggests that issuers of state and local government securities have an optimum capital goal—to obtain the lowest cost of capital over the desired repayment schedule—and that this goal is achieved through strategic choices. I discussed strategies built around the phenomena that issuers differ in their capacity to borrow and in borrowing costs. I also reviewed selected strategies for an issuer to manage its own financial agenda in the municipal market. Some issuer strategies have the benefit, if successful, of generating interest rate savings while other strategies have less precise economic benefits for the issuer. The research on debt strategies is sporadic at best. More empirical work is required.

While this chapter is only an exploratory discussion of issuer strategy, one point seems to emerge: issuers should follow deliberate capital strategies instead of allowing capital decisions to evolve out of inattention, being unduly swayed by others in the debt issuance process, or incremental decision making. A mistake in this management area stays with the community for many years to come, as long as the debt is outstanding.

References

Baber, William R., and Pradyot K. Sen. 1986. "The Political Process and the Use of Debt Financing by State Governments." *Public Choice* 48, no. 3: 201–215.

Bland, Robert L. 1984. "The Interest Savings from Optimizing Size and Frequency of Participation in the Municipal Bond Market." *Public Budgeting and Finance* 4 (Winter): 53–59.

———. 1985. "The Interest Cost Savings from Experience in the Municipal Bond Market." *Public Administration Review* 45 (January/February): 233–237.

———. 1987. "The Interest Cost Savings from Municipal Bond Insurance: The Implications for Privatization." *Journal of Policy Analysis and Management* 6, no. 2: 207–219.

Bond Buyer. 1991. *1991 Yearbook.* New York: Thomson.

Choate, Pat. 1980. *As Time Goes By: The Costs and Consequences of Delay.* Columbus, OH: Academy for Contemporary Problems.

Ciccarone, Richard A. 1992. "Municipal Disclosure: A Question of Intentions." *Municipal Finance Journal* 13, no. 1 (Spring): 68–71.

Cook, Timothy Q. 1982. "Determinants of Individual Tax-Exempt Bond Yields: A Survey of the Evidence." *Federal Reserve Bank of Richmond Economic Review* (May/June): 14–39.

Cuciti, Peggy. 1991. "Infrastructure and the Economy: Serious Debate in the Profession." *Municipal Finance Journal* 12, no. 4 (Winter): 73–81.

Davidson, R.B. 1991. "A Framework for Analyzing Municipal Quality Spreads." *Municipal Finance Journal* 12, no. 3 (Fall).

Doppelt, Amy. 1985. "Assessing Municipal Management." *Standard & Poor's Creditweek*, March 4.

Financial Control Board. 1984. *The Performance of New York City Bonds in the Secondary Market.* New York: New York State Financial Control Board.

Freeman, R. Edward. 1984. *Strategic Management: A Stakeholder Approach.* Boston, MA: Pitman.

Hildreth, W. Bartley. 1989. "Financing Strategy." In *Handbook of Strategic Management*, ed. Jack Rabin, Gerald J. Miller, and W. Bartley Hildreth. New York: Marcel Dekker, pp. 279–300.

Hsueh, L. Paul, and David S. Kidwell. 1988. "Bond Ratings: Are Two Better Than One?" *Financial Management* 17, no. 1 (Spring): 46–53.

Inzer, Robert B., and Walter J. Reinhart. 1984. "Rethinking Traditional Municipal Bond Sales." *Government Finance* 13 (June): 25–29.

Lamiell, Patricia. 1989. "Around the Nation: Nevada." *Bond Buyer* (January 24): 24.

Loviscek, Anthony L., and Frederick D. Crowley. 1990. "What Is in a Municipal Bond Rating?" *Financial Review* 25, no. 1 (February): 25–53.

Miller, Gerald J., and W. Bartley Hildreth. 1988. "The Municipal Debt Financing as a Network Political Economy: Network Stability and Market Efficiency." Paper presented at the Annual Meeting of the American Political Science Association, Washington, DC (September).

Moak, Lennox, L. 1982. *Municipal Bonds: Planning, Sale and Administration.* Chicago: Municipal Finance Officers Association.

National Council on Public Works Improvement. 1988. *Fragile Foundations: A Report on America's Public Works.* Washington, DC: Government Printing Office.

Office of Technology Assessment, Congress of the United States. 1990. *Rebuilding the Foundations: A Special Report on State and Local Public Works Financing and Management.* Washington, DC: Government Printing Office.

Palumbo, George, and Seymour Sacks. 1987. *Rural Governments in the Municipal Bond Market.* Washington, DC: Economic Research Service, U.S. Department of Agriculture.

Petersen, John E. 1989. *Information Flows in the Municipal Bond Market: Disclosure Needs and Processes.* Washington, DC: Government Finance Officers Association.

Peterson, George E. 1990. "Is Public Infrastructure Undersupplied?" In *Is There a Shortfall in Public Capital Investment?* ed. Alicia H. Munnell. Boston, MA: Federal Reserve Bank of Boston, pp. 113–130.

Peirog, Karen. 1992. "Mayor of Detroit Protests Moody's Ba1 Downgrade, Citing Unfairness." *Bond Buyer* (July 20): 1, 25.

Poterba, James M. 1986. "Explaining the Yield Spread Between Taxable and Tax-Exempt Bonds: The Role of Expected Tax Policy." In *Studies in State and Local Public Finance,* ed. Harvey S. Rosen. Chicago: University of Chicago Press, pp. 5–49.

Quigley, John M., and Daniel L. Rubinfeld. 1991. "Private Guarantees for Municipal Bonds: Evidence from the Aftermarket." *National Tax Journal* 44, no. 4, part 1 (December): 29–39.

Reid, Gary J. 1990. "Minimizing Municipal Debt Issuance Costs: Lessons from Empirical Research." *State and Local Government Review* (Spring): 64–72.

Sawicki, Theodore J. 1985. "The Washington Public Power Supply System Bond Default: Expanding the Preventure Role of the Indenture Trustee." *Emory Law Journal* 34: 157–199.

Sbragia, Alberta. 1979. "The Politics of Local Borrowing: A Comparative Analysis." Paper published by Center for the Study of Public Policy, University of Strathclyde, Glasgow, Scotland.

———. 1983. "Politics, Local Government, and the Municipal Bond Market." In *The Municipal Money Chase: The Politics of Local Government Finance,* ed. Alberta Sbragia. Boulder, CO: Westview Press, pp. 67–111.

Sharp, Elaine B. 1986. "The Politics and Economics of the New City Debt." *American Political Science Review* 80, no. 4 (December): 1271–1288.

South Carolina v. Baker. 1988. 485 U.S. 505.

Sullivan, Patrick J. 1983. "Municipal Bond Ratings: How Worthwhile Are They for Small Governments?" *State and Local Government Review* 15, no. 3 (Fall): 106–111.

U.S. General Accounting Office. 1983. *Trends and Changes in the Municipal Bond Market as They Relate to Financing State and Local Public Infrastructure.* Washington, DC: General Accounting Office.

Walters, Dennis. 1990. "Around the Nation: Nevada." *Muniweek* (October 15): 32.

Zimmerman, Dennis. 1991. *The Private Use of Tax-Exempt Bonds: Controlling Public Subsidy of Private Activity.* Washington, DC: Urban Institute Press.

CHAPTER 13

LITIGATION COSTS, BUDGET IMPACTS, AND COST CONTAINMENT STRATEGIES:

Evidence from California Cities

SUSAN A. MACMANUS

National surveys conducted in the early 1990s revealed that litigation costs were wreaking havoc on the budgets of many cities.[1] At that time, a number of local government officials across the United States projected that the trend would escalate as more individuals, businesses, and lawyers discovered the "rewards" of suing city hall with its assumed "deep pockets."

Naturally, most municipal officials vehemently disagree with the "deep pockets" characterization of their jurisdiction's financial conditions. They generally resent the fact that a government *has* to expend money to react to a lawsuit but a plaintiff does not need a "deep pocket" to sue. (Since a plaintiff normally hires an attorney who gets a share of the court award or settlement, usually from one-third to one-half, all that is needed is to find a lawyer willing to take a gamble.)[2]

Some describe aggressive litigating against government entities as exemplary of a "jackpot mentality" on the part of plaintiffs and their lawyers.[3] But those suing say that their actions are justified and one of the few ways to effectively "fight city hall" when it is unfair or unresponsive. Regardless of one's position, few would argue with the fact that litigation against government is now even more commonplace than at the beginning of the decade and hits some jurisdictions harder than others.

Litigation in California: Local Governments' Efforts to Publicize Cost Impacts

William Claiborne of the *Washington Post* has described California as ". . . one of the most litigious states in the nation, a place where filing a suit is almost as defining a pastime as surfing."[4] According to Claiborne, the state leads the nation in the number of lawsuits filed and its residents spend more on legal fees than any other state's residents. Nonetheless, it has been difficult to convince Californians or their elected representatives to approve proposals designed to put a brake on litigation incidences and costs.[5]

Some reform-minded local officials have maintained that citizens and legislators in California (and elsewhere) remain unaware of the degree to which lawsuits against local governments cost the taxpayers cold hard cash. Nor are they cognizant of the degree to which legal actions and

From *Public Budgeting & Finance*, vol. 17, no. 4 (Winter 1997), pp. 28–47. Copyright © 1997 by Blackwell Publishing. Reprinted with permission.

judgments have altered local spending priorities, often in a manner inconsistent with local budgetary preferences. Finally, the average citizen does not believe that government (local or otherwise) seriously seeks ways to control costs.

In an effort to enlighten the public and elected officials about the degree to which litigation costs are impacting California municipalities today and publicize the cost-containment efforts which have already been implemented, the League of California Cities conducted a mail survey of its 470 member cities in the summer of 1996. Forty-five percent (210 cities) responded.[6]

The survey instrument was patterned after a national survey conducted for the National Institute of Municipal Law Officers by the author in 1992 but adapted for California following input from various local officials. The results offer some valuable insights, and warning signals, to budget officials everywhere as there is little evidence that the litigation tidal wave has subsided. But more significantly, the results show that factors contributing to escalating litigation costs, and responses to them, vary considerably across cities in different size categories.

Budgetary Strains

The 1996 survey reveals that litigation costs are straining the budgets of many California cities, necessitating budget amendments, and in some cases prompting bond rating downgrades and/or changes in insurance method/carrier. Perhaps *the strain is best reflected in the willingness of many cities to settle cases they believe they could have won just to save money*—a rather unsettling pattern for many who see it as *contributing* to rising litigation costs over time.

Overall Impacts: Moderate to Large

The results show that in 33 percent of the 210 California cities responding to the survey, litigation costs have impacted their budgets "a lot" this year, in 53 percent, "a little," and in only 14 percent "not at all." In over half the cities (57 percent), litigation costs have escalated at a rate of 10 percent or more over the past two years. In 29 percent of the cities, the rate of increase has equaled or exceeded 30 percent. And in over one-third of the cities, legal costs exceeded half-a-million dollars (including judgments) last fiscal year.

Larger cities have been hit harder than smaller ones. For example, among cities of 100,000+ population, 53 percent say that their budgets have been impacted "a lot" by litigation compared to just 19 percent of those with populations under 10,000. (See Table 13.1, on p. 172.) Larger cities are more prone to lawsuits for a number of reasons: more people, greater population diversity (politically, racially, socioeconomically), more public employees, more government rules and regulations, and more lawyers, to mention a few.

Of the cities whose budgets have been impacted "a lot" by litigation, 80 percent report increases in litigation costs over the past two years in excess of 10 percent. In almost one-third of these cities, the rate of increase has exceeded 50 percent. (See Table 13.2, on p. 174.) In any event, the escalation rate has exceeded the inflation rate thereby putting considerable strain on these cities' budgets.

Budget Amendments Required

Previous research has shown that litigation-related costs are very difficult to forecast. They often emanate from unexpected events: national disasters, personal injuries sustained in accidents, civil disorders, federal or state mandates or court orders, among others. But when they happen, they often necessitate budgetary adjustments. For example, many California cities (43 percent) have had to amend their budgets at least once during the past fiscal year for litigation and judgment purposes. Of those having to amend their budget at least once (42.5 percent), nearly one-fourth (24 percent) have amended it three or more times.

Mid-year budget adjustments are not limited to minor changes. Of those having to amend, 27 percent described their amendments as "very large" relative to the original legal budget, 43 percent as "moderate," and less than one-third (29 percent) as "small."

Predictably, cities reporting that litigation has impacted their budgets "a lot" during the past fiscal year are more likely to have amended their budget than those whose budgets have not been impacted at all (71 percent v. 14 percent). Likewise, 89 percent of these heavily impacted jurisdictions describe the magnitude of their amendments as "moderate" or "very large." The need to amend has been greatest among cities in the 50,000–99,999 population bracket—both in terms of frequency and magnitude (Table 13.1).

Overall, these results suggest that the growing incidence of litigation has produced more uncertainty and flux in the annual budgetary process. Other research has also shown that allocation readjustments prompted by lawsuits often creates more interdepartmental friction inside city hall.

Some Potential for Impact on Bond Rating

The linkage between litigation-related fiscal "obligations" and bond ratings is well established. For years, bond rating firms have required governmental entities to list all outstanding litigation and estimate the potential cost of adverse rulings. Governments have always had trouble estimating the actual costs, especially as cases drag on, but in recent years, they have had even more difficulty predicting case outcomes. The changing composition and tenor of federal and state courts have resulted in more frequent, and more contradictory, interpretations of state and local government powers. To date, governments have tended to underestimate both the incidence and cost of adverse rulings.

It is not surprising, then, that some California municipalities (1 percent) blame legal costs for their recent bond rating downgrades or that even more (7 percent) expect such a consequence in the near future. Again, cities which report their budgets have been impacted "a lot" are the most likely to have had their bond ratings downgraded or to anticipate negative impacts on their bond ratings in the future because of rising litigation costs.

Some Impacts on Insurance Costs

The emergence of the risk management field in recent years has heightened local officials' awareness of the impact of lawsuits on insurance costs . . . and availability. And there *is* a relationship. Among California cities whose budgets have been impacted considerably by litigation costs but do not carry their own insurance, 46.9 percent say their insurance rates have been directly affected compared to just 15 percent of those not experiencing any litigation-related budget strain.

Initially, functions heavily reliant upon volunteers, such as libraries, parks and recreation, and social services, were identified as the most likely to create unnecessary liability exposure. But now concern about city liability for volunteers has spread to virtually every governmental function just as it has to the private sector. John Stossel, author of an ABC News special on lawyers, found that the city of Fresno, California, even stopped using volunteers to clean streets and that an Arizona restaurant stopped serving free dinners to poor people after being warned that it was "too risky."[7]

Table 13.1

Overall Effects of Litigation Costs by Population Size (percentaged vertically)

Effect	All % cited[1]	Below 10,000	10,000– 24,999	25,000– 49,999	50,000– 99,999	Over 100,000
			Population size—% cited			
Impact of litigation costs on budget—last year	n = 202	n = 47	n = 36	n = 51	n = 36	n = 32
A lot	32.2	19.1	33.3	33.3	38.9	53.1
A little	54.0	63.8	61.1	51.0	38.9	53.1
Not at all	13.9	17.0	5.6	15.7	22.2	6.3
% Increase in litigation costs (past 2 years)**	n = 199	n = 44	n = 37	n = 51	n = 36	n = 31
0	18.1	13.6	18.9	17.6	16.7	25.8
1–4	13.6	15.9	16.2	21.6	5.6	3.2
5–9	11.6	6.8	2.7	13.7	11.1	25.8
10–14	14.6	18.2	13.5	3.9	27.8	12.9
15–29	14.6	11.4	16.2	13.7	11.1	22.6
30–39	7.0	9.1	2.7	5.9	16.7	—
40–50	5.5	2.3	8.1	9.8	5.6	—
Over 50	15.1	22.7	21.6	13.7	5.6	9.7
Total litigation costs (last year)***	n = 204	n = 46	n = 37	n = 53	n = 36	n = 32
Less than $500,000	66.7	95.7	83.8	75.5	44.4	15.6
$500,000–$999,999	19.6	2.2	16.2	15.1	36.1	37.5
$1–5 million	11.3	2.2	—	7.5	16.7	37.5
$6–10 million	2.0	—	—	—	2.8	9.4
Over $10 million	0.5	—	—	1.9	—	—
Frequency of budget amendments (last year)*	n = 202	n = 46	n = 36	n = 52	n = 36	n = 32
0	57.4	63.0	50.0	48.1	69.4	59.4
1–2	33.7	30.4	44.4	44.2	8.3	37.5
3–4	5.4	4.3	2.8	5.8	11.1	3.1
5–6	1.5	—	—	1.9	5.6	—
7–10	1.5	—	2.8	—	5.6	—
Over 10	0.5	2.2	—	—	—	—
Magnitude of amendments	n = 83	n = 17	n = 18	n = 26	n = 11	n = 11
Small	30.1	41.2	11.1	42.3	18.2	27.3
Moderate	43.4	41.2	61.1	34.6	36.4	45.5
Large	26.5	17.6	27.8	23.1	45.5	27.3
Impact on bond rating (past three years)	n = 197	n = 44	n = 36	n = 50	n = 36	n = 31
No	92.4	93.2	86.1	88.0	97.2	100.0
Not yet (but very possible in the near future)	6.6	6.8	11.1	10.0	2.8	—
Yes	1.0	—	2.8	2.0	—	—
Direction of bond rating impact	n = 2	n = 0	n = 1	n = 1	n = 0	n = 0
Downgraded	100.0	—	100.0	100.0	—	—
% Cases settled just to save money	n = 201	n = 45	n = 36	n = 52	n = 36	n = 32
0	18.9	31.1	13.9	19.2	13.9	12.5
1–5	25.9	31.1	25.0	28.8	13.9	28.1
6–10	13.9	2.2	16.7	11.5	22.2	21.9
11–15	9.0	2.2	5.6	5.8	22.2	12.5
16–25	13.4	8.9	16.7	13.5	13.9	15.6
26–50	9.5	11.1	11.1	11.5	8.3	3.1
Over 50	9.5	13.3	11.1	9.6	5.6	6.3

Impact on insurance rates (past three years)	$n = 199$	$n = 46$	$n = 35$	$n = 51$	$n = 36$	$n = 31$
No	37.7	34.8	34.3	33.3	44.4	45.2
Not yet (but expected)	6.5	13.0	2.9	5.9	2.8	6.5
Yes	29.1	32.6	34.3	27.5	30.6	19.4
Not applicable (self-insured)	26.6	19.6	28.6	33.3	22.2	29.0
Direction of insurance cost impact*	$n = 52$	$n = 13$	$n = 11$	$n = 13$	$n = 10$	$n = 5$
Costs went up	88.5	100.0	81.8	100.0	80.0	60.0
Costs went down	11.5	—	18.2	—	20.0	40.0
Impact on insurance carrier	$n = 6$	$n = 0$	$n = 2$	$n = 26$	$n = 0$	$n = 2$
Changed carriers	83.3	—	100.0	100.0	—	50.0
Moved to self-insurance	16.7	—	—	—	—	50.0

Source: Mail survey of city managers in council-manager cities and city clerks in nonmanager cities conducted by the League of California Cities, July–September 1996.

Notes: [1]Percentages in the "All" column of this table may vary slightly from those reported for all cities in the text. The "All" figures cited in the text represent responses for all cities answering a particular effect question. The "All" figures in this table report statistics for the cities that provided responses to both the population size question *and* a specific effect question.

***The relationship between variables is statistically significant at the .001 level; ** at the 0.1 level; * at the .05 level.

Many governments have simply chosen to abandon certain activities rather than face loss of coverage by a private carrier or sharp increases in insurance costs. Others have been left with little choice but to pay the price, change carriers, join pools, or self-insure if political demands prevent abandonment of certain programs, services, or facilities.

Nearly 40 percent of the California cities that currently or at one time relied on private insurance carriers report that their jurisdiction's insurance costs have been affected by litigation over the past three years. Another 9 percent expect it to happen shortly. Among the cities whose insurance costs have been impacted, 89 percent say that they have gone up. Of those whose costs have escalated, 83 percent have moved to self-insurance and 17 percent have changed carriers. But regardless of whether a city insures itself or turns to some other arrangement, it is evident that litigation costs are affecting the true cost of insurance. Settling to save is seen by many in the private and public sectors as a practical way to make annual fiscal ends meet. One estimate is that 85 percent of all lawsuits in the private sector are settled before going to trial.[8] The 1992 National Institute of Municipal Law Officers survey reported over 81 percent of its member jurisdictions did the same.

The 1996 California survey affirms that this pattern still prevails. Over 80 percent of the respondent cities report settling at least some cases just to save money even in situations where city officials believe that they could have prevailed if costs were not a factor. Nearly one-fifth (19 percent) of the cities estimate that they "settle to save" more than 25 percent of their cases, another 62 percent report settling to save at least some cases, whereas only 19 percent report that they have not engaged in this practice.

Larger cities settle a great percentage of their cases as a cost-saving tactic. Eighty-seven percent of cities over 100,000 population report settling at least some cases to save compared to 69 percent of those below 10,000 population. And cities whose budgets have been hit hardest by litigation costs are more prone to settle to save than cities not impacted at all (86 percent vs. 64 percent).

A legislative analyst for the League of California Cities has summed up the situation well: "A number of cities will settle because even if they think they will prevail in court, the cost, the staff

Table 13.2

Overall Effects of Litigation Costs by Budget Impacts (percentaged vertically)

Effect	All %[1]	Impact of litigation on city budget		
		Not at all %	A little %	A lot %
% Increase in litigation costs (past 2 years)***	n = 201	n = 29	n = 106	n = 66
0	17.4	48.3	15.1	7.6
1–4	13.9	27.6	17.0	3.0
5–9	11.4	3.4	15.1	9.1
10–14	14.4	10.3	17.9	10.6
15–29	13.9	6.9	13.2	18.2
30–39	7.5	3.4	4.7	13.6
50–50	5.5	—	5.7	7.6
Over 50	15.9	—	11.3	30.3
Total litigation costs (last year)***	n = 206	n = 29	n = 110	n = 67
Less than $500,000	66.0	89.7	71.8	46.3
$500,000–$999,999	19.4	10.3	18.2	25.4
$1–5 million	12.1	—	8.2	23.9
$6–10 million	1.9	—	1.8	3.0
Over $10 million	0.5	—	—	1.5
Frequency of budget amendments (last year)***	n = 205	n = 28	n = 109	n = 68
0	57.6	85.7	67.9	29.4
1–2	33.2	14.3	28.4	48.5
3–4	5.9	—	2.8	13.2
5–6	1.5	—	0.9	2.9
7–10	1.5	—	—	4.4
Over 10	0.5	—	—	1.5
Magnitude of amendments***	n = 84	n = 4	n = 34	n = 46
Small	28.6	75.0	47.1	10.9
Moderate	44.0	25.0	41.2	47.8
Very large	27.4	—	11.8	41.3
Impact on bond rating (past three years)*	n = 201	n = 28	n = 107	n = 66
No	92.0	100.0	95.3	83.3
Not yet (but very possible in the near future)	7.0	—	3.7	15.2
Yes	1.0	—	0.9	1.5
Direction of bond rating impact	n = 2	n = 0	n = 1	n = 1
Downgraded	100.0	—	100.0	100.0
% Cases settled just to save money*	n = 203	n = 28	n = 109	n = 66
0	18.7	35.7	17.4	13.6
1–5	25.6	35.7	28.4	16.7
6–10	14.3	10.7	17.4	10.6
11–15	8.9	7.1	8.3	10.6
16–25	13.3	7.1	12.8	16.7
26–50	9.4	—	6.4	18.2
Over 50	9.9	3.6	9.2	13.6
Impact on insurance rates (past three years)*	n = 202	n = 29	n = 108	n = 65
No	37.6	55.2	39.8	26.2
Not yet (but expected)	6.9	3.4	3.7	13.8
Yes	28.7	10.3	29.6	35.4
Not applicable (self-insured)	26.7	31.0	26.9	24.6
Direction of insurance cost impact	n = 52	n = 3	n = 29	n = 20
Costs went up	88.5	66.7	86.2	95.0
Costs went down	11.5	33.3	13.8	5.0

Impact on insurance carrier	$n = 6$	$n = 0$	$n = 4$	$n = 2$
Changed carriers	16.7	—	25.0	—
Moved to self-insurance	83.3	—	75.0	100.0

Source: Mail survey of city managers in council-manager cities and city clerks in nonmanager cities conducted by the League of California Cities, July–September 1996.

Notes: [1]Percentages in the "All" column of this table may vary slightly from those reported for all cities in the text. The "All" figures cited in the text represent responses for all cities answering a particular effect question. The "All" figures in this table report statistics for the cities that provided responses to both the population size question *and* a specific effect question.

*** The relationship between variables is statistically significant at the .001 level; ** at the 0.1 level; * at the 0.5 level.

---

time, and the legal time they will have to put into that is in excess of the cost to settle."[9] But there are downsides to this approach as well. Many city legal officials acknowledge that it does not take long for some members of the plaintiffs bar to learn the dollar amount threshold that triggers a city's decision to settle. This threshold soon becomes a widely known figure and results in more lawsuits as attorneys file for judgments just below that figure for their clients. Thus, over time, the cumulative effect of more lawsuits may turn short-term saving into long-term liabilities.

Functional Areas Hit Hardest

Previously cited studies have found that certain municipal functions are more prone to be the objects of litigation than others. Activities with higher levels of direct employee interaction with individuals and businesses and/or those with large, diverse, unionized work forces seem to spark the most lawsuits.

California cities responding to the 1996 survey show this pattern persists. Respondents were asked: "Which of the following functional areas have been most negatively impacted (from a budget perspective) by litigation cost increases in your jurisdiction?" (multiple responses were possible). Of the 70 percent reporting at least one function impacted, the five most commonly cited in descending order are:

- Police   51.0 percent
- Streets   40.7 percent
- Employee salaries   34.5 percent
- Parks and recreation   30.3 percent
- Planning   22.1 percent

Over one-fifth also point to employee benefits and budget and finance.

The increase in the number of suits brought by employees, especially in cities reporting "a lot" of litigation-driven budgetary impact, explains the frequency with which the personnel (employee salaries and benefits) function is mentioned. This increase in employee-initiated lawsuits also parallels that observed in the private sector.[10]

Public infrastructure (streets, parks, and recreation) and utility (water, sewer) have been slightly more negatively impacted in mid-sized jurisdictions than in either the very smallest (under 10,000) or very largest (100,000+) cities. (See Table 13.3.) Mid-sized communities, often suburban in nature, have higher concentrations of Baby Boomer parents with kids. Suburban-dwelling Baby Boomers are generally more affluent than other cohorts, more knowledgeable of legal resources to government actions or inactions, and more willing to sue, especially if it is their child that is affected.

Table 13.3

Areas Negatively Affected by Litigation Cost Increases by Population Size
(percentaged vertically)

		Population size—% Cited				
	All %[1]	Below 10,000	10,000– 24,999	25,000– 49,999	50,000– 99,999	Over 100,000
Functional areas affected	(n = 144)	(n = 36)	(n = 27)	(n = 37)	(n = 23)	(n = 21)
Police	51.4	50.0	48.1	48.6	47.8	66.7
Fire	8.3	8.3	7.4	13.5	—	9.5
Prison/jails	1.4	—	—	—	8.7	—
Employee salaries	34.7	30.6	48.1	24.3	39.1	38.1
Water	9.0	2.8	11.1	10.8	17.4	4.8
Sewer	16.7	8.3	18.5	21.6	21.7	14.3
Elected officials	5.6	8.3	7.4	8.1	—	—
Convention centers/stadiums	0.7	—	3.7	—	—	—
Public transportation	2.8	2.8	3.7	2.7	—	4.8
Purchasing (contracting/ procurement)	10.4	5.6	14.8	10.8	17.4	4.8
Employee pensions	3.5	2.8	—	5.4	—	0.5
Solid waste services	4.2	2.8	3.7	2.7	8.7	4.8
Parks and recreation	30.6	25.0	33.3	37.8	26.1	28.6
Public housing	2.8	—	3.7	5.4	4.3	—
Economic development	13.9	5.6	11.1	16.2	21.7	19
Airport	2.1	2.8	—	—	4.3	4.8
Animal shelters	1.4	—	—	2.7	4.3	—
Planning	22.2	27.8	22.2	24.3	17.4	14.3
Employee benefits	20.8	13.9	33.3	16.2	17.4	28.6
Streets	41	33.3	48.1	51.4	21.7	14.3
Personnel (civil service)	16	5.6	18.5	16.2	30.4	14.3
Municipal courts	—	—	—	—	—	—
Budget and finance	20.8	11.1	14.8	27	30.4	23.8
Zoning	6.9	13.9	3.7	5.4	8.7	—
Legal	16.7	13.9	18.5	16.2	17.4	19.0
Emergency rescue	1.4	2.8	—	—	4.3	—
Other†	13.9	8.3	11.1	21.6	8.7	19.0

Source: Mail survey of city managers in council-manager cities and city clerks in nonmanager cities conducted by the League of California Cities, July–September 1996.

Notes: Respondents were asked, "Which of the following functional areas have been most negatively affected (from a budget perspective) by litigation cost increases in your jurisdiction?"

†Examples include: "capital projects/improvements," "reserves or general fund," "redevelopment."

Column percentages do not add to 100 percent due to the multiple response question format.

[1]Percentages in the "All" column of this table may vary slightly from those reported for all cities in the text. The "All" figures cited in the text represent responses for all cities answering the functional area question.

The "All" figures in this table report statistics for the cities that provided responses to both the population size question *and* the functional area question.

*** The relationship between variables is statistically significant at the .001 level; ** at the .01 level; * at the .05 level.

Factors Contributing Most to Rising Litigation Costs: Frivolous or Justified?

One of the first steps in devising viable cost containment strategies is to identify what factors appear to be driving up costs. The 1996 California survey asked respondents to identify "which of the following factors have contributed most to your jurisdiction's rising litigation costs over the past three years."

The five most-cited factors in descending order are:

• Increase in frivolous cases	52.7 percent
• Increased case complexity	49.5 percent
• Increased caseload	37.8 percent
• Higher incidence of employee suits	36.4 percent
• Greater need to rely on outside counsel	36.2 percent

Over 30 percent also cite the higher incidence of private citizen suits and attorney salaries as major contributing factors to rising litigation costs.

There are some significant differences across population size categories. (See Table 13.4.) Generally, the larger the city, the more likely is increased case complexity, federal and state court rulings, jury awards, increased reliance on expert witnesses; and higher incidences of employee and contractor-initiated lawsuits are identified as litigation cost-provoking.[11] For example, among cities over 100,000, increased case complexity (70 percent), employee suits (63 percent), and frivolous lawsuits (60 percent) are most oft-cited reasons. Among cities 25,000–49,999, they are: increased case complexity (54 percent), increased caseload (48 percent), frivolous cases (48 percent), and a greater need to rely on outside counsel (41 percent). Among cities under 10,000, it is frivolous cases (52 percent), the need to rely on outside counsel (48 percent), and attorney salaries (40 percent).

Frivolous lawsuits have long plagued the private sector.[12, 13] According to the president of the California Chamber of Commerce: "Frivolous lawsuits hold legitimate businesses hostage and force them to pay millions to avoid paralyzing court battles."[14] There is now evidence that these types of cases are having the same budgetary impact in the public sector. The joint push by business and government leaders for tort reform stems from the fact that many cases labeled "frivolous" involve personal injury claims by customers and employees.

Tort Claim Abuses

California municipal officials were asked to "provide any anecdotes that clearly typify tort claim abuses that your city has confronted during the past three years [including] cases that were settled out of court." Fifteen cities furnished such material.

The most common examples of tort claim abuses featured plaintiff allegations of: (1) city employee deficiencies (most often involving police officers, followed by personnel of civil service, and legal officials); (2) infrastructure inadequacies (especially streets, signs, lighting, sidewalks, and storm sewers); (3) failure to enforce existing regulations (rent control); and (4) environmental-related deficiencies prompting city employee illness.

Several survey respondents assert that abusive tort claims involving their municipality would not have gone as far as they did had the judge handling the case been more experienced, more knowledgeable of the law, less biased against the city, and less fearful of having his/her judgments overturned. Some respondents blame judges for making cities settle what they regard as frivolous tort cases.

Table 13.4

Factors Contributing to the Rising Costs over the Past Three Years by Population Size
(percentaged vertically)

		Population size—% Cited				
	All %[1]	Below 10,000	10,000– 24,999	25,000– 49,999	50,000– 99,999	Over 100,000
Factors identified	(n = 185)	(n = 42)	(n = 33)	(n = 45)	(n = 34)	(n = 30)
Attorney salaries	31.9	40.5	33.3	30.4	20.6	33.3
Increased caseload	37.8	28.6	24.2	47.8	47.1	40.0
Increased case complexity**	49.7	26.2	48.5	54.3	55.9	70.0
Lengthy appeals	22.7	19.0	24.2	26.1	17.6	26.7
Greater need to rely on outside counsel	36.8	47.6	27.3	41.3	38.2	23.3
Increase in frivolous cases	52.4	52.4	57.6	47.8	47.1	60.0
Increased cost of law journals and books	3.2	—	6.1	2.2	8.8	—
Liability insurance for legal personnel	2.2	7.1	—	—	2.9	—
Federal court rulings***	18.4	2.4	9.1	15.2	44.1	26.7
State court rulings**	15.7	2.4	15.2	13	35.3	16.7
Federal mandates	6.5	4.8	3.0	8.7	8.8	6.7
State mandates	7.6	4.8	6.1	6.5	8.8	13.3
Jury awards**	13.5	2.4	6.1	15.2	17.6	30.0
A very aggressive local plaintiffs bar	5.4	—	12.1	2.2	5.9	10.0
More intense local news media coverage of legal issues	7.6	2.4	9.1	2.2	14.7	13.3
Court reporting cases (reporter, transcripts)	4.9	—	3.0	4.4	11.8	6.7
Increased reliance on expert witnesses***	21.2	7.1	12.1	22.2	23.5	46.7
Higher incidence of employee suits*	36.4	26.2	33.3	28.9	38.2	63.3
Higher incidence of contractor suits**	10.3	2.4	6.1	4.4	23.5	20.0
Higher incidence of private citizen suits	31.5	33.3	39.4	35.6	17.6	30.0
Increase in number of attorneys involved in each case	20.7	16.7	24.2	17.8	26.5	20.0
Increase in number of adverse rulings	6.0	4.8	3.0	4.4	11.8	6.7
Increase in travel costs	3.3	7.1	3.0	4.4	—	—
Increase in number of cases attacking lost revenues (taxes, fees)	5.4	2.4	9.1	10.9	—	3.3
Cutback in services due to budget problems	10.3	4.8	15.2	6.5	11.8	16.7
Delayed infrastructure repairs resulting in more personal injury claims*	26.5	19.0	45.5	15.2	29.4	30.0
More reporting of large jury awards and settlements	11.4	2.4	9.1	17.4	11.8	16.7
Other†	10.3	7.1	12.1	8.7	11.8	13.3

Source: Mail survey of city managers in council-manager cities and city clerks in nonmanager cities conducted by the League of California Cities, July–September 1996.

Notes: Respondents were asked, "Which of the following factors have most contributed to your jurisdiction's rising litigation costs over the past three years? Check all applicable."

Column percentages do not add to 100 percent due to the multiple response question format.

*** The relationship between variables is statistically significant at the .001 level; ** at the .01 level; * at the .05 level.

†Examples include: "very aggressive local union," "escalating pool settlements," "court congestion," and "attorney solicitation/advertising."

[1]Percentages in the "All" column of this table may vary slightly from those reported for all cities in the test. The "All" figures cited in the text represent responses for all cities answering the cost contributor question.

The "All" figures in this table report statistics for the cities that provided responses to both the population size question *and* the cost contributor question.

Types of Cases Contributing Most to Rising Costs

In an effort to get even more precise information about the types of cases that tend to be the real "budget busters," officials in California cities were asked: "Which of the following types of cases have contributed *most* to your jurisdiction's rising litigation costs over the past three years?" (multiple responses were possible). Among the 91 percent who identified at least one type of case, the five most commonly cited in descending order are:

• Police liability	53.9 percent
• Personal injury	50.3 percent
• Worker's compensation	45.5 percent
• Land use/zoning	40.8 percent
• Civil rights	32.8 percent

Over one-fifth of the cities also cite torts (25.7 percent), environment (23.6 percent), and inverse condemnation (23.6 percent).

There are significant differences across population size categories in the types of cases seen as prompting rising litigation costs. As shown in Table 13.5, cities over 100,000 are considerably more likely than smaller cities to cite torts (50 percent vs. 14 percent), civil rights (63 percent vs. 17 percent), personal injury (70 percent vs. 29 percent), Americans with Disabilities Act [ADA] (33 percent vs. 2 percent), police liability (77 percent vs. 38 percent), Fourteenth Amendment (30 percent vs. 0 percent), and Fourth Amendment (23 percent vs. 2 percent) cases. Cities in the 25,000–49,999 range are the most likely to identify eminent domain cases (22 percent vs. 10 percent for both the smallest and largest cities).

The three types of cases most often identified by the very largest cities (over 100,000) are: police liability (76 percent), personal injury (70 percent), and civil rights (63 percent). For the very smallest, they are: land use/zoning (43 percent), police liability (38 percent), and workers' compensation (38 percent). For cities in the 25,000–49,999 range, personal injury (61 percent), police liability (56 percent), and workers' compensation (54 percent) are delineated.

The association between type of case and the degree of impact of litigation on the city budget is not quite as strong. The statistically significant differences appear with regard to tax, redistricting/elections, due process, and Fourteenth Amendment cases. Cities noting "a lot" of budgetary impact are more likely than those citing none to identify due process (17 percent vs. 10 percent) and tax (8 percent vs. 0 percent) cases. But the reverse is true for redistricting/election cases. Fourteenth Amendment cases are the most common among cities experiencing some litigation-driven budget impacts (12.4 percent).

The higher incidence of discrimination-based claims (race, gender, age, disability) observed in the 1996 survey than in the 1992 NIMLO survey can be viewed as a leading indicator of what will happen over the next decade. A number of government reports have already released statistics documenting an increase in the number cases claiming violations under the Americans with Disabilities Act, the Equal Employment Opportunity Act, the Civil Rights Act of 1991, and the Older Americans Act.[15]

The nation's graying and population diversification trends will continue to push age and racial concerns to the forefront. They will be felt first in larger, more diversely populated municipalities. Attention to these trends will help risk managers, fiscal officials, and policymakers develop strategies designed to minimize lawsuits from these increasingly litigious populations.

Table 13.5

Types of Cases Contributing Most to the Rising Litigation Costs over the Past Three Years by Population Size (percentaged vertically)

	All[1] %	Below 10,000	10,000–24,999	25,000–49,999	50,000–99,999	Over 100,000
			Population size—% Cited			
Type of case	(n = 189)	(n = 42)	(n = 35)	(n = 46)	(n = 36)	(n = 30)
Case Classification						
Civil	98.4	85.7	100.0	100.0	96.2	100.0
Criminal	1.6	4.3	—	—	3.8	—
Type						
First Amendment	8.5	4.8	2.9	8.7	11.1	16.7
Fourth Amendment*	6.9	2.4	2.9	4.3	5.6	23.3
Eighth Amendment	1.6	—	—	2.2	—	6.7
Fourteenth Amendment***	7.9	—	5.7	4.3	5.6	30.0
Fifteenth Amendment	0.5	—	—	2.2	—	—
Redistricting/elections	2.1	—	2.9	2.2	5.6	—
Environment**	23.8	23.8	5.7	21.7	44.4	23.3
Inverse condemnation	23.8	19.0	20.0	30.4	22.2	26.7
Police liability*	53.4	38.1	57.1	56.5	44.4	76.7
Labor	19	16.7	11.4	15.2	25	30.0
Workers' compensation	46.0	38.1	48.6	54.3	41.7	46.7
Employee early retirement	2.6	2.4	8.6	2.2	—	—
Tax	2.6	2.4	8.6	2.2	—	—
Torts***	25.9	14.3	11.4	19.6	41.7	50.0
Employee promotion complaints*	4.8	2.4	14.3	—	5.6	3.3
Due Process	9.5	14.3	2.9	8.7	8.3	13.3
Civil rights***	37.6	16.7	28.6	39.1	47.2	63.3
Antitrust	0.5	—	2.9	—	—	—
Preemption	0.5	—	—	—	—	3.3
Desegregation	—	—	—	—	—	—
Land use/zoning	40.7	42.9	51.4	41.3	25.0	43.3
ADA***	7.9	2.4	2.9	2.2	5.6	33.3
Personal injury**	50.8	28.6	48.6	60.9	50.0	70.0
Prosecution of ordinance violations	13.2	16.7	8.6	19.6	8.3	10.0
Employee disability	19.0	7.1	20.0	26.1	27.8	13.3
Employee pensions	3.7	2.4	5.7	4.3	—	6.7
Eminent Domain**	12.2	9.5	—	21.7	16.7	10.0
Employee salary complaints	2.6	—	2.9	2.2	5.6	3.3
Contracts	14.8	7.1	17.1	8.7	25	20.0
Other†	15.3	9.5	28.6	15.2	8.3	16.7

Source: Mail survey of city managers in council-manager cities and city clerks in nonmanager cities conducted by the League of California Cities, July–September 1996.

Notes: Respondents were asked, "Which of the following types of cases have contributed most to your jurisdiction's rising litigation costs over the past three years? Check all applicable."

Column percentages do not add to 100 percent due to the multiple response question format.

*** The relationship between variables is statistically significant at the .001 level; ** at the 01 level; * at the .05 level.

†Examples include: "general and sexual harassment," "wrongful discharge," "employment liability."

[1]Percentages in the "All" column of this table may vary slightly from those reported for all cities in the text.

The "All" figures cited in the text represent responses for all cities answering the case contributor question. The "All" figures in this table report statistics for the cities that provided responses to both the population size *and* the case contributor question.

Cost Containment Techniques Used over Past Three Years

The need to find ways to control litigation-related costs has been evident since the early 1990s. Earlier studies suggested that along with the more traditional method of finding ways to cut and/or readjust the budget "after the fact" (reactive approaches), cities would be well advised to investigate ways to prevent costs. Better risk management was one of the prevention-oriented recommendations.[16] The 1996 survey results suggest that many California cities took those recommendations to heart.

Respondents were asked: "Which of the following litigation cost containment techniques has your jurisdiction used over the past three years? Check all applicable." Among the 89 percent who reported using at least one technique, the five most commonly cited in descending order are:

• Improved risk management function	66.8 percent
• More willing to "settle" cases	29.4 percent
• Share costs with other public sector entities	26.7 percent
• Joined insurance pool	26.7 percent
• Reduced reliance on outside counsel	23.5 percent

Another one-fifth (21.9 percent) mention increased reliance on outside counsel as a way to contain costs.

Larger cities, more than smaller ones, have relied upon cost-saving strategies related to staffing patterns, material acquisition, and data distribution across departments. (See Table 13.6.) The very largest cities (over 100,000) are more prone than the very smallest (under 10,000) to increase the size of their in-house legal staff (44 percent vs. 3 percent) and reduce their reliance on outside counsel (50 percent vs. 11 percent), hire more paralegals (19 percent vs. 0 percent), rely more on part-time support staff (12 percent vs. 3 percent), reduce purchase of law books/journals (25 percent vs. 0 percent), and rely more on computer networks allowing access to documents, maps, data bases of other departments to save time and money (16 percent vs. 3 percent).

It is to be expected that larger cities have implemented more cost control actions than their smaller counterparts. As noted earlier, larger cities have experienced more fiscal stress as a direct consequence of litigation. And in comparison with smaller jurisdictions, their more extensive legal operations mean there are more areas to be pared back.

Conclusion

This 1996 survey of California cities, to which 210 cities responded, shows that litigation costs continue to strain the budgets of many California municipalities. Among the respondents, 86 percent report that litigation costs have impacted their budget this past fiscal year either "some" or "a lot."

For one-third of the California cities, the budgetary effects have been *quite substantial*, no matter whether measured in terms of overall impact, percent increase, frequency and magnitude of budget amendments, actual dollar costs, or the tendency to settle cases just to save money. Generally, the larger the city, the greater the strain litigation costs have put on the budget.

Rising litigation costs have also affected the cost of insurance in 40 percent of the cities who are not self-insured (driving it up in most). This has prompted many of those which have been negatively impacted to move to self-insurance (83 percent) or change carriers (17 percent).

The functional areas that have been most negatively impacted, as reported by the survey respondents, are: police (51 percent), streets (40.7 percent), employee salaries (34.5 percent), parks and recreation (30.3 percent), and planning (22.1 percent).

Table 13.6

Cost Containment Techniques Used over the Past Three Years by Population Size
(percentaged vertically)

	Population size—% Cited				
	All[1] %	Below 10,000	10,000– 24,999	25,000– 49,999	50,000– 99,999	Over 100,000
Technique employed	(n = 184)	(n = 36)	(n = 33)	(n = 48)	(n = 35)	(n = 32)
Reduce size of in-house legal staff	33.3	2.8	3.0	—	2.9	9.4
Increase size of in-house legal staff***	15.2	2.8	—	8.3	25.7	43.8
Greater reliance on outside counsel	22.3	22.2	21.2	16.7	34.3	18.8
Reduced reliance on outside counsel**	22.8	11.1	15.2	18.8	22.9	50.0
More willingness to "settle" cases	29.3	36.1	42.4	25.0	25.7	18.8
Improved risk management function**	67.9	55.6	84.8	81.3	60.0	53.1
Hire more paralegals	4.3	—	—	4.2	—	18.8
Improve distribution of new court rulings between legal departments and other line departments	4.9	—	3.0	6.3	2.9	12.5
Use student interns (undergraduate, law school)	3.8	—	3.0	2.1	8.6	6.3
Reduce training/continuing education for legal staff	1.6	—	3.0	—	—	6.3
Increase fees (e.g., reproduction costs)	1.1	—	—	2.1	—	3.1
Cost sharing with other public sector entities	27.2	26.0	33.3	37.5	25.7	9.4
More reliance on part-time support staff*	7.6	2.8	—	8.3	14.3	12.5
Reduce purchases of law books/journals**	12.0	—	12.1	14.6	8.6	25.0
Lobby state/federal government for tort reform	8.7	2.8	12.1	6.3	14.3	9.4
Join insurance pool	27.1	33.3	27.3	33.3	22.9	15.6
Abandon/privatize high litigation-yielding activities	5.4	2.8	6.1	8.3	2.9	6.3
Use more on-line data services (Lexis, Westlaw)*	12.0	8.3	3.0	10.4	8.6	31.3
Rely more on computer networks allowing access to documents, maps, data bases of other departments, thereby saving time (and money)**	10.3	2.8	—	10.4	17.1	21.9
Other†	10.9	2.8	12.1	14.6	8.6	15.6

Source: Mail survey of city managers in council-manager cities and city clerks in nonmanager cities conducted by the League of California Cities, July–September 1996.

Notes: Respondents were asked, "Which of the following litigation cost containment techniques has your jurisdiction used over the past three years? Check all applicable."

Column percentages do not add to 100 percent due to the multiple response question format.

*** The relationship between variables is statistically significant at the .001 level; ** at the .01 level; * at the .05 level.

†Examples include: "take proactive or preventive stance," "develop 'nonsettling' reputation," "develop safety programs," and "sexual harassment and ADA training."

[1]Percentages in the "All" column of this table may vary slightly from those reported for all cities in the text. The "All" figures cited in the text represent responses for all cities answering the cost containment question. The "All" figures in this table report statistics for the cities that provided responses to both the population size question *and* the cost containment question.

The five factors perceived by the most city officials as being responsible for rising litigation costs are: increase in frivolous cases (52.7 percent), increased case complexity (49.5 percent), increased caseload (37.8 percent), a higher incidence of employee suits (36.4 percent), and a greater need to rely on outside counsel (36.2 percent).

The types of cases which have sparked the greatest increase in litigation costs over the past three years are: police liability (53.9 percent), personal injury (50.3 percent), workers' compensation (45.5 percent), land use/zoning (40.8 percent), and civil rights (38.2 percent). One-fourth of the respondents also cited torts. The rank-orderings vary by size of the city. A higher percentage of big cities (over 100,000) than smaller ones blame rising costs on police liability, personal injury, civil rights, tort, Americans with Disabilities Act, Fourteenth Amendment, and Fourth Amendment cases.

The most common types of "frivolous" plaintiff allegations made in tort claims appear to be: (1) city employee deficiencies (especially of police officers); (2) infrastructure inadequacies; (3) failure to enforce existing regulations; and (4) environmental-related deficiencies prompting city employee illness. Some respondents attribute at least part of the blame for tort claim abuses on inexperienced or biased judges fearful of having their opinions overturned by a higher court.

There is considerable variation across the cities with regard to the type of case that has been *the* most costly. But the four most often identified are police liability (16 percent), land use/zoning (12 percent), personal injury (10 percent), and inverse condemnation (8 percent).

By far the most common litigation cost-saving technique utilized by California cities over the past three years has been improved risk management (cited by 66.8 percent). Other popular approaches have been to willingly settle more cases (29.4 percent), share costs with other public sector entities (26.7 percent), join an insurance pool (26.7 percent), and reduce reliance on outside counsel (23.5 percent). More larger than smaller cities report saving money by reducing reliance on outside counsel (and hiring more in-house counselors or paralegals).

In summary, this analysis of California cities' experiences with lawsuits over the past few years should signal to other cities across the United States that the number of lawsuits filed against municipalities continues to rise (especially frivolous ones) as do budgetary uncertainties. Forecasting when lawsuits will occur, how much they will cost, and the damage they will do to municipal insurance costs and credit ratings is extremely difficult. So too, is determining the long-term fiscal consequences of the current frenzy to settle lawsuits to save money in the short term.

This study also shows that more cases are being filed against municipalities by their own employees. Their suits, and those of many private citizens, often claim that a local government has violated some federal civil rights-related act. The nation's population trends (aging and diversifying, racially and ethnically) suggest such claims will escalate.

Finally, this study reveals that many cities have already discovered the utility of risk management strategies as a cost control mechanism. However, litigation costs remain rather unpredictable, uncontrollable, and unsettling for many localities.

Notes

The author wishes to thank the League of California Cities for funding this research and authorizing public dissemination of the results in this journal. The author also thanks Alice Johnson, MPA, for data entry and computer assistance.

1. See Susan A. MacManus, "Litigation: A Real Budget Buster for Many U.S. Municipalities," *Government Finance Review* 10 (February): 27–31; "The Impact of Litigation on Municipalities: Total Cost, Driving Factors, and Cost Containment Mechanisms," *Syracuse Law Review* 44 (1993): 833–860; "Litigation as a Budgetary Constraint: Problem Areas and Cost," *Public Administration Review* 55 (September/October 1993): 462–472 (with Patricia A. Turner).

2. Peter Passell, "Economic Scene: A California Initiative Would Put Lawyers to the Free-Market Test," *New York Times*, February 22, 1996, p. C-2.

3. William Claiborne, "Battle Over Lawsuits Raging in California," *Washington Post*, March 17, 1996, p. A-3.

4. Ibid.

5. In a light turnout election held in March 1996, California voters rejected three initiatives that would have made it more difficult to press civil lawsuits. Ibid.

6. A survey was mailed to the city manager in manager cities and the city clerk in nonmanager cities. Copies of the letter also went to risk managers, finance directors, and city attorneys. The usable response rate was 46 percent, which is quite good for mail surveys.

7. John Stossel, "Protect Us from Legal Vultures," *Wall Street Journal*, January 2, 1995, p. A-8.

8. Robert J. Samuelson, "Lawyer Leash Law," *Washington Post*, January 10, 1996, p. A-17.

9. Jay Lyman, "Claims Have Hiked City's Cost," *Glendale News-Press*, February 10, 1997, pp. A-1, A-8.

10. David Sommer, "Pink Slip No Longer Final Act," *Tampa Tribune*, April 7, 1996, p. 1, Florida/Metro section.

11. See Charles Mahtesian, "The Endless Court Orders," *Governing* (April 1997): 40–43.

12. *Black's Law Dictionary* defines a pleading as frivolous "when it is clearly insufficient on its face, and does not controvert the material points of the opposite pleading, and is presumably interposed for mere purposes of delay or to embarrass the opponent. A claim or defense is frivolous if a proponent can present no rational argument based upon the evidence or law in support of that claim or defense." Henry Campbell Black, ed., *Black's Law Dictionary with Pronunciations*, 6th ed. (St. Paul, MN: West, 1990), p. 668.

13. Many in the business community describe the situation as "an out-of-control legal system that spawns frivolous lawsuits. . . ." See Kirk Victor, "Looking to Limit Lawsuits," *National Journal* (March 8, 1997): 460–461.

14. B. Drummond Ayres, "California May Take Lead in Curbing of Lawsuits," *New York Times*, March 26, 1996, p. A-14.

15. Sommer, op. cit.; Knight-Ridder Newspapers, "It Is Now Easier to Sue for Age Bias," *St. Petersburg Times*, April 2, 1996, p. 1–A; David Segal, "Striking Gold in Those Bias Lawsuits," *Washington Post National Weekly Edition*, February 3, 1997, p. 29.

16. MacManus, "Litigation: A Real Budget Buster for Municipalities," p. 31.

PART 3

THE CHANGING WORLD OF PUBLIC PERSONNEL MANAGEMENT

Government at all levels is undergoing profound change caused by numerous forces that are constantly at work to cause this change. For example, the antigovernment political movement of the past two decades has resulted in pressure for governments to become smaller and more efficient, as well as to make government a less attractive career choice. Technological advances have made many jobs in the public sector obsolete while at the same time creating a need for numerous new ones. The privatization movement has shifted some traditional public sector functions to the private sector. Legal and constitutional issues have changed public personnel management dramatically during the past three decades, and created challenges for the public sector manager, such as equal employment opportunity for protected classes of citizens, violence in the workplace, drug testing, sexual harassment, and comparable worth.

Public personnel management has been critically affected by these changes because most governments spend anywhere from 50 percent to 90 percent of their budgets on personnel. Government is highly labor intensive, and, therefore, how this indispensable resource (personnel) is utilized and managed determines the success or failure of government. If a government does not effectively utilize and manage its personnel, it matters little how well it performs other functions for it is bound to fail. For this reason, knowledge and effective practice of personnel management is absolutely critical for public managers. The case studies, models, concepts, and management tools presented in Part 3 of this volume serve as a guide to the public manager through the turbulent world of public personnel management.

In chapter 14, Siegrun Fox Freyss presents two models for municipal human resource management systems and empirically tests the support for each model. The first "unidimensional" model is grounded on the assumption that cities are continually making small steps from a system founded on patronage toward a purely merit-based system. The other system, which is tested and supported using factor analysis and logistic regression, is termed "multidimensional" because it is defined as having four distinct personnel cultures: (1) affirmative action; (2) merit; (3) affirmative action for certain men; and (4) union. Freyss presents the various characteristics of each of these cultures, exploring the interrelationships among different municipal characteristics such as population, racial composition, geography, and form of government. It is important to the academician, practitioner, public official, and student of public administration to understand that personnel systems cannot be contained in neat packages. After identifying some of the personnel cultures that influence the human resource function at the local level, Freyss suggests two additional cultures that are emerging in the field. The first is termed a "democratic personnel system," which includes policies such as (p. 205) "total quality management, participatory management, team management" and a "flattened hierarchy." Freyss identifies the other emerging culture as a "competitive or market-driven personnel system" that is more aggressive in identifying talented job candidates, offering bonuses and merit pay and a wide variety of benefits, instituting broadbanding, and exploring privatization.

Steve Ballard and Gayle Lawn-Day (chapter 15) discuss the experiences of Norman, Oklahoma, in its attempt to achieve reform in its management of human resources, specifically in the area of affirmative action as a tool to achieve a representative bureaucracy. Although the reform movement failed, the case presents some interesting lessons for local government personnel management. Ballard and Lawn-Day present eight barriers that contributed to the failure of the local government reform. They also highlight the importance of the strong managerial support of the city manager. For the newly appointed city manager in this case, the urgency of the affirmative action reforms soon took a backseat to a host of other more politically controversial issues that quickly rose to the top of his agenda, which included labor negotiations, financial problems, and community conflicts. The case study addressed the "cumulative impact" (p. 215) of cultural barriers that the authors state "was perhaps more significant to the eventual political outcome than any other single factor" (p. 215). Obtaining "buy-in" and the lack of proper organizational communication were also addressed: "Perhaps the biggest failure in Norman was the failure of top management to communicate effectively with the rest of the organization. Thus, change and reform were identified with a very limited set of players rather than with the organization" (p. 216). The authors conclude that solutions to local government problems must be "community-based," legitimate and active enforcement is necessary, and women and minorities should organize and actively pursue broad-based policy changes.

As the Ballard and Lawn-Day article made clear, the departure of a city manager and the hiring of a new city manager are crucial turning points in municipal government. Richard Feiock and Christopher Stream (chapter 16) attempt to explain "the role that institutional constraints and community characteristics have on manager turnover" (p. 219). In contradiction to previous studies, these authors found that city managers with MPA degrees had slightly increased rather than decreased tenure. Their study showed no support for the relationship between a portable pension plan or different structures of political representation and tenure on their jobs. This study reinforces previous findings that "both the conflictual environment in which managers work and career characteristics" (p. 227), as well as "institutional arrangements" (p. 227), influence patterns of tenure for city managers. The presence of employment agreements was found to influence tenure in "an intervening manner rather than an additive manner" (p. 227).

Carole L. Jurkiewicz and Tom K. Massey (chapter 17) address the implications of employee satisfaction or dissatisfaction in "What Municipal Employees Want from Their Jobs Versus What They Are Getting." Many scholars believe that public sector employees are less motivated than private sector employees by financial rewards, and instead place a high value on the security provided by public employment and service to the public. These authors updated a 1976 study conducted in five cities in the Midwest by surveying these cities twenty years later to examine any changes that may have occurred since that time. The study was divided into two parts: what employees want from their jobs, and what employees receive from their jobs. Interestingly, the things that the employees "got" from their employment in local government remained largely unchanged. However, there were significant shifts in the profile of what employees desire from their municipal employment. The most significant shift was the *increased* desire for a "high salary." Other important shifts were the *decrease* in the importance of "working as part of a 'team'" and the "chance to benefit society." The authors concluded that the desires of public sector employees are increasingly mirroring private sector employees. The implication for human resource management is that in order to attract and retain quality employees, local governments cannot become complacent with their reward structure and must make a conscious effort to keep pace with the private sector.

As the large number of employees of the baby boom generation moves through the local government system, the needs and desires of the workforce will change. With the first group of individuals in this category turning fifty-five in 2001, how to manage an aging municipal workforce is a timely concern. Jonathan P. West and Evan M. Berman (chapter 18) discuss the "graying workforce" and what cities are doing throughout the country to address the needs of these valuable, experienced employees. Specifically, they address four areas: supportive workplace relations involving stress management, alternative work arrangements, and retirement needs; special training needs; career development; and performance appraisal issues including concern about age-bias. They found that the level of managerial professionalism, legal requirements, and fiscal issues are three factors in determining whether the policies are supported through the human resource function. West and Berman concluded that "some challenges have been well met by cities" (pp. 251–252) (such as grievance procedures, personnel policies, and labor agreements), while others (such as career revitalization, proficiency testing, and adaptation of training methods) still have not been adequately addressed. Instead of targeting programs to the needs of older workers, cities are addressing the needs of these individuals through the broad-based programs available to all employees. The authors urged municipalities to reassess proactively the four areas they discussed to protect against alienating this important group of public employees.

Municipal use of performance evaluation instruments for top management is addressed in the next article, written in 1986 by David N. Ammons and Arnold Rodriquez, and published here as chapter 19. These authors studied municipalities to determine the existence and frequency of satisfaction with performance appraisals used for department heads and key assistants. Interestingly, they found that only 59 percent of the respondents use a formal performance appraisal system for top management, 29 percent use an informal method, and more than 12 percent report no method of appraisal at all. The cities that did employ appraisals used them most commonly for "performance feedback" and "reward allocation." Of the cities using measures, most cities used Management by Objectives (MBO) either alone or in combination with other measures. This was especially true of the council-manager cities. Cities that used MBO reported a more frequent use of appraisals than those not using the technique. These cities also reported general satisfaction with the appraisals and suggested continued use. Of most concern to these authors was the relatively small amount of time spent on the process of performance measures. A majority of the cities reported spending less than 5 percent of a "person-year" on the process of evaluating upper management. The authors concluded this was an extremely small amount of time to dedicate to such a critical human resource management tool.

One issue that human resource management professionals have grappled with is the incorporation of values into the organizational culture. Evan M. Berman and Jonathan P. West (chapter 20) discuss how this effort has been sought through "the central notions that governmental organizations should *minimize ethical wrongdoing and increase responsiveness* to citizens, employees, and customers of government services" (p. 266). Personnel managers have provided both enforcement of compliance with ethics laws and policies and employee development training addressing issues involving employees, families, and customers. Their study demonstrates that the management of values is shifting away from the focus on compliance and will be increasingly focused on "building trust among employees and customers" (p. 274) in the years to come. This seems to be especially true in the areas of employee development where the goal is to increase the value of employees to the organization by fully utilizing the employees' talents and capabilities. According to the study, other significant future efforts will include "reducing work-related stress, providing timely feedback to employees, and providing individual career planning" (p. 274).

CHAPTER 14

MUNICIPAL GOVERNMENT PERSONNEL SYSTEMS:

A Test of Two Archetypical Models

SIEGRUN FOX FREYSS

For more than one hundred years local governments have received a combination of recommendations and mandates from the federal government, state agencies, courts, professional associations, and academicians for the implementation of proper personnel practices. The thrust of the suggested or required human resource policies has been portrayed to various degrees either as a unidimensional progression from the spoils system to the merit system, with professional standards slowly supplanting political considerations, or as a multidimensional field of four or more competing personnel systems, with the spoils system, merit system, collective bargaining system, and affirmative action system all vying for preeminence. Although both assumptions pervade the personnel literature, neither have been subjected to rigorous statistical analysis. Instead, the evidence regarding each model consists largely of conceptual analyses, case studies, and simple descriptive computations (Cayer 1991; Fox 1993).[1]

But as practitioners, consultants, and academicians look for ways to reinvent the public service in local government (Wilson 1989; Osborne and Gaebler 1992; Thompson 1993), as local jurisdictions are pressured to adopt competitive, more market-like administrative practices (Lan and Rosenbloom 1992), and as work organizations are transformed from modern to postmodern arrangements (Caldwell 1975; Clegg 1990), more needs to be known about existing conditions. Proposed solutions are more likely to be effectively implemented if they mesh with the organizational cultures in place.

The question addressed in this chapter is, which of the two models, if either, best reflects actual personnel practices—the continuum model or the competing systems model? Another possibility is also considered—that no coherent pattern can be empirically verified using the best data available, which is likely the set of responses gathered during the 1989 survey by the International City/County Management Association (ICMA). Following the usage in the ICMA questionnaire, the terms "personnel practices" and "personnel policies" are more or less applied interchangeably in this study.[2]

To test the linear progression model, an effort was made to develop a scale of professionalism, consisting of what the literature has identified as core professional personnel practices. But this procedure did not yield statistically strong findings. In contrast, factor analysis and subsequent logistic regression produced highly meaningful and statistically significant results in support of

From *Review of Public Personnel Administration*, vol. 15, no. 4 (Fall 1995), pp. 69–93. Copyright © 1995 by Sage Publications, Inc. Reprinted with permission.

the competing systems model. In the process, surprisingly, a personnel policy cluster or dimension not discussed in the personnel literature was also uncovered.

The Two Models in the Literature

The professional continuum model is the older conception of the two. It represents a linear process by which a successive addition of new professional personnel principles slowly replaces patronage and other deficient practices. The process begins in the late nineteenth century with the concept of merit system or civil service reform.[3] Originally, four primary principles were involved:

1. meritorious hiring based on competence;
2. political neutrality;
3. tenure in office; and
4. administration of the personnel function by a relatively independent civil service commission.

After the turn of the century, the scientific management school in the United States and the rational-bureaucratic model in Europe added job classifications and standardized pay scales to the notion of professional personnel practices (Van Riper 1958, 192–193). Over the years, other principles have been included to deal with such issues as the openness of examination processes, the certification of eligible applicants, the use of uniform disciplinary action, and the centralization of the personnel function in a staff agency. More controversial developments were the integration of veteran's preferences, collective bargaining, and EEO/affirmative action into the merit system, but according to advocates of the unidimensional model no insurmountable hurdles existed against their inclusion. One might call this model the optimistic one, in that its representatives believed in steady progress and the power of cooperation in overcoming possible incompatibilities.

Three types of literature constitute good sources to demonstrate the existence of the linear progression model. First, there are the professional publications on local government personnel improvements associated with the reform movement. Second, the hearings held in connection with the Intergovernmental Personnel Act of 1970 and subsequent amendments contain appropriate examples. And third, some of the academic literature, especially studies on the proper definition of the professional public administrator, tend to express the vision of a linear progression or optimistic view.

The reform movement was, of course, in support of the merit system and disseminated its preference through such organizations as the National Municipal League, founded in 1894 (now the National Civic League), and the International City Managers' Association (ICMA), started in 1894 (now the International City/County Management Association). Belief in progress through reform measures pervaded their writings. For instance, in his annual review delivered in 1911 and reprinted in the first issue of the *National Municipal Review*, the secretary of the National Municipal League pointed out that the growth of public functions had necessitated the departure from the spoils system and the introduction of the merit system. He acknowledged resistance to the change, but concentrated in his address on successful efforts (Woodruff 1912, 6–7). Writers on labor-management relations were given a voice in the publications of the League when they described the benefits of union cooperation with good government efforts (Galatas 1950, 79) or, vice versa, management cooperation with labor (Thompson 1975, 335).

Some articles written for ICMA publications expressed a similar optimism. Difficulties "in eradicating unsound features of public personnel legislation and administration" were described as temporary setbacks that were counterbalanced by encouraging trends elsewhere (Belsley 1938, 19). More recently, presenting the findings from ICMA surveys in an additive and descriptive way in the *Baseline Data Reports* and *Municipal Year Books* leaves the impression of compatibility among various local government personnel practices (Dahl and Wappel 1989; Cayer 1991; Fox and Fox 1991).

The Intergovernmental Personnel Act (IPA) of 1970 and subsequent amendments also generated arguments that reflected the professional continuum model. Individuals testifying at congressional hearings on behalf of the legislation argued that the New Federalism under the Nixon administration, with its devolution of responsibilities from the federal government to the state and local levels, would more likely be successful if local governments increased their management capacity, which could be accomplished through the adoption of merit systems. Moreover, members of the U.S. Civil Service Commission, union representatives, and EEO/affirmative action supporters assured the legislators that only minor adjustments would be required in the provisions of the act to accommodate their concerns (U.S. Senate 1967, 83, 236–237; U.S. House 1975, 25–26). Some speakers expressed reservations, but primarily about the speed of transition, not about likely incompatibilities (U.S. Senate 1969; U.S. House 1969; U.S. Senate 1975).

While practitioners tried to implement professional personnel standards, academicians grappled with the question of what professionalism actually meant in contemporary public administration (Rabin 1982). In retrospect, it appears some of the conceptual uneasiness expressed in various symposia articles on the issue of meaning stemmed from the effort to apply a unidimensional concept to a multidimensional phenomenon. When researchers studied public administrators closely to try finding a consensus about their role, to define their profession, and to discover an ideal of professionalism (Rabin 1982, 304), they assumed as their underlying paradigms a linear progression model where conflicts and incongruities could be kept to a relative minimum.

While conflicts among different personnel systems had been pointed out in passing for many years, the 1970s saw important publications analyzing these incompatibilities in a comprehensive way. The end of the linear and homogenous professionalism model is well summarized by Karl in a 1976 *Public Administration Review* article on the history of the professionalization of public administration:

> For the end of consensual politics, if one describes the past decade in those terms, is obviously painful and serious. The writers of the consensual era all sought in their various versions—and I would include what is called pluralism now among them—some concept of general truth which was distinct from the particular truths held by groups of interests or experts in various fields. (Karl 1976, 498)

The recognition that the assumptions of consensus and one truth were inadequate portrayals of reality lead to a multidimensional model representing conflicting personnel systems.

Mosher (1982) is perhaps the outstanding proponent of the competing personnel systems argument. He distinguishes among five competing claims: demand for management discretion; goals of the professions; civil service or merit principles; collective bargaining requirements; and EEO/affirmative action goals. The demands of these systems are all legitimate, in Mosher's view, in that they are all based on various aspects of democratic theory. Government by management discretion, for instance, implies such democratic concepts as public interest and public mandate (83, 94), and the notions of pluralism and representative bureaucracy (95–99). Government by the professions carries the benefit that professional knowledge is put in the service of the state and society (113). Government by merit principles involves competence, loyalty, continuity, and discipline (150–153). Government by collective bargaining is protected by the First

Amendment to the Constitution, has led to fairer employment practices (190–191), and offers the promise of greater personal democracy (216). Finally, government by EEO/affirmative action increases the likelihood for nondiscriminatory employment practices (223).

But while Mosher recognizes the legitimacy of these claims in principle and practice, he also acknowledges their limits and partial incommensurability. He therefore asks for moderation and concessions by all interests involved so that a balance can be struck and a workable democracy can be maintained (see, e.g., Mosher 1982, ix, 142, 212, 215, 216, 185, 224). One can call Mosher a transitional scholar from the modern to the postmodern epoch, in that he refuses to identify one best way for public personnel policies based on one universal truth. Instead, he urges the reader to accept the legitimacy of competing value claims. But one can also sense in his book an undercurrent of postmodern angst that the conflicting demands will spin out of control.

On a less ominous note, other researchers offer evidence that these competing systems can reach a modus vivendi. Perry, Wise, and Martin (1994, 48), for instance, describe the personnel policies of the city of Indianapolis and other jurisdictions in Indiana as an effective blending of elements of patronage and professionalism. Similarly, Stein (1994, 62) concludes from her research into the personnel practices of the city of St. Louis that merit and political considerations can form a continuum with accompanying advantages and disadvantages. Cohen and Eimicke (1994) present the public personnel system of New York City as a case of mutual accommodation between civil service and collective bargaining, unfortunately reinforcing each other in their tendencies toward overregulation. Lepper (1983, 238) looks at the arguments that declare merit systems and EEO/affirmative action incompatible, concluding that "merit and equal employment opportunity have the same objective: to ensure that selection is based on individual abilities and skills." Many more researchers could be cited to support the argument that the respective literature recognizes the existence of public personnel systems in conflict (see, e.g., Stanley 1972; Olufs 1985; Kearney and Sinha 1988; Graham 1990; Riccucci 1991).

A good summary of the competing personnel systems model is presented by Klingner and Nalbandian (1993, 4–19). The authors distinguish four clusters, most of which correspond with the typologies offered by Mosher (1982) and others:

1. political systems, where personnel decisions are primarily based on patronage and party loyalty,
2. civil service systems, where neutral competence is supposed to determine personnel decisions,
3. collective bargaining systems, where many employment conditions are set by contract negotiations, and
4. affirmative action systems where EEO/affirmative action regulations are supposed to ensure nondiscriminatory personnel actions.

Since the systems foster different values, attitudes, and employment practices, they can also be perceived as different organization cultures. This term will be favored in the description of the findings, because both the factor analysis and the logistic regression analysis results reported below provide evidence for substantial value and policy differences among personnel departments depending on their systemic culture.

Methodology

The 1989 survey by ICMA collected a large amount of data on local government personnel practices. It gathered information on:

1. adoption of formal merit systems;
2. administrative organization of the personnel function;
3. staffing and compensation procedures;
4. employee recruitment and selection policies;
5. affirmative action and equal employment opportunity issues;
6. employment benefits and regulations; and
7. performance appraisal systems.

The ICMA questionnaire yielded more than 300 variables, many of them of a dichotomous nature, because the answers only involved a simple "yes" or "no." The ICMA questionnaire asked respondents to exclude from their answers any personnel policy that applied solely to police, fire, education, or court personnel. This exclusion ensured that the data reflected the general staffing policies of the local jurisdiction and that the findings were not limited to special employment groups that have historically been treated separately.

As usual in survey research, the reliability of the measurement instrument is affected by the extent to which the respondents understand the many technical terms used in the questionnaire, and one has to assume a certain amount of random error in the answers. On the other hand, the validity of the measuring instrument, using content validity as criterion, seems to be assured. The questionnaire very appropriately captures the domain of municipal personnel practices (Hyman 1972; Kiecolt and Nathan 1985).

The survey was mailed to all cities with a population of 10,000 or more and to all counties with a population of 25,000 and above. Since the return rate for the cities was much higher (35.5%) for a total of 979 cases than for the counties (19.0%) for a total of 268 cases, only the cities were included for the statistical analysis in this chapter.

The number of cases actually used in each calculation was further affected by missing data. Since experimentation with various missing data treatment methods did not fundamentally change the findings, the study settled on pairwise as a compromise between listwise (which would have yielded only 135 cases) and mean/mode substitution, which of course would have resulted in the inclusion of all 979 cases. The findings would have been of questionable validity, however. To assess the representativeness of the 630 cases retained as a result of the use of the pairwise inclusion, the population groups in the factor analysis and in the ICMA sample were compared with the population groups in the whole country using the Census of Government data. As Figure 14.1 shows, the smallest cities in the survey, with a population of 10,000–24,999, are slightly underrepresented both in the ICMA data and in the factor analysis, while the larger jurisdictions are somewhat overrepresented. The differences may affect the findings, and one has to be cautious about external validity claims.

To test the unidimensional professionalism model, several variables identified by the literature as core professional personnel principles (Fox 1993; Sampson 1993) were selected from the data and subjected to a reliability analysis using Cronbach's alpha. After several iterations, involving adding and subtracting items, nine variables were retained covering the following policy areas:

1. merit system(s) in place;
2. management of the personnel function by a personnel department;
3. testing of applicants for job-related knowledge, skills, and abilities;
4. use of performance appraisals for various personnel actions;
5. pay raises based on merit pay;

194

Figure 14.1 Representation of Cities by Size in Factor Analysis and ICMA Survey (1989) in Comparison with Census of Governments (1987)

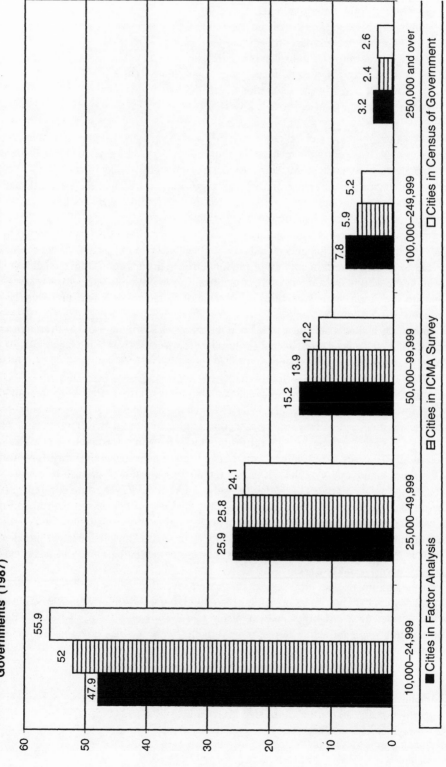

Source: ICMA (1989) and U.S. Bureau of Census (1991: 298).

6. affirmative action policy in place;
7. formal disciplinary procedure in place;
8. official grievance procedure available; and,
9. limits on partisan political activities.

Cronbach's alpha is a commonly used statistical procedure to test scale reliability, closeness of fit, or internal consistency of attitudinal and/or observational items. The coefficient can be interpreted as a type of correlation coefficient, with 0 indicating no fit and 1 a perfect fit. A coefficient of about .8 is generally considered the cutoff point for acceptance or rejection of the observation scale (Norusis 1990, 463–467). As is shown in the section on findings, the calculation of alpha did not yield statistically strong results, even when scale items were added or subtracted.

Testing of the alternative multidimensional model was done with factor analysis. This statistical procedure allowed for the identification of common dimensions or factors underlying the variables in the ICMA dataset. The first step involved the selection of meaningful variables from the close to 300 choices. Selection primarily depended on the nature of the variable. Factor analysis should be done with variables measured at the interval level, but nominal variables can also be used when they are in dichotomous form. This application to dummy variables has been demonstrated by Kim, Nie, and Verba (1977) and Muthen (1981). Many of the variables in the ICMA data set were either in dichotomous form, or could be meaningfully recoded into yes or no categories. This first step yielded forty-five variables.

The next phase required the computation of a correlation matrix to narrow the number of variables down to those that would create meaningful factors. The winnowing of appropriate variables was achieved with the Kaiser-Meyer-Olkin (KMO) measure of sampling adequacy and the examination of commonalities. In the end, fourteen variables were retained, which yielded a KMO measure of .828. Kaiser (1974) is generally accepted as the authority on this measure, and in his judgment a coefficient of about .8 indicates that the variables are fully acceptable for a factor analysis.

The principal component method was selected for the extraction phase, and the varimax rotation was used for the computation of the final factor matrix (Norusis 1990, 313–346). The number of factors extracted was determined from the initial statistics table. It indicated that four factors had eigenvalues greater than 1, which is considered the appropriate cutoff point for meaningful factors. The cumulative percentage of their variances accounted for 69.2 percent of the total variance. The factor loadings calculated for each variable made the interpretation of the four factors or dimensions rather obvious, as can be seen in the sections on "Findings." Factor loadings greater than .5 are considered very significant in interpreting an underlying factor (Hair, Anderson, and Tatham 1987, 249).

To examine the extent to which the four factors or dimensions influenced the implementation of various personnel policies, justifying the use of the terms "competing systems" or "system cultures," additional computations were conducted. They involved calculating factor scores for each jurisdiction and using them as independent variables in a logistic regression analysis with a wide range of personnel policies as the dependent variables. The factor scores could be conceived of as indicators of a community's core personnel system, and the logit analysis measured the effect of the core culture on employment policies, confirming or questioning the adequacy of the idea of distinct institutional preferences. The logit procedure was chosen over multiple regression because of the dichotomous nature of the dependent variables. In statistical terms the logit coefficients are estimates of the probability that an event will occur.

One final set of calculations was conducted to place the observed public personnel cultures in a demographic, geographic, and governmental context. The assumption was tested, using multiple regression analysis, that the prevalence of one or the other of the four personnel systems was dependent on the size of the jurisdiction and the percentage of minority residents. In other words, in this last section the factor scores or institutionalized personnel cultures were treated as dependent variables, and population and percentage of white residents were used as independent variables.

Moreover, two contingency tables were examined. One crosstabulation measured the association between geographical regions and factor scores/public personnel cultures. This statistical procedure tested previous findings which showed that union activities and the reform movement varied in their impact on municipal personnel policies depending on the geographical region, with unions supposedly being more active in the Northeast and Midwest, while merit system reform has had a stronger influence on the South and West (Dahl and Wappel 1989; Fox and Fox 1991).

The other contingency table estimated the association between form of government and personnel cultures. It tested the assumption that the council-manager form was more likely to have implemented merit-based employment policies than other types of cities.

The sequence of reasoning and quantitative analysis generated a substantial amount of statistically highly significant and quite consistent findings. The reader might feel overwhelmed by the many tables, but they all point to the same conclusion—municipalities exhibit distinct personnel system cultures. The systemic institutional conditions make it possible to estimate the probability that the jurisdictions will implement certain human resource policies. Moreover, the systemic personnel conditions vary in a statistically significant way by demographic, regional, and governmental characteristics.

First Finding: Weak Statistical Support for the Unidimensional Professionalism Model

The nine core personnel practices, mentioned in the Methodology section and used in the calculation of the scale reliability, yielded a Cronbach's alpha of .4160 (standardized item alpha = .4588). The addition or subtraction of other variables did not strengthen the alpha coefficient substantially. The alpha score can be treated like a correlation coefficient, and a result of .42 is generally identified as a weak relationship. A score of about .8 is needed to justify the claim of linearity (Norusis 1990, 463–467). In other words, the theoretical assumption that major professional personnel innovations, such as merit systems, performance appraisals, affirmative action plans, disciplinary procedures, and grievance policies, are homogenous and situated along a continuum is not supported by the statistical analysis of actual municipal practices.

Second Finding: Strong Statistical Support for Four Personnel Systems

Factor analysis, which examines the data for multidimensionality, provides a much more precise picture. As Table 14.1 shows, the analysis yields four meaningful factors or dimensions that summarize personnel practices in American municipal governments. The identity of the factors is revealed by the factor loadings. Coefficients of at least .5 indicate a very significant relationship with the personnel policies listed in the left-hand column.

The first factor can be called "affirmative action system" or, more precisely, "affirmative action for legally protected groups." It includes affirmative action policies for minorities, women, persons with disabilities, and older workers. Moreover, it covers the question "Are your AA goals integrated into the personnel plans and policies of each line department in your government?"

Table 14.1

Identification of Municipal Personnel Systems Based on Factor Loadings*
(Rotated Factor Matrix)

Variables	Factor 1	Factor 2	Factor 3	Factor 4
Affirmative action [AA] system				
(for legally protected groups)				
AA program for racial or ethnic minorities	.951			
Formal AA policy in place	.942			
AA program for women	.926			
AA program for persons with disabilities	.810		.258	
AA program for older workers	.603		.436	
AA goals integrated in line departments	.588			
Merit system				
Merit pay		.878		
Merit system		.877		
Pay raises tied to performance appraisal		.758		
AA system for certain men				
AA program for rehabilitated alcohol or			.863	
drug abusers				
AA program for ex-offenders			.842	
AA program for veterans	.423		.580	
Union system				
Recruitment requests to unions, trade, and				.768
professional associations				
Placement priority to laid-off employees				.767
Eigenvalue	4.820	2.190	1.580	1.090
Percent of variance explained	34.500	15.700	11.300	7.800
Cumulative variance	34.600	50.100	61.400	69.200

Source: ICMA (1989).
Notes: *Factor loadings of less than .2 not shown.
$N = 630$ cities, with a population of 10,000 and more.

(ICMA 1989, 4). The factor loadings are high to very high on the variables dealing with these personnel issues.

The second factor can be readily identified as "merit system." It combines variables that reflect the principles of merit and performance. More precisely, the variables deal with questions asking jurisdictions whether they have merit systems, use merit pay, and tie pay raises to performance appraisals. The findings from the logistic regression analysis, discussed below, shed further light on the policy preferences of this system culture.

Interestingly, the third factor also involves affirmative action, but for a different segment of the work force. Since it comprises affirmative action programs for rehabilitated alcohol or drug abusers, ex-offenders, and veterans, one might call this dimension, tongue firmly in cheek, "affirmative action for certain men." The inclusion of the male gender in the identification of this factor appears to be justified considering that the ratio of male to female alcoholics is about five to one (Keller, Steiner, and Clark 1994). The logit analysis below offers some more evidence that this factor reflects a male dominated personnel culture. However, no literature could be found describing it, and research into this phenomenon may be warranted. It is apparently not widespread, since only 8.9 percent of the jurisdictions included in the calculations had relatively high factor scores on this dimension.

The fourth factor is also easily recognizable, in that factor loadings are high on variables associated with union preferences. They include making "recruitment requests to unions, trade, and professional associations" and giving "placement priority to laid-off employees." The claim that this factor reflects union culture can also be strengthened by looking at the results of the logit analysis below.

Since the four factors explain 69.2 percent of the variation in the variables, a case can be made that the findings from the factor analysis provide empirical evidence in support of the competing personnel systems model.

Third Finding: More Statistical Evidence for the Existence of Different Personnel Cultures

The logistic regression analysis using the factor scores and other personnel policies strengthens the original interpretation of the four factors. To clarify the relationship, let us remember the conceptual meaning of factor scores in the context of this study. Because there are four factors, each jurisdiction gets four factor scores. They can be treated like indicators of the presence or absence of certain systemic characteristics. In the logit analysis, then, the factor scores are used as independent variables and other common personnel practices as dependent variables to estimate the probability of their occurrence. Statistically significant coefficients thus provide further evidence for or against the argument of four distinct personnel systems.

Table 14.2 (on pp. 200–201) contains the logit coefficients for forty-two personnel practices. The reader is reminded that the fourteen personnel policies that emerged as appropriate variables for the factor analysis and listed in Table 14.2 are not included in this discussion and in Table 14.2 since the correlations between these variables and factor scores are by calculation very high.

As Table 14.2 shows, the first column, reflecting an affirmative action culture, is significantly related to a variety of personnel practices that are fully compatible with such a culture. In the area of recruitment, requests to minority, female and other special interest organizations stand out; special considerations in the hiring process are apparently given to race or ethnicity; and career development and outreach programs tend to be in place to attract minority and women candidates. Finally, as one might expect, the probability of the affirmative action culture having a formal policy against sexual harassment is relatively high.

The second column of Table 14.2 lists the personnel practices that the logit analysis relates to the merit system culture in a statistically significant way. To confirm the appropriateness of this designation one can point to several sections in the table starting with compensation policies. The probability that the merit system culture hires above minimum pay level and offers bonuses for superior performance is relatively high. Under recruitment policies, the data confirm the expectation that this culture is strict with respect to nepotism rules. In the area of performance appraisal policies, the culture stands out as the only one strong on the use of formal performance appraisals. Moreover, it tends to base performance standards on job-related tasks and is likely to apply the most valid technique in the form of behaviorally anchored rating scales.

The appropriateness of the merit-system designation is also supported by the section on termination and retirement policies. The merit system culture prefers to base the order of layoffs on seniority and merit rather than strictly on seniority, which it tends to oppose judging from the negative sign.

Actually, the findings reflect the ambivalence with which practitioners and academicians tend to assess the merit system culture. On the one hand it is often equated with professionalism as such, and the large number of entries across most personnel functions justifies this designation. In other words, Table 14.2 clearly shows that the merit system culture is the most proactive personnel arena. Concerning fringe benefits, for instance, it is likely to offer such innovative employment programs as sick leave incentive plans, administrative and educational leave, tuition incentives to nonmanagement employees, flexible work hours, job sharing and part-time opportunities, cafeteria plans, and physical fitness programs.

On the other hand, the merit system culture has also been described as rigid and even reactionary when it adopts policies associated with the scientific management school, and the data confirm this inclination. Individual performance appraisals and personalized merit pay or bonuses have been called a throwback to Tayloristic management techniques, and they are considered incompatible with total quality management, according to Deming (1986) and subsequent scholars (Bowman 1994).

Some may argue that these policies are intended to make public sector employment competitive with the private sector. This observation is supported by the finding that hiring above minimum level seems to be a strong characteristic of this culture.

But other conservative tendencies can be observed in Table 14.2. A lack of progressivism can be implied from the finding that the merit culture shows little inclination to offer special programs benefiting women, minorities, and subordinates. Judging from the regression coefficients, the probability is low that the culture gives any special consideration to race or ethnicity in the hiring process or funds outreach programs to attract minority and women candidates. Concerning fringe benefits, the merit dimension is indeterminate with respect to unpaid maternity leave. And finally, with respect to discipline and grievance policies, the prevalence of this culture is no predictor of jurisdictions having instituted formal appeals processes in the case of disciplinary action or termination.

The union culture is discussed next. In many respects it is similar to the merit system dimension in that it tends to be proactive in innovative employment practices, but it apparently also embraces many of the policies favored by the EEO/affirmative action culture. Moreover, the regression coefficients are statistically significant for traditional union demands, justifying the claim that the fourth factor reflects a personnel system dominated by the union culture.

Compatible with the union dimension are compensation policies involving shift differential pay and hiring above minimum pay level. Also the recruitment and screening methods favored by this culture contain no surprises, especially when screening means the use of a centralized referral agency in the hiring process, minimum scores on tests, and the rule of "n" for certification. One would perhaps have expected this culture to be stronger on fringe benefits, but fully compatible are its emphasis on discipline and grievance policies and on termination and retirement policies. It apparently favors the possibility of appeals on disciplinary action and termination, and it supports labor-management committees. And the data confirm the union preference for a layoff order that is based strictly on seniority.

Finally, let's look at the culture that appears to favor affirmative action for certain men. It was given this name because of its high factor loadings on policies dealing with affirmative action programs for rehabilitated alcohol or drug abusers, ex-offenders, and veterans. The logit analysis confirms this label. The coefficients indicate that this employment culture is likely to give special consideration to veteran status in the hiring process, while opposing mothers in the workforce—it scores negatively on unpaid maternity leave. Overall, however, this personnel culture generates few statistically significant probability estimates, contributing little to the predictive capability of the model. This personnel system should therefore not be given too much weight.

In general, it needs to be pointed out that the lack of a statistically significant coefficient in Table 14.2 does not have to mean "no policy"; it only means that the implementation of the policy cannot be predicted by the respective personnel system. In the case of sexual harassment,

Table 14.2

Logit Analysis Involving Factor Scores and Various Personnel Policies

	Independent variables			
Dependent variables	1 AA system (for legally protected groups)	2 Merit system	3 AA system (for certain men)	4 Union system
Compensation policies				
Shift differential pay	.280**	−.007	−.001	.403***
	(.096)	(.094)	(.084)	(.085)
Hiring above minimum pay level	−.289	.664***	−.136	.587***
	(.172)	(.141)	(.131)	(.178)
Bonus for superior performance	−.068	.667***	−.108	.168
	(.101)	(1.27)	(.102)	(.092)
Cost of living adjustment tied to standard index	−.014	.263***	−.027	−.063
	(.096)	(.102)	(.091)	(.088)
Flexible salary step advancement	−.004	.305***	.019	.030
	(.089)	(.091)	(.081)	(.081)
Recruitment policies				
Public announcement of exam	.157	−.040	.199*	.517***
	(.089)	(.095)	(.102)	(.094)
Requests to minority, female and other special interest organizations	.668***	.164	−.070	.786***
	(.094)	(.095)	(.088)	(.096)
Internship program	.226	.385***	.068	.349***
	(.093)	(.102)	(.083)	(.082)
Centralized applicant referral	−.019	.180	.130	.342***
	(.104)	(.114)	(.089)	(.092)
Regulations on hiring relatives	.066	.430***	−.123	−.173
	(.100)	(.097)	(.089)	(.092)
Special screening methods				
Minimum score on tests	.109	.111	.031	.560***
	(.090)	(.093)	(.090)	(.094)
Assessment center	.087	.586***	−.027	.523***
	(.097)	(.118)	(.090)	(.086)
Rule of "n" certificate	−.065	−.108	.140	.270***
	(.086)	(.089)	(.085)	(.080)
Special considerations in hiring process				
Race or ethnicity	.656***	.082	.054	.330***
	(.132)	(.112)	(.092)	(.092)
Residency status of applicant	−.334***	−.393***	.045	.029
	(.107)	(.106)	(.104)	(.105)
Veteran status	.358***	−.164	.290***	.314***
	(.103)	(.097)	(.083)	(.086)
To attract minority and women candidates				
Career development program	.600***	.327*	.135	.499***
	(.164)	(.153)	(.102)	(.110)
Outreach programs	.744***	.038	.040	.566***
	(.109)	(.098)	(.084)	(.086)
Fringe benefits				
Sick leave incentive plans	−.019	.258**	−.102	.108
	(.090)	(.096)	(.090)	(.082)
Unpaid maternity leave	.095	.166	−.242**	.147
	(.103)	(.104)	(.093)	(.099)

Administrative leave	−.063	.555***	−.040	.256**
	(.097)	(.095)	(.091)	(.093)
Educational leave	.114	.336**	−.038	.105
	(.089)	(.093)	(.085)	(.082)
Tuition incentives to nonmanagement employees	.107	.477***	−.161	.176
	(.103)	(.099)	(.092)	(.101)
Flexible work hours	.062	.340***	.083	.277***
	(.089)	(.092)	(.087)	(.083)
Job sharing/part time	−.011	.250***	−.078	.207**
	(.091)	(.095)	(.088)	(.083)
Cafeteria plan	.085	.717***	−.099	.027
	(.107)	(.145)	(.109)	(.096)
Employee counseling program	.310***	.089	.216*	.522***
	(0.898)	(.091)	(.084)	(0.84)
Assistance for alcohol/drug problems	.369***	.221*	.118	.537***
	(.088)	(.092)	(.093)	(.091)
Physical fitness program	.157	.524***	−.052	.149
	(.121)	(.153)	(.113)	(.103)
Performance appraisal policies				
Formal performance appraisal in place	.105	1.240***	−.207	.105
	(.167)	(.165)	(.138)	(.169)
Behaviorally anchored rating scales	.047	.302**	−.023	.209*
	(.101)	(.114)	(.095)	(.089)
Performance standards based on job relatedness	.139	.463***	.062	.246*
	(.086)	(.090)	(.085)	(.083)
Involvement both of managers and employees in developing performance appraisal standards	.077	.394***	−.031	−.031
	(.092)	(.093)	(0.87)	(.085)
Formal appeals to appraisals	.055	.280**	.038	.142
	(.094)	(.105)	(.086)	(.084)
Discipline and grievance policies				
Possibility of appeals on disciplinary action	.184	.058	−.027	.416***
	(.113)	(.119)	(.113)	(.124)
Possibility of appeals on termination	.229*	.094	.143	.410***
	(.101)	(.106)	(.120)	(.110)
Labor-management committees	.071	−.151	.049	.476***.
	(.095)	(.095)	(.086)	(.085)
Termination and retirement policies				
Layoff order based strictly on seniority	.168	−.187*	.052	.542***
	(.092)	(.092)	(.084)	(.083)
Layoff order based on seniority and merit	.016	.455***	−.270**	.371***
	(.094)	(.111)	(.107)	(.085)
Shared work to avoid layoff	.431	.009	.307*	.467**
	(.254)	(.211)	(.129)	(.171)
Reduction of hours to avoid layoff	.261	.091	.281**	.344**
	(.158)	(.153)	(.100)	(.121)
Other personnel regulations				
Formal policy against sexual harassment	.534***	.216	.357	.200
	(.128)	(.130)	(.219)	(.137)
Formal AIDS policy	.425**	−.005	−.127	.261
	(.139)	(.124)	(.126)	(.106)
Formal smoking policy	.176*	−.048	−.109	.369***
	(.087)	(.092)	(.082)	(.86)

Source: ICMA (1989).
Notes: Figures are unstandardized logit coefficients; standard error in parenthesis. *N* varies between 557 and 630. *$p = -.05$; **$p = .01$; ***$p = .001$.

Table 14.3

Multiple Regression Analysis Showing the Influence of Population and Percentage of White Residents on the Four Personnel Cultures

Dependent variables factor scores	Independent variables	
	Population	% of White
Affirmative Action (AA) system		
(for legally protected groups)	.113**	.018
Merit system	.048	−.034
AA system (for certain men)	.130***	−.019
Union system	.287***	−.014

Sources: ICMA (1989).
Notes: Figures are beta coefficients (OLS). Minimum $N = 616$. $*p = .05$; $**p = .01$; $***p = .001$.

for instance, only the affirmative action culture shows some connection, but actually 82.6 percent of all cities participating in the ICMA survey have such a policy (Fox 1993, 20).

Fourth Finding: Relationships of Personnel Cultures to Demographic, Geographic, and Governmental Characteristics

This section explores possible connections between important jurisdictional characteristics and the four personnel cultures. The demographic characteristics tested are population and the percentage of white residents. As Table 14.3 shows, the size of the population influences the existence of three of the four cultures in a statistically significant way. The finding that size does not predict a merit system culture is noteworthy and deserves further study. Also, the observation that the percentage of white residents fails to predict the appearance of any of the systemic cultures invites additional research.

The testing of geographical characteristics leads to one expected finding and one surprise. As seen in Table 14.4, the merit culture shows a statistically significant and expected pattern in its distribution across the four regions of the United States. The South and West record a much larger percentage of high (.5–5.0) merit system factor scores than the North Central and Northeast regions. In contrast, although statistically significant, the union culture does not show the strength in the North Central and Northeast regions as one might have expected judging from previous research (Dahl and Wappel 1989).

As a final characteristic, the form of government—council-manager, mayor-council, or some other form such as commission—is reviewed for its possible association with the four personnel cultures. As presented in Table 14.5, the pattern is statistically significant for all four employment systems. The council-manager form is more likely to have high scores on the affirmative action culture and merit culture than the mayor-council form of government. One could continue testing the reasons for these observations, but the basic trend seems to hold. Municipalities do not exhibit a unidimensional professional standard on a scale from the spoils system to the merit system. Instead, their personnel policies cluster in such a way that four distinct personnel cultures emerge.

Implications

Local governments are expected to implement a variety of personnel policies. Some are court-mandated, some are required by federal law, some reflect the professional standards of the public

Table 14.4

Association of Geographical Region with the Four Personnel Cultures

Factor scores	North Central	Northeast	South	West	Row total
Affirmative Action (AA) system (for legally protected groups)					
−3.0 to .000	53.0	35.0	53.0	49.0	190.0
	27.9	18.4	27.9	25.8	30.2
	29.4	35.4	30.6	27.5	
.001 to .499	24.0	24.0	28.0	37.0	113.0
	21.2	21.2	24.8	32.7	17.9
	13.3	24.2	16.2	20.8	
			92.0	92.0	327.0
.5 to 5.0	103.0	40.0	92.0	92.0	327.0
	31.5	12.2	28.1	28.1	51.9
	57.2	40.4	53.2	51.7	
Cramer's V = .090; significance = .000					
Merit system					
−3.0 to .000	80.0	51.0	42.0	42.0	215.0
	37.2	23.7	19.5	19.5	34.1
	44.4	51.5	24.3	23.6	
.001 to .499	3.0	3.0	9.0	4.0	19.0
	15.8	15.8	47.4	21.1	3.0
	1.7	3.0	5.2	2.2	
.5 to 5.0	97.0	45.0	122.0	132.0	396.0
	24.5	11.4	30.8	33.3	62.9
	53.9	45.5	70.5	74.2	
Cramer's V = .182; significance = .000					
AA system (for certain men)					
−3.0 to .000	138.0	77.0	131.0	139.0	485.0
	28.5	15.9	27.0	28.7	77.0
	76.7	77.8	75.7	78.1	
.001 to .499	25.0	13.0	24.0	27.0	89.0
	28.1	14.6	27.0	30.3	14.1
	13.9	13.1	13.9	15.1	
.5 to 5.0	17.0	9.0	18.0	12.0	56.0
	30.4	16.1	32.1	21.4	8.9
	9.4	9.1	10.4	6.7	
Cramer's V = .037; significance = .943					
Union system					
−3.0 to .000	88.0	45.0	99.0	64.0	296.0
	29.7	15.2	33.4	21.6	47.0
	48.9	45.5	57.2	36.0	
.001 to .499	35.0	21.0	32.0	50.0	138.0
	25.4	15.2	23.2	36.2	21.9
	19.4	21.2	18.5	28.1	
.5 to 5.0	57.0	33.0	42.0	64.0	196.0
	29.1	16.8	21.4	32.7	31.1
	31.7	33.3	24.3	36.0	
Cramer's V = .117; significance = .008					
Column total	180.0	99.0	173.0	178.0	630.0
	28.6	15.7	27.5	28.3	100.0

Source: ICMA (1989).

Table 14.5

Association of Form of Government with the Four Personnel Cultures

Factor scores	Council-Manager	Mayor-Council	Other	Row total
AA system (for legally protected groups)				
−3.0 to .000	117.0	65.0	8.0	190.0
	61.6	34.2	4.2	30.2
	27.8	36.5	25.8	
.001 to .499	67.0	39.0	7.0	113.0
	59.3	34.5	6.2	17.9
	15.9	21.9	22.6	
.5 to 5.0	237.0	74.0	16.0	327.0
	72.5	22.6	4.9	51.9
	56.3	41.6	51.6	
Cramer's V = .0957; significance = .022				
Merit system				
−3.0 to .000	122.0	80.0	13.0	215.0
	56.7	37.2	6.0	34.1
	29.0	44.9	41.9	
.001 to .499	14.0	5.0		19.0
	73.7	26.3		3.0
	3.3	2.8		
.5 to 5.0	285.0	93.0	18.0	396.0
	72.0	23.5	4.5	62.9
	67.7	52.2	58.1	
Cramer's V = .112; significance = .003				
AA system (for certain men)				
−3.0 to .000	336.0	127.0	22.0	485.0
	69.3	26.2	4.5	77.0
	79.8	71.3	71.0	
.001 to .499	53.0	27.0	9.0	89.0
	59.6	30.3	10.1	14.1
	12.6	15.2	29.0	
.5 to 5.0	32.0	24.0		56.0
	57.1	42.9		8.9
	7.6	13.5		
Union system				
−3.0 to .000	186.0	96.0	14.0	296.0
	62.8	32.4	4.7	47.0
	44.2	53.9	45.2	
.001 to .499	108.0	23.0	7.0	138.0
	78.3	16.7	5.1	21.9
	25.7	12.9	22.6	
.5 to 5.0	127.0	59.0	10.0	196.0
	64.8	30.1	5.1	31.1
	30.2	33.1	32.3	
Cramer's V = .098; significance = .016				
Column total	421.0	178.0	31.0	630.0
	66.8	28.3	4.9	100.0

Source: ICMA (1989).

personnel field, and some emerge in competition with the private sector. Merit systems comprise the oldest set of principles, followed by collective bargaining, and EEO/affirmative action. Supporters of collective bargaining and affirmative action tend to argue that their demands are compatible with merit system principles, while others have described them as inherently in conflict. Scale analysis, using Cronbach's alpha, shows that the behavior of municipal personnel departments does not fall neatly on a continuum from the patronage system to the merit system with union preferences and EEO/affirmative action nicely folded in. Instead, factor analysis and logistic regression analysis reveal that personnel departments are dominated by certain systemic cultures, which lead them to emphasize certain values and practices.

These findings suggest several additional research questions. In light of the focus on reinventing government and the declining support for affirmative action, researchers and practitioners may wish to know how these cultures adapt to change. In all likelihood they will react differently to the introduction of policy innovations. The members of the Winter Commission have recognized this possibility and explored how cities dominated by union cultures respond to pressures for change. That research is published in *Revitalizing State and Local Public Service*, edited by Thompson (1993), and in the spring 1994 issue of the *Review of Public Personnel Administration*. The finding of four personnel cultures in this study suggests that similar case studies need to be conducted for the other three personnel systems to gain a more precise understanding of their potential for change. As Mosher (1982) and postmodern analysts (Caldwell 1975; Clegg, 1990) point out, in a fragmented society competing value claims cannot be avoided, but they can at least be made explicit so that a balance among them can be found.

The findings also suggest the need for more research of public personnel systems per se. To echo the argumentation by Morgan and Perry (1988), the literature has focused on constituent parts of civil service systems rather than on personnel systems as a whole and the relationship of personnel systems to the surrounding political and economic systems. One can, for instance, perceive the emergence of two more public personnel systems in the 1990s. One might be called the democratic personnel system and comprises policies like total quality management, participatory management, team management, flattened hierarchy, right to employer-financed training or at least regular time off for educational purposes, strengthened rights to freedom of speech and association, and legal protection of whistleblowers.

The other emerging public personnel system can be called the competitive or market-driven personnel system. It subsumes trends like more aggressive searches for qualified job candidates, merit pay and bonus pay, greater diversity in fringe benefits, abolition of detailed job classes and grades in favor of broadbanding, privatization, focus on the customer, and competitive bidding for government contracts involving public and private providers. Researchers conducting surveys of local governments may wish to ask questions probing for these developments so that the changes can be tracked in future statistical analyses.

Notes

1. The use of the term "human resources" has become more politically correct than "personnel," supposedly because it emphasizes the value of employees to the employer. In my view, this is an unfortunate choice and actually represents a throwback to the industrial model and scientific management, when human capital and other capital were treated with the same instrumental rationality. The term "personnel" at least has the stem "person" in it, which conveys more dignity. Nevertheless, the terms will be used interchangeably in this chapter.

2. It would be more precise to make a distinction between the terms "policies" and "practices," defining the former as the formal rules and the latter as the actual implementation of the rules. The survey instrument, however, did not aim for such a precision, and it would be wrong to second-guess the respondents whether they reported the official rules or actual procedures. An attempt to distinguish between the two terms was made in an earlier article using the same data set (Fox 1993).

3. "Merit system" and "civil service" refer to slightly different arrangements in the history of public personnel administration. But the argumentation in this article will not be hurt by ignoring the distinction. See also footnote (3) in Fox (1993, 23–24).

References

Belsley, G.L. 1938. "Personnel Administration." In *The Municipal Year Book 1938.* Chicago: International City Managers' Association.

Bowman, J.S. 1994. "At Last, an Alternative to Performance Appraisal: Total Quality Management." *Public Administration Review* 54, no. 2 (March/April): 129–136.

Caldwell, L.K. 1975. "Managing the Transition to Postmodern Society." *Public Administration Review* 35, no. 6 (November/December): 567–572.

Cayer, J. 1991. "Local Government Personnel Structure and Policies." In *The Municipal Year Book 1991.* Washington, DC: International City/County Management Association.

Cohen, S., and W. Eimicke. 1994. "The Overregulated Civil Service: The Case of New York City's Public Personnel System." *Review of Public Personnel Administration* 14, no. 2 (Spring): 11–27.

Clegg, S.R. 1990. *Modern Organizations. Organization Studies in the Postmodern World.* Newbury Park, CA: Sage.

Dahl, R.E., and J.F. Wappel. 1989. "Labor-Management Relations in Local Government: Current Practices." *Baseline Data Report* 21, no. 3. Washington, DC: ICMA.

Deming, W.E. 1986. *Out of the Crisis.* Cambridge, MA: MIT Press.

Fox, S.F. 1993. "Professional Norms and Actual Practice in Local Personnel Administration. A Status Report." *Review of Public Personnel Administration* 13, no. 2 (Spring): 5–28.

Fox, S.F., and C.J. Fox. 1991. "Merit Systems and Personnel Appraisals in Local Government." *Baseline Data Report* 22, no. 6. Washington, DC: ICMA.

Galatas, S.A. 1950. "Good Government and Labor." *National Municipal Review* 39, no. 2 (February): 79–82.

Graham, C.B. 1990. "Equal Employment Opportunity and Affirmative Action: Policies, Techniques, and Controversies." In *Public Personnel Administration. Problems and Prospects*, 2d ed., ed. S.W. Hays and R.C. Kearney. Englewood Cliffs, NJ: Prentice-Hall.

Hair, J.R., R.E. Anderson, and R.L. Tatham. 1987. *Multivariate Data Analysis*, 2d ed. New York: Macmillan.

Hyman, H.H. 1972. *Secondary Analysis of Sample Surveys: Principles, Procedures, and Potentialities.* New York: John Wiley.

International City Management Association. 1989. "Local Government Personnel Practices—1989." Washington, DC: ICMA. (Questionnaire).

Kaiser, H.F. 1974. "An Index of Factorial Simplicity." *Psychometrika* 39 (March): 31–36.

Karl, B.D. 1976. "Public Administration and American History: A Century of Professionalism." *Public Administration Review* 36, no. 5 (September/October): 489–503.

Kearney, R.C., and C. Sinha. 1988. "Professionalism and Bureaucratic Responsiveness: Conflict or Compatibility?" *Public Administration Review* 48, no. 1 (January/February): 571–579.

Keller, M., W.W. Steiner, and W.H. Clark. 1994. "Alcohol and Drug Consumption." *The New Encyclopaedia Britannica*, 15th ed. Chicago: Encyclopaedia Britannica.

Kiecolt, K.J., and L.E. Nathan. 1985. *Secondary Analysis of Survey Data.* Beverly Hills, CA: Sage.

Kim, J.-O., N. Nie, and S. Verba. 1977. "A Note on Factor Analyzing Dichotomous Variables: The Case of Political Participation." *Political Methodology* 4: 39–62.

Klingner, D.E., and J. Nalbandian. 1993. *Public Personnel Management: Context and Strategies*, 3d ed. Englewood Cliffs, NJ: Prentice-Hall.

Lan, Z., and D.H. Rosenbloom. 1992. "Public Administration in Transition?" *Public Administration Review* 52, no. 6 (November/December): 535–537.

Lepper, J. 1983. "Affirmative Action: A Tool for Effective Personnel Management." In *Public Personnel Administration. Problems and Prospects*, ed. S.W. Hays and R.C. Kearney. Englewood Cliffs, NJ: Prentice-Hall.

Morgan, E.P., and J.L. Perry. 1988. "Reorienting the Comparative Study of Civil Service Systems." *Review of Public Personnel Administration* 8, no. 3 (Summer): 84–95.

Mosher, F.C. 1982. *Democracy and the Public Service.* New York: Oxford University Press.

Muthen, B. 1981. "Factor Analysis of Dichotomous Variables: American Attitudes Toward Abortion." In *Factor Analysis and Measurement*, ed. D.J. Jackson and E.F. Borgatta. Beverly Hills, CA: Sage.

Norusis, M.J. 1990. *SPSS Base System User's Guide.* Chicago: SPSS, Inc.

Olufs, D.W. 1985. "The Limits of Professionalism." *Public Administration Quarterly* 9, no. 1 (Spring): 26–46.

Osborne, D., and T. Gaebler. 1992. *Reinventing Government.* Reading, MA: Addison-Wesley.

Perry, J., L.R. Wise, and M. Martin. 1994. "Breaking the Civil Service Mold." *Review of Public Personnel Administration* 14, no. 2 (Spring): 40–54.

Rabin, J. 1982. "Professionalism in Public Administration: Definition, Character and Values—A Symposium." *American Review of Public Administration* 15 (Winter): 303–412.

Riccucci, N.M. 1991. "Affirmative Action in the Twenty-first Century: New Approaches and Developments." In *Public Personnel Management. Current Concerns—Future Challenges*. New York: Longman.

Sampson, C.L. 1993. "Professional Roles and Perceptions of the Public Personnel Function." *Public Administration Review* 53, no. 2 (March/April): 154–160.

Stanley, D.T. 1972. *Managing Local Government Under Union Pressure*. Washington, DC: Brookings Institution.

Stein, L. 1994. "Personnel Rules and Reform in an Unreformed Setting." *Review of Public Personnel Administration* 14, no. 2 (Spring): 55–63.

Thompson, F.J., ed. 1993. *Revitalizing State and Local Public Service*. San Francisco: Jossey-Bass.

Thompson, Wayne E. 1975. "Labor-Management Focus: Improving Government Productivity." *National Civic Review* 64, no. 7 (July): 335–338.

U.S. Bureau of the Census. 1991. *Statistical Abstract of the United States, 1991*, 111th ed. Washington, DC: U.S. Government Printing Office.

U.S. House of Representatives. Committee on Education and Labor. 1969. Intergovernmental Personnel Act. 91st Cong., 1st Sess., November 17, 18, and 20.

U.S. House of Representatives. Committee on Post Office and Civil Service. 1975. Amendments to the Intergovernmental Personnel Act of 1970. 94th Cong., 1st Sess., March 3 and 5.

U.S. Office of Personnel Management. 1983. "Intergovernmental Personnel Act Programs; Standards for a Merit System of Personnel Administration." *Federal Register* 48, no. 44 (Friday, March 4): 9209–9212.

U.S. Senate. Committee on Government Operations. 1967. Intergovernmental Personnel Act of 1967. 90th Cong., 1st Sess., April 26, 27, and 28.

———. 1969. Intergovernmental Personnel Act of 1969. 91st Cong., 1st Sess., March 24, 25, 26, and April 1.

———. 1975. Amendments to the Intergovernmental Personnel Act. 94th Cong., 1st Sess., April 16.

Van Riper, P.O. 1958. *History of the United States Civil Service*. Evanston, IL: Row, Peterson.

Wilson, J.Q. 1989. *What Government Agencies Do and Why They Do It*. New York: Basic Books.

Woodruff, C.R. 1912. "American Municipal Tendencies." *National Municipal Review* 1, no. 1 (January): 3–20.

CHAPTER 15

AFFIRMATIVE ACTION IN MUNICIPAL GOVERNMENT:

Anatomy of a Failure

STEVE BALLARD AND GAYLE LAWN-DAY

Equal employment opportunity and affirmative action have become firmly institutionalized in American society over the past twenty-five years. A fundamental principle of this reform movement has been that reduction of legal barriers, by themselves, would be insufficient to overcome the past record of discrimination for women and minorities. "Affirmative Action" is viewed by many to be an apt description for public policy which unambiguously sought to encourage agencies to make fundamental changes in personnel decision-making.

The empirical evidence on minority utilization and gender diversifications suggests mixed results, however. Participation rates for women and some minority groups have increased somewhat, and several major jurisdictions can point to the reduction of longstanding employment-related barriers. However, on balance the record is one of creeping incrementalism (Huckles 1985). Continuation of occupational segregation, differential salary structures, and the virtual absence of role models for women and minorities at top management levels of municipal government strongly suggest that equal employment opportunity and affirmative action have had a limited influence on developing a representative bureaucracy.

This chapter examines a failed reform movement in a community which, according to conventional wisdom, should have been a prototype of reform in employment practices. Norman, Oklahoma, is a moderate-size, university community with a progressive self-image. A range of political and administrative conditions coalesced in the late 1980s to create a significant opportunity for progress toward modern employment practices. While significant reforms were initiated, very few were sustained. Three questions are addressed concerning this period of reform: (1) what was the relative importance of the various conditions influencing affirmative action and equal employment opportunity; (2) how did the reform movement become unraveled; and (3) what changes would be required to overcome barriers to affirmative action in similar communities.

Barriers to Affirmative Action

Public employment practices have been circumscribed by a variety of federal laws, executive orders, and court cases (Graham 1989; Nalbandian 1989; Redeker, 1986). This legal and regulatory structure has established two broad mandates for personnel practices in public agencies and

From *Review of Public Personnel Administration*, vol. 12, no. 3 (May–August 1992), pp. 5–18. Copyright © 1992 by Sage Publications, Inc. Reprinted with permission.

many private organizations. The concept of "equal employment opportunity," directed toward individual rights, is intended to eliminate discrimination in employment practices. "Affirmative Action," in contrast, entails proactive governmental initiatives to hire and promote members of groups ("suspect classifications") which have suffered job-related discrimination historically. The promise of affirmative action was fundamentally tied to the idea of representative bureaucracy; to be a success, change must occur at the aggregate level of employment, not just the individual level (Cayer and Sigelman 1980; Clynch and Gaudin 1982; Guy 1990; Slack and Sigelman 1987). In 1974, the Equal Employment Opportunity Commission (EEOC) stated that measurable results are expected, including ". . . yearly improvements in hiring, training and promotion of minorities and females in all parts of the organization" (EEOC 1974).

The general record across levels of government has been mixed[1] (Bremer and Howe 1988; Hopkins 1980; Lewis 1987; Kellough and Kay 1986). At the local level, past studies have identified a range of barriers. These include:

- "Covert discrimination" or cultural inertia—employment practices based upon the way they have traditionally been done (Guy 1990).
- Lack of political will, including the lack of political leadership and unprofessional administration (Stein 1988).
- The inability of primary constituents to effectively organize on behalf of affirmative action[2] (Neuse 1978; Reyfuss 1986).
- Bureaucratic inertia, organizational climate, and the routinization of affirmative action so as to minimize its importance or neglect the spirit of the law (Bremer and Howe 1988; Vertz 1985).
- Prejudice and discrimination, including stereotyping, tokenism, and occupational segregation (Cayer and Sigelman 1980; Guy 1990; Hopkins 1980; Kellough and Kay 1986; Lewis 1986).
- Lack of awareness, understanding, or commitment on the part of upper level management (Slack and Siegelman 1987).
- Conflict with merit principles and "public service efficiency"[3] (Graham 1989; Nalbandian 1989; Slack 1987).
- Lack of enforcement and/or a failure of the intergovernmental regulatory system (Perman 1988; Thompson 1984).

In Norman, four of these barriers were thought by reformers to be particularly important: (1) covert discrimination or cultural inertia; (2) lack of political will; (3) weak commitment of management; and (4) uninspiring organizational climate. Historically, little evidence existed that affirmative action had been a salient concern in municipal government and, during the twelve-year term of the prior city manager, city hall was operated along the lines of a traditional patronage system. The state government was understood to have a minimal commitment to affirmative action and equal employment opportunity, and few enforcement initiatives had been in evidence. However, change was to come to city hall as a consequence of the significant changes which were occurring in the political structure of the Norman community. This study began as an effort to examine whether these changes could overcome the political, cultural, and organizational inertia in city hall.

Research Setting and Approach

The community evaluated in this study has a relatively positive self-image, and in the late 1980s an unusual opportunity existed for reform. The community is heavily influenced by a public university and has a long history of considerable citizen participation in local affairs. Several civic groups and many members of the university community not only encouraged reform, but also participated directly in search committees for new management positions and in public discussions of the city's direction. These groups were instrumental in helping the council bring new management to the city in 1987, based on the widespread perception that the city had been ineffectively managed for the previous twelve years.

A new management team, with national credentials and sensitive to issues of professional personnel management, was brought to city hall. This team included the city manager and seven upper management positions. Since most members of the new management team were from out-of-state, they were thought to be less likely to be influenced by historical circumstance, cultural factors, or political barriers to equal employment opportunity or affirmative action.

Perhaps most importantly for our purposes here, the political will now clearly existed to pursue fundamental change and reform in the structure of city government. An unusual consensus existed between management and the city council about both substantive policy priorities and procedures for moving the city forward. As a result, the first mandate for the new administration was to restructure city government, bring professional managers into the top leadership positions, and improve the productivity and image of the city's workforce. These goals were unanimously agreed to by the nine-member council and discussed publicly. In addition, the composition of the city council suggested sensitivity to affirmative action goals. One member of the nine-member council was a minority and three others were women.[4] Finally, the authors were in unique positions as participant-observants; one was a member of the city council, the other a city employee who in time worked for the city manager and two division directors.

Information on E.E.O. and affirmative action developments was collected from three primary sources during a twenty-month period running from 1987 to 1989. First, the authors served as participant observants of the employment practices used throughout the city. Decision-making about employment policy, specific activities associated with personnel actions, and contacts from citizens and community groups interested in the reform movement were recorded. Second, the hiring processes for seven upper management positions were systematically monitored over a two-year period (1987–1989). These positions included the director of administrative services, director of public works, director of public safety, finance director, fire chief, police chief, and city attorney. In each case, the ratios of women and minorities applying were recorded, the qualified applicant pool was estimated, gender and race-sensitive advertising strategies were reviewed, and special circumstances that could have influenced the hiring process were assessed.

A third source of information was collected once hiring was completed. In-depth qualitative interviews were conducted by the authors with twenty-two municipal employees and staff of the regional EEOC. Given the sensitivity of many of the hiring and personnel decisions being made, it was not feasible to interview randomly. Rather, interviews were conducted with those most directly involved or affected, ranging from department heads to individuals whose careers were influenced or changed. Information collected in this manner was intended to provide a holistic perspective of the hiring process throughout the organization, to compare the attitudes of key participants regarding their commitment to affirmative action, and to evaluate the relative influence of internal and external barriers. .

Affirmative Action: Structure and Process

As the new management team was put in place in 1988, their impact on the affirmative action plan and decision-making about hiring was observed. They clearly recognized that cultural inertia and both overt and covert discrimination were obstructing reform of personnel practices. Structural problems with the affirmative action plan included improper analysis of the existing labor force and job pool and the absence of a feasible harassment and discrimination complaint system. More significantly, no effective system was in place to review and correct deficiencies in the plan. Indeed, the personnel director was in the position of policing himself insofar as he was also the affirmative action officer.

Evidence that the personnel department was not committed to a proactive approach to affirmative action was buttressed by the authors' review of several hirings. In each case, an assessment of progress to affirmative action goals was impeded by the city's failure to collect routine applicant demographic information. Consequently, the race and gender of the applicants had to be determined from resume data, or, in some cases, inferred from surname, affiliations, and other indirect indicators. Internal sources involved in the hiring process were instrumental in enriching the records with personal notes and observations. External sources such as affirmative action offices in other local organizations assisted in the development and verification of reasonable applicant pools as sources of comparison. They also provided scenarios and situations under which the nonattainment of affirmative action goals would be acceptable, both practically and theoretically. For example, the low number of minorities with advanced degrees in certain technical areas would prevent the employer from setting high job pool targets in that area.[5]

Information from qualitative interviews with municipal employees as well as observations made throughout the study indicated that three broad schools of thought existed within the organization during the time of our study: (1) those who preferred the traditional, largely patronage system; (2) those who supported equal opportunity employment but were unable or unwilling to express their views publicly, and (3) those supporting affirmative action and willing to take a public stance.

Support for affirmative action existed primarily with new employees who did not accept the organizational culture. Most of these were people in top management positions who had broad experience in municipal government in other geographical areas. This supportive group had the most political and management power, and their values about employment practices were incorporated into the hiring process during the period of this study. The struggle between the historical values of the organization and those of the new administration often took place in a covert manner. An undercurrent of tension was present in each interaction of the conflicting groups. As discussed below, the inability to reduce this tension was a significant factor in the demise of the reform movement.

Because of the support of the City Council and the attitudes of the new management team, extensive national advertising in trade and minority publications as well as contacts with minority trade organizations did take place. Even though such actions were publicly supported by the city manager, the resulting applicant pools were disappointing (see Table 15.1). For example, considering experience and education, about one-third of the qualified pool for most of the top management positions could have been female based on the percentage of the available national labor force. The resulting percentages fell in a range of zero percent to nine percent of qualified females in the pools. While considerable uncertainty exists about the composition of the qualified applicant pool, especially for some positions, Norman was able to attract only a few women to the search.

Two explanations can be made. First, many of the positions were in nontraditional fields with a low number of females in these jobs. The competition among employers to hire these qualified few may exclude those communities, including Norman, which offered mid-level salaries. Second, most of the senior managers believed that the Southwest, including Oklahoma, had a reputation for practicing traditional employment values with little commitment to affirmative action.

Table 15.1

Women Applying for Top Positions

Position	Percentage in pool	Percentage qualified in pool	Percentage interviewed
Director of public safety	0	0	0
Director of public works	0	0	0
Fire chief	0	0	0
Police chief	1	1	0
City attorney	15	9	1
Director of administrative services	8	1	0
Finance director	20	4	0

Note: Qualification was determined by comparing the job announcement and description to resume data.

The number of minorities applying for these positions was difficult, if not impossible, to obtain. City employees who reviewed the resumes and did preliminary screening estimated the maximum number of minority applicants at one or two per position. This was somewhat unexpected since a strong effort was made to attract these applicants. In the few jobs with qualified female and minority applicants, only one was interviewed. Based on observations and interviews with employees of the city, the potential women candidates frequently had national reputations that equaled or exceeded the males in question. Yet, all the hires were white males.

Finally, it became clear that the city did not fear the review or intervention by external forces such as the EEOC. The intergovernmental system exerted little influence on employment practices in Norman. EEO-4 forms and EEOC complaints were the only form of interaction discovered during the twenty-month research period. EEO-4 forms, filed yearly with the EEOC, delineate the number of minority and women in the various departments and job classes. An attempt was made to correlate the data on these forms to municipal employment records during the study period. It was discovered that these forms contained inflated figures for minority and female participation in the workforce. According to employees interviewed, such activities had been occurring over a lengthy time period during which there were no public repercussions.

EEOC complaints filed against the city were stalled and unanswered for as long as possible and usually died of inaction. Long-time employees of the city said publicly that this was the standard operating procedure to deal with these complaints. The personnel director adhered to the philosophy that if no information existed, the city could not be held accountable for its actions; therefore, he instructed his staff to avoid creating records of any action in the personnel process. As crude as this strategy was, it appeared to be effective since the EEOC did not press for further information in any of the cases.

Overcoming Cultural and Political Barriers

The Patronage System

How could such negative results be obtained in a political climate which had demanded reform? Respondents consistently identified cultural factors, both locally and within the state, as the key to developing an explanation. The most significant cultural factor was simply that affirmative action had never been seriously practiced, let alone a priority, in municipal government. Rather, employment in city hall was responsive to interests and pressures from the community. This practice was so entrenched that it had become widely accepted among municipal employees.

Virtually all respondents felt that women had a more difficult time than minorities in overcoming cultural barriers. Women were not allowed to maintain nontraditional positions with visible and important responsibilities. "Nontraditional" jobs are defined as those for which women had not been historically competitive. In Norman, these included most middle-management, supervisory, and upper-management positions.

Only four management positions were held by women; three of these were terminated within the twenty-month study period. Respondents cited their experience with women in their own areas. One official, responsible for over one-third of the labor force, had only three females in nontraditional jobs. He cited the difficulty experienced by these women in maintaining their position or their interest in municipal employment because of continuous attempts to reassign them to positions typically held by women. Another respondent was confronted by mid-level employees within his division who were opposed to having women occupy management jobs. Such actions, he was told, "went against God's will."

A startling examplecultural barriers concerned the practice of discouraging women from participating in training sessions. A trainer who questioned why no women signed up for a session on becoming a supervisor was informed that "women knew better than to go to training since they could not be supervisors anyway."

In an effort to overcome this history, the new city manager agreed to an organizational self-study. A nationally known organizational development specialist was asked to assist in defining employment goals and allocating staff resources. Extensive meetings with the council and upper and middle management were initiated. Again, these exercises were conducted in an atmosphere of constructive reform. The council participated enthusiastically, including in-depth individual sessions with the development specialist. Several division heads were among the strongest supporters of the self-study and were instrumental in generating cooperation among mid-level employees.

Unfortunately, two conditions conspired to impede the process. First, the city manager was absent during some of the final sessions. Thus, division heads were able to exert less influence on the city manager than they had hoped. Second, community-wide conflict between management and labor over the nature of employment contracts gradually reduced the positive climate of reform. The final recommendations of the organizational development specialist were largely ignored by the city manager, even though they were accepted by several division directors. In part, the city manager's response was caused by the pervasive political criticism which he faced; while he remained generally sympathetic to affirmative action, it was clearly a low priority by this time.

The Enforcement System

Respondents to the qualitative survey also believed that the intergovernmental system was of little value in helping the local reformers to overcome cultural and political barriers. Half of the respondents agreed that a lack of interest in affirmative action existed at the state and federal levels, resulting from both ideological differences between earlier administrations and the Reagan/ Bush administrations and from recent Supreme Court decisions. All but one of the respondents agreed that the values of the region also had a significant impact on the acceptability of affirmative action efforts and the intergovernmental process used to resist it. Many respondents in upper level management positions reported positive experiences in previous local government positions. However, one respondent felt that strong grassroots resistance existed to affirmative action nationally. She believed that in other geographical areas resistance and subversion was more subtle and more highly sophisticated.

The lack of a watchdog agency with enforcement powers was felt to be a significant weakness. Several respondents said that no incentive existed for compliance. The state EEOC was cited as extremely ineffective in both collective and individual action. Four individuals referenced personal experiences with the commission citing cases wherein complaints filed were either lost or poorly investigated.

Two specific complaints with the commission were the slowness and incompetence of the investigations. The two-year backlog of cases in the state EEOC as well as the lack of adequate training for the investigators contributed to this perception. Public educational sessions by the agency also hurt their image. At one session for managers in this municipality, the agency advocated the use of "common sense" rather than the understanding of either the spirit or the literal meaning of the legal system affecting employment practices.

The strong and frequently blatant resistance to affirmative action and equal employment opportunity resulted in a backlash in many of the professional organizations to which our respondents belonged. Over half of the respondents said that when representatives of these organizations learned of the turmoil in the city, they self-consciously directed their members away from employment in Norman. Managers employed at the city were contracted by out-of-state colleagues and employment agencies offering assistance in relocating.

Results of the Reform Movement

The patronage group had strong ties to the local community, a significant advantage in subverting most of the employment reforms initiated by the new management team. Within two years (by 1989), the make-up of the council had changed dramatically; four council members were replaced and the mayor narrowly won re-election.

Without question, labor-management relations were a key undercurrent of these elections. Difficulties between labor and management had become pervasive. The senior management team had become disenchanted with the city manager as he became increasingly isolated from the line employees. Several lawsuits were initiated which challenged hiring and retention decisions. Further, the manager, the council, and the three labor unions had reached an impasse regarding annual contracts. Within two and one-half years, the city manager and nearly all of his top appointments had left municipal government. Within this climate, lasting changes in personnel policies were difficult to sustain.

With respect to affirmative action, respondents believed that virtually no progress was made as a result of the reform movement. Eighty-six percent felt that, even at the end of the two-year study period, hiring and promotion decisions were based on individual values rather than any system of fair hiring practices. Education and training efforts, among the most significant initiatives of the reformers, met with both active and passive resistance. At one point, an employee with direct responsibility for affirmative action procedures made a written request for more training. The person was officially reprimanded by the personnel director for the request and was later dismissed from employment.

Even at the conclusion of the reform movement, new employees were predominantly white males with social or family connections to city personnel. One source involved in the hiring process was told by a superior "not to bother interviewing—just find out who the supervisor wants to hire and do it." Those hired on merit were often harassed to the point of voluntary termination. Minorities and women in nontraditional jobs were particular targets of these attacks.

Multiple attempts had been made by the new administration to eradicate these practices; however, as two of the top management respondents stated, "there were too many fires to put out."

Financial problems, citizen unrest, and union negotiation problems frequently superseded affirmative action problems. As a result, adherence to the spirit of affirmative action was virtually impossible. While the new management team did initiate an affirmative action plan, it required no outside review or technical assistance and many inaccuracies existed. In fact, the plan had not been completed by the end of the study period. In addition, without an organizational or community value system which supported the plan, both the letter and spirit of the law could be ignored.

Affirmative Action Policy in the 1990s

Previous studies of affirmative action have carefully documented a range of barriers to the development of gender diversification and minority utilization in the workplace. This case study, while not necessarily representative of affirmative action processes in municipal governments, suggests that each of the eight barriers had some influence on the failed reform effort in Norman, Oklahoma. Future studies which investigate the relative importance of these barriers would be a logical next step.

Even though all eight barriers were present in Norman, some were clearly more important than others. Two factors, the commitment of top management and political will, were not as significant as previous work suggests. At least in the beginning of the reform movement, both political will and commitment of management were strongly present. Neither, however, were sufficient to sustain the reform movement through implementation and both were eroded by the constituencies which coalesced to oppose the new management team. This study clearly suggests the primacy of cultural barriers to the development of effective affirmative action policy. While such factors are not necessarily critical during policy formation and adoption, their cumulative impact over the longer implementation process was perhaps more significant to the eventual political outcome than any other single factor.

This study also suggests that symbolic policy responses are easily overemphasized and generally ineffective. Symbolic responses include the affirmative action plan, appointment of a woman or minority as director of personnel, and ironically, the presence of the state EEOC. While a strong affirmative action plan and leadership by women/minority can be important elements in meeting affirmative action goals, they are not sufficient conditions.

Further, they can be impediments if a broader set of favorable conditions do not exist. Progress on affirmative action becomes virtually impossible if a woman or minority personnel director chooses to subvert the implementation process. In Norman, the presence of a black personnel director, with strong ties to the former city manager and the old patronage system, made challenges to specific implementation practices very difficult. In addition, it presented a significant barrier to the career advancement of women.

This study also illustrates quite well the extent to which the EEOC has become an almost completely symbolic organization; it presented only a minimal, reactive threat to the municipality as it engaged in backsliding on affirmative action programs. As Thompson so accurately predicted in 1984, the lack of intergovernmental support for equal rights and the severe weakening of the federal enforcement agencies would create the opportunity for widespread neglect of affirmative action goals. In the state in which our case study took place, the EEOC had neither the resources, the personnel, nor the credibility to oversee employment practices effectively. Since the EEOC has limited jurisdiction over affirmative action, policy reform should include the creation of multilevel oversight agencies. An independent affirmative action officer would quite likely have benefited the city in this situation.

This case, while hopefully not typical, does carry some implications for our understanding of both political reform and affirmative action policy. With respect to political reform, the council believed that it was in a very strong leadership position; it had the support of community elites, a strong electoral mandate, and internal consensus. Yet, these elements were not enough to sustain the reform movement. Some of the blame for this failure clearly rests with the council itself.

In retrospect, the council committed three large errors. First, in a rather classic manner, the council initiated *top-down* reform. Given the political history of the municipality, broad reform was not likely to occur without strong political leadership. Once initiated, however, the reform movement was not broadened to include the majority of municipal employees and more community groups. This failure to gain wider buy-in by affected groups became a critical weakness as the majority of employees, largely through their unions, gradually came to oppose reform and to influence the electoral process in a way inimical to progress on workforce diversity.

Second, the council failed to sustain and broaden the constituencies which helped support the reform movement. In part, this was simple miscalculation. The council incorrectly assumed that the activist community groups were representative of the larger community. In fact, they were only one of multiple constituencies who had become energized by the previous city administration; thus, their level of participation decreased as several of their reforms were adopted. The council was unable to broaden this base of support after the first years of the new administration. Equally significant, however, was the ineffectiveness of the council at sustaining core constituencies and related support groups. A more proactive approach to university constituents, women's groups, the state EEOC, or national organizations might have helped to counter the political muscle of the patronage groups.

This problem was exacerbated by the third council failure, the choice of city manager. Even though he had solid national credentials and had emerged from a very competitive hiring process, he was not the right manager for this community. In many ways, the council replaced the former city manager, a master politician, with a technocrat who had little inclination to market and communicate his reforms. While technical skills were instrumental in getting the new manager to town, they were clearly inadequate to deal with a very political, participatory community. Thus, the initial design of reforms, represented by attractive budget packages and rational reorganization systems, was successful. However, inadequate attention was paid to implementation and communication to the community-at-large. When the unions joined with the supporters of the old patronage system, insufficient political support existed to sustain the reforms.

Equally important was the failure of the senior management team to achieve broad organizational involvement. Perhaps the biggest failure in Norman was the failure of top management to communicate effectively with the rest of the organization. Thus, change and reform were identified with a very limited set of players rather than with the organization. Even when new division directors communicated within their division, and thereby developed an appreciation for the range of values present, it was difficult for this information to flow upward. In addition, even though affirmative action was frequently a salient issue, it could easily be superseded by other employment initiatives. Competency within city hall was much easier to discuss with city council than the idea of a representative bureaucracy.

Affirmative action programs must be pictured as operating in a complex, dynamic, political context. What solutions could be effective in such an environment? We see no way to achieve immediate advancement on affirmative action within an environment in which cultural barriers are so deeply ingrained. However, long-term policy reform may indeed be possible. Our experience in Norman would suggest that reform should begin with the recognition that supporters of affirmative action should not rely on the federal government or state enforcement agencies. While an effective EEOC would be beneficial, the twenty-five-year history of affirmative action shows in a compelling fashion how easily external enforcement mechanisms and negative sanctions can be dismantled.

Thus, we believe the solutions must be community-based. Building supportive relationships between the city leadership and the broader community would seem to be a prerequisite for employment reform in communities like Norman. While significant efforts were made to link top management to the council, it was mistakenly assumed that the council constituted a sufficient representation of the larger community. Since municipal governments both reflect and serve the community, the failure to develop adequate understanding and linkages to the diverse elements of the community in addition to the council was fatal. A workable management-council-community relationship was never established. While this failure affected many policy areas within the community, it was particularly debilitating to reform of employment practices since many participants in the organization who were opposed to affirmative action had closer links to the community than did top management.

One response to this problem, as well as the enforcement problem, is the constituency model. That is, women and minorities must become more active if there is any chance of overcoming the range of barriers addressed in this study. While it is unfortunate that the victims of past discrimination should bear the burden of policy change, it is also true that these groups do have access to government at the local level and, at least in Norman, a history of leadership on the council and in a broad range of community organizations. If they were to become effectively organized, the pressure for reform of employment practices could be initiated simply by making public the historical record. Once broad community involvement in municipal government is in place, it is much more likely that new reform opportunities will be successful.

Notes

1. Several studies report positive findings documenting slight to modest gains in participation rates of women and minorities (Bremer and Howe 1988; Lewis 1987; Huckles 1985; and Clynch and Gaudin 1982). However, evidence of discrimination, occupation segregation, or negligible progress also exists (Hopkins 1980; Guy 1990; Cayer and Sigelman 1980; and Lewis 1986).

2. Surprisingly, this factor has received sparse attention in the literature. For a discussion of the relationship of management ideologies of women and minorities to how group interests are represented, see Reyfuss 1986, 454–459. One study finds that women managers are more likely to favor constituent inputs to the administrative process than are men, but does not examine whether constituencies can help to improve personnel practices (Neuse 1978, 436–441).

3. Affirmative action is opposed, 2 : 1, if the manager considers it to be in conflict with merit principles (Slack 1987, 203).

4. This is important since research has shown that having women involved in the political structure benefits the hiring and promotion of women in municipal government (Warner and Steel 1989, 306).

5. Of course, an organization committed to affirmative action can take steps to increase these percentages. Such steps include working with community and public universities to promote minority participation in areas with historically low participation rates.

References

Bremer, K., and D. Howe. 1988. "Strategies Used to Advance Women's Careers in Public Service: Examples from Oregon." *Public Administration Review* (November/December): 959–961.

Cayer, N.J., and L. Sigelman. 1980. "Minorities and Women in State and Local Government." *Public Administration Review* (September/October): 443–450.

Clynch, E.J., and C. Gaudin. 1982. "Sex in the Shipyards: An Assessment of Affirmative Action Policy." *Public Administration Review* (March/April): 114–121.

Equal Employment Opportunity Commission. 1974. *Affirmative Action and Equal Employment: A Guidebook for Employers.* Washington, DC: EEOC.

Graham, B. 1989. "Equal Employment Opportunity and Affirmative Action Policies, Techniques, and Controversies." In *Public Personnel Administration: Problems and Prospects*, ed. S.W. Hays and R.C. Kearney. Englewood Cliffs, NJ: Prentice-Hall.

Guy, M. 1990. "Women in Management." In *Public Personnel Administration: Problems and Prospects*, ed. S.W. Hayes and R.C. Kearney. Englewood Cliffs, NJ: Prentice-Hall.

Hopkins, A. 1980. "Perceptions of Employment Discrimination in the Public Sector." *Public Administration Review* (March/April): 131–138.

Huckles, P. 1985. "Whatever Happened to Affirmative Action? Employment of Women in Los Angeles City Department of Water and Power, 1973–1983." *Review of Public Personnel Administration* (Fall): 44–58.

Kellough, J., and S. Kay. 1986. "Affirmative Action in the Federal Bureaucracy: An Impact Assessment." *Review of Public Personnel Administration* (Spring): 1–13.

Lewis, G. 1986. "Race, Sex, and Supervisory Authority in Federal White Collar Employment." *Public Administration Review* (January/February): 25–30.

———. 1987. "Changing Patterns of Sexual discrimination in Federal Employment." *Review of Public Personnel Administration* (Spring): 1–13.

Nalbandian, J. 1989. "The U.S. Supreme Court's Consensus on Affirmation Action." *Public Administration Review* (January/February): 38–45.

Neuse, Steven M. 1978. "Professionalism and Authority: Women in Public Service." *Public Administration Review* (September/October): 436–441.

Perman, F. 1988. "The Players and Problems in the EEO Enforcement Process: A Status Report." *Public Administration Review* (July/August): 827–833.

Redeker, J. 1986. "The Supreme Court on Affirmative Action: Conflicting Opinions." *Personnel* (October): 8–14.

Reyfuss, J. 1986. "A Representative Bureaucracy? Women and Minority Executives in California Career Service." *Public Administration Review* (September/October): 454–459.

Slack, J. 1987. "Affirmative Action and City Managers: Attitudes Toward Recruitment of Women." *Public Administration Review* (March/April): 203.

Slack, J., and L. Sigelman. 1987. "City Managers and Affirmative Action: Testing a Model of Linkages." *Western Political Quarterly* (December): 673–684.

Stein, L. 1988. "Dual Strands in Municipal Personnel Administration: Politics and Professionalism." *Review of Public Personnel Administration* (Spring): 37–48.

Thompson, F.J. 1984. "Deregulation at the EEOC: Prospects and Implications." *Review of Public Personnel Administration* (Summer): 41–56.

Vertz, Laura. 1985. "Women's Occupational Advancement and Mentoring: An Analysis of One Public Organization." *Public Administration Review* (May/June): 415–423.

Warner, R.M., and B. Steel. 1989. "Affirmative Action in Times of Fiscal Stress and Changing Value Priorities: The Case of Women in Policing." *Public Personnel Management* (Fall): 306.

CHAPTER 16

EXPLAINING THE TENURE OF LOCAL GOVERNMENT MANAGERS

RICHARD FEIOCK AND CHRISTOPHER STREAM

In recent years, considerable attention has been given to turnover in the executive ranks of local government. In particular, the issue of what factors account for turnover among local government managers has been the subject of several empirical analyses (DeSantis and Renner 1993; Renner 1990; DeHoog and Whitaker 1990; Whitaker and DeHoog 1991). Understanding and predicting manager turnover is not only important to the field of public management, it may have implications for public policy. Management researchers argue that administrative turnover leads to inconsistent organizational outcomes (Finkelstein and Hambrick 1990). Within the field of public administration, scholars have assumed that administrative turnover is significant because it indicates a loss of institutional memory and neutral competence (Heclo 1977; Wilson 1994; Hass and Wright 1989; Lewis 1991).

Only recently have the policy and management consequences of turnover among local government managers been systematically identified. Empirical studies indicate turnover may affect privatization, capital planning, debt financing, and public-private economic development projects because they presuppose minimal transaction costs and lengthy time horizons on the part of local leaders (Clingermayer 1995).

While tenure patterns of local government managers have generated considerable scholarly interest, this research has neglected the role that institutional constraints and community characteristics have on manager turnover. This study attempts to fill this lacuna by testing a model of manager turnover that includes community characteristics and institutional arrangements. We anticipate that this inquiry will provide valuable theoretical and practical information to account for turnover among local government managers. A more complete understanding of manager tenure is necessary to enrich the volume of existing anecdotal information. This not only may improve our knowledge of local governments but may also enrich our understanding of the theories of local institutions and administrative careers.

Executive Turnover in Local Government

Throughout much of U.S. history, it was common for administrative positions in American government to be filled by people who did not intend to make public service a career. Administrators gained their positions through patronage systems, which dispensed public employment to the followers of winning candidates and political parties. Turnover was a fact of life for many bureau-

From *Journal of Public Administration Research and Theory*, vol. 8, no. 1 (January 1998), pp. 117–131.

crats because their jobs depended on the uncertain outcomes of elections. During the last part of the nineteenth century, the civil service at all levels of American government began to incorporate policies that assured job security for many employees and placed a priority on retaining expert and professional personnel. Early in this century, the importance of careerism among public servants was stressed by scholars who helped build the intellectual foundations of public administration (Weber 1946). The municipal reform movement championed the institution of appointed, nonpartisan managers to promote efficiency and consistency in local administration.

Local government managers are professional city administrators who are often the highest-ranking civil servants in a city. Traditionally, the manager is hired by the council and is subject to removal at any time by a majority vote of the council. In the early days of the council-manager plan, most managers were civil engineers by training (Lineberry and Sharkansky 1974). Today, approximately three-fourths of local managers have been trained in graduate programs in public policy/administration (Barber 1988). Like many professionals in American society, city managers tend to be highly mobile: only a minority are from the cities in which they work (Renner 1990). A vast majority of managers (86 percent) were hired from outside the community they serve. The resumé of a typical manager might include work as an assistant manager, manager of a small community, and then similar posts in progressively larger or more prestigious communities (Barber 1988).

The Institutional Context of Local Public Management

The study of institutions has been of interest to scholars of urban management for decades (Salisbury 1969; Lineberry and Fowler 1967; Welsh and Bledsoe 1988; Ostrom, Bish, and Ostrom 1988; Stein 1990). Institutional constraints such as jurisdictional boundaries and the powers of office shape individual actions because they offer incentives to engage in certain behaviors and disincentives to behave in other ways. Institutions affect policy outcomes in predictable ways because they provide incentives for political exchange and affect the transaction costs of individual actions.

At a micro level, the contractual arrangements for employment of local executives influence individual choices in a similar way. For local managers, these arrangements offer incentives or disincentives to stay in their present positions and determine the transaction costs of moving. For councils, employment arrangements shape incentives to keep or replace managers. From this perspective both managers' and councils' choices can be viewed as the product of rational, self-interested calculations of benefits and costs.

Tenure and Termination of Managers

The literature on local government manager tenure indicates that managers leave for many reasons. In some instances they may leave after disagreements with city councils that create situations in which the managers are forced to either resign or be fired. The literature also points to managers who leave voluntarily because they decide to retire or pursue new career opportunities. Of course, managers also may decide to leave voluntarily because they perceive political turmoil on the horizon, such as an upcoming change of council membership or a new policy direction.

In a pioneering study of thirty-nine city manager turnovers in ten Florida cities from 1945 to 1959, Kammerer, Farris, DeGrove, and Clubok (1962) found that two-thirds of these were involuntary terminations by the council. They found that terminations were a direct result of political disputes. Political disagreements can also indirectly influence voluntary terminations, as managers decide to leave before the conflict escalates until they are fired by the council. Recent work by DeHoog and Whitaker (1990) accounts for city manager turnover in relation to what they describe as *push and pull factors*. Push factors are political conflicts that result in managers being either dismissed or asked to resign, or made so uncomfortable they choose to resign. These factors can include partisan political conflict as well as conflicts in the community that spill over onto the relationships between the manager and council.

Role conflict between managers and elected officials is another important push factor. Svara (1990) has categorized four dimensions of local government process: mission, policy, administration, and management. While ultimate responsibility for mission lies with the council and ultimate responsibility for management generally lies with the manager, responsibility for policy and administration typically is shared (Svara 1990). Conflict is likely to result when there are departures from established patterns in these roles, such as when council members intervene in personnel decisions.

Pull factors relate to professional and personal characteristics of individual managers that may lead them to move for career advancement. Previous researchers have sought to identify characteristics that indicate managers' openness to job offers and their likelihood of receiving and accepting these offers. The pull factors can include graduate training in public management and prior local government management experience. DeHoog and Whitaker (1990) contend that a manager who has an MPA [a Master of Public Administration degree] is likely to leave for reasons of professional advancement. They found that the holding of an MPA was positively related to turnover. The professionalization of local government management has led to greater levels of careerism (Renner 1990; Nalbandian 1991). Increases in the number of positions that managers hold over their careers correspond to increased professionalism. At the same time, the proportion of managers who are promoted to their positions from other positions in the same government has decreased (Renner 1990).

Past attempts to explain manager tenure based on conflict or ambition have systematically examined neither local government institutions that define the powers and contractual obligations of managers nor more macropolitical system structures. When political system institutions have been addressed in extant research these factors have been included as indicators of political conflict, not as institutional constraints. Even so, political institutions, particularly the formal structures of local governments, have proven to be consistent predictors of turnover (DeHoog and Whitaker 1990). Previous studies of manager turnover have paid particular attention to the relationship between the manager and mayor. Managers who serve under a form of government with an elected mayor are viewed as more likely to experience short tenure than those who serve under the traditional council-manager form. The expectation is that the presence of another city executive with substantive formal authority will increase potential for conflict and create an environment that is less conducive to long-term policy management. In some instances, the professional norms of managers may conflict with the interests of elected officials (Frederickson 1995). This expectation is consistent with Whitaker and DeHoog's (1991) finding that the presence of a popularly elected mayor is negatively associated with city manager tenure (see also Svara 1987 and 1990; Booth 1968). The institutional character of councils also can have implications for tenure decisions. Electoral institutions shape the incentive structures of local representatives. City manager tenure may be shorter under district-based representation because the chances for political conflict and strong expression of parochial interests are greater in district elections than in at-large elections (Clingermayer and Feiock 1995). To date, this literature has not examined the contractual arrangements that structure the employment of managers.

Employment Arrangements for Managers

The institutional arrangements and context of the employment of local executives can directly influence career choices. Over the past two decades, local government management career patterns and opportunities have been affected by the introduction of employment agreements between the manager and the governing body. Employment agreements clarify exit arrangements and related benefits. Such agreements typically call for periodic review of the manager's performance even if the contract is not for a fixed time period. In addition, the clarity of a predefined process avoids organizational disruption in situations in which a manager leaves (ICMA 1979; Green 1984). Many employment agreements include severance benefits. These benefits provide flexibility to both the managers and the council and influence their stake in either the continuation or termination of the existing employment situation. Councils that incur these costs might be less likely to terminate their manager because it is seen as costly to force the manager out of a job.

The International City and County Council Management Association (ICMA) has taken an active role in encouraging member cities to provide employment agreements. The 1980 report of the ICMA Future Horizons Committee noted the unique needs of city managers in relation to their job mobility and political vulnerability. The report advocated the use of employment agreements. One might expect that employment agreements would result in greater tenure because they clarify expectations and enhance communication between manager and council. Nevertheless, we contend that written employment contracts can reduce the tenure of managers because these contracts typically specify a limited duration of employment and call for periodic performance evaluation. Moreover, employment agreements with severance provisions may make it easier for some council members to vote for removal when they might otherwise have been constrained by concerns about the negative impact on the managers and their families.

The retirement benefits plan provided to an exiting manager, whether it is included in a written employment agreement or not, may also influence the decisions of managers and councils. A substantial minority of cities offer portable pensions. Schluckbier (1990) notes a trend by cities in North Carolina and Florida toward the use of the ICMA-Retirement Corporation portable pension program and other short-vested portable pensions. The anticipated impact of portable pensions is not clear. On one hand, it indicates a significant commitment to managers by councils; on the other hand, it may reduce managers' moving costs.

Research Design

DeHoog and Whitaker's (1990) examination of push and pull factors does not adequately test alternative explanations for manager tenure. Several of their work's limitations are addressed here. The DeHoog and Whitaker study provides important insights into the various push and pull factors and their interrelations, but it does not directly examine the factors that account for the tenure of city managers. Rather than measure the length of a manager's tenure, DeHoog and Whitaker rely on a dichotomous indicator of whether the manager was still present two years later. While they conduct a logit analysis of turnover, only summary statistics are reported and no multivariate results are included. Their description implies that no push variables are found to be significantly related to tenure in a multivariate test, and the explained variance of the model is low. Such results suggest the need for a more fully specified multivariate analysis in order to more systematically test which factors predict a manager's tenure. In addition to including push and pull factors, we need to add indicators of the institutional and contractual context discussed above and controls for the size and social characteristics of communities.

The data for this study are based on city managers' responses to a survey conducted during the summer of 1989 and follow-up data on their tenure through 1995. Surveys were sent to managers in 110 Florida cities with populations that exceed ten thousand. Completed surveys were returned by eighty-one managers, for a response rate of 74 percent. Subsequently, we followed the career patterns of these eighty-one managers over the next six years. Using ICMA directories, we identified the number of years managers remained in their positions.

The independent variables include measures of employment context, political institutions, political conflict, career patterns, and the size and income characteristics of the communities. The survey included several indicators of the employment arrangements. We make some initial hypotheses regarding what impact they may have.

The expected impact of provisions for written employment agreements is negative. Managers with written employment contracts are expected to have shorter tenures. Because employment agreements direct councils to conduct periodic reviews of managers, they may force councils to make decisions about retaining or terminating managers. The impact of portable pension plans on tenure is less clear because, while managers with pension plans may be mobile, provision of this benefit by a council may indicate they highly value the manager's service. The survey elicited information on these employment arrangements.

We also expect that managers' tenure will be shorter when there is role conflict between managers and councils. An index of managers' assessments of role conflict in the relationship between the council and the manager's office was constructed from survey responses to questions that asked whether the council rejected the manager's recommendations on service delivery or became involved in staff personnel decisions.[1] These areas correspond to administrative and management roles described by Svara (1990). Because council members' intervention in these areas could produce conflict between the manager and the council, we anticipate that less role conflict is associated with longer tenure.

We expected manager tenure to be shorter in cities where there are either partisan conflicts or significant conflicts among major interests in the community. As a measure of partisan conflict, respondents were asked to rank the importance of conflict between Democrats and Republicans. We constructed a community conflict index to gauge the possible conflictual environment within which the manager must operate. The index measured conflict based on race, ideology, income, and support for economic development.[2]

In order to examine whether manager tenure could be explained by pull factors relating to their ambition and career path, several professional characteristics of city managers were also constructed from the survey. The three indicators of ambition included for each manager are: total years of service in local management; number of previous city manager positions held; and possession of an MPA degree.

Two measures of the political system characteristics also were included. Managers were asked whether the mayors in their communities were directly elected or selected by councils. We expected that managers who work with directly elected political executives will experience shorter tenure. We also expected shorter tenure for managers who work in communities with district level council representation than for managers who work under electoral systems that provide at-large representation. If respondents indicated that all council members were elected at-large, the jurisdiction was classified as at-large. Any other responses (all district or mixed plans) were classified as district representation. We also added controls for the total population of the city and the percent of the population below poverty level. Using OLS regression techniques, these variables then were regressed on the tenure of local government managers.

Table 16.1

Predictors of Manager Tenure

Variable	B	Standard error	t
Role conflict	−.057417	.177247	−.324
Community conflict	−.543884*	.188881	−2.880
Partisan conflict	.923844	.660990	1.398
MPA degree	1.169222*	.516872	2.262
Years of service	.129169*	.061053	2.116
Number of positions	−.333340*	.158864	−2.098
Employment agreement	.263475	.588845	.447
Portable pension	−.331565	.643917	−.515
At-large election	−.010815	.506770	−.021
Elected mayor	.991417	.588084	1.686
Population	−.000003	.000003	−1.026
Poverty rate	.082573*	.040597	2.034
(Constant)	6.424913	2.438109	2.635
Multiple R	.60		
R square	.36		
Adjusted R square	.25		
Standard error	2.08		
F-statistic	3.20		
Significance of F	.001		
Number of cases	80		

*Significant at .05.

Summary of Findings

The average tenure for local government managers in Florida was 3.4 years, and twenty-eight (34 percent) were still in the same position six years later. The regression results were pleasing in that the model of manager tenure exhibits a better fit to the data than was reported in previous studies. Table 16.1 presents some evidence that conflict reduces manager tenure. Although partisan conflict and role conflict with the council do not have an effect, racial, ideological, and growth conflicts within the community significantly shorten a manager's tenure. Each additional conflict that was reported reduced tenure by about six months (.54 years).

With regard to managers' personal characteristics that can operate as pull factors, the evidence is even stronger. All three variables have significant effects, but one is not in the anticipated direction. Previous analysis found that managers with an MPA were more likely to experience turnover. Instead, we find that holding an MPA degree increased tenure by over one year. As we had expected, managers with longer service in public management had longer tenure. After we controlled for total service, we found that the more manager positions a respondent held the shorter their tenure.

We did not find any support for a relationship between employment institutions and manager tenure. Although the coefficient for the employment agreement variable was positive, it was not statistically significant. Likewise, provision of a portable pension plan also had no effect.

We did not find substantial support for political representation structures that influence tenure. Direct election of the mayor had a positive coefficient but fell short of statistical significance, and at-large elections had no influence on manager tenure. With regard to the community characteristics, the effect of population was small, but the proportion of the population below poverty level was associated with increased tenure.

Table 16.2

Tenure of Managers Under Employment Agreements

Variable	B	Standard error	t
Role conflict	−.067019	.189220	−.354
Community conflict	−.767424*	.234062	−3.279
Partisan conflict	.883588	.741394	1.192
MPA degree	1.497791*	.656729	2.281
Years of service	.306553	.090308	3.395
Number of positions	−.607395*	.163016	−3.726
Portable pension	1.769589*	.902662	1.960
At-large election	.184713	.622138	.297
Elected mayor	1.362890*	.730943	1.965
Population	−.000012	.000008	−1.375
Poverty rate	.095952*	.050509	1.971
(Constant)	6.629966	2.639128	2.387
Multiple R	.79		
R square	.62		
Adjusted R square	51		
Standard error	1.86		
F-statistic	5.42		
Significance of F	.0001		
Number of cases	48		

*Significant at .05.

This analysis provided a much stronger model to explain manager tenure than was previously available and accounted for 25 percent of the variation in tenure. Nevertheless, it is curious that the contractual provisions of employment had no influence on tenure. One reason that employment agreements do not influence manager tenure is that they may have an intervening or interactive effect on tenure. At the local level, institutional variables have exerted an intervening, rather than a direct, effect. In an early study of municipal spending policy, Lineberry and Fowler (1967) demonstrated that government structures did not directly influence spending levels. Instead, structure affected cities' responsiveness to economic conditions and spending demands. It is possible that, in a similar manner, the institutions of employment may shape the responsiveness of managers to push and pull forces.

To this point we have addressed only the additive effects of employment structure on manager tenure. To examine the intervening effect of employment agreements we split the sample and tested the model first for managers who work under employment agreements and then for managers who work without these provisions. If the employment arrangements have an intervening effect, we would expect the influence of push and pull factors on tenure to be different in the two samples.

The results of this analysis provided strong evidence that employment arrangements have an intervening effect on tenure. Despite the reduced number of cases, the adjusted R^2 for each of the smaller subsamples was actually higher than for all managers. Not only were there differences in which variables were significant, in some instances the relationship was in a different direction for managers who work without an employment agreement and those who work with such an agreement. Table 16.2 reports estimates of turnover for managers who work under an employment agreement, and Table 16.3 reports similar estimates for managers who do not have an employment agreement. Push factors exert more influence when managers work under an employment agreement. Community conflict has a particularly strong negative effect on managers who work

Table 16.3

Tenure of Managers Not Under Employment Agreements

Variable	B	Standard error	t
Role conflict	.135625	.303646	.447
Community conflict	−.461849	.301594	−1.531
Partisan conflict	−.343476	1.171424	−.293
MPA degree	1.346714	.718150	1.875
Years of service	.038390	.66375	.578
Number of positions	.645535*	.318793	2.025
Portable pension	−2.259431	.782046	.700
Elected mayor	−.717877	.795638	−1.620
Population	.000001	.000003	.367
Poverty rate	.111463*	.053113	2.099
(Constant)	4.643720	4.135335	1.123

Multiple R	.71
R square	.51
Adjusted R square	.26
Standard error	1.72
F-statistic	1.99
Significance of F	.08
Number of cases	33

*Significant at .05.

under this arrangement. The effect of this conflict is smaller, and it falls short of statistical significance for managers who work without employment agreements.

The intervening effect of employment arrangements is most dramatic with regard to the ambition or pull factors. Under employment agreements, the impact that an MPA has on extending tenure is more significant. For managers with an MPA, employment contracts may enhance tenure by reducing ambiguity about the manager's role. Also, total years of service has a strong positive effect on tenure that is absent for managers who do not work under these agreements. Finally, the number of previous city management positions that a manager held has a significant effect on tenure within both samples, but in opposite directions. For those who work under an employment contract, the more positions a manager had held the shorter his or her tenure. The number of previous positions increased tenure for managers in the other sample. This suggests that, for managers with a history of short tenure in previous management positions, employment agreements may facilitate their movement and at the same time provide a review mechanism that speeds their exit. The significance of interactive effects was confirmed by the F test comparing unexplained variance for a single equation "full model" that allows different slopes for cities using and not using employment agreements with a "restricted model" that imposes the restriction that the slopes are equal.

While at-large elections consistently had no effect, provision for a strong mayor had a positive effect on tenure of managers with employment agreements and had the predicted negative effect on managers without employment agreements, although this effect was not statistically significant. The percent of the population below poverty had a consistent positive effect on tenure.

Conclusion

There is a growing recognition of the importance of executive tenure and turnover for the performance of organizations in the private sector (Finkelstein and Hambrick 1990). While the tradition of professional city managers assumes that long tenure is associated with greater expertise and professionalism, not all would agree that longer tenure for public managers is necessarily desirable. Shorter tenures might even enhance administrative responsiveness. A better understanding of factors that predict the exiting of a city manager can help us begin to build a better understanding of both the causes and consequences of turnover.

The findings reported here build upon the firm foundation provided by previous research. We confirm the importance of both push and pull factors. We found, as other researchers have found, that both the conflictual environment in which managers work and career characteristics influence patterns of tenure. We add to this knowledge by demonstrating the importance of employment institutions in shaping a manager's choices and tenure. We found that the influence of push and pull factors is contingent upon and shaped by the context of the employment relationship. Of particular interest is the divergent effect of career paths on tenure. When cities hire managers who have moved around substantially in their careers, as is often the case in city management, the cities' choices of employment institutions may be especially important in determining how long they retain their managers. For managers with this career path, employment agreements may facilitate their movement and their advancement to positions in other cities.

Previous studies have explored the interrelationships among the variables that are linked to manager turnover, but they have not systematically applied institutional theories to questions regarding city manager tenure. This research has attempted to identify how tenure is influenced by the institutional rules that define the employment of a city manager. The evidence we report supports hypotheses that in addition to influence by push and pull factors, institutional arrangements also influence manager tenure. We find that employment agreements influence tenure, but in an intervening manner rather than an additive manner. We contend that the structure of employment institutions is important not only because it may structure personal incentives but because it may also either insulate managers from conflict in the community or propel them to the center of conflict.

Notes

An earlier version of this chapter was presented at the annual meeting of the Southern Political Science Association, Tampa, Florida, November 3–5, 1995.

1. The index of role conflict between the city manager and the council was based on two statements for which the city manager reported his or her level of agreement on a four-point scale with the following statements: (1) The council generally follows the manager's recommendations regarding services that the city should provide; (2) The council does not become involved in staff hiring or promotion decisions. Responses were coded so that higher values indicated council intervention.

2. Managers were asked: There are always conflicts in a community. How would you rate the importance of those listed below in your city? Whites vs. minorities; liberals vs. conservatives; low-income vs. high-income areas; and pro-growth vs. anti-growth interests. The rating scale was: 3 = very important, 2 = somewhat important, and 1 = not very important. We combined these responses as an additive index in which higher scores indicated more conflict in the community.

References

Barber, D.M. 1988. "Newly Promoted City Managers." *Public Administration Review* 48: 694–699.

Booth, D.A. 1968. "Are Elected Mayors a Threat to City Managers?" *Administrative Science Quarterly* 12: 572–589.

Clingermayer, James C. 1995. "Policy Implications of Leadership Turnover." *Policy Currents* 12 (May): 1–5.

Clingermayer, James C., and Richard C. Feiock. 1995. "Council Views Toward the Targeting of Council Benefits." *Journal of Politics* 57: 508–521.

DeHoog, Ruth, and Gordon Whitaker. 1990. "Political Conflict or Professional Advancement: Alternative Explanations of City Manager Turnover." *Journal of Urban Affairs* 12: 367–377.

DeSantis, Victor, and Tari Renner. 1993. "Contemporary Patterns and Trends in Municipal Government Structures." In *The Municipal Yearbook.* Washington, DC: ICMA, pp. 57–69.

Finkelstein, Sydney, and Donald C. Hambrick. 1990. "Top Management-Team Tenure and Organizational Outcomes." *Administrative Science Quarterly* 35: 484–503.

Frederickson, H. George. 1995. "The Architecture of Democratic Government: The Type III City." Unpublished manuscript.

Green, R.E. 1984. "Employment Agreements for Managers: Guidelines for Local Government Managers." Washington, DC: International City Management Association.

Hass, Peter J., and Deil S. Wright. 1989. "Administrative Turnover in State Government: A Research Note." *Administration and Society* 21: 265–277.

Heclo, Hugh. 1977. "OMB and Presidency: The Problem of Neutral Competence." *Public Interest* 38: 80–98.

International City Management Association (ICMA). 1979, 1984–90. *The Municipal Yearbook.* Washington, DC: ICMA.

———, Committee on Future Horizons. 1979. *New Worlds of Service.* Washington, DC: ICMA.

Kammerer, G.M., C.D. Farris, J.M. DeGrove, and A.B. Clubok, 1962. *City Managers in Politics: Analysis of Manager Tenure and Termination.* Gainesville: University of Florida Press.

Lewis, Gregory B. 1991. "Turnover and the Quiet Crises in the Federal Service. *Public Administration Review* 31: 328–43.

Lineberry, Robert L., and Edmund Fowler. 1967. "Reformism and Public Policies in American Cities." *American Political Science Review* 61: 701–16.

Lineberry, Robert L., and Ira Sharkansky. 1974. *Urban Politics and Public Policy,* 2d ed. New York: Harper and Row.

Nalbandian, John. 1991. *Professionalism in Local Government.* San Francisco, CA: Jossey-Bass.

Ostrom, Vincent, Robert Bish, and Elinor Ostrom. 1988. *Local Government in the United States.* San Francisco, CA: Institute for Contemporary Studies.

Renner, Tari. 1990. "Appointed Local Government Managers: Stability and Change." In *The Municipal Yearbook.* Washington, DC: ICMA.

Salisbury, Robert. 1969. "An Exchange Theory of Interest Groups." *American Journal of Political Science* 13: 1–32.

Schluckbier, Jack M. 1990. "Exit Experience and Opinions of Senior City Managers." Unpublished paper.

Stein, Robert M. 1990. *Urban Alternatives.* Pittsburgh, PA: University of Pittsburgh Press.

Svara, James H. 1987. "Mayoral Leadership in Council-Manager Cities: Preconditions versus Preconceptions." *Journal of Politics* 49: 207–227.

———. 1990. *Official Leadership in the City: Patterns of Conflict and Cooperation.* New York: Oxford University Press.

Weber, Max. 1946. *Max Weber: Essays in Sociology,* ed. and trans. by H.H. Gerth and C. Wright Mills. Oxford, UK: Oxford University Press.

Welsh, Susan, and Timothy Bledsoe. 1988. *Urban Reform and Its Consequences: A Study in Representation.* Chicago: University of Chicago Press.

Whitaker, Gordon P., and Ruth Hoogland DeHoog. 1991. "City Managers Under Fire: How Conflict Leads to Turnover." *Public Administration Review* 51, no. 2 (March/April): 156–165.

Wilson, Patricia A. 1994. "Power Politics and Other Reasons Why Senior Executives Leave the Federal Government." *Public Administration Review* 54: 12–19.

Chapter 17

WHAT MUNICIPAL EMPLOYEES WANT FROM THEIR JOBS VERSUS WHAT THEY ARE GETTING

Carole L. Jurkiewicz and Tom K. Massey

The more accurately public sector managers can answer the question of what motivates their employees, the more effective they will be at maximizing productivity, enhancing performance, and advancing the notion of public sector accountability (Cherniss and Kane 1987). Knowing the relevant dimensions of employee motivation is valuable information to anyone concerned with organizational performance (Locke 1991), as is the ability to make objective assessments of what employees want from their jobs and whether they feel they are getting it (Scully 1994). Whether it is formulating personnel policy or strategic plans or reengineering processes, keeping employees motivated is essential to reaching goals of productivity and efficiency (Emmert and Taher 1992).

Theoretical Orientation

Expectancy theory (Vroom 1964), one of the most widely accepted explanations of motivation, is rooted in the commonsense notion that individuals act in ways likely to maximize their rewards and minimize their costs. Essentially, within the organizational context, employees are the embodiment of classical economic theory. Social relationships are viewed as exchange processes in which employees engage in certain activities for which they expect certain outcomes. The strength of a tendency to act in a certain way depends on the intensity of expectation that an act will be followed by a particular outcome and on the attractiveness of that outcome to the individual. The outcomes can be viewed as either positive, negative, or neutral. The transaction is an economic one, and it is assumed that individuals have expectations and preferences regarding the rewards they will receive in exchange for their investment of time and resources. The applicability of these notions to public sector employees has been well documented (e.g., Gabris and Simo 1995; Perry and Porter 1982; Perry and Wise 1990) and empirically assessed (Perry 1996).

Homans (1958) is generally credited with explicating the fundamental concepts of social exchange theory, the basis of expectancy theory, in equating "organizational man" with "economic man." Related research by Thibaut and Kelley (1959) analyzed attraction to a group in terms of the rewards and costs to an individual that may be entailed by group membership. Adams (1963, 1965) built on these precepts by developing a more rigorous theory of social exchange. Adams's theory of equity proposes that in any exchange relationship, there exists the possibility that one or both of the individuals involved will feel that the exchange is inequitable. Equity is

From *Public Productivity & Management Review*, vol. 20, no. 2 (December 1996), pp. 129–138. Copyright © 1996 by Sage Publications, Inc. Reprinted with permission.

said to exist whenever the ratio of Person A's outcomes to inputs is equal to the ratio of Person B's outcomes to inputs. Similarly, inequity exists when these ratios are unequal (Mowday 1987). In each instance, the individual's perception of the situation determines its degree of equity, as opposed to some measure of objective criteria. Simon, Smithburg, and Thompson (1950) operationalized this concept by postulating that individuals will continue their participation in an organization as long as the rewards for doing so are perceived as having as great, or greater, a value than the contribution the individual is asked to make.

Using this theoretical orientation, as modified by Festinger's (1957) dissonance theory and described by Heimovics and Brown (1976), the exchange process in expectancy theory can be elaborated as follows: Inequality exists for individuals whenever they perceive a substantial gap between what they want from their work and what they are getting. In other words, when the relationship between an individual's "wants" and "gets" are inverse, the individual will seek some means to place them in balance. In such a circumstance, one can speculate that the individual will do the following:

1. modify either the "wants" or "gets" to bring them into balance;
2. seek other sources of "gets" that more closely parallel the "wants" or vice versa; or
3. choose to do little about either, with the possibility for attendant frustration, dissatisfaction, and retaliation.

In any case, one can presume that if inequity exists for an individual, that individual will be motivated to attend to the inequity at the expense of being motivated toward a particular organizational objective. The optimal point, then, exists when an individual perceives the exchange to be an equitable one, when presumably the focus of energies will be toward the organization's goals because, in turn, this will satisfy personal goals.

To determine if a state of disequilibrium exists, it is necessary to know the value placed on a set of potentially achievable outcomes by the individual in the workplace, as well as the relative attractiveness ascribed to the perceived rewards granted in exchange for the job done. Collectively, this information provides a picture of the general culture or subculture of an organization and indicates the homeopolarity of the exchange relationship.

Background for Study

In a 1976 study of public employees in five Midwestern suburban municipalities (Heimovics and Brown 1976), hereafter referred to as H&B, workers reported what they wanted from their jobs relative to what they felt they were getting from them. The findings of their study generally supported both the public's perception and the literature's contention that public employees are motivated in large part by an ethic of service, teamwork, and the promise of a stable and secure future—a contention as widely held today as it was twenty years ago (Clark and Wilson 1961; Flynn and Tannenbaum 1993; Kilpatrick, Cummings, and Jennings 1964; Maidani 1991; Nalbandian and Edwards 1983; Newstrom, Reif, and Monczka 1976; Rainey 1982; Solomon 1986). We revisited these municipalities, and new data were collected. The differences between the two results are illuminating.

Methodology

Four of the five original municipalities, as well as one supplemental municipality, participated in the study and allowed access to employees in each department: public works, fire, police, and administration. Each was situated in a suburban community on the perimeter of a large Midwestern

Table 17.1

Fifteen Work-Related Motivational Factors That Respondents Ranked in the Questionnaire

Chance to learn new things
Chance to benefit society
Freedom from pressures to conform both on and off the job
Opportunity for advancement
High prestige and social status
Freedom from supervision
Chance to use my special abilities
Variety in work assignments
Chance to engage in satisfying leisure activities (e.g., recreational, culture)
Friendly and congenial associates
Working as part of a "team"
High salary
A stable and secure future
Chance to exercise leadership
Chance to make a contribution to important decisions

metropolitan area with individual populations ranging from 21,000 to 48,000. Each had a council manager or council administrator form of government, and city budgets ranged from $7 million to $59 million, with a median of $15 million (figures are rounded). The city manager or administrator formally requested the cooperation of municipal employees in memo form in advance of the researcher's visit but were not on-site at the time the questionnaires were administered. Participation was effectively similar among cities and across departments, with the resulting number of usable questionnaires roughly the same as in the early study ($n = 271$ in H&B; $n = 278$ in the current study).

Response measures were collected using an anonymous self-administered questionnaire. Each instrument was administered in small on-site group sessions. In most cases, they were completed at the end of a regularly scheduled meeting. The balance was administered during meetings, arranged specifically for the purpose of completing the instrument.

Each respondent was first asked to rank the fifteen work-related motivational factors shown in Table 17.1 in terms of their relative importance to them on the job. This ranking comprised what will be called the "wants" profile. Next, without being able to refer to their first ranking task, respondents were asked to rank the same fifteen factors in the order that they felt these factors had been fulfilled in their present job. This ranking comprises what will be called the "gets" profile.

Results

Rankings of these motivational work factors in H&B some twenty years ago revealed an interesting pattern of "wants" and "gets." Revisiting these municipalities using the same methodology suggests that although the "wants" have shifted in relative importance, the "gets" have remained much the same. A picture thus emerges of cultural shifts in public sector organizations. Tabulating the rankings of "wants" for municipal employees in the current study and comparing those to the rankings of their counterparts in H&B, some interesting shifts can be observed. The comparative rank orders are shown in Table 17.2.

Although the lowest four ranked items remained virtually unchanged from the H&B study to the present one, more volatile shifts are recognizable in the middle and upper sectors. The most

Table 17.2

"Wants" Profiles for Municipal Employees

Heimovics and Brown study (1976)		Current study	
Rank	Motivational factor	Rank	Motivational factor
1	Chance to learn new things	1	A stable and secure future
2	Working as part of a "team"	2	Chance to learn new things
3	Opportunity for advancement	3	Chance to use my special abilities
4	A stable and secure future	4	High salary
5	Chance to benefit society	5	Opportunity for advancement
6	Chance to use my special abilities	6	Chance to make a contribution to important decisions
7	Friendly and congenial associates	7	Variety in work assignments
8	Chance to make a contribution to important decisions	8	Working as part of a "team"
9	Chance to exercise leadership	9	Friendly and congenial associates
10	Variety in work assignments	10	Chance to benefit society
11	High salary	11	Chance to exercise leadership
12	Freedom from pressures to conform both on and off the job	12	Freedom from supervision
13	Freedom from supervision	13	Freedom from pressures to conform both on and off the job
14	Chance to engage in satisfying leisure activities	14	Chance to engage in satisfying leisure activities
15	High prestige and social status	15	High prestige and social status

pronounced changes are the desire for a High salary (moved up seven ranks, from 11th to 4th), Working as part of a "team" (moved down six ranks from 2nd to 8th), and Chance to benefit society (moved down five ranks, from 5th to 10th). Notable changes also occurred for Chance to use my special abilities (from 6th to 3rd), Variety in work assignments (from 10th to 7th), and A stable and secure future (from 4th to 1st), all of which moved up three ranks. Minor shifts occurred for the following seven items, each of which moved up or down one or two ranks: Chance to learn new things, Freedom from pressures to conform both on and off the job, Opportunity for advancement, Freedom from supervision, Friendly and congenial associates, and Chance to exercise leadership. No shifts in rank occurred for Chance to engage in satisfying leisure activities and High prestige and social status, at ranks 14 and 15, respectively.

Examining the pattern of rankings in Table 17.3 for the current study and comparing them to those found in the H&B study, a much less dramatic shift occurs than what was witnessed for the pattern of the "wants" profile (see Table 17.2). Overall, no pronounced changes occurred for the rankings of what municipal employees reported they were getting in the H&B study versus the rankings of respondents participating in the current study. A few shifts in rankings can be seen, however, in Chance to use special abilities (moved up three ranks, from 6th to 3rd), Working as part of a "team" (moved down three ranks, from 2nd to 5th), and A Stable and Secure Future (moved up three ranks, from 7th to 4th). Minor changes also can be seen for nine additional factors, including Chance to benefit society, Opportunity for advancement, High prestige and social status, Freedom from supervision, Variety in work assignments, Friendly and congenial associates, High salary, Chance to exercise leadership, and Chance to make a contribution to important decisions. Three items—Chance to learn new things, Freedom from pressures to conform both on and off the job, and Chance to engage in satisfying leisure activities—were unchanged over time from the H&B study to the present one.

Table 17.3

"Gets" Profiles for Municipal Employees

Heimovics and Brown study (1976)		Current study	
Rank	Motivational factor	Rank	Motivational factor
1	Chance to learn new things	1	Chance to learn new things
2	Working as part of a "team"	2	Variety in work [assignments]
3	Variety in work assignments	3	Chance to use my special abilities
4	Chance to benefit society	4	A stable and secure future
5	Friendly and congenial associates	5	Working as part of a "team"
6	Chance to use my special abilities	6	Chance to benefit society
7	A stable and secure future	7	Friendly and congenial associates
8	Chance to exercise leadership	8	Chance to make a contribution to important decisions
9	Opportunity for advancement	9	Chance to exercise leadership
10	Chance to make a contribution to important decisions	10	Freedom from supervision
11	Freedom from supervision	11	Opportunity for advancement
12	Freedom from pressures to conform both on and off the job	12	Freedom from pressures to conform both on and off the job
13	Chance to engage in satisfying leisure activities	13	Chance to engage in satisfying leisure activities
14	High prestige and social status	14	High salary
15	High salary	15	High prestige and social status

In our comparison of what municipal employees report they want from their jobs and what they report they are getting, these descriptive indicators suggest a growing inequity in the exchange relationship over time. The pattern of responses diagramed in the bar graphs in Figure 17.1 and 17.2 depict this disparity quite clearly.

The first statistical test conducted on these sets of rankings was the nonparametric Spearman's rank correlation coefficient of association.[1] The interpretation of this measure is rather intuitive, because a Spearman's coefficient of zero would indicate no association (correlation) between the two sets of rankings. On the other hand, a coefficient of 1 would indicate that the two rankings are perfectly correlated.

The Spearman rank correlation coefficient for the "gets" rankings was .914, indicating a very high correlation between the rankings of the H&B study and the current one. The Spearman rank correlation coefficient for the "wants" score was only .721. In other words, these data suggest that the municipalities are delivering essentially the same reward structure as they did twenty years ago, but the desires of the workers have changed markedly over the same time period.

This disparity can be seen when the ranked correlation of the "wants" and "gets" profiles are compared within each study. The Spearman rank correlations comparing the rankings of "wants" and "gets" from H&B was .775, whereas the score comparing the rankings of "wants" and "gets" for the current group was .618. These results offer additional evidence that there is less agreement between what municipal employees report they want and what they get in the current group versus what they wanted and got two decades ago.

Discussion and Implications

The results indicate that what municipal employees want from their jobs has shifted dramatically over the past two decades, but what they are getting from them remains almost exactly the same.

234

Figure 17.1 Pattern of Responses: Wants Versus Gets for H&B

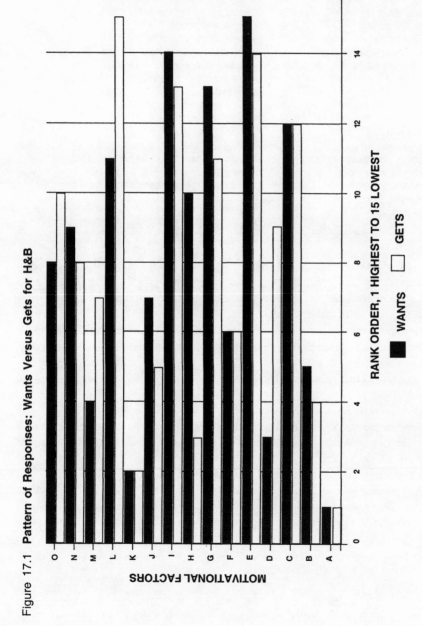

Notes: H&B = Heimovics & Brown (1976); A = Chance to learn new things; B = Chance to benefit society; C = Freedom from pressures to conform both on and off the job; D = Opportunity for advancement; E = High prestige and social status; F = Chance to use my special abilities; G = Freedom from supervision; H = Variety in work assignments; I = Chance to engage in satisfying leisure activities (e.g., recreational, cultural); J = Friendly and congenial associates; K = Working as part of a "team"; L = High salary; M = Stable and secure future; N = Chance to exercise leadership; O = Chance to make a contribution to important decisions.

Figure 17.2 **Pattern of Responses: "Wants" Versus "Gets" for Current Group**

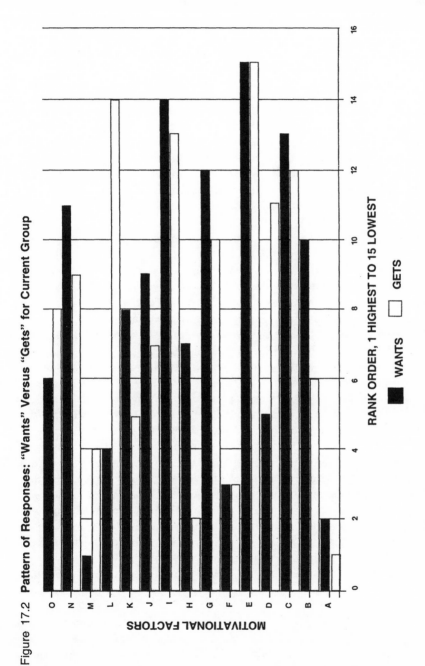

Notes: A = Chance to learn new things; B = Chance to benefit society; C = Freedom from pressures to conform both on and off the job; D = Opportunity for advancement; E = High prestige and social status; F = Chance to use my special abilities; G = Freedom from supervision; H = Variety in work assignments; I = Chance to engage in satisfying leisure activities (e.g., recreational, cultural); J = Friendly and congenial associates; K = Working as part of a "team"; L = High salary; M = Stable and secure future; N = Chance to exercise leadership; O = Chance to make a contribution to important decisions.

Table 17.4

"Wants" Factors That Have Increased in Importance over Time

A stable and secure future
Chance to use my special abilities
High salary
Chance to make a contribution to important decisions
Variety in work assignments
Freedom from supervision

The change in what employees want occurs most dramatically in the middle section of our list of motivational factors (see Table 17.4). This discrepancy may suggest a growing dissatisfaction among municipal employees regarding what they are getting from their jobs. Such value changes are not surprising, given the changes in the social context over the twenty-year interval, yet overall the gap between what municipal employees want and what they are getting has grown. These results also suggest a level of dissatisfaction that could affect morale, motivation, and productivity, in addition to hampering the ability of municipalities to recruit and retain preferred employees (Emmert and Taher 1992).

A positive supposition regarding employee commitment can be made from this study's findings in conjunction with Mathieu and Zajac (1990) and Mottaz (1988). They found that three factors included in our study—autonomy (G), challenge (F), and variety (H)—were positively correlated with organizational commitment in the public sector. The significance of the variety factor (H) in public sector employee motivation also has been supported by Emmert and Taher (1992). As this study reveals, these three factors are in relatively abundant supply in the municipalities studies. However, one factor in short supply for our group, significance (O), has been identified by many (Flynn and Tannenbaum 1993; Hackman and Oldham 1976; Mowday, Porter, and Steers 1982) as key to increasing employee motivation and behavioral involvement in their jobs in both the public and private sectors.

Although it is perhaps true, as many researchers suppose (e.g., Baldwin 1987; Gabris and Simo 1995; Rainey 1982, 1983; Rainey, Traut, and Blunt 1986), that public sector employees value monetary rewards less and social service more than do their private sector counterparts, our findings suggest that this distinction is relative indeed. Municipal employees in the current study responded that they are much less desirous of associative (teamwork) and altruistic (chance to benefit society) rewards from their work than they are with financial rewards and security (higher salary, stable and secure future), as well as personal growth (chances to learn new things, use special abilities, opportunities for advancement, and contributions to important decisions). So although it may be true that these factors are stronger motivators for employees in the private sector, their importance to employees in the public sector can be neither discounted nor dismissed. In fact, the data here suggest that the municipal employee profit of "wants" is growing to resemble more closely the profile of private sector employees, but their "gets" remain dissimilar (a notion advanced in Gabris and Simo 1995). A study comparing these two groups on this factor set could be illuminating indeed.

These data clearly suggest that municipal organizations need to assess the environmental and cultural factors that may be affecting the productivity of their largest single expenditure. Although budget difficulties are a constraining factor for most municipalities, many other elements common to private sector reengineering efforts may be altered to bring the "wants" and "gets" more closely in agreement. Creating opportunities for advancement, deemphasizing the motivational rhetoric of receiving a reward through benefiting society, and realizing that municipal employees face the same influences, reference groups, and external threats as private sector employees are just possible initial steps to improve the congruence between what is desired and received. Indeed, given evidence that the entrant quality of public sector employees surpasses that of entrants to the private sector (Crewson 1995), it is not surprising to see many similarities emerging across the two groups. Such an examination of "wants" versus "gets" by individual municipalities may, as many private sector companies have discovered, improve the quality of service and professionalism of the organization as a whole.

Note

1. Because these data are ordinal, and equal interval scaling cannot be assumed, the appropriate tests are nonparametric (see, e.g., Siegel 1956).

References

Adams, J. 1963. "Toward an Understanding of Inequality." *Journal of Abnormal and Social Psychology* 6: 422–436.
———. 1965. "Inequality in Social Exchange." In *Advances in Experimental Social Psychology*, vol. 2, ed. L. Berkowitz. New York: New York Press, pp. 267–299.
Baldwin, J.N. 1987. "Public vs. Private: Not That Different, Not That Consequential." *Public Personnel Management* 16, no. 2: 181–193.
Cherniss, C., and J. Kane. 1987. "Public Sector Professionals: Job Characteristics, Satisfaction, and Aspiration for Intrinsic Fulfillment Through Work." *Human Relations* 40, no. 3: 125–136.
Clark, P., and J. Wilson. 1961. "Incentive Systems: A Theory of Organization." *Administrative Science Quarterly* 6: 129–166.
Crewson, P.E. 1995. "A Comparative Analysis of Public and Private Sector Entrant Quality." *American Journal of Political Science* 39: 628–639.
Emmert, M.A., and W.A. Taher. 1992. "Public Sector Professionals: The Effects of Public Sector Jobs on Motivation, Job Satisfaction and Work Involvement." *American Review of Public Administration* 22, no. 1: 37–48.
Festinger, L. 1957. *A Theory of Cognitive Dissonance.* Evanston, IL: Row, Peterson.
Flynn, D.M., and S.I. Tannenbaum. 1993. "Correlates of Organizational Commitment: Differences in the Public and Private Sectors." *Journal of Business and Psychology* 8, no. 1: 103–116.
Gabris, G.T., and G. Simo. 1995. "Public Sector Motivation as an Independent Variable Affecting Career Decisions." *Public Personnel Management* 24, no. 1: 33–51.
Hackman, J.R., and G.R. Oldham. 1976. "Motivation Through the Design of Work." *Organizational Behavior and Human Performance* 16: 250–279.
Heimovics, R., and F.G. Brown. 1976. "Municipal Employee Behavior as an Exchange Process." *Midwest Review of Public Administration* 10, no. 4: 201–215.
Homans, G.C. 1958. "Social Behavior as Exchange." *American Journal of Sociology* (May): 597–606.
Kilpatrick, F., M. Cummings, and M. Jennings. 1964. *The Image of the Federal Service.* Washington, DC: Brookings Institution.
Locke, E.A. 1991. "The Motivation Sequence, the Motivation Hub, and the Motivation Core." *Organizational Behavior and Human Decision Processes* 50: 288–299.
Maidani, E.A. 1991. "Comparative Study of Herzberg's Two-Factor Theory of Job Satisfaction Among Public and Private Sectors." *Public Personnel Management* 20, no. 4: 441–448.
Mathieu, J.E., and D. Zajac. 1990. "A Review and Meta-analysis of the Antecedents, Correlates, and Consequences of Organizational Commitment." *Psychological Bulletin* 108: 171–194.
Mottaz, C. 1988. "Determinants of Organizational Commitments." *Human Relations* 41: 395–378.
Mowday, R.T. 1987. "Equity Theory Predictions of Behavior in Organizations." In *Motivation and Work Behavior*, ed. R.M. Steers and L.W. Porter. New York: McGraw-Hill, pp. 89–110.
Mowday, R.T., L.W. Porter, and R.M. Steers. 1982. *Employee-Organization Linkages.* New York: Academic Press.

Nalbandian, J., and J.T. Edwards. 1983. "The Values of Public Administration: A Comparison with Lawyers, Social Workers, and Business Administrators." *Review of Public Personnel Administrators* 4: 114–127.

Newstrom, J., W. Reif, and R. Monczka. 1976. "Motivating the Public Employee: Fact vs. Fiction." *Public Personnel Management* 5: 67–72.

Perry, J.L. 1996. "Measuring Public Service Motivation: An Assessment of Construct Reliability and Validity." *Journal of Public Administration Research and Theory* 6, no. 1: 5–17.

Perry, J.L., and L.W. Porter. 1982. "Factors Affecting the Context for Motivation in Public Organizations." *Academy of Management Review* 7: 89–98.

Perry, J.L., and L.R. Wise. 1990. "The Motivational Bases of Public Service." *Public Administration Review* (May/June): 367–372.

Rainey, N.G. 1982. "Reward Preferences Among Public and Private Managers: In Search of the Service Ethic." *American Review of Public Administration* 16, no. 4: 288–302.

———. 1983. "Public Agencies and Private Firms: Incentive Structures, Goals and Individual Rules." *Administration and Society* 15: 207–242.

Rainey, H.G., C. Traut, and B. Blunt. 1986. "Reward Expectancies and Other Work-Related Attitudes in Public and Private Organizations: A Review and Extension." *Review of Public Personnel Administration* 6, no. 3: 50–72.

Scully, J.P. 1994. "How to Really Change the Federal Government." *National Productivity Review* (Winter): 29–38.

Siegel, S. 1956. *Nonparametric Statistics for the Behavioral Sciences.* New York: McGraw-Hill.

Simon, H.A., D.W. Smithburg, and V.A. Thompson. 1950. *Public Administration.* New York: Knopf.

Solomon, E. 1986. "Private and Public Sector Managers: As an Empirical Investigation of Job Characteristics and Organizational Climate." *Journal of Applied Psychology* 71, no. 2: 247–259.

Thibaut, I., and H.H. Kelley. 1959. *The Social Psychology of Groups.* New York: John Wiley.

Vroom, V.H. 1964. *Work and Motivation.* New York: John Wiley.

CHAPTER 18

MANAGERIAL RESPONSES TO AN AGING MUNICIPAL WORKFORCE

JONATHAN P. WEST AND EVAN M. BERMAN

The concept of human capital emphasizes that employees are key organizational assets and that significant returns can be realized from investments in human potential (Becker 1993; Carnevale 1995; Hornbeck and Salamon 1991). There is a growing recognition on the part of those who analyze human capital that older workers are an important resource and that substantial organizational investments already have been made to help mature employees achieve their potential (Redwood 1990; Rosow 1990; Savoie 1990; NAB 1985; Robinson et al. 1985; Sterns et al. 1994; Lawler et al. 1993). To derive demonstrable returns on organizational human capital investments managers must give increased attention to the strategic management of older workers.

Diversity management has become somewhat of a buzzword among personnel specialists and public managers in the 1990s, reflecting the challenges facing human resource professionals as they manage a multicultural and maturing workforce of increasing gender and racial diversity (Bruce and Olshfski 1992; Kelly 1993). The challenge of dealing with aging workers has been called "an urgent policy issue" by some and "the forgotten diversity issue" by others (see, respectively, for example, Rosow 1990 and Capowski 1995). Despite its urgency, the "age" component of the diversity issue by-and-large has taken a back seat up to now because other competing issues are "screaming" louder (Dennis 1987; Barth et al. 1993; Buonocore 1992). As the baby boomers mature and assume more responsibility in organizations, however, the urgency of their concerns will bring more "screaming" and will likely require the careful crafting of managerial strategies which are tailored to respond to their particular needs.

The challenge of responding to an aging workforce is one facing managers in all sectors—private, nonprofit and public (see for example, Blocklyn 1987; Bove 1987; Johnson 1990; Elliott 1995). Within the public sector, HR managers at all levels—local, state, and federal—are increasingly conscious of the need to incorporate information about labor force trends into their strategic plans for making the best use of their human capital (Carnevale 1995; Halachmi 1992; West and Berman 1995). The focus of this study is on local government and the strategies used by municipal human resource managers (HRMs) to respond to an aging workforce. Prior research on this topic is more plentiful in the private sector than the public sector (Mirvis 1993), and studies of local government approaches are largely limited either to jurisdiction-specific case studies or survey data from a single state (Roberts 1995). This study provides the sort of nationwide observational base which is required to gain a better overall understanding of the strategic initiatives pursued by municipal government.

From *Review of Public Personnel Administration*, vol. 16, no. 3 (Summer 1996), pp. 38–58. Copyright © 1996 by Sage Publications, Inc. Reprinted with permission.

A few demographic and labor force facts further illustrate the significance of the "graying workforce" issue:

1. The first wave of baby boomers—those born in 1946—will be turning fifty-five by the year 2001 (thus meeting the classification of "older workers" used by BLS) (Capowski 1995).
2. The segment of the workforce fifty-five and older is projected to grow from 12.3 percent now to over 20 percent by 2020 (Barth et al. 1993), and it will increase at twice the rate of the rest of the population during the next decade (Strouse 1995).
3. The share of younger segments of the workforce—those in age categories eighteen to twenty-four and twenty-five to thirty-four—is declining (by the year 2000 these shares will decline 5 percent and 6 percent, respectively (Czaja 1995).
4. By the year 2000 the median age of employees will be nearly forty, and the middle-aged portion of the labor force (aged thirty-five to fifty-four) will comprise about 50 percent of the workforce (Kelly 1992).

Managerial responses and adaptations to current demographic and labor force trends are plentiful. Strategies developed by managers can be categorized into four key areas: (1) establishing supportive workplace relations; (2) providing training; (3) encouraging career development; and (4) objectively appraising skills and performance as a guide in HR decision making. These categories provide the framework for this chapter. Municipal governments use a variety of strategies within each of these groupings to address the needs of their older workers. They may be prompted to select such strategies by a combination of driving forces which are likely to increase the salience of this issue in some municipalities, but not in others. This chapter examines these strategies and forces in local government.

Framework

HRM plays a potentially crucial role in increasing the organizational effectiveness of local government by developing human capital through training, career development, performance management, and facilitating supportive workplace relations. Improved productivity, quality, and citizen satisfaction can result from such strategic initiatives by proactive HR management. Human resource managers who are aware of the present and future demographic makeup of their workforce will recognize the need to plan for the continued productive employment of current older workers. These older workers are a likely source of productivity gains based on skills training and upgrading if municipalities are willing to make investments in their development.

Supportive Workplace Relations

An important characteristic of high performing organizations is the presence of constructive workplace relations among employees and between management and labor (Carnevale 1992, 1995; Carnevale and Weschsler 1992). Such relations are often achieved by measures which ensure fair treatment, flexible policies and benefits, and which recognize the importance of balancing individual and organizational needs. Three focal areas have been identified that are especially important for achieving a supportive work environment for older workers: strategies which deal with stress and health, alternative work arrangements, and retirement-related assistance (Dennis 1987).

First, stress management is a strategy to help younger and older employees alike. Left unmanaged, stress leads to reduced productivity, increased errors, poor health and sometimes debilitating effects on individual and organizational performance (Cooper 1984). In-house stress management and/or referral arrangements via Employee Assistance Programs (EAP) can help to address these stress-related problems. While stress management and EAP programs constitute generic strategies (available to all employees), the availability of such efforts is likely to be especially appreciated by older municipal workers. To buttress stress management and EAPs, some cities encourage health promotion activities and/or wellness programs which provide a supportive environment for aging and other workers who are concerned about getting enough exercise, proper nutrition and thoughtful drug use, and learning relaxation methods (Tager 1987).

Second, alternative work arrangements include a host of strategies designed to provide flexibility and to balance individual and organizational needs (Tompkins 1995; Parker and Hall 1993). Job redesign is necessary to help older workers who have health problems which impede their ability to work. Job rotation or job transfers are a desirable option for aging workers who can no longer do physically demanding work, but who continue to have crucial job-related skills valued by the organization. Flexibility is also achieved by adapting leave policies (elder care, parenting), adopting flextime, making workplace adjustments due to functional losses (e.g., hearing or sight impairment), and redesigning equipment. Eldercare leave reduces a special strain on older workers who are the primary caregivers to incapacitated family members. Other adjustments are provided for workers who are near or past retirement age (part-time work options, reemployment of retirees, using retirees as volunteers) (Paul 1987). It is estimated that a third of all Americans, including substantial numbers of older workers are hired on a part-time, temporary, or contingent basis.

A third strategic focus for building supportive workplace relations is helping older workers meet their retirement needs. Employers can encourage and assist employees in their pension planning. Ideally, all workers should be aided by employers in assessing their financial needs early enough so that they can take appropriate steps. However, it is estimated that less than one-fourth of older workers have access to comprehensive retirement planning (AARP 1990). Another strategy consists of providing early retirement incentive programs. Although these strategies are often used in conjunction with downsizing objectives (which are often antagonistic to worker interest), the use of retirement incentives often contributes to meeting employees' retirement needs.

Training

The literature suggests that some employers are reluctant to offer training (or retraining) to older workers (Rosen and Jerdee 1985; Sonnenfeld 1978), and that some older workers are reluctant to make themselves available for such training or retraining (Sterns and Doverspike 1987). This latter disincentive stems from the possibility that an older trainee may be fearful of failing or feel inadequate to compete with younger trainers. Yet, all workers face a continuing need to acquire and update skills, to maintain high performance levels, and to avoid obsolescence; this is a special challenge to older workers.

A variety of training adaptations exists to better meet the needs of aging adult workers—adapting training by allowing more time, by emphasizing the familiar, and by better organizing information so that knowledge is developed step-by-step (Sterns and Doverspike 1987; Van Wart et al. 1993). Such adaptations are consistent with findings from learning theory which suggests that adults learn differently from children. The term "androgogy" has been applied to the teaching of adults, and those who popularized this approach have identified some special training-needs of older adults: the need to pay attention to the physical design and ergonomics of the training setting to ensure a comfort level promotive of learning; the need to rely on a variety of experiential instructional techniques rather than the traditional lecture format; and the need to acknowledge the value of an older worker's experience in the course of training, and to take into account how career stage progression may affect willingness to learn (Knowles et al. 1984). Informed municipal managers who are concerned about human capital issues adapt training and retraining programs for maturing adults in light of such findings regarding adult learning patterns.

Career Development

Older workers, as well as their younger colleagues, need to periodically update their skills to adapt to changes in their work environment. Employers facilitate such updating by aiding in skills assessment, skills development, and analysis of the tasks/skills mix (West and Berman 1993). They also encourage employees to develop annual career objectives, make available career counseling services, and assist in career planning and/or career revitalization programs (e.g., for the plateaued worker). Using the terminology of quality management, employers need to provide an environment of continuous learning opportunities for workers of all ages. This effort reflects a conscious decision to provide stimulating work assignments to employees and/or to enrich their jobs. It also involves decisions to capitalize on the wisdom and knowledge of senior workers by tapping them to mentor their more junior colleagues. Mentor programs which pair older and younger workers have been shown to increase communication among and across staff levels, and to facilitate the transfer of more subtle forms of knowledge from one generation to another. In an era of fiscal penny-pinching it is tempting (although unwise) for municipal officials to cut training and development programs which require short-term costs in exchange for uncertain and difficult to measure long-term payoffs. Doing so would disadvantage older employees as well as their younger coworkers, and would fail to heed the central message of the human capital specialists.

Performance Appraisal

Finally, age-bias is sometimes a problem when conducting performance appraisals (Sterns and Alexander 1987). To ensure that performance appraisal systems are valid, reliable, and age-neutral the literature increasingly supports use of objective performance measures (Lovrich 1995). Older workers as well as those in other age categories are greatly affected by the results of performance appraisals because they frequently influence salary decisions, training opportunities, prospects for transfer, and/or identification of candidates for layoff. Employers who are concerned about bias against older workers in performance appraisal increasingly rely on careful job analysis and performance standards to ensure that such appraisals are reasonable, relevant, and reliable.

To the extent that managers confront questions about the ability of older workers to perform at acceptable levels, organizations may rely on either mandatory or voluntary proficiency testing. Such tests allow managers to assess current skill and/or knowledge levels as a supplement to on-the-job performance ratings. The use of functional assessment or proficiency tests is necessary because chronological age is a poor predictor of worker performance, and the use of age as an aid in HR decision making is legally prohibited (for those in the forty to seventy age range) (Robinson et al. 1985; Davis and Dotson 1987). Another appraisal-related concern is that stereotypical thinking about aging may bias ratings against older workers, leading to inaccurate and disadvantageous assessments of their work performance. This suggests the need to train supervisors and managers to avoid rater bias in competing performance appraisals, and reinforces the need to make use of objective performance measures.

Driving Forces

The four areas comprising this framework—supportive workplace relations, training, career development, and performance appraisal—provide leverage points where managers can act strategically to recoup their investments in the human capital of their organizations. Thus, a key question concerns the extent to which cities make use of the strategies which are available. Typically, human capital policies are accorded a fairly low priority in local government (Orr 1992; Saltzstein 1995). Yet some organizations are inclined to act on these matters, others are not. What are the driving and restraining forces which stimulate or retard actions supportive of older workers (and workers in general)? Three categories of forces are considered: (1) managerial professionalism, (2) legal compliance, and (3) fiscal barriers.

Managerial professionalism is a vitally important factor shaping the strategic initiatives of communities. Some municipal management teams actively value and recognize the potential productivity gains to be realized by investing in older workers and press for the implementation of such strategies (Roberts 1995). Also, senior line managers charged with delivering a municipal service have an interest in human capital development and constitute a potential support base for older worker proposals. Where HR decisions are guided by a strategic plan and where labor costs assume substantial importance, a more coherent rationale exists for payoffs from HR investment strategies. Thus, an explanation based on managerial professionalism suggests that cities with HRM and senior managers who rate older worker issues as important, who operate with a strategic approach to human capital development, and who have economic concerns about labor costs are more likely to implement the desired strategies.

Legal compliance with provisions of the Age Discrimination in Employment Act and reaction to the litigation which followed provides an additional set of driving forces prompting local governments to think strategically about their aging workforce (Roberts 1995). By contrast, fiscal stress is a force which impedes development of new programs across the board (West, Berman, and Milakovich 1994; Wooldridge 1995), and thus mitigates against human capital development and special programs for aging workers (Barth et al. 1993). Cities that lack funds for training, early retirement incentives, advancement opportunities or adapting the workplace to older worker needs are likely to implement a narrower range of initiatives addressing the needs of their mature employees.

Methods

In 1995, a detailed survey was administered to human resource managers in all U.S. cities with populations of fifty thousand or more. The initial survey was developed based on a careful literature review and pretested on forty municipal personnel managers. The twelve-page survey contained questions about the municipal practices and strategies used by the city in dealing with older worker issues, the driving forces that led them to adopt aging worker policies, the barriers encountered, the attitudes of HR managers regarding older workers, and the nature of age discrimination charges filed against the city. Older workers are defined as all municipal employees who are at least fifty-five years of age. Respondents were told that this definition includes part-time workers, but excludes independent contractors and employees in service of other organizations.

Most of the response options use Likert scales. Open-ended questions were asked about specific accomplishments or obstacles facing the city.

Human resource managers were selected because they are most knowledgeable about the personnel policies and strategic initiatives of the city related to HRM generally, and about older worker issues in particular. The HR managers who responded to the survey were asked to indicate their familiarity with older worker issues in their city using a three-point scale—not familiar (0), familiar (1), and very familiar (2). Respondents said they were quite familiar (1.24) with such issues in their city. Over 66 percent of the surveys were completed by the named addressee; the remainder were completed by his or her designate.

A total of 544 surveys were mailed. After three follow-up mailings and telephone calls, 249 were returned for a 46 percent response rate. To examine the possibility of nonresponse bias, a telephone survey of fifty randomly selected nonrespondents was conducted. This latter survey found that responses between those completing the survey instrument and nonrespondents were similar. For example, 51 percent of respondents say their city uses retirees as volunteers compared to 54 percent of nonrespondents. Further, 32 percent of the respondent group say their city has been charged with age discrimination by older workers within the past five years; 33 percent of nonrespondents report such charges. These differences are very small. Based on these responses and based on the comparison of demographic characteristics, we find no evidence of a serious nonresponse bias.

Findings

To assess the importance of aging workers as a salient HRM concern, respondents were asked to rate the importance of older worker issues to their municipality's personnel management. Using a four-point scale (3 = very important; 2 = important; 1 = somewhat important; 0 = not important) respondents indicated that older workers are an important concern (1.79). A follow-up question asked whether the relative importance of older worker issues had changed in their city during the last five years. Using a seven-point scale which ranges from "decreased greatly" to "increased greatly" (7), the average response is "increased somewhat" (4.77). These responses suggest that, on average, older workers are relatively more experienced. The findings reported below document the strategic response of municipalities.

Supportive Workplace Relations

Table 18.1 shows strategies used by cities to create a supportive workplace environment. Health, stress, vigor, and longevity are important issues to older workers because they encounter unique stressors (e.g., caregiving responsibilities), are more vulnerable to serious illness, use health care facilities more frequently, and incur higher costs for disability and medical insurance. Four particular items deal with stress and health concerns. Employee Assistance Programs (EAPs) are used in nine out of ten cities. Health promotion activities are being implemented in three-fourths of our sample cities, and both wellness programs and stress management activities are present in two-thirds of these local governments. EAPs are helpful to older and younger workers alike because the diagnostic, counseling and referral services aid in coping with personal problems which impede work performance. Health promotion and wellness programs are welcomed by aging workers, especially if they address their special needs (e.g., health-screening, blood pressure monitoring). Such programs also have a "payoff" for organizations by encouraging a healthy, more productive, and less costly workforce (i.e., lower

Table 18.1

Strategies Dealing with Supportive Workplace Relations[a]

Supportive workplace relations	Use (%)	Large cities[b]	Small cities
Stress/Health			
Employee assistance programs (EAP)	93	94	91
Health promotion activities	77	77	77
Wellness program	65	63	66
Stress management	64	73	57**
Alternative work patterns			
Parenting leave	75	75	7
Job transfer	62	68	58
Elder care leaves	56	63	52
Workplace adjustments due to functional losses (e.g., hearing impairment)	54	60	50**
Flextime	52	60	45**
Part-time work options	51	57	47*
Using retirees as volunteers	51	54	50
Providing special equipment	48	50	46
Reemployment of retirees	42	49	36*
Job redesign	32	36	29*
Equipment redesign	29	33	27
Job rotation	20	23	18
Retirement			
Pension planning	72	68	74
Early retirement programs	60	63	57

Notes:

[a]Respondents were asked to identify generic strategies (available to all employees) that are used by older workers in their city. Cronbach alpha of three measures combined is 0.82.

[b]Large cities > 100,000; small cities < 100,000.

*10% significance; **5% significance; ***1% significance.

absenteeism, insurance costs, turnover, etc.). Large and small cities alike are investing in stress reduction and actions promoting healthy lifestyles for their workers, with large cities more frequently than smaller ones acting to manage stress.

On the second measure—alternative work patterns—there is greater variety in the specific strategies pursued by cities. Municipalities can offer flexible work schedules (e.g., flexible hours and/or part-time work), respond to episodic short-term time needs (e.g., parenting and elder care leaves), and provide longer-range time options (using retirees as volunteers). Flextime, which allows some latitude in deciding which days or hours to work, is an important incentive for older workers which may keep people working beyond retirement age. It is used in 52 percent of our sample cities. Part-time work options, available in 51 percent of cities, appeal to older workers who may need partial income, prefer a slower work pace, have increased family responsibilities, and who want to continue enjoying the benefits of work. Elder care leaves (56%) are more attuned to the needs of older workers who may have caregiving responsibilities for ailing parents, friends, or other relatives. Use of retirees as volunteers (51%) enables older workers to remain productive, maintain their work-related skills, and enjoy the stimulation and camaraderie found in the work setting.

Flexibility in work style requires municipalities to adapt to the special needs of older workers. Many cities have made such adaptations in selected areas, including workplace adjustments due to functional losses (54%), provision of special equipment (48%), and equipment redesign (29%).

Functional losses for older workers may include hearing or sight impairment or loss of physical mobility; adjustments or special equipment might require telephone amplifiers, computer screen magnifiers, and clutter-free work environments which allow for use of assistive devices (e.g., wheelchair, cane, walkers). Redesign of equipment might be necessary when, for example, age-related physical problems (e.g., arthritis) require modification in the word processing work station (chairs, table) or use of voice-activated software. Other adaptations might result from more traditional HR strategies such as job transfer (62%), job redesign (32%), and job rotation (20%). Job transfers may prolong the working life of older workers by reassignment to a slower paced, less physically or mentally demanding position. Job redesign could help a mature worker if the newly designed job was a better "fit" with the current skills of the employee (e.g., if worker health problems limit their ability to work). Job rotation would enable competent older workers to provide supervision, guidance, and instruction to less experienced, skilled and knowledgeable younger employees. Large cities are more likely than small cities to use flextime strategies.

Retirement and pre-retirement programs such as pension planning and early retirement incentives—the most popular method of downsizing—are used by a majority of cities (72% and 60%, respectively) and their rate of use is similar in both large and small cities.

Training

Table 18.2 reports findings for three separate measures—training, career development, and performance appraisal. Paralleling trends in the private sector (Rhine 1984), local governments rely heavily on work-education programs such as tuition assistance for training (73%). In most instances this is a wise investment for employers of older workers because such employees are more likely to remain with the organization than their younger "job-hopping" colleagues. Training-related strategies that are more tailored to the needs of older workers are less frequently used, however. Job retraining, an important requirement for middle-aged and aging workers, especially those affected by technological change, is found in just three out of ten cities. Furthermore, there is little evidence that training programs are being adapted to meet the specific needs of older workers. A third of the sample cities adapt training by seeking active participation by trainees (35%), even fewer make allowances for older workers by providing more time to complete work (19%), by better organizing training information (23%), or by emphasizing the familiar (21%). These findings mirror those from the private sector which report that companies make few adjustments for the learning styles of older employees (Barth et al. 1993).

Career Development

Governments have traditionally lagged behind the private sector in career planning and management. A majority of cities (56%) are current providing the kind of continuous learning opportunities for their employees which are stressed in the quality management and employee development literature. Similarly, structured programs stressing skills development exist in only half (52%) of the sample cities. Despite the growing need for a highly skilled municipal workforce, only a limited number of cities are systematically assessing employee skills (29%) and analyzing the tasks/skills mix (39%). Half of the cities surveyed encourage employees to prepare annual development objectives (52%); however, other career-related strategies are used less often. Using older workers as mentors could have the beneficial result of having a more fruitful mix of younger and older workers within each work unit, but use of this strategy is limited to a quarter (24%) of the sample cities. Older workers could profit by human capital investments in career revitalization (11%), career counseling (27%), and career planning (19%), but these approaches to workforce

Table 18.2

Strategies Dealing with Training, Development, and Performance[a]

Strategies	Use (%)	Large cities	Small cities
Training (alpha = .79)			
Tuition assistance for training	73	81	68
Adapting training by seeking active participation	35	31	37
Motivating workers for training opportunities	34	30	37
Job retraining	33	36	31
Adapting training by better organizing information	23	23	23
Adapting training by emphasizing the familiar	21	21	22
Adapting training by allowing more time	19	16	20
Career development (alpha = .81)			
Providing continuous learning opportunities	56	58	55
Skills development	52	55	49
Annual development objectives	52	55	49
Analysis of tasks/skills mix	39	42	37
Stimulating work assignments	31	30	32
Job enrichment	30	28	32
Skills assessment	29	28	30
Career counseling	27	32	23
Older workers as mentors	24	21	27
Career planning	19	21	18
Career revitalization programs	11	12	10
Performance appraisal (alpha = .67)			
Objective performance measures	67	72	63
Appraisal for salary decisions	59	56	61
Appraisal to identify training opportunities	40	41	39
Appraisal to identify transfer opportunities	23	24	22
Appraisal for layoff	19	20	18
Mandatory proficiency testing	18	17	18
Voluntary proficiency testing	9	7	10

Notes:
[a]Respondents were asked to identify generic strategies (available to all employees) that are used by older workers in their city.
    *10% significance; ** 5% significance; *** 1% significance.

development are seldom found in local government. There are no significant differences between large and small cities in career development activities.

Performance Appraisal

The final human capital strategy is performance appraisal. Objective performance measures are relied upon in two-thirds of cities, and appraisals are used for salary decisions in six out of ten cities. Cities make less use of appraisal results to identify candidates for training (40%), for job transfers (23%), or for layoffs (19%). A supplement to measurements of on-the-job performance which is relevant to older workers is the use of skills testing. Very few cities are conducting either mandatory or voluntary proficiency testing (18% and 9%, respectively).

Use of Strategies by City Size, Government Type, and Region

Table 18.3 examines the use of these four sets of strategies in cities which vary by city size, form of government, and geographic region. To ensure that the four measures are reliable, Cronbach

Table 18.3

Municipal Strategies for Older Workers (percent of organizations reporting generic strategies used to deal with older worker issues)

	N	Supportive workplace relations	Training	Career development	Performance appraisal
Size					
Over 1,000,000	6	0.33	0.26	0.18	0.24
500,000 to 999,999	8	0.55**	0.54	0.50	0.41
250,000 to 499,999	24	0.45	0.45	0.45***	0.38
100,000 to 149,999	65	0.37	0.38	0.28	0.30
50,000 to 99,999	142	0.36	0.42	0.32	0.32
Government					
Mayor-council	93	0.36	0.40	0.31	0.28**
Council manager	149	0.39	0.44	0.36*	0.36**
Other	3	0.28	0.09	0.12	0.23
Region					
Northeast	36	0.26***	0.27***	0.18***	0.17***
North Central	57	0.41	0.46	0.34	0.29*
South	82	0.35	0.38	0.30	0.33
West	70	0.44***	0.48***	0.41**	0.42***
Total	245	0.38	0.41	0.32	0.32

Note: The index numbers are fractions of the number of items used in each category. For example, 33% of the items reported in Table 18.1 regarding supportive workplace relations are used in cities over one million.
    *10% significance; **5% significance; ***1% significance.

alpha is used. It is found that the coefficient of these four measures are: supportive workplace relations (.82), training (.79), career development (.81), and performance appraisal (.67). This suggests acceptable to high reliability. Findings are consistent with the patterns shown in Tables 18.1 and 18.2 in that there is little variation by city size, the only exceptions being the greater likelihood of cities with populations between 500 thousand and one million to adopt strategies promoting supportive workplace relations, and cities with populations of 250 thousand to 500 thousand to adopt career development strategies. By contrast, a consistent (although statistically weak) pattern is evident with regard to form of government, with council-manager cities more frequently featuring all four sets of strategies than mayor-council cities. This finding might be explained by the greater emphasis given to professionalism in council-manager cities because strategic investments in human capital are consistent with a professional and longer-range approach to municipal management. Variations by region are also evident, with cities in the Northeast adopting these strategies less frequently than those in the other three regions, and with cities in the West adopting such strategies most frequently across-the-board. Similar patterns of regional variation have been found in other studies of municipal innovation (see ICMA 1992, 1993, 1994).

Aspiration Gap

One way to assess the present and future importance of older worker issues for municipal governments is to examine the aspiration gap. The aspiration gap is defined as the difference between policies and practices currently in use (reality) and the percent of organizations reporting that important improvements are required (aspiration) in a particular area in the next five years. When

Table 18.4

Aspiration Gap

	Aspiration gap (%)	Improvement required (%)
Adopt a policy for older workers	+24	33
Adapt appraisals to the conditions of older workers	+22	27
Provide outplacement assistance	+15	36
Use mediators in age discrimination suits	+7	23
Use arbitrators in age discrimination suits	+5	18
Ombudsman	+2	17
Check performance appraisal for age bias	−2	33
Train raters to avoid age bias	−16	35
Policies which make retirement attractive after 20+ years	−19	32
Use proficiency tests	−24	23
Adopt a seniority policy	−33	16
Examine employment policies for age bias	−50	25
Negotiate labor-management contracts	−52	10
Open door policies	−69	9
Grievance procedures	−87	8

Note: The aspiration gap is defined as the difference between the percent of cities currently using the following policies and practices and the percent of organizations reporting that important improvements are required during the next five years.

the gap is high and the difference is positive (as in the case of the need to adopt a policy for older workers), the issue appears to be an emerging or increasing concern. By contrast, if the gap is high and the difference is negative, as in the need to adopt grievance procedures (gap = .87 percentage points) the issue might be an adequately addressed or waning problem. However, because an issue is referred to as waning does not necessarily mean it will be unimportant in the future. Results reported in Table 18.4 show the distribution of items having a positive versus a negative gap. Those items where the gap is positive and moderately large—suggesting the need for future improvements beyond past accomplishments—include the need to adapt appraisals to the needs of older workers, to adopt a policy for older workers, and to provide outplacement assistance. Other items where the gap is positive but smaller include the use of third parties (mediators, arbitrators) in age discrimination suits.

A large negative gap (ranging from 40 percent to 87 percent) occurs for four items—adoption of grievance procedures, open door policies, examination of employment policies for age bias, and negotiation of labor-management contracts. These employee relations issues have been adequately addressed in most local jurisdictions making them less salient in the future. Other items where the gap is negative, indicating less need for future action than occurred in the past, deal with adoption of a seniority policy, use of proficiency tests, initiatives which make retirement attractive after two decades, and reducing age bias by training raters and checking performance appraisals.

Driving Forces

What factors help explain why some cities adopt older worker strategies and other cities do not? All four of the indicators of managerial professionalism are significantly related to these strategic initiatives (Table 18.5). Interest by the municipal HRM and by other senior managers is a signifi-

Table 18.5

Determinants of Older Worker Strategies

Determinants	Supportive workplace relations	Training	Career development	Performance appraisal
Senior managers	.120**	.217***	.192***	.120**
HRM	.110**	.157***	.157***	.061
Costs of employees	.112**	.183***	.133***	.058
Strategic planning	.088*	.173***	.168***	.088*
Changes in laws	.062	.123**	.102**	.054
Lack of funds (barrier)	.037	.100**	−.003	.038
Policy	.241***	.344***	.313***	n/a
Lawsuits	.059	.044	.054	.056

Note: Association with driving forces and barrier of older worker strategies (tau-c).
* 10% significance; ** 5% significance; *** 1% significance.

cant determinant across the range of strategies. This highlights an important finding: profession-alism does matter when it comes to responding to the needs of older workers. Two other indicators of managerial professionalism are correlated with three of the four sets of dependent variables measures—the cost of employees and strategic planning. Cities which stress the importance of labor-related costs of municipal employees are also more willing to make human capital invest-ments of the types summarized by our measures (with the exception of performance appraisal). We speculate that rather than seeking to save costs by having higher-paid older workers dropped from the city payroll through downsizing, far-sighted HRMs seek to recoup their full investment in competent and experienced older workers by retaining, retraining, and developing them. Also those who emphasize a strategic HR planning approach are more likely to see merit in the human capital perspective. These findings related to managerial professionalism are consistent with results from private sector research where it has been shown that the best predictors of HRM innovativeness are a company's willingness to invest in people and long-term goals together with supportive interest of top management (Lawler et al. 1993).

The link between legal compliance and municipal concern with older worker issues is less clear. Legal changes are correlated with training and career development, but not with other measures. Similarly, the presence of active lawsuits is not correlated with any measure. While compliance with statutory law (ADEA and its amendments) and sensitivity to litigation cannot be ignored by HRMs, action on a wide range of older workers issues is prompted more by other forces.

One surprising finding is the greater the financial stress (i.e., lack of funds as a barrier) the more likely a city is to rely on training strategies. While this finding contradicts conventional wisdom, it may be explained in part by our operationalization of "lack of funds" as a composite measure including lack of funds for various practices. It could be that cities facing funding constraints will choose to invest their limited resources in training rather than other competing options (e.g., early retirement incentive programs, accelerated advancement, adaptations to the workplace). There is limited support in the private sector literature for the special treatment accorded to training; it has been noted that "training was more likely to be treated with kid gloves than to be singled out for deep cuts" in current circumstances (Gordon 1991).

Finally, cities which clarify age-related policies in connection with decisions regarding per-formance appraisal are more likely to implement the three sets of strategies regarding older workers (performance appraisal is excluded from this analysis). HR departments which eliminate age-bias from appraisal instruments, train raters to avoid age bias, and adopt flexible assessment procedures demonstrate a commitment to age-neutral decision making, and this guiding HR philosophy of sensitivity to aging worker issues apparently prompts support for other strategic initiatives on behalf of older employees.

Accomplishments and Obstacles

Two open-ended question were included as part of the survey. The first asked respondents to reflect on their city's experience with older-worker programs to date, and to indicate what they consider to be their city's greatest accomplishments. Six items accounted for a majority of responses to this question. The most frequently mentioned response, not surprisingly, is the practice of the city to treat all employees equally and fairly regardless of the workers' demographic group. Retention of older workers is the next most frequently mentioned item. This is followed closely by reemploying retirees in full- and part-time work, and by a well-funded retirement or pension plan. Taken together, these four items account for 45 percent of all open-ended answers to this question. Five other frequently registered responses deal with early retirement incentive programs, active volunteer programs, compliance efforts under EEO and ADEA, dissemination of pre-retirement information, and revised paid benefit schemes. Less frequently mentioned are downsizing activities that were carried out without reducing services or mandating layoffs, and the absence of age-discrimination complaints. There are multiple responses in twelve additional categories, including: increased age awareness, wellness programs, the value placed on older workers, elder care, accommodation given to employees regardless of age, the presence of seniority-based systems, job redesign, employment training programs for older workers, improvement of health care plans, tuition reimbursement funds, the absence of mandatory retirement age, and workplace adjustments due to functional losses. The remaining 12 percent of responses are jurisdiction-specific accomplishments which a particular city claimed (e.g., placing displaced older workers in funded, vacant positions).

The second open-ended question asks about the greatest obstacles that have been encountered in implementing programs for older workers. Once again, a few items account for the bulk of responses. By far the most common response is the lack of funds, followed by lack of awareness, lack of interest, lack of priority, and lack of staff. Responses in these five categories account for 69 percent of the answers to the question concerning obstacles. The inflexibility of union contracts is mentioned by five HR managers. Downsizing of government, lack of information on the growing needs of an aging workforce, lack of job openings available to older workers, lack of priority given to training, and the absence of age-specific programs were obstacles mentioned by a few. The remaining 15 percent of responses pertain to specific barriers which are problematic for one city, but not mentioned by respondents from other municipalities (e.g., fear of reverse discrimination charges). Table 18.6 contains quotes in the respondents' own words regarding their accomplishments and the obstacles they encounter in dealing with older worker issues.

Summary and Conclusion

The aging of the American workforce is relevant to managers, especially human resource managers, in all institutions of American society, including local governments. While the full impact of labor force trends will not be felt until the next century when the baby boomers enter the ranks of "older workers," clear-thinking and farsighted managers are recognizing the need to plan and act now to deal with current issues and anticipate those of the future. Some challenges have been well

Table 18.6

[Comments on Accomplishments and Obstacles]

Selected comments about accomplishments:

"Reemployment of retirees in part-time work situation. We can meet an organizational need with a dependable, trained employee who can enjoy greater leisure time and work for the city as well in a productive capacity."

"Implementation of a diversity action plan concentrating on minorities, females, aged workers, and appreciating difference each group brings to the city's objectives."

"We have integrated workers in our workforce regardless of age at the time of employment and we have successfully kept employees considerably past normal retirement age (62–65) when they were still very valuable and productive."

"We've never [had] any age discrimination complaints during my seven years of employment with the city. Age is never an issue in selection for employment or promotions internally. An employee's desire for retirement is usually the driving force in leaving. We have not yet experienced lay-offs or mandatory reductions-in-force. We have one employee that is seventy-nine years old, and several over sixty-five."

"The ability to continue to employ an older workforce that is properly trained and promotable."

Selected comments about obstacles:

"Not enough people see this issue as a priority—workforce tends to concentrate completely on tasks at hand and little on such productivity issues as aging workforce."

"A general lack of monies available for programs targeting special groups of any sort whether older, minority, female, and so forth. Mandated special programs take most of the funds, and communities most concerned to have monies spent to reduce crime, graffiti, gangs, and so on."

"Lack of information on growing needs of aging workforce, and union contracts which do not provide flexibility."

"Union contracts can be restricting because all individuals within that bargaining unit are entitled to the same provisions."

"The biggest obstacles are resistance to technological change (training, etc.) and reinventing government (organizational change)."

"Fear of reverse discrimination charges by younger employees if program is geared toward older workers."

met by cities, others are yet to be satisfactorily confronted (e.g., career revitalization, proficiency testing, adapting training methods). Research reported here suggests that most needs of older workers are currently being addressed via generic strategies which are available to all workers rather than by specifically tailored programs adapted to their unique needs.

Among the proactive steps public sector managers and personnel specialists in local government might consider are the following: (1) Assess current policies and practices regarding training and retraining of older workers to ensure that they can compete on an equal footing with their younger coworkers and prolong their productive employment; (2) apply the findings from the field of androgogy (the art and science of helping adults learn) by training the trainers to recognize that older workers learn differently than younger workers and by encouraging trainers to experiment with new and appropriate training techniques and methods; (3) reexamine performance appraisal instruments and methods to ensure that they are age-neutral and bias free; (4) examine health and retirement benefits to minimize disincentives to continued employment beyond retirement age; (5) evaluate career management practices to ensure that there is no bias against investing in older workers and move aggressively to retain older workers by accommodating their career needs; (6) educate older workers regarding the alternative work arrangements which are currently available (eldercare, part-time work, flextime, job transfers, workplace adjustments, equipment redesign, etc.) in many municipalities; and (7) remove any artificial barriers (e.g., unnecessary training and experience requirements) so that older workers are not disadvantaged in competing for current and future jobs. While many of these steps have been advocated and tried in selected private and public sector settings (Barth et al. 1993; AARP 1990), local government human resource managers are well positioned to promote their application more broadly at the municipal level.

Future scholarly research is needed to identify the special problems older government employees encounter at work and to assess the effectiveness of different strategies for dealing with aging workers. Since municipal governments are rather labor-intensive, human capital strategies make good sense as a way to increase productivity, achieve high performance organizations, and remain responsive to employee needs. While problems such as age discrimination may be somewhat less common in government than in the private sector (Roberts 1995), bias charges are nonetheless often filed, and frequently these claims arise in reaction to objectionable avoidable actions taken by public sector employers. What are these avoidable objectionable actions, how widespread are they, and how can they be minimized? If local government managers and supervisors hold inaccurate stereotypes of older workers, what impact does that have on their willingness to support such strategies as skill upgrading, alternative work arrangements and retraining for older workers? Are cities doing anything to adjust supervisor/managerial mindsets, to minimize the problem of age bias, and to encourage management of older workers in an age-neutral way? Case studies are needed to document successful efforts to address the needs of older city workers, such as training programs which incorporate adult learning theory into the design and execution of classes, career revitalization programs for plateaued workers, older-worker mentor programs, and reemployment of retirees. Human capital investments do bring payoffs for both individuals and organizations. While the return on the investment in older workers might be shorter-lived than that in younger workers, future research could give us a better fix on the short-term benefits derived from investing in a valuable municipal asset—the mature worker.

References

American Association of Retired Persons (AARP). 1990. *Resourceful Aging: Today and Tomorrow.* Arlington, VA: AARP. Volume 4, Work/Second Careers, Conference Proceedings.

Barth, M.C., W. McNaught, and P. Rizzi. 1993. "Corporations and the Aging Workforce." In *Building the Competitive Workforce*, ed. P.H. Mirvis. New York: John Wiley, pp. 156–200.

Becker, G.S. 1993. *Human Capital: A Theoretical and Empirical Analysis.* Chicago: University of Chicago Press.

Blocklyn, P.L. 1987. "The Aging Workforce." *Personnel* 64: 16–19.

Bluestone, I., R.J.V. Montgomery, and J.D. Owen. 1990. *The Aging of the American Work Force.* Detroit: Wayne State University Press.

Bove, R. 1987. "Retraining the Older Worker." *Training and Development Journal* 41: 77–78.

Buonocore, A.J. 1992. "Older and Wiser: Senior Employees Offer Untapped Capabilities." *Management Review* 81: 49–51.

Bruce, W., and D. Olshfski. 1993. "The New American Workplace." In *Public Productivity Handbook*, ed. M. Holzer. New York: Marcel Dekker, pp. 425–443.

Capowski, G. 1995. "Ageism: The New Diversity Issue." In *Business Ethics*, ed. J.E. Richardson. Guilford, CT: Dushkin, pp. 79–84.

Carnevale, D.G. 1992. "The Learning Support Model: Personnel Policy Beyond the Traditional Model." *American Review of Public Administration* 22: 19–36.

———. 1995. "Human Capital and High Performance Organizations." In *Public Personnel Administration*, ed. S.W. Hays and R.C. Kearney. Englewood Cliffs, NJ: Prentice-Hall, pp. 133–144.

Carnevale, D.G., and B. Weschsler. 1992. "Trust in the Public Sector: Individual and Organizational Determinants." *Administration and Society* 23: 471–494.

Cooper, C.L. 1984. "Sources of Occupational Stress Among Older Workers." In *Aging and Technological Advances*, ed. P.K. Robinson, J. Livingston, and J.E. Birren. New York: Plenum Press, pp. 209–219.

Czaja, S.J. 1995. "Aging and Work Performance." *Review of Public Personnel Administration* 15: 46–61.

Davis, P.O., and C.O. Dotson. 1987. "Job Performance Testing: An Alternative to Age Discrimination." *Medicine and Science in Sports and Exercise* 19: 179–185.

Dennis, H., ed. 1987. *Fourteen Steps in Managing an Aging Workforce.* Lexington, MA: Heath.

Elliott, R.E. 1995. "Human Resource Management's Role in the Future Aging of the Workforce." *Review of Public Personnel Administration* 15: 5–17.

Gordon, J. 1991. "Training Budgets: Recession Takes a Bite—1991." *Training* 28: 37–45.

Halachmi, A. 1992. "Evaluation Research: Purpose and Perspective." In *Public Productivity Handbook*, ed. Marc Holzer. New York: Marcel Dekker, pp. 213–225.

Hornbeck, D.W., and L.M. Salamon. 1991. *Human Capital and America's Future: An Economic Strategy for the '90s.* Baltimore, MD: Johns Hopkins University Press, pp. 213–225.

International City/County Management Association (ICMA). 1992. *Municipal Yearbook.* Washington, DC: ICMA.

———. 1993. *Municipal Yearbook.* Washington, DC: ICMA.

———. 1994. *Municipal Yearbook.* Washington, DC: ICMA.

Johnson, P. 1990. "Our Aging Population—The Implications for Business and Government." *Long Range Planning* 23: 55–62.

Kelly, J. 1992. "The Rising Tide of Older Workers." *Nation's Business* 80 (September): 22.

Kelly, R. 1993. "Diversity in the Public Workforce: New Needs, New Approaches." In *Revitalizing State and Local Public Service*, ed. F. Thompson. San Francisco, CA: Jossey-Bass, pp. 197–222.

Knowles, M.S. and Associates. 1984. *Androgogy in Action: Applying Modern Principles of Adult Learning.* San Francisco, CA: Jossey-Bass.

Lawler, E.E., S.G. Cohen, and L. Chang. 1993. "Strategic Human Resource Management." In *Building the Competitive Workforce*, ed. P.H. Mirvis. New York: John Wiley, pp. 31–60.

Lovrich, N. 1995. "Performance Appraisal: Seeking Accountability and Efficiency Through Individual Effort, Commitment, and Accomplishment." In *Public Personnel Administration: Problems and Prospects*, ed. S.W. Hays and R.C. Kearney. Englewood Cliffs, NJ: Prentice-Hall, pp. 105–120.

Mirvis, P.H. 1993. *Building the Competitive Workforce.* New York: John Wiley.

National Alliance of Business (NAB). 1985. *Invest in Experience: New Directors for an Aging Workforce.* Washington, DC: NAB.

Orr, M. 1992. "Urban Regimes and Human Capital Policies: A Study of Baltimore." *Journal of Urban Affairs* 14: 173–187.

Parker, V.A., and D.T. Hall. 1993. "Workplace Flexibility: Faddish or Fundamental." In *Building the Competitive Workforce*, ed. P.H. Mirvis. New York: John Wiley, pp. 122–155.

Paul, C.E. 1987. "Implementing Alternative Work Arrangements for Older Workers." In *Fourteen Steps in Managing an Aging Workforce*, ed. H. Dennis. Lexington, MA: Heath, pp. 113–119.

Redwood, A. 1990. "Human Resources Management in the 1990s." *Business Horizons* 33: 74–80.

Rhine, S.H. 1984. *Managing Older Workers: Company Policies and Attitudes.* New York: Conference Board.

Roberts, G.E. 1995. "Age Related Employment Issues in Florida Municipal Governments: Are Municipalities Preparing for Change?" *Review of Public Personnel Administration* 15: 62–83.

Robinson, P.K., S. Coberly, and C.E. Paul. 1985. "Work and Retirement." In *Aging and the Social Sciences*, ed. R. Binstock and E. Shanas. New York: Van Nostrand Reinhold, pp. 503–527.

Rosen, B., and T.H. Jerdee. 1985. *Older Employees: New Roles for Valued Resources.* Homewood, IL: Dow Jones-Irwin.

Rosow, J.M. 1990. "Extending Working Life." In *The Aging of the American Workforce*, ed. I. Bluestone, R.J.V. Montgomery, and J.D. Owen. Detroit: Wayne State University Press, pp. 399–420.

Saltzstein, A. 1995. "Personnel Management in the Local Government Setting." In *Public Personnel Administration: Problems and Prospects*, ed. S.W. Hays and R.C. Kearney. Englewood Cliffs, NJ: Prentice-Hall, pp. 37–53.

Savoie, E.J. 1990. "The Aging of Organizations: Strategic Issues." In *The Aging of the American Workforce*, ed. I. Bluestone, R.J.V. Montgomery, and J.D. Owen. Detroit: Wayne State University, pp. 275–420.

Sonnenfeld, J. 1978. "Dealing with the Aging Work Force." *Harvard Business Review* 56: 80–90.

Sterns, H.L., and R.A. Alexander. 1987. "Performance Appraisal of the Older Worker." In *Fourteen Steps in Managing an Aging Workforce*, ed. H. Dennis. Lexington, MA: Heath, pp. 85–93.

Sterns, H.L., G.V. Barrett, S.J. Czaja, and J.K. Barr. 1994. "Issues in Work and Aging." *Journal of Applied Gerontology* 13: 7–19.

Sterns, H.L., and D. Doverspike. 1987. "Training and Developing the Older Worker: Implications for Human Resource Management." In *Fourteen Steps in Managing an Aging Workforce*, ed. H. Dennis. Lexington, MA: Heath, pp. 97–110.

Strouse, C. 1995. "Older Workers Fight for Acceptance." *Miami Herald*, March 12, p. 16A.

Tager, R.M. 1987. "Stress and the Older Worker." In *Fourteen Steps in Managing an Aging Workforce*, ed. H. Dennis. Lexington, MA: Heath, pp. 55–66.

Tompkins, J. 1995. *Human Resource Management in Government*. New York: HarperCollins.

Van Wart, M., N.J. Cayer, and S. Cook. 1993. *Handbook of Training and Development for the Public Sector*. San Francisco, CA: Jossey-Bass.

West, J.P., and E.M. Berman. 1993. "Human Resource Strategies in Local Government: A Survey of Progress and Future Directions." *American Review of Public Administration* 23: 279–297.

West, J.P., and E.M. Berman. 1995. "Strategic Human Resource and Career Planning." In *Public Personnel Administration: Problems and Prospects*, ed. S.W. Hays and R.C. Kearney. Englewood Cliffs, NJ: Prentice-Hall, pp. 73–88.

West, J.P., E.M. Berman, and M.E. Milakovich. 1994. "Total Quality Management in Local Government." In *ICMA Municipal Yearbook*. Washington, DC: ICMA, pp. 14–25.

Wooldridge, B. 1995. "Overcoming Obstacles to Public-Sector Improvement Efforts." In *Quality Management Today*, ed. J.P. West. Washington, DC: ICMA, pp. 37–50.

CHAPTER 19

PERFORMANCE APPRAISAL PRACTICES FOR UPPER MANAGEMENT IN CITY GOVERNMENTS

DAVID N. AMMONS AND ARNOLD RODRIGUEZ

The extensive literature on performance appraisal indicates the importance of that topic in the management of organizations—public sector and private. Much of the literature, however, is devoted to essays extolling the virtues of "good" performance appraisal, descriptions of innovative and not-so-innovative appraisal techniques, and case studies describing the experiences of selected organizations in the application of particular performance appraisal practices.

Relatively little attention has been directed toward documenting the level of use of presumably popular performance appraisal techniques, the objectives for which they have been implemented, and their perceived effectiveness in the public sector in general or city government in particular. Still less attention has been directed toward the methods, objectives, and effectiveness of appraisal of the performance of upper management in city government—department heads, mayoral assistants, and assistant city managers. The purpose of this chapter is to address this deficiency through the examination of appraisal practices for evaluating the performance of upper management employees in 122 medium and large United States cities.

Data for the study were obtained from a mail survey of chief administrators in 170 selected United States cities with 1980 populations of 65,000 or more.[1] The survey, which was conducted in the spring of 1984, produced 122 responses for a response rate of 72 percent.

The questionnaire, addressed to municipal government chief executives, requested information on the nature of performance appraisal for upper management, the degree of formality of any such practices, techniques used, objectives of the appraisal process, level of subordinate participation, the amount of staff time committed to the process, and the level of satisfaction with current practices. Most respondents addressed all of these matters.

Respondents' Characteristics

Only one of the questionnaires was returned anonymously. Of the remaining 121 cities, 80 operate under the council-manager form of government (66.1 percent), 36 are mayor-council form (29.8 percent), and 5 are commission form (4.1 percent). The 1980 populations of the responding cities ranged from 65,047 to 2.97 million people. The mean population among respondents was 224,402. Municipal employment ranged from 350 to 35,000, with a mean of 2,737 employees.

From *Public Administration Review*, vol. 46, no. 5 (September/October 1986), pp. 460–467. Copyright © 1986 by American Society for Public Administration. Reprinted with permission.

Table 19.1

Formality of Performance Appraisal Process for Upper Management in Major U.S. Cities (N = 122)

	N	%
Formal, documented appraisal	72	59.0
Informal appraisal, with person-to-person interaction	34	27.9
Informal appraisal, without person-to-person interaction		
No appraisal	15	12.3
Total	122	100.0

Respondents were asked to identify themselves by title on the questionnaire. Chief executives (i.e., mayor or city manager) constituted 41.3 percent of the respondents; chief administrators (e.g., chief administrative officer, city administrator, etc.), 11.6 percent; principal assistants (e.g., assistant city manager, assistant to the mayor, etc.), 23.1 percent; personnel department officials, 20.7 percent; and other city officials, 3.3 percent.

Formality of Appraisal

Previous studies have reported the widespread existence of formal appraisal systems. Two often-cited private sector studies indicate that between 80 and 89 percent of all private companies have formal appraisal systems.[2] In the public sector, a survey of fifty large city governments in the late 1970s indicated the existence of formal appraisal systems in 74 percent of the cases, and a 1981–82 review of state government appraisal practices revealed the existence of formal systems in 94 percent of the states.[3]

Each of the above-mentioned studies reported the incidence of formal appraisal systems for employees in general. In contrast, lower percentages of private corporations have reported the use of formal systems for appraising the performance of managerial employees. A study of 293 private companies by Lazer and Wikstrom produced findings suggesting a lower likelihood of formal appraisal as one climbs the corporate ladder: 74 percent of the companies reported the use of formal appraisal systems for lower management (supervisors, foremen, etc.), 71 percent reported use of such systems for middle management, and 55 percent reported formal appraisal systems for top management (chief executive or president and those reporting immediately to them).[4]

In general concurrence with Lazer and Wikstrom's private sector findings, only 59 percent of the city governments responding to the survey upon which this chapter is based reported formal systems for the appraisal of the performance of upper level managers (Table 19.1). Informal appraisal was reported by 28.7 percent, while 12.3 percent of the cities reported no appraisal system whatsoever for upper management.

Appraisal Objectives

Many managers and academic proponents of performance appraisal expect a great deal from the process. The sweeping nature of such expectations is demonstrated at the federal level in the language of the United States Civil Service Reform Act of 1978: "Each agency shall develop one or more performance appraisal systems which (1) provide for periodic appraisals of job performance of employees; (2) encourage employee participation in establishing performance objectives; and (3) use the results of performance appraisal as a basis for training, rewarding, reassigning, promoting, demoting, retraining, and separating employees."

Table 19.2

Management Performance Appraisal Objectives in Major U.S. Cities

	Objectives						
Objective	Primary	Second	Third	Fourth	Fifth	Sixth	Total
Allocation of rewards	23.9	28.4	15.9	5.7	0.0	0.0	73.9
	(21)	(25)	(14)	(5)	(0)	(0)	(65)
Identification of skill deficiencies	8.0	25.0	17.0	3.4	1.1	0.0	54.5
	(7)	(22)	(15)	(3)	(1)	(0)	(48)
Feedback	60.2	22.7	4.5	1.1	0.0	0.0	88.6
	(53)	(20)	(4)	(1)	(0)	(0)	(78)
Promotional potential	0.0	2.3	11.4	6.8	0.0	0.0	20.5
	(0)	(2)	(10)	(6)	(0)	(0)	(18)
Workforce planning	0.0	0.0	0.0	0.0	2.3	1.1	3.4
	(0)	(0)	(0)	(0)	(2)	(1)	(3)
Other	8.0	0.0	2.3	1.1	0.0	0.0	11.4
	(7)	(0)	(2)	(1)	(0)	(0)	(10)
Totals	100.0	78.4	51.1	18.2	3.4	1.1	
	(88)	(69)	(45)	(16)	(3)	(1)	

At the state level, Feild and Holley surveyed personnel directors with statewide performance appraisal systems and found support for the following purposes in descending order: promotions, demotions and/or layoffs; manpower planning and utilization; salary adjustments; communication between supervisors and subordinates; determination of management development needs; validation of selection and promotion procedures; and updating position descriptions.[5] More recently, Tyer found state personnel director support for the following purposes of appraisal in state government, again in descending order: communication between supervisor and subordinates; salary adjustments; manpower planning; promotions, demotions, layoffs; updating position descriptions; validation of selection and promotion procedures; and determination of management development needs.[6]

Lazer and Wikstrom found discrepancy between the stated objectives of performance appraisal systems for corporate executives and the reported uses of appraisal information. Based upon frequency of mention, the apparent objectives of upper corporate management appraisal systems, in descending order, were performance measurement, management development, performance improvement, compensation administration, feedback, identifying potential, manpower planning, and communications. In terms of actual usage, however, performance feedback and compensation administration were the most frequently cited uses of upper management appraisal information (73 percent and 63 percent of the responding companies reporting those usages, respectively), followed by identification of management development needs (54 percent), promotion decisions (50 percent), manpower planning (34 percent), and validation of selection procedures (13 percent).[7]

Participants in the survey of city governments were asked to indicate whether any of five common objectives for performance appraisal or an open-ended "other" response were considered to be the primary objective of their management appraisal system, the secondary objective, and so forth. Among those responding to this question, 60.2 percent indicated that performance feedback was their primary objective, and 23.9 percent indicated that the proper allocation of rewards was the main purpose of their system (Table 19.2). In fact, 82.9 percent and 52.3 percent regarded feedback and reward allocation, respectively, to be among their top two objectives, paralleling to a remarkable degree the private sector findings of Lazer and Wikstrom. Despite recurring warnings by many authors that reward and development objectives conflict with one another in the appraisal process,[8] almost three-fourths of the responding cities placed rewards allocation among their top four appraisal objectives along with such development objectives as performance feedback and determination of promotion potential.

Techniques Utilized

Various appraisal techniques have been adopted in public and private sector organizations in hopes of achieving appraisal objectives while addressing concern over rater bias. The traditional appeal of adjectival and numeric rating scales, made popular no doubt by their simplicity, has begun to give way to seemingly more objective, performance-based techniques used either solely or in combination with rating scales.

Studies of general employee appraisal practices in the private sector suggest that heavy reliance on trait-based rating scales has dipped sharply during the past decade from one out of every two companies to one out of five—though many more continue to appraise performance based upon traits in combination with behavior or results.[9] Findings in the public sector have been similar. In the mid-1970s, Feild and Holley reported that 62 percent of the state governments with statewide performance appraisal systems were relying exclusively on numeric rating scales, 5 percent entirely on graphic rating scales, 16 percent on combinations of rating scales with other systems, 13 percent on essay evaluation, and 5 percent on checklists of job behaviors.[10] Among large city governments in the late 1970s, Lacho, Stearns, and Villere found 18 percent relying exclusively on graphic rating scales, 68 percent using graphic rating scales in combination with essay appraisals, 7 percent using a goal-setting system, 5 percent using essay appraisals, and 2 percent using a combination of essay and critical incident.[11]

Private corporations report extensive use of objective-setting or Management by Objectives (MBO) systems for appraising upper management performance. While such systems were reportedly used by 63 percent of the respondents in the Lazer-Wikstrom study, sometimes in combination with other systems, less extensive usage was reported for essay appraisals (36 percent), rating systems (conventional or graphic: 10 percent), rating systems (conventional or graphic: 10 percent; behavior anchored: 9 percent), critical incident systems (11 percent), checklists (behavioral: 8 percent; trait: 9 percent; forced choice: 2 percent), and forced distribution (10 percent) and other ranking or comparison systems.[12]

Among municipalities responding to the 1984 survey, 35.1 percent reported using MBO alone and reporting the existence of a managerial appraisal system of some kind in their organization (Table 19.3). Almost 65 percent reported using MBO either alone or in combination with other techniques, once again paralleling the findings for corporate executive appraisal systems. The second most frequently used appraisal technique for managerial employees was the rating scale, with 16.2 percent of the municipal respondents reporting use of that technique alone and 33.8 percent reporting its use in some form. The third most frequently cited management appraisal system was behaviorally anchored rating scales (BARS). BARS was reportedly used alone by 12.2 percent of the respondents and used in combination with other appraisal systems by another 16.3 percent.

Appraisal Frequency

The frequency of performance appraisal differs from organization to organization, but most conduct performance appraisals on an annual basis.[13] More frequent performance appraisal or

Table 19.3

Techniques Used in Managerial Performance Appraisal in Medium and Large U.S. Municipalities

	Employee comparison/ ratings	MBO	Direct indexes	Rating scale	BARS	Critical incident
System used alone	35.1		16.2	12.2	2.7	
	(26)		(12)	(9)	(2)	
Used in combination with						
Employee comparison/ratings only			1.4			
	(1)					
MBO only			8.0	6.8	4.1	
	(6)	(5)	(3)			
Direct indexes only				1.4		
	(1)					
Rating scale only	1.4	8.1	1.4			
	(1)	(6)	(1)			
BARS only		6.8				
	(5)					
Critical incident only		4.1				
	(3)					
Multiple techniques	2.7	10.8	1.4	6.8	9.5	6.8
	(2)	(8)	(1)	(5)	(7)	(5)
Total	4.1	64.9	2.7	33.8	28.4	13.5
	(3)	(48)	(2)	(25)	(21)	(10)

Notes: 1. This table includes only the seventy-four cities reporting the use of specific performance appraisal techniques. Cities failing to provide such information or reporting that no managerial appraisal system exists in their organization were excluded from all computations.

2. Percentages sum to more than 100.0, since a given combination of appraisal techniques is credited to the column of each technique.

Descriptions:

Employee comparison/ratings—The manager (or chief administrator, or mayor) lists and ranks assistants and/or department heads according to performance.

Management by objectives (MBO) or Goals/results approach—The manager and assistants/department heads jointly set objectives, and the employee's performance is rated based upon achievement of objectives.

Direct indexes—The manager sets specific, quantifiable measures or standards, and assistants/department heads are evaluated against the standards.

Rating scale—Appraisal is based on a set of traits and the degree to which they describe the assistant or department head.

Behaviorally anchored rating scale (BARS)—Appraisal is based on a set of behavioral statements and the degree to which they describe the assistant or department head's performance.

Critical incident—The manager documents positive and/or negative events.

review sessions have been found to be associated with several desirable organizational characteristics, including goal clarity and favorable attitudes.[14] Greater feedback frequency seems especially important for organizations using MBO. Survey responses from 30 cities using MBO in 1979 indicated that 14 (46.7 percent) had annual performance reviews, while 16 (53.3 percent) conducted reviews on a more frequent basis—10 (33.3 percent) twice yearly and 6 (20 percent) quarterly.[15]

The 1984 survey respondents, only part of whom were associated with organizations using MBO systems for management appraisal, reported somewhat less frequent appraisals than those responding to the study of thirty MBO cities, but higher frequencies than reported for employee performance appraisals in organizations in general—especially public sector organizations. While major studies have indicated that 52 to 92 percent of private firms and 80 to 91 percent of state and local government organizations have annual performance appraisials,[16] only 58.9 percent of the 1984 municipal respondents reported limiting appraisals of upper management assistants and department heads to a once-a-year basis. Other commonly cited frequencies were "twice yearly" (24.3 percent), "quarterly" (7.5 percent), "monthly" (3.7 percent), and "other" (5.6 percent). Presumably, contributing to this relatively high frequency of review sessions, at least in comparison to other surveys of public sector organizations, were the relatively extensive use of MBO systems among the responding jurisdictions and the focus of this study on appraisal practices for upper management employees as opposed to employees in general.

Satisfaction with Appraisal System

Several previous studies have examined the level of satisfaction with appraisal systems, often gauged in terms of perceived effectiveness. A review of assessments, however, suggests only modest levels of unequivocal satisfaction but at least enough general satisfaction to sustain the notion that regular performance appraisal is important. For example, 28 percent of the respondents to a survey of American Society for Personnel Administration members in three regions reported that their appraisal systems were working "very well";[17] 22 percent of the respondents in a survey of key industrial firms indicated that they were "highly satisfied" with their appraisal systems, while 69 percent were merely satisfied and 9 percent were unsatisfied;[18] 140 personnel administrators attending two conferences of the American Society for Personnel Administration produced an average rating of their managerial appraisal systems' effectiveness of 3.6 on a 7-point scale ranging from 0 for "not effective at all" to 6 for "effective to a very great extent";[19] 71 percent of 123 survey respondents thought their corporate executive appraisal systems were effective, and 29 percent thought they were ineffective;[20] 13 percent of the respondents to a 1979 survey of municipal personnel directors strongly agreed with the statement that "there is a performance evaluation system that fairly and thoroughly measures the quality of employees' work" in their organization, while 42 percent merely agreed, 23 percent disagreed, 6 percent strongly disagreed, and 16 percent were undecided;[21] and 21.1 percent of the respondents to a 1981–82 survey of state personnel directors evaluated their appraisal systems as very effective, while 63.2 percent thought they were somewhat effective and 15.8 percent thought they were not very effective.[22]

A slim majority of our municipal respondents were either generally satisfied (44.6 percent) or very satisfied (11.6 percent) with their management appraisal systems. Very nearly one-third (32.2 percent) reported mixed feelings regarding their level of satisfaction. Relatively few reported being generally dissatisfied (9.9 percent) or very dissatisfied (1.7 percent) with current appraisal practices.

Respondents tended to perceive somewhat higher levels of satisfaction among assistants and department heads who were the subjects of the appraisal systems than they felt themselves. They perceived more than 70 percent of the subordinate managers to be either "generally satisfied" (61.9 percent) or "very satisfied" (8.8 percent), 22.1 percent to be "indifferent or neutral," 7.1 percent to be "generally dissatisfied," and no group of assistants and department heads to be "very dissatisfied" with current appraisal practices. While it is possible that such perceptions are inflated, respondents report a generally high level of participation by assistants and department heads in the identification and development of performance standards, measurements, and objectives for their jobs—the kind of participation that may be expected to produce greater satisfaction

Table 19.4

Use of Selected Appraisal Techniques for Upper Management in Medium and Large U.S. Municipalities, by Organization Size and Form of Government

	Less than 1,000 employees	1,000– 2,499 employees	2,500– 7,499 employees	7,500 employees or more	Council- manager form	Mayor- council form	Commission form
N	25	27	15	7	52	17	4
Employee comparison/ratings							
Alone	0	0	0	0	0	0	0
	(0)	(0)	(0)	(0)	(0)	(0)	(0)
Combination	0	2	1	0	1	2	0
	(0)	(7.4)	(6.7)	(0)	(1.9)	(11.8)	(0)
MBO							
Alone	10	6	7	3	21	3	1
	(40)	(22.2)	(46.7)	(42.9)	(40.4)	(17.6)	(25)
Combination	8	9	4	1	19	2	1
	(32)	(33.3)	(26.7)	(14.3)	(36.5)	(11.8)	(25)
Direct indexes							
Alone	0	0	0	0	0	0	0
	(0)	(0)	(0)	(0)	(0)	(0)	(0)
Combination	0	1	0	1	2	0	0
	(0)	(3.7)	(0)	(14.3)	(3.8)	(0)	(0)
Rating scale							
Alone	6	4	1	1	5	7	0
	(24)	(14.8)	(6.7)	(14.3)	(9.6)	(41.2)	(0)
Combination	4	6	2	1	11	2	0
	(16)	(22.2)	(13.3)	(14.3)	(21.2)	(11.8)	(0)
BARS							
Alone	1	5	2	1	4	3	2
	(4)	(18.5)	(13.3)	(14.3)	(7.7)	(17.6)	(50)
Combination	4	6	2	0	10	1	1
	(16)	(22.2)	(13.3)	(0)	(19.2)	(5.9)	(25)
Critical incident							
Alone	0	1	1	0	2	0	0
	(0)	(3.7)	(6.7)	(0)	(3.8)	(0)	(0)
Combination	1	4	2	1	5	3	0
	(4)	(14.8)	(13.3)	(14.3)	(9.6)	(17.6)	(0)

Note: Numbers in parentheses = %.

with management systems in general.[23] More than 86 percent of the respondents indicated that assistants and department heads provide "considerable" (53.8 percent) or "full" (32.7 percent) assistance in the development of most standards, measurements, or objectives for their job. Much smaller percentages of the respondents indicated very little participation (9.6 percent) or no participation at all (3.8 percent).

Organization Size, Form of Government, and Appraisal Techniques

Little variation in managerial appraisal techniques is evident in comparison across varying organization sizes (Table 19.4). MBO, either used alone or in combination with other systems, is the favored technique in each of the surveyed organization size categories, though it should be noted that small cities were excluded from this study. Rating scales and BARS compete for a distant second and third, each being favored over the other in two organization size categories.

Table 19.5

Aggregate Time Allocated to the Managerial Appraisal Process by All Persons Involved

	N	%
Less than 5 percent of a "person-year"	65	55.6
Between 5 and 15 percent of a "person-year"[a]	48	41.0
Between 15 and 25 percent of a "person-year"[a]	3	2.6
More than 25 percent of a "person-year"[a]	1	0.9
Total	117	100.1

Notes:
[a]One "person-year" (or "staff-year") is the equivalent of one person working full time for one year, whether actually attributable to one person or more (e.g., one "person-year" would be allocated to a project when two persons were assigned to that project, each on a half-time basis).

Much greater variation in appraisal techniques was found among different forms of local government. MBO was reportedly used alone by 40.4 percent of council-manager cities and in combination with other systems by another 36.5 percent (Table 19.4). In contrast, 17.6 percent of the mayor-council cities reported using MBO alone, and 11.8 percent reported use of MBO in combination with other systems.

Rating scales were found to be more popular among mayor-council cities, with 41.2 percent reporting the use of rating scales alone for management appraisals and 11.8 percent reporting use of rating scales in combination with other systems. Only 9.6 percent of council-manager cities reported using rating scales alone, while 21.2 percent use rating scales in combination with other systems.

Time Allocation

Respondents were asked to estimate the aggregate amount of time in "person-years" devoted by them and by members of their staffs to the evaluation process for upper management during a typical year. (One "person-year" or "staff-year" is equivalent to the time that would be devoted by one person working full time on a given assignment.) They were asked to include time for information gathering, review sessions, goal planning, and related activities.

More than half (55.6 percent) of the respondents reported that they and their staffs spend less than 5 percent of a person-year on the appraisal of upper management performance (Table 19.5). Forty-one percent reported spending between 5 and 15 percent of a person-year, and 2.6 percent reported spending between 15 and 25 percent of a person-year. Less than 1 percent of the respondents reported spending more than 25 percent of a person-year in aggregate on the appraisal of upper management performance.

Conclusion

Researchers reporting the results of performance appraisal surveys of a different, often more general, nature than the one reported here have observed trends toward attempting to tie both appraisal and pay more closely to measurable performance,[24] toward more collaborative appraisal tems and greater employee participation in the establishment of performance targets,[25] and away from "person-based" or "trait-based" rating systems.[26] Part of the incentive for change is a desire to improve organizational performance; much of it is a desire to avoid potential legal problems resulting from a legally indefensible system.[27] These characteristics are reflected in this study's findings regarding the relative favor in which MBO appraisal systems are evidently held for upper management review in medium and large cities and in the reported level of subordinate participation in the appraisal process and related activities.

The appraisal process for upper management takes a variety of forms in major U.S. cities. No single format can be considered typical, though MBO as a sole system or in combination with others is reportedly in wide use among those cities having formal, documented appraisal systems. A high level of satisfaction with current appraisal practices is perceived for the assistants and department heads affected by those practices, with greater reservations, though still generally favorable attitudes, reported by the respondents themselves.

Despite the generally optimistic tone evident in relatively high levels of reported satisfaction with current management appraisal practices, a few troublesome aspects of the survey findings suggest serious deficiencies in the state of managerial performance appraisal in major U.S. cities. First, only 59 percent of the 122 responding cities report that managerial assistants and major department heads are evaluated on a formal, documented basis. While 29 percent report that such evaluation occurs on an informal basis, more than 12 percent indicate that no formal or informal mode of performance appraisal for upper management exists in their organization. In an era of public concern over value received for tax dollars, a systematic means of appraising and improving managerial performance would seem an integral part of serious performance management.

Second, approximately 16 percent of those jurisdictions reporting the use of specific managerial appraisal techniques reported full reliance on rating scales. Although such scales offer administrative convenience, their tendency to be trait-centered and highly subjective rather than performance-based makes such heavy reliance questionable at best.

Third, perhaps the most revealing indication of the state of managerial performance appraisal is the extremely modest amount of executive and staff time devoted to the process. Nalbandian has observed that "the basic impediment to effective performance appraisal is not the technique used, but the motivation of those called upon to evaluate others."[28] When a majority of executives report that they and their staffs spend less than 5 percent of a person-year on the upper management appraisal process and more than 96 percent report spending 15 percent of a person-year or less, the depth of such motivation may be called into question.

Notes

1. The city of Arlington, Texas, while examining its own management appraisal system in 1984, conducted the survey upon which this chapter is based and made the raw data available to the authors. Although the sample receiving questionnaires was not selected randomly in the technical sense, sample bias is thought to be modest since there was no apparent effort to influence findings through selection or exclusion and since the sample constitutes more than half of the entire universe of cities above the chosen population threshold. Of the 302 U.S. cities of 65,000 population or greater in 1980, 170 (56 percent) were mailed questionnaires. Responses were received from 72 percent of the sample (or 40 percent of all cities of 65,000 population or greater). The authors gratefully acknowledge the cooperation of the city of Arlington in making these data available.

2. Glen H. Varney, "Performance Appraisal—Inside and Out," *Personnel Administrator* 17 (November–December 1972): 15–17; Alan H. Locher and Kenneth S. Teel, "Performance Appraisal—A Survey of Current Practices," *Personnel Journal* 56 (May 1977): 245–254.

3. Kenneth J. Lacho, G. Kent Stearns, and Maurice F. Villere, "A Study of Employee Appraisal Systems of Major Cities in the United States," *Public Personnel Management* 8 (March–April 1979): 111–125; and Charlie B. Tyer, "Employee Performance Appraisal in American State Governments," *Public Personnel Management* 11 (Fall 1982): 199–212. "Formal system" includes the one city in the Lacho, Stearns, and Villere study reporting department-level appraisal systems, and "no formal system" includes the three cities awaiting approval of a system at the time of the survey. "Formal system" includes statewide and decentralized systems noted in the Tyer study.

4. Robert I. Lazer and Walter S. Wikstrom, *Appraising Managerial Performance: Current Practices and Future Directions* (New York: Conference Board, 1977), p. 6.

5. Hubert S. Feild and William H. Holley, "Performance Appraisal: An Analysis of State-Wide Practices," *Public Personnel Management* 4 (May–June 1975): 145–150.

6. Tyer, "Employee Performance Appraisal."

7. Lazer and Wikstrom, *Appraising Managerial Performance*, p. 11.

8. See, for example, Michael Beer, "Performance Appraisal: Dilemmas and Possibilities," *Organizational Dynamics* 9 (Winter 1981): 24–36.

9. Kenneth S. Teel, "Performance Appraisal: Current Trends, Persistent Progress," *Personnel Journal* 59 (April 1980): 296–316; Locher and Teel, "Performance Appraisal: A Survey of Current Practices"; and H. John Bernardin and Lawrence A. Klatt, "Managerial Appraisal Systems: Has Practice Caught Up to the State of the Art?" *Personnel Administrator* 30 (November 1985): 79–86.

10. Feild and Holley, "Performance Appraisal."

11. Lacho, Stearns, and Villere, "A Study of Employee Appraisal Systems of Major Cities."

12. Lazer and Wikstrom, *Appraising Managerial Performance*, p. 22. Percentages sum to more than 100 percent due to combination usage of various systems.

13. Robert A. Zawacki and Robert L. Taylor, "A View of Performance Appraisal from Organizations Using It," *Personnel Journal* 55 (June 1976): 290–292, 299; Tyer, "Employee Performance Appraisal"; and Lazer and Wikstrom, *Appraising Managerial Performance*, pp. 23–24.

14. John M. Ivancevich, James H. Donnelly, and Herbert L. Lyon, "A Study of the Impact of Management by Objectives on Perceived Need Satisfaction," *Personnel Psychology* 23 (Summer 1970): 139–151; P.P. Fay and D.N. Beach, "Management by Objectives Evaluated," *Personnel Journal* 53 (October 1974): 767–769; Stephen J. Carroll, Jr., and Henry L. Tosi, "The Relationship of Characteristics of the Review Process to the Success of the 'Management Objectives' Approach," *Journal of Business* 44 (July 1971): 299–305; John C. Aplin, Jr., Charles G. Schoderbek, and Peter P. Schoderbek, "Tough-Minded Management by Objectives," *Human Resource Management* 18 (Summer 1979): 9–13.

15. Perry D. Moore and Ted Staton, "Management by Objectives in American Cities," *Public Personnel Management* 10 (Summer 1981): 223–232.

16. Zawacki and Taylor, "A View of Performance Appraisal"; Locher and Teel, "Performance Appraisal: A Study of Current Practices"; Lazer and Wikstrom, *Appraising Managerial Employees*, p. 24; Lacho, Stearns, and Villere, "A Study of Employee Appraisal Systems of Major Cities"; and Tyer, "Employee Performance Appraisal."

17. Varney, "Performance Appraisal."

18. Zawacki and Taylor, "A View of Performance Appraisal."

19. Bernardin and Klatt, "Managerial Appraisal Systems."

20. Lazer and Wikstrom, *Appraising Managerial Employees*, p. 43.

21. Jonathan P. West, "City Personnel Management: Issues and Reforms," *Public Personnel Management* 13 (Fall 1984): 317–334.

22. Tyer, "Employee Performance Appraisal."

23. See, for example, Nicholas P. Lovrich, Jr., Paul L. Shaffer, Ronald H. Hopkins, and Donald A. Yale, "Do Public Servants Welcome or Fear Merit Evaluation of Their Performance?" *Public Administration Review* 40 (May/June 1980): 214–222.

24. Teel, "Performance Appraisal: Current Trends, Persistent Progress"; and Tyer, "Employee Performance Appraisal."

25. Zawacki and Taylor, "A View of Performance Appraisal"; and West, "City Personnel Management," p. 332.

26. Tyer, "Employee Performance Appraisal."

27. For recommendations regarding the adoption of legally defensible appraisal systems, see, for example, Ronald W. Clement and Eileen K. Aranda, "Performance Appraisal in the Public Sector: Truth or Consequences?" *Review of Public Personnel Administration* 5 (Fall 1984): 34–42; and Shelley R. Burchett and Kenneth P. De Meuse, "Performance Appraisal and the Law," *Personnel* 62 (July 1985): 29–37.

28. John Nalbandian, "Performance Appraisal: If Only People Were Not Involved," *Public Administration Review* 41 (May/June 1981): 394.

CHAPTER 20

VALUES MANAGEMENT IN LOCAL GOVERNMENT

EVAN M. BERMAN AND JONATHAN P. WEST

Values in government have received much attention in recent years. Of particular interest have been the central notions that governmental organizations should *minimize ethical wrongdoing* and *increase responsiveness* to citizens, employees, and customers of government services. Governments use a variety of strategies to further these values, including employee training, reward structures, top management exemplars, and program design. These strategies are of particular importance to personnel administrators because they often manage employee training and are partially responsible for enforcing standards of wrongdoing. Personnelists also have a broader responsibility to ensure that public managers act in ways that inspire and increase trust in their intentions and abilities (Edwards and Bennett 1987; West, Berman, and Cava 1993).

Personnel administrators who address these concerns must combine their more traditional "compliance officer" role with that of consultation and facilitation of organizational processes. This dual-role evolution of the personnel function is widely discussed (Nalbandian 1981; Bowen and Greiner 1986; Carnevale 1992; Tsui 1987). The facilitative role for personnelists in "values management" involves building and sustaining a shared set of beliefs among employees that is beneficial to the organization, its members and the public. Values are formed, implicitly or explicitly, in an ongoing communication and education process that supplements traditional compliance functions.[1]

Notwithstanding the heightened importance of minimizing wrongdoing and increasing responsiveness in government, we know very little about progress in these areas at the local government level (Menzel 1992). The nation's 2,711 cities are obviously highly diverse in their approaches and results (Menzel 1992; West, Berman, and Cava 1993). While the literature contains references to "ethics management" and responsiveness to employees and customers in particular jurisdictions or agencies (Bonczek 1992; Osborne and Gaebler 1992; Thompson 1988; Denhardt 1993; Varley 1990), and to studies of the value orientations of administrators (Bowman 1990; Menzel 1992; 1993a; Stewart and Sprinthall 1991, 1993), there are no systematic studies that profile activities to promote these values across cities (see West, Berman, and Cava 1993). This study addresses this gap in the literature by providing a systematic assessment of the contemporary values management activities of cities, focusing on objectives, strategies, and relations to selected outcomes.

Framework

Values management is increasingly recognized as an important area of public administration. Both the International City and County Management Association (ICMA) and the American

From *Review of Public Personnel Administration*, vol. 14, no. 1 (Winter 1994), pp. 6–23. Copyright © 1994 by Sage Publications, Inc. Reprinted with permission.

Society for Public Administration (ASPA) have published books recently focusing on the management of values in public organizations (Kellar 1988; Richter, Burke, and Doig 1990). Values are defined as the ideals, beliefs and commitments which bind members of an organization and provide standards for interpersonal relations and preferred modes of conduct (Ladd 1993; Rokeach 1973). The task of values management is the clarification and promotion of such values. Some examples of organizational values are avoiding sexual harassment and conflict of interest, and meeting the needs of customers and constituents. Values are part of the organizational culture, which in turn is defined as the shared beliefs and the norms and practices of an organization. The latter are common or pervasive ways of acting that are found in organizations and which give meaning to values through application and specification. Most values have many norms and practices that are associated with them. For example, norms about sexual harassment often specify particular language and communications that must not occur.

This study is concerned with values, but restricts its analysis to the study of (1) formal policies and programs that embody values; (2) organizations rather than individual actors and agents (e.g., employees); and (3) public service values that are related to wrongdoing and responsiveness. Regarding responsiveness, it should be noted that this study does not directly address the broader social values that government seeks to foster in its policies and programs—such as promoting social justice, democratic representation, or other major tenets of contemporary democratic governance.

In recent years, moral wrongdoing has become associated with "ethics," although in fact most definitions of ethics include standards of both right and wrong conduct. The ASPA and ICMA Codes of Ethics include both categories of behavior (Kellar 1988). However, in practice, organizations often fail to agree on meaningful standards of right behavior, only specifying those standards of wrong conduct that are dictated by higher levels of government, the law or survival. Such standards are frequently stated in the negative, as proscriptions. This study adopts this commonly followed narrow interpretation of ethics as prescriptive of prohibitions, and limits its focus to those standards of conduct adopted by an organization (rather than by individuals) (Menzel and Benton 1991; Menzel 1993a; Truelson 1991).

Responsiveness, as a value, is concerned with meeting the needs of members of an organization and the customers it serves. Concern about responsiveness is consistent with democratic theory and represents an important theme in quality management and workforce diversity programs (Cohen and Brand 1993; Kanter 1986; Copeland 1988). Increasing responsiveness is also associated with building and maintaining trust and loyalty between government and employees, and between agencies and citizens and customers. The presumption is made that when stakeholder needs are being met, their commitment and support for the agency responsible increases as a consequence. Ethics programs alone often fail to increase levels of trust, but complementary efforts to increase responsiveness can help. The need to increase trust is evident from events such as tax revolts and other manifestations of negative public attitudes toward government (National Commission on the Public Service 1989; Kettering Foundation 1991; Ehrenhalt 1993). Responsiveness is also a theme in recent popular books that emphasize the development of "community" in the workplace and "cooperation" with interests outside the organization. In a sense, efforts to increase trust and loyalty through heightened responsiveness may be regarded as attempts to balance self-interest in stakeholder relations with that of building community and commitment toward mutual objectives (Denhardt 1993; Gurwitt 1992; Luke 1991; Menzel 1993b).

Minimizing wrongdoing and increasing responsiveness are reflected in many different, specific actions. Some of these actions are shown in Figure 20.1. Examples of traditional ethical concerns are reflected in such wrongdoings as acceptance of unauthorized gifts, fraud, waste and abuse uncovered by whistleblowers, and conflicts of interest; the more recent concerns of sexual harassment and noncompliance with municipal codes of ethics are also among the actions covered in values management efforts. Included as ethics, but not as wrongdoing, are EEO policies of comparable worth and affirmative action. The absence of such corrective policies typically does not imply legal wrongdoing, but rather failure to address the problems of gender-based pay inequity and other forms of discrimination may be considered unethical. The right column is labeled "responsiveness" and is subdivided into three stakeholder groups. Concerns about employees focus on (1) ensuring a positive job experience through stress reduction and increased empowerment; and (2) helping employees to acquire new skills that ensure their competitiveness in the job market. Concerns about employees' families focus on the balance of family/work relations through assistance with child and elder care. By addressing these issues, employers may hope to increase the commitment and loyalty of their workforce.[2] Concerns about clients and constituents focus on the quality of service, and whether services meet needs.

Progress and compliance are also important issues in values management. Statements of principles and conduct alone do not ensure progress in the above areas: Indeed, the idea of ethics in particular is often ridiculed for this reason. To the extent that values are managed through programs, progress can and should be measured. Compliance involving minimizing wrongdoing is often mandated by law, which requires specific fact finding, reporting, and training activities. Progress is frequently measured by the number of reported violations. Compliance pertaining to responsiveness is seldom legally mandated, though a few cities have adopted policies that require agencies to provide service through quality management. Progress is frequently measured by the availability of such programs. But even in the case of minimizing wrongdoing, where compliance is legally mandated, progress in training and enforcement (two important concerns of personnelists) typically requires substantive commitment by city administrators and other senior managers to ensure success. Consequently, progress and compliance are a matter of policy (see e.g., Balk 1985; Burke and Black 1990).

What range of strategies do organizations use to enhance value management? Historically, U.S. values have emphasized the importance of upbringing as a determinant of character, often to the exclusion of values management by institutions (Thompson 1988). At times the moral view of key executives influences the moral character of institutions (Cooper and Wright 1992). This tendency has been reflected in the selection of important government officials and judges. However, institutions are beginning to take seriously the possibility of deliberate and systematic management of values (Andrews 1989). In this regard, however, an important distinction needs to be made between formal and informal approaches. Formal approaches to values management involve legal documents, training requirements, and personnel actions relating to recruitment and promotion. Informal approaches involve the public praising of role models and frequent use of positive reinforcement, and they are behaviorally based in their conceptualization. Regular communication and feedback about standards and ethics, preferably from the top executives as role models, as well as voluntary training programs for the promotion of new ethical activities are typical examples of an informal system in action. Both formal and informal approaches help to improve the organizational culture in institutions (Menzel 1992; Murphy 1988).

Previous studies in the human resource management field (Dresang 1978, 1982; Mushkin and Sandifer 1979; O'R. Hayes 1977; Layden 1980; Greiner 1980; West 1984, 1986) suggest that jurisdictional characteristics (city size, geographic region, form of government) may affect the development of and progress in the above value management areas. Based on the available literature, it is suggested that progress is furthered by the availability of a larger resource base in

Figure 20.1 **Values Management in Organizations**

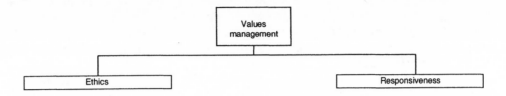

Values management

Ethics

Responsiveness

Minimizing wrongdoing
Conflict of interest. Avoiding pursuit of interests or activities which conflict with the conduct of official duties
Whistle blowing: Disclosing information by employees of government fraud, waste and abuse

Unauthorized gifts: Avoiding solicitation or acceptance of gifts which might influence the performance of official duties
Sexual harassment: Avoiding an offensive work environment through sexually oriented comments or actions

Complying with code of ethics: Monitoring and enforcing compliance with a municipality's code of ethics.
Fairness in job assignments: Avoiding job assignments based on criteria other than experience or qualifications

EEO policy
Affirmative action: Adopting a corrective program to aid those adversely affected by discrimination based on age, race, religion, sex or handicap.
Comparable worth: Adopting a corrective policy to overcome pay inequities resulting from sex-segregated jobs and pay discrimination based on sex

Employees
Fully using employees' skills: increasing commitment to employees' career needs by using all of an employee's skills
Immediate feedback: Providing immediate feedback to employees in order to increase job satisfaction and future performance
Empowerment: Placing trust in employees to make more decisions in the workplace
Development objectives: Setting annual development goals to ensure employee growth and conformance with future organizational goals
Reducing work-related stress: Improving job satisfaction and lowering health risks by reducing on-the-job stress

Families
Providing elder care: Increasing commitment to employees by providing elder care leave
Providing child care: Increasing commitment to employees by providing child care leave and programs

Customers
Quality of service: Showing commitment to stakeholders by increasing responsiveness to their needs
Feedback from constituencies: Increasing amount of feedback from constituencies, and use of such information
Meeting needs of customers: Ensuring that services meet the expectations and needs of customers and constituencies.

Source: See text references.

bigger cities; by the heightened professionalism that is associated with the council-manager form of government; and by the innovative tendencies which characterize Western cities (McGowan and Poister 1983; Saltzstein 1990; Cayer 1991). The literature also suggests that values management is associated with efforts to increase quality and productivity. Denhardt (1993) writes that total quality management (TQM) assumes values of increased responsiveness and trust in employee decision-making abilities. Such an assumption suggests that the absence of many forms of ethical wrongdoing is a prerequisite to effective implementation of TQM because trust and wrongdoing are largely mutually exclusive constructs.

The Survey

In the spring of 1992, a detailed survey was sent to human resource directors in all municipalities with a population over 25,000.[3] The questions, based on a review of the literature, were initially pretested on a sample of forty municipal managers. Following modifications, the nationwide survey was administered. The individuals contacted in each city were identified through the International City/County Management Association (ICMA), the professional association of administrators serving cities, counties, regional councils and other local governments. ICMA provided its most current list of human resource directors of such cities. A total of 1,171 surveys were mailed to all persons on the list. After follow-up mailings and telephone calls, 427 were returned for a 36 percent response rate. The response group closely matches the population as a whole, and no significant nonresponse bias is present.[4]

Both the literature and our pilot survey show that nearly all organizations use various approaches to attain the values management objectives stated in Figure 20.1. Thus, of interest is adequacy of results rather than policy per se.[5] Other focal concerns are future needs and formal or informal strategies for implementing value management.

Results

Using the categories shown in Figure 20.1, Table 20.1 reports recent progress in attainment of objectives for cities. On average, 59 percent of the respondents believe that adequate progress has been made in these areas of values. However, there are considerable differences between item groups: items of minimizing wrongdoing and client satisfaction rated, respectively, 73 and 75 percent, whereas equal employment opportunity rated 63 percent. Ties with families and employee development rated only 36 and 39 percent, respectively. Customer satisfaction seems exceptionally high to us, which may reflect the fact that respondents are personnel managers who function in a staff role and who may be more insulated from customer/citizen contact than their line manager counterparts. Alternatively, it may be that recent progress indeed has been adequate, but that much more needs to be done. Differences within groups are small, with the exception of "complying with a code of ethics."

Table 20.2 reports the value aspiration gap. The "aspiration gap" is defined as the difference between past progress on the attainment of value objectives, reported in Table 20.1, and the percent of organizations reporting that important improvements are required during the next five years. Where the gap is high, the issue is thus an emerging or rising concern. Table 20.2 shows that the gap exceeds 50 percentage points for three items: fully using employees' skills, providing immediate feedback for employees, and reducing job-related stress. For example, the adequacy of results achieved in "fully using skills" is deemed adequate in 35 percent of cities (Table 20.1), while the same item is identified as requiring future improvement by 94 percent of the respondents (Table 20.2); the difference or "aspiration gap" is 59 percent. As discussed, progress on these issues increases the loyalty and commitment of employees by addressing important employee concerns, and personnel administrators regard these issues as increasingly salient to value management in coming years.

A negative gap indicates that the issue is either a mature or waning problem. Five of the eight traditional issues of ethics wrongdoing fall into this category: Accepting unauthorized gifts is clearly seen as a waning issue. While eight out of ten cities report adequate results in avoiding conflict of interest, seven out of ten indicate that further improvements are required in the future. Hence, "conflict of interest" might be interpreted as an important, mature issue, but not an emerging one. These findings suggest that the objectives of personnel administrators are likely to shift substantively from concerns of wrongdoing to those of employee development as a focus for building trust. This will require investments in employee development.

This study examines the use of various strategies in selected areas of ethics management and responsiveness.[6] Table 20.3 shows that cities use a mix of formal and informal strategies for this purpose. Informal strategies are more frequently used, specifically exemplary moral leadership of senior managers (73 percent of cities) and elected officials (57 percent). This strategy is followed by formal strategies of protecting whistleblowers (59 percent), approval of outside activities (56 percent) and financial disclosure (53 percent). In addition, about four in ten of the cities provide

Table 20.1

Recent Progress in Values Management: Evidence from a Nationwide Survey of City Personnel Directors (*N* = 427)

	%
Minimizing wrongdoing (average 73%)	
Conflict of interest	82
Whistleblowing	76
Unauthorized gifts	85
Sexual harassment	73
Complying with code of ethics	45
Fairness in job assignments	79
Equal employment opportunity (average 63%)	
Comparable worth	53
Affirmative action	72
Ties with families (average 36%)	
Providing elder care	27
Providing child care	46
Employee development (average 39%)	
Fully using employees' skills	35
Immediate feedback	37
Empowerment	41
Development objectives	43
Reducing work-related stress	37
Client/customer satisfaction (average 75%)	
Quality of service	79
Feedback from constituencies	67
Meeting needs of customers	79

Notes: Survey of cities of 25,000+ population conducted during spring 1992.
Percent of organizations reporting that adequate results have been achieved in the following areas during the last five years.

Table 20.2

The Values Management Aspiration Gap: Evidence from a Nationwide Survey of City Personnel Directors (*N* = 427)

	Aspiration gap	Improvements required (%)
Fully using employees' skills	+59	94
Reducing work-related stress	+52	89
Immediate feedback	+51	88
Development objectives	+41	84
Providing elder care	+37	64
Empowerment	+33	74
Complying with code of ethics	+30	75
Feedback from constituencies	+17	84
Providing child care	+15	61
Quality of service	+13	92
Sexual harassment	+11	84
Meeting needs of customers	+11	90
Affirmative action	+9	81
Comparable worth	-2	51
Whistleblowing	-10	66
Fairness in job assignments	-10	69
Conflict of interest	-12	70
Unauthorized gifts	-34	51

Note: The "Aspiration Gap" is defined as the difference between past progress and the percent of organizations reporting that important improvements are required during the next five years.

Table 20.3

Strategies for Ensuring Progress Toward Selected Traditional Values Management Objectives: Evidence from a Nationwide Survey of City Personnel Directors ($N = 427$)

	Cities (%)
Formal approaches	
Protecting whistleblowers for valid disclosures	59
Requiring approval of outside activities	56
Requiring financial disclosures	53
Use of proportionate penalties in ethical matters	41
Required familiarity with the code of ethics	29
Mandatory ethics training courses for all employees	29
Making ethics a criterion in hiring and promotion	27
Lengthening budgeting cycles to avoid short-time horizons	13
Raise employee pay to reduce temptations	11
Mandatory ethics training courses for violators	6
Informal approaches	
Exemplary moral leadership by senior management	73
Exemplary moral leadership by elected officials	57
Voluntary ethics training courses	41
Regular communication to employees about ethics	29
Monitoring adherence to the code of ethics	28
Making counselors available for ethical issues	22
Periodic rereading of the code of ethics	15
Surveying employees' opinions about ethics	7
Mean items[1] = 4.6	

Notes: [1]Mean number of items in the above list reported by organizations. See n. 6.

Percent of cities using the following strategies for ensuring progress toward traditional values management objectives (i.e., minimizing wrongdoing).

voluntary ethics training courses. Other strategies are used in only a minority of cities, including those based on adopting and implementing a written code of ethics. While the adoption of codes of ethics has received much discussion in business administration, the adoption of similar codes by cities is perhaps less relevant because of the long tradition of codes of ethics by professional organizations (for example, ICMA and ASPA), and also because many legislative bodies have formulated specific guidelines of conduct. Indeed, from the results of a separate question it can be noted that only 41 percent of cities have adopted a code of ethics, and that only 29 percent of those cities require familiarity with their code of ethics.

Which cities are experiencing the greatest progress in attaining the objectives of value management? Table 20.4 reports the percentage of cities indicating that adequate results have been achieved in the four general areas during the last five years. The data are broken down by city size, form of government, and geographic region. Survey results suggest that larger cities are the most likely to achieve adequate results in EEO, employee development and minimizing wrongdoing. As hypothesized above, cities in the West are more likely to adopt employee development programs, as well as child/elder care programs. However, it is also seen that cities in the Northeast are less likely than those in the South, West, and North Central regions to implement employee development programs. Cities with council-manager forms of government are more likely than those with mayor-council forms to achieve progress in client satisfaction, minimizing wrongdoing, as well as implementing employee development programs.

Table 20.5 provides tentative evidence that progress in the several value management objectives

Table 20.4

The Values Management Objectives of Municipal Governments: Results of a Nationwide Survey of Municipal Personnel Directors

	N	EEO	Minimizing wrongdoing	Ties with families	Employee development	Client satisfaction
Size						
Over 500,000	15	75	73	39	54	75
250,000–500,000	15	87**	83*	35	45	76
100,000–250,000	53	63	71	36	29	73
50,000–100,000	124	61	74	34	39	77
25,000–50,000	220	62	74	38	39	75
Government						
Mayor-council	121	65	70	38	34*	70**
Council-manager	288	63	76	36	41*	79***
Commission	12	54	57	32	31	67
Other	6	58	73	33	46	50
Region						
Northeast	56	60	73	33	31*	74
North Central	112	60	72	38	36	68***
South	131	65	74	30**	39	80
West	128	65	76	43**	44**	77
Total	427	63	74	36	39	75

Notes: *10 percent significance (compared to group mean); **5 percent significance (compared to group mean); ***1 percent significance (compared to group mean).

Percent of organizations reporting that adequate results have been achieved in the following areas during the last five years.

may be related to subsequent productivity improvement and other favorable outcomes (see Balk 1985; Burke and Black 1990; Denhardt 1993). Findings reported in the table suggest that the attainment of value management objectives, with the exception of child/elder programs, is positively associated with self-reported, actual cost reduction and improvement in the quality of municipal services. Table 20.5 reports the Wald chi-square estimates of logistic regressions based on respondents' assessments. The independent variables are multi-item scales based on the groupings in Table 20.1. The Cronbach alpha reliabilities of the items shown are all better than 0.7 (the EEO group is omitted because of a reliability score below this threshold).

These findings are tentative, of course, in the absence of independent, objective measures of municipal productivity in our cities. Also, while the logistic regressions include intercept, city size and form of government, other potential determinants of outcomes are not considered. Thus, only evidence of association is claimed; no claim of causation is made. Carefully detailed case studies would be necessary to substantiate claims that the attainment of value management objectives leads to the enhancement of municipal productivity in a variety of settings. Our survey results also suggest that value management programs, with the exception of child/elder programs, are associated with increased constituency responsiveness and meeting employee needs.

Discussion and Conclusion

This study responds to the need for systematic information about values management efforts being made in local government. Perhaps the most significant finding is that municipal personnel directors think that duplicating their cities' past efforts in values management is inadequate

Table 20.5

Association of Values Management Efforts with Productivity and Other Favorable Outcomes: Evidence from a Nationwide Survey of Municipal Personnel Directors (N = 427)

	Productivity outcomes[1]		Other outcomes[1]	
	Cost reduction (Wald sign chi-square)	Quality improvement (Wald sign chi-square)	Constituency responsiveness (Wald sign chi-square)	Employee needs (Wald sign chi-square)
Values management[2]				
Objectives				
Minimizing wrongdoing	29.**+	41.**+	25.**+	38.**+
Ties with families	0.+	0.+	0.+	11.**+
Employee development	33.**+	31.**+	25.**+	66.**+
Client[3] satisfaction	46.**+	57.**+	43.**+	34.**+

Notes:
[1]Logistic regression results. See text for explanation of this statistical procedure. Sign is the interpreted parameter estimate.

[2]The reliabilities of the independent variables are as follows: minimizing wrongdoing = 0.76; ties with families = 0.85; employee development = 0.76; client satisfaction = 0.71. The "EEO" group is omitted because of a low reliability score.

[3]To avoid possible bias, this measure excludes "quality of service" in the quality improvement regression, and "feedback from constituents" in the constituency responsiveness regression.

*5 percent significance; **1 percent significance.

Legend:
Cost reduction = reducing the cost of services.
Quality improvement = improving the quality of services.
Constituency responsiveness = improving responsiveness to constituencies.
Employees needs = meeting the personal needs of employees.

to meet future challenges. Values management is shifting from minimizing wrongdoing to building trust among employees and customers of public services. Specifically, further progress is needed in responsiveness to the career management and development needs of employees. Given the technological and demographic changes in the workplace, it is perhaps not surprising that employee development activities are the items where the gap is greatest between what municipal personnel directors identify as past results and what they indicate are priority concerns for future improvements. This observation is consistent with other studies showing that seven of ten American workers are underemployed—that is, employees feel that they are relatively unchallenged in their jobs, unrewarded for their work, and are not fully utilizing their capabilities (Coil 1984).

Public personnel management must support organizational needs by ensuring the basic competence of employees in requisite skills, and then helping to empower employees to use these skills effectively. These are important and growing concerns in the views of human resource directors. The most salient issues in coming years are fully using employee skills, reducing work-related stress, providing timely feedback to employees, and providing individual career planning. Such issues represent the expanding frontiers of contemporary HRM. They raise important questions for personnel managers to consider. What career planning assistance programs offer the human resource function the best ways to make a strategic contribution through the motivation and retention of key managers and employees? What methods provide career development and challenge in the absence of multiple organizational layers that once offered more frequent and incremental promotion opportunities? How can public personnel managers best work with others to prevent, detect, and manage stress in their work settings? What individual and organizational strategies are most helpful in stress management? Can career and developmental needs be met in ways that increase organizational effectiveness? What effect do career planning and employee developmental programs have on the likelihood and frequency of employee exit?

The cities that lead in making progress on values management also tend to be those municipalities that emphasize addressing the needs of their employees and meeting their customers' expectations. This study finds positive evidence of the mutually reinforcing influences of quality improvement and values management. Such a finding would seem to connect with efforts under way to "reinvent government," and suggests that these efforts may succeed best in cities where trust exists between government and its employees, and among government and citizens and constituencies.

What are the implications of this study for academic research? This study provides a snapshot of the current value management objectives in American local governments. Future research needs to establish the extent to which values are successfully implemented, and the extent to which personnelists are adding the strategic, support-oriented role to their longstanding compliance officer role. A better understanding is needed of the most effective mix of formal and informal strategies in actually minimizing wrongdoing and maximizing governmental responsiveness. Additional research is also needed to determine the impact of the various trust-building employee development innovations and family-sensitive policies on individual workers and on organizational performance. Career-related concerns are compounded for many organizational members by the increased demands of child and elder care, as the growth in dual-income families and families with single heads-of-households continue. Although the above are "off-the-job" concerns, to what extent do these pressures contribute to reduced performance? Absenteeism? Employee exit? What responses by the human resource department are appropriate in respecting the privacy of employees? Are these approaches cost-effective in the face of intense budget pressures? Hard data are needed that address the tradeoffs between organizationally sponsored work/family experiments and employee needs. And, with a slower growth in the public sector workforce in the 1990s, current concerns over "rightsizing" may give way to increased attention to securing and retaining an optimal workforce. The ability of public personnel managers and others to address both these current and future pressures may be the ultimate strategic contribution.

Notes

1. Thus, it would be inaccurate to view values management as primarily or exclusively concerned with instrumental manipulation of values to minimize wrongdoing or to change or imprint values for the benefit of particular groups, such as top management. Such an orientation views values management as a "control mechanism" with public managers and personnelists ensuring compliance with prescribed values. A more contemporary view of values management has leaders and managers assuming a supportive role oriented to developing constructive stakeholder relations, to communicating a vision of the organization, and to building trust among its members and customers.

2. Obviously, employers have other reasons as well for providing these programs, such as increased job complexity and health care costs. While these are important reasons, addressing these employee issues also increases loyalty and commitment, which has been widely noted. It is also noted that while investments in skills increase the "exit" option for employees, employers are likely to take this calculated risk because of increased job complexity and because of regulations stressing minority and female hiring and the need for appropriate career objectives and promotion paths.

3. Surveys were sent directly to municipal personnel directors. In 92 percent of the cases the address labels

provided by ICMA listed the personnel director by name and by title; in 8 percent the title of personnel director was listed along with the address but no name was provided. Our pilot study and follow-up interviews suggest in many cities personnel directors are indeed the most informed on ethics matters, in both breadth and depth, because of their responsibilities in ethics training and enforcement. We leave it to subsequent studies to survey employees, city managers, agency directors and other appropriate personnel in order to deal with issues of self-reporting bias in this target group.

4. The following table shows that the sample closely matches the population as a whole. We find little evidence of a serious nonresponse bias problem. Size and form of government are relevant measures by which to compare the sample and the population (see framework).

Size	All cities population (%)	Survey sample (%)	Form of government	All cities population (%)	Survey sample (%)
> 250,000	11.6	7.0	Mayor-council	36.8	28.3
100,000–249,999	12.2	12.4	Council-manager	57.0	67.5
50,000–99,999	28.3	29.0	Commission	3.8	2.8
25,000–49,999	47.9	51.5	Other	2.4	1.4

Notes: N = 1,171. See also Table 20.4, left column.

5. Sample survey questions are the following:

   A. "Please evaluate the following objectives. Please indicate whether adequate results have been accomplished in the last five years."
   B. "Please indicate whether improvements are required over the next five years."
   C. "Which of the following strategies are currently used for ensuring an ethical climate in your organization? Circle the particular response. If you are uncertain, please go to the next item."

   Items with regard to questions A and B are stated in Table 20.2. Question A is also the basis for Tables 20.2, 20. 4, and 20.5. Items with regard to question C are stated in Table 20.3.

6. The use of values management strategies in efforts to increase responsiveness are not examined because these are more varied and tied to human resource management and client/quality management. This list in Table 20.3 also notably excludes strategies that deal with sexual harassment, comparable worth, and fairness in job assignment.

References

Andrews, K.R. 1989. "Ethics in Practice." *Harvard Business Review* 89, no. 5: 99–104.
Balk, W.L. 1985. "Productivity Improvement in Government Agencies: An Ethical Perspective." *Policy Studies Review* 4, no. 3: 475–483.
Bonczek, S.J. 1992. "Ethical Decision Making: Challenge for the 1990s: A Practical Approach for Local Government." *Public Personnel Management* 21, no. 1: 75–88.
Bowen, D.E., and L.E. Greiner. 1986. "Moving from Production to Service in Human Resource Management." *Organizational Dynamics* 15, no. 1: 34–45.
Bowman, J.S. 1990. "Ethics in Government: A National Survey of Public Administrators." *Public Administration Review* 50, no. 3: 345–353.
Burke, F., and A. Black. 1990. "Improving Organizational Productivity: Add Ethics." *Public Productivity and Management Review* 14, no. 2: 121–133.
Carnevale, D. 1992. "The Learning Support Model: Personnel Policy Beyond the Traditional Model." *American Review of Public Administration* 22, no. 1: 19–34.
Cayer, N.J. 1991. "Local Government: Personnel Structure and Policies." In *1991 Municipal Yearbook*, ICMA. Washington, DC: International City/County Management Association.
Cohen, S., and R. Brand. 1993. *Total Quality Management in Government.* San Francisco, CA: Jossey Bass.
Coil, A. 1984. "Job Matching Brings Out the Best in Employees." *Personnel Journal* 63, no. 1: 54–60.

Cooper, T.L., and N.D. Wright. 1992. *Exemplary Public Administrators.* San Francisco, CA: Jossey Bass.

Copeland, L. 1988. "Learning to Manage a Multicultural Work Force." In *Personnel Practices for the '90s,* ed. J. Matzer. Washington, DC: ICMA.

Denhardt, R. 1993. *The Pursuit of Significance.* Belmont, CA: Wadsworth.

Dresang, D.L. 1978. "Public Personnel Reform: A Summary of State Government Activity." *Public Personnel Management* 7, no. 5: 287–294.

———. 1982. "Diffusing of Civil Service Reform: The Federal and State Governments." *Review of Public Personnel Administration* 2, no. 2: 35–47.

Edwards, G., and K. Bennett. 1987. "Ethics and HR: Standards in Practice." *Personnel Administrator* 32, no. 12: 62–66.

Ehrenhalt, A. 1993. "The Utter Uselessness of 1990s-Style Corruption." *Governing* 6, no. 5: 8–9.

Greiner, J.M. 1980. "Incentive for Municipal Employees: An Update." In *1980 Municipal Yearbook, ICMA.* Washington, DC: International City Management Association.

Gurwitt, R. 1992. "A Government That Runs on Citizen Power." *Governing* 6, no. 3: 48–54.

Kanter, R.M. 1986. "The New Workforce Meets the Changing Workplace." *Human Resource Management* 25, no. 4: 515–537.

Kellar, E.K., ed. 1988. *Ethical Insight: Ethical Action.* Washington, DC: International City Management Association.

Kettering Foundation. 1991. *Citizens and Politics: A View from Main Street America.* New York: Kettering Foundation.

Ladd, C.E. 1993. *The American Polity.* New York: Norton.

Layden, D. 1980. "Productivity and Productivity Bargaining: The Environmental Context." *Public Personnel Management* 9, no. 4: 244–256.

Luke, J.S. 1991. "New Leadership Requirements for Public Administrators: From Managerial to Policy Ethics." In *Ethical Frontiers in Public Management,* ed. J.S. Bowman. San Francisco, CA: Jossey Bass.

McGowan, R.P., and T. Poister. 1983. "Personnel Related Management Tools in Municipal Administration." *Review of Public Personnel Administration* 4, no. 1: 78–95.

Menzel, D.C. 1993a. "The Ethics Factor in Local Government: An Empirical Analysis." In *Ethics and Public Administration,* ed. H.G. Frederickson. Armonk, NY: M.E. Sharpe.

———. 1993b. "Through the Ethical Looking Glass Darkly?" Unpublished paper prepared for delivery at the Annual Conference of the Florida Political Science Association.

Menzel, D.C. 1992. "Ethics Attitudes and Behaviors in Local Governments: An Empirical Analysis." *State and Local Government Review* 24, no. 3: 94–102.

Menzel, D.C., and J.E. Benton. 1991. "Ethics Complaints and Local Government: The Case of Florida." *Journal of Public Administration Research and Theory* 1, no. 4: 419–436.

Murphy, P.E. 1988. "Implementing Business Ethics." *Journal of Business Ethics* 7, no. 12: 907–915.

Mushkin, S.J., and F.H. Sandifer. 1979. *Personnel Management and Productivity in City Government.* Lexington, MA: Lexington Books.

Nalbandian, J. 1981. "From Compliance to Consultation: The Changing Role of the Public Personnel Administrator." *Review of Public Personnel Administration* 1, no. 2: 37–51.

National Commission on the Public Service. 1989. *Leadership for America.* Washington, DC: National Commission on the Public Service.

O'R. Hayes, F. 1977. *Productivity in Local Government.* Lexington, MA: Lexington Books.

Osborne, D., and T. Gaebler. 1992. *Reinventing Government.* Reading, MA: Addison-Wesley.

Richter, W.T., F. Burke, and J.W. Doig, eds. 1990. *Combating Corruption, Encouraging Ethics.* Washington, DC: American Society for Public Administration.

Rokeach, M. 1973. *The Nature of Human Values.* New York: Free Press.

Saltzstein, A. 1990. "Personnel Management in the Local Government Setting." In *Public Personnel Administration,* ed. S.W. Hays and R.C. Kearney. Englewood Cliffs, NJ: Prentice-Hall.

Stewart, D.W., and N.A. Sprinthall. 1991. "Strengthening Ethical Judgment in Public Administration." In *Ethical Frontiers in Public Management,* ed. J.S. Bowman. San Francisco: Jossey Bass.

———. 1993. "The Impact of Demographic Professional and Organizational Variables and Domain on the Moral Reasoning of Public Administrators." In *Ethics and Public Administration,* ed. H. George Frederickson. Armonk, NY: M.E. Sharpe.

Thompson, D.F. 1988. "The Possibility of Administrative Ethics." In *Ethical Action: Ethical Insight,* ed. E.K. Keller. Washington, DC: ICMA.

Truelson, J.A. 1991. "New Strategies for Institutional Controls." In *Ethical Frontiers in Public Management*, ed. J.S. Bowman. San Francisco, CA: Jossey Bass.

Tsui, A.S. 1987. "Defining the Activities and Effectiveness of the Human Resources Department: A Multiple Constituency Approach." *Human Resource Management* 26, no. 1: 35–69.

Varley, P. 1990. "Affirmative Action in Pasadena." In *Ethics and Politics*, ed. A. Gutmann and D. Thompson. Chicago: Nelson Hall.

West, J.P. 1984. "City Personnel Management: Issues and Reforms." *Public Personnel Management* 13, no. 3: 317–334.

———. 1986. "City Government Productivity and Civil Service Reform." *Public Productivity Review* 10, no. 1 (Fall): 45–59.

West, J.P., E.M. Berman, and A. Cava. 1993. "Ethics in the Municipal Workplace." In *1993 Municipal Yearbook, ICMA*. Washington, DC: International City/County Management Association.

PART 4

MAKING LOCAL GOVERNMENTS MORE PRODUCTIVE AND RESPONSIVE

Local governments have been under intense pressure over the past several decades to do more with less. Citizens have revolted at proposals to pay increased taxes but they have consistently requested more and better services from their local governments. Elected officials and professional public administrators on the local level have felt the pressure to improve the quality and efficiency of their governments. Because of the demands placed on them and the fiscal restrictions they face, local officials have turned to numerous new approaches to improve service delivery, cut costs, and prepare for the future.

The public administration literature has been in the forefront of reporting on the efforts of local governments to use processes and techniques to improve local government management. Beyond reporting, scholars have encouraged practitioners to adopt these management approaches in the confidence crisis they confront with their constituents. Because there are so many local governments in the United States and because they are relatively adaptable, they are often the testing grounds for new approaches in government. Insofar as public managers are judged on their ability to make their organizations effective, efficient, and responsive, they are open to trying new management ideas that will lead to their success. The chapters included in Part 4 of the book reflect broad attempts to improve local government management over the past three decades.

Harry P. Hatry of the Urban Institute described the challenges and issues of productivity measurement for local governments in a 1972 *Public Administration Review* article (published here as chapter 21) that would have been timely thirty years later. Hatry cited the pressures at the time on local governments to maximize productivity, that is "to make the local government dollars go as far as possible" (p. 283). Rising prices and expenditures coupled with spiraling inflation placed considerable pressure on local governments in the early 1970s to improve productivity. Hatry argued that local governments had to be concerned with productivity measurement in order to identify problem areas and priorities for improvement efforts, determine progress toward targets or goals, and establish and implement employee incentive plans. He recognized that productivity measurement is very difficult to utilize effectively in local government because workload measurements do not address differences in service quality, variances in reporting, or the numerous variations of local practices, laws, and demands of local jurisdictions. Hatry concluded, "Much closer examination is needed to determine why certain jurisdictions appear to be doing better. Once this is accomplished, the insights gained may be used to help improve the poorer performing jurisdictions" (p. 289).

One tool for improving the effectiveness of local governments is goal setting or management by objectives. Louise G. White explores efforts to improve the ability of city council members to provide guidance to their governments through goal setting (chapter 22). She identifies the frustration that city councilors feel from "pothole politics," or the obsession with specific problems brought to them by constituents, rather than dealing with the long-term needs of their cities.

White suggests that councilors have three immediate needs: to set long-term goals, to function effectively as a group, and to work more effectively with the administrative staff. Based on her review of numerous case studies, she describes four strategies that local officials could employ to improve their ability in policymaking. All of the strategies dealt with group processes rather than individual skills. For example, collaborative relationships and teamwork, policymaking and goal setting, brainstorming for alternative solutions, and organizational development over an extended time period are the approaches that build on each other to maximize the effectiveness of city councilors as policymakers.

In the late 1970s and early 1980s, local governments faced severe fiscal pressures because of high inflation, decreases in federal assistance, and a national economic recession. Practitioners and public administration scholars turned their attention to what Charles Levine described as "cutback management." In chapter 23, Richard G. Higgins, Jr. reviews the challenges facing local governments during this period and concludes that "the fiscal pressures that governments face (particularly at the local level) make the stakes in the productivity game even higher" (p. 304). He points out that governments, like the private sector, had always operated with the mindset of continued growth. Now, because of fiscal stress, they were facing cutback management or "doing more with less." Higgins identified three responses of local governments to the crisis of the time: generate more revenue, change the administration of programs through productivity improvements designed to maximize existing resources, or make selective or across-the-board cuts in services. To illustrate these responses, Higgins presented case studies of Syracuse and Charlotte—one a Northern declining city with a strong mayor government and the other a thriving Sunbelt metropolis with council-manager government. Despite their apparent differences, both cities employed the three responses Higgins identified to combat the fiscal stress they faced.

Over the past two decades, the public administration literature has included many efforts to introduce the concept of strategic planning to local government management. Strategic planning has been viewed by many authors as an effective way for local governments to deal with the unstable environment that created the need for cutback management. Gregory Streib, who described the process in local government as strategic decision making, argues (chapter 24) that the four management functions are often in a state of disassociation in local government. For strategic decision making to succeed, all four management functions—leadership, human resources, management skills, and external support—must be integrated because strategic decision making requires integration; it does not produce integration. Streib postulates a "kind of universal law governing the feasibility of strategic decision making: *the greater the need for strategic decision making, the less likely that strategic decision making will be possible*" (p. 320). Only a minority of local governments has the level of leadership required for strategic decision making, even though most have the management skills to be successful. However, insofar as elected officials comprise the human resource base and there is constant turnover among elected officials, it is unlikely that long-term consistency and support of strategic decision making will take place. External support for strategic decision making is the most difficult to maintain of all four management functions, according to Streib, who concludes: "strategic decision making, as commonly described, is simply too demanding for many local governments to use effectively" (p. 325).

In the late 1980s, total quality management (TQM) was introduced in local governments after its success in the private sector was well established. In chapter 25, Jonathan P. West, Evan M. Berman, and Michael E. Milakovich survey council-manager governments to determine the level of usage of TQM. They estimated that approximately one-fourth of council-manager cities were using this management technique, which is characterized by a commitment to improving service to customers and constituents. The authors identified three tasks of leadership essential to TQM implementation: transformational, transactional, and representational. Transformational leadership tasks include "formulating and communicating new, visionary goals" (p. 331, Table 25.1) and instilling in the organization a commitment to the customer or constituent. Transactional leadership tasks involve gaining commitments from organizational members for new programs and policies either voluntarily or through coercion. Transactional leaders often have to develop pockets of excellence that will spread to the rest of the organization. Representational leadership is the process of gaining support for TQM from the primary stakeholders, such as members of city council or key community leaders.

West, Berman, and Milakovich found that the most common causes for cities to implement TQM were interest and support of city managers, budget pressures, and public complaints. Because city managers are responsible for the effectiveness of city services and their professional standing depends on successful implementation of modern management practices, they generally play the role of transformational leader in their city governments.

Herbert A. Marlowe, Jr., Ronald Nyhan, Lawrence W. Arrington, and William J. Pammer argue (chapter 26) that the forces of change in our governments and in society are real and long term. The various re- movements—reinvention, reengineering, and restructuring—reflect the need for local governments to respond to the forces of change. The authors identify five elements that are the major forces behind the call for governmental change: the collapse of consensus, the emergence of messy problems, the transformation of the global economy, the crisis of citizenship and self-interest, and the loss of social capital. Current governmental structures and attitudes are not sufficient to deal with the major forces of change and the result will be a fiscal and service delivery crisis. Public confidence in government's ability to address the messy problems society faces is very low, according to the authors. In addition, there is very little interest in government service because of the deriding taken by public servants from elected officials and citizens. The authors state: "Our local governmental structures were not designed to solve messy problems" (p. 344) that are enumerated as urban and social decay, environmental issues, energy shortages, agriculture's loss of topsoil, and fiscal problems, including the federal deficit and the nation's lack of investment in infrastructure. They conclude that it is not enough for local governments to be efficient and effective but they must address the fundamental question of purpose: "what do we want government to be effective at?" (p. 348) To determine purpose, Marlowe, Nyhan, Arrington, and Pammer argued that we must engage in visioning, direction setting, and public policy consensus building. This futuring process will provide the missing ingredient to the re- movement—purpose.

CHAPTER 21

ISSUES IN PRODUCTIVITY MEASUREMENT FOR LOCAL GOVERNMENTS

HARRY P. HATRY

Productivity recently has become the object of rejuvenated interest. National concern over rising prices without apparent rises in output has been a major cause. This inflation pinch has been felt severely in the local government sector of the economy where expenditures have been increasing at a rapid pace. Pressures to make the local government dollars go as far as possible—through increased productivity—appear likely to continue over the next few years at least.

The attempt to keep costs down and to improve efficiency has always been a task of local government management. The revival of concern over productivity simply reflects the heightened challenges on local governments today to meet the demands for services within very tight cost-revenue constraints.

Why should local governments worry not only about productivity, but also about productivity measurement? Productivity measurement itself involves added cost. Ultimately, productivity measurement has to be justified as helping to lead to improved productivity. Following are some specific uses of local government productivity measurement, first, for that carried out by local officials, and next, for that carried out by federal or state officials.

Productivity measurement generated locally can help to:

1. *Identify problem areas and priorities for improvement efforts.* The measures will afford a perspective on the current level of productivity and how it is changing over time for various services.
2. *Determine progress toward targets or goals.* Individual programs aimed at increasing productivity need to be evaluated. Local officials may be tempted to "fiat" annual increases in productivity, such as 5 percent per year, but this would be meaningless without means to measure actual accomplishment.
3. *Establish and implement employee incentive plans.* Measurable productivity changes can be considered as items for bargaining between labor and management.

Comparative productivity measures of local governments can help federal and state officials to:

1. *Identify overall nationwide (or state) trends as a basis for setting priorities for resource allocations.* Funds, research, and technical assistance can then be assigned more specific targets for improving local productivity.

From *Public Administration Review*, vol. 32, no. 6 (November/December 1972), pp. 776–784. Copyright © 1972 by American Society for Public Administration. Reprinted with permission.

2. *Give national attention to productivity improvement opportunities.* For example, productivity measurement can be included in evaluations of demonstration or experimental projects; then local officials generally can be alerted to successful new approaches (and to failures that may be avoided). Also, high performers can be identified and others encouraged to emulate them.

In summary, productivity measurement can help governments to identify priority areas needing attention and the degree to which specific actions have helped. Unless governments continually monitor productivity, they will lack feedback to determine whether their courses of action have been successful and whether they should be continued in the future or modified.

Productivity measurement will be particularly useful if the following three types of comparisons are made:

1. Comparisons over time—to provide information on trends and progress, if any. Lacking external standards, a government's own past history can be used.
2. Comparisons with other jurisdictions, particularly those with similar characteristics—to provide some baseline against which a government can measure its own performance.
3. Comparisons among operational units within a jurisdiction, such as among solid waste collection crews, police precincts, or social service offices—so the more productive units can be recognized (and their methods duplicated) while the less productive units can be given the necessary attention to improve their performance.

What Is Productivity Measurement?

Productivity measurement essentially means relating the amount of inputs of a service or product to the amount of outputs. Traditionally this has been expressed as a ratio such as number of units produced per man-hour. National productivity measurements for the private sector have been made for many years. This is not as easily accomplished for the local government sector because its "products" primarily fall into the classification of services; hard-to-measure *quality of service* then becomes an essential ingredient of output along with physical output measurements such as "number of cases processed" or "tons of solid waste collected." Even in the private sector, productivity measurement efforts have failed to measure services adequately.

Thus, a principal difficulty in productivity measurement for local government services is in defining and measuring output, a familiar problem to public administrators. Some government services such as utilities do have physical outputs, but here, too, quality is an important aspect. For example, treating so many million gallons of water or sewage is important, but the quality of the treated water or effluent is an equally important dimension.

Solid waste collection offers a more typical and subtle example. Suppose that tons of solid waste collected is used as the measure of output. Then merely shifting from backdoor to curbside collection can increase *workload* productivity (tons collected per man-hour) significantly. However, the quality of the service to the public will have been diminished; that is, part of the collection activity—transporting the garbage from door to curb—has been shifted to the customer. Furthermore, obtaining the tons of garbage collected fails to indicate whether the streets are clean. A city could show an increase in total tonnage collected (or in the tonnage collected per man-hour) while the streets were actually getting dirtier.

Perverse measurement is another serious problem. Governments need to avoid leading employees to take actions that make the measurements "look good," but which may be against the public interest. For example, the "number of arrests per policeman" seems like one highly plausible measure of police productivity. Using this measure by itself in productivity incentive plans, however, would generate considerable temptation to increase the number of arrests at the expense of arrest quality. Another example: overemphasis on waste tonnage collected might tempt collectors to look for heavy objects, to douse waste with water, and so on. Clearly, local officials want to avoid such perversities and need to seek productivity measurement procedures that reduce their likelihood.

Thus, simplistic notions of productivity measurement should be treated with great caution. Rather, it seems advisable to consider a multiple set of measurements for each service. These should include workload measures, quality measurements, and other local condition factors that could affect the interpretation of the findings. Table 21.1 provides an illustrative set of such measures for a number of local government services.

Current State of Measurement

The current state of productivity measurement for local government is poor—both at the individual local government level and at the national level. Little has been done. A surprising number of local governments apparently do not even systematically keep workload measurement data on many of their services. Fewer seem to examine systematically and regularly their unit cost data, for example, cost per unit of workload. The inverse of unit cost data, workload per unit of cost, is a productivity measure. Seldom are these reported for local government services.

Measurement of service effectiveness to include quality aspects of services—how they serve the citizens of the jurisdiction—is quite rate in many, if not most, local services. Only in very recent years have local governments (and state and federal as well) begun to take steps to correct this deficiency. Many governments are now beginning to develop "performance measurement" systems. Without the consideration of quality in service effectiveness, productivity measurement is too likely to be deficient if not actually perverse.

In addition, there is currently little effort by the federal government to measure productivity of local government services—either to provide comparative city-by-city data or nationwide aggregates.

Measuring the Amount of Input

Thus far, this discussion has focused on measurement of output, but input measurement is also an integral part of productivity measurement.

Three general options are available: first, a measure of manpower such as man-hours or man-years of effort; second, cost in constant dollars, that is, dollars evaluated in terms of some base year price; and third, cost in current dollars without deflating for price level changes.

Man-hours is the classical productivity measurement. It has the virtue of focusing on the output of specific employees, and to this extent is certainly useful. However, it has some major limitations. It does not reflect potential tradeoffs with other input factors such as capital items. For example, a city might choose to purchase a more automated piece of equipment, such as a new waste collection vehicle with a mechanical arm to pick up garbage cans. The additional capital investment is likely to reduce collection manpower, but raise vehicle maintenance costs. Thus, productivity in terms of output per unit of collection manpower would show an increase, but productivity in terms of dollars, constant or current, might show a substantially different picture.

Table 21.1

Illustrative Set of Workload Measures, Quality Factors, and Local Condition Factors That Should Be Considered in Productivity Measurement[a]

Selected service functions[b]	Illustrative "workload" measures[c]	Illustrative quality factors (i.e., measures of citizen impact) that should be considered in interpreting productivity[d]	Illustrative local conditions factors that should be considered in interpreting productivity
1. Solid waste collection	Tons of solid waste collected	Visual appearance of streets / "Curb" or "backdoor" collection / Fire/health hazard conditions from solid waste accumulation / Service delays	Frequency of collection / Private vs. public collection / Local weather conditions / Composition of the solid waste (including the residential-commercial-industrial mix; type of waste, etc.)
2. Liquid waste treatment (sewage)	Gallons of sewage treated	Quality level of effluent, e.g., "BOD" removed and remaining after treatment / Water quality level resulting where dumped	Initial quality of waterway into which the sewage effluent is released / Community liquid waste generation characteristics
3. Law enforcement (police)	Number of surveillance hours / Number of calls / Number of crimes investigated	Reduction in crime and victimization rates / Crime clearance rates, preferably including court disposition / Response times / Citizen feeling of security	Percent of low-income families in population / Public attitude toward certain crimes
4. Law enforcement (courts)	Number of cases resolved	Number of convictions; number of plea-bargain reduced sentences / Correctness of disposition / Delay time until resolution	Number and types of cases
5. Health and hospital	Number of patient-days	Reduced number and severity of illnesses / Conditions of patients after treatment / Duration of treatment and "pleasantness" of care / Accessibility of low-income groups to care	Availability and price of health care / Basic community health conditions
6. Water treatment	Gallons of water treated	Water quality indices such as for hardness and taste / Amount of impurities removed	Basic quality of water supply source

Service function	Workload measures	Effectiveness measures	External factors
7. Recreation	Acres of recreational activities Attendance figures	Participation rates Accessibility to recreational opportunities Variety of opportunities available Crowdedness indices Citizens' perceptions of adequacy of recreational opportunities	Amount of recreation provided by the private sector. Number of individuals without access to automobiles; and the available public transit system Topographical and climate characteristics Time available to citizens for recreation activities
8. Street maintenance	Square yards of repairs made	Smoothness/"bumpiness" of streets Safety Travel time Community disruption: amount and duration Dust and noise during repairs	Density of traffic Density of population along roadway Location of residences, homes, shopping areas, recreational opportunities, etc.
9. Fire control	Fire calls Number of inspections	Fire damage Injuries and lives lost	Local weather conditions Type of construction Density of population
10. Primary and secondary education	Pupil-days Number of pupils	Achievement test scores and grade levels Continuation/drop-out rates	Socioeconomic characteristics of pupils and neighborhood Basic intelligence of pupils Number of pupils

Source: Hatry and Fisk (1971), pp. xvi–xvii.

Notes:

[a]More extensive lists of workload measures and quality factors (often called measures of effectiveness or evaluation criteria) can be found in references number 1, 6, 9, 10, 16, 17, and 26 of the Bibliography in *Improving Productivity and Productivity Measurement in Local Governments*.

[b]Numerous subfunctions each with its own submeasures could also be identified. However, care should be taken to avoid going into excessive, unuseful detail.

[c]Dividing these by total dollar cost or by total man-days yields workload-based productivity measures.

[d]Such local conditions as population size and local price levels are relevant to all service functions.

The example just cited illustrates another caution. If a government hires personnel for maintenance activities, such additional manpower, it can be argued, should also be considered in evaluating the changed productivity. In addition, if the government decides to contract out for the maintenance work rather than hire its own personnel, its productivity, if measured solely on a per man-hour basis, will appear improved.

Another example: what are the productivity considerations when a local government employs computers for preparing the payroll and for tax and utility billing? The number of clerical personnel is typically reduced. Yet additional higher paid personnel for the computer and various other computer-related expenses may be required. In net, the computer-related costs may have absorbed much, if not all, of the dollar savings. Actually, the primary payoff may be an increased quality of output, both in terms of accuracy (fewer payroll mistakes to raise the ire of employees) and quicker payroll and billing, as well as the ability to do more things and provide more information with the computer.

Thus, government productivity in the big-picture sense is not just a function of manpower but of the other cost elements as well. It seems necessary for governments also to express productivity in terms of dollars.

The third option listed above, output per *current* dollar, is not normally labeled a productivity measurement. Economists would press for the use of cost deflators to provide *constant* dollars. This has the virtue (or drawback depending on one's outlook) of removing the effects of price changes. Local officials are, however, also concerned with actual current costs, including any price rises.

Thus, local governments probably will want to use all three forms of input measures to obtain a better perspective on productivity.

Input measurement can also prove inadequate or misleading unless it includes *all relevant man-hours or dollars*. Employee fringe benefits, related maintenance costs, facility costs, and the like should all be taken into account. The handling of indirect and shared joint costs is a dilemma which affects this problem as well as many other cost analysis issues.

In making productivity measurement decisions, a government needs to address the question: the productivity of whom or what? For example, for some purposes a government would likely be interested in the productivity of specific collection crews. For other purposes, local officials would probably also need a more complete picture of the entire waste collection department. If the local government develops an agreement to share productivity gains with employees (and this may become a reality for at least some local governments), the government would want to estimate the actual net gains after consideration of such expenses as improved equipment and increased maintenance costs. This would permit the productivity resulting from these investments to be allocated equitably.

As will be discussed in the next section, when a city's performance is to be compared against others, an additional problem arises—that of commonality of reporting practices. For example, some governments may typically include employee fringe benefits as part of employment costs; others may normally keep them separate.

Intercity Comparisons

Dependable, meaningful data on other, similar governments can help to provide targets or standards for a jurisdiction. In the United States, comparative productivity data on local government services for individual cities or counties is not generally available. There is information available on expenditures and manpower for various services such as that collected by the U.S. Bureau of the Census and by the International City Management Association. However, on the output side there is little meaningful comparative information.

Possibly only in the police crime control area is there at least partial output information. There the federal government has undertaken to obtain crime and arrest data using common definitions. Adherence to the reporting requests is dependent on voluntary compliance by individual local governments. The resulting data has come under considerable attack for its insufficiencies and for lack of common data collection practices in at least some cities.

A major effort to obtain commonality is needed for adequate comparative productivity analysis. Federal agencies might provide a basis for comparison by undertaking periodic tabulations of service data in a sampling of local governments, rather than attempting to cover all governments each year.

Assuming commonality of data, a further question is: What jurisdictions are sufficiently similar to provide fair comparisons? Hundreds of characteristics differentiate the various cities and counties, with each jurisdiction as unique as is each human being. Yet categories can narrow the band of significant differences for certain purposes. The little data that is currently collected on local governments, such as fiscal data, is generally grouped by population category. Demographic, socioeconomic, organizational, and miscellaneous characteristics abound—climate; central city vs. suburban vs. rural area; form of government (e.g., manager-council vs. elected executive); racial composition; household income; class mix; and so forth.

There is surprisingly little theory or research on how such characteristics should be expected to affect efficiency, effectiveness, or productivity of specific local services. For example, convincing analyses of the economies or diseconomies of scale for local government services is sparse indeed.

Each particular public service needs to be examined in light of its own characteristics. For example, in solid waste collection, housing density, as a proxy for how close together pickup points are, would instinctively seem to be an important productivity factor. Yet the little available analysis presents conflicting evidence.

What seems clear, however, from existing data sources is that major city-to-city productivity differences often do exist. This is true even after allowing for variations in selected service and community variables. An examination of solid waste collection data from a special 1971 survey indicated that for once-a-week curbside or alley pickup the tons collected per man varied from 940 to 1,900. Tons collected per $1,000 expended varied from 41 to 90. Based on 1970 police data, the number of clearances of reported crimes per police employee ranged from 1 to 7 among cities of approximately 100,000 population.

While a portion of such wide ranges may result from different data collection practices, real productivity differences appear to exist after adjusting for these practices. What is not known is how much of the remaining differences are due to inherent local characteristics not found elsewhere and how much due to better practices by some of the jurisdictions.

Much closer examination is needed to determine why certain jurisdictions appear to be doing better. Once this is accomplished, the insights gained may be used to help improve the poorer-performing jurisdictions.

Examples

To illustrate some of the major issues in productivity measurement, two examples are presented in the following sections: one on solid waste collection and the other on police crime control. The first is a relatively easy local service for productivity measurement; the second is considerably more difficult.

Solid Waste Collection

Inspection of data indicates that solid waste collection may be too complex to measure as such. It needs to be broken down further to distinguish residential-commercial trash and garbage collection from street cleaning activities. The former also can usefully be divided so that residential and commercial collections are measured separately. Otherwise different or changing proportions of these activities can result in apparent productivity changes that are in reality due to the particular mix of activities.

Two basic output measures for workload productivity of waste collection seem appropriate: total tons collected and number of units (e.g., households) served. However, level-of-service factors also need to be considered: pickup location and frequency of collection are examples. Considerably more difficult to measure are the quality factors, cleanliness of streets and citizen satisfaction with collection services. Few cities currently collect data on either of these quality aspects, although they are clearly significant. Procedures have been developed that enable local governments to make such measurements—through systematic visual inspection rating systems for street cleanliness, and through citizen surveys for indications of satisfaction.

If the level- (or quality) of-service aspects change substantially from one year to the next, these may cause major changes in workload productivity. Thus, if a city changes to curb from backdoor pickup, one would expect a significant increase in tons collected per man-hour. This change is not an improvement in productivity as defined in the broad sense. When evaluating one city's performance against those of other cities, these factors should again be considered. Cities might be grouped by selected quality and level-of-service characteristics, or more complicated adjustments may be made to provide a basis for comparability.

Table 21.2 illustrates the type of data and computations that could be made.

Police Crime Control

Measuring police productivity presents many conceptual difficulties. There appear to be two major purposes of police crime control: deterring crime and, given that it has not been deterred, apprehending criminals. There is currently no effective way to measure how many crimes have been deterred by governmental actions, such as by increasing the size of the police force.

Apprehension productivity is more tangible. The "number of arrests per policeman or per dollar" is an obvious productivity measurement. As already noted, this measure could lead to perversities if used alone. It does not consider the issue of the quality of the arrest. A partial way to account for quality of arrest for felonies is to examine the percentage of arrests that "survive" preliminary hearings in the court of limited jurisdiction (normally the first court into which a felony is placed). In addition, percentage of arrests that lead to convictions can also be used as an indicator of the full productivity of arrests. Note, however, that both these factors, the second more so than the first, involves the performance of other parts of the criminal justice system in addition to the police.

Other productivity information can be obtained by examining clearance rates (that is, the percentage of reported crimes that lead to an arrest) perhaps divided by dollars (or employees) per capita.

Note that such measurements as "number of calls answered per man-year" seem of limited usefulness as measures of productivity, although they may be of interest to city management for other purposes.

A critical input measurement difficulty is trying to separate manpower costs for traffic control

Table 21.2

Illustrative Productivity Measurement Presentation: Solid Waste Collection Example

	1970	1971	Change
Data			
1. Tons of solid waste collected	90,000	100,000	$10,000
2. Average street cleanliness rating[a]	2.9	2.6	−0.3
3. Percent of survey population expressing satisfaction with collection[b]	85%	80%	−5
4. Cost (current)	$1,200,000	$1,500,000	+$300,000
5. Costs (1970 dollars)	$1,200,000	$1,300,000	+$100,000
Productivity measures			
6. Workload per dollar (unadjusted dollars)	75 tons per thousand dollars	67 tons per thousand dollars	−11%
7. Workload productivity (1970 dollars)	75 tons per thousand dollars	77 tons per thousand dollars	+3%
8. Output index: $\frac{(1) \times (2) \times (3)}{(4)}$ (unadjusted dollars)	0.185	0.139	−25%
9. Productivity index: $\frac{(1) \times (2) \times (3)}{(5)}$ (1970 dollars)	0.185	0.160	−14%

Source: Improving Productivity and Productivity Measurement in Local Governments, Harry P. Hatry and Donald M. Fisk, The National Commission on Productivity, 1971, p. 19.

Notes:

[a]Such rating procedures are currently in use in the District of Columbia. The rating in line 2 is presumed to be based on a scale of "1" to "4," with "4" being the cleanest.

[b]The figures in line 7 indicate some improvement in efficiency, but line 6 suggests that cost increases such as wages have more than exceeded the efficiency gains. Productivity has gone down even further on the basis of decreases in the street cleanliness ratings and decreased citizen satisfaction. However, such indices have to be studied carefully and interpreted according to local circumstances to be fairly understood.

from those for crime control. The same personnel may have both functions. On the output side, problems include apparent inaccuracies in reported crime rates and vague or conflicting definitions of certain crime categories. There is also the problem of which crimes to consider in measuring crime and clearance rates. For example, the FBI uses such classifications as "Part I and Part II" crimes, "Index" crimes, "property crimes," and "crimes of violence."

Summary

Productivity measurements are important devices for letting a local government know its current status. They reveal, after action is taken, how successful it has been. Measurements can help to identify new procedures or approaches that are worth pursuing, and those that are not. Used in dealings with employees, they can provide a basis for incentive plans and the sharing of benefits of increased productivity.

Unfortunately, the state of the art of productivity measurement for local government services is disappointing. The temptation is and will be great to stick with the more readily available and traditional workload type of measurements. But used alone these measurements can lead to perversities and misallocations of effort. The collecting and at least arraying of various quality considerations should also be undertaken and used in interpreting workload productivity calculations. Single, readily available, physical measurements, tempting as they may be, should be viewed with a jaundiced eye. Inevitably, for a government to obtain a reasonable perspective of its productivity for any service, it will need multiple measurements.

Effort by the federal government seems vital if adequate comparative data on local government productivity in the United States is to be provided. A set of common definitions and, to the extent possible, common data collection practices need to be provided for each public service to encourage at least reasonable comparability of data—both of the input figures (man-years and dollars) and of outputs.

Many new productivity improvement approaches need to be tried out in local governments if productivity is to be improved. These include a number of approaches used in the past by industry such as value engineering, time and motion studies, employee incentive plans (possibly for supervisory as well as supervised employees), various cost reduction programs, and new technological and procedural changes. Whether funded by federal, state, or local governments, these attempted innovations need proper evaluation of their net effects on productivity. The governments undertaking the tests need this information. In addition, widespread and rapid dissemination of the results, at least of those innovations with most potential, is highly desirable. However, without adequate measurement, so-called evaluations are likely to be little more than public relations stories by the sponsors and of minimal practice use.

The current lack of effective means to seek out potential innovations, to give them thorough and objective evaluation, and to effectively disseminate the findings is restraining local governments from helping themselves and from reducing waste of resources. Adequate productivity measurement tools would do much to fill part of this gap.

Bibliography

This chapter is based primarily on research undertaken by the Urban Institute for the National Commission on Productivity and the U.S. Department of Housing and Urban Development on various aspects of measuring the effectiveness of local government services and on measuring local government productivity.

For some recent attempts to identify local government service quality measurements, see the following publications:

Blair, Louis H., and Alfred I. Schwartz. *How Clean Is Our City: Measuring the Effectiveness of Solid Waste Collection Operation.* Washington, DC: Urban Institute, 1972.

Hatry, Harry P., and Diana R. Dunn. *Measuring the Effectiveness of Local Government Services: Recreation.* Washington, DC: Urban Institute, 1971.

Hatry, Harry P., and Donald M. Fisk. *Improving Productivity and Productivity Measurement in Local Governments.* Washington, DC: National Commission on Productivity, 1971.

Urban Institute and the International City Management Association. *Improving Productivity Measurement and Evaluation for Local Governments.* Washington, DC: National Commission on Productivity, 1972.

Webb, Kenneth, and Harry P. Hatry. *Obtaining Citizen Feedback: The Application of Citizen Surveys to Local Governments.* Washington, DC: Urban Institute, 1972.

Winnie, Richard E., and Harry P. Hatry. *Measuring the Effectiveness of Local Government Services: Local Transportation.* Washington, DC: Urban Institute, 1972.

CHAPTER 22

IMPROVING THE GOAL-SETTING PROCESS IN LOCAL GOVERNMENT

LOUISE G. WHITE

Case studies and reports on council-manager government over the past decade indicate that councilors are frustrated in their efforts to make policy and establish goals for their communities. Two different surveys by the National League of Cities in 1973 and in 1979 indicate a general malaise. The major problems cited were excessive time demands, internal conflict, pressures from citizens and staff, and an inability to establish priorities and goals.[1] Whereas some councils have tried and succeeded in using the budget as a planning device, many find themselves responding to community issues in an ad hoc fashion, and being unable to set priorities or guidelines. Councilors refer to the prevalence of what some call "pothole politics." They feel consumed by responding to specific demands—to fix potholes here and there—and have little time for developing a long range maintenance policy or transportation system.[2] One observer notes that councilors are frustrated when they merely adapt to circumstances and want to be able to determine their community's future.[3] Another finds that "a growing number of council members feel the need to get into a position of control rather than reaction."[4]

To the extent that council members feel dissatisfied and constrained in carrying out their policy-making role, the task of administrators—managers and agency heads—may be made more difficult. Efforts to be more efficient and to make more rational decisions may be stymied by a council that feels shut out of a central policy function. It is not surprising, therefore, that the same case studies indicate that managers have played a major role in encouraging and helping councils improve their capacities, often by assisting them in establishing special training events to develop goal-setting skills. Many of these efforts have been evaluated positively, and even enthusiastically by both participants and external consultants.[5]

As case studies of such capacity-building efforts accumulate, however, two related questions have been raised. The first is whether goal-setting is consistent with the political role of councils. Legislators, after all, need to retain an ability to respond to constituent interests, and bargain over various policy issues. Statements of legislative goals may generate opposition and impede this activity. Council members may believe that merely participating in a process to rationalize policy formation would force them to be more public about their commitments than they can afford to be. And, if there is a continuing turnover on a council, members may be less likely to invest themselves in looking at issues beyond their immediate term of office. Efforts to rationalize legislative procedures are therefore pragmatically difficult, and also would be inappropriate if they insulated policy making from political pressures.

From *Public Administration Review*, vol. 42, no. 1 (January/February 1982), pp. 78–83. Copyright © 1982 by American Society for Public Administration. Reprinted with permission.

The second question deals with the content of the training. Reports indicate that many of the capacity-building events for councilors have been based on training models developed for administrative units, generally referred to as organization development or OD strategies. The issue is whether training models developed for administrative organizations are also appropriate for elected legislative bodies such as local councils.

In order to place these two questions in context, this chapter will begin by describing some of the dimensions of the frustration which councilors are experiencing, and some of the reasons for it. Next it will examine approaches to capacity building as described in various case studies. Finally, it will address the two questions raised above about the ability of a political body to establish goals, and about the appropriateness of organization development training models for political bodies.

Reasons for Council Frustrations

The problems councils face are systemic in nature. According to one observer, "the people involved are better qualified, more earnest, and more dedicated than ever before. The problem stems from the governmental resources and institutions with which they have to work, and the state of the art of the process of governance."[6] There are three broad areas of difficulty: first, increased demands at a time of shrinking resources; second, an ambiguity over the nature of the policy-making process and the respective roles of councilors and administrators; and third, inadequacies in current training practices.

Pressures Versus Resources

There has been a marked escalation of pressures and demands on councilors, who increasingly find themselves drawn into coping with conflict.[7] More issues are being defined as public problems with which the government must deal, and citizens continue to be vocal in pressing their demands. Often these demands reflect neighborhood interests rather than broad community goals; in these cases the role of citizens diffuses the policy process. Even as citizen pressures increase and often direct the council to parochial concerns, councils find their resources shrinking. Thus they have to choose which interests they will satisfy, rather than being able to distribute broadly the benefits of policies.[8]

Intergovernmental relations have also complicated the tasks of councils. Consider the following points:

- The shift toward a greater reliance on block grants places added responsibilities on local officials by forcing them to deal with issues formerly handled by federal agencies.[9] The Reagan administration's intention to decentralize and devolve more policy-making, financial, and operational responsibilities to the state and local levels, will only increase these burdens.
- These added responsibilities are coinciding with a decline in resources. In addition to voter mandated constraints on property taxes and other local revenue sources, the Reagan administration and Congress are making severe cutbacks in federal aid, and there is every indication that the states will do likewise.
- One observer notes that intergovernmental relations have been marked by an "increasing density and complexity";[10] while the implications of Reagan's policies are still unclear, they are unlikely to reduce significantly this complexity.

• Recent court decisions make state and local officials liable if their statutory actions violate federal guarantees of individual rights. Two observers note that "The rulings are likely to dampen state and local government enthusiasm for taking innovative and adaptive approaches toward program management, for the prospect is that the more they exercise ministerial flexibility, the greater the probability their administration of that program will be challenged."[11]

The Policy-Making Role Conflict

The second problem is an ambiguity over who is responsible for policy making. This is the role recently described as "policy management," which involves "providing guidance and leadership," and requiring the government "to develop priorities and establish commitments."[12] Traditionally, it was assumed that councils would perform this role, and that a council-manager form of government would leave the legislators "time and energy for the consideration of the broader problems with which the elected representatives were appropriately prepared to cope."[13] This view was expressed in 1940; since then academicians and practitioners alike have agreed that it is both unrealistic and undesirable to attempt to separate policy making or political decisions from administrative activities. Most attention, however, has focused on the implication of this conclusion for the role of administrators, and the fact that they play a larger role in setting and redefining policies than the reformers believed.[14] (In a recent survey, councilors reported that administrative staff is almost as likely as they are to initiate policy—38 and 41 percent, respectively.[15]) The importance of the role of managers in policy making has encouraged efforts to make the policy process more rational, and emphasis has been placed on managers' decision-making and evaluation skills, as well as their ability to hold lower-level officials accountable.[16]

In the face of this focus on the manager's policy management activities, the council's role in making policy and setting goals has been given less attention. In some communities councils have made efforts to use the budgets to set priorities, establish master plans, or implement various growth control mechanisms in order to maintain some control over decision making. On balance, however, it appears that administrators have actually expanded their roles and increased their capacity vis-à-vis elected officials.[17] In part managers have been able to do this because it is perceived that they can be more efficient than legislative bodies. Goal setting as a political process is admittedly incremental, and appears to move slowly, and to be inadequate to meeting the problems which communities face. It is also suspect because it is subject to pressures from special interests.

As a result of these views the task of goal setting has been subtly redefined. It is less apt to refer to actions by legislators to establish priorities; instead it usually refers to the use of specific managerial tools, such as management by objectives (MBO).[18] Hence the role of councils in setting policy for their community or of actually governing has been downplayed. In its place, councilors find they spend most of their time responding to specific citizen pressures and overseeing administration.[19]

These changes in the roles of councilors and managers have the potential for generating conflict between them, and several case studies of council-manager governments indicate that such tensions are very real.[20] As managers expand their policy-making role, councilors resent their intrusion into this arena. Alternatively, as councilors emphasize an ombudsman and oversight role they will tend to constrain and antagonize the manager.

Current Training Practices

The third problem is that local councils are ill-equipped to provide "guidance and leadership." They are typically run by nonprofessionals, who generally have no training or experience in the government. A 1979 survey of council members indicates that 88 percent are part-time.[21] The demands on their time can be overwhelming, and the presumption that they have the necessary expertise raises unreasonable expectations. It is interesting, therefore, that most of the training activities that are offered by the federal government are technical in nature, and are designed for administrators.[22] Generally this emphasis has also been true of federal agency programs to increase local capacity, such as HUD's Financial Management Capacity Sharing Program.[23] Even when nonadministrators are included, little training has been available which focused on the policy-making role; rather it has dealt with management techniques, personal skills in time management, and communications, or it has provided training in substantive policy areas. Several of the state and local interest groups—like the National Association of Regional Councils, National League of Cities, and International City Management [Managers'] Association have begun to expand training activities for individual legislators through workshops and seminars on an open enrollment basis. These are limited, however, insofar as they do not deal with the council as a governing body.

A review of the training activities offered to local governments by the Virginia State Office of Personnel and Training is illustrative of state and local priorities. This type of training is significant because it has been the conduit of federal funds from the 1970 Intergovernmental Personnel Act (IPA). Almost all "requests for proposals" (RFPs) going out to universities from local governments in Virginia over the past three years dealt with training for administrators and usually focused on supervisory and interactive skills for individuals. Among these there have been only a handful of requests for training which included councils, and all of these have been very recent.

How Councils Define Their Needs

The above discussion suggests that councilors are frustrated because:

- Increasing demands confront them with policy choices;
- Responsibility for policy making is diffuse and often ambiguous; and
- They have not received help in developing a capacity to set long range policy.

In order to illustrate how councils have responded to these frustrations, thirty-two cases in which councils have tried to improve their decision-making processes were reviewed. In addition to written reports, telephone interviews were held with participants in twelve of these.[24]

The case studies suggest that councilors define three immediate needs: (1) to set long-term goals; (2) to function effectively as a group; and (3) to work more effectively with the administrative staff.

Goal Setting. When councilors were asked how effectively they performed certain tasks, the two which ranked lowest on their list were "establishing priorities," and "setting long-term goals." Whereas 97 percent felt they were effective in responding to citizen needs, only 50 percent felt they dealt adequately with goal setting.[25] In several of the cases, goal setting was viewed as a way for the council to develop a unique role for itself, in addition to allowing it to be more effective.[26]

Group Process. The survey cited above also documents the second need. When the councilors were asked about their job frustrations, the problem mentioned most frequently was "conflict with other members" (33 percent).[27] In various reports problems were defined in terms of the need to "communicate better," "increase trust," "take time out for reflection," or "negotiate more effectively." Several note that unless councilors can work together effectively as a body, they will have a hard time holding their own with administrators. According to Stephen Burks, formerly of the National League of Cities, a "council that can't act as a body is easily manipulated, or sometimes bypassed, by a strong mayor or a strong manager."[28]

Work with Staff. Finally, reports indicate that both councilors and administrators feel a need to improve their ability to work together effectively; the phrase which recurs in nearly every article and case study is "team building." The reasoning here is that typically each party feels that it is better able to protect the "public interest" and thus resents any presumed interference by the other. Each also wants to gain public visibility and political credit for dealing with local problems. Misunderstandings, competition, and confusion are often the result. The need therefore is to reintegrate the policy process in such a way that the council can participate more effectively in the work of department heads. According to one manager: "The problems and issues are much too complex and difficult for councils to work in the policy areas without a full understanding of the administrative issues. . . . Equally important many administrative issues are much too politically sensitive for the manager to proceed without keeping councils fully informed."[29] Two trainers who have worked closely with local governments in Virginia observe that: "A 'team' concept, emphasizing mutual support and interaction between the legislative group and the administrative staff is necessary to develop a fully effective government."[30]

Strategies to Deal with Needs

Just as the needs they define revolve around group interaction and organizational dynamics, the strategies that councilors have chosen deal primarily with group processes rather than individual skills.[31] The strategies fall into four patterns.

One approach emphasizes the importance of establishing collaborative relationships and teamwork among the council members and with the manager. It focuses on interpersonal dynamics, and draws from studies of organizational behavior which show that members from different groups frequently stereotype each other and then have difficulty communicating, and tend to become very formal and critical. By contrast, this approach encourages cooperation and communication, and helps both groups feel they are part of a single team.[32]

The second approach extends this team-building model to include policy-making and goal-setting skills. Typically, it draws from the same organizational models as the team-building approach, but it adds an emphasis on policy making. It deals with helping members share perceptions about goals, and then turn them into specific objectives. It tries to be sensitive to the issue of political feasibility by stressing the importance of arriving at some consensus on the goals and priorities.

A third strategy also focuses on goal setting but it relies on cognitive activities rather than on team building or on group interaction. It uses structured group exercises which force members to generate alternative goals or programs, and then prioritize them. Discussions, therefore, revolve around selecting among competing proposals rather than on interpersonal communication or on building consensus.[33]

A fourth strategy involves the council in a more extended process of organizational development. It is concerned with the council as an ongoing organization; therefore the emphasis is on processes for setting policy and goals and on organizational activities and procedures.

The vast majority of council activities reviewed were based on either the first or second strategy—a "team-building" or "goal-setting" model. The next section draws from these cases to offer some general observations about the experiences, describes a "typical" training event, and summarizes some evaluative comments by two participants.

A Typical Training Event

A remarkably consistent pattern was evident in the majority of cases and reports, underscoring the extent to which the training strategies were based on similar models of group behavior.

- Almost all of the cases were in council-manager systems, and the initiative came from the manager. The manager had had a positive experience with training events for his staff, and provided the impetus for a retreat which would include the council.
- Most of the cases combined an emphasis on personal interaction and role definitions with goal-setting exercises.
- All had outside facilitators.
- Most occurred right after elections of new council members.
- Council members usually felt the weekend was risky in that it might raise uncomfortable interpersonal issues, and efforts were made to reassure them.
- Respondents almost always felt "positive" and cited better communication as the major outcome.
- Sunshine laws were seen as a problem, but in no case was press coverage harmful. Usually after the retreat was explained, the press agreed to do a background story, but not to cover the actual sessions.

Phase I. Data Gathering. External consultants are brought in to plan some training with the councilors, and to help them clarify their needs and expectations. Next the consultants gather data from the participants, both councilors and administrators. Usually the data gathering involves individual interviews; some are supplemented by a questionnaire. Questions focus on what problems the members perceive and what frustrations they experience. Often the consultant observes a council meeting. The data is then organized in some manner and used at a conference. Sometimes, it is circulated among members prior to the conference for revisions. This phase usually includes efforts to reassure the participants and to explain procedures and probable outcomes.

Phase II. Off-site Meeting, Retreat. In every case the actual training was offered in a retreat setting, usually lasting two days. The schedule always included some social occasions, times for relaxing, and an emphasis on getting to know each other.

1. Participants begin by sharing perceptions about some problem. For example, staff and council may meet separately, with each group focusing on such questions as "What do you like best and least about our relationships?" Responses are put on newsprint, shared with both groups, and discussed. Alternatively the facilitator reports the data collected prior to the conference. The procedure then is to break down into groups and react to this information, sorting out areas of agreement and disagreement.
2. The next step is to break into small groups to define problems. These usually emerge from the above discussions. The sessions can either focus on policy problems or on process ones. Often the assignment was to come up with a list of the major policy problems in the community. The results were then reported to the entire group, and an effort was made to come to some general consensus or ranking of the problems.

3. Less frequently, a session is designed to clarify the difference between goals and objectives. Participants do exercises which show them how to break goals down into specific and measurable objectives.

4. A problem-solving session is commonly held, in which members are given a chance to actually design a solution or approach to a specific problem. For example, they develop an action plan which lays out specific tasks to deal with a problem: who is responsible, by when, and what follow-up is needed? Often they are divided into small groups with a mix of elected officials and administrators.

Phase III. Follow-up Activities. About a third of the cases involved a follow-up activity. Reports indicate that it is easy to let this phase slide due to pressure of business, and that a real effort is necessary to schedule sessions to monitor what progress has been made. One council agreed to meet for an informal breakfast prior to their formal sessions to maintain some of the communication and sharing that occurred during the retreat. Others have scheduled sessions six months later to review their progress since the retreat.

Evaluations of the training have been uniformly positive. Two trainers who conducted retreats in Virginia noted that expectations were clarified, often specific solutions were obtained, and members realized the extent to which they respected one another and could in fact effectively communicate. "In a broader sense these team building efforts gave each local government team a whole unit perspective and a very real sense of their power to make good things happen more often. The long-range effects will be influenced by their increased ability to use more effective communications, to clarify roles, and to solve real problems."[34] The interviews with those who had participated in the training confirm these results. Even those who were initially wary of the design found the experience reassuring and helpful.

Improving the Policy Process

The first three strategies—team building, goal setting, structured group processes—were usually designed as a single event. The fourth strategy—organizational change—by contrast tries to involve local councilors in a more extensive and continuing effort to improve their organizational processes. Typically these include retreats, and many of the elements described above, but they are designed as parts of a broader attempt to redesign the policy process and the council as an organization.

One example of such an effort is provided by the "Policy Leadership Project" of the NLC. This project was designed to encourage councils to embark on a long-range effort to diagnose their needs and improve their procedures. A formal relationship is established between the council and some external group, often a university, which works closely with professionals at NLC. Their function, as described by one of the consultants, is to "serve as facilitators, to gather and feed back data on council processes to council members, to conduct workshops, and to locate resources in matters the councils wish to improve or change. The staff does not, however, identify the problems or prescribe the solutions. Because the council itself must decide what needs doing, members develop a high degree of commitment to the work plans they conceive."[35] Frequently a retreat training event is included, but there is also a broader range of sessions and activities included which involve ongoing processes. The NLC requires the external relationship in order to promote "stability and objectivity," and they are now encouraging institutions of higher education to develop similar projects in their own states.[36]

A review of the six projects noted that in three of the cities the council chose to emphasize "basic improvements in council organization and procedure." The other three cities adopted strategies designed to deal with "council decision making and interpersonal communication processes."[37] In evaluating the NLC project Stephen Burks underscored the importance of two factors. One is the active support of such training by at least a few council members. The second is a local resource which can provide training on a short-term and practical basis. Without these two conditions, councilors will have little incentive to invest themselves in an activity which from their view has no guaranteed or immediate pay-off.[38]

Goal Setting and Political Reality

At the outset two questions were raised—to what extent is it appropriate for representative political bodies to engage in goal-setting efforts and do the training strategies which councils adopt enable them to effectively deal with conflict and political agendas? It is suggested that these can be translated into a single proposition—goal-setting strategies are appropriate if they include a concern for helping councilors deal with political conflict and competing interests, or at the least if they do not obscure potential conflict.

The problem is that many of the strategies in the cases described above are based on models originally designed for making management more effective, rather than for representing and aggregating different interests. Golembiewski and Sink have cautioned against a simple transfer of organization development models to elected bodies. They cite the role of constituent interests, the reality of public scrutiny, the short time frames of council decisions, and the turnover in leadership as factors which limit the relevance of these traditional group process models.[39] Robert Luke, Jr. offers a similar warning and cites one trainer who concluded that "I feel strongly the political process is not a management process; that an elected council is not an organization."[40] The point is that training appropriate for managers may not always be appropriate for politicians.

One problem is that existing group process models assume the value of cooperation and consensus building. Political processes, however, stress that it may be legitimate to use power to promote a position. Many of the cases reviewed here reported efforts to remove politics from the discussions, or to stay away from hot issues.[41] In this sense the strategies did not help the councils enhance their political roles, and may have encouraged a false consensus. One report of a retreat which was not successful concluded that the consultants had been so oriented toward collaboration that they disregarded the extent of conflict among the members; they assumed a hierarchical organization model, and thus they failed to diagnose the extent to which power was dispersed among the group; and they were so influenced by a process model that they failed to see that the basic problem was poor performance by the council members, and not a lack of communication.[42]

If sensitivity to political dimensions is often lacking, the reports also suggest that the goal-setting process itself does not necessarily conflict with the political role of councils and their need to be responsive to community demands. In general those participating in goal-setting activities did not attempt to establish hard and fast positions. Rather, council members would brainstorm about a wide range of policy issues and political demands. Typically they would come up with a broadly inclusive list, and then select one or two goals for immediate attention, rather than try to settle the entire political agenda. Their emphasis was on identifying several goals they could agree on and designing some immediate action steps, not on making a premature closure on sensitive policies or ignoring competing interests.

According to one review of council development strategies by Wolf and Wolf, sometimes it is appropriate to focus on group and organizational effectiveness, while at other times political dynamics need to be emphasized. When the issue is posed in this manner, it is clear that training needs will vary with the situation. The authors go on to argue that council activities fall into three stages:

- An initial stage in which the major task is for councilors to learn to work together;
- A longer middle stage in which they focus on implementing their goals;
- A third stage prior to reelection in which electoral strategies become paramount.

They conclude that training needs will vary with the degree of politicization on any particular council, as well as the stage they are in at the time. "Once political questions predominate, particularly in the third stage, the applied behavioral science techniques are a less appropriate kind of an intervention," and a council would do better to turn to a political consultant. Such an approach might be designed to help members build coalitions or work with constituent groups, rather than focus on internal processes.[43] Its purpose would be to increase the skills of councils to negotiate more effectively with all those who share responsibility for decision making.

The fourth strategy—dealing with councils as organizations—seems to have the greatest potential to help them develop their policy management role while being sensitive to their representative role. Emphasizing the council as an organization enables councilors to focus on a variety of processes, including those of collecting information from citizens as well as communicating with administrators and following through on implementation. It makes a connection between internal processes and relations with the community. For example, a study of an ongoing organizational development process in Pensacola, Florida, noted that they have tried to equip "the city organizational internally for greater exposure and responsiveness to public needs of all kinds. This has meant an orientation toward both greater internal cohesiveness and the skill of problem-solving."[44] This fourth strategy encourages councils to diagnose their problems and develop some specific remedial actions. In this context, goal setting emerges as one of several processes which councils may choose to develop, and would be placed in a broader definition of capacity building.

The Wolfs' schema is a useful reminder that training strategies need to be designed for a particular context and situation. The case studies attest to the fact that many councils feel a need to deal with their internal processes, and confirm that team-building strategies have been valuable in many instances. At the same time it is true that these same approaches do not help councilors develop their political capacity, their ability to work more effectively with citizen groups, to build coalitions, or enhance their power base. In part this failing can be traced to the fact that present training strategies are primarily based on collaboration and consensus-building models which were originally developed within an organizational context. The emerging skepticism about these models, and the developments of several variations is therefore a welcome sign.

Notes

I am grateful to John Cole, director of the George Mason University Public Management Institute, for enabling me to do this research and for his several contributions to the analysis. I also thank Richard Stillman for reviewing and commenting on this chapter, and Stephen Burks for sharing material from the National League of Cities. The reviewers were most perceptive in their comments and suggestions. The responsibility of course is my own.

1. Raymond Bancroft, "American Mayors and Councilmen: Their Problems and Frustrations" (Washington: National League of Cities, 1974), pp. 6, 58–60; "A National Survey of City Council Members: Issues in Council Leadership" (Washington, DC: National League of Cities, 1980). See also William Jones and C. Bradley Doss, "Local Officials' Reaction to Federal Capacity Building," *Public Administration Review* 38, no. 1 (January/February 1978): 64–69.

2. Thomas Grubisich, *Washington Post*, March 27, 1980.

3. Leo Penne, "Cities Seek Policy Making Approaches to Shape Events, Not React to Them," *National League of Cities Special Report* (November 6, 1978).

4. Robert Saunders, "Improving City-Council Policy Making Skills" (Washington, DC: National League of Cities, February 1980), p. 3.

5. In particular see the essays in Stephen Burks and James Wolf, *Building City Council Leadership Skills* (Washington, DC: National League of Cities, 1981).

6. J. Wright, "Building the Capacities of Municipal Government," *Public Administration Review* 35, no. 6 (November/December 1975): 748–754; Louis Garcia, "Improving the Governing Ability of City Councils," *Western City* (September 1976): 11–13, 43.

7. Lawrence Landry, "City Councils as Policy Maker," *National Civic Review* (December 1977): 553–557; Saunders, op. cit.; Sanford Skaggs, "View from the Elected Official," *Public Management* 59 (September 1977): 8; Paul Scott and Robert MacDonald, "Local Policy Management Needs: The Federal Response," *Public Administration Review* 35, Special Issue (December 1975): 786–794.

8. Stan Altman, "Performance Monitoring Systems for Public Managers," *Public Administration Review* 39, no. 1 (January/February 1979): 79. A 1979 survey of councilors found that the second greatest frustration reported was "interest group pressure," cited by 32.9 percent of the sample. *A National Survey of City Council Members* (Washington, DC: National League of Cities, 1980), p. 20.

9. Carol Van Horn, "Evaluating the New Federalism," *Public Administration Review* 39, no. 1 (January/February 1979): 17–22; Christopher Lindley, "Changing Policy Management Responsibilities of Local Government," *Public Administration Review* 35, no. 6 (November/December 1975): 794–797; Michael Deeb, "Municipal Council Members," *National Civic Review* (September 1979): 411–416.

10. Catherine H. Lovell, "Evolving Local Government Dependency," *Public Administration Review* 41, Special Issue (January 1981): 201; *State of Maine v. J. Thiboutot*, US 65 L Ed 2d 555, 100 S Ct., 1980.

11. Walter Croszyk, Jr. and Thomas Madden, "Managing Without Immunity: The Challenge for State and Local Government Officials in the 1980s," *Public Administration Review* 41, no. 2 (March/April 1981): 268.

12. Philip Burgess, "Capacity Building and the Elements of Public Management," *Public Administration Review* 35, Special Issue (December 1975): 709.

13. Harold Stone, Don Price, and Kathryn Stone, *City Manager Government in the United States* (Chicago: Public Administration Service, 1940), p. 165.

14. Richard Stillman, "The City Manager: Professional Helping Hand or Political Hired Hand?" *Public Administration Review* 37, no. 6 (November/December 1977): 659 [published here as chapter 2]; Altman, op. cit., p. 79.

15. A National Survey of City Council Members (Washington, DC: National League of Cities, 1980), p. 14.

16. Clarence Stone, "The Implementation of Social Programs," *Journal of Social Issues* 36, no. 4 (1980): 15–34.

17. Charles Dunn, "The City Council: How to Be a Team Player," *Nations Cities* (June 1975); Robert Rycroft, "Selecting Policy Evaluations Criteria," *Midwest Review of Public Administration* 12 (June 1978): 87–89; Alan Saltzstein, "City Managers and City Councils," *Western Political Quarterly* 27 (June 1974): 275–293.

18. For example, see Charles Usher and Gary Cornia, "Goal Setting and Performance Assessment in Municipal Budgeting," *Public Administration Review* 41, no. 2 (March/April 1981): 229–235.

19. Kenneth Prewitt, *The Recruitment of Political Leaders* (Indianapolis, IN: Bobbs-Merrill, 1970).

20. Thomas Wells, "Council-Manager Relations," *Virginia Town and City* (June 1975): 5–7. See also David Booth, "Council Manager Government in Small Cities," *Public Management* 55 (November 1977): 7–9; and Robert Kipp, "Mayors and Councils—The New Breed," *Public Management* 55 (September 1977): 2–4.

21. National League of Cities, "The National Survey of City Council Members: Issues in Council Leadership" (Washington, DC: National League of Cities, 1980), p. 11.

22. Lawrence Landry, "Council Member Training Sessions," *Nations Cities* (April 1975); Anthony Brown, "Technical Assistance to Rural Communities: Stop Gap or Capacity Building?" *Public Administration Review* 40, no. 1 (January/February 1980): 18–23.

23. U.S. Department of Housing and Urban Development, *Financial Management Capacity Sharing Program* (Washington, DC: U.S. HUD, Office of Policy Development and Research, September 1979); Garcia, op. cit., p. 11; Charles R. Warren and Leanne R. Aronson, "Sharing Management Capacity: Is There a Federal Responsibility?" *Public Administration Review* 41, no. 2 (May/June 1981).

24. Published descriptions include the following: James Giese, "The Cacapon Retreat," *Municipal Maryland* (July 1976): 9–11; Steve Hays et al., "Goal Setting and Team Management," *Western City* (August 1978):

8–9; R. Horgan, "Streamlining City Council Agendas," *Nations Cities* (August 1975); Karen Marsters, "Goal Setting in River City" (Washington, DC: National League of Cities, n.d.); Landry, "Training Sessions," op. cit.; John Runyon, "The Management 'Retreat,'" *New Jersey Municipalities* (October 1978): 41–42; Stephen Burks and James Wolf, *Building City Council Leadership Skills* (Washington, DC: National League of Cities, 1981) contains seven case studies. Other cases come from responses to RFPs which describe the training events.

25. *A National Survey*, 1980, p. 20.

26. Scott and MacDonald, op. cit., p. 790.

27. *A National Survey*, 1980, p. 20.

28. National League of Cities, "How Can City Councils Learn to Work Effectively?" (July 17, 1978).

29. Arthur Mendonsa, "Council-Manager Relations and the Changing Community Environment," *Public Management* 55 (September 1977): 7.

30. William Giegold and Richard Dunsing, "Team-Building in the Local Jurisdiction: Two Case Studies," *Public Administration Review* 38, no. 1 (January/February 1978): 60. For a good background on organizational development see Edward Schein, "Process Consultation: Its Role in Organization Development," in *Organizational Development* (Reading, PA: Addison Wesley, 1969).

31. Stephen Burks, "A National Perspective on City Council Capacity Building," in Burks and Wolf, op. cit., p. 5.

32. Giegold and Dunsing, op. cit., p. 60. See also Floyd Hyde, "A Municipal Management System" (Washington, DC: Floyd Hyde Associates, n.d.); and the following articles by Chris Becker: "Goal Setting by the Governing Body" (Washington, DC: International City Management Association, 1977); "Council-Manager Retreat," *Management Information Systems Reports* (January 1978); "Elected Official-Chief Administrator Conference: Post Activity Analysis," mimeo (March 23, 1979); "Getting Elected Is Just the Beginning," *Public Management* (July 1979): 10–14; Robert Luke, "Alternative Approaches and Techniques in City Council Leadership Development Training," in Burks and Wolf, op. cit., pp. 16–26.

33. James Coke and Carl Moore, "Coping with a Budgeting Crisis," in Burks and Wolf, op. cit., pp. 66–74; Kay Waldo and F. Brown, "The Council Does Long-Range Planning in Liberty, Missouri," in Burks and Wolf, op. cit., pp. 75–88; John Ostrowski, Louise White, and John Cole, "Structured Group Processes and Goal Setting," Public Management Institute, George Mason University, May 1981.

34. Giegold and Dunsing, op. cit.

35. Saunders, op. cit., p. 3.

36. During 1979 six cities were chosen to engage in the project: Memphis, Tennessee; Wichita, Kansas; Charleston, South Carolina; Long Beach, California; Akron, Ohio; Albuquerque, New Mexico. NLC staff, under the direction of Steve Burks are currently using these experiences to develop training materials for other councils. Periodic reports have been issued by the NLC describing these projects.

37. Burks, op. cit., p. 8.

38. Ibid., pp. 9–11.

39. Robert Golembiewski and R. Sink, "What Is the Status of Urban OD Applications? Testing Common Wisdom," *Journal of International Public Administration* 1 (1979): 1–12.

40. Fred Fisher cited in Luke, op. cit., p. 25.

41. James Wolf and Linda Wolf, "Policy and Leadership Effectiveness," in Burks and Wolf, op. cit., p. 150.

42. F. Brown and Gary Combs, "'Retiear' Said the Council of Richland," in Burks and Wolf, op. cit., pp. 44–65.

43. Wolf and Wolf, op. cit., pp. 151–154, 149.

44. R.K. Ready and Frank Farson, "Who Pitched That Inning?" in Joseph Uveges, *The Dimensions of Public Administration*, 2d ed. (Boston: Holbrook Press, 1975), pp. 75–91.

CHAPTER 23

STRATEGIES FOR MANAGEMENT OF DECLINE AND PRODUCTIVITY IMPROVEMENT IN LOCAL GOVERNMENT

RICHARD G. HIGGINS, JR.

Nearly all of the options that are available to governments in cutback (decline) situations involve productivity considerations.[1] In recent years we have witnessed numerous accounts of how managers have attempted to:

- Stretch available personnel and equipment;
- Provide more services each year with little or no growth in budgets; and
- Substitute one input factor for another.

In ways that are sometimes subliminal, productivity improvement has always been with us; nearly all managers think of their tasks in terms of efficiency and effectiveness as they relate to service delivery.

What is different about the environment of the late 1970s and the 1980s is that the fiscal pressures that governments face (particularly at the local level) make the stakes in the productivity game even higher. As one author has stated:

> The existence of a cutback climate creates both opportunities and problems for productivity improvement. On one hand, efforts to improve productivity appear to be a reasonable way to try to cope with fiscal limitations. On the other hand, resource constraints and attitudes associated with the cutback climate may make it difficult to use improvement methods.[2]

The pressures for productivity improvement at the local government level have never been greater than they are at the present time. Traditional federal funding sources are rapidly drying up, and unstable economic conditions are increasing the demand for public services and reducing local government revenues. Improving productivity has become increasingly important for local governments, not as an answer to all financial problems, but as one approach to maximizing the resources that are still available to meet the needs of citizens.

Fiscal Stress and Cutback Management

Evidence of the factors of fiscal stress (weakened tax base, tax and expenditure limits, and reduced levels of federal assistance) is present in nearly all United States cities as we move into

From *Public Productivity Review*, vol. 13, no. 4 (Winter 1984), pp. 332–352. Copyright © 1984 by Jossey-Bass. Reprinted with permission.

the "crisis" period of the 1980s. While the term "crisis" is not a new one as it applies to either urban problems or fiscal federalism,[3] it is a very different type of crisis or stress situation this time.

> The fiscal crisis has made impossible the high expenditure approach to solving the social problems of urban America. Attention has been forced away from expansionary policies of program development and capital projects toward policies of *revenue generation, increased program productivity*, and expenditure cutbacks.[4]

The challenge before public managers to deal with the "cutback/retrenchment" period ahead is a very difficult one. Nearly all government institutions (at all levels) as well as private sector organizations were built and sustained under practices and theories grounded in assumptions of growth in both resource availability and organizational capacity.

> Put squarely, without growth, how do we manage public organizations? We have no ready or comprehensive answers to this question, only hunches and shards of evidence to serve as points of departure. Under conditions and assumptions of decline, the ponderables, puzzles, and paradoxes of organizational management take on new complexities. For example, organizations cannot be cut back by merely reversing the sequence of activity and resource allocation by which their parts were originally assembled.[5]

The intricate relationships between the government and the domestic economy add an additional layer of complexity. For example, there is the problem of inflation, which causes government expenditures to rise annually just to maintain existing service levels while at the same time its effect on the economy creates additional clients for public programs (social service, unemployment compensation, mass transit, etc.), as well as reducing the government's revenue raising capacity to provide the necessary services (at current or expanding levels). The challenge of "doing more with less" for an extended period of time will force governmental decision-makers to engage in comprehensive examinations of their objectives and exhaustive searches for new means of achieving the objectives judged to be essential.

In the past, crises and emergencies in the public sector have been of short duration and confined to a relatively small number of organizations. The current fiscal pressures are being felt throughout the society and show little sign of being short-term. The unprecedented level of business failures in the private sector indicates that the problems of organizational decline and retrenchment management are not issues for public sector consideration alone. Private sector management theorists have recently discovered that there is definite paucity in theory and research into how organizations, public and private, deal with the forces of decline and the necessary adjustments to new and usually lower levels of organizational activity. In many ways the "preoccupation with growth" mentality has caught up with both the practitioner and academic communities.[6] A growing number of researchers have felt that many of the traditional distinctions between private and public sector management have been overstated.[7] This has spawned both interdisciplinary and intersectoral searches for alternatives to the generic concept of organizational decline. The focus of this chapter is on the nature of fiscal management and productivity improvement strategies for cities, but the author will borrow from the literature of management theory where it is particularly appropriate.

Local Government Responses

Like any other organizational entity, a local government can be viewed as a system with the function of converting *inputs* (revenue and other resources) into *outputs* (public sector goods and services). A threat to the organization's operation necessarily must be met with some response in the form of changing the external input-output arrangement or the internal conversion process.

At the local level, the traditional response to a threat such as resource scarcity (fiscal areas) has been to increase taxes or tap other revenue sources (inputs) and/or reduce service expenditure levels (outputs). The administration of programs (conversion process), when carefully examined, can provide cost-savings that may be sufficient to cushion the effect of fiscal stress. While changes in administrative procedures and service delivery modes may not provide all the solutions, they may deserve more attention as an idle option between revenue generation and service reductions. Cities have found that changes in program administration (some quite logical and painless) allow them to avoid major reductions in service levels.

The level of the threat embodied in the current fiscal crisis situation facing many United States cities will likely require a strategy that combines changes on all three fronts. There have been numerous accounts in recent years of how cities have endeavored to:

1. Generate more revenue either from traditional or new sources;
2. Change the administration of programs through productivity improvements and other measures designed to maximize the utility of existing resources; and
3. Make selective or across-the-board cuts in services.

Local government officials have always been involved in these functions, but the current situation for many cities has created a much greater sense of urgency. For many cities, whatever can be done in the way of new revenue generation and program/administrative process changes will still not prevent service expenditure reductions and employee terminations.

Many cities have experienced either all or part of this dilemma for a decade or more.[8] The 1980s outlook on fiscal stress is that it has multiple causes (economic, political, and social) and that it is present at all levels of government (federal, state, and local). These two dimensions create a situation that is much more serious and long-term in nature than previous "crises" (real or perceived). Fiscal austerity is the rule of the day across the country. Conservative approaches to government activity, whether generated by public officials or the citizenry, have taken hold in the "rich" states as well as the "poor" ones.[9] The fact that real expenditure growth (from own funds) was halted at the state and local levels before President Reagan came into office has been obscured by the effects of inflation.[10] All of the evidence seems to be pointing to a contractionary period at the local government level that is unlikely to be of short duration.

The approach taken here will be to summarize some of the actions that cities have taken in the three response areas (options):

1. Revenue generation;
2. Productivity improvement (program/administrative process changes); and
3. Expenditure reductions.

Then the strategies of two cities, Charlotte, North Carolina, and Syracuse, New York, will be described and compared. The central question will be: *How are local governments responding to the forces of fiscal stress, and cutback management,* as defined by Charles H. Levine, ". . . managing organizational change toward lower levels of resource consumption and organizational activity?"[11]

Revenue Generation

Not long ago, the first revenue option that a city manager or mayor would pursue would be intergovernmental assistance. Federal grants to state and local governments have peaked and are currently on a course of precipitous decline in real terms. The current national economic situation has had a variable effect on the economies of the fifty states (the rich versus poor dichotomy), which leaves open the question of whether states can or will come to the aid of troubled cities. The general consensus is that cities should be prepared to view their revenue problems as situations that they must solve themselves. The situation that cities face in the traditional category of "own source revenue" is described by Robert J. Cline and John Shannon:

> Particularly significant is the accelerating decline in the share of municipal revenue raised through property taxes and the sharp upswing in user fees and other nonproperty tax revenues. The property taxes' relative decline can be partly attributed to the adoption of new state constraints on local expenditures and revenues during this period. Proposition 13 in California and Proposition 2½ in Massachusetts are examples of limitations that actually rolled back property tax rates and further limited the rate of increase in the local property tax base. . . . The upsurge in the use of service charges reflects the most logical way for local policymakers to reconcile the need for more revenue with the realities of voter resistance to increased property tax levels.[12]

In the quest for diversity in local revenue mix, city officials have been particularly aggressive in pursuing user fees and charges as well as increasing municipal borrowing (both short- and long-term).

At present there are many studies of the development of user charges and fees as a meaningful revenue source for local governments. Some services formerly provided without charge to residents were considered general responsibilities of government and costs were met from general taxes. However, as costs have increased, as property tax collections have leveled off, and as grants from federal and state governments have declined, many cities are examining the question of which public services should be provided free to all residents as distinguished from those that can be financed from user charges. Charges and fees have long been advocated by public finance economists as an "opportunity for a more efficient allocation and a more equitable distribution of public services."[13] But until recently they have been used quite sparingly for services such as utilities, library operation, and parks and recreation. In a major survey on the increased importance of charges and fees, the International City Management Association (ICMA) discovered that their role in city finance had grown from 23.7 percent of local tax revenue in 1970–71 to 31.6 percent in 1978–80.[14] At present, user charges are particularly important revenue items for small and medium size jurisdictions. The major service categories for which user charges are being implemented are sewage, airports, hospitals, and water provision. User charges and fees are major items for cities in states particularly hard hit by tax and expenditure limitations. The ACIR study of California (after Proposition 13) and Massachusetts (after Proposition 2½) reveals significant increases in this area.[15]

During the annual budget review in Detroit, agencies must explain why operating costs *cannot* be met by fees and charges rather than general fund revenues. A secondary development to the revived interest in charges and fees may be a change in the way they are administered. Jay Abrams comments:

> As communities increasingly come to recognize the gains to be realized from the adoption of fees and charges, so too, will they need to become more sophisticated in the setting of these fees. In the past, cities often set fees that bore no relation to the cost of producing the service and which often acted as a very poor rationing mechanism for the use of city

services. This situation might change as cities see charges as an increasingly important method of financing government services.[16]

Many of the local government services that are increasingly being supported by fees and charges for operating expenses (sewage, water, hospitals, etc.) have traditionally been supported by municipal borrowing. One of the most unfortunate legacies of the fiscal problems of United States cities is the long-term burdens that high debt service payments inflict on current expenditure options. The current condition of the capital infrastructure of many cities (roads, bridges, and public facilities) has forced many managers to borrow more and at higher rates in order to meet current maintenance requirements. The current penchant for new and largely unsecured forms of short-term borrowing is cause for a great deal of concern in the municipal finance community.[17]

But as John Peterson points out, city officials appear to have very little latitude at the present time:

> But, unfortunately, many of the same economic circumstances that have led to the deteriorating support for capital spending from federal grants and current revenues have reflected themselves in very unattractive credit market conditions, making borrowing a volatile and expensive means of raising funds for capital projects.[18]

An example of this problem is the "crowding out" thesis, which has become well known in recent years. This thesis refers to the effect of increasingly large federal deficits on the credit market during periods of restrictive monetary policy. In effect, federal borrowing raises the cost of borrowing for other actors (among them local governments) and forces many out of the market altogether.

Productivity Improvement: Program/Administrative Process Changes

Public sector productivity is traditionally defined as the relationship between the quantity and/or quality of public services produced and the amount of resources required to produce them. Productivity improvement occurs when service levels (quality and quantity) can be maintained despite declining resources, or in some instances where service levels are actually increased in the face of stable or declining resource consumption.[19] A recent survey concerning the use of productivity improvement in local government units lists the range of techniques in use:[20]

- The utilization of advanced technology;
- The use of outside resources;
- Consolidation and reorganization;
- Revision of operating procedures; and
- Improvement of employee performance.

This category of response to fiscal stress includes a number of opinions that cities could consider to avoid major reductions in expenditure levels. Most of the options here are either *service related* (changes in the content or form of service delivery) or *nonservice* (changes in administrative or central management procedures such as budgeting, purchasing, and information management). The literature on public sector productivity improvement is growing rapidly, and it includes a wide range of options in both of these categories.

Despite the attention in both literature and practice, the "challenge" of providing either

(a) more/better services for the same unit cost or (b) the same quantity and quality of services at lower unit costs is still very much with us.[21] The pressures for productivity improvement or more broadly-defined cost-effective modes of service delivery have never been greater for local governments than at the current time. The "do more with less" situations that cities increasingly find themselves in have drastically changed the traditional thinking about municipal budgeting. Techniques such as zero base and decremental budgeting are in place where managers no longer can assume current funding levels as a base for next year's estimates. Managers now must be concerned with defining minimum service levels which are considerably below current funding levels.

In a related area, fiscal pressures have forced city officials to re-think the traditional notion of service delivery (i.e., reliance on city employees). Increasingly, local government officials are providing public services without actually delivering (producing) the services. There are two major options that cities have devised to deal with the high costs of necessary services; intergovernmental agreements and using the private sector.

Intergovernmental agreements with either counties or nearby cities are on the increase for many programs in the health and human services area. Public safety (police, fire, and ambulance) provision is another area where local governments often pool resources. Contracting services out to the private sector is quite common at the city level in the areas of streets and sanitation, facilities maintenance, data processing, and information management.

In addition to these options, many local governments combine the traditional and new approaches to service delivery in ways such as volunteers supporting paid library staff or using existing city employees as bus drivers and trash collectors to augment the "private" provision of these services.

It should be noted that there are legal, political, and practical limitations to wholesale adoption of some of the options labeled alternative service delivery approaches. The point being made here is that these options deserve attention. A recent ICMA survey documents the fact that despite their limitations, these options and many others have not escaped the attention of managers and mayors across the country.[22]

Expenditure Reductions

When all else fails, cities are faced with expenditure reductions, service interruptions, and employee terminations. Events such as school closings, capital construction and maintenance delays, social service benefit cuts, and municipal employee R.I.F.'s are occurring all across the country. As mentioned before, fiscal problems are present in regions such as the urban South which were thought to be better insulated than the traditionally hard-pressed areas of the Northeast and industrial Midwest. Given the large scale of this forced experiment with cutback/retrenchment management, there is a growing body of literature involved with the analysis of municipal retrenchment issues.

In the beginning, most of the literature was devoted to the economic and demographic conditions that were considered *causes* of fiscal stress. Much of this literature (mid-1970s vintage) was devoted to examination of the New York City experience and was concerned with the extent to which other cities were likely to follow suit. In the interim period, there have been fiscal problems in other cities (although none of the scale of New York City) and to this date the examination of the nature of fiscal stress is a very active research area. As a result of the number and variety of cities experiencing fiscal stress, a new research area has emerged that is the examination of the *response* to fiscal stress, that is, the process and outcomes of urban retrenchment. At first, the research in this area was of a theoretical and hypothetical nature. It is well known that it is much easier to theorize about local governments than to actually study them in a systematic manner. But even with the difficulties associated with comparative urban research, individuals are going out into the field and conducting research studies on the nature of the strategies that cities have implemented to respond to fiscal stress as well as the distributional (service-related) consequences of cutbacks.[23]

An important point to be made here is that it is assumed that a city official will be concerned with decisions regarding what programs to cut and how only after other avenues (alternative revenue sources, managerial improvements, etc.) have been tried and found insufficient to support existing expenditure requirements.

The two most common cutback approaches are the "across-the-board cuts" and cutting weak or vulnerable programs. Jeremy F. Plant and Louise G. White describe these options as follows:

a. *Across-the-board cuts*—fixed percentage cuts applied to all (or most) agencies or programs. This strategy is an easily applied and often used tool; it is usually the "line of least resistance" . . . such a strategy has the merit of apparent equity and hence may be easier to sell to staff and the public.

b. *Cutting vulnerable programs*—a search for those programs which have been instituted most recently, which have had bad publicity, or which have a narrow constituency.[24]

Most researchers and practitioners acknowledge the weaknesses of both of these approaches to cutback decisions. A more comprehensive, program-centered system of linking city resources with overall goals and objectives to guide retrenchment decisions is usually beyond the political and managerial means of city officials. To do this, managers must be able to build alliances with other officials, the community, and other levels of government. As Charles H. Levine and others[25] have noted, coalition building in the era of declining resources is a very difficult proposition inasmuch as there are few "slack resources" to serve as rewards for cooperation.

One of the key measures associated with the ability to effect necessary cutback decisions is the concept of political power. The extent to which there is a strong, vocal constituency serviced by a particular program is a major determinant of whether the program will survive the austerity cuts.[26] In many instances, services without strong interest group support are also judged to be nonessential or low priority functions. It should be noted, however, that many cities have already either reduced or eliminated the weaker, nonessential programs and are now faced with the much more difficult decisions of how to reduce expenditures in the stronger, essential city services. While the judgment as to which services are essential/nonessential strong/weak varies from city to city, the problems of dealing with this phenomena are much more general in nature.

An even more important factor in designing an effective retrenchment strategy is the degree to which city officials recognize these fiscal problems and respond quickly, effectively, and decisively. As Levine et al. explain, there is a sequence of responses associated with fiscal stress which captures the essence of many of the difficulties facing distressed cities:

An early formulation of the process developed the idea of a *three-stage response* to fiscal stress in which the first set of responses includes ignoring the problem and utilizing delaying tactics; the second set of responses involves *rationing services and stretching resources in the face of resistance from many competing sources*; and the third set of responses involves *deep selective cutbacks and efforts to smooth operations after the cuts.*[27]

The division of the level of fiscal stress and resulting response stages is a very useful tool for comparative urban policy research. While the use of three stages (rather than four or five) may be restrictive, the evidence supports the notion that there are certain characteristics that cities exhibit in the early stages of fiscal stress that are quite different from those exhibited in a deeper and more long-term situation. A three-stage response approach will be used in the analysis of the two cities under study here.

Charlotte, North Carolina

Retrenchment Strategy

Despite the characterization of Charlotte as a healthy city, officials are aware of the problems of urban fiscal stress and some of the factors that could be characterized as growing pains. Among these problems are:

- Declining federal assistance which impacts Charlotte most seriously in the area of Mass Transit service;
- The concern over inflation and unemployment affects both the expenditure and revenue (sales tax) side of the city's budget equation; and
- Although the city has added both population and economic activity through annexation, it has incurred the requirement of providing city services (police, fire, water, sewage) to large and less dense population areas.

Perhaps the greatest problem that the city faces is the dominant conservative position taken by the citizenry as it relates to government in general and taxes in particular. The Charlotte area, as well as the State of North Carolina, had a tradition of fiscal conservatism that predates the national movement of the late 1970s. So even where there appears to be a comfortable tax margin, city officials are much more prone to seek other revenue alternatives. City officials over the years have been very wary of the dangers of overreliance on federal assistance. This approach has led officials (both appointed and elected) to view projects funded by federal grants as "quasi-luxuries" in the sense that they should be prepared to either do without the service or finance it by some other means. For example, the current and previous city managers have made it a policy to use revenue sharing funds for capital rather than operating purposes and disperse the funds to a variety of programs. The only service areas likely to be particularly hard-hit will be transportation (the city operated bus system) and sewage and water system construction.

It would appear that the conservative fiscal position that Charlotte adopted during the growth period of federal grants will serve it well during the decline period.

The city's retrenchment strategy includes elements of the three traditional responses outlined earlier:

- Search for new revenue;
- Productivity improvement (program/administrative process changes); and
- Service cuts and terminations.

Revenue Generation

1. At present the city has measures pending before the State legislature that would add an additional 1 percent to the local sales tax proceeds (currently at 4 percent) as well as

institute a hotel/motel occupancy tax for Charlotte-Mecklenburg. Both of these revenue sources would be shared by the city and the county. There appears to be genuine concern as to whether they will win legislative approval.

2. Residential and commercial property values were reassessed during the past year. The most conservative projections indicate a 20 percent increase in property tax revenue as a result of rising values. There is discussion at the county level of reducing the tax rate for the next budget year.

3. The city is currently engaging in a major study of the degree of utilization of existing fees and charges, as well as functions which could support new user charges.

4. The city is in a relatively good borrowing situation (both in terms of bond rating and debt ratio), which can support construction efforts previously financed with federal assistance. However, voter approval is necessary for all major borrowing issues, even for public enterprise operations.

Productivity Improvement: Program/Administrative Process Changes

1. The city instituted the Management by Objectives (MBO) system nearly a decade ago. This has made it possible for the city to better assess its revenue situation as it relates to its programmatic goals and objectives. The budget process does not exhibit the conflict and rancor sometimes present in other jurisdictions.

2. The city is in the process of negotiating with the county to merge administrative data processing and payroll information systems. The possibility of merging the dispatch systems for all of the city and county emergency personnel (city policy and fire, county police, and county emergency medical services) is also being investigated.

3. The city and county have merged the animal control and animal shelter operations that they previously operated separately. The new combined service will be run by the city using its facility, and most of the county staff was absorbed into the new operations.

4. The city-county bus system has been operated by a private sector firm for the past five years. Private sector contractors also manage a number of public facilities under the direction of a governing board of city, county, and private sector officials.

Service Cutbacks and Employee Reductions

Compared to most cities, Charlotte has experienced very few problems in this area. It has, however, instituted several measures under the MBO system to prioritize services in the event of serious deterioration in the city revenue structure.

1. There is a "general" employee hiring freeze in effect. This has resulted in a slight reduction in the number of employees over the past two years. Most of the reduction is due to attrition, but there have been layoffs in both transportation and public works.

2. There have been some social service programs (vocational training, counseling, and aid to the elderly) that the city has either terminated or turned over to the community service organizations for operation.

3. The only major change in level of service delivery is a reduction in the frequency of residential trash collection, leaves pickup, and street sweeping. Even this relatively minor reduction in services was initially met with citizen resistance.

Syracuse, New York

Retrenchment Strategy

To Syracuse, like most older Northeastern cities, the terms fiscal austerity and cutback management are not new ones. Declining population, tax-base erosion, high property taxes, loss of
economic strength to the suburbs, and all the associated socioeconomic problems of urban areas
have been experienced and more or less managed in Syracuse since the 1950s.

In the 1960s, spending in Syracuse was primarily for established programs, with only incremental budget increases due to inflation. The search for new revenue was directed at negotiating
the sharing of resources from items such as sales tax with the county. Less effort was made to seek
federal funds, because of the city administration's aversion to dependence on the federal government. Services cut were those which were least visible, or whose reduction could go unnoticed by
city residents for a period of time, such as capital improvements, equipment replacements, and so
forth. The major emphasis was on keeping taxes as low as possible.

The 1970s marked a change in management style and strategy for the city, as government
funding was actively sought. The strategy deployed consisted primarily of the creation of a
strong, semi-independent office, whose purpose was to obtain federal and state aid (the Office of
Federal and State Aid Coordination, known as OFSAC). Concurrently with the emphasis on
obtaining federal aid, productivity improvements were pursued; and reviews were made to determine if fees and user charges could be implemented or increased. Taxes were increased each year,
and new taxes were reviewed for implementation, although none were actually approved.

In 1977, however, the city reached its constitutional taxing limit. Budget adjustments were
made by across-the-board cuts for supplies, travel, and equipment. Politically weak programs
were funded at levels that allowed little more than a perfunctory performance of responsibilities.
Expenditure shifts to the capital budget and onto the county tax levy occurred where possible.
Federal and state monies allowed the city to continue and even to grow in certain program areas.
The tax limitation was subsequently eased by the state, but most of the practices brought about
by this limitation are still in effect. By 1980, the city had eliminated, by transferring to the
county, all the easily shifted programs, such as Health, Social Services, and planning. City staff
had been trimmed since 1970, so that all departments worked with a lean staffing arrangement.
Efficiency had been emphasized throughout the city; innovative tradeoffs of equipment for
personnel had been pursued in major departments such as Fire and Public Works.

When the 1980s began, the city had few options to cut costs. Using Levine's idea of a three-
stage response to fiscal stress, Syracuse had long been rationing services and stretching resources,
the second stage. Syracuse began moving toward the third stage of deep selective cuts with the
advent of the current federal aid reductions. The city administration had been preparing for this
eventuality since the late 1970s by setting up federally funded programs to function independently of regular city budgeting and administration. The separation of noncity funded programs
from city funded programs has made adjustments due to federal aid reductions "easier" to accomplish. Whole programs could disappear quickly with little disturbance to core city programs.
Departments such as Community Development were separated and funded by the city into those
areas that required funding by city mandate and those that did not. If the funding was no longer
available from federal sources the programs would be dropped, and the city would take over full
funding for only its mandated functions.

While it is possible to separate out those programs that were not city funded programs, it
is more difficult to take the steps to terminate workers. However, in 1981 these steps began.

Department heads drew up lists of programs and jobs to be eliminated and timetables that would stretch resources as far as possible. Departments that had been dependent in large measure on federal funding sources began shifting their work effort to objectives more in keeping with reduced staff and budgets. OFSAC, after losing about two-thirds of its work force, began shifting its efforts toward state lobbying and county issues.

Internally, the city reviewed possible consolidation plans for several departments and possible consolidation arrangements with the county. Specific programs were reviewed for reductions or outright elimination. Strong stands were taken concerning wage and salary increases. Property taxes were increased and a new round of review was undertaken to determine whether new taxes or charges were feasible. There were no across-the-board cuts. Those departments that were determined to be nonessential or politically weak were cut. It was decided that certain core services must be maintained. The departments providing these services received priority funding, although most departmental budgets were allowed only minimal increases, and certain budgets were actually cut.

While the primary thrust of Syracuse's strategy continues to be the seeking of outside revenue sources, the focus was shifted from a federal lobbying effort to a state and county effort. Issues concerning reimbursements for services provided to the state and county received increased attention. Syracuse continued to increase property taxes, fees and licenses, and user charges. Plans were also made for increased use of charges, particularly in those services used by noncity residents. Budgets were reduced in certain programs by reducing hours of operation, changing emphasis from active (programming) to maintenance functions, and postponement of capital improvements.

Syracuse has made use of a wide range of traditional retrenchment strategies, although some, such as user charges, departmental consolidation, and contracting of services, could be used to a greater extent. Many of these strategies, such as increasing property taxes, seem to intensify the problems of the city. The strategies that remain require in most instances state government as well as voter approval. Given the recent publicity concerning the problems of cities coping with cutbacks and the desire of residents to continue a broad range of services, it is possible that they will be implemented. Recent controversy with the county concerning nonresident use of city services and tax exempt properties also make the implementation of certain nontraditional strategies more likely now than previously would have been the case. Among these options are:

- Instituting user charges for tax exempt properties;
- Instituting an income tax or seat (facilities) tax; and
- Seeking county takeover of the city school district and increasing the local utilities tax.

There are signs that even though the city rejects the concept of metropolitan government, it will not be able to support the broad range of services now provided with local revenue sources, and metropolitan government on county terms will be the most likely outcome.

Concluding Observations

The first and most evident observation to be made about Syracuse and Charlotte is that they are in very different fiscal and political situations. Syracuse, a city in decline, has been forced to deal with the problems associated with all three stages of fiscal stress/cutback management (as described by Levine). Charlotte, on the other hand, has felt few serious fiscal pressures, due in large part, to a healthy economy which fiscally (but not politically) could support an expansion rather than a contraction of municipal services. While Charlotte has pursued retrenchment strategies in all of the categories mentioned, the level of urgency does not compare to that of cities such as Syracuse. Charlotte has instituted some changes in revenue structure and managerial processes, and is prepared to respond further if the local fiscal situation deteriorates further (in the Levine schema, Charlotte would be somewhere between stages one and two). In contrast, Syracuse has gone through the entire cycle of cutback stages and is currently in a position where more "rationing and stretching" and outside (county or state) assistance is necessary to avoid deeper service cuts.

Even with the obvious differences in fiscal conditions, governmental processes, and overall political cultures, there are some common areas present in the retrenchment strategies developed by both Syracuse and Charlotte.

1. Both cities are seeking to diversify their revenue mix—in response to federal aid reductions and also as a means to hold down local property taxes. Ironically, the citizen acceptance of property tax increases is greater in Syracuse.
2. Both jurisdictions are attempting to change their management processes and service delivery arrangements through the traditional methods (budget reforms, service consolidations, productivity improvements, etc.).
3. Based on this comparative analysis, there is mixed support for the notion that there is a sequence of retrenchment management responses which is associated with the perceived level of fiscal stress. The Syracuse case provides initial support for this concept. However, both cities exhibit a tendency to resort to combined responses at all three levels rather than exhausting (1) new revenue source options before proceeding to (2) process changes and (3) service reductions.

Even in jurisdictions as dramatically different in political and fiscal terms as Charlotte and Syracuse the importance of productivity improvement for municipal management is apparent. While the range of techniques and their sophistication varies, it is clear that productivity improvement is given top priority consideration by local government managers in both growing and declining regions. As stated previously, the combination of high service demands and scarce resources has forced this point home for government officials at all levels. The evidence here illustrates the point that concerns for effectiveness and efficiency are present at all three stages of retrenchment strategy development.

In recent years the public administration community has played a vital role in disseminating information about the value of productivity improvement to governmental management at all levels. It is no small coincidence that many journal articles, conference proceedings, and workshops have been dedicated to this theme over the past decade. Despite this attention, there are still many local managers who are unaware of the value of productivity improvement management; or where they are aware they are unable to afford the investment in more sophisticated computer and technological innovations. Equally important are the obstacles presented by employee or political interest group opposition to changing either existing administrative processes or service delivery arrangements. One area that needs much more attention in the future is the important linkage between productivity improvement efforts and other administrative processes such as municipal budgeting and personnel management.

This also would appear to be an area where greater cooperation between state and local governments would be appropriate. Many of the management problems that plague cities and counties are also concerns for managers at the state level. In most instances, state resources to be devoted to exploring new and existing productivity efforts are greater than those at the local level. This potential state-local partnership of mutual value could take the form of information dissemination, workshop and technical assistance exchanges, and perhaps joint acquisition and use of the more sophisticated technology of the field.

The problems created by the forces of fiscal austerity and cutback management at the local level are indeed difficult ones. But experience across the country has shown these problems to be manageable. As long as the public administration practitioner and research communities continue their efforts at devising new managerial and problem-solving tools, the situation will never be as bleak as it seems.

Notes

1. For an extensive anthology of public sector productivity theory and practices, see *Productivity Improvement Handbook for State and Local Government*, George J. Washnis, ed. (New York: John Wiley, 1980).

2. Elaine Morley, "Using Productivity Improvement as a Managerial Strategy During a Period of Retrenchment" (paper presented at the 1983 Annual Meeting of the American Society for Public Administration, April 17, 1983), p. 2.

3. There is a large body of literature on the history of crisis situations in both urban policy and fiscal federalism. See David B. Walker, *Toward a Functioning Federalism* (Cambridge, MA: Winthrop, 1981); Gary A. Tobin, ed., *The Changing Structure of the City: What Happened to the Urban Crisis* (Beverly Hills, CA: Sage, 1979); Jesse Burkhead and Guthrie S. Burkhead, "Yet Another Crisis in Fiscal Federalism?" *The Ways and Means Report* (Albany, NY: New York Assembly Ways and Means Committee, summer 1981).

4. Charles H. Levine, Irene S. Rubin, and George G. Wolohojian, *The Politics of Retrenchment: How Local Governments Manage Fiscal Stress* (Beverly Hills, CA: Sage, 1981), p. 11, emphasis added.

5. Levine, "Cutback Management," *Public Administration Review* 38, no. 4 (July/August 1978): 317.

6. See David A. Whetten, "Organizational Decline: A Neglected Topic in Organizational Science," *Academy of Management Review 1980* 5, no. 4 (1980): 577–588; Victor V. Murray and Todd D. Jick, "Strategic Decision Responses to Hard Times in Public Sector Organizations," *Academy of Management Proceedings* (1981): 339–343.

7. The generic management movement grew in response to the position that despite important differences in context, business and government management have many structural and process features in common. The current emphasis on resource scarcity in both sectors once again calls us to examine the nature of the similarities between public and private sector management. See Barry Bozeman and Jeffrey D. Straussman, "Organizations' 'Publicness' and Resource Management Strategies" (paper presented at the Conference on Organization Theory and Public Policy, State University of New York at Albany, New York, April 1–2, 1982).

8. The fiscal problems of American cities were in evidence even before the 1974–75 New York crisis. See, for example, *City Financial Emergencies: The Intergovernmental Dimension*, Report A-42 (The Advisory Commission on Intergovernmental Relations, Washington, DC, July 1973).

9. See Robert J. Cline and John Shannon, "Municipal Revenue Behavior After Proposition 13."

10. Real local expenditure from own funds actually peaked in 1974, and at the state level real expenditure peaked in 1976. To further illustrate the change in fiscal federalism as well as the effects of inflation, it should also be noted that in real terms federal aid to state and local governments peaked in 1978.

11. Levine, "More on Cutback Management: Hard Questions for Hard Times," *Public Administration Review* 39, no. 2 (March/April 1979): 180.

12. Cline and Shannon, "Municipal Revenue Behavior After Proposition 13," p. 22.

13. See Selma J. Mushkin and Charles L. Vehorn, "User Fees and Charges," in *Managing Fiscal Stress: The Crisis in the Public Sector,* ed. Charles H. Levine (Chatham, NJ: Chatham, 1980).

14. Maurice Criz, "The Role of User Charges and Fees in City Finance," *Urban Data Service Report* 14, no. 6 (Washington, DC: International City Management Association, June 1982).

15. Cline and Shannon, "Municipal Revenue Behavior After Proposition 13."

16. Jay H. Abrams, "Local Government Finance: Realities and Directions," *Public Budgeting and Finance* 11, no. 1 (Spring 1982): 7.

17. In the aftermath of New York City and Cleveland, the nature of local government borrowing practices has received more intense scrutiny by federal government officials, the research community, and particularly bond rating agencies. The ratio of short- to long-term debt has become a generally recognized measure of fiscal health (or the lack thereof).

18. John E. Peterson, "Creative Capital Financing in the State and Local Sector," *Public Budgeting and Finance* 2, no. 4 (Winter 1982): 74.

19. The broader definitions of productivity currently include considerations of service quality and satisfaction of citizenry expectations (effectiveness) as well as the optimal relationship of outputs to inputs (efficiency).

20. W. Maureen Godsey, "Productivity Improvement in Small Local Governments," *Urban Data Service Reports* 14, no. 7 (Washington, DC: International City Management Association, July 1982), p. 4.

21. Nancy C. Hayward, "The Productivity Challenge" in *Managing Fiscal Stress: The Crisis in the Public Sector*, ed. Charles H. Levine, pp. 259–268.

22. Martha A. Shulman, "Alternative Approaches for Delivering Public Service," *Urban Data Service Reports* 14, no. 10 (Washington, DC: International City Management Association, October 1982).

23. This is the purpose behind the *Fiscal Austerity and Urban Innovation Project*, a nationwide effort to gather data on the retrenchment behavior of all U.S. cities with populations in excess of 25,000. See Terry Nichols Clark, ed., *Urban Policy Analysis* (Beverly Hills, CA: Sage, 1981).

24. Jeremy F. Plant and Louise G. White, "The Politics of Cutback Budgeting: An Alliance Building Perspective," *Public Budgeting and Finance* 2, no. 1 (Spring 1982): 66.

25. See Levine, "More on Cutback Management: Hard Questions for Hard Times," in Levine, Rubin, and Wolohojian, *The Politics of Retrenchment.*

26. See Murray and Jick, "Strategic Decision Responses."

27. Levine, Rubin, and Wolohojian, "Managing Organizational Retrenchment: Preconditions, Deficiencies, and Adaptations in the Public Sector," *Administration and Society* 14, no. 1 (May 1982): 120–122.

CHAPTER 24

APPLYING STRATEGIC DECISION MAKING IN LOCAL GOVERNMENT

GREGORY STREIB

Strategic decision making was first introduced to government in the form of strategic planning which had already developed a considerable track record in the private sector. Many authors promoted the technique as a way to help governments cope with an increasingly unstable environment (McConkey 1981; Dodge and Eadie 1982; Eadie 1983; Bozeman 1983; Stevens 1984; Sorkin, Ferris, and Hudak 1984; Denhardt 1985; Maxwell 1990). While there are many variations on the strategic decision-making theme (Bryson and Roering 1987; Bryson 1988), most approaches contain the following components:

- A mission statement that establishes goals and objectives
- An environmental scan to identify key factors and trends important for the future
- An organizational scan to identify the organization's strengths and weaknesses
- Identification of strategic objectives and implementation
- Reviews and updates to monitor implementation and assess effectiveness.

While the strategic decision-making bandwagon has scarcely slowed in recent years, questions have arisen about the normative implications of applying a results-oriented private sector tool to the process-dominated world of government (Swanstrom 1985, 1987), and about the practical value of the strategic process (Gargan 1984, 1990; Streib and Poister 1989; Streib 1991). Even former supporters have voiced concerns. Bryson and Roering (1988, 995), for example, recently stated that "whatever the merits of strategic planning in the abstract, normal expectations have to be that most efforts to produce fundamental decisions and actions in government through strategic planning will not succeed." Defenders have argued that the usefulness of the strategic process can be greatly increased by fusing efforts to establish meaningful strategic objectives with traditional management control functions (Ansoff, DeClerck, and Hayes 1976; Schendel and Hofer 1979; Ansoff 1984; Steiss 1985; Montanari, Daneke, and Bracker 1990). The resulting hybrid known as strategic management, is a dynamic process that can facilitate the integration of organizational and individual goals (Korten 1984; Bracker and Pearson 1980). Others have argued that circumstances will often require focusing strategic efforts on a limited number of issues (Ansoff 1980; Eadie and Steinbacher 1985; Eadie 1985, 1986), or some type of incremental process (Quinn 1980; Hayes 1985; Methe and Perry 1990).

From *Public Productivity & Management Review*, vol. 15, no. 3 (Spring 1992), pp. 341–354. Copyright © 1992 by Jossey-Bass. Reprinted with permission.

This chapter argues that whereas authors have been right to question the usefulness of strategic decision-making techniques for government applications, no one has yet to illuminate fully the difficulties involved in effective use of this demanding technique. Failure to recognize the obstacles to effective strategic decision making could encourage wasted effort. Government officials need to understand fully the complexities of these techniques before they can decide if they are appropriate for their needs. A secondary goal of this chapter is to suggest some ways to employ management resources more effectively.

The Challenge of Integration

Although many view strategic decision making as a new innovation, it remains a comprehensive, integrative approach with roots in the same systems perspective as such widely recognized management failures as PPBS [Planning, Programming and Budgeting System] and ZBB [Zero-Base Budgeting] (Gargan 1984, 1990; Swanstrom 1985, 1987; Montanari and others 1990; Klay 1990). Even though many authors view the focus on strategies as avoiding the frailties of synoptic analysis (Lindblom 1979; Ansoff 1984; Steiss 1985; Bryson 1988; Klay 1990), as conventionally portrayed, the process must still pull together a variety of management functions if it is to produce significant benefits. You cannot have a partial strategic decision-making process; you either have the whole, unified process, or you have nothing. Bryson and Roering (1988) noted that "effective strategic planning is like a quilt. You need all of the pieces before you can stitch together an interesting pattern" (1002).

The pieces that comprise a successful strategic effort are difficult to define (Eadie 1986, 1990; Shapek and Richardson 1990), but the following four management functions are critical:

1. Leadership: the ability of key actors to initiate, organize, and direct a strategic effort
2. Human resources: the ability of supportive individuals to help make important decisions and implement necessary programs and policies
3. Managerial skills: the ability to establish effective control over management process and provide analytical support for strategic efforts
4. External support: the ability to satisfy external demands on the organization with limited disruption of internal processes, the willingness of external actors to provide vigorous support for decisions made as a part of the strategic process, and the financial means to handle the costs of developing a strategic effort.

Skillful execution of these four management functions does not give an organization the ability to make effective use of strategic decision making. It is only after integrating these functions that an organization has the potential to develop a successful strategic effort. Without integration, an organization will not be able to focus its efforts on specific strategic objectives. Figure 24.1 illustrates the relationship between the management functions and the ability to make effective use of strategic decision making. In this disassociated state, clear paths exist for integration, but steady progress toward integration is necessary in all areas, more or less simultaneously, if strategic potential is to be attained. Until strategic potential has been attained, there is little chance that an organization can successfully develop a strategic decision-making effort.

Figure 24.2 illustrates the transition to total strategic potential. In the left-hand part of the figure we see the situation where all management functions have begun to assume some basic elements of strategic thinking. An organization at this stage has long since achieved a high level of skill in all management functions and displays some minimal progress toward integrating

Figure 24.1 **Management Functions in a State of Disassociation**

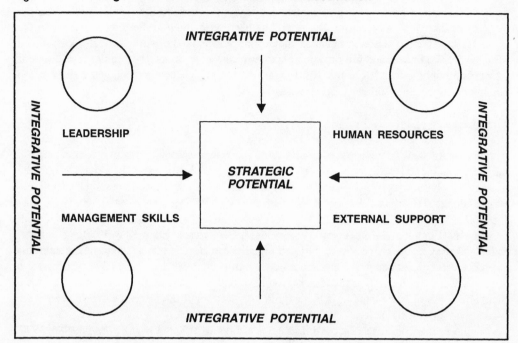

these functions. Despite this accomplishment, however, an organization at this stage would not have achieved total strategic potential. It is at this stage that all management functions are totally integrated and effective strategic decision making is possible. Organizations at this stage may incorporate many strategic decision-making concepts in their activities, but they need not ever develop a large-scale strategic decision-making effort.

The figures help to emphasize the difficulties involved in strategic decision making. It is likely that there are many local governments that cannot skillfully perform at least one of the management functions, and many more that are not able to proceed to integration. Unfortunately, these are the very local governments that might turn to strategic decision making to enhance the effectiveness of their organization. These governments might achieve better results by focusing their energy on management problems or integration, rather than engaging in some type of strategic decision-making exercise. This analysis suggests what might be considered a kind of universal law governing the feasibility of strategic decision making: *the greater the need for strategic decision making, the less likely that strategic decision making will be possible.*

It should be stressed that this assessment says nothing about the overall merit of strategic processes. This analysis suggests that techniques such as strategic planning and strategic management may be more difficult than many local government officials realize, but it does not offer any wisdom concerning the overall merit of these techniques. The existing research indicates that local governments have a positive opinion of strategic decision making (Gargan 1984; Streib and Poister 1989; Streib 1991), but all studies to date have raised questions about the ability of local governments to use these techniques effectively. The desirability of strategic decision making is not the issue. At this time many local governments are contemplating a strategic effort, and the officials involved need to understand the type of commitment that will be necessary. The

Figure 24.2 **Management Functions Moving Toward Total Strategic Potential**

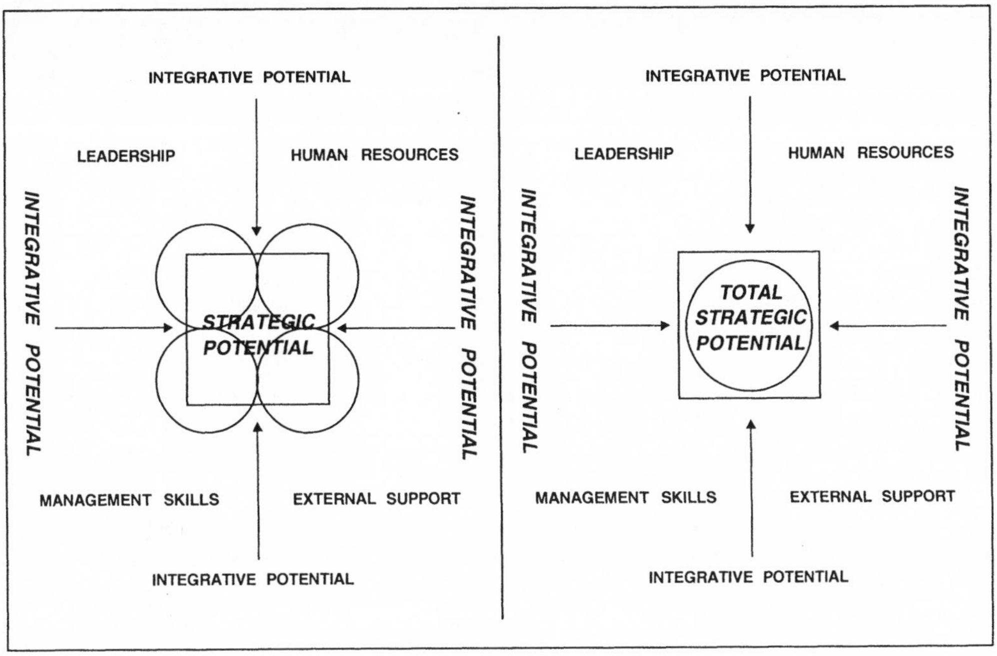

challenge of developing strategic potential will be explored by taking a closer look at the four management functions discussed above.

Meeting Leadership Needs

Few authors have discussed the implementation of public sector strategic decision making without emphasizing the need for vigorous, competent leadership. Olsen and Eadie (1982), for example, argued that the chief executive officer was the organization's preeminent strategist, and that even neutrality on the part of this individual was enough to cripple a strategic decision-making effort. Hosmer (1982, 47) summarized the importance of leadership in the following passage: "Leadership is important; it is not an outmoded concept from a less scientific and more romantic age, and there is a need for leaders, properly defined, within an organization to make strategic planning something more than 'muddling through' or an incremental process."

Another perspective on leadership in the strategic decision-making process stresses the need for a single individual to accept primary responsibility for the success of a strategic management effort. After a study of eight different types of governmental units, Bryson and Roering (1988, 1000) concluded that "successful initiation of strategic planning" required "a strong process champion."

Other useful leadership characteristics include the ability to work effectively with elected officials and senior managers (Eadie 1986, 1990), the ability to work on the formulation of strategic goals and implementation (Hosmer 1982), and some type of unifying, comprehensive vision (Bryson 1988). Bennis and Nanus (1985) found that the ability to define and pursue an attractive organizational future was a key component of effective leadership. This argument was echoed by Kouzes and Posner (1987), who found that the ability to articulate a desirable future was one important aspect of moving organizations to do extraordinary things. Although there is no reason to believe that effective strategic decision making requires a leader with all of the characteristics that various authors have listed, the writing to date does suggest that accomplishing extraordinary things requires an extraordinary leader. As Klay (1900, 435) noted, "strategic management places a momentous burden on leaders."

Given the nature of the challenge, there is some reason to question the extent to which the public sector (or private, for that matter) possesses the level of leadership necessary to achieve in local governments.

There are many local government forms, but virtually all of them exhibit some type of friction between elected officials and appointed administrators. To some, this may indicate the need for an integrative mechanism such as strategic decision making. However, as discussed above, strategic decision making *requires* integration, it does not *produce* integration. Strategic decision making will only be possible in local governments if elected and appointed officials can first establish constructive working relationships. Eadie (1986, 2) argued that in council-manager governments the city manager needed to assume the role of "chief executive officer" and "accept responsibility for designing and supporting a strong council role in policy formulation" in order to make strategic decision making possible.

The existing literature gives little reason to doubt the ability of city managers to exhibit a leadership role in policy matters (Adrian 1958; Stone, Price, and Stone 1940; Newell and Ammons 1987; Svara 1989), and it is possible that mayors in council-manager governments could aid in enhancing the relationship between the manager and the council. But it seems unrealistic to expect elected and appointed officials to maintain a shared vision of their respective roles and community goals over an extended period. This is true simply because elections and staff changes are likely to disrupt even the best working relationships.

Other forms of municipal government are even less likely to offer the comprehensive leadership required for strategic decision making. In mayor-council governments, for example, there is some evidence that the mayor is likely to spend more time on politics and less on management and policy than a city manager (Newell and Ammons 1987). While many of these governments possess a general manager who administers the executive function, these individuals also fail to assume the "responsibility which is found in the position of city manager" (Anderson 1989, 25). The prospects for strategic decision making are even less promising for county governments, where the prevalence of commission governments (Snider 1952; Duncombe 1966; Blake, Salant, and Boroshok 1989), weaker appointed managers (Cape 1967), and power fragmentation among constitutional row officers could stifle integration (Advisory Commission on Intergovernmental Relations 1981; DeSantis 1989; Streib and Waugh [1991]). Upton (1981) clearly captured the challenge of county management when he stated that it was like "goin' bear huntin' with a switch" because of the lack of executive authority (Upton 1981).

Given the nature of the challenge, it is likely that only a minority of local governments possess, and can maintain, the level of leadership required by strategic decision making. If this is the case, strategic decision making is likely to be less effective than might be expected. Or more likely, the benefits would be short-lived, coming to a halt when leadership support crumbled. It also must be remembered that even when effective leadership exists, the other three components of strategic potential are still important. For example, a supportive human resource base would be essential to a successful strategic decision-making effort. This management function will be discussed further in the next section.

Meeting the Need for Human Resources

Strategic decision making places significant burdens on an organization's human resources. In a local government context this includes members of the elected policy body and support staff.

Apart from skill needs, success requires the attitudes and cognitive factors that support human relationships and encourage the acceptance of the new tasks that would accompany a strategic effort. These factors amount to what Eadie (1990) has called what an organization "will do."

Many writers view the human resource needs of strategic decision making as largely intangible. For example, Methe and Perry (1990, 44) noted that "to a great extent strategic management processes are cognitive. They are driven by the personal knowledge, perceptions and limitations of organizational actors, rather than purely, or even primarily, rational and objective processes." Many authors argue that organizations must possess a culture of success that drives its members to strive continually to maintain and expand organizational performance.

In an organization that can maintain a high level of strategic potential, there is likely to be a mutually supportive relationship between the leader and the human resource base. It is difficult to envision a high level of strategic capacity in one area and not the other. The question of which of these two factors precedes the other is likely to vary from one form of government to another, though the leader who seeks to build up human resources to achieve strategic capacity would have to cope with a variety of forces that threaten productivity and motivation (Greiner and others 1981; Ammons 1985). Of course, in the case of a city manager, an elected city council would constitute most of the human resource base, and significant alterations would probably be impossible.

Failure to maintain a high level of integration between leadership and human resources would likely lead to a condition that Shapek and Richardson (1990) have described as a responsibility gap. This results from the natural tendency of elected officials, who have primary responsibility for policy implementation, to ignore long-range concerns in favor of short-term solutions. Close cooperation between elected officials and administrators could help to avoid this difficulty. Also, the lack of cooperation could create a high level of confusion that would eventually lead to chaos (Alchian 1950). As Methe and Perry (1990) have pointed out, the greater the level of disagreement, the greater the resources expended in bargaining. At some point, this would make the strategic decision-making process too time consuming to be practical.

Meeting the Need for Management Capacity

The literature suggests that effective use of strategic decision making requires a high level of management skill. This perspective is very different from the traditionally low-key approach to local government capacity that adopted the guiding principle, you are only as good as you have to be (Gargan 1981). While use of strategic decision making does not imply a commitment to perform at a higher level than is necessary, the spirit of the technique denotes a perception that organizations must seek the highest possible levels of efficiency and effectiveness to survive in a hostile environment. There is an implicit assumption that strategic decision making would not be needed in a nonthreatening environment (Sorkin, Ferris, and Hudak 1984).

The literature suggests that organizations seeking to master strategic decision making should have skill in the following areas:

- Basic management technology consisting of managerial experience and expertise and the management processes necessary to accomplish organizational objectives (Lenz 1980, 1981). This could include such activities as financial management (payroll, accounting, inventory, purchasing, and the like), personnel management, and contract management (Eadie 1990).
- The capacity to develop and analyze materials that would be part of conventional long-range planning (Eadie 1986, 190).

- Management control techniques that could be used to steer an organization toward the achievement of long-term objectives (Carlson 1978; Eadie 1990). As a part of this process, organizations need the ability to monitor current and proposed strategic actions against key external factors and the organization's internal environment (Shapek and Richardson 1990). Many consider effective use of management by objectives to be an essential part of a strategic management effort (Steiss 1985; Klay 1990).
- An organizational structure that does not impede the flow of strategic information. Such barriers could "impede or enhance an organizational strategy implementation in the same way that organizational culture affects the process" (Shapek and Richardson 1990, 224).

While the existing research does not adequately deal with all forms of local government, there is substantial evidence that local government officials possess a high level of management skill (Poister and Streib 1989; Streib and Poister 1989), and that they are generally confident about their abilities to govern effectively (Waugh and Streib 1990). If a government attained the requisite leadership and human resource base, it is unlikely that management skill would pose a considerable barrier to effective strategic decision making. The final component of strategic potential, however, deals with an area that may pose significant difficulties.

Meeting the Need for External Political Support

The literature on strategic decision making stresses the importance of the relationship between an organization and its stakeholders (Lenz 1980, 1981; Nutt and Backoff 1987). Stakeholders are defined as "any person, group, or organization that can place a claim on an organization's attention, resources, or output, or is affected by that output" (Bryson 1988, 52). To a local government, support from stakeholders could translate into a broad base of support for programs and policies. Negotiation with stakeholders can be an essential part of establishing organizational goals and objectives (Lindblom 1959; Mintzberg 1979). This type of highly political activity is an inescapable part of the strategic process (Pettigrew 1977).

The political nature of the strategic decision-making process presents problems for local government officials because many factors that influence stakeholders' attitudes are beyond their control. There is no question that "general economic, political, and social conditions and their rates of change" are not amenable to influence by an organization (Methe and Perry 1990, 42). In this complex environment it would be very difficult to achieve the level of agreement on policy issues, or even basic values, that would be essential to maintaining the strategic process. As noted above under the heading of human resources, environmental turbulence can greatly limit the ability of an organization to maintain the strategic process. The amount of negotiations needed to sustain the effort would eventually become unacceptable.

On a much more basic level, it is more likely that day-to-day citizen demands consume enough organizational energy to limit the ability of many local governments to consider any type of strategic decision making (Eadie 1990). Evidence from a recent study of council-manager governments by Streib (1991) offers some support for this argument. In this study, even those municipalities that had made extensive use of strategic decision making reported that diverse external political pressures were a threat to their efforts.

Of all four management functions, external political support is probably the most difficult to maintain. This is particularly true in the present era, because citizens do not hold government in high regard and continue to demand increased services from local governments that have declining resources. Furthermore, it must be emphasized that engaging in strategic decision making is not likely to promote citizen support; strong external political support is necessary before a local government has the potential to develop an effective strategic decision-making effort.

Conclusion

Although this chapter has illustrated many difficulties involved in the use of strategic decision-making techniques, it is not intended as an attack upon strategic thinking. The idea that local government officials should work to envision the role of their organization within a dynamic environment is very valuable. Trouble arises when this simple notion becomes an elaborate decision-making exercise driven by the premise [that] the local government can be molded and shaped to reach the specific objectives of a small group of individuals.

The central theme of this chapter is that strategic decision making, as commonly described, is simply too demanding for many local governments to use effectively. The approach has a great deal in common with the synoptic model of decision making that authors such as Lindblom (1959, 1979) rallied against. Furthermore, pursuit of strategic decision making without the achievement of total strategic potential is likely to yield unsatisfactory results. Gabris (1989, 161), for example, noted that such efforts often coupled "halcyon expectations" with "insufficient knowledge" to produce "frustrating, marginal, or disappointing outcomes." By emphasizing the potential for unsatisfactory results, this article may help local government officials make an informed choice about whether they should begin a strategic decision-making effort.

Given the difficulty of the strategic decision-making process, there may be a tendency to seek alternatives that limit the need for integration (incrementalism) or the scope of the effort (strategic issue management). Incremental approaches limit the need for integration by allowing strategies to emerge from a series of "strategic formulation subsystems" (Quinn 1980, 16). Each of these subsystems involves different groups of individuals and focuses around a specific issue or activity. While such an idea corresponds to the fractionalized decision making found in government, the catch is that this approach requires a powerful leader able to maintain integration. Nevertheless, this approach may be useful in local governments that have at least one skillful individual with a strong desire to develop and manage a strategic decision-making effort. A cautionary note is that this individual should expect to spend a great deal of time bargaining with and among the various subsystems and external political forces, since the process would not have developed from an integrated environment.

Eadie (1990, 169) advocated the use of "strategic issue management," which he said would help an organization to develop a "dynamic strategic change agenda" that would "keep an organization in balance with its ever-changing environment." The key to this approach is that the change agenda does not deal with the full range of organizational activities. This approach would be ideal for an organization that faced only a few easily identified problems, though integration would still be needed among the individuals working to solve these problems. Also, this approach could not focus the efforts of the entire organization, as could a more comprehensive approach (Ansoff 1980). Given these shortcomings, it would be incorrect to view this approach as a substitute for other strategic decision-making techniques.

The basic principle of seeking to make use of the strategic concept without falling into the trap of synopsis is never to expect strategic decision making to "build" organizational capacity, and never to seek "completeness" (Lindblom 1979, 519). For local government applications, the most effective approaches are likely to be those that seek to do little more than establish some general objectives, most of which can be expected to be modified at some future date. This type of effort would be consistent with what Gabris (1989) presented as "strategic goal setting."

In the final analysis, the greatest contribution of strategic decision making has probably been to popularize the idea of strategic thinking. While this concept has a long history, it has yet to play a major role in government decision making. In time, a level of consensus will develop on how best to apply strategic thinking to the local government environment. In the meantime, local government managers would be wise to consider the barriers to effective use of strategic decision making in its current form.

References

Adrian, C. 1958. "Leadership and Decision Making in Manager Cities." *Public Administration Review* 18: 208–213.

Advisory Commission on Intergovernmental Relations. 1981. *State and Local Roles in the Federal System.* Washington, DC: Advisory Commission on Intergovernmental Relations.

Alchian, A. 1950. "Uncertainty, Evolution, and Economic Organization." *American Economic Review* 58: 211–221.

Ammons, D.N. 1985. "Common Barriers to Productivity Improvement in Local Government." *Public Productivity Review* 9: 292–310.

Anderson, E. 1989. "Two Major Forms of Government: Two Types of Professional Management." *The Municipal Yearbook.* Washington, DC: International City Management Association.

Ansoff, H.I. 1980. "Strategic Issue Management." *Strategic Management Journal* 1: 131–148.

———. 1984. *Implementing Strategic Management.* Englewood Cliffs, NJ: Prentice-Hall.

Ansoff, H.I., R.P. Declerck, and R.I. Hayes, eds. 1976. *From Strategic Planning to Strategic Management.* New York: Wiley.

Bennis, W., and B. Nanus. 1985. *Leaders: The Strategies for Taking Charge.* New York: HarperCollins.

Blake, R.J., T.J. Salant, and A.L. Boroshok. 1989. *County Government Structure.* Washington, DC: National Association of Counties.

Bozeman, B. 1983. "Strategic Public Management and Productivity: A 'Firehouse' Theory." *State Government* 56: 2–7.

Bracker, J.S., and J.N. Pearson. 1980. "Planning and Financial Performance of Small, Mature Firms." *Strategic Management Journal* 7: 219–224.

Bryson, J.M. 1988. *Strategic Planning for Public and Nonprofit Organizations: A Guide to Strengthening and Sustaining Organizational Achievement.* San Francisco, CA: Jossey-Bass.

Bryson, J.M., and W.D. Roering. 1987. "Applying Private-Sector Strategic Planning in the Public Sector." *Journal of the American Planning Association* 53: 9–22.

———. 1988. "Initiation of Strategic Planning by Governments." *Public Administration Review* 48: 995–1004.

Cape, W.H. 1967. *The Emerging Patterns of County Executives.* Lawrence: University of Kansas Governmental Research Center.

Carlson, T.S. 1978. "Long Range Strategic Planning: Is It for Everyone?" *Long Range Planning* 11: 54–61.

Denhardt, R.D. 1985. "Strategic Planning in State and Local Government." *State and Local Government Review* 17: 174–179.

DeSantis, V.S. 1989. "County Government: A Century of Change." *The Municipal Yearbook.* Washington, DC: International City Management Association.

Dodge, W.R., Jr., and D. Eadie. 1982. "Strategic Planning: An Approach to Launching New Initiatives in an Era of Retrenchment." *MIS Report* 14, no. 9: 1–13.

Duncombe, H.S. 1966. *Modern County Government.* Washington, DC: National Association of Counties.

Eadie, D.C. 1983. "Putting a Powerful Tool to Practical Use: The Application of Strategic Planning in the Public Sector." *Public Administration Review* 43: 447–452.

———. 1985. "Strategic Agenda Management: A Marriage of Organizational Development and Strategic Planning." *National Civic Review* 74: 15–20.

———. 1986. "Strategic Issue Management: Improving the Council-Manager Relationship." *MIS Report* 18: entire report.

———. 1990. "Identifying and Managing Strategic Issues: From Design to Action." In *Handbook of Strategic Management*, ed. J. Rabin, G.J. Miller, and W.B. Hildreth. New York: Marcel Dekker.

Eadie, D.C., and R. Steinbacher. 1985. "Strategic Agenda Management: A Marriage of Organizational Development and Strategic Planning." *Public Administration Review* 45: 424–430.

Gabris, G.T. 1989. "Educating Elected Officials in Strategic Goal Setting." *Public Productivity and Management Review* 13, no. 2: 161–175.

Gargan, J. 1981. "Consideration of Local Government Capacity." *Public Administration Review* 41: 649–658.

———. 1984. "An Assessment of the State of the Art in Strategic Planning by City Governments." Unpublished report. Urban University Program, Kent State University.

———. 1990. "Strategic Management in City Government: Continuing the Interplay of Rationality and Politics." In *Handbook of Strategic Management*, ed. J. Rabin, G.J. Miller, and W.B. Hildreth. New York: Marcel Dekker.

Greiner, J.M., H.P. Hatry, M.P. Koss, A.P. Millar, and J.P. Woodward. 1981. *Productivity and Motivation: A Review of State and Local Government Initiatives.* Washington, DC: Urban Institute Press.

Hayes, R.H. 1985. "Strategic Planning: Forward in Reverse." *Harvard Business Review* 63: 111–119.

Hosmer, L.T. 1982. "The Importance of Strategic Leadership." *Journal of Business Strategy* 3, no. 2: 4–21.

Klay, W.E. 1990. "The Future of Strategic Management." In *Handbook of Strategic Management*, ed. J. Rabin, G.J. Miller, and W.B. Hildreth. New York: Marcel Dekker.

Korten, D.C. 1984. "Strategic Organization for People-Centered Management." *Public Administration Review* 44: 341–343.

Kouzes, J.M., and B. Posner. 1987. *The Leadership Challenge: How to Get Extraordinary Things Done in Organizations.* San Francisco, CA: Jossey-Bass.

Lenz, R. 1980. "Environment, Strategy, Organization Structure and Performance." *Strategic Management Journal* 1: 209–226.

———. 1981. "Determinants of Organizational Performance: An Interdisciplinary Review." *Strategic Management Journal* 2: 131–154.

Lindblom, C.E. 1959. "The Science of 'Muddling Through.'" *Public Administration Review* 19: 79–88.

———. 1979. "Still Muddling, Not Yet Through." *Public Administration Review* 39: 517–526.

McConkey, D.D. 1981. "Strategic Planning in Nonprofit Organizations." *Business Quarterly* 3: 24–33.

Maxwell, J. 1990. "Strategic Management: A Framework for the Management of Change." *Boardroom Files* 9: 22–24.

Methe, D.T., and J.L. Perry. 1990. "Incremental Approaches to Strategic Management." In *Handbook of Strategic Management*, ed. J. Rabin, G.J. Miller, and W.B. Hildreth. New York: Marcel Dekker.

Mintzberg, H. 1979. *The Structuring of Organizations.* Englewood Cliffs, NJ: Prentice-Hall.

Montanari, J.R., G.A. Daneke, and J.S. Bracker. 1990. "Strategic Management for the Public Sector: Lessons from the Evolution of Private-Sector Planning." In *Handbook of Strategic Management*, ed. J. Rabin, G.J. Miller, and W.B. Hildreth. New York: Marcel Dekker.

Newell, C., and D.N. Ammons. 1987. "Role Emphasis of City Managers and Other Municipal Executives." *Public Administration Review* 47: 246–243.

Nutt, P.C., and R.W. Backoff. 1987. "A Strategic Management Process for Public and Third-Sector Organizations." *Journal of the American Planning Association* 53: 44–57.

Olsen, J.B., and D.C. Eadie. 1982. *The Game Plan: Governance with Foresight.* Washington, DC: Council on State Planning Agencies.

Pettigrew, A.M. 1977. "Strategy Formulation as a Political Process." *International Studies on Management and Organization* 7: 78–87.

Poister, T.H., and G. Streib. 1989. "Management Tools in Municipal Government: Trends over the Past Decade." *Public Administration Review* 49: 240–248.

Quinn, J.B. 1980. *Strategies for Change.* Homewood, IL: Irwin.

Schendel, D.E., and C.W. Hofer. 1979. *Introduction to Strategic Management.* Boston, MA: Little, Brown.

Shapek, R., and W.D. Richardson. 1990. "Strategic Capability." In *Handbook of Strategic Management*, ed. J. Rabin, G.J. Miller, and W.B. Hildreth. New York: Marcel Dekker.

Snider, C.F. 1952. "American County Government: A Mid-Century Review." *American Political Science Review* 46: 66–80.

Sorkin, D.L., N.B. Ferris, and J. Hudak. 1984. *Strategies for Cities and Counties: A Strategic Planning Guide.* Washington, DC: Public Technology.

Steiss, A.W. 1985. *Strategic Management and Organizational Decision Making.* Lexington, MA: Lexington Books.

Stevens, J.M. 1984. "Strategic Public Management and Productivity Improvement: A Symposium." *Public Productivity Review* 8: 195–373.

Stone, H.A., D.K. Price, and K.H. Stone. 1940. *City Manager Government in the United States.* Chicago: Public Administration Clearinghouse.

Streib, G. 1991. "Strategic Decision Making in Council-Manager Governments: A Status Report." In *The Municipal Yearbook.* Washington, DC: International City/County Management Association.

Streib, G., and T.H. Poister. 1989. "Established and Emerging Management Tools: A 12–Year Perspective." In *The Municipal Yearbook.* Washington, DC: International City Management Association.

Streib, G., and W.L. Waugh. [1991.] "Probing the Limits of County Reform in an Era of Scarcity." *Public Administration Review* [15, no. 3: 378–395].

Svara, J.H. 1989. "Policy and Administration: City Managers as Comprehensive Professional Leaders." In *Ideal and Practice in Council-Manager Government,* ed. H.G. Frederickson. Washington, DC: International City Management Association.

Swanstrom, T. 1985. "Strategic Planning for Cities: A Preliminary Evaluation." Paper presented at the annual meeting of the American Political Science Association, New Orleans, Louisiana.

———. 1987. "The Limits of Strategic Planning for Cities." *Journal of Urban Affairs* 9: 139–157.

Upton, H.G. 1981. "Bear Huntin' with a Switch." *Public Management* 63: 5–7.

Waugh, W.L., and G. Streib. 1990. "County Officials' Perceptions of Local Capacity and State Responsiveness After the First Reagan Term." *Southern Political Review* 18: 27–50.

CHAPTER 25

IMPLEMENTING TQM IN LOCAL GOVERNMENT:

The Leadership Challenge

JONATHAN P. WEST, EVAN M. BERMAN, MICHAEL E. MILAKOVICH

Total quality management (TQM) has become increasingly important in government in recent years. TQM is a set of principles, tools, and processes for managing and improving the quality of government services (Keehley 1992). The many applications of TQM in local government include efforts in police departments, fire services, waste management, personnel management, transportation, public works, parks, and utilities (Galloway 1992; Osborne and Gaebler 1992). Local governments may find TQM attractive because it helps departments better understand the needs of their communities. Public agencies can thereby avoid designing their services exclusively around the customers who are most vocal in their complaints. TQM also allows administrators to contain costs and improve services. This is important to local governments that face increased responsibilities, decreased revenues, and public cynicism about their capabilities (Sensenbrenner 1991).

This chapter reports the results of a survey of city managers and chief administrative officers (CAOs) about the strategies local governments use in implementing TQM. These experiences contain important lessons for other administrators, as well as for academics who are interested in testing theories about change in organizations. Although the literature contains some case studies about TQM at the local level, there are no systematic efforts that profile these activities across the nation's cities. This study responds to such a need.

TQM as Public Administration

TQM is a relatively modern productivity improvement strategy that is characterized by a commitment to meeting the needs of customers and constituents. Citizens are currently demanding more custom-tailored, timely, and cost-effective services, and the objectives of TQM are consistent with these goals (Denhardt 1993). The efficacy of TQM depends not on the use of esoteric tools, but rather on organizational change, empowerment, and systematic analysis. Empowerment gives public officials the latitude to identify and respond to the needs of individual customers without seeking time-consuming approvals. Systematic analysis involved both systemwide perspective of agency outputs and a logical ordering of problems, approaches, and priorities. Milakovich (1991) notes that TQM could challenge traditional administrative systems that are designed to control rather than empower, and to provide uniform services rather than adaptability.

From *Public Productivity & Management Review*, vol. 17, no. 2 (Winter 1993), pp. 175–189. Copyright © 1993 by Jossey-Bass. Reprinted with permission.

Although some argue that TQM has assumed cultlike status among its followers, it is neverthe-less important to note continuities with previous productivity improvement approaches (Walters 1992). Its immediate predecessor is organizational excellence, which focuses on similar objec-tives of action-orientation, closeness to citizens, employee orientation, flatter organizational structures, a clear set of values, and entrepreneurship (Duncan, Ginter, and Capper 1991). Also, both TQM and organizational excellence deal with employee resistance to change, improving the quality of daily work by reducing uncertainty and fear about expectations and rewards. Perhaps the most important differences between organizational excellence and TQM are that the latter focuses on customers rather than on professional criteria for determining excellence and emphasizes continuous improvement in outcomes, cost reduction, and a systematic perspective.

TQM is not without its critics. One concern is that TQM may be undemocratic by focusing on paying customers rather than citizens or constituents. Public agencies must be responsive to the needs of constituents (Frederickson 1992). This is especially relevant to areas such as parole programs, road taxes, and solid waste management, in which the interests of customers and constituents sharply diverge (Swiss 1992). Another concern is the possibility that TQM might impose service uniformity. Early TQM efforts involved manufacturing, and in these applications, product uniformity was desirable. The contrasting idea that services must be tailored to the needs of individual customers is perceptively captured by Johnston (1993), who writes that "If you treat everyone the same, what varies is satisfaction. To achieve equal satisfaction, you must vary treatment" (29). More contemporary applications of TQM in services recognize the need for customization and individualized treatment to increase customer satisfaction.

Tasks of Leadership

Successful implementation of TQM involves substantial leadership challenges. The scope of change is large, especially for departments that have been steeped in traditional styles of top-down management, management by objectives, procedure rather than goal-oriented processes, and fear-based styles of employee management. In this chapter, leadership is examined as an *organizational* phenomenon, that is, as a set of strategies public managers undertake to imple-ment change, rather than as the activities or characteristics of leaders who help implement TQM. These municipal leadership tasks are analytically distinguished as *transformation, transaction,* and *representation*. These distinctions encompass the full spectrum of required leadership tasks, and are defined in Table 25.1.

Transformational tasks involve the analysis and implementation of new goals and processes that are specific to TQM (Behn 1989). Ideas about transformational change are based on struc-tural-rational theories of organizations. They involve the values, goals, structures, boundaries, communication and information systems, and rewards and expectations of organizations (Kotter 1990). In TQM, some of the most important transformational tasks are as follows: instilling throughout the organization a sense of commitment to the customer, which is often achieved by using surveys to identify customer needs and then acting on the results; ensuring rewards for meeting customer needs; training and assisting employees and managers in their own empower-ment and using new techniques to measure performance and analyze problems; increasing coor-dination among units; and providing incentives for continuous improvement in all of the above areas (Grady 1992).

Given these objectives, *transactional* leaders concern themselves with ensuring that TQM methods, strategies, and principles are adopted by organizations (Burns 1978). The idea of trans-actional leadership is founded on theories of exchange and expectancy, which discuss how effective leadership requires acceptance by those being led (Fairholm 1990). Early studies in the

Table 25.1

Leadership Definitions

Transformational leadership: The process of formulating and communicating new, visionary goals that respond to fundamental and often currently unmet human and organizational needs, desires, and expectations. Transformational leadership sometimes provokes unquestioned following, but it usually requires transactional leadership.

Transactional leadership: The process of obtaining commitment from organizations and individuals for new programs and policies. Transactional leadership involves either voluntary acceptance (achieved through processes of mutual accommodation and exchange, often involving present or future benefits and promises), or coercion (involving manipulation, deceit, or threats).

Representational leadership: The process of obtaining support and legitimation from stakeholders of the organization for its results, objectives, and processes. Representation involves substantial education efforts and political boundary-spanning.

Source: Adapted from Burns (1978).

management of change point out that acceptance of change is a negotiation and communication process between top management and employees: employees must understand the need for change and believe that change is better than the status quo (Linden 1990). Recent studies also find that employees must be actively involved in the change process. In a study by Beer, Eisenstat, and Spector (1990), top management provided employees with task-aligned resources to solve problems and facilitated future problem-solving by providing information about solutions to all employees. Only after the new methods had been broadly accepted did top management attempt to institutionalize these changes through reward structures.

The need for transactional leadership poses important constraints on the speed of transformational leadership (Badaracco and Ellsworth 1989). Leaders cannot speed up change by imposing newfound ideas of quality and customer service upon the organization. Instead, they must follow the logic of transactional change by building pockets of commitment in the organization and expending these pockets in subsequent stages throughout the organization. Previous cases of TQM implementation suggest that such processes take a minimum of three years to bear fruit, and from five to seven years to reach maturity (Bowman and French 1992). As the results of more cases in various policy areas are published, the learning curve may shorten the time required for application.

Finally, *representational* leadership addresses the need for acceptance of TQM by external professional, political, and community groups. Recognizing that representational leadership distinguishes public from business administration, some local governments have created community quality councils composed of local government officials, administrators, business leaders, school spokespersons, health care providers, hospitality industry representatives, and other members of the community (Lusk, Tribus, and Schwinn 1989). Support from city councils is also critical in TQM implementation because it helps overcome the short time horizons of political appointees, minimize resistance to change among senior managers who are accustomed to traditional systems, reduce the fear of middle-level appointed officials by providing assurances about rewards and expectations, and provide financial support for initial TQM efforts.

Study

During the summer of 1993, a survey was sent to city managers and CAOs regarding the use of TQM in their municipalities. The survey was pretested on a group of fifty city managers and, following modifications, was sent to managers of all cities with a population over 25,000. These managers and municipalities were identified with the assistance of the International City/County Management Association (ICMA). A total of 1,211 surveys were mailed. After four waves of mailing and telephone calls, 433 usable responses were received. To evaluate the extent to which responses were obtained from all cities that implement TQM, a telephone survey of one hundred randomly selected nonrespondents was conducted. This survey found that 14 percent of nonrespondents used TQM, which suggests that the repeated mailings adequately reached cities that use TQM. It follows that $(1,211 - 433) \times 0.14 = 109$ cities that use TQM are not represented in the respondent group. Because 237 of the 433 respondents use TQM in their jurisdiction, the effective response rate among cities that use TQM is $237 / (237 + 109) = 68.5$ percent.

In addition, close to one hundred telephone interviews were conducted with city managers regarding TQM efforts in their cities. Detailed results from this study, only a portion of which are reported here, will be published in ICMA's *Municipal Yearbook 1994*.

In the survey, *quality improvement* is defined narrowly to include productivity and quality improvement efforts that meet all of the following criteria: commitment to customer-driven quality; employee participation in quality improvement; actions based on facts, data, and analysis; commitment to continuous improvement; and systemic perspective. The term *QI* was used in favor of TQM in order to avoid misinterpretation of bias. Recognizing that not all quality improvement efforts may meet these standards, a second definition was used: *customer service* was broadly defined as performance objectives that emphasize responsiveness to customers and that include a systematic method of assessing customer satisfaction. This latter definition is intended to identify efforts that are not strictly TQM, but otherwise embody the spirit of customer orientation.

The following sections discuss the nature of TQM applications in cities, followed by separate discussions of transformational, transactional, and representational strategies used by cities, and the reasons that cities implement TQM.

Nature of TQM Applications

Table 25.2 shows the implementation of TQM and customer service in local government. As expected, the most frequent implementation was in police work, recreation, parks, budgeting, and personnel services. (In nearly all cases, the percentage of customer service applications is about twice the percentages for TQM.) Transit and museums are areas of municipal service with low rates of TQM implementation, which may indicate that some of these functions are not provided by local government. On average, cities that implement TQM do so in 7.7 of the twenty-one functional areas shown in Table 25.2. There is very little difference in the number of areas in which TQM is used between large and small cities that use TQM (8.9 versus 7.2). These figures suggest that TQM is well established in local government. In fact, the data show that 26 percent of cities use TQM in at least one application in one functional area. Respondents reported that half of these efforts were implemented before 1990, and the other half in recent years.

Many TQM applications involved administrative services. Typical TQM examples of administrative applications involve streamlining paperwork processes in fleet scheduling and repair, reducing customer inquiries due to unclear tax forms and other paperwork, minimizing operator errors in transcribing customer-provided information into computers, and decreasing time in processing personnel requisitions (from initial requisition to opening of position). The results show that TQM is frequently used in municipal administrative services. These findings provide empirical support for a general assertion in the literature linking TQM action and administrative services (Barzelay 1992). This finding in municipal government is not surprising because administrative services are among the fastest growing costs in service delivery.

Table 25.2

TQM in Local Government: Survey Responses

Functions	TQM (%)	Customer service (%)
Police	37	60
Recreation	32	56
Parks	31	52
Budgetary reporting	31	39
Personnel services	31	44
Streets	29	51
Water/sewer	29	47
Solid waste	28	44
Fire	28	46
Fleet/vehicles	26	36
Data processing	26	37
Traffic	24	43
Buildings	20	30
Emergency services	19	33
Libraries	17	32
Animal control	14	32
Tax collection	14	29
Transit	13	24
Convention centers	9	15
Public health	9	15
Museums	6	12

Note: Based on considerations explained in the methods section, the number of cities that use TQM for each function can be calculated as the above percentage times 632 (433 respondents / 0.685 estimated response rate for cities using TQM). Hence, in the population of 1,211 cities that have populations over 25,000, it is estimated that 234 police forces use TQM.

However, many TQM efforts are focused on other objectives. For example, the city of Hollywood, Florida, increased collections from parking tickets by making it easier for violators to pay: the parking ticket is also a self-addressed envelope. Several cities conducted a baseline survey of citizen needs and complaints. The city of Mountain View, California, uses "citygrams" whereby citizens raise questions, make suggestions, register complaints, and offer plaudits about city services. Some municipal recreation programs have been designed to meet the needs of users, who are now paying a user fee. In many cities, fleet repair activities are now coordinated with the departments that use the vehicles. Several cities have also created customer service units in their public works and planning departments. Many efforts also deal with increasing the life of street pavement and minimizing the cost and duration of street repair work. In College Station, Texas, street maintenance and repair crews are empowered so that tasks that used to require a formal work order are now finished on the spot by crew members. The variety in TQM efforts is considerable.

Variety in TQM activities is reflected within cities as well as across jurisdictions. This is highlighted in a 140-page report that was forwarded to us along with a completed survey. The report was issued by one southern city in the sample. It summarized 780 productivity and "rightsizing" initiatives implemented from 1990 to 1992. These TQM efforts included technology improvements; work process changes; use of volunteers; and renewed attention to grants, contracting, public–private partnerships, staff-resource sharing, and development of fee structures. This city estimated $38.5 million in savings, $4.1 million in estimated revenue increases, and $8.8 million in grants received. Six approaches tell how they did it: customer needs assessments and surveys, reorganizations and consolidations, system redesign, process improvements, technology improvements, and service enhancements. Clearly, competent management was committed to a multifaceted approach to TQM in this city.

The range of TQM activities across cities is reported in the next three sections. The framework of leadership strategies—transformational, transactional, and representational—provides structure to the discussion.

Transformational Strategies

As shown in Table 25.3, the most frequently used transformational strategies are identifying customer needs (87 percent) and increasing coordination among units (80 percent). Cities use a variety of ways to identify customer needs. Results of the survey show that about half of cities that use TQM use systematic customer and community surveys, which provide governments with information about service satisfaction and community needs. However, cities also use other approaches to collect customer information, such as customer contact reports and focus groups. Focus groups are groups of citizens that provide feedback and suggestions for improvement of government services.

The second most frequently used strategy is increased coordination. The lack of coordination among services is a frequent target of citizen complaints because it causes delays, inconsistency, and duplication. Coordination is frequently improved by direct intervention of the city manager or CAO, who has the authority to make departments cooperate.

The emphasis on results rather than mere activity or effort was evident from managers' responses to open-ended survey questions. For example, one manager penned on his survey, "We began our efforts in 1989 using a highly structured process that demanded activity. We have evolved to a less rigid, results-oriented process that involves managers as team members and leaders and links to the corporate strategy." Another transformational manager whose city also started a TQM program in 1989 wrote that before starting a continuous improvement program, ". . . every department focused on effort and not results. To counter this, we implemented the following key programs: (1) team building; (2) established a line item account for TQM; (3) redefined roles and missions; (4) focus groups with employees, elected officials, residents, community and business leaders as appropriate, and (5) improved communications with newsletters focusing on quality, economy, responsiveness, and service to educate employees and residents."

Table 25.3 also provides evidence that the use of these transformational strategies is positively associated with increased levels of TQM implementation in cities. In these regressions, the dependent variable is the number of functions in which TQM is implemented in cities that implement TQM. This is a stringent measure of the efficacy of strategies, because a particular strategy (such as obtaining support from influential citizens) may facilitate TQM implementation in a particular department without facilitating its use across functions. Thus, the lack of evidence of an association between the number of functions implementing TQM and the use of a particular strategy cannot be interpreted as total inefficacy of the strategy. Table 25.3 shows that cities that identify customer needs and increase coordination among services are likely to implement TQM across more functions. Also, although reformulating mission statements and monitoring internal performance are also widely used strategies, these strategies are not statistically associated with increased levels of TQM. This is consistent with conventional wisdom. Merely formulating new slogans will not produce change, nor will increased monitoring of performance, which is a traditional management activity. These latter are necessary, but not sufficient to effect change.

Table 25.3

Leadership Strategies in Cities Using TQM

Independent variables	Use in cities (%)	Intercept	Coefficient	Standard error
Transformational strategies				
Identifying customer needs	87	6.69	3.29	1.25[c]
Increased coordination among units	80	7.07	3.05	1.06[c]
Monitoring internal performance	77	9.04	0.70	1.03
Reformulating mission statements	73	8.60	1.40	0.96
Training in techniques	70	8.45	1.60	0.93[a]
Budgets for quality improvement	54	7.97	2.61	0.89[c]
Visiting other sites	45	8.95	1.45	0.87[a]
Benchmarking	40	8.68	2.02	0.89[b]
Rewards for group performance	31	8.98	1.75	0.93[c]
Transactional strategies				
Recognition of achievement	77	8.49	1.58	1.02
Mid-level implementation teams	66	8.49	1.72	0.90[a]
Pilot project	54	8.61	1.82	0.86[b]
Grass roots initiatives	52	8.66	1.50	0.87[a]
Monitoring employee satisfaction	50	9.09	1.05	0.86
Consistency in the use of new performance measures	48	8.46	2.33	0.85[c]
Top-down planning	46	8.65	2.03	0.86[b]
Assessing unit readiness for change	37	9.08	1.63	0.90[a]
Developing a plan for cultural change	31	8.89	2.46	0.95[c]
Representational strategies				
Obtaining support from council members	77	7.52	2.75	1.00[c]
Obtaining support through community participation	56	8.36	2.44	0.85[c]
Obtaining support from influential citizens	46	8.60	2.38	0.88[c]
Obtaining support from other political leaders	42	8.89	2.00	0.86[b]

Notes: The last three columns show the result of regression analyses in which each strategy is regressed against the level of TQM implementation (as measured by the number of TQM-using functions) in each city. By convention, a level of 1 or 5 percent significance, shown by the footnotes, implies that such a relationship exists between the use of this strategy and increased diffusion of TQM. For relationships that are statistically significant, the coefficient is a measure of efficacy.
[a] 1 percent significance, [b] 5 percent significance, [c] 10 percent significance.

Table 25.3 also shows strategies that are less often used. For example, only 40 percent of cities use benchmarking as part of their TQM process. Benchmarking is an activity whereby performance is assessed against identical services in other cities, past performance, criteria of customer satisfaction and needs, and standards of professional performance. Benchmarking is a very aggressive means of monitoring and improving performance, and it is statistically related to increased levels of TQM ($p < 0.05$). Another such technique is site visits. Site visitation promotes learning from other municipalities, which can prompt action and prevent duplication of efforts. A third strategy is providing budgets for TQM. It is generally recognized that TQM is costly, at least in the initial stages, and should be viewed as an investment. Cities that budget for TQM provide necessary resources. Budgeting for productivity improvement is also a way of signaling commitment to TQM strategies. Finally, training in techniques is linked to implementation of quality initiatives. Such training covers a variety of skills for analysis of processes, data gathering, and process improvement (Wood 1992).

This study also found that top management support for TQM is a critical requirement for realizing transformational strategies. Not surprisingly, top management support is significantly associated with city adoption of the above strategies ($p < 0.01$). In one of the sample cities, the CAO required all departments to develop annual flow charts of at least two work processes and undertake a process improvement effort in at least one. All department heads serve on a process improvement team. Study findings show that top management support is also significantly associated with obtaining support from other senior managers in city government, whose support is also associated with adoption of the above strategies ($p < 0.05$). Clearly, change starts at the top. The TQM training activities recently initiated by the American Society for Public Administration (ASPA) and ICMA should be evaluated as a positive development.

In sum, six transformational strategies were identified that are positively and significantly associated with the level of TQM implementation: identifying customer needs, increasing coordination, adopting budgets for TQM implementation, training in techniques, visiting other sites, and benchmarking. These findings are consistent with a recent General Accounting Office (1992) study that surveyed federal TQM efforts. For example, GAO found that 69 percent of federal installations that use TQM have procedures to identify customer needs, 55 percent provide training to employees and managers in the use of new techniques, and 30 percent use benchmarking as part of their TQM efforts. However, at the time of the GAO study, the federal government had implemented TQM in 36 percent of its installations, whereas only 26 percent of local governments had implemented TQM at the time of this study.

Transactional Efforts and Results

To be effective, transformational strategies often need to be accompanied by transactional strategies. This helps to ensure acceptance by organizations. Cities must consider the overall philosophy or strategy for achieving transformational change, as well as specific actions to initiate employees in TQM and overcome resistance. The survey assessed three overall strategies: top-down planning, midlevel implementation teams, and support of grass roots initiatives. The survey shows that the use of midlevel implementation teams is the most frequently used (66 percent), followed by grass roots (52 percent) and top-down planning (46 percent). As the sum of percentages indicates, these strategies can be combined.

As discussed earlier, the logic of midlevel implementation teams is that they create pockets of successful TQM efforts, which are subsequently emulated throughout the organization. Transactionally, they are important because they involve employees, middle managers, and sometimes senior managers. Initial efforts are often small or well-bounded, which allows top management to empower employees and middle managers to implement strategies in a manner that is not threatening to the rest of the organization. Grass roots efforts are similar in that they change by small steps, but differ in that middle management may or may not be included. Despite the "grass roots" label, top management frequently encourages initiatives from employees regarding specific problems, who are then provided with resources to deal with them. Thus, grassroots is not always a passive or bottom-up approach. Finally, top-down planning involves hands-on activities of the city manager or CAO to ensure implementation. A problem with exclusive reliance on top-down implementation is that this strategy is not designed to change the city's organizational culture. Table 25.3 shows that all three strategies are significantly associated with increasing the level of TQM.

To overcome employee resistance, cities rely primarily on recognizing achievement, using new performance measures consistently, monitoring employee satisfaction, and assessing a unit's readiness for change. A principal source of employee resistance is fear of change (especially of losing one's job), capricious use of rewards and punishments by management, or not being able to meet new expectations. These strategies assist in addressing such concerns. For example, achievement can be recognized, as it was in one of the sample cities, by issuing certificates of completion to TQM trainees, having receptions for process improvement teams, holding recognition ceremonies, and allowing TQM teams to make presentations directly to the city manager or CAO. Monitoring employee satisfaction provides information about employees' concerns, which are then addressed. To dispel fear and address workers' concerns, one city added rumor control to the agenda of regular staff meetings, used employee focus groups, and issued employee newsletters addressing quality issues. Consistency in the use of measures not only alleviates concerns about erratic management behavior, but it also creates predictability in practice. Such measures can relate to unit as well as individual performance. Examples of unit performance measures might be percent of departments or agencies using TQM teams, dollars saved, and measurable increases in employee and customer satisfaction. Assessments of unit readiness and plans for cultural change are less often used, but they are positively associated with increased levels of TQM implementation.

Representational Strategies

Representational strategies are used as frequently as transformational and transactional strategies. TQM proponents generally seek to obtain support from city council members. The importance of city council support was learned the hard way by one city in the sample. Because the city failed to involve the governing body in the quality transformation, council members viewed TQM initiatives negatively when they were approached by resistant managers. Early involvement of the council and other elected officials in TQM would likely minimize such problems. Many cities also use community planning councils, which are a source of new ideas for improvement of city services. For instance, in one city, recommendations of the community council were adopted to train taxi drivers to be more friendly and helpful in their conversations with passengers arriving at the airport. Because of these suggestions, taxi drivers now welcome travelers to this city and provide information about hotels and upcoming events.

Leadership strategies of all three types—transformational, transactional, and representational— are widely used in cities. The following section examines why cities are turning to TQM.

Reasons for Implementing TQM

What causes cities to implement TQM? Figure 25.1 reports the importance of various reasons for promoting implementation of TQM in large and small cities. The same driving forces that are thought to be important in large cities are considered important in smaller cities as well. Interest of city managers and CAOs is the most important reason cities implement TQM. The effectiveness of city services is the primary concern of city managers and CAOs, who are prompted by their professional associations to use modern management methods. Recognition for applying modern methods also increases their competitiveness in the job market for municipal executives. For example, in one municipality, the city manager retired after championing TQM as the city's transformational leader. Commitment by the mayor and the city council to the fledgling quality improvement initiatives led them to add "familiarity with TQM" as a crucial qualification when screening candidates to fill the city manager's vacancy. The findings also show that some city managers use TQM in response to budget pressures. TQM promises to decrease costs while increasing quality.

Figure 25.1 **Reasons for Implementing Total Quality Management (TQM)**

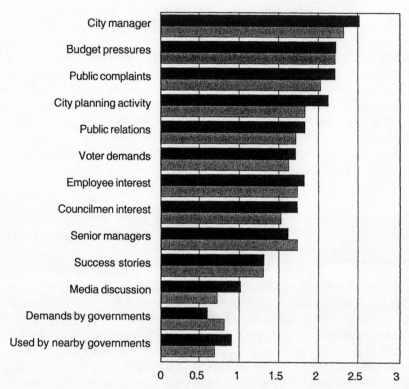

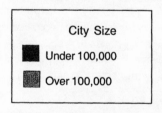

Scale: 3 = very important; 2 = important; 1 = somewhat important; 0 = not important.

Responding to public complaints is also a very important reason for implementing TQM. One city manager stated that he ordered a department head to implement TQM in order to move persistent public complaints about agency services off his agenda. It is interesting to note that although public complaints are important, voter demands are less so. Administrative reform is seldom a hot voter topic. Administrators cannot count on positive TQM results to satisfy voters and elected officials. In other words, TQM is not a panacea for the political needs of elected officials.

City and community planning activities are another reason for implementing TQM. An illustration comes from the city of Virginia Beach, Virginia, recipient of an award from the U.S. Senate Productivity Award Board. In 1992, the city adopted a strategic plan for the long-term cultural transformation of municipal government. The plan spells out core values and quality principles and establishes four goals: organization commitment, discipline of knowledge, visibility of efforts, and process formation support. Other Virginia governments (cities, counties, and school boards) have asked to use the plan, which Virginia Beach willingly provided in hopes that a uniform approach would develop for Virginia governments, all of which are under pressure of increased service demands and tight budgets.

Summary and Conclusions

About one in four cities now use TQM in at least one function; half of these efforts are less than three years old. The most frequent applications are in police work, parks, recreation, budgeting, and personnel services.

The most important reasons for implementing TQM are city manager interest, public complaints, and budget pressures. These reasons are important in both large and small cities.

TQM cannot be implemented by decree or through top-down management alone. Leaders must create pockets of commitment throughout the organization. TQM implementation requires initial successes of pilot projects and project implementation teams involving employees and midlevel management.

Obtaining support from council members and the community is essential to the continued success of TQM throughout the municipal government.

TQM implementation depends critically on leadership from top appointed and elected officials. Leaders must commit to improved municipal service delivery to respond to customers and constituents, and implement this vision by identifying customer needs, increasing coordination among units, and monitoring internal performance. Some important processes for achieving these objectives are delegating responsibility to the lowest levels (empowerment), using pilot projects, redesigning reward structures and ensuring consistency in their use, and recognizing achievement. Local government leaders who have the vision to promote quality transformation in their communities, who use transactional skills, and who act to ensure that critical stakeholders' views are represented, are changing the way municipal services are delivered to citizens.

References

Badaracco, J.L., and R.R. Ellsworth. 1989. *Leadership and the Quest for Integrity.* Boston, MA: Harvard Business School Press.

Barzelay, M. 1992. *Breaking Through Bureaucracy.* Los Angeles: University of California Press.

Beer, J., R. Eisenstat, and B. Spector. 1990. "Why Change Programs Don't Produce Change." *Harvard Business Review* (November–December): 158–166.

Behn, R.D. 1989. "Leadership Counts." *Journal of Public Policy Analysis and Management* 8, no. 3: 494–500.

Bowman, J., and B. French. 1992. "Quality Improvement in a State Agency Revisited." *Public Productivity and Management Review* 16, no. 1: 53–64.

Burns, J.M. 1978. *Leadership.* New York: HarperCollins.

Denhardt, R.B. 1993. *The Pursuit of Significance.* Belmont, CA: Wadsworth.

Duncan, W., P. Ginter, and S. Capper. 1991. "Excellence in Public Administration: Four Transferable Lessons from the Private Sector." *Public Productivity and Management Review* 14, no. 3: 227–236.

Fairholm, G. 1990. "Leadership." In *Public Sector Management*, ed. M. Whicker and T. Areson. New York: Praeger.

Frederickson, H.G. 1992. "Painting Bull's-Eyes Around Bullet Holes." *PA Times* 15, no. 11: 9.

Galloway, R.A. 1992. "Quality Improvement and the Heightened Self-Esteem: The Brighton Police Story." *National Productivity Review* (Autumn): 453–461.

Grady, D.O. 1992. "Promoting Innovations in the Public Sector." *Public Productivity and Management Review* 16, no. 2: 157–171.

International City/County Management Association. 1994. *Municipal Yearbook*. Washington, DC: ICMA.

Johnston, K.B. 1993. *Beyond Bureaucracy: A Blueprint and Vision for Government That Works*. Homewood, IL: Business One Irwin.

Keehley, P. 1992. "TQM for Local Government." *Public Management* (August): 10–16.

Kotter, J.P. 1990. "What Leaders Really Do." *Harvard Business Review* (May–June): 103–111.

Linden, R.M. 1990. *From Vision to Reality: Strategies of Successful Innovators in Government*. Charlottesville, VA: LEL Publishers.

Lusk, K., M. Tribus, and C. Schwinn. 1989. "Creating Community Quality Councils: Applying Quality Management Principles in a Political Environment." Paper presented at the William G. Hunter Conference, Madison, Wisconsin, April 19.

Milakovich, M. 1991. "Total Quality Management in the Public Sector." *National Productivity Review* 10, no. 2: 195–204.

Osborne, D., and T. Gaebler. 1992. *Reinventing Government*. Reading, MA: Addison-Wesley.

Sensenbrenner, J. 1991. "Quality Comes to City Hall." *Harvard Business Review* (March–April): 64–75.

Swiss, B. 1992. "Adapting Total Quality Management to Government." *Public Administration Review* 52, no. 4: 356–362.

U.S. General Accounting Office. 1992. *Quality Management: Survey of Federal Organizations*. Washington, DC: U.S. General Accounting Office, October, Document GAO/GGD–93–9BR.

Walters, J. 1992. "The Cult of Total Quality." *Governing* (May): 38–42.

Wood, P. 1992. "How Quality Government Is Being Achieved." *National Productivity Review* 11, no. 2: 257–264.

CHAPTER 26

THE *RE-ING* OF LOCAL GOVERNMENT:

Understanding and Shaping Governmental Change

HERBERT A. MARLOWE, JR., RONALD NYHAN,
LAWRENCE W. ARRINGTON, AND WILLIAM J. PAMMER

Reinvention, re-engineering, and restructuring are some of the many approaches to governmental change that begin with the prefix *re*. These efforts are responses to the fact that many local governments are nearing a fiscal and service delivery crisis. The voices decrying the weaknesses and failures of public organizations are strong and perhaps growing (Osborne 1992). Four primary factors are contributing to this crisis.

First, public confidence in government as a problem-solving mechanism is low (Heise, Gladwin, and McLaughen 1991). The public employee is derided by the pejorative term *bureaucrat* and is not viewed as a productive person contributing to society (Hubbell 1991). Elected officials have publicly criticized their staffs in order to shift blame and to vent their frustration over the complexity and seeming intractability of socioeconomic problems (Arrington and Marlow 1992). Thus, it is understandable that the self-image of the public employee is low. Osborne and Gaebler (1992) report that only 5 percent of Americans surveyed would choose government as their preferred career. Only 13 percent of top federal employees would encourage their children to go into public service as a career.

In addition to the lack of public confidence, government employees face other serious problems. Chief among these are the ongoing fiscal crises that drain the energy and lower the expectations of public organizations (Spitzer 1991). These fiscal crises restrict the choices available to public managers to where and when to cut back, instead of which problems to address. Furthermore, the perception of public employment as a stable career has diminished as layoffs and furloughs become more prevalent as budget-balancing mechanisms (MacManus 1992).

Another problematic factor is the growing complexity of the issues the public sector is asked to solve. Public schools, for example, are asked not only to teach but also to assume the role of family and social worker for our children. Environmental agencies are asked to solve problems we did not have or did not recognize a generation ago, often without the data needed to determine the ripple effect of those solutions. Human service agencies are asked to solve highly complex social problems with minimal funding, poorly trained staff, and a public attitude of NIMBY [not in my backyard] to creative solutions that would affect local communities. Although government work still has some relatively straightforward elements (such as pothole repair or animal control), the policy dimensions are increasing in complexity.

From *Public Productivity & Management Review*, vol. 17, no. 3 (Spring 1994), pp. 299–311. Copyright ©
1994 by Jossey-Bass. Reprinted with permission.

A fourth factor challenging public organizations is a general societal malaise and sense of fundamental disorder, including a lack of mission and ideological consensus (Wildavsky 1988). Borgmann (1992) argues that the current public mood is one of sullenness. He contends there is a lack of public will for self-discipline or self-government, a lack of willingness to engage reality. This results in a posture of debilitation, an inability to experience real joy or real pain, and a lack of vigor and integrity. He further argues that professional and technological leaders have responded with a hyperactivity that, although energizing, is ultimately destructive because of its narrowness and misplaced energy. Goldfarb (1991) describes this malaise as public cynicism. Krugman (1992) argues that we live in an age of diminished expectations. Whereas we once expected an increasing standard of living, many now would be content to maintain the standard they currently have, and expect no more (Peterson 1991).

These four factors, coupled with low productivity growth and quality issues in the public sector, give rise to tension, frustration, and hopelessness. They shape a widely shared belief that all the institutions of our society, including government, must change dramatically if they are to remain viable (Deal 1985; Kimberly and Quinn 1984). As a consequence, there is a sense among elected officials, public employees, and the public that local government needs a major overhaul (Pammer 1990; Walters 1992).

In response, there has been an extensive and growing national movement for governmental change. Proposed solutions have taken numerous forms, under various names. With the exception of the quality approaches—total quality management (TQM) and continuous process improvement (CPI)—most begin with the prefix *re*. We maintain that the various approaches to *re-ing* government, including TQM, CPI, and other approaches, must be integrated into a comprehensive approach to governmental change. In addition to offering models for change, such an approach should identify the genesis of the current call for change [and] provide a model for the future direction of governments. This chapter is an attempt to develop an approach that meets these three criteria.

Genesis of the Call for Governmental Change

Calls for government reform do not occur in societal vacuums. Because governments are created to serve the public, their mission, role, and validity all emanate from the society at large. The search to understand the calls for governmental change must therefore begin with an understanding of social change.

In a society as diverse and complex as that of the United States, any attempt to delineate a dynamic model of current forces for social change is bound to be incomplete. Even within the identified elements of any proposed model, many nuances and dimensions are omitted. Within these limitations, the following five elements are the major forces behind the call for governmental change.

- The collapse of consensus
- The emergence of messy problems
- The transformation of the global economy
- The crisis of citizenship and self-interest
- The loss of social capital.

The Collapse of Consensus

America's political economy is in the midst of an identity crisis. There is little confidence in the institutions of government or the direction of the national economy. The crosscurrents creating

America's instability are found in a growing distrust of the assumptions underlying its historical growth strategy. There is public disenchantment with the promises and fruits of that strategy. America's political structure—its governmental architecture and the major policies underlying it—were designed to promote the nation's growth, particularly at state and local levels. As the scheme for developing America is questioned, so are the political institutions and policies that were designed to support it. America's governments lack public confidence because public support for the traditional means and ends of the national political economy has declined.

A breakdown in the process of political consensus is preceded by a collapse of social consensus. What is meant by social consensus?

From a national perspective, *social consensus* means that there is a broadly shared agreement within society about the national identity and purpose. Hunter defines this as a broad level of agreement as we face the issues of "deciding who we as a nation have been, coming to grips with who we are now, and defining what we should aspire to become in the future" (1991, 108). On the local level, the issues are much the same, phrased in terms of local identity. Who are we? Who do we wish to be? If the social consensus is collapsing, how can we rebuild a broad agreement, a new workable level of social consensus?

To address these issues, we must determine what comprises a social consensus. How is a consensus developed? Once developed, how does it fragment or disintegrate? Once we understand how consensus evolves and disintegrates, we are in a better position to build a new social consensus.

What comprises a social consensus? The foundation of a social consensus lies in three domains: the paradigms or myths by which we order and interpret our world and our place in it, the shared values or sources of moral authority that underlie our common life, and our vision for the future, which is an expression of our hopes, fears, and desires. The degree of shared agreement about these three interrelated domains is a direct measure of the degree of social consensus in a society or community.

According to Gardner (1990, 112),

> A community lives in the minds of its members in shared assumptions, beliefs, customs, ideas that give meaning, ideas that motivate. And among the ideas are "norms" or "values." In any healthy and reasonably coherent community, people come to have shared views concerning right and wrong, better and worse—in personal conduct, in governing, in art, whatever. They decide for their time and place what things they will define as legal or illegal, virtuous or vicious, good taste or bad. They have little impulse to be neutral about such matters. . . . In a pluralistic community there will be, within the broad consensus that enables the community to function, many and vigorous conflicts over specific values. At best that is a sign of vitality, at worst it is the price of pluralism. But conflict is one thing; disintegration is something else. When the community's broad consensus disintegrates or loses its force, the society sickens. People no longer find meaning in their lives. Nothing holds together.

Gardner observes that in a given community, group, or organization, values decay over time. Values are kept alive through a process of regeneration. "Each generation must rediscover the living elements in its own tradition and adapt them to present realities" (1990, 37). Leaders must concern themselves with reaffirmation of values if this regeneration is to take place.

The Emergence of Messy Problems

Simply put, American society faces five messy problems: urban and societal decay, environmental stress and degradation, energy restrictions, infrastructure failings and a serious agricultural predicament, and fiscal difficulties. Our governments are not designed and structured to handle these problems.

Before these five messy problems and their relationship to perceived governmental ineptitude are introduced, a definition of the terms is warranted. A messy problem has the following characteristics:

- Its boundaries are unclear. Its beginning and end are not obvious.
- The exact nature of the problem is ill-defined. There are many different perspectives and definitions of the problem.
- Messy problems are comprised of a number of smaller, interrelated problems whose interactions are often fuzzy or unknown.
- Actions to remedy a messy problem often have unforeseen consequences, some of which can be negative.
- Messy problems overlap in obvious and in unknown ways with other messy problems.
- Messy problems cannot be solved in isolation from other messy problems.
- The solutions to messy problems require a mix of technological, social, economic, paradigm shift and value examination activities.
- The solutions to messy problems require paradoxical solutions at micro and macro levels as well as redefinitions of institutional and personal responsibility. Messy problems cannot be solved from the inside, nor can they be solved unless individuals take responsibility for them.

What is so messy about messy problems? Why can't we solve messy problems in the same way we have solved so many other problems as a nation? There are several reasons.

Our local governmental structures were not designed to solve messy problems. Rather, they had such straightforward tasks as designing road networks, administering charities, and building water and sewer lines. Second, messy problems cut across institutional and sector boundaries. These problems cannot be easily assigned to any one institution, nor can they be solved alone by either the public or private sectors. Messy problems require entirely new institutional configurations. Third, the problems themselves weaken our ability to solve them. For example, federal and state governments delegate many messy problems to local governments, but because of their messy fiscal problem, they send no money to assist in local problem solving. Fourth, these problems exist over a fundamental social, psychological, and moral crisis that has weakened our ability to perform the very tasks needed to resolve messy problems. These messy problems coexist with this fundamental crisis in a symbiotic relationship that combines them and further weakens our problem-solving capacity.

Solutions to these messy problems require all our problem-solving intelligence and more. The first step is analysis: clear, critical thinking about these problems, their relationship to each other, and to the underlying fundamental crisis. The fundamental approach is systems thinking coupled with chaos and complexity concepts. The next steps involve the creation of new problem-solving structures and processes more suited to messy problems.

Urban and societal decay are one messy problem facing our society. This is physically expressed in the infrastructure decay of our inner cities and of first- and second-ring suburbs. It is socially expressed in crime rates, drug problems, violence, and family deterioration. Our social life is under enormous stress. Environmental issues are the second messy problem. Globally, the current levels of consumption and industry are not ecologically sustainable, yet our economies are based on continuing growth in consumption.

Energy shortages are the third messy problem. Industrial, consumer societies require concentrated energy sources. Currently, our primary energy sources are nonreplenishable. Use of these energy sources is likely to rise unless a major technological breakthrough occurs or the cost of energy from nonrenewable sources exceeds the costs from renewable sources.

The fourth messy problem is agriculture. Farmers are losing 24 billion tons of topsoil each year (Brown 1993). It is estimated that world yields from the seas peaked at one hundred million tons in 1989 and will never exceed this number (Brown, Kane, and Ayres 1993).

Our fifth messy problem is fiscal. One aspect of this problem is the federal deficit and its rippling effect throughout the economy. A second aspect is our decaying infrastructure. Our current national infrastructure needs are estimated at $4.5 trillion. Our scheduled capital expenditures for infrastructure from federal, state, and local sources over the next twenty years is $2.5 trillion.

The Transformation of the Global Economy

Many contemporary scholars and social critics have observed that the global political economy is undergoing a massive transformation. Many terms have been used to describe this transformation. It has been described as the emergence of a new paradigm, a power shift to a new world order, and, in the words of Harvard political economist Robert Reich, "a transformation that will rearrange the politics and economics of the coming century" (Reich 1991).

Reich is particularly insightful in his description of the transformation and its implications:

> There will be no national products or technologies, no national corporations, no national industries. There will no longer be national economies, at least as we have come to understand that concept. All that will remain rooted within national borders are the people who comprise a nation. Each nation's primary assets will be its citizens' skills and insights. Each nation's primary political task will be to cope with the centrifugal forces of the global economy which tear at the ties binding citizens together—bestowing ever greater wealth on the most skilled and insightful, while consigning the less skilled to a declining standard of living. As borders become evermore meaningless in economic terms, those citizens best positioned to thrive in the world market are tempted to slip the bonds of national allegiance, and by so doing disengage themselves from their less favored fellows. (3)

A brief summary of major events in the global economy during the past four decades will set the stage for our discussion. At the end of World War II, the United States emerged as the dominant political, military, and economic force in the world. By 1950, the Soviet Union emerged as the United States' ideological, military, technological, and economic rival. Containment of communism in Eastern Europe and (after the fall of Cuba) in Central America became the dominant U.S. political and economic policy objective. The 1960 presidential election of John F. Kennedy revolved around promises to "get the country moving again" in the face of Soviet achievements. The Cuban Missile Crisis and the construction of the Berlin Wall occurred shortly after Kennedy's election, and were seen as ominous signs of the imperatives of the bipolar struggle. By mid-decade, the seeds of American involvement in Vietnam would be sown, marking the beginnings of a decade-long national tragedy.

Thurow (1992) describes the essence of what happened next in the bipolar struggle:

> Two oil shocks and the discovery that the Chinese dragon was a friendly dragon—if not an ally, at least not an enemy—temporarily diverted attention away from the Soviet Bear in

the mid-1970s. But with a Soviet buildup in the 1970s, ... the American humiliation in Iran, and the USSR's invasion of Afghanistan, the bear was back—bigger, badder, and more dangerous than ever. In response to the glimpse of this enormous bear in the woods, President Ronald Reagan doubled America's military budget in the first half of the 1980s. ... Suddenly, the bear disappeared. The Berlin Wall came down, East and West Germany were united, democracy and capitalism arrived in the formerly communist countries of Middle Europe, the Red Army withdrew to the east, the Warsaw Pact was abrogated, the Soviet Union split asunder, and communism ended in Europe, its birthplace. (12)

The bipolar world has collapsed, and in the aftermath a new multipolar political economy has emerged. Thurow notes, "In broad terms there are now three relatively equal contenders—Japan; the European Community, centered around its most powerful country, Germany; and the United States" (33). It is difficult for many Americans to come to grips with what has happened to the nation's status in the world community. In 1950, the per capita GNP of the United States was four times that of West Germany and fifteen times that of Japan. The United States has plummeted from being the world's largest net creditor to its largest net debtor. The rules of the global political economy and America's place in setting and following them have changed. The happy consensus that stabilized the U.S. political economy during its years of dominance has collapsed. This consensus rested on a bargain among the major players in the political economy: business, government, labor, and the public. The major institutions of the U.S. political economy were structured to produce the fruits of the bargain in a world dominated by the United States. The political economy at the foundation of the bargain promised and, for a time, produced economic prosperity and general political stability. Then, for reasons we are only beginning to understand, global forces were unleashed, causing the bargain to fall apart.

The entire structure of the U.S. political economy is undergoing a transformation whose guiding values, principles, methods, and direction have sparked a national debate of unprecedented intensity. The debate extends from the boardroom to the classroom, where calls for massive institutional restructuring strike at the ways and means of conducting the business of the nation, if not its very purpose.

The Crisis of Citizenship and Self-Interest

The issues discussed so far are critical and difficult problems. Our understanding of these issues is debatable and specific solutions are often controversial, inadequate, or counterproductive. The lack of knowledge, the lack of money, the lack of priority all stand in the way of solving these issues. Yet a more fundamental barrier exists. That barrier is a crisis in citizenship, responsibility, and purpose. What are the dimensions and ramifications of that crisis?

Political discourse is currently centered on narrow self-interest. Although self-interest must be part of any public debate, to focus only on one's immediate self-interest is to invite societal destruction. What we must regain is de Tocqueville's concept of self-interest rightly understood.

Related to the narrowing of self-interest is the diminishment of the responsibilities of citizenship. Governments subtly and unintentionally promote this diminishment when they overemphasize the public as customer. Unlike the private sector, who will, for a price, give customers whatever they want, the public sector often has to mediate between differing and inherently conflicting desires and wishes. Customers focus on their desires and wishes and how they can be expeditiously satisfied. Citizenship requires a focus on the common good and the long-term benefits and costs.

Related to these questions is the more fundamental issue of responsibility. One of the unfortunate consequences of the bureaucratic state is the diminishment of individual responsibility. When government takes "responsibility," it all too often produces paternalistic programs that weaken the ethos of individual responsibility. Although this dynamic is generally cast as a liberal (institutional responsibility, systemic failure) versus conservative (personal responsibility, individual failure) political debate, the greater issue is our failure to effectively couple institutional and personal responsibility. By breaking this dynamic linkage, the responsibility debate has degenerated into one of political philosophy instead of addressing the greater issue of how to develop more responsible institutions and persons.

The Loss of Social Capital

One of the critical dynamics underlying American society is the loss of social capital. *Social capital* is the network of relationships that allows people to proceed with projects on the basis of some level of trust; these informal arrangements allow quick action when needed. This loss is exhibited in various ways, including the weakening of family life, the deterioration of urban neighborhoods and older suburbs, and the unique dynamics associated with high-growth communities. This loss of social capital is critical because as Putnam (1993) has found, social networks and their resulting social capital are the key determinants of economic development and local quality of life.

There are a number of reasons for this loss of social capital. It is important to note that even as social capital is lost in one sector of our society, it is being generated in others. Although we may be losing traditional downtowns to the Wal-Marts of the world, electronic networks are linking millions of people. One of the strengths of American society is its social, physical, and intellectual mobility. Freedom is often defined as the ability to move up based on one's efforts as well as the ability to relocate anywhere in the nation if one has the money. This high degree of mobility is certainly a key element of a dynamic society.

Mobility has its price, however. This price is best seen in high-growth areas where the population nearly doubles over a decade. One consequence of this high rate of growth is that the established social infrastructure is overwhelmed with new faces, new groups, new perspectives on issues. Whether one terms the existing social infrastructure the *establishment* or the *old boy network*, the existing social network is often overwhelmed by growth.

The price of mobility is also seen in one of the unfortunate consequences of the desegregation movement. As middle-class blacks won the freedom to live where they wished, many chose to leave traditional black neighborhoods. As they did so, the traditional social structure of the black community was weakened, leading in part to many of the difficulties black neighborhoods face today.

The price paid for this change is not simply a few individual egos. The nation is weakened economically because it lacks the social capital that is so often the precursor of financial and human capital. The social problem-solving capacities of groups at all levels is diminished. Lacking access through adequate social capital, individuals concentrate, however falsely and shortsightedly, on efforts to maximize their immediate self-interest. In essence, this loss of social capital returns us to the root issue of loss of citizenship.

Futuring Model for Purposing Government

A key element of the quality movement and the *re-ing* of government is to increase effectiveness and efficiency. As financial restrictions tighten, efficiency becomes even more critical. As public policy makers and administrators seek to raise public confidence, effectiveness is critical. However, it is not enough that the sole criteria for governmental change be effectiveness and efficiency, significant as those two qualities are. The more fundamental question is what do we want government to be effective at? There is a missing component to the *re-ing* of government. That component is purpose.

To answer this question, we must move beyond the world of management consultants and public sector productivity experts. We must move into the world of visioning, direction setting, and public policy consensus building. How do we create a consensual vision for the future upon which we can redesign government?

The futuring process must move beyond global vision statements that are so generic and positive that they are in essence pabulum. Instead, the process should produce the following outputs:

- An intellectual platform that provides a comprehensive understanding of the current and developing changes affecting the community.
- A strategic analysis that examines a community's strengths and weaknesses, assesses realistic opportunities and threats, and delineates which features it wants to maintain, which features it wants to add, and what needs to be eliminated from the community.
- A vision statement that expresses how the community wishes to be unique. In economic terms, it is a vision of what will give the community competitive advantage in the marketplace.
- An action agenda that identifies critical, root actions and prioritizes those actions.
- An implementing structure that provides a follow-up mechanism. This structure should be the encompassing model through which partnering efforts occur.

This process should provide a community agenda into which governmental bodies can direct their efforts. It will provide the *re-ing* movement's missing component: purpose. Government is now being redesigned to become more productive and more effective for the ends established during the futuring process.

Systemic, Equilibrium Approach to Governmental Change

Having developed a model for conceptualizing environmental change and a system for developing appropriate purposes for government at the local level, the stage is set to develop a model for governmental change. There are two key components to the model. This first is that governmental change must be systemic in scope. The second is that governments are living organisms whose change processes model those of other living organisms. Each component is discussed below.

Figure 26.1 details an organizational design model, overlaid with the various *re*-efforts. The key to the model is that the various elements are linked as a dynamic system so that change in one area affects the others or may be negated by other elements. Element-focused approaches to organizational change are bound for either failure or minimal impact. Changes in decision-making systems are meaningless if the reward system is not commensurately changed. Changes in structure, particularly those that move the boxes on the organization chart, are often viewed internally as meaningless. This perception is most often accurate because no other element of the organizational design has been changed.

Any element-based approach is a piecemeal approach. Although valuable in itself, perhaps, it cannot lead to the fundamental rethinking required of governmental entities. For that reason, the most appropriate model is the systemic model.

Figure 26.1   **Redesigning Government**

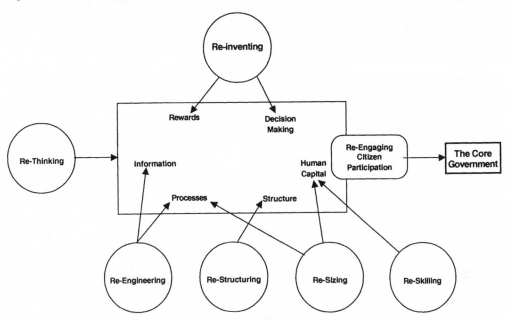

The second component is the *punctuated equilibrium paradigm* (Gersick 1991). This paradigm conceptualizes change as an alternation between long periods when stable infrastructures permit only incremental adaptation, and brief periods that permit intense change. The punctuated equilibrium paradigm consists of three components: the deep structure of the organization, equilibrium periods, and intense change periods.

Gersick notes that the validity of change theories is dependent upon the nature of the organization. The punctuated equilibrium paradigm provides a model to explain the dynamics of change as well as to guide intervention strategies for change. For most of an organization's life, there is a state of equilibrium in which incremental adaptations are made. However, there are opportunities for intense, fundamental change in the deep structure of the organization. These periods of intense change allow for fundamental changes in governmental operations and structure, underlying values, power relationships, and control systems. The punctuated equilibrium paradigm appears to be particularly applicable to governmental agencies characterized by high levels of stability and are typically difficult to change.

The equilibrium paradigm model offers several relevant change strategies. One is the deliberate creation of organizational niches that provide stability and protection to let new systems develop. Several organizations are deliberately employing this variant of the "skunk works," groups of employees engaged in creative projects on an unofficial basis (Marlowe and Nyhan 1993). Another change strategy is the creation of crisis. In many ways, the tax revolt may be viewed as a crisis-provoking event that punctuates the organizational equilibrium (Marlowe and Arrington 1993). The third strategy is that of incremental change. Governments are changing at micro levels every day. In this strategy, the accumulation of these micro-level changes promotes a broader range of change. The final change strategy is a cognitive shift. The basic purpose and operational paradigm of governance is called into question. This cognitive reframing generates the force for change (Marlowe, Hoffman, and Bordelon 1992).

Conclusion

The *re-ing* of government arose from profound and extensive societal forces. For this reason, one should not mistake enchantment or disillusionment with techniques for change as reasons to advocate or resist the rethinking of government. These fundamental forces override individual interest, technique, or unique political issues. The forces for change are real and long term.

If we are to engage these forces productively, we must first seek to understand them. Building on that understanding, we must then engage in a futuring process to repurpose our governments. Within those efforts, the efforts of governmental change can proceed.

Note

This chapter was presented at the Sixth National Public Sector Productivity Improvement Conference, Scottsdale, Arizona, September 10, 1993.

References

Arrington, L., and H.A. Marlowe. 1992. "The Governing Crisis." Paper presented to the Florida Association of Counties 1992 Conference, Marco Island, Florida, June.

Borgmann, A. 1992. *Crossing the Postmodern Divide.* Chicago: University of Chicago Press.

Brown, L.R. 1993. *State of the World.* New York: W.W. Norton.

Brown, L.R., H. Kane, and E. Ayres. 1993. *Vital Signs.* New York: W.W. Norton.

Deal, T. 1985. "Cultural Change." In *Gaining Control of the Corporate Culture*, ed. R. Kilmann, M. Saxton, and R. Serpa. San Francisco, CA: Jossey-Bass, pp. 292–331.

Gardner, J.W. 1990. *On Leadership.* New York: Free Press.

Gersick, C. 1991. "Revolutionary Change Theories: A Multi-Level Exploration of the Punctuated Equilibrium Paradigm." *Academy of Management Review* 16: 10–36.

Goldfarb, J.C. 1991. *The Cynical Society: The Culture of Politics and the Politics of Culture in American Life.* Chicago: University of Chicago Press.

Heise, J., J. Gladwin, and D. McLaughen. 1991. *FIU/Florida Poll.* Miami, FL: FIU Press.

Hubbell, L. 1991. "Ronald Reagan as President Symbol Maker: The Federal Bureaucrat as a Loafer, Incompetent Buffoon, Good Ole Boy, and Tyrant." *American Review of Public Administration* 21: 237–253.

Hunter, J.D. 1991. *Culture Wars: The Struggle to Define America.* New York: Basic Books.

Kimberly, J., and R. Quinn. 1984. *New Futures: The Challenge of Managing Corporate Transitions.* Homewood, IL: Dow Jones-Irwin.

Krugman, P. 1992. *The Age of Diminished Expectations.* Cambridge, MA: MIT Press.

MacManus, S. 1992. *Budget Strategies Among Florida Local Governments.* Tampa: University of South Florida.

Marlowe, H.A., and L.A. Arrington. 1993. Paper presented to the Charlotte County Board of Commissioners. Port Charlotte, Florida, May.

Marlowe, H.A., and R.C. Nyhan. 1993. "Changing the Deep Structure of a Public Organization: Using the Punctuated Equilibrium Paradigm to Guide Productivity and Quality Improvement Programs." In *Productivity and Quality Management Frontiers IV*, ed. D.J. Summanth, R. Poupart, and D.S. Sink. Norcross, GA: Industrial Engineering and Management Press, pp. 597–606.

Marlowe, H.A., S.H. Hoffman, and S. Bordelon. 1992. "The Application of Organizational Development Processes to Downsizing: A Cognitive View." *Journal of Managerial Psychology* 7: 22–32.

Osborne, D. 1992. "Beyond Left and Right: A New Political Paradigm." *The Responsive Community* 2: 26–41.

Osborne, D., and T. Gaebler. 1992. *Reinventing Government.* Reading, MA: Addison-Wesley.

Pammer, W.J. 1990. *Managing Fiscal Strain in Major American Cities: Understanding Retrenchment in the Public Sector.* New York: Greenwood.

Peterson, I. 1991. "Americans See Dimmer Prospects." *Miami Herald*, November 4, p. 5–A.

Putnam, R.D. 1993. *Making Democracy Work.* Princeton, NJ: Princeton University Press.

Reich, R.B. 1991. *The Work of Nations.* New York: Alfred A. Knopf.

Spitzer, K. 1991. *Florida Local Government Revenue and Expenditure Forecasts, 1991–2000*, vol. 1. Tallahassee: Florida Association of Counties.

Thurow. L. 1992. *Head to Head: The Coming Economic Battle Among Japan, Europe, and America.* New York: William Morrow.

Walters, J. 1992. "The Shrink Proof Bureaucracy." *Governing* 5: 32–39.

Wildavsky, A. 1988. "Ubiquitous Anomie: Public Service in an Era of Ideological Dissensus." *Public Administration Review* (July/August): 753–755.

PART 5

CITIZEN INVOLVEMENT: OPPORTUNITIES FOR PARTICIPATION

One of the basic premises of democratic governance is that individuals elected to political office by the citizenry should represent the concerns and interests of the governed. This expectation of representation seems to be especially poignant at the local level where elected officials are physically and often emotionally closer to the citizens they represent. The best local government management practices require an understanding of local citizen preferences; however, achieving this "understanding" is quite challenging. Traditional public hearings are not likely to solicit the representative input eagerly sought by elected officials and public managers. As municipalities are challenged to do more with less, public officials find increased pressure to make sure that city policy and financial decisions are representative of the interests and concerns of a diverse population.

The chapters included in Part Five address a number of ways that local government is reaching out to its citizens and attempting to improve its services in a way that is reflective of the desires of its citizens. There are a number of formal and informal approaches being used to solicit citizen input that are not addressed in this section. However, these chapters present important concepts and ideas to consider when examining citizen involvement at the local level.

As critical players in the management of local government, city managers can influence the creation of avenues that incorporate citizen input into the goals and policies of city government. Because the most important and influential decisions are made at the top of an organization, the influence of gender and management style on the way citizen input is used is especially fundamental at this level. In their article, "Gender and Local Government: A Comparison of Women and Men City Managers" (published here as chapter 27), Richard L. Fox and Robert A. Schuhmann highlight gender differences and similarities in male and female approaches to political leadership, the policy process, and decision making. In particular, they conclude that female city managers are more likely to incorporate citizen feedback into their management style and to "emphasize communication in carrying out their duties as a manager" (p. 369) than are their male counterparts. In light of the limited research on the role of gender in local government management, this chapter addresses an interesting aspect of an emerging trend of increasing numbers of female city managers.

Entrepreneurial innovation and creative leadership approaches often emerge from citizen-driven pressure on municipalities to solve community problems. In chapter 28, Paul Teske and Mark Schneider find that entrepreneurial city managers are more widespread than suggested by the few highly publicized city managers. Specifically, these authors note that when the local citizenry call for change and the elected officials do not offer policies to address the issues, a large number of city managers address a variety of challenging issues in innovative ways in spite of constraints and challenges they face. With their intimate knowledge of their city's structure and municipal operations, city managers are uniquely able to look within their organization to find ways "to improve the efficiency of their workforce by promoting teamwork and inspiring their workers" (p. 385) and to look outside the organization "by adopting approaches that are in good currency, such as user fees and privatization" (p. 385).

Incorporating citizen sentiment into local government management is an ongoing issue of interest and concern to both academics and practitioners in public administration. Although public involvement is a worthwhile goal, incorporating constructive input is often quite challenging especially when the city already has a negative image. In chapter 29, "Dealing with Cynical Citizens," Evan M. Berman suggests that public administrators can be involved "in shaping public attitudes" (p. 389). His findings of a national survey addressing the attitudes of citizens toward their local governments reveal that cities that actively participate in efforts to promote a positive image through communication and education, citizen involvement, and a reputation of professionalism and excellence have less cynical citizens than those that do not. He concludes, "manifestations of cynicism should not be understood as the result of misunderstandings or as the result of systemic or isolated ethical wrongdoing" (p. 398). Instead, he finds that the issues of citizen cynicism and trust are grounded in the management of government.

One way that a growing number of municipalities are building citizen input into the processes of local government management and policymaking is with citizen surveys. As a measurement of public sentiment, citizen surveys offer representative feedback from the entire citizenry rather than from a few active and vocal citizens. Thomas I. Miller and Michelle A. Miller examine the results from 261 local government citizen surveys in an attempt to identify any commonalities and explain any differing results. They find that, for the most part, citizens felt good about the services their cities provide. This was especially true in cities that were "midsized with residents who were wealthier and were more likely to commute to a metropolitan job center" (p. 418). One interesting finding was that the consistently best-rated services were fire, library, and trash collection and the most poorly rated services were animal control, planning, and street repair. This finding was consistent across local governments regardless of survey type, quality, or how recently the survey had been conducted. In addition, satisfaction was not related to the amount citizens paid for the services. Although the role of management practices was not addressed by the data, this chapter clearly addresses the issues of service provision and citizen satisfaction that are so crucial to public administration at the local level.

CHAPTER 27

GENDER AND LOCAL GOVERNMENT:

A Comparison of Women and Men City Managers

RICHARD L. FOX AND ROBERT A. SCHUHMANN

Do women city managers view their role differently than their male counterparts? Do women offer a style of city management different from men? Does the inclusion of women in the highest positions of administrative power alter the nature of representation in city government? These questions have been largely overlooked in explorations of the local government landscape. In this chapter we address these questions by presenting the results of a national survey of over 500 men and women city managers in the United States. Our central finding in this investigation is that women managers are more likely than their male counterparts to embrace a style of management that relies on citizen input. This finding may have broad implications for the development of local public policy and for the type of representation that exists in city-level bureaucracies.

Gender and Political Leadership

In an effort to better frame the significance of gender influences on the behavior of city managers it is important to first take cues from two broad bodies of literature—the literature showing influences of gender on the behavior of public officials and the literature focusing on the importance of the city management position to local government. There is an expanding body of sociopsychological and political science literature that suggests women have political attitudes and societal orientations that differ in meaningful ways from those of men. Further, there is a body of scholarship that argues convincingly that public administration broadly conceived is a high gendered environment (Stivers 1993, 1990; Ferguson 1984). While it is also important not to overstate gender differences, it is increasingly evident that men and women often bring different leadership qualities, agendas, priorities, and methods of conceptualizing policy issues to their professional roles.

Many investigators have relied upon Carol Gilligan's (1982) path-breaking but controversial book, *In a Different Voice*, as the basis for establishing potential differences between the leadership, management, and political behaviors of women and men. Gilligan's central assertion is that men and women "construe social reality differently," leading to the creation of distinctively male and female voices (171). According to Gilligan, the female voice embraces the ideals of responsibility, caring, and interconnectedness, while the male voice embraces adherence to rules and individualism (172–173). Other sociopsychological investigations, including some conducted

From *Public Administration Review*, vol. 59, no. 3 (May/June 1999), pp. 231–242. Copyright © 1999 by American Society for Public Administration. Reprinted with permission.

by Gilligan herself, have further refined her initial arguments (Gilligan, Lyons, and Hammer 1990; Gilligan et al. 1988; Belenky et al. 1986).

Based in part, on these conceptions of gender differences, a growing number of studies of elected officials, public administrators, and private managers have explored the professional behavior of men and women and found important differences. For example, in studies of elected officials, Thomas (1994) found that women state legislators placed high priorities on policies that concern women, family, and children, while male legislators focused on business and economic legislation. At the national level, Clark (1998) studied the voting records of women and men in the U.S. House of Representatives and concluded that on certain issues, such as abortion and the environment, gender is an important determinant of how a member of Congress votes. In a study of leadership style, Rosenthal (1998) found that women committee chairs in state legislatures were much more task oriented than their male counterparts (176) (see also Carey, Niemi, and Powell 1998; Kathlene 1998; Berkman and O'Connor 1993; Reingold 1992; Dodson and Carroll 1991; Tolleson Rinehart 1991; Saint-Germain 1989).

In terms of the management style of appointed or merit employees, the research on gender influences in the public sector seems less well developed than the literature on elected officials. Further, we found that most of the attention has focused on state- and federal-level administrators (e.g., Borelli and Martin 1997; Guy 1992). One of the few broad-scale empirical examinations of gender and municipal administration was Ruth Ann Burns's (1979) *Women in Municipal Management: Choice, Challenge and Change.* Here, Burns studied 590 women and men from all levels of city administration, including assistant managers, finance directors, and department heads. She found differences between women and men in a number of areas, such as professional ambition, definition of the role of manager, and support networks. Debra Stewart (1990) also conducted extensive research on gender in city government, although not specifically with city managers. Stewart notes that women are underrepresented in executive roles within most departments of city government; however, she finds that women are more highly represented in agencies with programs requiring educational backgrounds traditionally associated with women. In addition, Stewart contends ": . . . female advancement in management is curtailed because women describe themselves, and are described by men, as having self-concepts that make them less suitable than men for management" (208). A similar finding has been found in a study of public managers in the federal government (Naff 1995) (see also Duerst-Lahti and Kelly 1995; Duerst-Lahti and Johnson 1992).

Finally, studies of private sector managers, such as Rosener's (1995), have found that women show a pattern of leadership that differs from the top-down, controlling style often associated with men. Rosener notes that women encourage participation, share power and information more readily, enhance the self-worth of those around them, and tend to energize others (11–13). In another study of managerial style, Helgesen (1990) found that women executives tended to see themselves as being in the "middle of things" (45). Women preferred to be not at the top, but in the center of a "web of inclusion" (43–60). Lunneborg (1990) found that women exhibit a number of stylistic characteristics that may set them apart from their male management counterparts in important ways. Some of these characteristics include a higher level of intuition about people, an interest in offering more praise to employees, a greater interest in giving orders "kindly," a greater sensitivity to subordinates' needs, a higher level of compromise and conciliation, and a different approach to teamwork (see also Billing and Alvesson 1994).

While the applicability of these bodies of literature to questions of city management must be handled carefully, these investigations provide an important starting point for evaluating potential gender differences among city managers.

City Manager Influence in the Municipal Policy Process

The second important body of relevant literature concerns the role of the city manager in questions of local governance. In principle, a city manager is the chief executive officer of a municipality whose prime directive is to manage the day-to-day affairs of the city. In reality, the city manager's role is much different and more complex (e.g., Montjoy and Watson 1995; Golembiewski and Gabris 1995).

As a professional orthodoxy emerged after the turn of the century, the city manager was seen as a value-neutral administrator and nonpolitical actor in the development and implementation of public policy. The elected officials (i.e., the city council and the mayor) were tasked with policy development and the city manager would implement that policy in the most efficient, effective, "professional" manner possible. (This is not to say that there was no policy role for the city manager. See Svara 1998.) This value-neutral role was, in part, an effort to face the increased challenges brought about by the changing municipal government landscape, characterized by an increased demand for municipal services and a heightened level of technical competence required to provide them. This early role was also a plank in the municipal reform movement in response to the graft and corruption seen (or perceived) in many cities. To achieve this latter goal, the council-manager plan sought to depoliticize municipal administration. This nonpolitical role also fit well with the "precepts of representative democracy" (Nalbandian 1991, 51) where elected officials establish public policy and nonelected, "expert" public officials implement it. Whether city managers could operate in such a politically sterile fashion has been a matter of much debate. What is clear is that this politics-administration dichotomy was part of the administrative *zeitgeist*.

A number of distinguished scholars are noted for tearing down this dichotomy, particularly as the construct relates to city management (e.g., Svara 1998, 1991, 1990, 1985; Nalbandian 1989; Ammons and Newell 1988; Newell and Ammons 1987). It is impractical to believe that city managers were ever simply considered apolitical chief executive officers. As harbingers of important municipal information, managers must influence the policy development process. They participate through the data they bring before city councils, the recommendations they make, and the particular lens through which they view city problems. As DeSantis, Glass, and Newell (1992) note, "[t]he value systems of city managers stem from their personal background, education and training, and personal and professional relationships" (447). Thus, a manager's value system affects how he or she views a problem (or whether it is viewed as a problem at all). As Denhardt (1981) notes, "what is observable, then, is always related to the awareness of the actor. . . . In our everyday relationships with one another, we can never fully separate our perceptions of that which is objective from that which is subjective" (104). At the very least, city managers approach their role from a value-laden position that influences their decision making. At the very most, city managers are active participants in policy development.

In a study of more than 500 municipal executives, Newell and Ammons (1987) found that 61.6 percent of city managers indicated that their most important role involved policy and politics. Administrative activities, on the other hand, were most important for only 38.5 percent (252). Additional support for the important policy-making role of city managers was found in a study carried out by Renner (1990). Here, in a survey of over sixteen hundred local government managers, 75 percent reported that they always participate in the formulation of municipal policy (51).

Lockard captures an important summary of the city manager's significance in local government. He notes, "[t]he city manager is among other things, chief administrator, chief legislator, political chief, symbolic and ceremonial head of the community, chief of public safety, and chief negotiator with other governments" (cited in Loveridge 1971, 31). Although this statement was made over thirty years ago, it remains reflective of the importance of the city manager position in municipal governance.

Methods and Data Collection

In an effort to explore the managerial styles of women and men city managers we utilized mail survey techniques. The survey sample was drawn from the International City/County Management Association's (ICMA) 1996 listing of city officials. The survey was carried out during 1997, with the majority of responses received by the end of the year. The ICMA compiles data on virtually all cities in the United States, including the type of government structure, the name of the city manager, and the city's location and size. The sample included only current city and town managers. Assistant managers were not included in this study. As the number of women city managers included in this list is relatively small, we chose to survey the entire population—a total of 435. We then developed a list of their male counterparts by closely matching each female city manager with a corresponding male manager from the same geographic region and from a similar-sized city from within that region. Our goal was to have two samples of cities, roughly equal in size—one managed by men and the other managed by women. The final number of male managers selected was 440. Combining this with our sample of women managers, our sample total consisted of 875 city managers.

In surveying the managers we devised a four-page questionnaire combining both open- and closed-ended questions. Our objective was to understand how each manager conceived of his or her role, what issues they viewed as important, and what important decisions they had made as a city manager. We also asked several questions about the demographics of the city and the political environment in which they worked. We first sent a copy of the instrument with a cover letter asking for each city manager's participation in the project. We did not mention our interest in gender differences in the letter. One week after the initial mailing we sent a reminder postcard to each survey recipient. Two weeks later we mailed a second copy of the survey and another letter urging participation from those who had not yet responded. All managers were assured of complete anonymity.

Of our original sample of 435 women managers, twenty-five managers were no longer in the position, reducing the possible number of respondents to 410. We received surveys from 251 for a response rate of 61.2 percent. In our original sample of 440 male managers, six no longer were in the position and dropped out of the pool. Of the 434 remaining male managers, we received 284 surveys for a response rate of 65.4 percent. Table 27.1 shows the demographics of cities and the relevant characteristics of managers that were included in the final sample.

Table 27.1 reveals similarities between the sample of women and men managers in their age, average number of years in the current position, the city's budget, the city's population, and the number of employees in their organization. There were also some important differences in the samples as well. Men were in the city management profession longer and had higher incomes. Women managers lived in the cities they were managing longer. Lastly, and perhaps most importantly, there were clear differences in the education levels of the city managers. More men had Masters degrees and more women had completed only high school.

In addition to demographic characteristics presented above, we collected information about the political environments of the cities. We asked managers to self-report their personal political ideology and assess the ideologies of the mayor, the city council, and the community. In part, the

Table 27.1

Demographics of Cities for the Men and Women City Managers in This Study

	Women (246)	Men (278)
Mean city size	24,412.0	20,798.0
Mean annual budget	$32,097,477.0	$24,965,441.0
Mean number of city employees	240.0	199.0
Mean years in city management profession	10.3***	13.5
Mean years in current position	6.3	7.1
Mean years lived in city	21.1***	16.0
Mean salary	$54,170.0***	$60,579.0
Mean age	47.9	47.8
Level of education		
High school	21.8%***	7.9%
A.A.	13.1%	7.6%
B.A.	24.2%	24.5%
Masters	35.7%***	58.1%
Doctorate	1.6%	.7%

Notes: Difference of means test comparing men and women managers, $*p < .10, **p < .05, ***p < .01$.

reason for attempting to assess political ideology was to limit the possibility of confusing gender differences with ideological differences. Using a seven-point ideology scale (1 = extremely liberal, 2 = liberal, 3 = somewhat liberal, 4 = moderate, 5 = somewhat conservative, 6 = conservative, and 7 = extremely conservative) women managers rated themselves as more liberal than men. The mean for women was 4.01 and the mean for men was 4.40 (significant at $p < .01$). Women city managers also gave their council and mayor a more liberal rating than men gave to their elected officials (both significant at $p < .05$). There were no significant differences in how men and women rated the ideology of the communities in which they worked. Overall, the data suggest that women managers operated in more liberal political environments than men. Thus, as we investigate the behavior of men and women city managers, we must be certain to consider education, ideology, and other job-related factors in our analysis.

Findings and Analysis

The findings reported in this chapter are broken into three sections. The first section addresses managers' motivations for pursuing a career in city government. The second deals with how men and women city managers define the role and responsibilities of the city manager. The third assesses the decision making styles of women and men city managers. Throughout this comparison differences emerge that suggest women are more likely to encourage citizen input and community involvement in the decision making process.

Motivations for Employment in City Government

In an open-ended question we asked managers why they pursued careers in city government. We felt this would tell us how managers conceived of the role of city manager and whether (or in what way) they valued their position. Among the responses provided by all managers, we found ten common answers that fell into three categories. The first was labeled *employment opportunities*. In it we included all responses in which managers asserted that they were only in the position

Table 27.2

Motivations for a Career in City Management

	Women (193)	Men (254)
Employment opportunities		
"Needed a good job"	14.0%**	21.3%
"Fell into it"	9.3***	2.8
Climbing career ladder	7.8	4.3
Commitment to the field		
"Like/love politics"	9.3	6.7
"Find work challenging"	22.8	18.5
Specific policy motivation	7.3	8.3
Commitment to public service		
"Public service"	69.4	68.1
"Help community"	28.5***	15.4
"Make a difference"	19.2*	26.0
"Work with /serve citizens"	28.5**	18.5

Notes: Entries indicate the percentage of managers who identified that area as a primary motivation. Difference of means test comparing men and women managers, $*p < .10$, $**p < .05$, $***p < .01$.

because of their need for employment. We included in this category those who said they "liked the salary and benefits," those who said they "fell into it" by chance, and those who said being city manager was merely a result of climbing the career ladder." The second category was labeled *commitment to the field*, and here we included managers who said they "liked or loved politics," those who said they "find this type of work challenging," and those who expressed interest in a specific public policy issue they hoped to address as a manager. The third category included all answers that alluded to an individual's *commitment to public service*. The notion of public service was expressed in a number of ways. Many managers used the exact words "public service," without any additional explanation. Others referred to the need to "help the community," or the desire to "make a difference," or the desire to "work with people and serve the citizens." Table 27.2 compares the responses of men and women city managers.

To test whether there were clear gender differences on some of the responses in Table 27.2, we conducted logistic regression analysis of each of the ten responses. The following variables were included in the equations: sex of the manager, level of education, ideology, salary, and a measure of how significant the job is to the manager. Table 27.3 presents these results.

Our findings indicate that four of the ten responses showed a statistically significant difference between men and women. Women managers were less likely than their male counterparts to enter the profession because of their desire for a "good salary" or "good benefits." Women managers were more likely than men to say that they simply "fell into" the profession. These results suggest women may assert a slightly lower level of political ambition than their male colleagues. Further, women and men responded similarly in terms of their commitment to the field of city management. Managers of both sexes mentioned a love for politics, the challenge of the work, and commitment to a specific area of public policy in similar proportions.

Roughly 70 percent identified "public service" as an important motivation for entering the city management profession. However, some important differences emerged in how men and women managers defined the meaning of public service. Women were more likely to define public service in terms of helping to improve the community, and were much more likely to use

Table 27.3

Logistic Regression Models for Motivations for Entering the City Management Professions

	Employment categories				Public service responses			Profession responses		
	Fell in	Career ladder	Benefits	Public service	Help community	Citizen welfare	Make a difference	Love work	Challenge	Specific policy
Manager sex	-.95* (.53)	-.62 (.48)	.61** (.30)	.02 (.24)	-.69*** (.27)	-.23 (.28)	.42* (.26)	-.50 (.38)	-.27 (.25)	0.11 (.40)
Level of education	-.62*** (.22)	.02 (.20)	-.04 (.13)	.05 (.11)	.03 (.12)	.12 (.14)	.08 (.13)	.30 (.19)	.11 (.12)	-.05 (.19)
Manager ideology	-.27 (.17)	.24 (.18)	-.04 (.10)	-.13 (.09)	-.03 (.09)	-.19* (.10)	-.11 (.09)	.09 (.14)	-.01 (.09)	.17 (.15)
Salary	1.3E-05 (1.0E-05)	-2.6E-05* (1.4E-05)	-1.9E-05** (7.6E-06)	1.6E-05*** (5.9E-06)	2.8E-06 (5.8E-06)	-9.9E-07 (6.1E-06)	7.4E-06 (5.4E-06)	1.1E-06 (9.7E-06)	-4.1E-06 (5.9E-06)	8.0E-06 (8.7E-06)
Significance of job	.11 (.34)	-.01 (.33)	.21 (.20)	-.49*** (.17)	-.35* (.20)	-.20 (.21)	-.01 (.19)	-.10 (.30)	-.21 (.20)	.06 (.29)
CONSTANT	-.85 (1.40)	-.15 (2.78)	.67 (1.55)	.91 (.95)	-.31 (.97)	-.50 (1.10)	-1.59* (.92)	-3.40*** (1.13)	-.93 (.71)	-3.72*** (1.12)
Log-likelihood	151.40	156.29	363.03	480.81	409.36	373.05	437.32	230.40	426.19	225.47
N	413	413	413	413	413	413	413	413	413	413

Notes: Independent variables were coded 0 (did not mention the motivation) and 1 (did mention the motivation).

"Sex of manager"—0 = woman, 1 = man.

"Level of education"—coded for the highest degree completed, 1 = high school, 2 = A.A., 3 = B.A., 4 = M.A., 5 = Doctoral degree.

"Manager ideology"—self-identified on a 7-point scale, 1 = extremely liberal, 2 = liberal, 3 = slightly liberal, 4 = moderate, 5 = slightly conservative, 6 = conservative, 7 = extremely conservative.

"Salary"—self-identified ranging from $8,000 per year to $150,000 per year.

"Significance of job"—self-reported, 1 = very significant, 2 = significant, 3 = somewhat significant, 4 = little significance, 5 = no significance.

Standard error in ( ). T-test significance levels, *$p < .10$, **$p < .05$, ***$p < .01$.

the word "community" and "citizen" in their definition. They saw public service as the rather contextual community-oriented matter of doing whatever it takes to improve the welfare of the citizens. Men, on the other hand, were more likely to say that they wanted to "make a difference" or "get something done." The feeling of personal accomplishment at achieving a specific and recognizable goal was important to them. This might include improving productivity in the office or successfully starting a new city program.

Comparing typical responses of men and women managers further illustrates how managers defined their public service motivations. We chose three women and three men with similar levels of education, from similarly sized cities, and from the same geographic region. Below are the three responses from the women managers:

"I became very involved in my children's school. I worked on all sorts of educational issues with broad implications. This experience gave me an interest in public service and what it means to help people."

"I became a city manager because I wanted to improve residents' quality of life and I wanted to get people involved in the political process."

"I had a desire to make a difference in my community. I just had a strong interest in working with, and serving, citizens."

These three responses share the similar feature of stating a desire to help people. The notion of public service for these women managers is defined in terms of service to citizens and community involvement. When these responses are contrasted with typical responses of male managers, clear differences emerge in their meaning of public service. Several male responses include:

"I am committed to public service and always have been."

"I got involved because I wanted to make a difference in how government works. I wanted to make government and the process more efficient—especially in terms of managing city finances."

"I felt I could get a lot done and make a lot of positive changes."

These responses do not demonstrate the same level of specificity in explaining the meaning of public service as those generally offered by women managers. This difference is supported by the constructs of masculine and feminine attitudes that Gilligan (1982) lays out—with women focusing on community and context and men focusing on individual accomplishment. A similar gender difference in defining public service has been found in a study of men and women congressional candidates (Fox 1997).

Although men and women managers in our sample offered both types of responses in explaining their motivations, women managers were more likely than men to refer to citizen welfare and community. The gender difference in the public service response begins to illustrate that some men and women conceive of community, citizen involvement, and public service differently.

Defining the Job of City Manager

We next asked managers how they defined the role of the city manager and how they viewed their most important responsibilities. We asked two types of questions. The first was an open-ended question asking managers to list what they saw as the most important responsibilities of a city manager. Second, we asked a series of closed-ended questions about the role of a city manager. Turning first to the open-ended questions, we again identified three broad types of responses. The first type focused on the responsibilities associated with managing the fiscal condition of the city. This included activities such as balancing the budget, encouraging economic development, and writing grant proposals. The second category of response focused on the manager as an administrator. This included activities such as managing the city staff, supervising the implemen-

Table 27.4

Primary Responsibilities of a City Manager (in percent)

	Women (207)	Men (260)
Fiscal responsibilities		
Balancing the budget	61.4	64.6
Economic development	8.7	8.5
Seeking out grants	4.8	3.2
Administrative responsibilities		
Managing personnel	45.9	43.1
Administer city services	25.1	28.8
Long-term planning	11.1	16.2
Policy development	16.4	18.5
Communication responsibilities		
Communicate with citizens	28.4**	9.2
Communicate with elected officials	43.1*	34.6
Motivate staff	5.1**	1.5

Notes: Entry indicates the percentage of managers who identified that area as a primary motivation. Difference of means test comparing men and women managers, $*p < .10$, $**p < .05$, $***p < .01$.

tation of city services, long-term planning, and policy development. The third category included various types of communication, including efforts to communicate with citizens, elected officials, and staff. Table 27.4 presents a comparison of how the respondents defined their jobs.

Again, for each of these ten responses we conducted logistic regression analysis using the following variables: sex of the manager, level of education, ideology, salary, and a measure of how significant the job is to the manager. Table 27.5 presents the results of the equations.

There were no significant differences between men and women city managers in terms of the first two areas outlined, fiscal and administrative responsibilities. However, gender differences began to emerge in the third category, communication responsibilities. Women managers were significantly more likely than men to state that communicating with citizens, communicating with elected officials, and motivating the staff are primary responsibilities of a city manager. The following are some typical ways women managers described their duties as facilitators of communication:

"A big part of the job is making sure that all of the members of the city council and the mayor are getting along and talking to each other."

"Communication with the public and making sure that residents know what we are doing and making certain we know how the public feels. . . ."

"I am constantly trying to open up the lines of communication between the government and the people."

Women managers more frequently offered these types of responses, providing evidence that women place greater emphasis than men on community input and citizen involvement in decision making, as well as on fostering interaction among various groups and actors in the community. In addition to gender differences, Table 27.5 also reveals that the salary level of the manager has a significant relationship to how he or she defines the job. Managers with lower salaries are more likely to include balancing the budget and economic development as primary responsibilities. Managers with higher salaries are more likely to mention communication with the government officials and motivating the staff.

Table 27.5

Logistic Regression Models for Primary Responsibilities of City Managers

	Fiscal responsibilities			Administrative responsibilities				Communication responsibilities		
	Balance budget	Economic development	Grants	Manage personnel	Administer services	Planning	Policy development	Communica-tion with citizens	Communica-tion with government	Motivate office staff
Sex of manager	.13	-.03	-1.53	-.11	.21	.27	.04	-.37*	-.29	-1.48*
	(.22)	(.37)	(1.24)	(.21)	(.24)	(.32)	(.28)	(.22)	(.22)	(.76)
Level of education	.07	.26	.10	.10	.01	-.09	.31**	-.12	.12	.00
	(.10)	(.17)	(.45)	(.10)	(.11)	(.14)	(.13)	(.10)	(.10)	(.33)
Manager ideology	-.09	-.02	.33	-.05	.00	.09	.00	.04	-.08	.14
	(.08)	(.13)	(.38)	(.07)	(.08)	(.11)	(.10)	(.08)	(.08)	(.24)
Salary	-1.1E-05**	-1.6E-05*	.00	1.8E-06	-2.5E-06	6.6E-07	2.3E-06	4.6E-07	1.3E-05***	2.1E-05*
	(4.9E-06)	(9.45E-6)	(4.6E-05)	(4.8E-06)	(5.4E-06)	(6.9E-06)	(6.0E-06)	(5.0E-06)	(5.0E-06)	(1.2E-05)
Significance of job	-.10	-.14	.46	-.21	.08	.26	.11	-.04	-.25	.53
	(.16)	(.27)	(.61)	(.16)	(.17)	(.22)	(.20)	(.16)	(.17)	(.52)
CONSTANT	.74	-1.38	1.64	-.63	-.94	.95	-2.68***	.26	-1.13	-4.50
	(.83)	(1.53)	(8.50)	(.95)	(.81)	(1.84)	(6.70)	(.85)	(.77)	(3.45)
Log-likelihood	551.33	250.86	37.96	581.22	504.76	327.93	392.62	536.16	539.75	88.49
N	429	429	429	429	429	429	429	429	429	429

Notes: Independent variables were coded 0 (did not mention the responsibility) and 1 (did mention the responsibility).
"Sex of manager"—0 = woman, 1 = man.
"Level of education"—coded for the highest degree completed, 1 = high school, 2 = A.A., 3 = B.A., 4 = M.A., 5 = Doctoral degree.
"Manager ideology"—self-identified on a 7-point scale, 1 = extremely liberal, 2 = liberal, 3 = slightly liberal, 4 = moderate, 5 = slightly conservative, 6 = conservative, 7 = extremely conservative.
"Salary"—self-identified ranging from $8,000 per year to $150,000 per year.
"Significance of job"—self-reported, 1 = very significant, 2 = significant, 3 = somewhat significant, 4 = little significance, 5 = no significance.
Standard error in ( ). T-test significance levels, *p < .10, **p < .05, ***p < .01.

Table 27.6

Influence of Various Factors on the Decision Making of Women and Men City Managers

	Women (257)	Men (282)
How important are the following factors in influencing how you make decisions as city manager?		
Doing what I think is best for the city	1.59	1.67
Budgetary constraints	1.32***	1.52
Treating citizens equally	1.66	1.66
Treating citizens fairly	1.37	1.46
Demands of the city council	1.76	1.69
Demands of the mayor	2.34	2.67
Whether the decision is in accord with city norms	1.80***	2.08
Relying on my own experience	2.37	2.27
The political consequences	2.89	2.96
Public opinion	2.14*	2.27
Input of my staff	2.15**	2.02

Notes: Entries represent the mean scores based on a 1–5 scale with 1 = "very important," 2 = "important," 3 = "somewhat important," 4 = "little importance," and 5 = "no importance."

Difference of means test comparing men and woman managers, $*p < .10$, $**p < .05$, $***p < .01$.

In a series of closed-ended questions, we asked more specifically how men and women defined the role of the city manager. One question asked whether men and women considered themselves "entrepreneurial city managers." We defined an entrepreneurial city manager as one who attempts to create or shape city policies (see Teske and Schneider 1994). Ninety-three percent of men identified themselves as entrepreneurs and only 76 percent of women did likewise (significant at $p < .01$). When respondents were asked to assess their level of agreement and disagreement with several statements about the proper role of the city manager, women were more likely than men to say the role of city manager should be administrative and not policy oriented, 69 percent to 57 percent (significant at $p < .01$). Women were also more likely than men to assert that city managers should remain neutral on controversial city issues, 47 percent to 29 percent (significant at $p < .01$). What emerges is a portrait of a woman city manager who is a facilitator of community relations, while men are more entrepreneurial and emphasize individual responsibility.

Decision Making and the City Manager

The final area that we will address in this chapter is the decision making process of men and women city managers. In many regards decision making might be considered the essence of managerial and administrative style. Performing the job of city manager is often a sequence of decisions, small and large. To understand the decision making of managers we employed two approaches. First, we presented managers with a list of eleven possible influences on decision making and asked them to rate on a scale from one to five how important each item was for making decisions. A typical five-point scale was used with "1" indicating highest importance and "5" indicating no importance. Table 27.6 presents the mean score for each factor for men and women.

We found statistically significant differences between the responses of men and women managers on four of the eleven influences. More women than men managers said that budgetary constraints, accordance with city norms, and public opinion were most important in their decision making process. Men placed greater weight than women on input from their staff in making decisions. These differences are consistent with the patterns that are developing throughout this analysis. Women's greater consideration of city norms and public opinion coincides with their emphasis on preserving the community and serving the wishes of the residents. The greater adherence to budgetary constraints is consistent with the less entrepreneurial approach women take to the position. Overall, the differences identified in Table 27.6 are very small. However, closed-ended questions of this nature often obscure subtle gender dynamics.

In an attempt to understand the subtleties involved in managerial decision making, we presented managers with two hypothetical scenarios, both common to the task of city management. The first asked managers how they would resolve the dilemma of providing city services against constituents' cries for reduced taxation. The second scenario asked managers how they would handle a personnel problem. The two scenarios were presented in the mail survey as follows.

Scenario Number One

Your city is in dire need of a new recreation facility. Acquiring a new building is going to be costly. However, the residents of the city are demanding that the tax burden be reduced. How would you handle this situation? How would you balance the needs of the city with the stated desires of the citizens?

Scenario Number Two

There is an effective and popular department head on your staff, but over the last couple of years he has developed a bad reputation with the city council. The elected officials are urging you to fire him. How would you handle this situation? Do you think you would ultimately fire this individual?

Responses

Managers chose a variety of approaches to handle the dilemma in the first hypothetical scenario, but we were able to code answers into six categories. The six common approaches and how they were coded are listed below:

1. Seek Alternative Funding—usually meant applying for state and federal grants or raising the money in some way that did not include tax increases.
2. User Fees—the recreation center would pay for itself retroactively by charging users.
3. Low-Cost Alternative—these were solutions that would save money, such as sharing the facility with neighboring cities or trying to find space to rent.
4. Gather More Information—many managers wanted more information about why the recreation center was necessary before they would offer a recommendation about how to work through the dilemma.
5. Public/Private Partnership—this response usually included some form of corporate sponsorship for the center.
6. Involve Citizens—these responses include such things as a call for a referendum or the formation of a citizen committee.

Table 27.7 illustrates how women and men managers employed these various approaches. For the results of both hypothetical decision making scenarios (presented in Tables 27.7 and 27.8) we

Table 27.7

Hypothetical Decision Making Number 1: Services Versus Revenue

	Women (206)	Men (250)
Seek alternative funding	64.1%	58.0
User fees	13.1	14.4
Low-cost alternative	20.4*	14.1
Gather more information	16.0	16.4
Public/private partnership	31.0	34.0
Involve citizens	57.8***	43.6

Notes: Entries indicate the percentage of managers who identified that particular option.

Columns do not add up to 100 percent because some managers mentioned two or three options and combined some of the options.

Difference of means test comparing men and women managers, $*p < .10, **p < .05, ***p < .01$.

Table 27.8

Hypothetical Decision Making Number 2: Personnel Issue

	Women (200)	Men (243)
Willingness to fire		
Definitely will not fire	58.0%	50.6%
Fire as last resort	7.0	7.0
Fire with serious efforts	17.4	20.6
Fire	.5	2.5
Resolution plan		
Urge to quit	8.5	5.8
Gather more information	19.9*	26.7
Devise plan to rehabilitate employee	22.9*	16.0
Work as an intermediary between employee and council	51.2***	38.6
Facilitate/moderate direct communication between employee and council	23.9**	14.8

Notes: Entries indicate the percentage of managers who identified that particular option. Columns do not add up to 100 percent because some managers mentioned two or three options and combined some of the options. Difference of means test comparing men and women managers, $*p < .10, **p < .05, ***p < .01$.

conducted logistic regression analysis of the variables to test whether gender remained significant in light of the other possible explanatory variables such as level of education and ideology. In the analysis, gender remained the only significant variable (regression analysis not shown).

Overall, women would resolve the recreation facility scenario differently than men. If we break down the numbers further than what is shown in Table 27.7, we find that 31 percent of women said the issue should go before the citizens for a vote while only 15 percent of men said the same. Again we can turn to the statements of several of the women managers to illustrate.

"The first thing I would do would be to set up a citizen advisory committee and have the citizens research the problem and present their recommendations to the council."

"Communicate pros and cons with the citizens and encourage a citizen group to work with the city to seek solutions."

"Conduct a citizen survey to determine desires of the community, not just those [citizens] who show up at meetings."

Women managers' preference for citizen involvement was further corroborated when the managers were asked specifically about the degree to which they incorporated citizen input into their decision making process. Managers were asked to rank on a five-point scale how, when making decisions, they balanced their own professional expertise with citizen input. On the scale, a rating of "1" indicated total reliance on citizen input in decision making, a rating of "5" indicated total reliance on the managers' own expertise, and a rating of "3,"—the center point of the scale— indicated a perfect balance. The mean score for male managers was 3.51 and the mean score for female managers was 3.03 (significant at $p < .01$).

In the hypothetical scenario concerning the employee, managers were asked to decide how they would deal with an employee who by all professional measures was deemed effective or "good" but that the city council wanted to fire. There were two components to this question and the responses were broken down by: (1) the relative likelihood of firing the individual, and (2) the means by which the manager would attempt to address the situation. In the first component, managers offered several clear types of responses including: "definitely would not fire," "would likely fire," or "would urge the employee to quit." An additional response, "fire as last resort," refers to those managers who said they would do everything in their power to save the employee, but that they would not lose their own job over the issue. A final response, "fire with serious efforts," refers to those managers who said they would try to work with the employee, but might ultimately resort to termination if the situation did not improve.

The second component of this question focused on how the manager would attempt to address the problem. Answers to this part of the scenario were coded into four categories. The coding scheme is defined below:

1. Gather More Information—these responses indicated a manager's desire to acquire more information before acting.
2. Devise Plan to Rehabilitate Employee—these were any responses in which the manager identified a specific course of action to improve the employee's image.
3. Work as an Intermediary Between Employee and Council—in these responses the manager would work as a go-between to repair the relationship between the employee and city council members.
4. Facilitate Direct Communication Between Employee and Council Members—in these instances, unlike category number three, the manager attempts to bring the employee and the council together to smooth over their differences.

Table 27.8 shows how responses broke down according to gender.

On the question of whether the manager would fire the employee, there were only small gender differences. Women managers were somewhat less likely to choose the option of firing, while men were slightly more likely to say they would terminate the employee. However, in terms of what specific actions managers would take in attempting to resolve the situation, there are clear differences between the sexes. Men are more likely to say they want to obtain more information about the situation, while women are more likely to try to devise a specific plan to help rehabilitate the employee.

The final two types of responses reveal that women managers are more likely than men to attempt to facilitate communication between the employee and the city council with the hopes of salvaging the image of the employee. In the first case women are more likely than men to act as an intermediary between the employee and council members. In illustrating this approach, one woman manager stated her strategy: "I'd work with the department head and each council mem-

ber to define specific problems and resolve them . . . 90 percent of these problems are communication." In another example a woman manager said she would ". . . interview the department head.
Then I would interview each council member and work as a go-between to resolve the differences." In these instances women managers are attempting to resolve the situation by working as
mediator. In the second scenario, women city managers are more likely than men managers to
suggest that all of the aggrieved parties sit down together and work things out directly. One
woman manager noted that the first thing she would do is "hold an employee/council conference
to air differences." Another said she "would have him or her [the employee] meet individually
with council members to try to build relationships." Again, the emphasis by women managers on
facilitating communication is consistent with the constructs of masculine and feminine voices, as
conceived by Gilligan (1982).

Summary of Findings and Conclusion

This study's central finding is that women city managers are more likely than men city managers
to incorporate citizen input and to be concerned with community involvement in their decisions.
This finding emerged when women stated their motivations for involvement in city administration, when they defined their primary responsibilities as a manager, and, most importantly, when
they explained how they made decisions. A second major finding, which is consistent with the
first, is that women managers tend to emphasize communication in carrying out their duties as a
manager. This includes communication with citizens, as revealed in how women defined their job
responsibilities, and with elected and unelected government officials, as evidenced by women's
decision making practices. A third finding, which is less well developed but appeared in several
areas, is that women are less likely than men to see themselves as policy entrepreneurs and more
likely to see their role as a manager and facilitator. This result emerged from questions concerning
policy making and policy entrepreneurship.

In the end, we found that the interaction between gender and the position of city manager is
greater than we might have expected. This is particularly important since local government
actors have received only light attention in the gender politics literature. Thus, future examinations of city managers and the city management profession will need to consider the possible
importance of manager gender. Further, the role of gender in city administration may have increased importance as more and more women are poised to become chief executive officers in
cities across the United States.

Beyond making contributions to the respective literatures, there are two broad implications of
our findings. First, there appears to be a distinct "feminine voice" in the politics of city management
and this voice is underrepresented in the city management profession. Women are significantly
more likely than men to display the "feminine voice" traits. The serious problem in terms of
representation and legitimacy arises in that women compose only 11 percent of chief administrators
in city government. Compounding this problem is the circumstance that unlike other political
venues where the number of women is steadily on the rise, the percentage of women city managers
has been slow to change over the past ten years (Schuhmann and Fox 1998; Szymborski 1996).

A second implication is that women appear more likely to promote traditional democratic
processes, that is, making citizens an important part of the decision making process. Women in
this study were more likely to value citizen input and would prefer to be in the middle of a "web"
of interactions rather than to be on top of the hierarchy. At the local level of government, public
officials have more chances to share decisions with the community. Women managers seem more
likely to take advantage of these important opportunities. Encouraging citizen participation is

clearly an important issue because the legitimacy of governmental power is at stake. Krislov and Rosenbloom (1981) argue that from the point of view of democratic values, "legitimation is conveyed through governmental representation of the public and by public participation in government" (21). We found that women managers seem to utilize skills that further the democratic principle of "governing by the people." The skills and values that women managers demonstrate can only help to advance the legitimacy of government—in this case, local-level bureaucracy.

References

Ammons, David N., and Charldean Newell. 1988. "'City Managers Don't Make Policy': A Lie; Let's Face It." *National Civic Review* 77, no. 2: 124–132.

Belenky, Mary Field, Bluthe McVicker Clinchy, Nancy Rule Goldberger, and Jill Mattuck Tarule. 1986. *Women's Ways of Knowing*. New York: Basic Books.

Berkman, Michael B., and Robert E. O'Connor. 1993. "Do Women State Legislators Matter? Female Legislators and State Abortion Policy." *American Politics Quarterly* 21: 201–124.

Billing, Yvonne, and Mats Alvesson. 1994. *Gender, Managers, and Organizations*. New York: Walter de Gruyter.

Borelli, MaryAnne, and Janet M. Martin, eds. 1997. *The Other Elites*. Boulder, CO: Lynne Rienner.

Burns, Ruth Ann. 1979. *Women in Municipal Management: Choice, Challenge, and Change*. Eagleton Institute of Politics, Rutgers, NJ: Center of the American Woman and Politics.

Carey, John M., Richard G. Niemi, and Lynda Powell. 1998. "Are Women State Legislators Different?" In *Women and Elective Office*, ed. Sue Thomas and Clyde Wilcox. New York: Oxford University Press.

Clark, Janet. 1998. "Women at the National Level: An Update on Roll Call Voting Behavior." In *Women and Elective Office*, ed. Sue Thomas and Clyde Wilcox. New York: Oxford University Press.

Denhardt, Robert B. 1981. *In the Shadow of Organization*. Lawrence: University Press of Kansas.

DeSantis, Victor S., James J. Glass, and Charldean Newell. 1992. "City Managers, Job Satisfaction, and Community Perceptions." *Public Administration Review* 52, no. 5: 447–453.

Dodson, Debra, and Susan J. Carroll. 1991. *Reshaping the Agenda: Women in State Legislatures*. Eagleton Institute of Politics, Rutgers, NJ: Center for the American Woman and Politics.

Duerst-Lahti, Georgia, and Cathy Marie Johnson. 1992. "Management Styles, Stereotypes, and Advantages." In *Women and Men of the States: Public Administrators at the State Level*, ed. Mary E. Guy. Armonk, NY: M.E. Sharpe.

Duerst-Lahti, Georgia, and Rita Mae Kelly. 1995. *Gender Power, Leadership, and Governance*. Ann Arbor: University of Michigan Press.

Ferguson, Kathy E. 1984. *The Feminist Case Against Bureaucracy*. Philadelphia, PA: Temple University Press.

Fox, Richard L. 1997. *Gender Dynamics in Congressional Elections*. Thousand Oaks, CA: Sage.

Gilligan, Carol. 1982. *In a Different Voice: Psychological Theory and Women's Development*. Cambridge, MA: Harvard University Press.

Gilligan, Carol, Nona P. Lyons, and Trudy J. Hanmer, eds. 1990. *Making Connections: The Relational Worlds of Adolescent Girls at Emma Willard School*. Cambridge, MA: Harvard University Press.

Gilligan, Carol, Janie V. Ward, Jill McLean Taylor, and Betty Bardigie, eds. 1988. *Mapping the Moral Domain: A Contribution of Women's Thinking to Psychological Theory and Education*. Cambridge, MA: Harvard University Press.

Golembiewski, Robert T., and Gerald Gabris. 1995. "Tomorrow's City Management: Guides for Avoiding Success Becoming Failure." *Public Administration Review* 55, no. 3: 240–246.

Guy, Mary E., ed. 1992. *Women and Men of the States: Public Administrators at the State Level*. Armonk, NY: M.E. Sharpe.

Helgesen, Sally. 1990. *The Female Advantage*. New York: Doubleday.

Kathlene, Lyn. 1998. "In a Different Voice: Women and the Policy Process." In *Women and Elective Office*, ed. Sue Thomas and Clyde Wilcox. New York: Oxford University Press.

Krislov, Samuel, and David H. Rosenbloom. 1981. *Representative Bureaucracy and the American Political System*. New York: Praeger.

Loveridge, Ronald O. 1971. *City Managers in Legislative Politics*. New York: Bobbs-Merrill.

Lunneborg, Patricia W. 1990. *Women Changing Work.* New York: Greenwood.

Montjoy, Robert S., and Douglas J. Watson. 1995. "A Case for Reinterpreted Dichotomy of Politics and Administration as a Professional Standard in Council-Manager Government." *Public Administration Review* 55, no. 3: 231–239.

Naff, Katherine C. 1995. "Subjective vs. Objective Discrimination in Government: Adding to the Picture of Barriers to the Advancement of Women." *Political Research Quarterly* 48: 535–557.

Nalbandian, John. 1989. "The Contemporary Role for City Managers." *American Review of Public Administration* 19, no. 4: 261–278.

———. 1991. *Professionalism in Local Government.* San Francisco, CA: Jossey-Bass.

Newell, Charldean, and David N. Ammons. 1987. "Role Emphases of City Managers and Other Municipal Executives." *Public Administration Review* 47: 246–253.

Reingold, Beth. 1992. "Concepts of Representation Among Female and Male State Legislators." *Legislative Studies Quarterly* 17: 509–537.

Renner, Tari. 1990. "Appointed Local Government Managers: Stability and Change." In *The Municipal Yearbook 1990.* Washington, DC: International City Management Association, pp. 41–52.

Rosener, Judy. 1995. *America's Competitive Secret.* New York: Oxford University Press.

Rosenthal, Cindy Simon. 1998. "Getting Things Done: Women Committee Chairpersons in State Legislatures." In *Women and Elective Office,* ed. Sue Thomas and Clyde Wilcox. New York: Oxford University Press.

Saint-Germain, Michelle A. 1989. "Does Their Difference Make a Difference? The Impact of Women on Public Policy in the Arizona Legislature." *Social Science Quarterly* 70: 956–968.

Schuhmann, Robert A., and Richard L. Fox. 1998. "Women Chief Administrative Officers." In *The Municipal Yearbook.* Washington, DC: International City/County Management Association.

Stewart, Debra W. 1990. "Women in Public Administration." In *Public Administration: The State of the Discipline,* ed. Naomie B. Lynn and Aaron Wildavsky. Chatham, NJ: Chatham House.

Stivers, Camilla. 1990. "Towards a Feminist Perspective in Public Administration Theory." *Women and Politics* 10, no. 4: 49–65.

———. 1993. *Gender Images in Public Administration: Legitimacy and the Administrative State.* Newbury Park, CA: Sage.

Svara, James H. 1985. "Dichotomy and Duality: Reconceptualizing the Relationship Between Policy and Administration in Council-Manager Cities." *Public Administration Review* 45: 221–232.

———. 1990. *Official Leadership in the City.* New York: Oxford University Press.

———. 1991. "Council and Administrator Perspectives on the City Manager's Role: Conflict, Divergence, or Congruence." *Administration and Society* 23, no. 2: 227–246.

———. 1998. "The Politics-Administration Dichotomy Model as Aberration." *Public Administration Review* 58, no. 1: 51–58.

Szymborski, Lee. 1996. "Why Are There So Few Women Managers?" *Public Management* 78, no. 12: 11–15.

Teske, Paul, and Mark Schneider. 1994. "The Bureaucratic Entrepreneur: The Case of City Managers." *Public Administration Review* 54: 331–340 [published here as chapter 28].

Thomas, Sue. 1994. *How Women Legislate.* New York: Oxford University Press.

Tolleson Rinehart, Sue. 1991. "Do Women Leaders Make a Difference? Substance, Style and Perceptions." In *Gender and Policy Making,* ed. Debra Dodson Eagleton. Rutgers, NJ: Center for the American Woman and Politics.

CHAPTER 28

THE BUREAUCRATIC ENTREPRENEUR:

The Case of City Managers

PAUL TESKE AND MARK SCHNEIDER

Unelected bureaucrats regularly influence the implementation of public policies. Some entrepreneurial bureaucrats play an even more important role in shaping policy agendas and in formulating new policy. Such bureaucratic entrepreneurship, however, generally has been treated by scholars as a chance occurrence rather than as a phenomenon that can be explained systematically (Wilson 1989).

We conceive of bureaucratic entrepreneurs as actors who help propel dynamic policy change in their community.[1] Like other entrepreneurs, they engage in the act of "creative discovery" by creating or exploiting new opportunities to push forward their ideas (Schneider and Teske 1992; Kirzner 1973; Schumpeter 1942). While some social scientists have started to develop more systematic theories of entrepreneurship, most studies still rely heavily on biographical studies of leaders whose actions produced innovative or unexpected policy changes (Caro 1974; Lewis 1980; Doig and Hargrove 1987; Kirchheimer 1989; Weissert 1991). According to Wilson, such studies show that the personalities and actions of individual executives are critical to explaining innovative bureaucratic change. In turn, Wilson (1989, 227) argues: "It is not easy to build a useful social science theory out of 'change appearances.'" However, we believe that the emergence of entrepreneurial city managers in the decentralized American system of local government can be related systematically to community characteristics (see Mohr [1969] who relates bureaucratic innovation to organizational characteristics).

Suburban governments have been buffeted by major changes in recent years, including reductions in intergovernmental aid, citizen demands for new services and lower taxes, questions about the value of growth, and the increasing costs of basic service delivery. Many of these factors require local governments to respond with innovative policies. As a result, some entrepreneurial leaders in government have begun to introduce and implement new policy ideas, improve the efficiency of existing programs, and redirect bureaucratic behavior to meet these challenges. Osborne and Gaebler (1992, 16) argue that of all levels of governments in the United States, *local* governments have the most innovative, propelled by the combination of property tax revolts, cuts in intergovernmental aid during the early 1980s, and the 1982 recession. As we shall illustrate, sometimes city managers emerge to play this entrepreneurial role in local government.

Recently, scholars have analyzed the process of policy innovation in state and local governments, documenting a "bottom-up" process of political and managerial entrepreneurship in

From *Public Administration Review*, vol. 54, no. 4 (July/August 1994), pp. 331–340. Copyright © 1994 by American Society for Public Administration. Reprinted with permission.

American government (Eisinger 1988; Altshuler and Zegans 1990; Golden 1990; Sanger and Levin 1992; Osborne and Gaebler 1992). These studies are concerned mostly with policy innovations. In contrast, our focus is on the actors who promote and implement such innovations.

In local government, entrepreneurial leadership is most likely to come from elected politicians in the community, such as mayors and council members. But high-level bureaucratic employees, such as city managers, also emerge as entrepreneurs. Because most of the entrepreneurial bureaucrats that we identified in our research were city managers, we focused specifically on them. City managers, as the chief operating officers of their communities, are a well-defined professional group, and they share similar training in public administration (Kammerer 1964). The activities of city managers were fairly comparable in the suburban communities in our sample.

Explaining the Emergence of Entrepreneurial Managers

City managers work in complex environments. Local economic and fiscal conditions are constantly changing, and the preferences and policy demands of politicians and citizens also change. Local bureaucrats and politicians may present roadblocks to city managers trying to change policy directions. While these problems present challenges, they also create opportunities for innovative and creative policy entrepreneurship. As Hargrove (1989, 79) notes: "the central act of creative leadership is to provide plausible strategies of action in an ambiguous environment." In exercising such leadership, entrepreneurial managers face two worlds: an internal world defined by demands of managing the local bureaucracy and a complex external world defined by the political, legal, and economic milieu in which cities exist. The goals, strategies, and constraints entrepreneurial managers face differ across these two domains.

Internal issues relate to the ability of managers to motivate public sector employees to perform more efficiently. A critical task for every government manager is to get workers to comply with organizational goals. For entrepreneurial managers seeking change, the need to motivate workers to overcome inertia and be more productive is even greater.

External issues are defined by the constraints and opportunities presented by the changing environment communities face and by the need managers have to interact with local politicians, interest groups, actors in higher levels of government, and the media to create coalitions and constituencies supporting new policies.

The Goals of City Managers

The concept of opportunity is critical to the study of entrepreneurship: What conditions affect the likelihood that an entrepreneur will be found in a particular locality? What goals do entrepreneurial managers pursue?

Most economic theories argue that the pursuit of profits drives the entrepreneurial process and that the supply of entrepreneurs increases with the potential for these entrepreneurial profits (Ricketts 1987). Unlike business entrepreneurs, who can usefully be modeled as single-mindedly pursuing monetary profits, public sector bureaucrats pursue a combination of goals (Downs 1967; Wilson 1989). Clearly, city managers are interested in their own careers, which usually means moving up to a larger city with a higher salary, control over more resources, perhaps more autonomy, and greater prestige within the profession (Kammerer 1964; Barber 1988). But career advancement and attendant higher salaries are not sufficient to understand why some city managers are more entrepreneurial than others. Managers are also motivated by the desire to achieve specific policy goals, by solving problems, and by a desire for public service (DeSantis, Glass, and Newell 1992).

Absent the dominant goal of monetary profits as driving the emergence of entrepreneurs, political scientists have had trouble developing insight into how and why entrepreneurs are called forth. Kingdon (1984) describes policy entrepreneurs as constantly shopping around for windows of opportunity through which to push their preferred policy ideas. Kingdon (1984) and Walker (1981) both stress the importance of policy communities in determining which ideas have currency. Local managers are often involved in professional networks from which they learn about new policy ideas and to which their professional egos are tied (Oakerson and Parks 1988; Ammons and Newell 1989). Baumgartner and Jones (1991) argue that the outcome of political debates can vary with the venue in which the debates occur, and that successful policy entrepreneurs shop around for the most favorable venue. Although these studies focus on the strategies of entrepreneurs, they do not identify systematically the conditions under which they emerge.

The Internal World of the Entrepreneurial Manager

Whatever their specific goals, entrepreneurial managers face constraints, particularly in getting subordinates to implement new policies successfully. Although entrepreneurs play a critical role in importing and formulating new policies, ultimately their success is tied to how well policies are carried out. Mazmanian and Sabatier (1983) argue that leadership is the only bureaucratic variable crucial to successful policy implementation.

According to Miller (1992), all managers, including those advocating entrepreneurial changes, have two basic approaches to persuade and motivate workers to implement their policies. The first, associated with Max Weber and Frederick Winslow Taylor and related to today's principal/ agent models (Moe 1984), focuses on control and hierarchy to achieve an optimal mix of incentives and monitoring techniques to influence subordinates. But even the most clever employment contract cannot overcome the problems of shirking, which are far more severe in the public sector than in private firms (Wilson 1989; Miller 1992; and Brehm and Gates 1993).

An alternate approach, harking back to Chester Barnard and Philip Selznick, postulates that control mechanisms are not enough to guarantee achievement of the leader's goals. Leaders must master motivational and/or rhetorical skills to inspire workers to work toward organizational goals. Ouchi (1980) argues, for example, that the problem of "performance ambiguity" (endemic to the delivery of local public goods) is best managed by transforming the operating units of an organization into the equivalent of a "clan" united by "organic solidarity." Wilson (1989, 156) argues that the best solution to shirking is to inculcate in workers a shared sense of mission, even if there are no financial payoffs. In suburban governments, city managers usually cannot motivate workers with financial rewards, and they do not have large personal staffs to monitor bureaucratic behavior closely. Consequently, entrepreneurial managers must motivate subordinates using their own interpersonal skills.

The External World of the Entrepreneurial Manager

Many scholars of bureaucratic leadership argue that external relations may be even more important than internal implementation strategies. Lynn (1990) notes that entrepreneurial managers are more likely to focus on external agency issues, while nonentrepreneurial administrators focus mostly inward. Wilson (1989, 203) summarizes studies of successful executives: "all had one thing in common: They found or maintained the support of key external constituencies."

Entrepreneurs often try to develop technical expertise within their organization to provide a potent resource to bargain with external constituents and their elected sovereigns (Miller and

Moe 1983; Niskanen 1975). As reform ideas and professionalization have become more wide-spread, city managers have gained power and autonomy (Ammons and Newell 1989; Nalbandian 1989), which has not been countered by a similar professionalization of city council or mayoral staff support (Protasel 1988). Thus, compared to changes at the national level, the relative lack of full-time potential political overseers supported by large staffs, may give local bureaucrats more discretion to use expertise and to engage in entrepreneurial behavior.

City managers face important constraints, including economic conditions that limit their options (Peterson 1981; Schneider 1989). They also face political limits imposed by the actions of politicians and interest groups (Svara 1990). Reduced intergovernmental aid, stagnating prop-erty tax revenues, and mandates imposed by higher levels of government (Lovell et al. 1979; ACIR 1985) can further constrain entrepreneurial opportunities.

Politically, bureaucratic entrepreneurship may also be limited because the range, complexity, and size of local programs are less than at higher levels of government. The relatively small size of the voting public may also allow voters to hold bureaucrats more directly accountable. Local interest groups can also constrain managers by ringing "fire alarms" to which politicians will attend (McCubbins and Schwartz 1984), while the openness of local governments allows indi-vidual citizen demands to act as constraints (Sharp 1986). This combination of economic, finan-cial, and political factors can limit entrepreneurial behavior by managers.

Successful entrepreneurial managers learn to overcome such limits. Sanger and Levin (1992, 111) argue that successful entrepreneurs use "a conscious underestimating of bureaucratic and political obstacles" (see also Hirschman 1967). While the economic approach to human behavior assumes fixed preferences, a crucial feature of politics is that preferences can be changed (Wilson 1980; Jones 1989). Entrepreneurial managers may be able to change the preferences of other actors who otherwise might constrain them and manipulate policy agendas (Hammond 1986; Hammond, Hill, and Miller 1986; Riker 1986).

Clearly, scholars need to synthesize many disparate themes to develop a more systematic theory of bureaucratic entrepreneurship. Development of better theory also must take place in conjunction with empirical evidence about where entrepreneurs are found and what they do. In the following section, we analyze the conditions that increase the likelihood of finding an entrepreneurial city manager. To understand how and when city managers can emerge as entre-preneurs, we compare these conditions to the factors associated with the absence of entrepreneur-ial leadership and with the emergence of entrepreneurs in elected offices.

Where Do Entrepreneurial City Managers Emerge?

In our research, we started with a database consisting of more than 1,400 incorporated suburban communities in fifty-five metropolitan areas in over twenty states. These suburbs were comparable in size and small enough for a city manager to act in an entrepreneurial fashion. We asked city clerks, who are knowledgeable about the politics of their communities, whether or not their commu-nity had been led by an entrepreneur in the past decade who had helped propel a dynamic policy change. We also asked the clerks about other political conditions in their community. We received usable responses from 956 clerks, of which 27 percent named an entrepreneur in their community. Of the 257 entrepreneurs named, 49 (almost 20 percent) were city managers.[2] Most of the other entrepreneurs identified in our survey were mayors or members of the local council who must stand for periodic elections. We called these individuals "political entrepreneurs." We matched our survey responses with information on population, employment, and services from various government cen-suses and with information on local taxes and fiscal conditions gathered from county and state reports.

In contrast to a large literature that focuses on the achievements of a few dynamic individuals or that presents examples of innovative policy change, we were interested in developing a more systematic foundation for entrepreneurship that could be tested in the context of a large sample of local governments. It is not easy to go beyond the examples provided in studies developed by Osborne and Gaebler (1992) or by the Ford Foundation–JFK School of Government Innovation Awards (Barzelay 1992). To gather such information, we decided that city clerks would be the most credible respondents to provide us with a sample of entrepreneurs. For several reasons, we are confident that the names put forward by the clerks are valid. First, city clerks are close observers of community politics, and they are trained to respond to public inquiries. About one-quarter of the clerks nominated an entrepreneur, so in the aggregate they clearly did not just pick someone for the sake of providing a response to our query nor did they seem to avoid naming anyone because it was too much work. Second, the clerks provided us with specific information about what the entrepreneurs they named actually did; these activities were almost always examples of dynamic change in policy relative to older practices in their own community. The entrepreneurs for whom we have prepared more detailed case studies developed innovations that were covered in important regional and national newspapers (e.g., *Wall Street Journal*, *New York Times*, *Chicago Tribune*, *Boston Globe*) that normally do not focus on suburban politics. Third, we created a validation sample, surveying clerks in neighboring jurisdictions about whether the nominated entrepreneur was appropriately cited. Of those nearby clerks who felt they had adequate information concerning the politics of the neighboring city, about three-fourths verified the nomination of the entrepreneur. Finally, we had to consider whether there would be a better source of entrepreneurial nominations. Clerks nominated mayors, council members, city managers, private citizens, and business leaders; many of these individuals would have been missed if we had asked for self-nominations from only elected leaders. In short, we believe that our method successfully identified individuals proposing dynamic change in their communities.

To understand better the incentives and goals of bureaucratic entrepreneurs, we wanted to identify the conditions associated with their emergence. Our first concern was with the possible effects of region. As is well known, municipalities in the South and West are more likely to have a city manager than are cities in other parts of the country.[3] However, entrepreneurial city managers are not regionally distributed: once the distribution of city managers is controlled, entrepreneurial city managers are not more likely to be found in any given geographic region.

Absent a regional pattern of emergence, we turned next to the effects of local conditions. Although our interest was in bureaucratic entrepreneurs, they should not be studied in isolation. Thus, not only did we identify those conditions that led to the emergence of local entrepreneurship, but we identified the circumstances associated with the emergence of *bureaucratic entrepreneurs* compared to the emergence of *political entrepreneurs*.[4]

We believe that in some communities citizens seek dynamic political or policy change and do not care much who provides the impetus for change. In some of these communities, depending on the structure and context of local politics, entrepreneurial politicians will emerge to satisfy citizen demand. When they do not, entrepreneurial managers might step forward to satisfy the underlying demand for change.

A growing literature shows several possible relationships between mayors and managers. Sometimes city managers are the dominant policy makers, sometimes mayors are, and at other times neither is particularly active (Morgan and Watson 1992 and Svara 1990). In some circumstances, elected mayors and managers are competitive. As Whitaker and DeHoog (1991, 162) note: "elected mayors may be more likely to oppose the manager (to see him or her as a rival leader) and elected mayors may be more able to build popular support for their opposition to the manager." The most fundamental difference between them is that managers do not face the need to be elected to office directly by the voters of their city. The basis of their political support differs from that of politicians, and their allegiance may be as much to professional norms about performance as it is to political pressures from elected officials (Gormley 1989).

Thus, the literature (Stillman 1977; Browne 1985; Svara 1990; Morgan and Watson 1992) and our theoretical expectations suggest that political structural variables might influence whether or not a city manager acts as a bureaucratic entrepreneur. In Table 28.1, we present a multinomial logit analysis identifying the political structural conditions under which entrepreneurial managers or entrepreneurial politicians are likely to emerge, controlling for the four major geographic regions defined by the U.S. Bureau of the Census.[5] The structural variables include whether or not the suburban community has an office of city manager and a mayor's office. In addition, we measure the length of the mayor's term and the competitiveness of mayoral and council elections, as assessed by the clerk in a given suburb (on a 1–5 scale). Our dependent variable takes on three values: 0 when no entrepreneur was cited in that community (as was true in the majority of communities, 699), 1 when an entrepreneurial politician was cited (in 208 cases), and 2 when an entrepreneurial manager was cited by the clerk (in 49 cases).

The results show that if a community has a mayor (as is the case in nearly 90 percent of our communities), it is significantly less likely that a city manager will emerge as an entrepreneur. Using a sensitivity analysis, we found that if no communities had mayors, the average likelihood of finding an entrepreneurial manager would more than double, from .052 to .123 (Table 28.3). Of course, a community must have an office of city manager for an entrepreneurial manager to emerge.[6] If all communities had city managers, *ceteris paribus*, the average likelihood of an entrepreneurial manager emerging would almost double from .052, the same mean, to .091.

As the right-hand portion of Table 28.1 shows, political entrepreneurs are *more* likely to emerge when a community has a mayor's office, when the mayoral races are more competitive, and when the mayor's term is shorter. We believe that all of these factors increase the opportunities for political entrepreneurs to capture the office of mayor. Note that the probability of a political entrepreneur emerging is *not* significantly affected by whether or not a suburb has a city manager. This suggests that citizens seek political entrepreneurship first. Indeed, even most city managers prefer that mayors take an active policy leadership role (Wikstrom 1979, 273). If a political entrepreneur does not emerge, an entrepreneurial manager is more likely to emerge to promote change.

Elsewhere, we have shown that local demographic factors, such as race and growth, can create new political cleavages or "dimensions" upon which entrepreneurs can organize political alliances and thus significantly affect the probability that an entrepreneurial politician will emerge (Schneider and Teske 1992). In contrast, these same demographic characteristics do not affect the probability with which an entrepreneurial city manager emerges.[7] Entrepreneurial managers head existing organizations with resources and technical expertise and do not usually need to create new political alliances to support their policy innovations. However, other important factors affect the emergence of entrepreneurial managers.

In Table 28.2 we present a separate multinomial logit analysis exploring how the interest group environment and local fiscal conditions in a community affect the emergence of entrepreneurs. Entrepreneurial city managers are significantly more likely to emerge in municipalities where local public sector workers are highly paid relative to the prevailing private sector manufacturing wages in that region.[8] In contrast, a more heavily unionized local municipal work force reduces the probable emergence of an entrepreneurial manager. Strong unions may

Table 28.1

Multinomial Logit Analysis: The Impact of Political Structure on the Emergence of Entrepreneurs

Variable	Entrepreneurial managers			Entrepreneurial politicians		
	Coefficient	SE	p > t	Coefficient	SE	p > t
City manager	3.07	.75	.00*	−.08	.18	.63
Mayor	−.95	.56	.09*	.82	.40	.04*
Competitiveness of mayor	−.16	.11	.15	.13	.06	.02*
Mayor term	.34	.38	.36	−.34	.19	.07*
Competitiveness of council	−.01	.13	.93	.01	.07	.91
Northeast	−.20	.54	.71	−.10	.29	.72
North Central	.28	.49	.57	.08	.27	.77
South	.39	.53	.47	−.27	.32	.42
Constant	−4.21	.94	.00	−2.23	.45	.00

Sources: The dependent variable and first five independent variables come from the authors' survey of city clerks. The regional variables are defined by the U.S. Bureau of the Census.

Notes: Chi square = 68; *p < .01; total N = 903.

N of entrepreneurial managers = 49. Mean predicted value = .052.

N of entrepreneurial politicians = 201. Mean predicted value = .216.

City manager and mayor = 1 if city has office; 0 otherwise. The competitiveness of the mayoral and council races is measured on a 1–5 scale, with 5 most competitive. Mayor term = 1 if > 2 years; 0 if # 2 years.

Table 28.2

Multinomial Logit Analysis: The Impact of External Groups Strength and Fiscal Conditions on the Emergence of Entrepreneurs

Variable	Entrepreneurial managers			Entrepreneurial politicians		
	Coefficient	SE	p > t	Coefficient	SE	p > t
Chamber of commerce	.15	.16	.35	.08	.09	.34
Taxpayer groups	−.48	.16	.00*	−.11	.09	.21
Neighborhood groups	.02	.16	.89	.16	.09	.08*
Pay ratio	.45	.19	.02*	.05	.11	.66
Union	−.33	.18	.07%	−.06	.11	.59
Debt/PC	.18	.17	.28	.20	.11	.05*
Northeast	−.47	.57	.41	−.42	.30	.16
North Central	−.03	.52	.95	−.01	.28	.98
Constant	−.172	.73	.02	−1.42	.42	.00

Sources: Union, Debt/PC, and the nominator of Pay ratio are from 1982 Census of Governments. The denominator of Pay ratio is from the Bureau of Labor Statistics. Each of these three measures is converted into a z-score based on the MSA pattern. The variable has a regional mean of zero and standard deviation of one, and measures the condition in a specific community relative to the metropolitan area average (e.g., Schneider 1989).

Notes: Chi square = 37; *p < .01. Total N = 685 (less than in Table 28.1 because data for some communities were missing).

N of entrepreneurial managers = 49. Mean predicted value = .060; N of entrepreneurial politicians = 201. Mean predicted value = .228.

The Chamber of Commerce, taxpayer, and neighborhood variables are the reported strength of local Chamber of Commerce, taxpayer, and neighborhood groups with a range of 1–5, with 5 the strongest value.

Pay ratio = the ratio of the average public sector wage to the average Metropolitan Statistical Area manufacturing wage.

Union = the percentage of municipal workers that are unionized.

Debt/PC = the total debt of the community divided by population.

Table 28.3

Sensitivity Analysis: The Impact of Changing Significant Variables from Tables 28.1 and Table 28.2 on the Probability of an Entrepreneurial Manager Emerging (with other variables held *ceteris paribus*)

	Variable	Mean	Predictions	
			High extreme	Low extreme
From Table 28.1	Mayor	.052	.123	.048
	Council-manager	.052	.091	.005
From Table 28.2	Taxpayer	.060	.117	.022
	Pay ratio	.060	.170	.016
	Union	.060	.129	.013
	Taxpayer, pay ratio, and union jointly	.060	.505	.001

Notes: The mean prediction on an entrepreneurial manager emerging is .052 in Table 28.1 and .059 in Table 28.2. In this sensitivity analysis, we vary the significant variables to extreme values above and below their own means, and let the other variables assume their values, holding their influence constant.

From Table 28.1, if there were no mayor in any community (mayor is set to 0) the likelihood of an entrepreneurial manager emerging would increase to .123, while if every community had a mayor (mayor set to 1), the likelihood would fall to .048. Similarly, if all communities had a city manager, the likelihood would increase to .091, while if no community had a city manager, the likelihood would fall to nearly zero (which is true by definition).

From Table 28.2, taxpayer group strength, the public/private pay ratio and union percentage are varied to their extremes to determine the impact on the emergence of entrepreneurial managers with the impact of other variables held constant. In the last row, all three of these variables are set to their extreme values at the same time.

oppose entrepreneurial managers who seek to cut costs, privatize local services, or otherwise disrupt the existing modes of service delivery. These same factors do not affect the probability of finding a political entrepreneur.

Municipal unions are an important internal group, but entrepreneurs also need political support from external interest groups. In local politics, some groups, such as the Chamber of Commerce, represent concentrated interests, other groups, such as taxpayer groups, represent dispersed citizens, while yet others, such as neighborhood groups, represent citizens in specific geographic areas.

Morgan and Watson (1992, 441) note that for local executives informal power relates not only to "style and personality, but also to the ability to exercise a range of political brokerage skills" across political groups. We found that when taxpayer groups in a community were relatively *weak*, and thus unlikely to represent the citizens' interest in constraining taxes, an entrepreneurial city manager was more likely to emerge to do so. In contrast, entrepreneurial politicians were more likely to emerge when neighborhood groups are important, showing their need for geographic electoral support. In short, entrepreneurial city managers were more likely to emerge to address efficiency issues, such as pay scales for government workers and taxes, particularly when local interest groups had not been able to address these issues effectively through elected politicians. To make this argument more concrete, the sensitivity analysis in Table 28.3 shows that, *ceteris paribus*, very weak taxpayer groups or very weak municipal unions can more than double the likelihood of finding an entrepreneurial manager. In contrast, very high public pay ratios triple that probability.[9] Moreover, when these three factors are combined at their extreme values, the likelihood of an entrepreneurial manager emerging changes from virtually zero (.001) to more than 50 percent (.505).

The importance of local government efficiency issues in the emergence of entrepreneurial city managers may also help explain the policies these managers pursue. Entrepreneurial managers are significantly more likely than entrepreneurial politicians to support new user fees, development impact fees, and contracting out for services.[10]

Actions of Entrepreneurial Managers

Morgan and Watson (1992, 438) argue that when mayors are not leading policy: "city managers may be compelled to play an active policy role, largely by necessity, but their leadership is likely to be less publicly visible and more formally constrained than would be the case for directly elected officials." To test these propositions and others discussed in other recent work on entrepreneurial policy development, such as Osborne and Gaebler (1992) and Barzelay (1992), we next examined in more detail the actions of entrepreneurial managers, the constraints on their behavior, and their strategies for success.

To gather more detailed information on the personalities, career lines, and strategic approaches of the entrepreneurial managers, we sent a follow-up survey to the forty-nine city clerks who named an entrepreneurial city manager in our first survey. We received thirty-one useable responses, providing us with detailed information on 63 percent of the city managers named as entrepreneurs. Although this is not a large sample, our entrepreneurial managers matched closely to demographic information reported by the International City/County Management Association (ICMA) for a much larger sample of the nation's city managers, in terms of age, gender, race, education, and political preferences. We present the following descriptive information as suggestive of patterns of local entrepreneurship and as indicative of themes for further research.

New Ideas and Forces for Entrepreneurship

Existing work argues that entrepreneurs have strong needs to achieve. For example, Hargrove and Glidewell (1990) cite a strong personal incentive or a strong belief in specific policies, wide-ranging government experience, an open-minded evaluation process, an attraction to experimentation, and a willingness to risk failure. Similarly, Sanger and Levin (1992) find that entrepreneurs create personal missions, take risks, have a bias toward action and purposely underestimate constraints.

City managers are more likely to be innovative when they previously worked in another city and if they have a broader professional orientation (Wilson 1989; Carlson 1961; Rosenthal and Crain 1968). Of the thirty-one entrepreneurial managers in our sample, 67 percent played important roles in professional organizations. In their prior employment, 62 percent had been city managers in another town, while only 20 percent had moved up within their town's government, and 10 percent came from the private sector. Thus, nearly two-thirds of these entrepreneurs followed a city manager career track, and a similar percentage were active in professional organizations.

What was the origin of the new policies these entrepreneurial managers proposed? As noted by Oakerson and Parks (1988), professional organizations are among the most important sources of new managerial ideas (approximately 75 percent of the clerks suggested that the entrepreneurial city manager got his/her ideas from such organizations). This was followed by newspapers (69 percent) and by other communities (64 percent). In contrast, local politicians and entrepreneurial city managers engage in limited cross-fertilization—only 21 percent of the clerks named local politicians as an ideas source, a result supported by Morgan and Watson's (1992) findings on the limited amount of mayor/manager team leadership in smaller communities.

We also asked clerks to identify the forces that entrepreneurial city managers were responding to in their introduction of new ideas and policies. Congruent with other studies of entrepreneurs (Lewis 1980; Hughes 1986), the single most common reason given was the city manager's own leadership (60 percent). But managerial entrepreneurship is not totally self-motivated. City managers respond to demands from local politicians (43 percent) and from citizens (40 percent). Thus, entrepreneurial managers get their ideas mainly from professional organizations, newspapers, and other communities, but the force that pushes them actually to introduce the ideas is most often their own leadership, buttressed by demands from politicians or citizens.

Compared to entrepreneurial politicians, entrepreneurial managers are much less likely (3 percent versus 21 percent) to introduce policy ideas that are very different from ideas in circulation in their metropolitan region. Many of the innovations managers introduce are defined by their professional networks and norms. In contrast, political entrepreneurs sometimes argue for radical changes to create a winning electoral coalition, proposals that need not stand rigorous tests of professional scrutiny.

Constraints on Entrepreneurial Managers

Armed with their ideas and their abilities, entrepreneurial managers face constraints. Congruent with arguments presented by Peterson (1981) and Schneider (1989), the city clerks suggested that the most binding constraints on the innovative behavior of managers were financial and economic. Fully 78 percent of our respondents cited both tax limitations and growing fiscal problems as constraints on city managers, which DeSantis, Glass, and Newell (1992, 449) also find to be important in their analysis of a larger sample of city managers. The intergovernmental system imposed further limits on the behavior of managers: 54 percent cited intergovernmental mandates, and 46 percent cited changing intergovernmental aid as constraining factors. Local politicians (cited by 53 percent) were obviously important constraining factors on the freedom of city managers, especially since they ultimately hire and fire managers.

In both the political and managerial domains, entrepreneurs need a coalition of existing or new groups to support their policies. Entrepreneurial managers are more likely to work within the existing political power structure than are entrepreneurial politicians, who must challenge and alter it to be successful (Schneider and Teske 1992). Most entrepreneurial managers head existing organizations and do not have to build or maintain organizations as often as politicians. Thus, compared to political entrepreneurs, entrepreneurial managers in our sample are less likely to be the catalysts behind the formation of new neighborhood or taxpayer groups. But entrepreneurial managers are as likely as entrepreneurial politicians to rely on new business groups, a traditional part of the power elite of most communities (Logan and Molotch 1987; Stone 1989).

Entrepreneurial Strategies

To overcome constraints, city managers need effective internal and external strategies. The ability to motivate subordinates to higher levels of performance is the most important internal task of an entrepreneur (Miller 1992; Brehm and Gates 1993). Teamwork is the dominant approach used by most entrepreneurial city managers. We asked the clerks whether the entrepreneur stressed a teamwork strategy or hierarchy, or some mix of the two: 6 percent cited all teamwork, 58 percent cited mainly teamwork, 33 percent cited an even mix of the two approaches, only 3 percent cited mainly hierarchy, and no one suggested all hierarchy. Similarly, the ability to inspire or motivate workers was rated "much better" or "better than the average city manager or similar local official" for 84 percent of the entrepreneurs, while the ability to monitor and control workers was similarly rated for only 65 percent of the sample (using the same 5-point scale). Rather than relying only on monitoring and control, entrepreneurial city managers try to inculcate a sense of mission through teamwork.

Without having to run for office, much of the work of entrepreneurial managers is not subject to rigorous public examination, allowing managers to limit the scope of political debate, by defining issues as technical (Baumgartner 1989). On the other hand, some policies *require* an expansion of scope when key politicians are opposed and an entrepreneurial manager believes there is broad political support in the community. The main strategy of entrepreneurial managers is to handle issues quietly, behind the scenes (true for 70 percent). Only 22 percent of respondents said that the entrepreneur's main strategy for handling issues was to go public, supporting the picture of entrepreneurial city managers working with existing power structures rather than trying to overturn them.

In building support, entrepreneurial city managers call on a wide range of the tools available to them. Of our respondents, 86 percent rated the entrepreneur's use of strategic information as "substantial" or "very substantial," 77 percent so rated the use of bureaucratic or technical expertise, 54 percent for the use of local media, and 40 percent for the use of rhetoric. Following Riker's (1986) description of how entrepreneurs can inject an added "dimension" to political debates in order to create new coalitions, fully 90 percent of the entrepreneurial managers had used new ideas or issues to create support across groups; and 66 percent linked two seemingly unrelated issues to create broader support.

Entrepreneurial managers need to be salespeople for new policies, not only to the citizenry but to elected politicians. We found that 42 percent of the entrepreneurial managers took political heat to shield politicians very or fairly often, 33 percent did so sometimes, while 25 percent rarely or never did so. Entrepreneurial managers were even more generous in sharing credit for policy innovations: 66 percent shared credit very or fairly often, while 24 percent shared credit only sometimes, and 10 percent rarely or never shared credit. By helping politicians look good, entrepreneurial managers may be cementing alliances with local politicians and in so doing building up credit that can be used to loosen political constraints on their efforts to implement innovative policies.

We recognize that thirty-one is a relatively small number of entrepreneurial city managers. Thus the information presented in the last section should be taken as suggestive of patterns of entrepreneurship, especially since we cannot compare it directly to managers in communities without an entrepreneurial city manager. Still, these thirty-one responses do represent 53 percent of all of the entrepreneurial managers named from a nationwide sample of nearly one thousand suburban clerks. Their actions document dimensions of entrepreneurial behavior that are congruent with existing studies of bureaucratic managers who are active in policy development.

As noted earlier, to verify our aggregate data and to develop further insights into the entrepreneurial process in local government, we constructed a series of case studies of individuals nominated as entrepreneurs. Here, we present two case studies of entrepreneurial managers (see *Cases in Point* [Boxes 28.1 and 28.2]). Robert Healy, from the relative large suburban city of Cambridge, Massachusetts, illustrates the power an entrepreneurial manager can develop and how this power can be used to handle fiscal stress in innovative ways. Our second case, that of Paul Leonard, from the much smaller suburb of Perkasie, Pennsylvania, shows how an entrepreneurial manager can help solve pressing local problems with a solution that provides an innovative model for the nation.

Our survey and case study results also suggest strategies for other city managers who would

Box 28.1
Case in Point

The case of Robert Healy, the city manager of Cambridge, Massachusetts, a large suburban city just across the Charles River from Boston, illustrates several of the themes of our research. Healy was hired as city manager in 1982. Perhaps Healy's most important challenge was dealing with the fiscal environment, specifically cuts in property tax revenue mandated by Massachusetts's Proposition 2½.

According to the *Boston Globe* (February 13, 1990): "In 1981, after passage of Proposition 2½, the city's bond rating was suspended by rating services that believed the measure to limit property taxes would make it difficult for Cambridge to make bond payments. The city rebounded, however, and its bond rating rose several times."

Healy was a major force behind the rebound. In the first year of mandated cuts in 1982, Healy was able to juggle the budget and find a few sources of surplus from previous years, allowing budget cuts to be made without too much pain for most of Cambridge's citizens. In 1983, Proposition 2½ mandated a 15 percent cut in property tax revenue. With a preliminary budget proposal to the city council and community, Healy showed the extreme budget cuts that would be necessary to achieve this reduction: "The fat that people talk about does not exist in the city's budget. Next year, the public works department will barely be able to collect the rubbish."

This bleak vision of the future pushed the Cambridge city council toward action and also led to the formation of a citizen's initiative designed to force a referendum vote, which, under the rules of Proposition 2½ could postpone the 15 percent cut for one year if two-thirds of the community voters voted twice to do so. Healy supported this referendum and it indeed met the stringent requirements for enactment. Thus, the 1983 budget was funded at the level of the previous year and cuts were put off until more fundamental changes could be made. With this success and others, the *Boston Globe* noted about Healy: "The walls outside his office are decorated with awards from professional groups such as the Governmental Finance Officers Association of the United States and Canada."

Healy, now [fifty-seven] years old, and a Cambridge resident since birth, first came to work for the former city manager in 1974. With two decades of experience, he has also been able to innovate in other areas. He was a leading player in attracting commercial growth in the 1980s, which led to some antigrowth opposition. Healy argues that growth is linked to services and taxes: "I think balanced and controlled development have been important to the financial health of this city."

As an entrepreneur with innovative ideas, Healy attracts controversy. One councilor said: "His power under the charter is immense. He can set policy in areas that never reach the council. So, it is extremely important that he be held accountable." But another councilor noted that Healy can be a team player: "He tends to carry out policy that he believes is supported by the majority of the council."

Healy recognizes that he is controversial: "This is a complicated, diverse city and any decision you make is going to have 50 percent against and 50 percent for." The *Globe* noted that Healy "says he has had to make unpopular decisions that have not endeared him to neighborhoods, but believes this is the nature of the job."

Thus, Healy's case illustrates some of the constraints and opportunities that entrepreneurial managers faced in the 1980s. By going well beyond their simple job description, they were able to motivate change, when politicians could not or would not do so.

like to develop innovative policy. In their popular book, *Reinventing Government*, Osborne and Gaebler (1992) develop ten principles of entrepreneurial organizations. Their strategies of empowerment, a focus on customer (citizen) needs, decentralization and teamwork, and leveraging actors in the private marketplace (strategies echoed in Barzelay 1992) also are reflected in our survey results and in the case studies of these entrepreneurial city managers.

Box 28.2
Case in Point

Another innovative local manager identified in our survey was Paul Leonard of Perkasie, Pennsylvania, a rapidly growing borough of 6,200 people, twenty-five miles north of Philadelphia. Perkasie faced a major solid waste disposal problem in the late 1980s. Leonard's solutions were innovative enough to be reported on the front page of the *Wall Street Journal* in a story by Bill Paul, "Pollution Solution: Pennsylvania Town Finds a Way to Get Locals to Recycle Trash" (June 21, 1989).

As in may other jurisdictions, waste disposal was a growing problem as the borough's cost per ton skyrocketed 900 percent from 1981 to 1987. According to the *Journal:* "When town leaders proposed an incinerator, public opposition killed the idea."

Given this manifestation of the not-in-my-backyard (NIMBY) syndrome, Perkasie needed a solution. But as the *Journal* noted: "federal and most state environmental officials haven't yet found a way to reduce the waste stream. Perkasie, it seems, is ahead of them."

As Leonard said: "We've let Adam Smith lead the way." As Osborne and Gaebler (1992) and others have advocated, Leonard led Perkasie to try market incentives. According to the *Journal:* "Despairing of getting federal or state help, Mr. Leonard, the borough manager, decided to experiment. Although it wasn't the first community to try per-bag fees, Perkasie apparently is the first to have linked such fees with the threat of fines, a powerful incentive to recycle."

Leonard's innovation proved successful. After implementation of the program, the amount of garbage that needed to be disposed by Perkasie dropped by more than 50 percent, as people recycled as much as possible. Leonard acted as a "cheerleader" to develop a positive attitude about recycling in Perkasie: "We're not going to let the big guys dump on us anymore. Why should we pay to dispose of trash that companies needlessly produce?"

As with many successful entrepreneurs, Leonard is not yet satisfied. According to the *Journal:* "Leonard says he doesn't even want plastic garbage bags. He is considering switching to a heavy duty paper bag." Although recycling is not his only area of responsibility, manager Leonard addressed the community's most pressing problem with an innovative solution that has earned him national attention.

Conclusions

American suburban governments are part of a diverse and open system filled with opportunities for entrepreneurial behavior. Several different types of actors can emerge as entrepreneurs to drive change in local policies. In our survey, fully 20 percent of the entrepreneurs named were city managers. But only about one in every eleven city managers in the sample was named as an entrepreneur. City managers are most likely to seize the opportunity to motivate dynamic change when the local political climate does not breed entrepreneurial politicians.

Given the professional and political differences between entrepreneurial city managers and local politicians, it is not surprising that the coalitions entrepreneurial managers build and the specific policies they advocate differ from those of politicians. Managers are more likely to focus on narrowly concentrated coalitions of power holders rather than on broader political interests. Moreover, entrepreneurial city managers are relatively more cautious in their policy proposals and more likely to advocate new ideas that have been "vetted" by their professional associations. In contrast, political entrepreneurs are more likely to advocate untried ideas (such as no-growth policies) and to create a broader mass political base in the community (for example, by helping in the creation of new neighborhood based groups).

These differences in strategies are rooted in the definitions of success different types of entrepreneurs seek. City managers seek to enhance their professional reputation and career mobility, which can best be achieved by successfully implementing professionally approved policies that leaders or city managers in other municipalities will recognize and respect. In contrast, entrepreneurial politicians seek to win broad electoral support, often introducing completely new ideas or organizing new groups to challenge the status quo within their own community.

All entrepreneurs face constraints. City managers are often dependent on the actions of either a mayor or city council for the adoption of their policies. Indeed, managers are dependent on these political actors for their jobs. The growing fiscal problems of local government and an increasingly harsh intergovernmental milieu may present even stricter limits on the freedom of city managers to implement new policies. Given these limits, entrepreneurial city managers try to increase the efficiency of local service delivery by adopting approaches that are in good currency, such as user fees and privatization. Entrepreneurial city managers also turn inward, trying to improve the efficiency of their work force by promoting teamwork and inspiring their workers to implement more efficient policies.

Existing biographical case studies provide some insight into the expected emergence and behavior of bureaucratic entrepreneurs. But this research leaves many gaps that will be closed only with broader empirical evidence. Such efforts should shift the focus away from biographical studies of a few rare individuals toward the identification of systemic factors that encourage the entrepreneurial behavior of city managers and other high-level bureaucrats.

Notes

1. We use the term "public entrepreneur" to refer to an actor who helps to propel dynamic policy or political change in the community. We call entrepreneurs operating in elected office, political entrepreneurs, and those in full-time career positions, bureaucratic entrepreneurs. Frequently the policies public entrepreneurs advocate are innovative and they often must exercise considerable leadership skills to be successful. But the defining characteristic of the entrepreneur is to be the agent for change that is far more than incremental *relative to the policies and politics of the community in the past.* Thus, the policies or innovations that define an entrepreneur in one community may be well established in another community and not provide dynamic change. In addition, our focus is on the emergence of entrepreneurial individuals more than the emergence of innovation more generally in bureaucratic organizations, as in Mohr (1969).

2. Since this is the first large scale survey of suburban municipalities, it is impossible to say whether the 27 percent rate of entrepreneurship is high or low. However, in a comparative study of economic development strategies in close to two hundred cities, Clarke (1990) finds "innovative" programs in 5–21 percent of the cities surveyed. Since her numbers are for individual programs, it is not unreasonable to assume that a joint set of programs that might define an entrepreneur will be found in the proportion of cities we report. Morgan and Watson (1992, 442) also find that 32 percent of city managers report policy innovation as one of their top three roles.

3. Nearly 60 percent of the communities responding to our survey have city managers, with a range from almost 90 percent in the western communities to only 25 percent in New England.

4. Although we allowed more than one entrepreneur to be named, and several clerks did so, most of the respondents named only one in the 1980s. We do not see this as a major problem, however, because a community may not have room for more than one entrepreneur at one time. If political entrepreneurs do emerge in a community, managers are still needed to implement innovative policies, but implementation of entrepreneurial policy developed by politicians should not by itself qualify a city manager as an entrepreneur. Morgan and Watson (1992) found that it was rare for powerful mayors and managers to coexist in the same city.

5. Multinomial logit is an appropriate technique given an unordered dependent variable that takes on more than two values (e.g., 0, 1, 2). See Aldrich and Nelson (1984) or Maddala (1983) for a methodological description of the technique. A positive coefficient on an independent variable indicates an increase in the likelihood that an entrepreneur will emerge in a community with that characteristic, holding all other variables constant.

6. Of the 956 communities that responded to our survey, about 60 percent have city managers. Thus, it is reasonable to include as an independent measure a variable indicating whether or not a community has an office of city manager to explain the emergence of entrepreneurial politicians, and, since we utilized the same exact set of independent variables for both, the emergence of entrepreneurial managers.

7. We do not report these negative results here, but they are available from the authors upon request.

8. It is possible that a high pay ratio means that a community has higher quality workers, including the city manager. In this case, one could argue that the higher wages are attracting more talented managers who are more likely to be entrepreneurial. While we cannot yet rule out this possibility, we find the efficiency interpretation more plausible, but recognize that the two factors could be working simultaneously.

9. The average likelihood of an entrepreneurial manager emerging in this analysis is .06. If all communities had very weak taxpayer groups, the average likelihood would increase to .117. Similarly, if all communities had municipal labor forces that were not unionized (as 34 percent of the communities in the sample actually do have), the average likelihood would increase to .129. If all communities had public/private pay ratios equal to the largest ratio in the sample (which is 168/100), the average likelihood of an entrepreneurial manager emerging would increase to .17.

10. Based on a simple chi-squared test, managerial entrepreneurs are significantly more likely than political entrepreneurs to pursue each of these strategies at $p < .02$.

References

Advisory Commission on Intergovernmental Relations (ACIR). 1985. *Significant Features of Fiscal Federalism, 1984*. Washington, DC: Government Printing Office.

Aldrich, John, and Forrest Nelson. 1984. *Linear Probability, Logit, and Probit Models*. Newbury Park, CA: Sage.

Altshuler, Alan, and Marc Zegans. 1990. "Innovation and Creativity: Comparisons Between Public Management and Private Enterprise." *Cities* 23 (February): 16–24.

Ammons, David, and Charldean Newell. 1989. *City Executives: Leadership Roles, Work Characteristics, and Time Management*. Albany: State University of New York Press.

Barber, Daniel. 1988. "Newly Promoted City Managers." *Public Administration Review* 48, no. 3: 694–699.

Barzelay, Michael with Babak Armajani. 1992. *Breaking Through Bureaucracy: A New Vision for Managing Government*. Berkeley: University of California Press.

Baumgartner, Frank. 1989. "Strategies of Political Leadership in Diverse Settings." In *Leadership and Politics*, ed. Bryan Jones. Lawrence: University Press of Kansas, pp. 114–134.

Baumgartner, Frank, and Bryan D. Jones. 1991. "Agenda Dynamics and Policy Subsystems." *Journal of Politics* 53: 1044–1074.

Brehm, John, and Scott Gates. 1993. "Donut Shops and Speed Traps: Evaluating Models of Supervision on Police Behavior." *American Journal of Political Science* 37: 555–581.

Browne, William. 1985. "Municipal Managers and Policy: A Partial Test of the Svara Dichotomy-Duality Model." *Public Administration Review* 45, no. 5: 620–622.

Carlson, R.O. 1961. "Succession and Performance Among School Superintendents." *Administrative Science Quarterly* 6: 210–227.

Caro, Robert. 1974. *The Power Broker: Robert Moses and the Fall of New York*. New York: Random House.

Clarke, Susan. 1990. "Local Autonomy in the Post-Reagan Period." Paper presented at the annual meeting of the American Political Science Association, San Francisco.

DeSantis, Victor, James Glass, and Charldean Newell. 1992. "City Managers, Job Satisfaction, and Community Problem Perceptions." *Public Administration Review* 52, no. 5: 447–453.

Doig, Jameson, and Erwin Hargrove, eds. 1987. *Leadership and Innovation: A Biographical Perspective on Entrepreneurs in Government*. Baltimore, MD: Johns Hopkins University Press.

Downs, Anthony. 1967. *Inside Bureaucracy*. Boston, MA: Little Brown.

Eisinger, Peter. 1988. *The Rise of the Entrepreneurial State*. Madison: University of Wisconsin Press.

Golden, Olivia. 1990. "Innovation in Public Sector Human Services Programs: The Implications of Innovation by 'Groping Along.'" *Journal of Policy Analysis and Management* 9: 219–248.

Gormley, William. 1989. *Taming the Bureaucracy: Muscles, Prayers and Other Strategies*. Princeton, NJ: Princeton University Press.

Hammond, Thomas. 1986. "Agenda Control, Organizational Structure, and Bureaucratic Politics." *American Journal of Political Science* 30: 379–420.

Hammond, Thomas, Jeffrey Hill, and Gary Miller. 1986. "Presidential Appointment of Bureau Chiefs and the 'Congressional Control of Administration' Hypothesis." Paper presented at the annual meeting of the American Political Science Association, Washington, DC.

Hargrove, Erwin. 1989. "Two Conceptions of Institutional Leadership." In *Leadership and Politics*, ed. Bryan Jones. Lawrence: University Press of Kansas, pp. 57–83.

Hargrove, Erwin, and Jon Glidewell. 1990. *Impossible Jobs in Public Management*. Lawrence: University Press of Kansas.

Hirschman, Albert. 1967. "The Hiding Hand Principle." *Public Interest* (Winter): 10–23.

Hughes, James. 1986. *The Vital Few: The Entrepreneur and American Economic Progress*. New York: Oxford University Press.

Jones, Bryan, ed. 1989. *Leadership and Politics: New Perspectives in Political Science*. Lawrence: University Press of Kansas.

Kammerer, Gladys. 1964. "Role Diversity of City Managers." *Administrative Sciences Quarterly* 8: 421–442.

Kingdon, John. 1984. *Agenda, Alternatives, and Public Policies*. Boston, MA: Little, Brown.

Kirchheimer, D.W. 1989. "Public Entrepreneurship and Subnational Government." *Polity* 22: 108–122.

Kirzner, Israel M. 1973. *Competition and Entrepreneurship*. Chicago: University of Chicago Press.

Lewis, Eugene. 1980. *Public Entrepreneurship: Toward a Theory of Bureaucratic Power*. Bloomington: Indiana University Press.

Logan, John R., and Harvey Molotch. 1987. *Urban Fortunes*. Berkeley: University of California Press.

Lovell, C. et al. 1979. *Federal and State Mandating on Local Governments: An Exploration of Issues and Impacts*. Washington, DC: National Science Foundation.

Lynn, Lawrence. 1990. "Managing the Social Services Net: The Job of Social Welfare Executive." In *Impossible Jobs in Public Management*, ed. Erwin Hargrove and John Glidewell. Lawrence: University Press of Kansas, pp. 133–151.

Maddala, G.S. 1983. *Limited Dependent and Qualitative Variables in Econometrics*. New York: Cambridge University Press.

Mazmanian, Daniel, and Paul Sabatier. 1983. *Implementation and Public Policy*. Glenview, IL: Scott Foresman.

McCubbins, Matthew, and Thomas Schwartz. 1984. "Congressional Oversight Overlooked: Police Patrols versus Fire Alarms." *American Journal of Political Science* 28: 165–179.

Miller, Gary. 1992. *Managerial Dilemmas: The Political Economy of Hierarchies*. Cambridge, UK: Cambridge University Press.

Miller, Gary, and Terry Moe. 1983. "Bureaucrats, Legislators, and the Size of Government." *American Political Science Review* 77: 297–322.

Moe, Terry. 1984. "The New Economics of Organization." *American Journal of Political Science* 28: 739–777.

Mohr, Lawrence. 1969. "Determinants of Innovation in Organizations." *American Political Science Review* 63: 111–126.

Morgan, David, and Sheilah Watson. 1992. "Policy Leadership in Council-Manager Cities: Comparing Mayor and Manager." *Public Administration Review* 52, no. 5: 438–446.

Nalbandian, John. 1989. "The Contemporary Role of City Managers." *American Review of Public Administration* 19: 261–279.

Niskanen, William. 1975. "Bureaucrats and Politicians." *Journal of Law and Economics* 18: 617–643.

Oakerson, Ronald, and Roger B. Parks. 1988. "Citizen Voice and Public Entrepreneurship: The Organizational Dynamic of a Complex Metropolitan County." *Publius* (Fall): 91–112.

Osborne, David, and Ted Gaebler. 1992. *Reinventing Government: How the Entrepreneurial Spirit Is Transforming the Public Sector*. Boston, MA: Addison-Wesley.

Ouchi, William. 1980. "Markets, Bureaucracies and Clans." *Administrative Sciences Quarterly* 25: 129–141.

Peterson, Paul. 1981. *City Limits*. Chicago: University of Chicago Press.

Protasel, G.J. 1988. "Abandonments of the Council-Manager Plan: A New Institutionalist Perspective." *Public Administration Review* 48, no. 4: 807–812.

Ricketts, Martin. 1987. *The New Industrial Economics*. New York: St. Martin's.

Riker, William. 1986. *The Art of Political Manipulation*. New Haven, CT: Yale University Press.

Rosenthal, David, and Robert Crain. 1968. "Structure and Values in Local Political Systems: The Case of Fluoridation Decisions." In *City Politics and Public Policy*, ed. James Q. Wilson. New York: Wiley, pp. 217–242.

Sanger, Mary Bryna, and Martin Levin. 1992. "Using Old Stuff in New Ways: Innovation as a Case of Evolutionary Tinkering." *Journal of Policy Analysis and Management* 11: 88–115.

Schneider, Mark. 1989. *The Competitive City: The Political Economy of Suburbia*. Pittsburgh, PA: University of Pittsburgh Press.

Schneider, Mark, and Paul Teske. 1992. "Toward a Theory of the Political Entrepreneur: Evidence from Local Government." *American Political Science Review* 86: 737–746.

Schumpeter, Joseph. 1942. *Capitalism, Socialism, and Democracy.* New York: Harper and Row.

Sharp, Elaine. 1986. *Citizen Demand Making in the Urban Context.* University: University of Alabama Press.

Stone, Clarence N. 1989. *Regime Politics.* Lawrence: University Press of Kansas.

Stillman, Richard. 1977. "The City Manager: Professional Helping Hand, or Political Hired Hand?" *Public Administration Review* 37, no. 6: 659–670.

Svara, James. 1990. *Official Leadership in the City: Patterns of Conflict and Cooperation.* New York: Oxford University Press.

Walker, Jack. 1981. "The Diffusion of Knowledge, Policy Communities and Agenda Setting." In *New Strategic Perspective on Social Policy*, ed. John Tropman. London: Pergamon, pp. 46–71.

Weissert, Carol S. 1991. "Policy Entrepreneurs, Policy Opportunities and Legislative Effectiveness." *American Politics Quarterly* 19: 262–274.

Whitaker, Gordon, and Ruth Hoogland DeHoog. 1991. "City Managers Under Fire: How Conflict Leads to Turnover." *Public Administration Review* 51, no. 2: 156–165.

Wikstrom, Nelson. 1979. "The Mayor as a Policy Leader in the Council-Manager Form of Government: A View from the Field." *Public Administration Review* 39, no. 3: 270–276.

Wilson, James Q. 1980. *The Politics of Regulation.* New York: Basic Books.

———. 1989. *Bureaucracy: What Government Agencies Do and Why They Do It.* New York: Basic Books.

CHAPTER 29

DEALING WITH CYNICAL CITIZENS

EVAN M. BERMAN

Widespread concern exists about public cynicism toward government (Gore 1994; Dubnick and Rosenbloom 1995; Greider 1992; Lipset and Schneider 1987; Ruscio 1995; Cisneros and Parr 1990). Manifestations of public cynicism include pervasive beliefs that government policies and public officials are corrupt, inept, or out to take advantage of citizens (Johnson 1993). Such disillusionment causes alienation and disengagement and is therefore of key interest to public administration and processes of democratic governance. Yet, little is written about the role of public administrators in shaping public attitudes. Much of what is written focuses on typologies of citizen roles (Frederickson 1991; Luton 1993) and administrative processes for managing citizen involvement (Stivers 1994; Thomas 1993; Box 1992).

This chapter responds to the need for a theory of citizen cynicism that is relevant to public administration. It also reports on the results of a national survey among city managers and chief administrative officers about perceptions of trust in local government. It finds that cities that foster positive citizen attitudes through a variety of strategies of participation, information, and reputation experience less cynicism than cities that do not. The effect of community conditions on trust is also examined.

A Theory of Cynicism

Cynicism is discussed in general terms in the literatures of trust and social capital. Many authors argue that all human relations and exchanges (economic, political, and social) require trust that promises will be honored, and that individuals are not taken advantage of (Coleman 1990; Putnam 1993; Bellah et al. 1991; Mansbridge 1990). Trust is seen as purposive, a lubricant of relations. It also provides a sense of belonging that serves the emotional needs of individuals. Cynicism is defined as low trust, specifically, a pervasive "disbelief in the possibility of good" in dealing with others (Damon 1995; Barber 1983; Merton 1957). Cynicism increases social distance and diminishes the public spirit (Gore 1994). "Social capital" refers to the number of trusting and mutually supportive relationships that members of a group draw on in realizing their economic, social, and political aims (Loury 1987).

Individuals in groups with low levels of social capital often have too few interdependent relations to achieve their goals and are likely to experience disenfranchisement. Disappointment over unrealized goals contributes to cynical attitudes, which, in turn serve as barriers to forming productive relations, thus causing social capital to further erode in a vicious circle.

From *Public Administration Review*, vol. 57, no. 2 (March/April 1997), pp. 105–112. Copyright © 1997 by American Society for Public Administration. Reprinted with permission.

Cynical attitudes toward government often center on the integrity, purpose, and effectiveness of government and its officials (Starobin 1995; Durant 1995; O'Connell, Holzman, and Armandi 1986; Jurie 1988). The literature makes a distinction between ardent cynicism and milder forms. Ardent cynicism is usually linked to ideological beliefs that are highly critical of government, for example, "government is always out to get the ordinary citizen." Facts are used selectively to justify claims that "nothing ever changes" and that authorities use smoke and mirrors to appease and mislead the masses. Milder expressions of cynicism are often characterized by beliefs that are less critical of government (e.g., "government tries its best, but it just doesn't have the resources"), and by beliefs that give greater weight to facts (e.g., "government doesn't deliver on its promises: the roads are still not fixed"). Because of the greater dependence on facts, the milder form of cynicism may be more open to influence by reason.[1]

Theories of human motivation and behavior adapted from organizational behavior (McClelland 1985; Bianco 1994; Robertson and Tang 1995) suggest that citizens question their relationship with government and experience disenfranchisement when the following conditions are present: (1) citizens believe that local government is using its power against them or otherwise not helping them; (2) citizens do not feel part of local government, or they feel misunderstood or ignored, and (3) citizens find local government services and policies to be ineffective. When citizens experience these feelings intensely, when they believe, for example, that government is plotting to exploit and brainwash citizens, they become ardently cynical and withdraw from government. When they experience these feelings moderately, believing, for example, that "things aren't done because government doesn't care much about us," they may develop milder forms of cynicism.

Analysis suggests that many citizens develop slightly negative orientations about their local governments. Citizens see government taxing them, charging them fees, and fining them, while granting special favors to special interests. They are often less informed about government's role in providing environmental programs, quality education, and economic development planning. Their negative experiences of government often outweigh positive ones. Although citizens often do have positive encounters with agencies (Goodsell 1994), such experiences are incidental, discounted, and do not reflect the full range of citizen contacts that shape public opinion about government power. Also, few citizens normally experience a sense of affiliation with government; indeed, many seldom even think of it.[2] In addition, many citizens become aware of local government services only after they fail. While many services do work, such problems as traffic congestion, overcrowded public schools, and a lack of public safety are frequently cited as evidence of government failure and incompetence. Widespread ideologies of privatization also suggest that government is an ineffective producer. Citizens frequently discount positive outcomes, which are viewed as legal entitlements or "due" to them in exchange for paying taxes.

This theory of cynicism suggests three goals for public administration strategies to reduce public cynicism.[3] The goal of the first set of strategies is to show that government uses its power to help citizens, rather than to harm them or be indifferent. Many citizens are not aware of local government activities and how these activities help further their own aims. The lack of such awareness reduces trust. There is thus a need to reach out and explain what government does and how it serves the interests of citizens, for example, through persistent, diverse, and consistent information campaigns such as mailings (Wheeler 1994; Garnett 1992; Denton and Woodward 1990).

The second set of strategies aims to incorporate citizen input into public decision-making. Traditional public hearings often fail to attract much citizen participation, except in unusual, crisis-laden situations. Citizen surveys, panels, and focus groups are alternative participation strategies (Glaser and Bardo 1994; Giancoli 1993; Chrislip 1993; Buckwalter, Parsons, and Wright 1993; Bacot et al. 1993; International City/County Management Association 1989;

Table 29.1

Perceptions of Citizen Trust in Local Government

	Percent of cities with response of "agree" of "strongly agree"[a]
A. Statements	
Government services meet citizen needs	69.7
Government treats citizens fairly	63.0
Government does not take advantage of citizens	59.8
Government is competent	56.1
Government officials are honest	46.3
Government fulfills its promises	43.0
Government understands citizen needs	41.6
Government can be trusted	41.5
B. Analysis[b]	
Mean response "somewhat agree" or less	33.6
Sub: Mean response "somewhat disagree" or less	8.3
Mean response between "somewhat agree" and "agree"	43.0
Mean response "agree" or more	23.4
Sub: Mean response three or more "strongly agree" responses	9.0
Total	100.0

Notes: [a]Responses are based on a seven-point Likert scale, ranging from "strongly agree" to "strongly disagree."

[b]Analysis excludes the general item "government can be trusted." See text for discussion.

National League of Cities 1995; Streib 1992). Of course, citizens must be aware of government using these strategies.

A third set of strategies aims to enhance the reputation of local government for competency and efficiency. This strategy has two components: good performance and effective communication of that performance. Communication is necessary because citizens may be unable to evaluate the cost and quality of government services unless they are provided with information (International City/County Management Association 1992; Stipak 1977).

In addition to strategies, this study also examines community conditions that affect cynicism. Cities with large affluent populations and high economic growth rates have lower levels of citizen cynicism than cities without these factors because these conditions enable higher levels of government services (Beck et al. 1987). Smaller cities are associated with lower levels of citizen cynicism because they allow for greater participation and direct communication between officials and citizens (Haeberle 1993). Public attitudes are also shaped by halo effects that stem from personal well-being, for example, "I feel good about this place." Social conditions such as high crime rates and discord among community groups may increase the level of public cynicism due to government's real or perceived failures in these areas.

Findings

Current Levels of Cynicism

Respondents assessed various statements about cynicism in their jurisdictions (Table 29.1). The methodology box [Box 29.1] discusses in detail the validity of these perceptions. In the opinion of city managers, most citizens "agree" or "strongly agree" that services meet their needs (69.7 percent), that local government treats citizens fairly (63.0 percent), and that it does not take advantage of citizens (59.8 percent). However, fewer citizens believe that local government is

Box 29.1
Methodology

During the summer of 1995, a national survey was administered to city managers and chief administrative officers, who provided perceptions of citizen trust in their cities. The survey was pretested on thirty-five city managers and was sent to all cities with populations over 50,000. A total of 502 surveys were mailed. After three waves of mailings and telephone calls, 304 usable responses were received, for a response rate of 61 percent (304/502 = .605 = 61 percent). In addition, over sixty interviews were conducted with respondents about trust and cynicism in their cities.

To examine the possibility of nonresponse bias, a telephone survey of forty randomly selected nonrespondents was conducted. Responses were compared across ten randomly selected survey items, but no significant, major differences were found between these populations. Neither are there significant differences between the demographic characteristics of respondents and nonrespondents. To ensure the accuracy of responses, further interviews were conducted with respondents who indicated very high or very low levels of trust. However, very few changes resulted from these interviews.

Respondents are very knowledgeable about citizens' attitudes in their jurisdictions; 94 percent report daily interaction with citizens. They have worked, on average, 20.3 years in government, 8.5 years as a city manager or chief administrative officer, and 9.7 years in the city for which they are responding.

Respondents used a variety of sources in forming their opinions (mean = 7.1). The most frequently used sources are citizen complaints (used by 87 percent of respondents), conversations with citizens (85 percent), local newspapers (84 percent), conversations with elected officials (82 percent), conversations with managers (79 percent), voting results (77 percent), local radio and TV (65 percent), and surveys of citizens (62 percent). Using a four-point scale, of "not familiar" (0) to "very familiar" (3), city managers also report that they are familiar with citizen attitudes (mean = 2.6).

This study also examined biases resulting from respondents' knowledge of citizen attitudes and, perhaps, from a desire to present their city in a favorable light. Comparison with other surveys suggests estimates that are consistent with this study. Specifically 42 percent of the *General Social Survey's* (National Opinion Center 1987) national sample of 1,394 residents responded to the question "how much of the time do you think you can trust local government here in (your city)?" with "almost never" and "only some of the time." Similarly, 41 percent of an ABC/*Washington Post* sample of 1,518 residents responded to the same question in this manner (ABC 1990). Also, to the following item on the 1993 survey conducted by the Advisory Commission on Intergovernmental Relations—"Overall, how much trust do you have in your local government to do a good job in carrying out its responsibilities"—35 percent (of 1,028) responded by stating "none at all" or "not very much." These direct assessments suggest a range of 35 to 42 percent concerning citizen cynicism. These results are consistent with the current study's estimate of 34 percent, allowing for sampling errors, differences in questions, survey year, and respondent groups. A fourth poll, conducted by Harris between 1973 and 1986, found higher dissatisfaction. Based on the question "As far as people in charge of running local government are concerned, would you say that you have a great deal of confidence, only some confidence or hardly any confidence at all in them?," 72 percent to 83 percent indicate "only some" or "hardly any" confidence. However, using only three response categories contributes to this high negative rating. By contrast, the other polls all have four categories. Harris has discontinued asking this question. The measure of cynicism also behaves similarly to that of the *General Social Survey* with regard to city size and region.

The current study also examined whether cynical city managers are more likely to view citizens' attitudes as cynical. Respondents' negativism was measured by responses to the general statements "most people would tell a lie to get ahead," and "life is just a game." These measures are frequently used in clinical counseling (Corcoran and Fischer 1987).

On a scale of 3 (strongly agree) to –3 (strongly disagree), the mean values of these two items are, respectively, –1.0 and –1.6. These results suggest that respondents are more optimistic than pessimistic. This result is consistent with Kanter and Mirvis (1989), who report that cynicism is lowest among middle-aged managers. Although the construct of cynicism is associated with the measure "most people would tell a lie to get ahead" ($p <$ .05), controlling for the level of respondents' negativism does not change the statistical significance of the study results. Eliminating extreme pessimists and extreme optimists from the dataset increases the percentage of cynical cities from 33.6 percent to only 34.7 percent but does not affect the statistical findings in this study.

Further analysis also shows that the subjective assessment of crime is consistent with objective crime statistics. However, despite these procedures and findings, the data are perceptions of citizen cynicism, and they do not substitute for assessments that are made by citizens themselves.

competent (56.1 percent), is honest (46.3 percent), fulfills its promises (43.0 percent), understands citizen needs (41.6 percent), and can be trusted (41.5 percent). These low ratings reflect negative assessments across different concerns and are therefore lower than specific ratings.[4]

An index variable, trust, was constructed based on the above items to determine the level of cynicism. This construct has high internal reliability (Cronbach alpha = 0.18). One-third of respondents (33.6 percent) have mean responses that fall within the range of "disagree" to "somewhat agree." Such cities are classified as having "cynical" citizen attitudes. These low ratings imply problems of trust because a city that only "somewhat" meets citizen needs cannot be viewed as an effective partner in helping citizens to achieve their goals. About one-quarter of cynical cities (or 8.3 percent of all respondents) have average ratings of "somewhat disagree" or less. Citizen attitudes in these cities are called "ardently cynical." Changing these cutoff points does not affect the number of ardently cynical cities and those with widespread cynical attitudes, but only those that are on the margin.[5] Further interviews with respondents in ardently cynical cities corroborated the presence of dark attitudes. Specific concerns included the use of government power (e.g., lack of consideration for minorities), a lack of openness in decision-making processes, catering to special interests, and the ineffectiveness of local government in solving important community problems such as traffic congestion and crime.

Municipal Strategies

Cities use a variety of strategies that affect citizen trust (Table 29.2). Although information strategies are widely used (group mean = 60.4 percent), the nature of information provided through these strategies varies. Only a little over half of the cities explain how government meets citizen needs (57.1 percent) and the purpose, benefits, and results of taxes (55.1 percent). Even fewer explain how government fairly balances different community interests (34.8 percent).

Cities also use a range of strategies to enhance their reputation for good management. Communicating awards of distinction (76.3 percent) and encouraging managers to make positive statements about the city (70.5 percent) are common. Half of the cities use media campaigns (50.4 percent), although follow-up interviews suggest that many of these are targeted toward businesses, rather than citizens. Few cities respond to negative comments in the media (39.2 percent), and even fewer inform citizens of high ethical standards in municipal government (25.7 percent).

Participation strategies are also widely used. Citizen participation through public hearings and open meeting policies is widespread (respectively 97.5 percent and 94.7 percent), a finding

Table 29.2

Municipal Strategies in Dealing with Citizens

	Use (%)	Association with cynicism[a]
All	61.2	−2.25**
Two or more strategies from each group	68.9	−2.91***
A. Information		
Informing citizens of changes in rules and programs	82.3	+
Mailings to explain what government does	72.5	−1.66*
Information about service performance	63.9	−1.85*
Mailings to explain how government meets citizen needs	57.1	+
Mailings to explain the purposes, benefits and results of taxes	55.1	+
Mailings to explain how government fairly balances different interests	34.8	−1.85*
Group mean	60.4	−2.15**
B. Participation		
Conduct public hearings	97.5	−
Adopt open meeting policies	94.7	−
Use citizen panels for controversial issues	73.4	−2.29**
Use surveys to elicit citizen preferences	57.8	+
Use voter referenda or ballots	50.0	−2.55**
Group mean	74.4	−2.34**
C. Reputation		
Seeking awards of national or regional distinction	76.3	−
Managers making positive statements	70.5	+
Using campaigns to portray a positive image	50.4	−1.78*
Respond to negative comments in the media	39.2	−
Demonstrate commitment to ethics through sanctions	32.2	+
Regularly informing citizens of high ethical standards in city	25.7	+
Group mean	49.0	−0.83

Notes: [a]The measure of cynicism is based on administrators' perceptions. Associations based on *t*-tests. A plus sign indicates a variable that significantly contributes to the index variable. The index consists of the eleven variables that are not individually associated with cynicism. See text for further discussion.
$*p < .10, **p < .05, ***p < .01$.

which reflects that such participation is often mandated by law. Other strategies are the use of citizen surveys to identify citizen preferences (57.8 percent), voter referenda (50.0 percent) and citizen panels (73.4 percent). Many cities now survey citizen preferences, and some report these poll results and accomplishments through mailings. Citizen panels are also widely used. In some cities, they are a principal strategy for engaging citizens at both city and neighborhood levels (e.g., Seattle).

The use of a range of strategies is significantly associated with lower cynicism ($p < .01$). These results are shown in Table 29.3. Using fewer than 40 percent of the strategies listed in Table 29.2 and not using at least one strategy from each of the three "sets" was defined as using a narrow range of strategies. The perceived level of cynicism, according to respondents, is indicated as "low trust" in Table 29.3. This result is robust using a wide range of category definitions. Given that these data reflect the quantity and not quality of efforts, this finding can be regarded as a rough but stringent estimate of the relationship between strategies and cynicism. Further analysis shows that the effect of strategies is strongest on reducing cynicism when cynicism is high.[6]

Table 29.3

Municipal Strategies and Association with Cynicism

		Number of strategies	
		Low	Medium/High
Level of trust	Low	37 (50.7%)	65 (28.1%)
	Medium/High	36 (49.3%)	166 (71.9%)

Chi square = 12.1, $p < 0.01$.

Note: Column percentages are shown.

The individual strategies are analyzed in the following manner. First, six of the seventeen strategies have a significant negative association with cynicism (Table 29.2). These strategies are informational mailings about what government does, levels of service performance, the use of mailing to explain how government balances interests, the use of citizen panels and voter referenda, and media campaigns. Second, to examine the significance of the eleven remaining strategies, an index was constructed of these strategies. This index (alpha = 0.77) is also significantly associated with decreases in cynicism ($p < .05$). Third, the significance of each of these eleven remaining variables is determined by examining the effect of their elimination from the index variable. A "plus" in Table 29.2 indicates that dropping a variable significantly decreases the statistical significance of the index variable ($p < .05$ or better).[7] Seven of these eleven strategies are significant in this manner. Fourth, Table 29.2 also shows that the group index variables of information ($p < .05$) and participation strategies ($p < .05$) are significantly associated with decreased cynicism. These tests support propositions made above that strategies affect cynicism. However, the composite measure of reputation is not associated with cynicism. Two possible explanations are that these efforts are not yet fully developed in many cities and that they are targeted at economic development, which concerns a business audience. Fifth, Table 29.2 shows that the index variable of all strategies is significantly associated with decreased cynicism ($p < .05$), as is the measure of using any two strategies from each group ($p < .01$). In this regard, reputational strategies do make a significant contribution to the statistical significance of the latter measure. Table 29.4 reports cynicism and the use of strategies by city size, region, and form of government.[8]

Interviews and comments support the importance of using a range of strategies. Interviews with respondents in cities with low levels of trust identify the use of public hearings, public access broadcasts of council meetings, a few citizen advisory panels, annual reports, and sporadic surveys of citizen attitudes as important cynicism-reduction initiatives. By contrast, interviews and survey comments by respondents in "high trust" cities identify the use of a much broader range of strategies. In addition to the standard strategies, these cities use dozens of citizen task forces and focus groups, have strategies to respond immediately to citizen queries and complaints, use surveys to identify citizen preferences (in addition to attitudes), have regular meetings with neighborhood activists, prepare bimonthly newsletters, and consistently explain what government does and how it meets citizen needs. In some cities, over 300 citizen panels and advisory boards are used. Many of these arise from neighborhood activism, and they increase the dialogue between city hall and community leaders (Adler and Blake 1990). In Arvada, Colorado,

Table 29.4

Cynicism and Trust-Enhancing Strategies by Size, Region, and Form of Government

Characteristics	Population	Sample	Cynicism	Information	Participation	Reputation	Outcomes
Size							
Over 500,000	24	13	0.33	0.69	0.76	0.61	0.9
250,000–499,999	36	26	0.41	0.71	0.80	0.57	0.74
100,000–249,999	127	89	0.42*	0.62	0.77	0.50	0.83
50,000–99,000	315	176	0.32*	0.58	0.72	0.47	1.03
Region							
Northeast	88	46	0.46***	0.53*	0.69	0.47	0.73
North Central	119	73	0.37	0.60	0.74	0.51	0.81
South	131	86	0.28**	0.57	0.73	0.50	1.13**
West	164	99	0.37	0.67*	0.78	0.47	0.91
Government							
Mayor-council	181	103	0.35	0.60	0.70	0.52	0.94
Council manager	311	199	0.33	0.62	0.77	0.48	0.94
Other	9	2	0.00	0.75	0.80	0.42	1.31
Total	502	304	0.34	0.60	0.74	0.49	0.94

Notes: The index numbers indicate the fraction of strategies implemented (based on the number of survey items), the fraction of cities that are classified as cynical, and the average rating of outcomes (based on a seven-point Likert scale, see Table 29.7). The t-tests compare the mean of each subgroup against the mean of the remaining observations.

    * 10 percent significance (compared with group mean, *t*-test);

   ** 5 percent significance (compared with group mean, *t*-test);

 *** 1 percent significance (compared with group mean, *t*-test).

city officials schedule meetings with residents at their homes. These cities also often use various reputational strategies. Some cities have "pride" programs, through which local governments increase community awareness among neighborhoods or targeted groups such as children. These and related efforts, also help to balance the negative media coverage of local events.

Although performance awards have received much attention in recent years, respondents have mixed assessments regarding their value. In cities such as Phoenix, Glendale, and Scottsdale (all in Arizona), national and state awards for service excellence are seen as very positive. "Before, people did not even acknowledge that we did things like pick up trash until something went wrong. Now, the press gives the city more respect, the neighborhood associations know they are dealing with a competent entity . . . and people take pride that the city is moving in a positive direction." Respondents in other cities that have won awards state that "awards are a nice pat on the back, but they have little effect on citizen attitudes. . . . It is an ongoing helpful attitude from city hall that the citizens value." Another respondent stated that "the thing of importance is having many citizen and neighborhood groups, openness, low crime, and pleasant parks, good services, etc." This ambivalent assessment of awards is consistent with the findings in Table 29.2, that the strategy of touting awards is not significantly associated with decreasing public cynicism.

Conditions and Outcomes

Table 29.5 confirms that the level of perceived cynicism is greatly affected by economic and social conditions. Cities with well-educated populations and above average economic growth rates have less cynicism toward government (both $p < .01$). Conversely, cities with large poor populations are more cynical about local government ($p < .01$). Table 29.5 also shows a variety of social conditions that affect cynicism. Cities with low crime rates have less public cynicism, as do cities in which citizens take pride in their city, and in which community groups cooperate well together (all $p < .01$). Cities where members of the council and the media are cynical experience greater levels of public cynicism (both $p < .01$). Cities in which citizens have a historically strong interest in municipal affairs are also associated with less cynicism ($p < .05$). These results are robust, even when controlled for economic conditions. For example, low crime rates are associated with increased trust, controlled for the level of economic growth.

Consistent with the above framework, the results in Table 29.6 show that both conditions and strategies are associated with trust. The logistic regression shows that using more strategies is significantly associated with trust after controlling for economic and social conditions. The implication is that public managers who seek to build a positive climate of public trust should aim to improve community conditions *and* use a broad range of information, participation, and reputation strategies. Table 29.7 shows the subjective ratings of municipal objectives. These are positive, albeit low. Satisfaction with outcomes is significantly and positively associated with the level of trust and with the use of a range of trust-enhancing strategies (both $p < .01$). The impact of cynicism on municipal outcomes is widely recognized by respondents: "Cynical attitudes among citizens and council members have made it very difficult to undertake new efforts. We spend a lot of time dealing with citizen complaints. We are not focused on what we should be doing." However, many respondents acknowledged the value of carefully cultivating a climate of trust to ensure positive results: "We have adopted policies of involving our citizens in just about everything. We are now reaping the benefits."

Discussion

Democracy requires a degree of trust that we often take for granted (Bellah et al. 1991). The continuing slide of citizen trust suggests that new approaches are needed to regain public confidence. To

Table 29.5

Local Conditions: Association with Cynicism

Conditions	Present (%)	Association with cynicism[a]
A. Economic conditions		
Population is relatively well educated	62.7	−3.58***
Economic growth is above regional average	54.0	−3.46***
Over 20 percent of population is poor	47.4	4.22***
Population has many retirees	41.3	−1.68
Large income disparities	28.8	−0.85
Population is largely affluent	27.9	−0.16
B. Social conditions		
Citizens take pride in their city	86.3	−3.81***
Citizens respect ordinances	86.0	−2.72***
Citizens support government by volunteerism	83.9	−1.85*
Councilpersons are cynical	73.4	4.45***
Citizens have historically strong interest in municipal affairs	72.6	−2.41**
Community groups cooperate well together	71.1	−3.27***
City has low crime rate	65.6	−2.94***
Media is cynical about local government	61.9	4.80***
A majority of the population consists of minorities	24.7	2.45***

Notes: [a]The measure of cynicism is based on administrators' perceptions. Associations based on t-tests.
  $*p < .10; **p < .05; ***p < .01$.
  Negative associations indicate decreases in cynicism. Statistical tests are based on t-tests.

Table 29.6

Logistic Regression Predicting Cynicism

Dependent variable: cynicism

Independent variables	Maximum likelihood estimate	Standard error
Intercept	−2.263	1.075**
Strategies	−0.365	0.184**
Northeast	0.272	0.631
West	−0.090	0.443
South	−0.760	0.461*
Size	0.234	0.261
Economic conditions	−0.226	0.142*
Social conditions	−0.280	0.110***

$-2 \text{ Log } L = 33.30 \ (p < 0.001)$.
Note: $* = p < .10; ** = p < .05; *** = p < .01$.

this end, manifestations of cynicism should not be understood as the result of misunderstandings or as the result of systemic or isolated ethical wrongdoing. Rather, this chapter suggests that cynicism and trust are deeply rooted in the management of government-citizen relations. Public administration matters. To restore trust, citizens must come to increase their commitment to the purpose of government. Specifically, they must believe that government serves their needs, that they can affect decision-making, and that government is able to deliver. Public administration

Table 29.7

Outcomes of Trust

Municipal objectives	Rating[a]	Association with	
		Cynicism	Strategies
Getting citizens to participate in neighborhood watch groups	1.6	1.37	1.52
Getting citizens to abide by the law	1.3	−4.24***	2.45**
Getting citizens to participate in community affairs	1.1	−1.06	2.30**
Getting citizens to be supportive of local government	0.9	−5.08***	3.04***
Getting citizens to accept new regulations	0.7	−3.12***	2.17**
Getting citizens to adopt civic values	0.6	−4.40***	1.63
Getting citizens to accept new taxes	0.2	−3.50**	1.15
All	0.9	−4.61***	3.10***

Note: [a]All data are based on administrators' ratings. Scale: −3 (very dissatisfied) to 3 (very satisfied) with municipal accomplishments concerning the above objectives. Statistical tests based on *t*-tests.

affects these outcomes. Cities that use frequent information, participation, and reputation strategies experience less cynicism, even when we take into account a broad range of community conditions.

This study finds that cynicism is present in about one-third of all cities with populations over 50,000, and that about one-quarter of these have widespread, "ardently" cynical attitudes (Table 29.1). Although cynicism about local government is not ubiquitous, it is frequent. Managers who seek to affect the level of trust might begin by considering the impact on public attitudes of all communications that citizens receive about city agencies and jurisdictions. In this regard, what do citizens know and believe about the performance and relevance of municipal services? Managers might then use the measures of cynicism reported in Table 29.1 as an instrument for assessing citizen attitudes in their own jurisdictions. Such surveys provide further evidence for administrators' perceptions, can be linked to local conditions, and can identify citizen preferences for information and participation strategies. The strategies reported in Table 29.2 provide a benchmark of such efforts. Consideration of the latter will lead some jurisdictions to broaden and enhance their efforts, and to develop multifaceted and durable strategies.

This study advances our understanding of cynicism as a phenomenon that is linked to unsatisfied citizen needs. However, much further research is needed on the subjects of trust and social capital in public administration. Specifically, careful case studies are needed of jurisdictions or agencies that have turned around negative public attitudes. Detailed attention is required to the strategies, contexts, and actors' abilities. For example, culture's role in causing cynicism, resisting anticynicism strategies, and protecting against ardent cynicism needs more study. The efficacy of different strategies might also be examined in greater detail, focusing, for example, on the psychology of citizen perception and on the impact of strategies on the formation of social capital in communities. Finally, in public administration it is often assumed that managers who seek to serve the public interest also develop the skills to ensure trust. But this study suggests that ensuring the public trust is not a simple task. A broad range of strategies are needed. It would be useful to know how public administrators perceive their tasks of increasing trust and dealing with cynicism. A role also exists in public administration education to ensure that students have adequate skills and perspectives in this area. Undoubtedly, in many public settings, greater efforts are needed to combat cynicism. The time has come to ensure that agencies receive the public support they deserve.

Notes

1. In recent years, skepticism has sometimes been contrasted with cynicism. Skepticism is defined as negative views that are open to influence by reason, whereas cynicism is associated with stubborn beliefs. The fact/belief dichotomy is false because all persons rely on both beliefs and facts in forming their opinions. Within psychology, both are seen as degrees of negativism. Various authors state that cynical beliefs are also consistent with personal orientations that are political, that is, "us-versus-them" (Bolman and Deal 1982), and narcissistic or self-centered (Lasch 1979).

2. Survey respondents illustrated this point in various ways. One city manager stated "Most people just aren't interested. After a hard day of work, most people just want to be entertained, and many city issues just aren't that exciting. It is hard to compete with *NYPD Blue*."

3. This study does not imply that all cynicism is undesirable. The notion of checks and balances is built around distrust. The present concern is that the level of cynicism is too high. It is unlikely that efforts to reduce cynicism will result in too little cynicism.

4. This analysis shows the dangers of relying on broad measures of trust. Table 29.1 shows that more respondents meet citizen needs than understand citizen needs. This may suggest that although citizens perceive services to be effective, other needs are unaddressed. Respondents might also rely on their own understanding of citizen needs, while being uncertain what these needs are.

5. No respondents strongly disagreed with all statements. Changing the cutoff point to 1.5 on the Likert scale increases the number of cities to 40.5 percent, and changing it to 0.5 reduces this number to 29.5 percent. Adopting the standard of one or more negatively rated items increases the number of cities to 39.4 percent. About 93 percent of observations of the previous group are part of this latter group.

6. OLS regressions using continuous variables of trust and the number of strategies result in lower levels of significance ($p < .05$), reflecting lower levels of association at the higher end of both scales. Because this study focuses on cynicism, or low trust, the approach shown in Table 29.3 is more appropriate.

7. This is determined by F-tests of the difference between the residual sum of squares of models involving the full and reduced index as a predictor of trust.

8. It has been suggested that the fact that some cities have strategies to reduce cynicism might affect administrators' perception of cynicism. In the final analysis, the possibility of a halo effect is related to validity, which is discussed in the Methods Box [29.1]. In this regard, personal optimism (which is consistent with halo effects) does not affect the statistical results, and interviews corroborate assessments of very high or low cynicism.

References

ABC/Washington Post. 1990. *Poll of 1,518 Citizens.* January.

Adler, Sy, and Gerald F. Blake. 1990. "The Effects of a Formal Citizen Participation Program on Involvement in the Planning Process: A Case Study of Portland, Oregon." *State and Local Government Review* (Winter): 37–43.

Advisory Commission on Intergovernmental Relations. 1993. *Changing Public Attitudes on Government and Taxes.* Washington, DC: Advisory Commission on Intergovernmental Relations.

Bacot, Hunger, Amy S. McCabe, Michael R. Fitzgerald, Terry Bowen, and David H. Folz. 1993. "Practicing the Politics of Inclusion: Citizen Surveys and the Design of Solid Waste Recycling Programs." *American Review of Public Administration* 23, no. 1: 29–41.

Barber, Benjamin. 1983. *The Logic and Limits of Trust.* New Brunswick, NJ: Rutgers University Press.

Beck, Paul A., Hal G. Rainey, Keith Nichols, and Carol Traut. 1987. "Citizen Views of Taxes and Services: A Tale of Three Cities." *Social Science Quarterly* 68 (September): 223–243.

Bellah, Robert N., Richard Madsen, William M. Sullivan, Ann Swidler, and Steven M. Tipton. 1991. *The Good Society.* New York: Vintage Press.

Bianco, William T. 1994. *Trust: Representatives and Constituents.* Ann Arbor: University of Michigan Press.

Bolman, Lee G., and Terrence E. Deal. 1982. *Modern Approaches to Understanding and Managing Organizations.* San Francisco, CA: Jossey-Bass.

Box, Richard C. 1992. "The Administrator as Trustee of the Public Interest." *Administration and Society* 24 (November): 323–345.

Buckwalter, Doyle, Robert Parsons, and Norman Wright. 1993. "Citizen Participation in Local Government: The Use of Incentives and Rewards." *Public Management* 23 (September): 11–15.

Chrislip, David D. 1993. "The Failure of Traditional Politics." *National Civic Review* 82 (Summer): 234–245.

Cisneros, Henry G., and John Parr. 1990. "Reinvigorating Democratic Values: Challenge and Necessity." *National Civic Review* 79 (September/October): 408–413.

Coleman, James S. 1990. *Foundations of Social Theory.* Cambridge, MA: Belknap Press.

Corcoran, Kevin, and Joel Fischer. 1987. *Measures for Clinical Practice: A Sourcebook.* New York: Free Press.

Damon, William. 1995. *Greater Expectations.* New York: Free Press.

Denton, Robert E., and Gary C. Woodward. 1990. *Political Communication in America.* Westport, CT: Praeger.

Dionne, E.J. 1991. *Why Americans Hate Politics.* New York: Simon and Schuster.

Dubnick, Mel, and David Rosenbloom. 1995. "Oklahoma City." *Public Administration Review* 55 (September/October): 405–406.

Durant, Robert F. 1995. "The Democratic Deficit in America." Paper presented at the 56th Annual Research Conference of the American Society for Public Administration, July 22–26, San Antonio, Texas.

Fairholm, Gilbert W. 1994. *Leadership and the Culture of Trust.* Westport, CT: Praeger.

Frederickson, H. George. 1991. "Toward a Theory of the Public for Public Administration." *Administration and Society* 22 (February): 395–417.

Garnett, James L. 1992. *Communicating for Results in Government: A Strategic Approach for Public Managers.* San Francisco, CA: Jossey-Bass.

Giancoli, Donald. 1993. "Citizen Survey Use in Lauderhill, Florida." Paper presented at the Southeastern Conference on Public Administration, October, Cocoa Beach.

Glaser, Mark A., and James W. Bardo. 1994. "A Five-Stage Approach for Improved Use of Citizen Surveys in Public Investment Decisions." *State and Local Government Review* 26 (Fall): 161–172.

Goodsell, Charles. 1994. *The Case for Bureaucracy,* 3d ed. Chatham, NJ: Chatham House.

Gore, Al. 1994. "Cynicism or Faith." *Vital Speeches* (October 1995): 645–649.

Greider, William. 1992. *Who Will Tell the People: The Betrayal of American Democracy.* New York: Simon and Schuster.

Haeberle, Steven H. 1993. "Community Type and Citizen Responses to Government." *State and Local Government Review* 15 (Winter): 16–23.

Harris, Louis. 1973–1986. Confidence in Government Surveys, various years. Polls of approximately 1,500 citizens.

International City/County Management Association. 1989. *Solving Community Problems by Consensus.* MIS Report. Washington, DC: International City/County Management Association.

———. 1992. Practical Promotion: Strategies for Improving Services and Image. MIS Report. Washington, DC: International City[/County] Management Association.

Johnson, Peter. 1993. *Frames of Deceit: A Study of the Loss and Recovery of Public and Private Trust.* New York: Cambridge University Press.

Jurie, Jay. 1988. "Bureaucracy and Higher Education: The Redefinition of Relevance." *Scholar and Educator* 12 (Fall): 80–91.

Kanter, Donald L., and Phillip H. Mirvis. 1989. *The Cynical Americans: Living and Working in an Age of Discontent and Disillusion.* San Francisco, CA: Jossey-Bass.

Lasch, Christopher. 1979. *The Culture of Narcissism.* New York: Norton.

Lipset, Seymour M., and William Schneider. 1987. *The Confidence Gap: Business, Labor and Government in the Public Mind.* Baltimore, MD: Johns Hopkins University Press.

Loury, Glenn. 1987. "Why Should We Care About Group Inequality?" *Social Philosophy and Policy* 5 (Spring): 249–271.

Luton, Larry S. 1993. "Citizen-Administrator Connections." *Administration and Society* 25 (May): 114–134.

Mansbridge, Jane J., ed. 1990. *Beyond Self-Interest.* Chicago: University of Chicago Press.

McClelland, David C. 1985. *Human Motivation.* Glenview, IL: Scott Foresman.

Merton, Robert K. 1957. *Social Theory and Social Structure.* Glencoe, IL: Free Press.

National League of Cities. 1995. *The State of America's Cities.* Washington, DC: National League of Cities.

National Opinion Research Center. 1987. *General Social Survey.* Storrs, CT: Roper.

O'Connell, Brian J., Herbert Holzman, and Barry R. Armandi. 1986. "Police Cynicism and the Modes of Adaptation." *Journal of Police Science and Administration* 14 (September): 307–313.

Putnam, Robert D. 1993. *Making Democracy Work*. Princeton, NJ: Princeton University Press.

Robertson, Peter J., and Shui-Yan Tang. 1995. "The Role of Commitment in Collective Action: Comparing the Organizational Behavior and Rational Choice Perspectives." *Public Administration Review* 55 (January–February): 67–80.

Ruscio, Kenneth P. 1995. "Trust, Democracy, and Public Management: A Theoretical Argument." Paper presented at the Trinity Symposium for Public Management Research, July, San Antonio, Texas.

Starobin, Paul. 1995. "A Generation of Vipers: Journalists and the New Cynicism." *Columbia Journalism Review* 33 (March/April): 25–33.

Stipak, Brian. 1977. "Attitudes and Belief Systems Concerning Urban Services." *Political Opinion Quarterly* 41 (Spring): 41–55.

Stivers, Camilla. 1994. "The Listening Bureaucrat: Responsiveness in Public Administration." *Public Administration Review* 54 (July–August): 364–369.

Streib, Gregory. 1992. "Professional Skill and Support for Democratic Principles." *Administration and Society* 24 (May): 22–40.

Thomas, John C. 1993. "Public Involvement and Governmental Effectiveness: A Decision-Making Model for Public Managers." *Administration and Society* 24 (February): 444–469.

Wheeler, Kenneth M., ed. 1994. *Effective Communication. Municipal Management Series*. Washington, DC: International City/County Management Association.

CHAPTER 30

STANDARDS OF EXCELLENCE:

U.S. Residents' Evaluations of Local Government Services

THOMAS I. MILLER AND MICHELLE A. MILLER

> *Nothing appears more surprising to those who consider human affairs with a philosophical eye than the easiness with which the many are governed by the few. . . . When we inquire by what means this wonder is effected, we shall find that . . . the governors have nothing to support them but opinion. It is therefore, on opinion only that government is founded; and this maxim extends to the most despotic and most military governments as well as the most free and popular*
> (David Hume 1711, as quoted in Neumann-Noell 1979, 145).

When George Gallup was a young man making his reputation as a political pollster, he met skeptics who ". . . thought we were an evil force which might lead the country straight to Hell—or direct democracy, which they regarded as equally terrifying" (Gallup 1957). Since then, survey methods have been refined, gained (sometimes grudging) respect, and had their applications broadened to include far more than prediction of presidential elections.

Citizen surveys—local government surveys of residents—are offshoots of the seed planted by early twentieth century pollsters. Surveys concerning citizens' needs, behaviors, characteristics, policy preferences, service evaluations, and hopes and dreams fill libraries and offices of city and county governments.

Among the many types of locally sponsored surveys, the most useful tool for local government administrators arguably is the survey that elicits citizens' assessments of city services—the evaluative survey. The evaluative survey casts the citizen as a consumer whose attitudes about service delivery (in the absence of free market competition) represent government's only bottom line (Brown and Pyers 1988).

The evaluative survey also has been characterized as a measure of local government effectiveness (Usher and Cornia 1981), productivity (Folz and Lyons 1986), impact (Brudney and England 1982), responsiveness and equity (Hatry and Blair 1976), performance (Ostrom 1982), and output (Fisk and Winnie 1974).

The literature on citizen surveys covers more than survey uses and importance. It tells how to do surveys (Daneke and Klobus-Edwards 1979; Hatry and Blair 1976), how to interpret them (Parks 1984), how many are done (Streib 1990), and how flawed and even dangerous they are (Stipak 1979; MacNair et al. 1983; Miller 1987; Herbers 1990).

From *Public Administration Review*, vol. 51, no. 6 (November/December 1991), pp. 503–512. Copyright © 1991 by American Society for Public Administration. Reprinted with permission.

Box 30.1
Data

Surveys from forty states were represented. No surveys were received from Alaska, Hawaii, New Hampshire, Vermont, Rhode Island, North Dakota, West Virginia, Mississippi, Nevada, or New Mexico. Altogether, 3,206 evaluative questions about quality of local government services were coded from the 261 citizen surveys (one survey from each jurisdiction). About twelve service evaluation questions were coded, on average, for each citizen survey. The 261 jurisdictions had populations totaling about 41,521,000 in 1985.

The surveys were collected through a six month process of mail and personal contacts. All cities with over fifty thousand population in 1985 were mailed a request to participate, and each was asked to inform about other candidates for inclusion. Newspapers in large cities were contacted directly, and a newspaper data base was searched.

Missing from the studies of citizen surveys is an analysis of what they say. When academic studies do examine what surveys say, they tend to concentrate on findings from national probability samples (see for example, *Public Opinion Quarterly*) or on survey results that provide special meaning to theory (*Social Indicators Research*). Local evaluative surveys, sitting in planning directors' files, on public library shelves, and conference tables across the country are largely ignored.

This chapter summarizes the results of surveys of residents' evaluations of local government services. This summary provides qualitative results in a common metric so that norms for perceptions about service delivery can be used by local government administrators to compare their own residents' perceptions to those of other places where evaluative surveys have been done.

The evaluative surveys that we collected comprise a ponderous body of data that have been ignored for practical reasons and presumptions about quality and generality. Even if the results of local government evaluative surveys are important to local administrators, one might wonder what possible use Padukah's results could be to the residents of Tallahassee.

Residents' evaluations of local government services are rarely understood in the context of evaluations of like services provided elsewhere. Norms of citizens' perceptions are needed as benchmarks against which local government administrators can compare their community's ratings. In the absence of clear prescriptions about what constitutes acceptable thresholds for residents' evaluations of local services, we refer to these norms as standards.

What is an acceptable standard for residents' perceptions of local government services? Is a "Good" evaluation for police good enough? Can more be expected from a street repair service that gets only "Fair" evaluations? The absence of normative data about service evaluations means that an important ingredient is lacking from the information that feeds public policy. Reference to how others are doing fuels political debate. Are we getting our fair share of legislators, tax dollars, wages, Rhodes scholars, protection from crime, clean streets, and good libraries?

This study is a meta-analysis (Glass et al. 1981; Rosenthal 1984; Hunter and Schmidt 1990), a quantitative integration of outcomes from existing research. In the fifteen years since Glass coined the term "meta-analysis" in an address to the American Educational Research Association, this way of quantitatively summarizing individual research studies has become the method of choice in a wide variety of disciplines.[1]

For this study, we focus on service evaluations integrated from 261 citizen surveys administered within the last ten years to more than 215,000 people living in American cities, counties, and townships. The results of these surveys were used to represent the opinions of more than 40 million U.S. residents about quality of local government services or quality of community life. (See Box 30.1.)

Table 30.1

Three Cities' Questions About Street Repair and the Citizens' Responses

City	Question	Scale (percent)				
Telluride, CO	"Rate the quality of street repair"[a]	5 (3)	4 (8)	3 (26)	2 (30)	1 (33)
Orlando, FL	"Some of the following situations may exist in your neighborhood . . . Poor street or sidewalk repair."[b]	0 (61)		3 (15)	2 (11)	1 (13)
Glendale, CA	"Do you feel that the street repair is better than, worse than, or about the same as in other cities?"	Better (52)		About same (37)		Worse (11)

Note: [a]Telluride: 1 = lowest; 5 = highest. [b]Orlando: 0 = not a problem; 1 = problem that concerns respondent most; 3 = problem that concerns respondent least.

Search for the Common Threads

Examples of results from three different communities where residents were asked to rate street repair appear in Table 30.1. They represent the usual kinds of variation in more than three thousand questions integrated in this meta-analysis.[2]

How can sense be made of responses to such diverse questions? Similarities in questions and responses can be understood better if citizens' attitudes are recorded on a single scale. One way to make better sense of responses indicated on scales of different size and with different wording is to calculate the average score on each scale and to put those averages onto a single scale, say, ranging from 0 to 100, where the worst evaluation is zero and the best evaluation is 100. This conversion can be accomplished easily and it works for all evaluative survey scales.

By placing all responses onto a 0 to 100 scale with units called Percent to Maximum (PTM) (see Table 30.2), we made it easier to compare diverse scales. However, the PTM scale cannot, by itself, correct for overall differences expected from one kind of question versus another. (See Box 30.2.)

The difference for PTM rating can be seen in a simple example. Say only 10 percent of the population of Archtip, Iowa, has negative opinions about police service. When the community responds to the same questionnaire using two different four-point scales, one symmetrical and one skewed with more positive than negative options, the responses on the symmetrical scale show a higher PTM than those on the scale with a positive skew as shown in Table 30.2. All the positive evaluations must be "squeezed" into the two positive ratings at the top of the symmetrical scale (see Table 30.3).

This example demonstrates that intrinsic differences in question options can influence results (PTM ratings) independent of the service being evaluated or the degree of satisfaction with the service. Not only do positively biased scales get lower PTM than symmetrical scales, but two-point scales tend to evince higher PTMs than three-, four-, or five-point scales. Evaluative questions seeking comparisons of service quality to other jurisdictions or other times tend to receive lower PTMs than questions without relative referents. We used multiple regression analyses to develop statistical controls to adjust for the intrinsic differences in PTM found among different types of questions (see Box 30.3).

Table 30.2

Conversion of a Five-Point Scale to Percent to Maximum (PTM)

Scale	High 5	4	3	2	Low 1
Percent responding at each point on the scale	3	8	26	30	33
Average rating on the 5-point scale (mean = 2.18)*	5	4	3	2	1
Distance from the bottom of the scale to the top (distance = 29.5%)**	100			2.18 ↕ 29.5%	

Notes: *Mean is the weighted average of responses calculated as follows: $((3 \times 5) + (8 \times 4) + (26 \times 3) + (30 \times 2) + (33 \times 1))/100$.
**Distance is calculated as follows: $((\text{Mean} - 1)) \times 100$ or $((2.18 - 1)/(5 - 1)) \times 100$.

Table 30.3

Hypothetical Distributions of Opinion About Police Where Only 10 Percent of the Population Thinks III of Service Received

Scale type	Scale and responses (percent)				PTM
Symmetrical	Very satisfied 30	Satisfied 60	Dissatisfied 5	Very dissatisfied 5	72
Skewed positive	Excellent 30	Good 40	Fair 20	Poor 10	63

Findings

Outcomes of Service Evaluations

The overall average adjusted PTM across all service ratings coded for this study is shown in Figure 30.1 on a thermometer scale that ranges from 0 PTM to 100 PTM. The thermometer is labeled 0 for Very bad; 25, Bad; 50, Neither good nor bad; 75, Good; and 100, Very good.

In a scale with any number of options, 100 PTM is the top anchor, 0 is the bottom, and 50 occurs in the middle. The location of the intermediate options depends on the number of option points to be inserted. If Figure 30.1 had been characterized as a four-point scale with no middle, "Good" and "Bad" would occur at 66 PTM and 33 PTM, respectively. On a five-point scale, "Good" occurs at 75 PTM and "Bad" at 25 PTM. We chose the five-point display since it gives a slightly more conservative interpretation of results. That is, 63 PTM is closer to "Good" on the four-point scale than on the five-point scale. This does little damage to our interpretation of how good ratings are and the conservative approach has no affect whatever on comparison of PTM among services, cities, or any other categorization of the data.

Across all service evaluations, the average adjusted PTM was 67.2, not much below the 75 rating for "Good" showing that, on average, citizens thought well of their local government services. For more than a quarter of all questions, ratings averaged well above "Good" (79 PTM). Most of citizens' evaluations were above the scale midpoint of 50. Only about 25 percent of all

Box 30.2
Percent to Maximum (PTM) Scale

Take the Telluride, Colorado, street repair evaluation as an example (shown in Table 30.2). The average rating on street repair in Telluride is 29.5 percent of the distance along a scale that runs from 0 percent, meaning the worst evaluation, to 100 percent, meaning the best evaluation.

We have called each conversion to the uniform 100 percentage-point scale "percent to max" (PTM) because each reflects the distance in percentage units from the lowest possible evaluation to the maximum possible evaluation, regardless of the question wording or the width of the original scale.

Although conversion to PTM inflicts no violence on mean scores, standard deviations of each service evaluation are not taken into account, which often occurs when scores from different scales are converted to a standard metric. Z scores, expressions of the mean in standard deviation units, would, by definition, equal zero in every case because we are dealing with mean scores for each service question. The coefficient of variation, the standard deviation divided by the mean, was thought to be too cumbersome and too susceptible to the problems described for d scores.

D scores, a metric common to many meta-analyses, could have been calculated by deviating the scale mean score around the scale center and dividing by the standard deviation of responses to the question. We were uncomfortable with the interpretive requirement of d scores that, ceteris paribus, would give worse service evaluations when there was more diverse community opinion about service quality. For example, city XYZ gives police the following percent for each rating on a five-point scale: $0 = 10, 1 = 20, 2 = 20, 3 = 20, 4 = 30$. City ABC evaluates police as follows: $0 = 40, 1 = 0, 2 = 0, 3 = 0, 4 = 60$. Both get a PTM = 60, but the d score for XYZ, where opinion is more homogeneous, is .29 while the d score for ABC is .20.

Furthermore d scores are typically constructed by expressing in standard deviation units the difference in the means of two random variables. The only way to construct d scores in this case, since two groups were not being compared, would have been to deviate the mean of the single random variable (community service evaluations) around a constant, the scale center. This could create some inappropriately large d scores because the mean of the single random variable is more likely to be farther from the scale center than from another mean derived by similar methods.

Still, more must be done to diminish the influence of question wording on responses. The conversion to PTM allows each outcome to be measured on the same scale but all the scales must be adjusted to the same starting point so that fair comparisons of service evaluations across different types of questions are possible.

Guidance about how to make those adjustments was provided by the vast literature on response effects. (McNemar 1946; Cantril 1947; Payne 1951; Hilton 1976; Kalton et al. 1978; Schuman and Presser 1981; Ayidiya and McClendon 1990.) The literature revealed two meta-analyses of survey findings (Sudman and Bradburn 1974; Fox et al. 1988) whose authors also had faced the problems of quantitatively integrating results from surveys conducted for different reasons, using different methods and question wording and applied to different kinds of respondents. These authors chose d scores as their outcome metric because the literature they were integrating was experimental and had a treated and a control group that could be compared.

Most research focused on wording (and other) effects in questions about sweeping controversial policies (abortion, gun control) and almost none of the literature examined response consequences in surveys about local government services.

Nevertheless, split ballot experiments have helped to reveal specific instances where manipulation of question order, use of "Don't Know," question balance, middle-option wording, and phone vs. in-person administration have led to different responses. These variables were treated as possible correlates of service evaluations and each was either statistically controlled or tested by other means.

(continued)

408

(*Box 30.2 cont'd*)

Variables not controlled in the regression model were type of survey administration, examined by comparing outcomes of phone and mailed surveys; and question order, examined by correlating question outcome with question number, which was usually a close approximation of the location of each item. The simple correlation between question order and outcome was $r = .11$ across all questions, suggesting that questions asked later in surveys were slightly more likely to have lower PTM scores. The relationship accounted for about 1 percent of the variance in outcomes. There was no significant relationship between type of administration and outcome as seen in the following tabulation for jurisdictions with over 10,000 population.

Type of administration	Mean adjusted PTM	SD	Number of jurisdictions
Mail	74.2	10.1	62
Phone	75.7	10.1	81

Box 30.3
Adjusting for Differences Among Questions

By simultaneously controlling for number of scale options, symmetry of scale options, demand for a referent (absolute or relative) and existence of "Don't Know" as an option, we were able to determine the independent effect of scale anchor wording. Similarly, the independent effects of the other question characteristics were determined, which gave the number of PTM points needed to adjust for several characteristics of the questions. Because sample size accounted for less than 1 percent of the variance in PTM ($r = .09$), our analyses weighted by sample size and unweighted were essentially the same. Regression of PTM onto dummy variables for number of scale options, scale wording, scale symmetry, scale referent, and whether "Don't Know" was permitted yielded a Multiple $R = .39$.

Although we understand that adjusted PTM scale scores will even out a good deal of the roughness in comparisons among different original rating scales, the adjustments are not perfect. The confounding of scale types and points means that few instances exist of two-point scales with anchor wording of "Excellent" and "Poor." Consequently, it is difficult—even with a mathematical model—to disentangle completely the effects of scale wording and scale size.

In fact, because some overadjustments occurred for a few specific scales, adjusted PTM ranged above 100 in 29 cases of the 3,823 survey questions. To control for overadjustment we imposed a criterion separate from scale characteristics on all adjustments. Points given to an unadjusted PTM could not exceed one-half the distance between the unadjusted PTM and 100. For example, if a question on garbage collection received a PTM of 70, its adjusted PTM could not exceed 85 ([100–70] / 2 = 15).

No unadjusted low scores (44 PTM or less) were affected by this cap on adjustment, but the closer the unadjusted score was to 100, the greater the decrease in permissible adjustment. We assumed that citizens would be less affected by scale anomalies when services were seen to be excellent, so big adjustments at the upper end of the PTM scale would give unneeded and undeserved advantage to services already perceived as very good. Few scores were capped by more than five points, and, of course, no adjusted PTM was able to advance beyond 100.

We applied the regression weights to convert all 3,206 service evaluations to a scale that had four or five forced choice options, was symmetrical, permitted "Don't Know," and had as anchor wording "Satisfied/Dissatisfied" (S/D), "High/Low" (H/L), "Good/Bad" (G/B), "Agree/Disagree" (A/D) or "Good/Poor" (G/P). The standard question form was absolute, that is respondents were not asked to compare a service to one in another location or another time.

Figure 30.1 **Average Adjusted Percent to Maximum (PTM) for All Local Government Services**

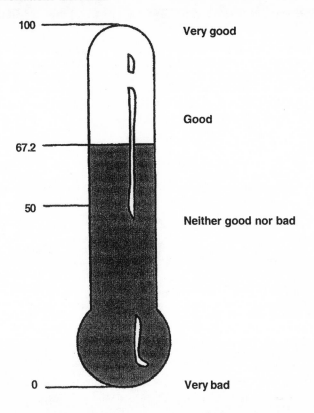

Mean = 67.2

Standard deviation = 16.1

N questions = 3,206

Median = 69

25th percentile = 57

75th percentile = 80

evaluations were below a PTM of 56. This finding is particularly important for the administrator who hesitates to conduct a citizen survey for fear that citizens will vent their spleen on bureaucrats in city hall. It is also important because it provides some validation of our method by confirming globally positive evaluations of government described in recent piecemeal examinations of surveys about local government service delivery (Goodsell 1983).

Evaluations of Different Services

Services were placed in the following eight broad categories. Evaluations of these are shown in Table 30.4.[3]

Table 30.4

Average Adjusted Percent to Maximum (PTM) for Eight Categories of Community Services

Service category	PTM	Number of questions	SD
Cultural and arts programs	76.7	133	15.2
Public safety	75.1	493	13.8
Support services	67.8	309	13.4
Parks and recreation	71.5	311	15.6
Public utilities	69.5	469	13.7
Public works/transportation	62.8	894	16.7
Health and human services	62.6	467	15.6
Planning and growth management	55.4	130	15.6

Cultural and Arts Programs: library, entertainment, arts, museum, zoo.

Public Safety: fire, emergency medical service, police, traffic enforcement, police patrol, crime prevention.

Support Services: government, overall city services, general maintenance/cleanliness, maintenance of city buildings, courtesy of city employees, delivery of information by city employees.

Parks and Recreation: parks/recreation/open space facilities or programs, number and quality of parks, recreation, open space, swimming pools, baseball fields.

Public Works/Transportation: maintenance of traffic signs, clean or maintained sidewalks, weed control, code enforcement, animal control, parking, parking garages, streets in general, street repair/maintenance, street cleaning, snow removal, traffic in general, timing of traffic lights, traffic safety, traffic noise, traffic volume, traffic congestion/flow in neighborhoods and on major streets, traffic speed, trash collection, bus/transit service, municipal airport, alternate mode travel.

Health and Human Services: social services, services to seniors, handicapped, minorities, youth/teens, women, health services, education/schools, housing, municipal court.

Planning and Growth Management: economic development, general growth, quality of growth, speed of growth, zoning, planning.

Cultural and arts and public safety programs ranked among the best services. The worst average ratings went to planning and growth management. However, even with planning and growth management, the average citizen evaluation was above the scale midpoint.

Evaluations of individual services are shown in descending order of average adjusted PTM in Table 30.5. These evaluations provide normative benchmarks against which jurisdictions can compare their locally provided services. Only services evaluated in sixty or more jurisdictions are shown. Only one evaluative question was coded for any service in a given jurisdiction. Where several questions were asked about a single service, the results of all these questions were averaged before they were coded for analysis.

The best-rated services were fire, library, and trash collection, and the worst rated were animal control, street repair, and planning.

Table 30.5

Summary of Average Ratings of the Services Evaluated by Sixty or More Jurisdictions

Service	Average adjusted PTM	SD	Number of jurisdictions
Fire	81.1	12.4	168
Library	79.3	13.9	104
Trash	78.0	11.5	142
Water/sewer	73.5	12.0	119
Parks	72.3	15.1	65
Police	71.8	12.8	182
To seniors	69.5	15.2	63
Schools	69.4	13.7	92
Sewer	69.1	12.7	72
Parks/recreation	68.5	17.2	83
Open space/recreation	68.0	15.4	89
Snow removal	67.0	13.6	73
Street lighting	66.9	10.6	60
Street cleaning	66.6	10.7	67
General maintenance	66.1	12.4	79
Health services	64.1	15.3	70
Code enforcement	62.3	14.0	62
Bus/transit	61.9	15.8	71
Animal control	60.3	15.6	63
Street repair	58.5	14.6	126
Planning/zoning	57.5	11.5	75

Stability of Differences in Service Evaluations

How confident should we be that these service evaluations will hold across many cities? We have used thousands of service evaluations from 261 jurisdictions. Although conclusions drawn from a broad sample have benefits, using evaluations of different services from different cities presents problems.

Differences in Service Evaluations in Cities Where the Same Services Were Rated

Table 30.6 contains the results of a series of analyses in which the entire database of service evaluations was culled to identify sets of cities in which the same services were evaluated. These analyses provide an important control not found in the larger analysis where comparisons among service evaluations permitted variations in question wording or the services evaluated. In this analysis, different service ratings cannot be attributed to different survey samples, methods, question wording, or date of administration.

As the number of evaluated services rose, the number of jurisdictions in which all the services were evaluated declined. Only five cities evaluated fire, library, police, streets, trash, water/sewer, and parks/recreation, but fifty-three cities evaluated fire, police, streets, and trash. Not only were service differences very stable across cities, but the reliability of city differences was very strong, too.[4]

All five subsets of quality ratings placed the services in approximately the same order as that calculated using all the data in the study. Furthermore, except for the subset based on five cities (where all the services were rated poorly), the adjusted PTM averaged almost the same as that found for each service in the entire study. Whether from the entire database or

Table 30.6

Comparison of Service Evaluations (Mean Adjusted Percent to Maximum [PTM]) in a Subset of Jurisdictions Where the Same Services Are Measured

| Services | Number of cities measuring all services reported | | | | | | | | | | Comparison results from entire survey | | |
| | 5 | | 15 | | 27 | | 37 | | 53 | | | | |
	PTM	SD	PTM	SD	PTM	SD	PTM	SD	PTM	SD	PTM	SD	Number of jurisdictions
Fire	75	21	82	15	83	14	84	13	82	11	81	12	168
Water/sewer	75	4	80	7	80	10			79	9	74	12	119
Trash	71	18	79	13	78	19	79	17			78	12	142
Library	64	35	77	22	73	16	73	16	73	14	79	14	104
Police	56	29	69	21							72	13	182
Parks/recreation	55	32									72	15	65
Street repair	44	18	53	16	55	16	55	15	56	16	59	15	126

subsets of 15, 27, 37, or 53 communities, street repair averaged about 20 PTM lower than library. Fire beat police by about 7 to 10 points. Trash haul received 3 PTM points less than fire but about the same as libraries.

To test further the robustness of our conclusions about the relative size of service-evaluation differences, we performed other analyses. We averaged results without any regression adjustment; averaged the percent of respondents in option categories with positive wording (e.g., Excellent, Good, Fair); looked at average results for questions with only EGFP scales; looked at calculating d scores instead of PTM; and created a regression adjustment procedure that was more elaborate than the original.

All results were very similar. The evaluations of fire and trash exceeded "Good" on the evaluation scale; police were reliably lower and street repair was rated only marginally above the middle—neither good nor bad. The magnitude and order of findings for the eight service categories, with a few small exceptions, also remained unchanged (Table 30.7).

Critics might argue that it is unfair to include in norms results from surveys done poorly, by mail or, a long time ago. Implicit in such criticism is the assumption that such surveys would show different results than those that are done well, or conducted over the phone, or are more recent.

Residents' service evaluations were, on average, very similar (and not statistically significantly different) whether higher or lower response rates were obtained, or good survey methods were used, phone or mail was used, questions came early or late in the survey, or the survey was conducted in the last four years.

While the consistent differences among service ratings provide strong evidence about the reliability of residents' perceptions of service quality, they are not necessarily synonymous with differences in observed quality of service delivery. We suspect, like Stipak (1979), that no simple monotonic relationship exists between perceptions about service delivery and actual quality of service. Part of our research included case studies of the best and worst rated services where, if anywhere, differences in actual service delivery should be apparent.

We uncovered important differences at the extremes of impressions about service: the worst street repair ratings were given to communities with dirt roads (none of the best had dirt roads); the best snowplow rating went to a community where residential streets were plowed (no residential streets were plowed in the worst rated communities); the worst fire service ratings were given to communities with small volunteer fire departments (few of the best had only volunteers).

Having suggested that consistency of perceptions about service quality may not always reflect reliable differences in observed service delivery, we must also say that the consistency of service evaluation differences across jurisdictions—library was consistently better than street repair—does not require the existence of some immutable law of government or psychology. It is obvious that there is plenty of room for movement in ratings of every service (Table 30.5).

Although we suspect it would be rare to find a community with better evaluations of street repair than library (in part because of consumers' different emotional and physical associations with the two services), exceptions will exist.

Predicting Service Excellence

We attempted to account for cities' different service evaluations by examining seven of the services most frequently rated: fire, police, trash haul, library, street repair, parks and recreation, water and sewer. Why was police service rated higher in some locales than others? Would wealthy communities do better? Would communities with older residents get worse evaluations than communities with younger residents?

Table 30.7

Summary of Major Results Using Different Analyses (Adjusted Means with Explanation)

	M&M mean[a]	NR mean[b]	EGFP mean[c]	% + mean[d]	53 mean[e]	R^2 mean[f]	d scores for EGFP[g]
Individual services							
Fire	81.1	81.8	84.2	83.3	82.2	81.9	87.8
Trash haul	78.0	77.9	77.4	80.9	79.4	78.0	81.3
Police	71.8	71.6	71.7	74.6	72.8	72.5	76.6
Street repair	58.5	59.5	61.3	58.4	55.9	60.0	61.0
ICMA categories							
Cultural and arts (CA)	76.7	76.2	79.4	76.5	—	77.0	85.6
Public safety (PS)	75.1	75.7	77.2	75.9	—	75.8	81.9
Parks and recreation (PR)	71.5	71.8	71.7	74.6	—	72.0	78.8
Public utilities (PU)	69.5	69.1	71.9	67.4	—	70.4	71.7
Support services (SS)	67.8	69.8	68.1	72.2	—	67.5	72.8
Public works/transportation (PT)	62.8	63.5	63.3	60.7	—	63.5	67.7
Health and human services (HHS)	62.6	60.7	63.7	61.1	—	63.7	73.5
Planning and zoning (PZ)	55.4	54.4	53.1	52.4	—	56.5	63.3

Notes:

[a]Results from this study; average adjusted PTM.

[b]Derived from conversion of results to the same scale, PTM; a linear adjustment of each mean from its own scale (e.g., 1–5) to a 0–100 scale. No regression adjustments were made. For each category, 8.1 was added to control for the fact that unadjusted results were on average 58.2 PTM while adjusted results were 66.3 PTM. This way, column 2 can be compared to column 1.

[c]Results from Excellent, Good, Fair, Poor (EGFP) scales only, the largest subset of scale types. No regression adjustment was made. Because these scales averaged 13.9 points lower than all the adjusted scores (the average for EGFP scales was 52.; for adjusted scales it was 66.3), 13.9 was added to each category of results to make it comparable to our results.

[d]Derived from averaging the sum of all responses to positively worded scale options (E + G + F). Because the average for percent positive results was 7.9 points higher than for our adjustment (74.2 for % + vs. 66.3 for us) 7.9 was subtracted from all averages.

[e]Results came from fifty-three jurisdictions in which fire, trash haul, police, and street repair were rated. The same question was usually asked, for example, only the service name was changed, otherwise the wording of the question and scale options were the same. The same method of data collection was used in each jurisdiction, and resident with the same incomes, ethnic makeup, and so on, answered all four questions in each jurisdiction. These results keep constant the way questions were asked, who was asked and how the survey was conducted, so they provide substantial confirmation of the larger study where these characteristics were allowed to vary.

[f]Derived from conducting the regression adjustments using a more elaborate model that included over seventy predictor variables compared to our model that included only ten predictor variables.

[g]d scores were calculated for all EGFP scales to see how d scores might compare to PTM. With no regression adjustment, we subtracted the observed mean for each question from 2.5 (the scale midpoint) and divided by the standard deviation (SD) of responses to each question. Resulting d scores were converted to comparable scales for comparison to the other six columns of this table by the following: For each category, we multiplied the observed average d score by the average within question SD and added that to 2.5. From this product, we subtracted 1 (to change the EGFP scale from 1–4 to 0–3) and divided the entire result by 3 (the new scale max). This gave the unadjusted PTM equivalent for EGFP scales to which we added 13.9 (the difference between the average EGFP—51.4—and the average adjusted PTM—66.3). Observed d scores follow: Their magnitude and order confirm other results except in the case of HHS which did relatively better by this method. Fire = 1.09; Trash = .71; Police = .48; Streets = −.11. ICMA categories: CA = .93; PS = .73; PR = .59; PU = .29; SS = .37; PT = .14; HHS = .36; PZ = −.02.

Predictor data came, most often, from the 1987 Census of Local Governments provided on electronic medium from the International City Managers' Association (ICMA). Data included total number of government employees, number of government employees in specific depart-ments (for fire and police only), total government expenditures (overall and for each service except library), population, number of white residents, serious crimes, and measures of residents' education, income, age, and length of residency. All raw predictor data were converted to data per capita (except, of course, population itself).

For each of the seven services, Table 30.8 displays the simple correlations between each predictor and the average adjusted service ratings. Table 30.9 summarizes the multiple correlations, which included specific subsets of predictors.[5]

The zero-order correlations between service ratings and community characteristics in Table 30.8, indicate that proximity to a metropolitan job center (as measured by a greater percent of residents who commute out), community wealth (as measured by a smaller percent of residents in poverty or greater resident income per capita), and education were consistent predictors of higher service evaluations (except for library ratings and ratings of water/sewer).

The reasons for such findings may be that well-to-do, better educated, white residents of suburbs may actually receive better services than people in other kinds of communities. Furthermore, moderate-sized suburbs have fewer services to manage than, say, metro areas where there are airports, museums, zoos, or ports. Therefore, while resources per capita are no greater, the management of resources is more tractable.

Of course, a plausible alternative explanation forsakes the putative causal link between perceived service delivery and actual service delivery. The relatively diminished problems of crime, poverty, air pollution and traffic in well-off suburbs may lead to a better quality of life, which colors residents' impressions of all local government services.

Whatever the cause of the correlations observed among community characteristics and service evaluations, the most interesting results may be the absence of correlation between service evaluations and measures of personnel per capita or expenditures per capita. For overall expenditures per capita, expenditures per capita for specific services, overall employees per capita, or the number of police or firefighters per capita, the correlations with service ratings were close to zero and, when significantly different from zero (but still small), they were as likely to be negative—worse ratings associated with higher expenditures or staff per capita—as positive (Table 30.8).

We combined several community characteristics in multiple regression analyses, attempting to account for as much variance in survey evaluations as possible. Even the multiple regression models did not perform well (Table 30.9). In the cases of street repair and police, where Multiple R's were significant and substantial, the predictability of service ratings using several independent variables was only moderately enhanced beyond the simple correlations of service rating with location near a metropolitan center or with residents' wealth.

Because of the complexities of integrating disparate survey results, this study represents only the first step toward providing local governments with the benchmarks for comparison with their citizens' evaluations of local government services. As the value of norms for citizens' perceptions about service quality becomes more apparent to local government managers, we hope there will be greater uniformity in survey questions and methods so that the precision of norms will improve incrementally over time.

Summary and Conclusions

Our study found that citizens thought well of local government services in America. The average evaluation of all city services was close to the "Good" category on a five-point scale that ranged from "Very Bad" to "Very Good." Even the city service with the worst evaluation received an average rating above the scale midpoint.

The individual services of local government that received the best evaluations were fire,

Table 30.8

Simple Correlations of Service Area Ratings with Selected Jurisdiction Characteristics

	Government employee rate[a]	Expenses per capita[b]	Population	Percent white	Serious crime rate	Percent with at least 16 years education	Money income per capita	Families below poverty	Percent who work outside city	Median age of population	Percent in college	Median length of residency[c]	Government rate[d]	N[e]
Fire														
r	.0474	.0279	.0675	-.0536	.0401	.2277	.2166	-.1027	.1537	.1263	.0882	.0293	.154	88–166
p	.328	.398	.195	.269	.334	.004	.006	.116	.038	.070	.156	.387		
Police														
r	-.2176	-.0338	-.0008	.2212	-.3690	.2136	.3418	-.3868	.3590	.1169	.0071	.1344	-.113	104–180
p	.010	.348	.496	.003	.000	.004	.000	.000	.000	.076	.466	.043		
Trash														
r		.0557	.1255	.0851	-.2739	.1012	.2614	-.2267	.2233	.1677	-.0312	-.0056	-.126	100–142
p		.288	.068	.181	.003	.136	.002	.007	.008	.034	.369	.475		
Library														
r			-.0474	-.1672	.0302	.0300	.0414	.0338	.0952	.2688	-.0276	.0921	-.085	69–104
p			.317	.068	.403	.393	.354	.380	.197	.006	.402	.189		
Street maintenance														
r		-.1546	.0502	.1056	-.2204	.2815	.4237	-.3594	.5111	.0764	-.0887	-.1436	-.160	99–126
p		.059	.288	.137	.014	.001	.000	.000	.000	.213	.178	.067		

													N
Parks and recreation													
r	.2332	.0652	.2750	-.2095	.4108	.4683	-.4135	.2793	.1112	.2574	-.1620	-.127	173–235
p	.001	.160	.000	.003	.000	.000	.000	.000	.059	.000	.009		
Water and sewer													
r	.0651	.1242	-.1266	-.0917	.0943	-.0152	-.0274	-.0068	-.0653	.0512	.0640	-.113	79–119
p	.282	.089	.111	.211	.179	.442	.396	.474	.263	.311	.250		
All services													
r	.067	-.051	.068	-.112	.175	.212	-.200	.179	.034	.075	-.071	-.143	2,529–3,794
p	.000	.000	.000	.000	.000	.000	.000	.000	.000	.000	.000		

Notes:

r = simple correlation.

p = significance of correlation coefficient.

[a]Fire and police personnel per 100,000 population.

[b]Expenditures for each service per 100,000 residents.

[c]Predicted from 1980 census.

[d]Government rate: overall government personnel per 1,000 population.

[e]N varies between rages shown since not all characteristics were available for every jurisdiction.

Table 30.9

Summary of Attempts to Predict Service Evaluations for Different Jurisdictions

Service	Multiple R	Adjusted R^{2*}	N	Significance
Street repair	.66	.40	98	<.001
Police	.60	.31	92	<.001
Library	.40	.10	66	.03
Parks/recreation	.38	.04	50	.22
Fire	.37	.06	80	.09
Trash haul	.31	.05	93	.11
Water/sewer	.21	.03	72	.71
All services	.27	.07	2,563	<.001

Note: *Percent of variance accounted for by all predictors.

library, and trash haul. The worst-rated services were animal control, street repair, and planning. The differences among service quality ratings were very stable from one community to another, across well or poorly conducted surveys, whether conducted by mail or phone, and whether a recent or older survey. Results were also stable across several methods of developing norms.

A 70 PTM rating indicated exceptionally positive perceptions of street repair but very poor perceptions of library service and worse than average police work. The service quality ratings found in jurisdictions across the United States can provide the comparisons needed for any locale to make the most meaningful interpretation of its citizens' evaluations of local services.

And what can be done with these results? Suppose Archtip, Iowa, residents give animal control and library the same evaluation, say, 75 PTM (adjusted) or "Good" on the standard symmetrical scale. Before these comparative data were available, the survey results might have been interpreted as follows: Both animal control and library service were considered "Good" by Archtip residents. Although that interpretation is not wrong, an important dimension can now be added. Archtip residents gave their library a rating that put it among 25 percent or 30 percent of the worst libraries compared to other cities in the nation where library service was rated. At the same time, Archtip residents' ratings of animal control showed that service to be among the top 10 percent or 15 percent of all cities where animal control was rated.

The communities in which residents felt that they received the best services tended to be midsized with residents who were wealthier and were more likely to commute to a metropolitan job center. The fact that community economic well-being and location may influence service ratings will excite few administrators, because, like weather, managers cannot do much about such things. No evidence in existing data indicates that residents of cities with better-rated services paid more per capita than residents of cities where services were given worse ratings or that they were served by more government personnel per capita. Better service ratings may come with better management techniques that could not be captured in existing data about characteristics of local jurisdictions. Further research using predictors derived from local management practices should help shed light on this murky area of public management.

Notes

1. The first book written about the results of a meta-analysis concerned psychotherapy and psychotropic drug therapy experiments (Smith, Glass, and Miller 1980). Numerous meta-analyses have been conducted in the area of educational psychology (Kulick et al. 1979; Smith 1980; Hunter et al. 1979). Meta-analysis has become so popular in the field of medicine that the *New York Times* published an article on it with a flow chart titled, "How to Do a Meta-analysis" (Altman 1990), and graduate studies in public health include course work on meta-analysis.

2. Most meta-analyses summarize experiments by quantifying the difference between two groups or among many groups investigated in a single study. Outcomes of specially treated groups are compared to control groups and the differences, in standard units, become the elements of the meta-analysis. In our meta-analysis, no such comparisons were made because we were not dealing with data from experiments but we were only estimating the degree of satisfaction with service delivery.

3. The following table shows the adjustments required to simulate a four- or five-point symmetrical scale with "Don't Know" permitted and anchor wording "Satisfied/Dissatisfied" (S/D), "High/Low" (H/L), "Good/Bad" (G/B), "Agree/Disagree" (A/D), or "Good/Poor" (G/P). Question or scale is absolute. The adjustments represent the regression coefficients derived from the regression equation.

If Scale	Make this adjustment to PTM	
Has 2 points	Subtract	10.1 PTM points
Has 3 points	Subtract	0.1 PTM points
Has 6 points or more	Add	4.6 PTM points
Is relative	Add	8.6 PTM points
Prohibits "Don't Know"	Subtract	4.7 PTM points
Is skewed positive	Add	10.8 PTM points
Is skewed negative	Add	6.0 PTM points
Anchors worded E/P*	Add	4.3 PTM points
Anchors worded anything but E/P, S/D, H/L, G/B, A/D, or G/P	Add	6.3 PTM points

*E/P means Excellent/Poor.

4. For each subset of cities (with numbers of cities in the subsets equaling 5, 15, 27, 37, and 53), a mixed model repeated-measures analysis of variance was performed with cities as the random factor and services as the fixed factor. Reliability of city differences as measured by Cronbach's alpha ranged from .85 to .89 (this means that, within each city, the differences between service ratings were very similar), and for every subset of jurisdictions (except the subset of five cities where $p < .05$), the differences between services were statistically significant beyond $p < .0001$.

5. The predictors used for regression equations

	Work/out[a]	Population[b]	Income[c]	Employees/Service[d]	Expenditure/Service[e]	Employees[f]	Expenditures[g]
Street repair	X	X	X		X	X	
Police		X	X	X	X	X	X
Library	X	X	X		X		
Parks/recreation	X	X	X		X	X	
Fire		X	X	X	X	X	X
Trash haul	X	X	X		X	X	
Water/sewer	X	X	X			X	X

Notes:

[a]Work/out = percent of population that commutes to nearby metropolitan area.

[b]Population = Total 1985 or 1987 estimated population.

[c]Income = 1985 money income per capita.

[d]Employees/Service = Number of employees per capita for a specific service (e.g., police/10,000 population).

[e]Expenditure/Service = Expenditure per capita on each specific service: for street repair, highway expenditures were used; for water/sewer, sewer expenditures were used.

[f]Employees = Total government employees per 1,000 population.

[g]Expenditures = Total government expenditures per 1,000 population.

References

Altman, Lawrence, K. 1990. "New Method of Analyzing Health Data Stirs Debate." *New York Times*, sect. B. (Science), August 21, pp. 5B, 9B.

Ayidiya, Stephen A., and McKee J. McClendon. 1990. "Response Effects in Mail Surveys." *Public Opinion Quarterly* 54: 229–247.

Brown, Richard E., and James B. Pyers. 1988. "Putting Teeth into the Efficiency and Effectiveness of Public Services." *Public Administration Review* 48, no. 3 (May/June): 735–742.

Brudney, Jeffrey, L., and Robert E. England. 1982. "Urban Policy Making and Subjective Service Evaluations: Are They Compatible?" *Public Administration Review* (March/April): 127–134.

Cantril, Handley C. 1947. *Gauging Public Opinion*. Princeton, NJ: Princeton University Press.

Daneke, Gregory, A., and Patricia Klobus-Edwards. 1979. "Survey Research for Public Administrators." *Public Administration Review* 39, no. 5 (September/October): 421–426.

Fisk, Donald, M., and Richard E. Winnie. 1974. "Output Measurement in Urban Government: Current Status and Likely Prospects." *Social Science Quarterly* 54, no. 4: 725.

Folz, David, H., and William Lyons. 1986. "The Measurement of Municipal Service Quality and Productivity: A Comparative Perspective." *Public Productivity Review* 40 (Winter): 21–33.

Fox, Richard J., Melvin R. Crask, and Kim Jonghoon. 1988. "Mail Survey Response Rate: A Meta-Analysis of Selected Techniques for Inducing Response." *Public Opinion Quarterly* 52: 467–491.

Glass, Gene V., Barry McGaw, and Mary Lee Smith. 1981. *Meta-Analysis in Social Research*. Beverly Hills, CA: Sage.

Gallup, George. 1957. "The Changing Climate for Public Opinion Research." *Public Opinion Quarterly* 21, no. 1: 23–27.

Goodsell, Charles T. 1983. *The Case for Bureaucracy*. Chatham, NJ: Chatham House.

Hatry, H.P., and L.H. Blair. 1976. "Citizen Surveys for Local Governments: A Copout, Manipulative Tool or a Policy Guidance and Analysis Aid?" In *Citizen Preferences and Urban Public Policy*, ed. Terry N. Clark. Beverly Hills, CA: Sage.

Herbers, John. 1990. "They're Taking the Public Out of Public Policy Making." *Governing* (February).

Hilton, Robert. 1976. "On Question Wording and Stability of Response." *Social Science Research* 5: 39–41.

Hunter, John E., and Frank L. Schmidt. 1990. *Methods of Meta-Analysis*. Newbury Park, CA: Sage.

Hunter, J.E., F.L. Schmidt, and R. Hunter. 1979. "Differential Validity of Employment Tests by Race: A Comprehensive Review and Analysis." *Psychological Bulletin* 86: 721–735.

Kalton, Graham, Martin Collins, and Lindsay Brook. 1978. "Experiments in Wording Opinion Questions." *Applied Statistics* 27, no. 2: 149–161.

Kulick, J.A., C.C. Kulick, and P.A. Cohen. 1979. "A Meta-Analysis of Outcome Studies of Keller's Personalized System of Instruction." *American Psychologist* 34: 307–318.

MacNair, Ray H., Russell Caldwell, and Leonard Pollane. 1983. "Citizen Participants in Public Bureaucracies-Foul-Weather Friends." *Administration and Society* 14, no. 4: February.

McNemar, Quinn. 1946. "Opinion-Attitude Methodology." *Psychology Bulletin* 43: 289–364.

Miller, T.I. 1987. "The Nine Circles of Citizen Survey Hell." *Management Science and Policy Analysis* 4, no. 3 (Spring): 26–32.

Neumann-Noell, Elisabeth. 1979. "Public Opinion and the Classical Tradition." *Public Opinion Quarterly* 43, no. 2: 143–156. (Quoted in Hume, 1711.)

Ostrom, Elinor. 1982. "The Need for Multiple Indicators in Measuring the Output of Public Agencies." *Policy Studies Journal* 2, no. 2.

Parks, Roger. 1984. "Linking Objective and Subjective Measures of Performance." *Public Administration Review* 44 (March/April): 118–127.

Payne, Stanley L. 1951. *The Art of Asking Questions*. Princeton, NJ: Princeton University Press.

Rosenthal, Robert. 1984. *Meta-Analytic Procedures for Social Research*. Newbury Park, CA: Sage.

Schuman, Howard, and Stanley Presser. 1981. *Questions and Answers in Attitude Surveys*. New York: Academic Press.

Smith, M.L. 1980. "Sex Bias in Counseling and Psychotherapy." *Psychological Bulletin* 87: 392–407.

Smith, M.L., G.V. Glass, and T.I. Miller. 1980. *Benefits of Psychotherapy*. Baltimore, MD: Johns Hopkins University Press.

Stipak, Brian. 1979. "Citizen Satisfaction with Urban Services: Potential Misuse as a Performance Indicator." *Public Administration Review* 39 (January/February): 46–52.

Streib, Gregory. 1990. "Dusting Off a Forgotten Management Tool: The Citizen Survey." *Public Management* (August): 17–19.

Sudman, Seymour, and Norman M. Bradburn. 1974. *Response Effects in Surveys*. Chicago, IL: Aldine.

Usher, Charles L., and Gary C. Cornia. 1981. "Goal Setting and Performance Assessment in Municipal Budgeting." *Public Administration Review* 41, no. 2 (March/April): 229–235.

INDEX

ABOUT THE EDITORS

Douglas J. Watson is the city manager of the City of Auburn, Alabama, and a visiting professor at Auburn University. He has served as Auburn city manager since 1982 and holds a master of public administration from the University of Georgia and a doctorate from Auburn. He is the author or editor of five books and over thirty journal articles. Dr. Watson serves on the editorial boards of four journals, including the *Public Administration Review* and *State and Local Government Review*. He is the recipient of a number of honors for his work, including the National Public Service Award from the American Society for Public Administration and the L.P. Cookingham Award for Career Development and the Orin F. Nolting International Award from the International City/County Management Association.

Wendy L. Hassett has ten years of experience in local government management, currently as the assistant city manager of the City of Auburn, Alabama. She holds a master of public administration degree and a doctorate in public administration and public policy from Auburn University. She is co-author of articles in *Public Administration Review*, *Public Works Management and Policy*, and *Journal of Public Budgeting, Accounting & Financial Management*. She has written a chapter in the forthcoming book, *Gender and Work in Comparative Perspective* and co-written a chapter in *Innovative Governments: Creative Approaches to Local Problems*.